An Introduction to SOLIDWORKS® Flow Simulation 2015

John E. Matsson, Ph.D.

SDC
Publications

SDC Publications
P.O. Box 1334
Mission, KS 66222
913-262-2664
www.SDCpublications.com
Publisher: Stephen Schroff

ISBN-13: 978-1-58503-934-0
ISBN-10: 1-58503-934-9

Printed and bound in the United States of America.

Acknowledgements

I would like to thank Stephen Schroff and Mary Schmidt of SDC Publications for their help in preparing this book for publication.

About the Author

Dr. John Matsson is a Professor of Engineering and Chair of the Engineering Department at Oral Roberts University in Tulsa, Oklahoma. He earned M.S. and Ph.D. degrees from the Royal Institute of Technology in Stockholm, Sweden, in 1988 and 1994, respectively and completed postdoctoral work at the Norwegian University of Science and Technology in Trondheim, Norway. His teaching areas include Finite Element Methods, Fluid Mechanics, Heat Transfer, Manufacturing Processes, Principles of Design and Special Topics. He is a member of the American Society of Mechanical Engineers ASME Mid-Continent Section and also a member of the American Society of Engineering Education (ASEE). Please contact the author jmatsson@oru.edu with any comments, questions, or suggestions on this book.

Notes:

Table of Contents

Notes:

Chapter 1 Introduction

SOLIDWORKS® Flow Simulation Introduction

SOLIDWORKS Flow Simulation 2015 is a fluid flow analysis add-in package that is available for SOLIDWORKS in order to obtain solutions to the full Navier-Stokes equations that govern the motion of fluids. Other packages that can be added to SOLIDWORKS include SOLIDWORKS Motion and SOLIDWORKS Simulation. A fluid flow analysis using Flow Simulation involves a number of basic steps that are shown in the following flowchart in figure 1.1.

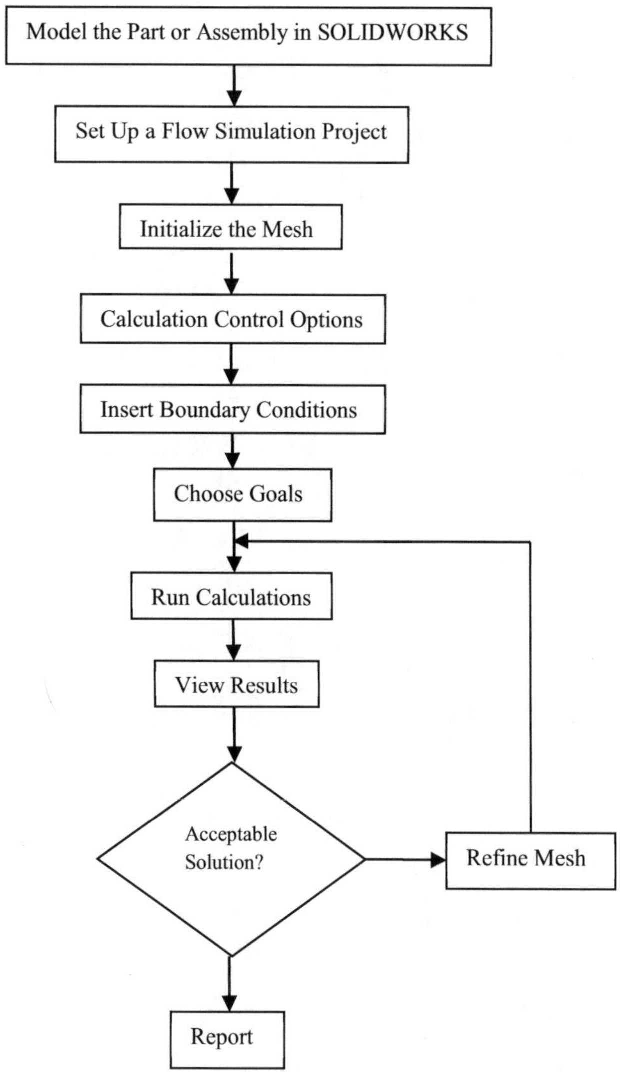

Figure 1.1 Flowchart for fluid flow analysis using SOLIDWORKS® Flow Simulation

Setting Up a SOLIDWORKS® Flow Simulation Project

The process of setting up a Flow Simulation project includes the following general setting steps in order: choosing the analysis type, selecting a fluid and a solid and settings of wall condition and initial and ambient conditions. Any fluid flow problem that is solved using Flow Simulation must be categorized as either internal bounded or external unbounded flow. Examples of internal flows include flows bounded by walls such as pipe and channel flows, heat exchangers and obstruction flow meters. External flow examples include flows around airfoils and fuselages of airplanes and fluid flow related to different sports such as flows over golf balls, baseballs and soccer balls. Furthermore, during the project setup process a fluid is chosen as belonging to one of the following six categories: gas, liquid, non-Newtonian liquid, compressible liquid, real gas or steam. Physical features that can be taken into account include heat conduction in solids, radiation, time-varying flows, gravity and rotation. Roughness of surfaces can be specified, and different thermal conditions for walls can be chosen including adiabatic walls or specified heat flux, heat transfer rate or wall temperature. For a more complete list of possible settings, see table 1.1.

General Settings						
Analysis type	Internal	External				
Physical Features	Heat Conduction in Solids	Radiation	Time-dependence	Gravity	Rotation	
Fluids	Gases	Liquids	Non-Newtonian Liquids	Compressible Liquids	Real Gases	Steam
Flow Types	Laminar	Laminar and Turbulent	Turbulent			
Solids	Alloys	Glasses and Minerals	Metals	Non-Isotropic Solids	Polymers	Semi-conductors
Wall Thermal Condition	Adiabatic Wall	Heat Flux	Heat Transfer Rate	Temperature		
Thermodynamic Parameters	Pressure	Temperature	Density			
Velocity Parameters	Velocity in X direction	Velocity in Y direction	Velocity in Z direction			
Turbulence Parameters	Turbulence Intensity	Turbulence Length	Turbulence Energy	Turbulence Dissipation		

Table 1.1 List of different general settings in SOLIDWORKS® Flow Simulation

Meshing in SOLIDWORKS® Flow Simulation

The SOLIDWORKS Flow Simulation mesh consists of cells in the form of rectangular parallelepipeds. The Flow Simulation mesh can contain basic cells of three different types: fluid cells, partial cells and solid cells; see figure 1.2. Basic cells can be split during the process of refinement. During refinement, each basic cell is split in eight smaller cells with the same volume; see figure 1.2. Therefore, the volume of each refined cell is only 1/8 of the original volume. There are a maximum of seven refinement levels that can be set in the calculation control options. A table of the different available mesh settings is summarized in table 1.2. An essential part of any computational study of fluid flows is to vary the density of the computational mesh and study whether the solution converges as the mesh is refined. However, it should be remembered that a fine mesh in fluid flow simulations may require a substantial amount of RAM and that calculations can take a very long time to reach convergence.

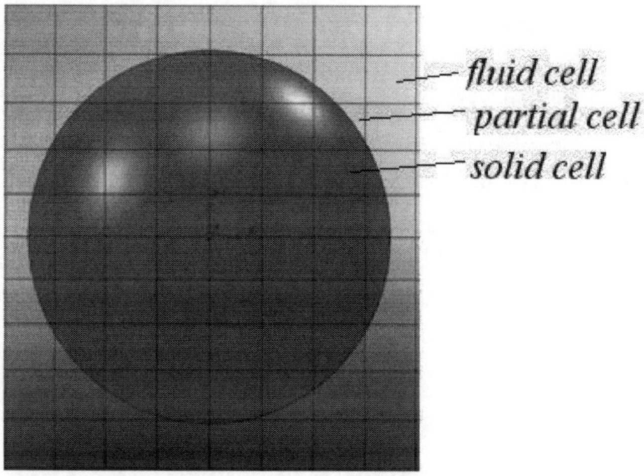

Figure 1.2 Different types of mesh cells

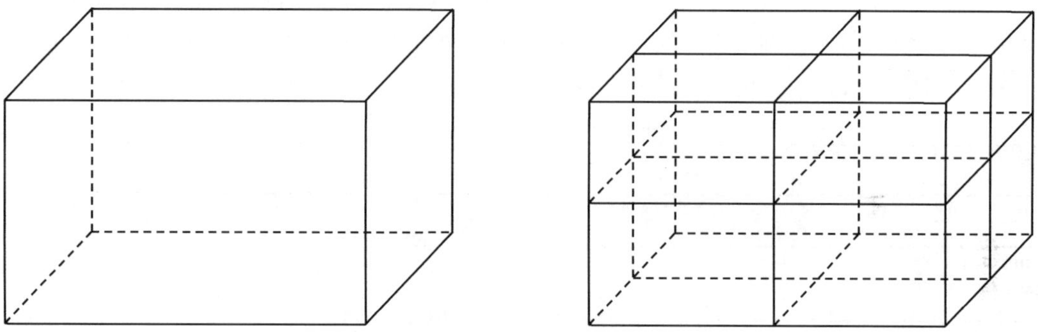

Figure 1.3 Refinement of a rectangular parallelepiped

Mesh Settings				
Automatic Settings	*Level of Initial Mesh*	*Minimum Gap Size*	*Minimum Wall Thickness*	
Manual Settings	*Basic Mesh*	*Solid/Fluid Interface*	*Refining Cells*	*Narrow Channels*
	Number of Cells per X <1001	Small Solid Features Refinement Level < 8	All Cells	Number of Cells
	Number of Cells per Y <1001	Curvature Refinement Level < 8	Fluid Cells	Refinement Level
	Number of Cells per Z <1001	Tolerance Refinement Level < 8	Partial Cells	Minimum Height
			Solid Cells	Maximum Height

Table 1.2 List of mesh settings in SOLIDWORKS® Flow Simulation

There are also a number of six control planes available in Flow Simulation that can be used to optimally contract or expand the mesh in order to assure that details and features of the geometry will be captured by the computational mesh.

The computational mesh is recommended to be constructed in the following order:

a) Start by using the automatic mesh setting. Set the minimum gap size and minimum wall thickness to appropriate values.
b) Turn off automatic settings and set your own basic mesh values with both the small solid features refinement level and the curvature refinement level set to zero. Disable the narrow channel refinement.
c) Increase both the small solid features refinement level and the curvature refinement level in steps and enable the narrow channel refinement.

Calculation Control Options

There are a number of ways in which you can control your calculations; see table 1.3. As shown in the table the finishing conditions include refinement number, iterations, calculation time and travels. Travel is defined as the number of iterations related to the propagation of a perturbation through the computational domain. In the value drop down box of the calculation control options, it is possible to choose whether calculations will stop when one of the finishing conditions is satisfied or when all of them are satisfied. The maximum number of travels depends on the specific goals that are used in the calculations, result resolution level and the type of problem that is studied.

Calculation Control Options			
Finish Conditions	*Saving*	*Refinement*	*Advanced*
Minimum Refinement Number	Save Before Refinement	Disabled	Flow Freezing
Maximum Iterations	Periodic Saving	Level = 1 - 7	Notify when calculation is finished
Maximum Calculation Time	Tabular Saving		
Maximum Travels			

Table 1.3 List of mesh settings in SOLIDWORKS® Flow Simulation

Inserting Boundary Conditions

Boundary conditions are required for both the inflow and outflow faces of internal flow regions with the exception of enclosures subjected to natural convection. Visualization of boundary conditions can be shown with arrows of different colors indicating the type and direction of the boundary condition. The boundary conditions are divided in three different types: flow openings, pressure openings and walls; see table 1.4.

Boundary Conditions								
Flow Openings	Inlet Mass Flow	Inlet Volume Flow	Inlet Velocity	Inlet Mach Number	Outlet Mass Flow	Outlet Volume Flow	Outlet Velocity	Outlet Mach Number
Pressure Openings	Environment Pressure	Static Pressure	Total Pressure					
Wall	Real Wall	Ideal Wall						

Table 1.4 List of available boundary conditions in SOLIDWORKS® Flow Simulation

Each boundary condition has a number of parameters related to it that can be set to different values. The available parameters for each boundary condition are shown in table 1.5.

Boundary Conditions	Flow Parameters	Thermodynamic Parameters	Turbulence Parameters	Boundary Layer	Wall Parameters	Wall Motion	Options
Inlet Mass Flow	√	√	√	√			√
Inlet Volume Flow	√	√	√	√			√
Inlet Velocity	√	√	√	√			√
Inlet Mach Number	√	√	√	√			√
Outlet Mass Flow	√						√
Outlet Volume Flow	√						√
Outlet Velocity	√						√
Outlet Mach Number	√						√
Environment Pressure		√	√	√			√
Static Pressure		√	√	√			√
Total Pressure		√	√	√			√
Real Wall					√	√	√
Ideal Wall							√

Table 1.5 List of available parameters for different boundary conditions in SOLIDWORKS® Flow Simulation

The flow parameter depends on the boundary condition but includes velocity, Mach number and mass and volume flow rate. The direction of the flow vector can be specified as normal to the face, as swirl or as a 3D vector. The thermodynamic parameters include temperature and pressure. For the turbulence parameters you can choose between specifying the turbulence intensity and length or the turbulence energy and dissipation (k-ε turbulence model). The boundary layer is set to either laminar or turbulent. You can also specify velocity and thermal boundary layer thickness for the inlet velocity boundary condition as well as specify the core velocity and temperature. For the real wall boundary condition you can specify the wall roughness together with wall temperature and heat transfer coefficient. The real wall also has an option for motion in the form of translational or angular velocity.

Choosing Goals

Goals are criteria used to stop the iterative solution process. The goals are chosen from the physical parameters of interest to the user of Flow Simulation. The use of goals minimizes errors in the calculated parameters and shortens the total solution time for the solver. There are five different types of goals: global goals, point goals, surface goals, volume goals and equation goals. The global goal is based on parameter values determined everywhere in the flow field, whereas a point goal is related to a specific point inside the computational domain. Surface goals are determined on specific surfaces, and volume goals are determined within a specific subset of the computational domain as specified by the user. Finally, equation goals are defined by mathematical expressions. Table 1.6 is showing 48 different parameters that can be chosen by the different types of goals.

GG: Global Goal, SG: Surface Goal, VG: Volume Goal					***PG: Point Goal***
Parameter	*Minimum*	*Average*	*Maximum*	*Bulk Average*	*Value*
Static Pressure	*GG, SG, VG*	*GG, SG, VG*	*GG, SG, VG*	*GG, SG, VG*	*PG*
Total Pressure	*GG, SG, VG*	*GG, SG, VG*	*GG, SG, VG*	*GG, SG, VG*	*PG*
Dynamic Pressure	*GG, SG, VG*	*GG, SG, VG*	*GG, SG, VG*	*GG, SG, VG*	*PG*
Temperature of Fluid	*GG, SG, VG*	*GG, SG, VG*	*GG, SG, VG*	*GG, SG, VG*	*PG*
Density	*GG, SG, VG*	*GG, SG, VG*	*GG, SG, VG*	*GG, SG, VG*	*PG*
Mass Flow Rate			*GG, SG*		
Mass in Volume			*VG*		
Volume Flow Rate			*SG*		
Velocity	*GG, SG, VG*	*GG, SG, VG*	*GG, SG, VG*	*GG, SG, VG*	*PG*
X-Component of Velocity	*GG, SG, VG*	*GG, SG, VG*	*GG, SG, VG*	*GG, SG, VG*	*PG*
Y-Component of Velocity	*GG, SG, VG*	*GG, SG, VG*	*GG, SG, VG*	*GG, SG, VG*	*PG*
Z-Component of Velocity	*GG, SG, VG*	*GG, SG, VG*	*GG, SG, VG*	*GG, SG, VG*	*PG*
Mach Number	*GG, SG, VG*	*GG, SG, VG*	*GG, SG, VG*	*GG, SG, VG*	*PG*
Turbulent Viscosity	*GG, SG, VG*	*GG, SG, VG*	*GG, SG, VG*	*GG, SG, VG*	*PG*
Turbulent Time	*GG, SG, VG*	*GG, SG, VG*	*GG, SG, VG*	*GG, SG, VG*	*PG*
Turbulent Length	*GG, SG, VG*	*GG, SG, VG*	*GG, SG, VG*	*GG, SG, VG*	*PG*
Turbulent Intensity	*GG, SG, VG*	*GG, SG, VG*	*GG, SG, VG*	*GG, SG, VG*	*PG*
Turbulent Energy	*GG, SG, VG*	*GG, SG, VG*	*GG, SG, VG*	*GG, SG, VG*	*PG*
Turbulent Dissipation	*GG, SG, VG*	*GG, SG, VG*	*GG, SG, VG*	*GG, SG, VG*	*PG*
Heat Flux	*GG, SG*	*GG, SG*	*GG, SG*		
X-Component of Heat Flux	*GG, SG*	*GG, SG*	*GG, SG*		
Y-Component of Heat Flux	*GG, SG*	*GG, SG*	*GG, SG*		
Z-Component of Heat Flux	*GG, SG*	*GG, SG*	*GG, SG*		
Heat Transfer Rate			*GG, SG*		
X-Component of Heat Transfer Rate			*GG, SG*		
Y-Component of Heat Transfer Rate			*GG, SG*		
Z-Component of Heat Transfer Rate			*GG, SG*		
Normal Force			*GG, SG*		
X-Component of Normal Force			*GG, SG*		
Y-Component of Normal Force			*GG, SG*		
Z-Component of Normal Force			*GG, SG*		
Force			*GG, SG*		
X-Component of Force			*GG, SG*		
Y-Component of Force			*GG, SG*		
Z-Component of Force			*GG, SG*		
Shear Force			*GG, SG*		
X-Component of Shear Force			*GG, SG*		
Y-Component of Shear Force			*GG, SG*		
Z-Component of Shear Force			*GG, SG*		
X-Component of Torque			*GG, SG*		
Y-Component of Torque			*GG, SG*		
Z-Component of Torque			*GG, SG*		
Temperature of Solid	*GG, SG, VG*	*GG, SG, VG*	*GG, SG, VG*		*PG*
Melting Temperature Exceed	*SG, VG*	*SG, VG*	*SG, VG*		*PG*
Mass Fraction of Air	*GG, SG, VG*	*GG, SG, VG*	*GG, SG, VG*	*GG, SG, VG*	*PG*
Volume Fraction of Air	*GG, SG, VG*	*GG, SG, VG*	*GG, SG, VG*	*GG, SG, VG*	*PG*
Mass Flow Rate of Air			*SG*		
Volume Flow Rate of Air			*SG*		

Table 1.6 List of available parameters for different goals in SOLIDWORKS® Flow Simulation

Viewing Results

Results can be visualized in a number of different ways as indicated by table 1.7.

Result Settings								
Results	Cut Plots	3D-Profile Plots	Surface Plots	Isosurfaces	Flow Trajectories	Particle Studies	XY Plots	Point , Surface and Volume Parameters

Table 1.7 List of available results in SOLIDWORKS Flow Simulation

Limitations of SOLIDWORKS® Flow Simulation

It is important to know the limitations of SOLIDWORKS Flow Simulation before you start the process of modeling your engineering problem. The limitations include the following common flow situations that can't be studied in the present version of SOLIDWORKS Flow Simulation: chemically reacting flows, free fluid surface flows, fluid mixing flows, multi-phase flows and moving model parts. However, it should be pointed out that motion of walls can be specified as boundary conditions in SOLIDWORKS Flow Simulation. An example of this is shown in chapter 5 where we study Taylor-Couette flow between rotating cylinders.

References

[1] SOLIDWORKS Flow Simulation 2015 Solving Engineering Tasks

[2] SOLIDWORKS Flow Simulation 2015 Technical Reference

[3] SOLIDWORKS Flow Simulation 2015 Tutorial

Notes:

Chapter 2 Flat Plate Boundary Layer

Objectives

- Creating the SOLIDWORKS part needed for the Flow Simulation
- Setting up Flow Simulation projects for internal flow
- Setting up a two-dimensional flow condition
- Initializing the mesh
- Selecting boundary conditions
- Inserting global goals, point goals and equation goals for the calculations
- Running the calculations
- Using Cut Plots to visualize the resulting flow field
- Use of XY Plots for velocity profiles, boundary layer thickness, displacement thickness, momentum thickness and friction coefficients
- Use of Excel templates for XY Plots
- Comparison of Flow Simulation results with theories and empirical data
- Cloning of the project

Problem Description

In this chapter, we will use SOLIDWORKS Flow Simulation to study the two-dimensional laminar and turbulent flow on a flat plate and compare with the theoretical Blasius boundary layer solution and empirical results. The inlet velocity for the 1 m long plate is 5 m/s, and we will be using air as the fluid for laminar calculations and water to get a higher Reynolds number for turbulent boundary layer calculations. We will determine the velocity profiles and plot the profiles using the well-known boundary layer similarity coordinate. The variation of boundary-layer thickness, displacement thickness, momentum thickness and the local friction coefficient will also be determined. We will start by creating the part needed for this simulation; see figure 2.0.

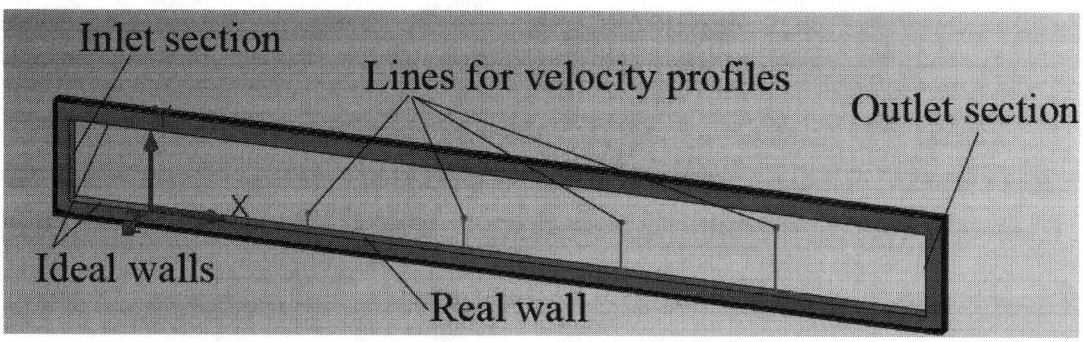

Figure 2.0 SOLIDWORKS model for flat plate boundary layer study

Creating the SOLIDWORKS Part

1. Start by creating a new part in SOLIDWORKS: select **File>>New** and click on the **OK** button in the **New SOLIDWORKS Document** window. Click on **Front Plane** in the **FeatureManager design tree** and select **Front** from the **View Orientation** drop down menu in the graphics window.

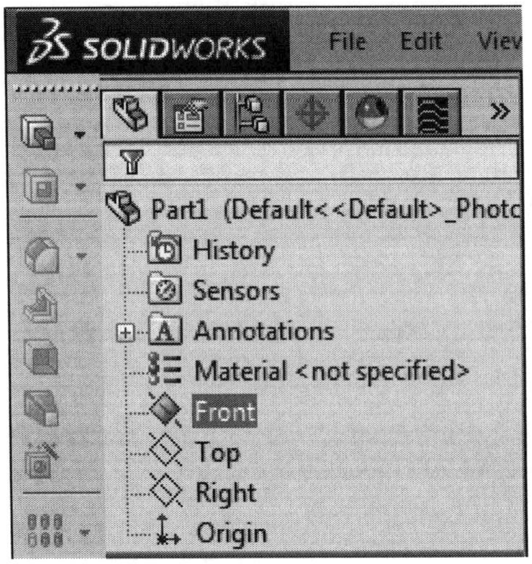

Figure 2.1a) Selection of front plane

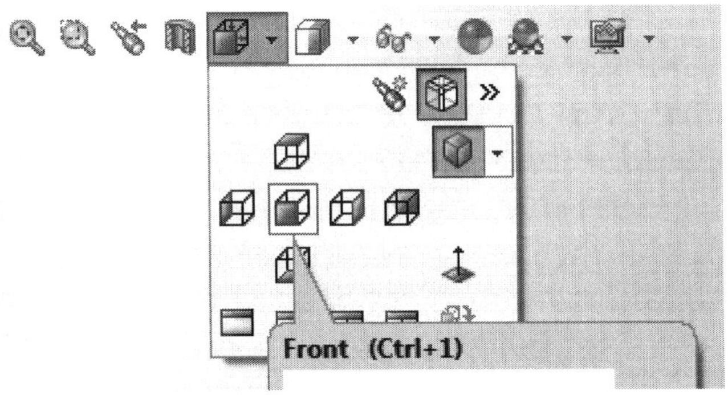

Figure 2.1b) Selection of front view

2. Click on the **Sketch** tab and select **Corner Rectangle**.

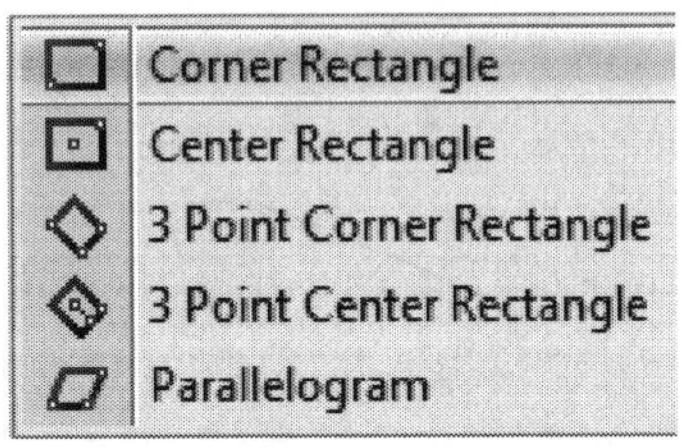

Figure 2.2 Selecting a sketch tool

3. Make sure that you have **MMGS** (millimeter, gram, second) chosen as your unit system. You can check this by selecting **Tools>>Options** from the SOLIDWORKS menu and selecting the **Document Properties** tab followed by clicking on **Units**. Click to the left and below the origin in the graphics window and drag the rectangle to the right and upward. Fill in the parameters for the rectangle: 1000 mm wide and 100 mm high. Close the Rectangle dialog box by clicking on ✓. Right click in the graphics window and select **Zoom/Pan/Rotate>> Zoom to Fit**.

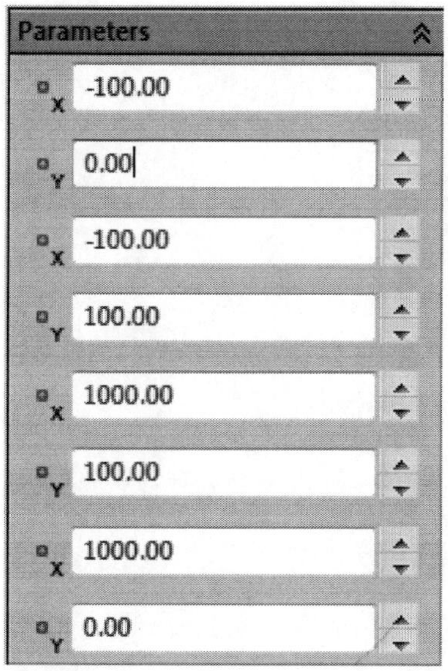

Figure 2.3a) Parameter settings for the rectangle

Figure 2.3b) Zooming in the graphics window

4. Repeat steps **2** and **3** but create a larger rectangle outside of the first rectangle. Dimensions are shown in Figure 2.4.

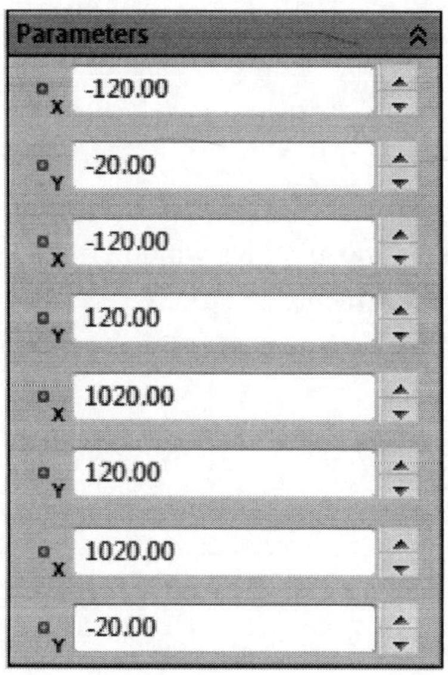

Figure 2.4 Dimensions of second larger rectangle

5. Select **Extruded Boss/Base**. Check the box for **Direction 2** and click **OK** to exit the **Boss-Extrude Property Manager**.

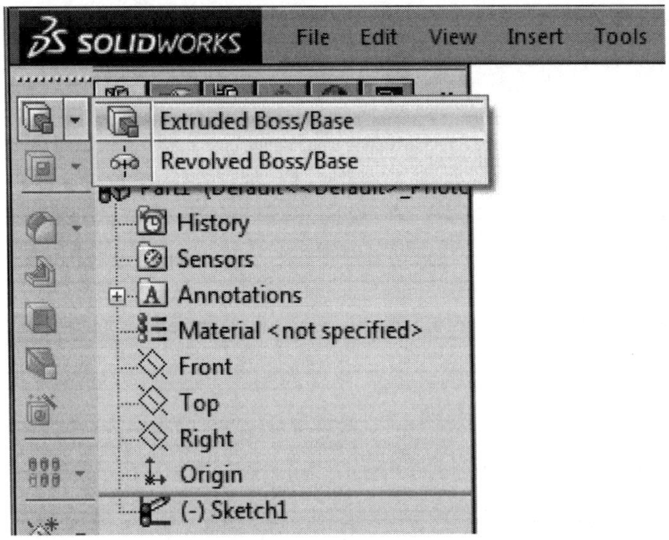

Figure 2.5a) Selection of extrusion feature

Figure 2.5b) Closing the property manager

6. Select **Front** from the **View Orientation** drop down menu in the graphics window. Click on **Front Plane** in the **FeatureManager design tree.** Select the **Line** sketch tool.

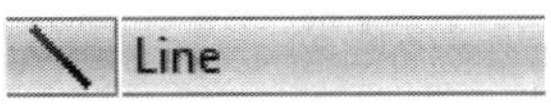

Figure 2.6 Selection of the line sketch tool

7. Draw a vertical line in the Y-direction in the front plane starting at the lower inner surface of the sketch. Set the **Parameters** and **Additional Parameters** to the values shown in the figure. Close the **Line Properties** dialog and the **Inert Line** dialog.

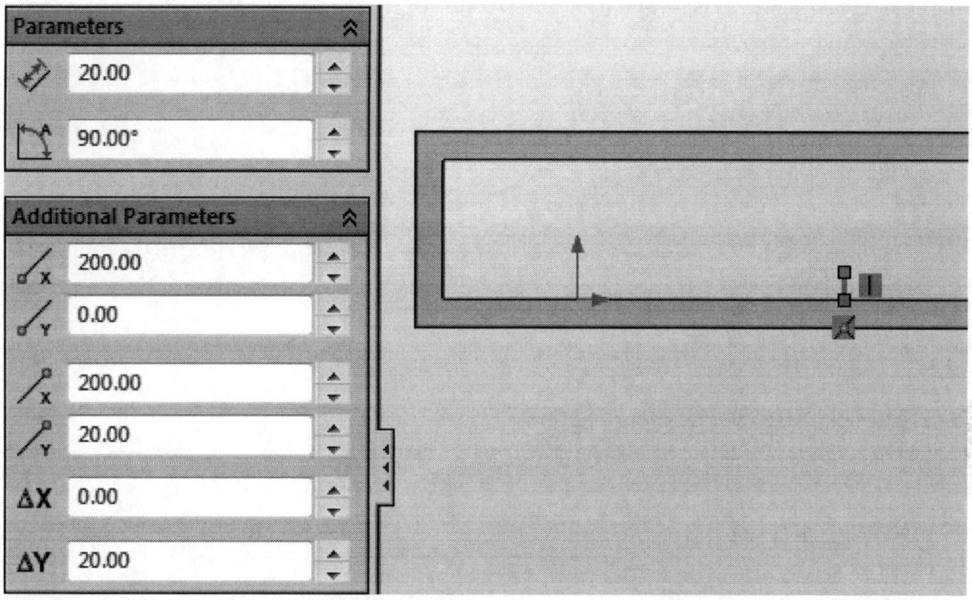

Figure 2.7 Parameters for vertical line

8. Repeat step **7** three more times and add three more vertical lines to the sketch: the second line at X = 400 mm with a length of 40 mm, the third line at X = 600 mm with a length of 60 mm and the fourth line at X = 800 mm with a length of 80 mm. These lines will be used to plot the boundary layer velocity profiles at different streamwise positions along the flat plate. Close the **Line Properties** dialog and the **Insert Line** dialog. Save the SOLIDWORKS part with the following name: **Flat Plate Boundary Layer Study 2015**. Rename the newly created sketch in the **FeatureManager design tree**; see figure 2.8. Click on the **Rebuild** symbol in the SOLIDWORKS menu.

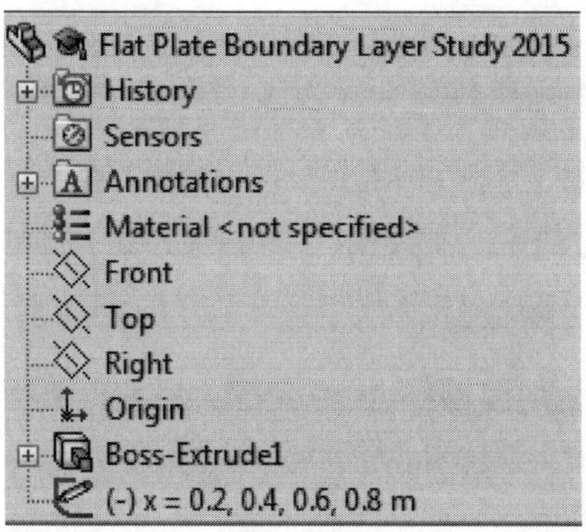

Figure 2.8 Renaming the sketch for boundary layer velocity profiles

9. Repeat step **6** and draw a horizontal line in the X-direction starting at the origin of the lower inner surface of the sketch. Click on **Origin** in the **FeatureManager design tree** to find the location of the origin. Set the **Parameters** and **Additional Parameters** to the values shown in the figure and close the **Line Properties** dialog and the **Insert Line** dialog. Rename the sketch in the **FeatureManager design tree** and call it **x = 0 – 0.9 m**. Click on the **Rebuild** symbol.

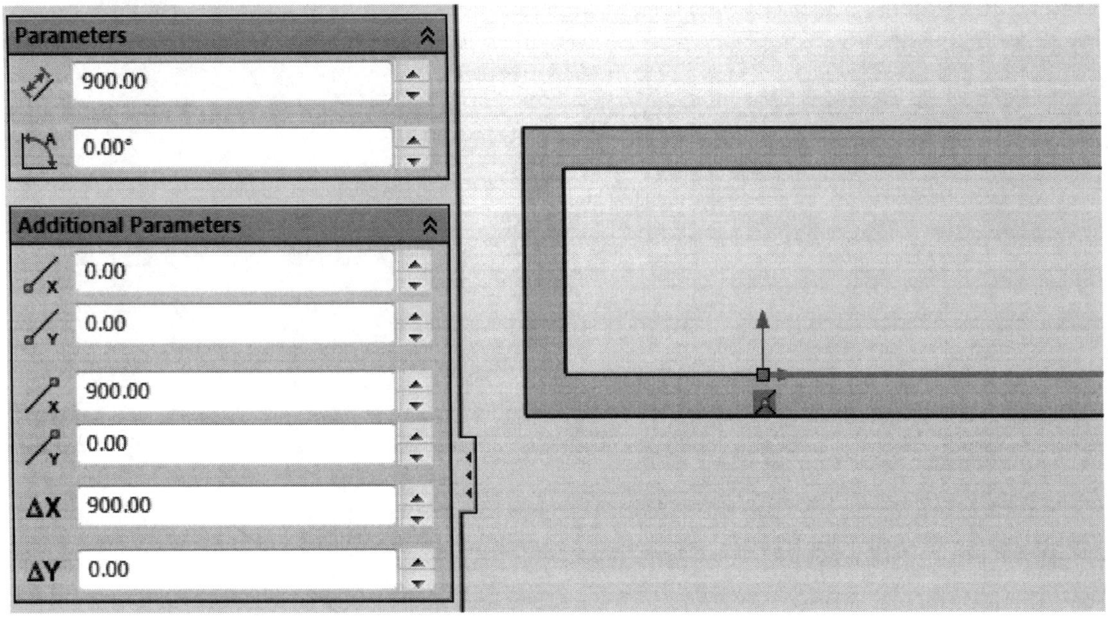

Figure 2.9 Adding a line in the X-direction

10. Next, we will create a split line. Repeat step **6** once again, but this time select the **Top Plane** and draw a line in the Z-direction through the origin of the lower inner surface of the sketch. It will help to zoom in and rotate the view to complete this step. Set the **Parameters** and **Additional Parameters** to the values shown in the figure and close the dialog.

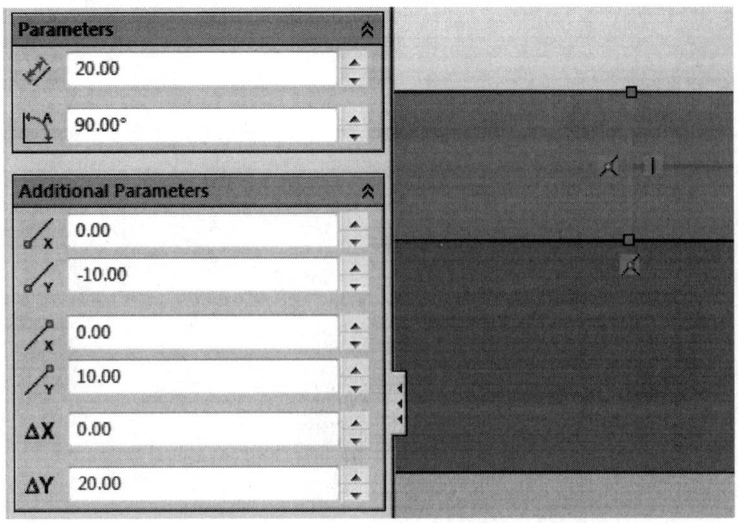

Figure 2.10 Drawing a line in the Z-direction

11. Rename the sketch in the **FeatureManager design tree** and call it **Split Line**. Click on the **Rebuild** symbol once again. Select **Insert>>Curve>>Split Line…** from the SOLIDWORKS menu. Select **Projection** under **Type to Split**. Select Split Line for **Sketch to Project** under **Selections**. For **Faces to Split**, select the surface where you have drawn your split line; see figure 2.11b). Close the dialog. You have now finished the part for the flat plate boundary layer. Select **File>>Save** from the SOLIDWORKS menu.

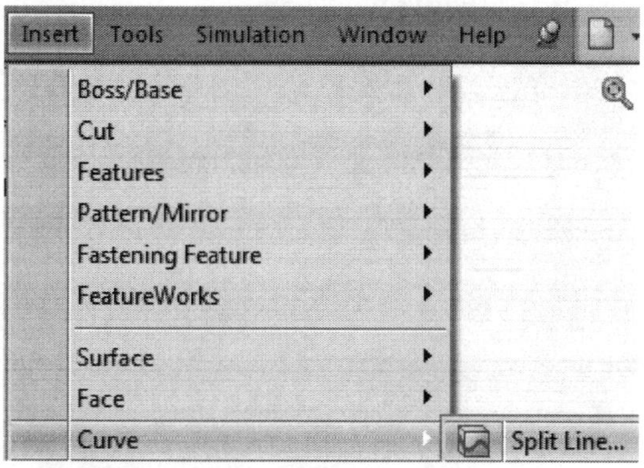

Figure 2.11a) Creating a split line

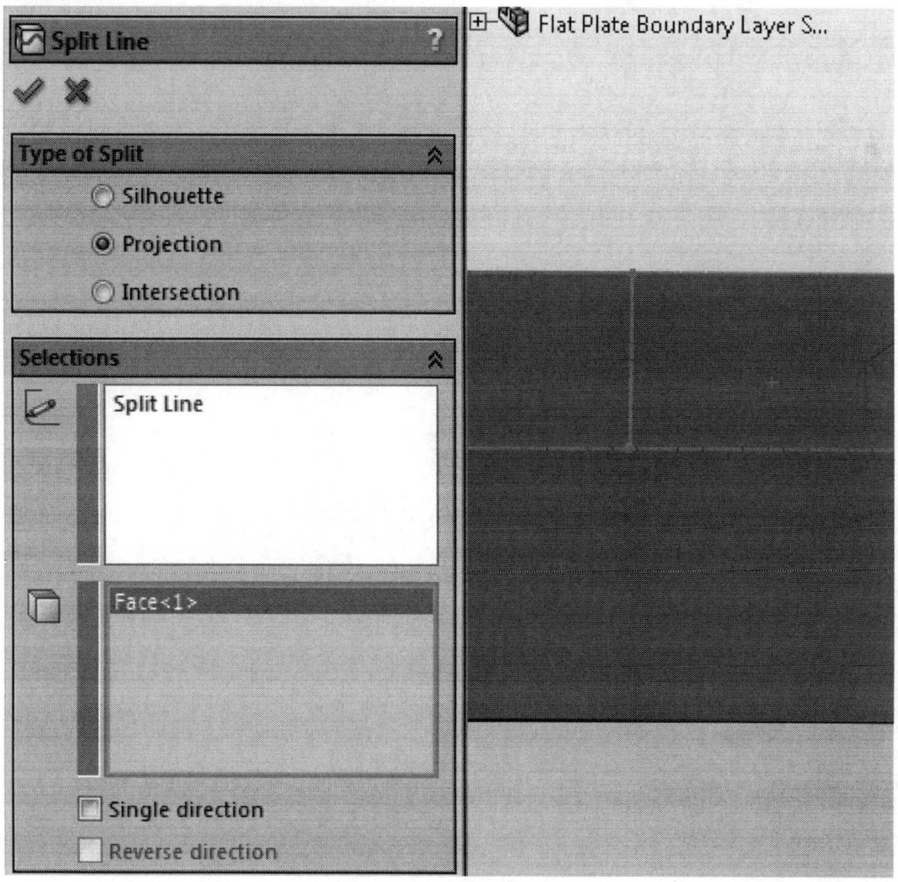

Figure 2.11b) Selection of surface for the split line

Setting Up the Flow Simulation Project

12. If Flow Simulation is not available in the menu, you have to add it from SOLIDWORKS menu: **Tools>>Add Ins…** and check the corresponding **SOLIDWORKS Flow Simulation 2015** box. Select **Tools>>Flow Simulation>>Project>>Wizard** to create a new Flow Simulation project. Enter Project name "**Flat Plate Boundary Layer Study**." Click on the **Next >** button. Select the default **SI (m-kg-s)** unit system and click on the **Next>** button once again.

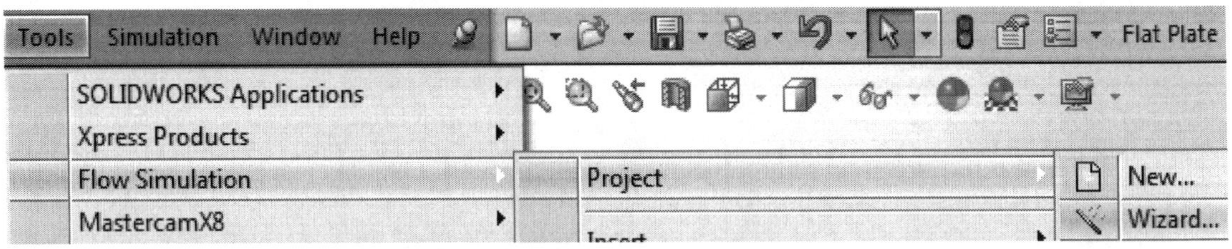

Figure 2.12a) Starting a new Flow Simulation project

Figure 2.12b) Creating a name for the project

13. Use the default **Internal Analysis type** and click on the **Next>** button once again.

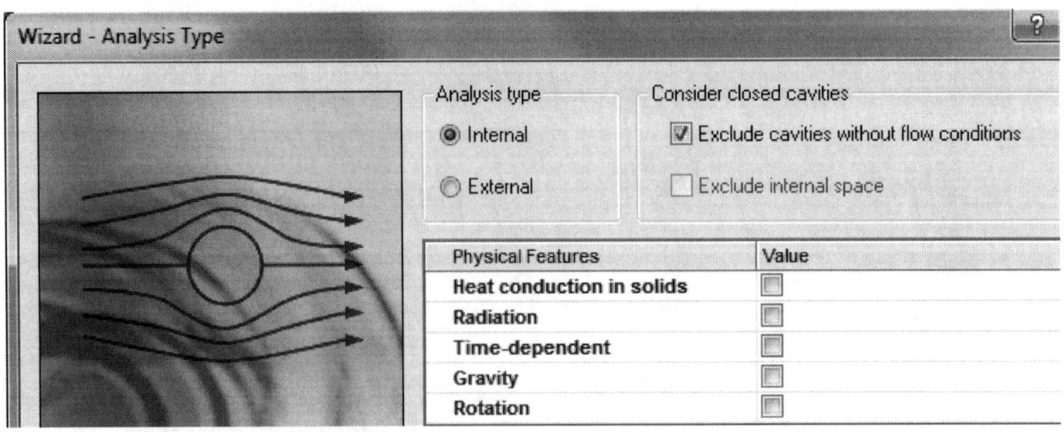

Figure 2.13 Excluding cavities without flow conditions

14. Select **Air** from the **Gases** and add it as **Project Fluid**. Select **Laminar Only** from the **Flow Type** drop down menu. Click on the **Next** > button. Use the default **Wall Conditions** and click on the **Next** > button. Insert **5 m/s** for **Velocity in X direction** as **Initial Conditions** and click on the **Next** > button. Slide the **Result resolution** to **8**. Click on the **Finish** button. You will get a fluid volume recognition failure message. Answer Yes to this and all other questions and create a lid on each side of the model.

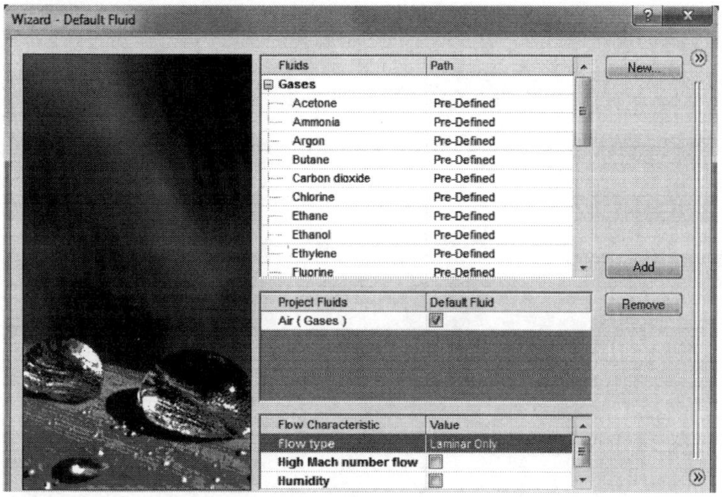

Figure 2.14 Selection of fluid for the project and flow type

15. Select **Tools>>Flow Simulation>>Computational Domain…**. Click on the **2D simulation** button under **Type** and select **XY plane**. Close the **Computational Domain** dialog .

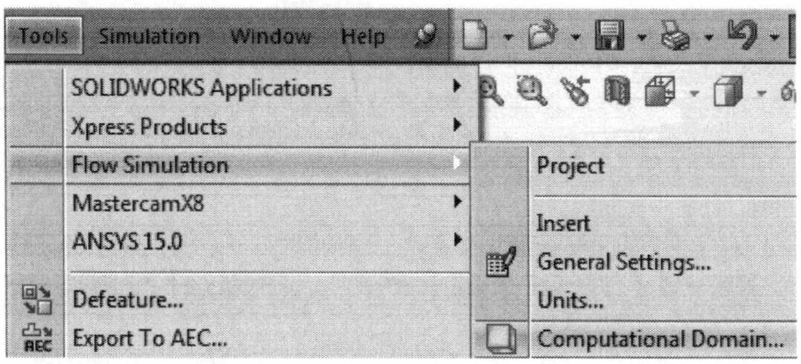

Figure 2.15a) Modifying the computational domain

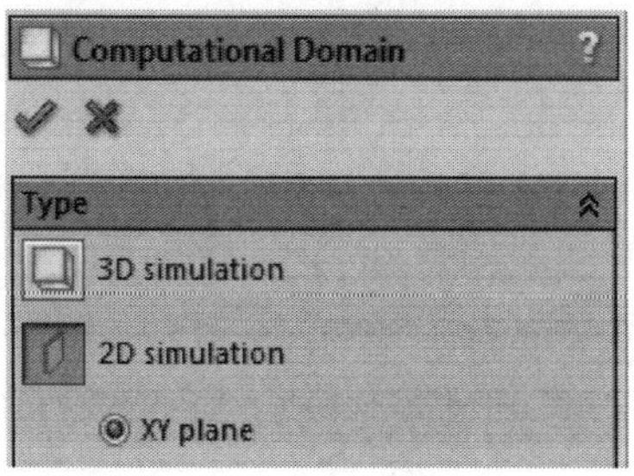

Figure 2.15b) Selecting 2D simulation in the XY plane

16. Select **Tools>>Flow Simulation>>Initial Mesh…**. Uncheck the **Automatic setting** box at the bottom of the window. Change the **Number of cells per X:** to **300**, the **Number of cells per Y:** to **200**, and the **Number of cells per Z:** to **1**. Click on the **OK** button to exit the **Initial Mesh** window.

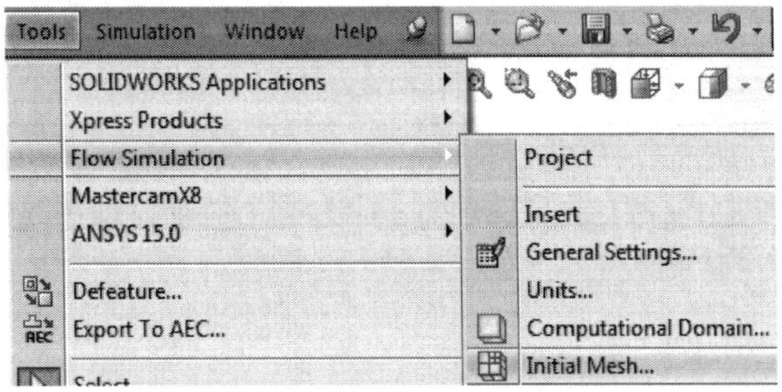

Figure 2.16a) Modifying the initial mesh

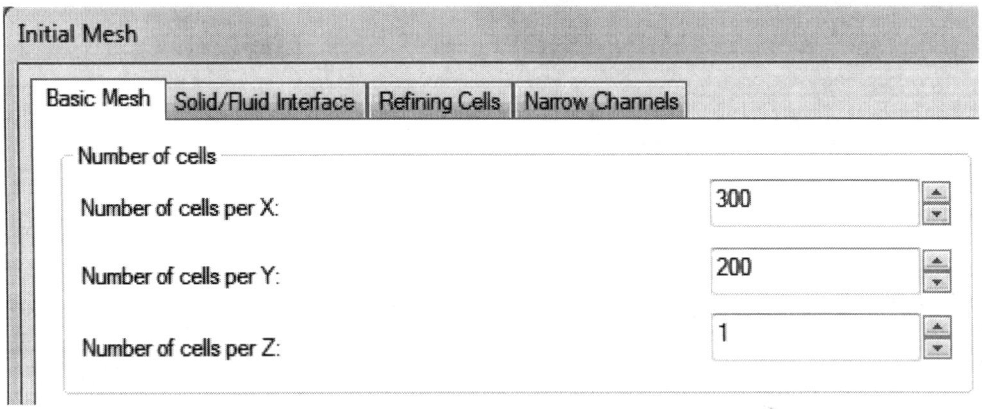

Figure 2.16b) Changing the number of cells in two directions

Selecting Boundary Conditions

17. Select the **Flow Simulation analysis tree** tab, open the **Input Data** folder by clicking on the plus sign next to it and right click on **Boundary Conditions**. Select **Insert Boundary Condition…**. Select Wireframe as the **Display Style**. Right click in the graphics window and select **Zoom/Pan/Rotate>>Zoom to Fit**. Once again, right click in the graphics window and select **Zoom/Pan/Rotate>>Rotate View**. Click and drag the mouse so that the inner surface of the left boundary is visible. Right click again and unselect **Zoom/Pan/Rotate>>Rotate View**. Right click on the left inflow boundary surface and select **Select Other**. Select the Face corresponding to the inflow boundary. Select **Inlet Velocity** in the **Type** portion of the **Boundary Condition** window and set the velocity to **5 m/s** in the **Flow Parameters** window. Click **OK** to exit the window. Right click in the graphics window and select **Zoom to Area** and select an area around the left boundary.

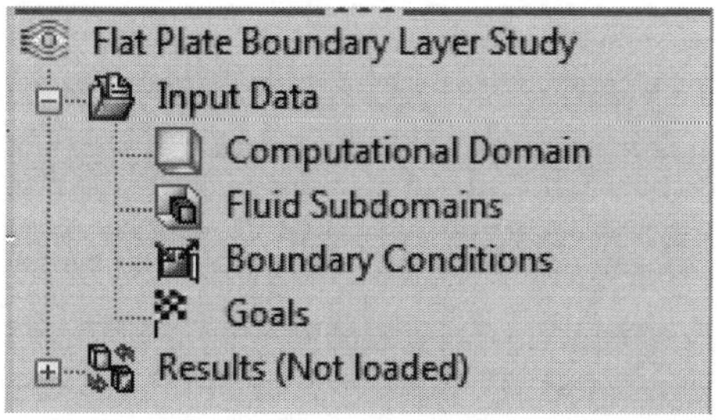

Figure 2.17a) Inserting boundary condition

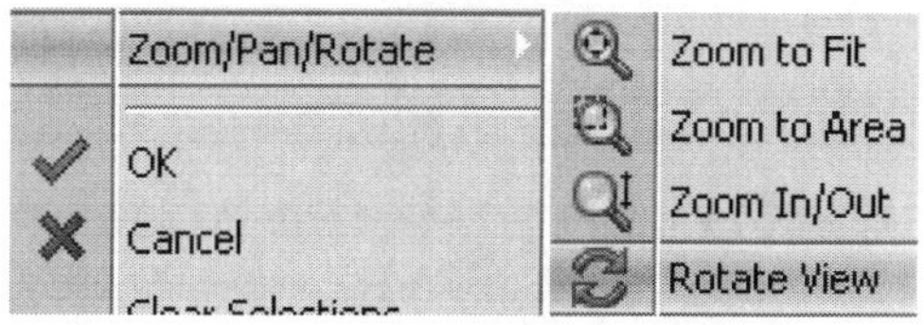

Figure 2.17b) Modifying the view

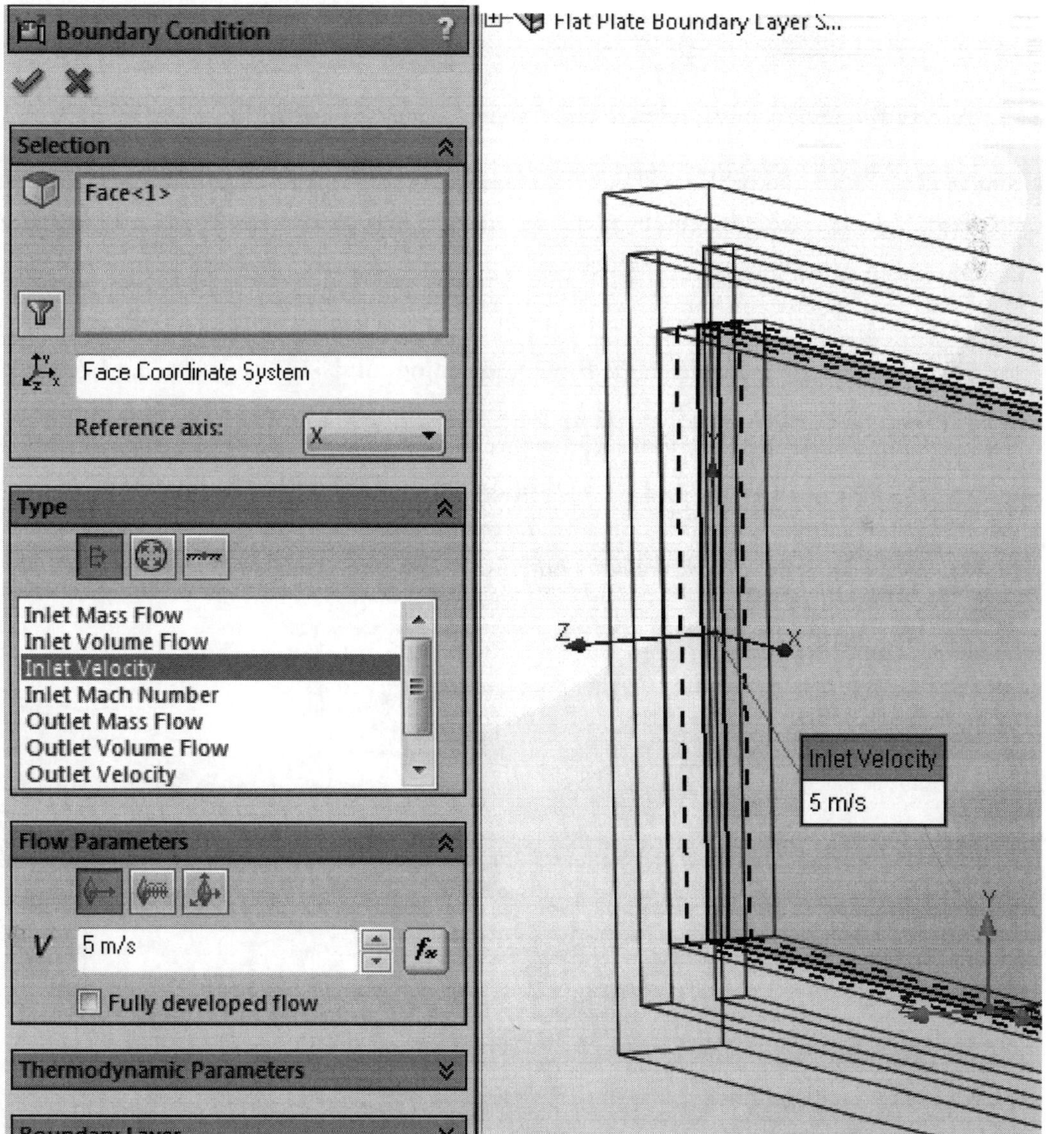

Figure 2.17c) Velocity boundary condition on the inflow

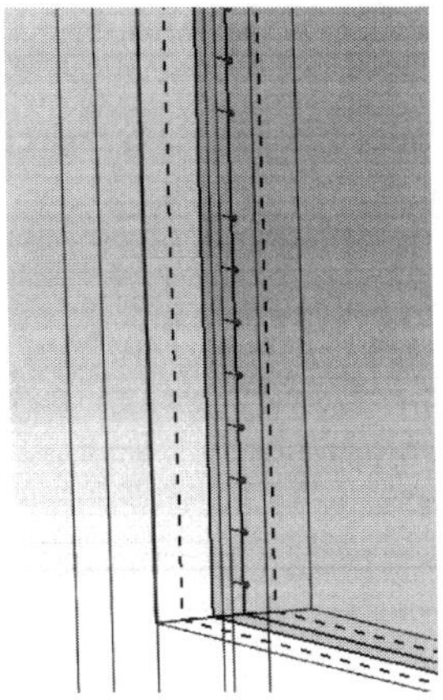

Figure 2.17d) Inlet velocity boundary condition indicated by arrows

18. Red arrows pointing in the flow direction appear, indicating the inlet velocity boundary condition; see figure 2.17d). Right click in the graphics window and select **Zoom to Fit**. Right click again in the graphics window and select **Rotate View** once again to rotate the part so that the inner right surface is visible in the graphics window. Right click and click on **Select**. Right click on **Boundary Conditions** in the **Flow Simulation analysis tree** and select **Insert Boundary Condition…**. Right click on the outflow boundary surface and select **Select Other**. Select the Face corresponding to the outflow boundary. Click on the **Pressure Openings** button in the **Type** portion of the **Boundary Condition** window and select **Static Pressure**. Click OK to exit the window. If you zoom in on the outlet boundary, you will see blue arrows indicating the static pressure boundary condition; see figure 2.18b).

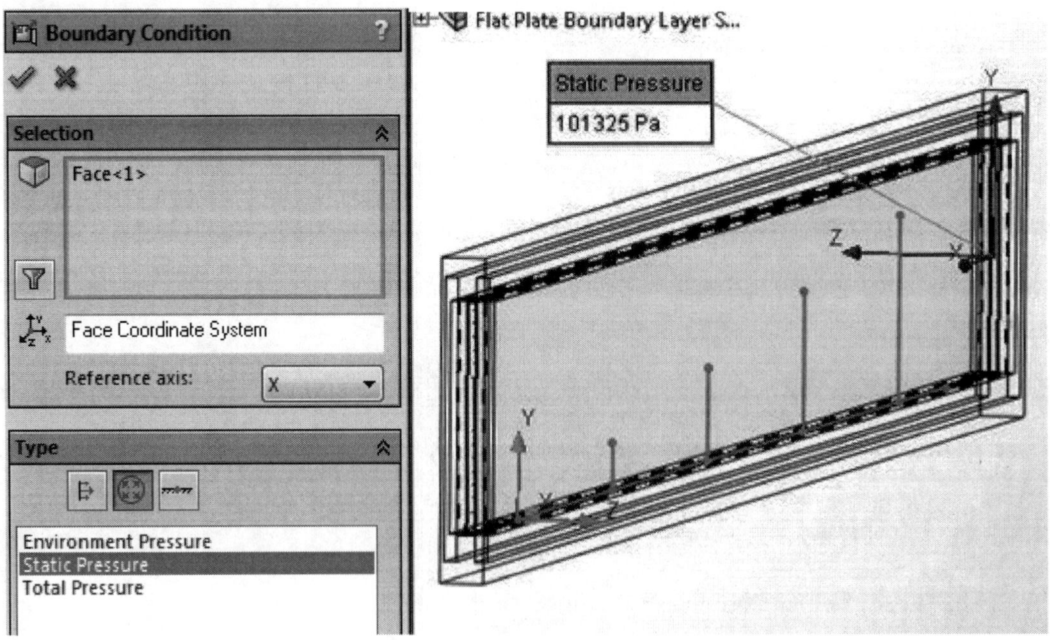

Figure 2.18a) Selection of static pressure as boundary condition at the outlet of the flow region

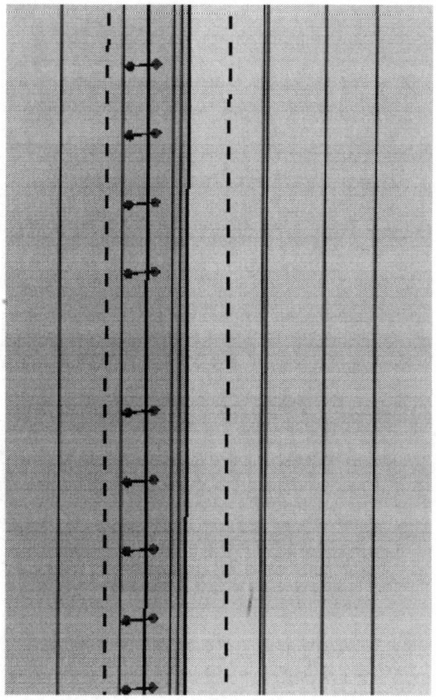

Figure 2.18b) Outlet static pressure boundary condition

19. Enter the following boundary conditions: **Ideal Wall** for the lower and upper walls at the inflow region; see figures 2.19. These will be adiabatic and frictionless walls.

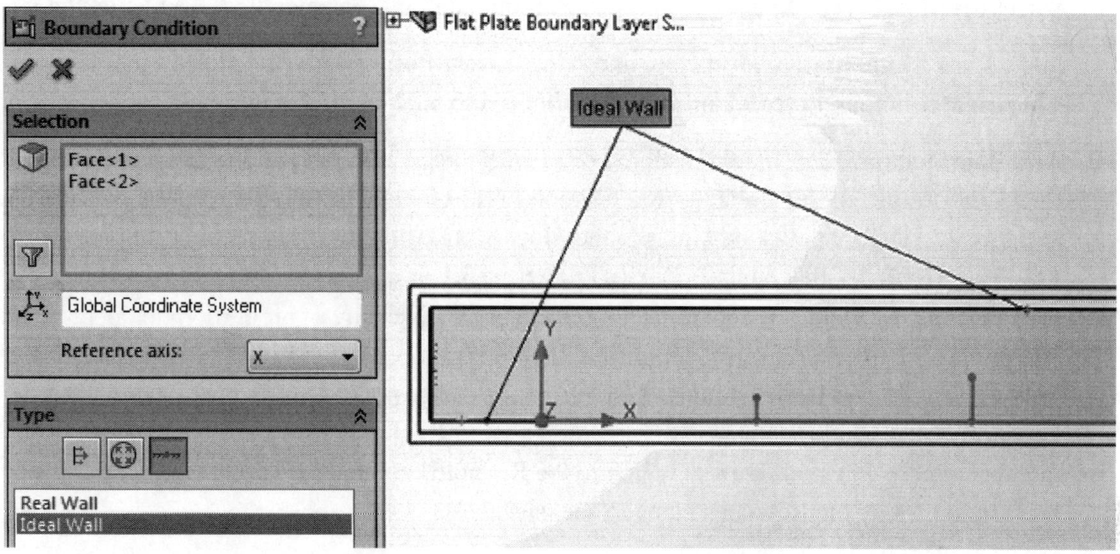

Figure 2.19 Ideal wall boundary condition for two wall sections

20. The last boundary condition will be in the form of a **Real Wall**. We will study the development of the boundary layer on this wall.

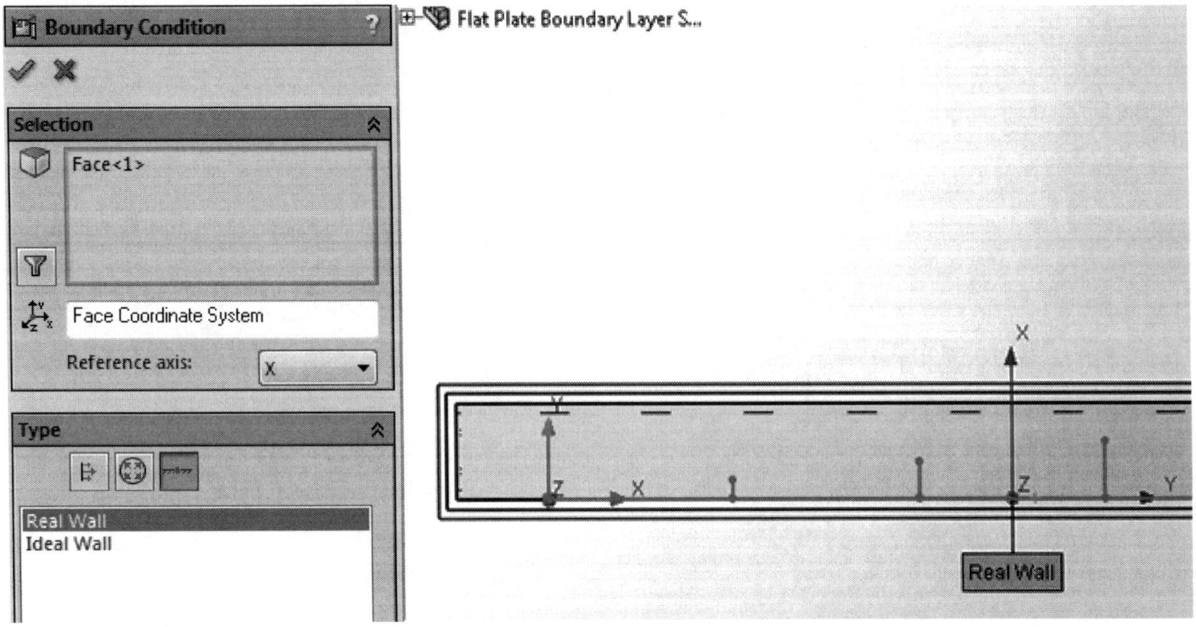

Figure 2.20 Real wall boundary condition for the flat plate

Inserting Global Goals

21. Right click on **Goals** in the **Flow Simulation analysis tree** and select **Insert Global Goals….** Select **Friction Force (X)** as a global goal. Exit the **Global Goals** window. Right click on **Goals** in the **Flow Simulation analysis tree** and select **Insert Point Goals….** Click on the **Point Coordinates** button. Enter **0.2 m** for X coordinate and **0.02 m** for Y coordinate and click on the **Add Point** button. Add three more points with the coordinates shown in figure 2.21e). Check the **Value** box for **Velocity (X)**. Exit the **Point Goals** window. Rename the goals as shown in figure 2.21f). Right click on **Goals** in the **Flow Simulation analysis tree** and select **Insert Equation Goal….** Click on the **Velocity (X) at x = 0.2 m** goal in the **Flow Simulation analysis tree**, multiply by $x = 0.2$ m and divide by the kinematic viscosity of air at room temperature (ν = 1.516E-5 m^2/s) to get an expression for the Reynolds number in the **Equation Goal** window; see figure 2.21g). Select **Dimensionless LMA** from the dimensionality drop down menu. Exit the **Equation Goal** window. Rename the equation goal to **Reynolds number at x = 0.2 m**. Insert three more equation goals corresponding to the Reynolds numbers at the three other ***x*** locations. For a definition of the Reynolds number, see page 2-21.

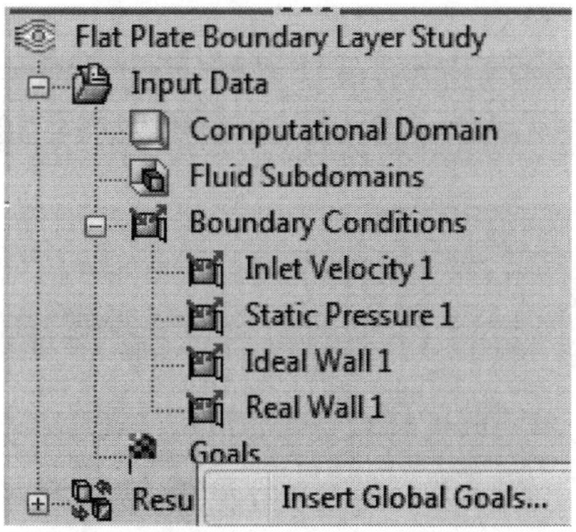

Figure 2.21a) Inserting global goals

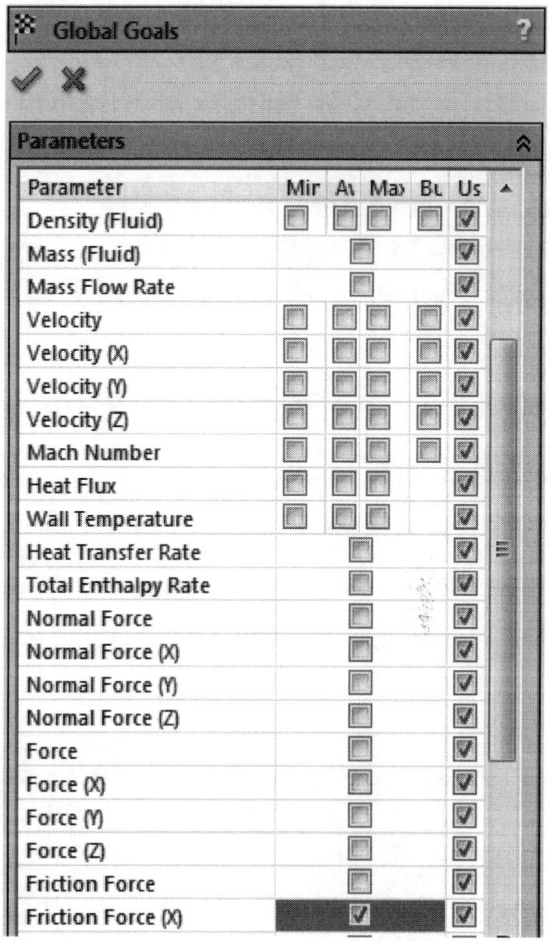

Figure 2.21b) Selection of shear force

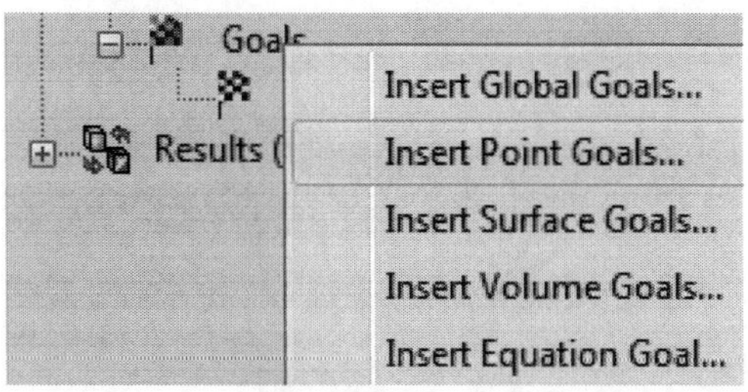

Figure 2.21c) Inserting point goals

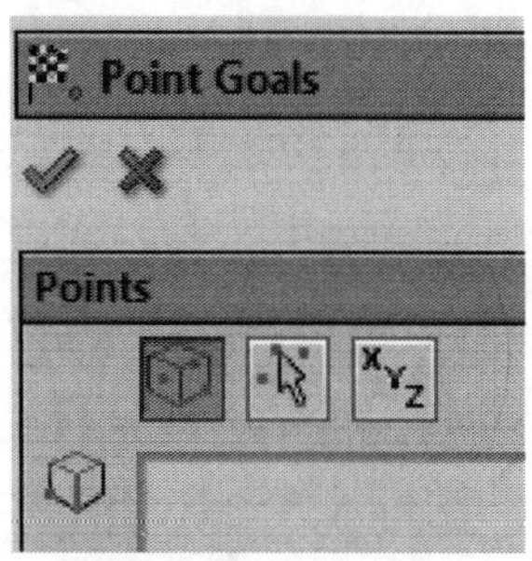

Figure 2.21d) Selecting point coordinates

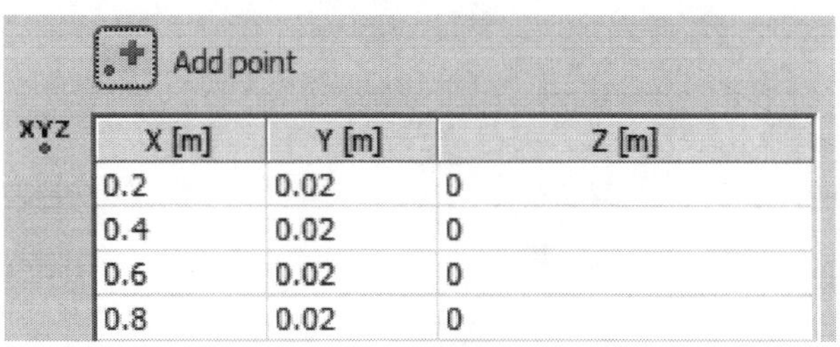

Figure 2.21e) Coordinates for point goals

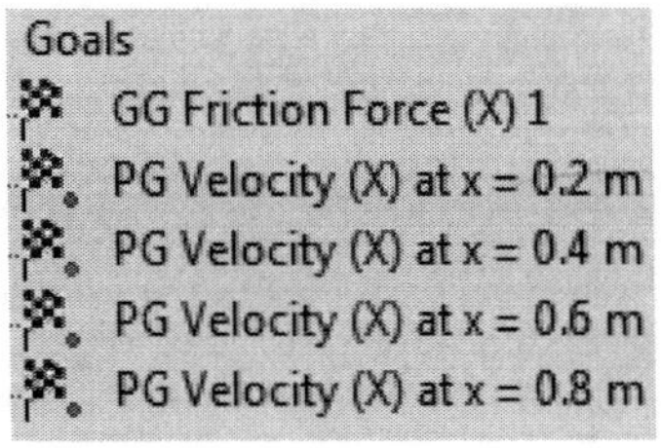

Figure 2.21f) Renaming the point goals

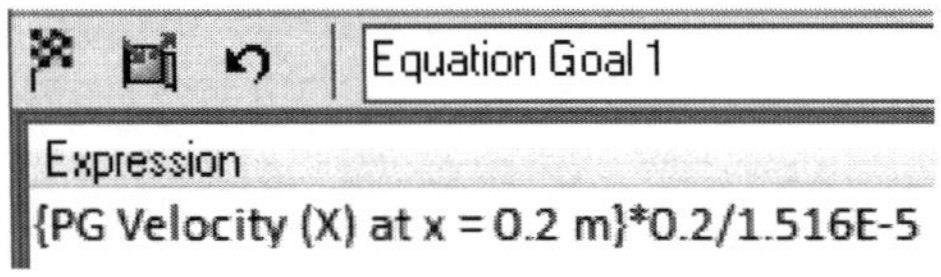

Figure 2.21g) Entering an equation goal

Running the Calculations

22. Select **Tools>>Flow Simulation>>Solve>>Run** from the SOLIDWORKS menu to start the calculations. Click on the **Run** button in the **Run** window. Click on the goals button in the **Solver** window to see the **List of Goals**.

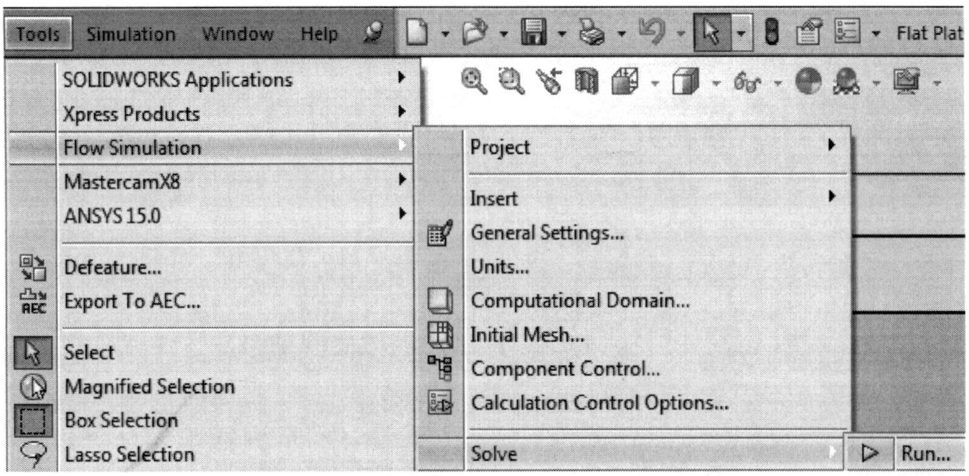

Figure 2.22a) Starting calculations

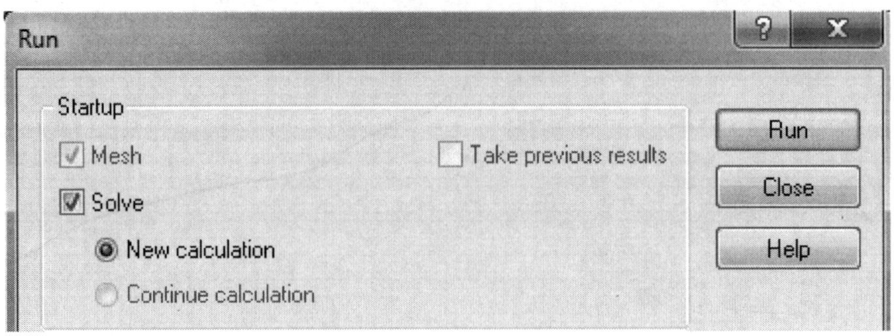

Figure 2.22b) Run window

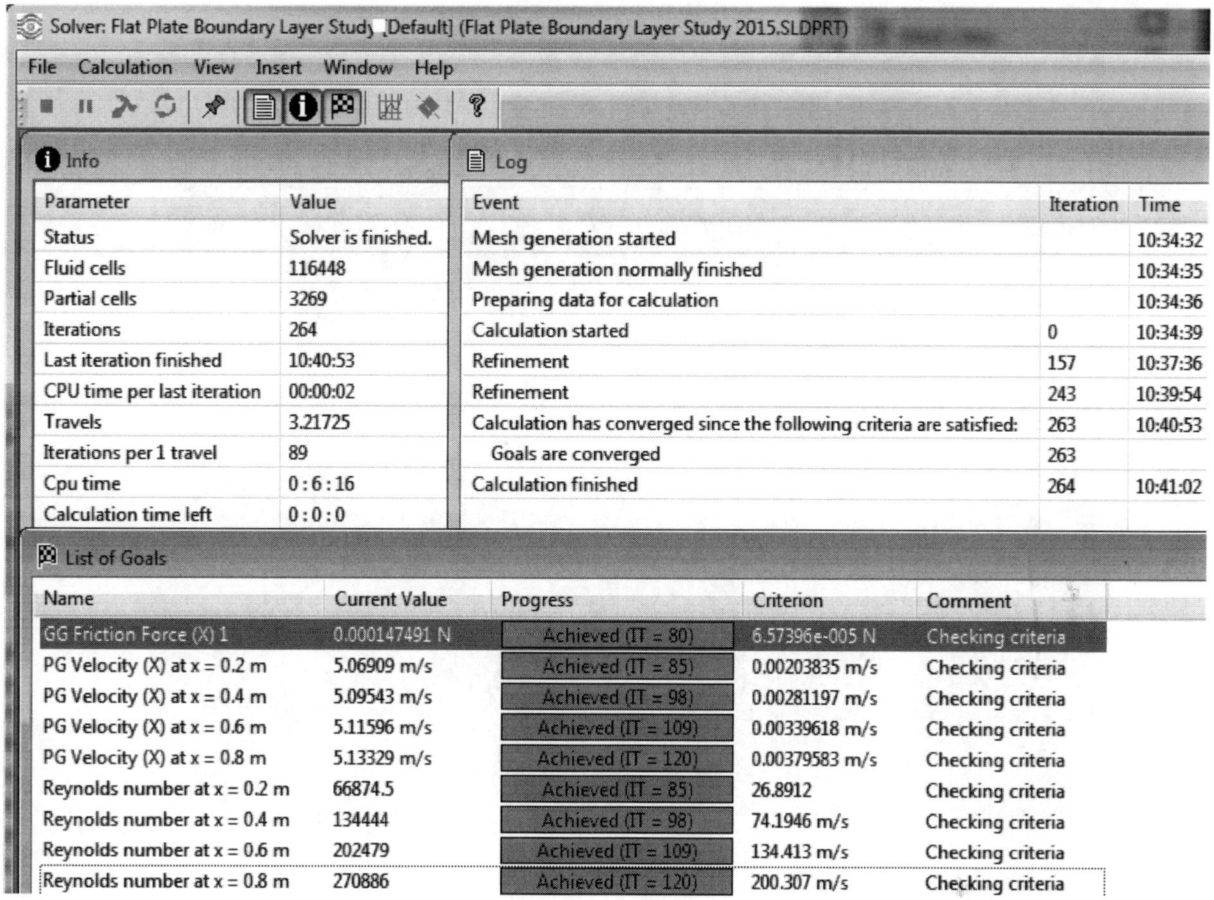

Figure 2.22c) Solver window

Using Cut Plots to Visualize the Flow Field

23. Right click on Cut Plots in the **Flow Simulation analysis tree** under **Results** and select **Insert…**. Select the **Front Plane** from the **FeatureManager design tree**. Slide the **Number of Levels** slide bar to 255. Select **Pressure** from the **Parameter** drop down menu. Click OK to exit the **Cut Plot** window. Figure 2.23a) shows the high pressure region close to the leading edge of the flat plate. Rename the cut plot to **Pressure**. You can get more lighting on the cut plot by selecting **Tools>>Flow Simulation>>Results>>Display>>Lighting** from the SOLIDWORKS menu. Right click on the **Pressure Cut Plot** in the **Flow Simulation analysis tree** and select **Hide**. Repeat this step but instead choose **Velocity (X)** from the **Parameter** drop down menu. Rename the second cut plot to **Velocity (X)**. Figures 2.23b) and 2.23c) are showing the velocity boundary layer close to the wall.

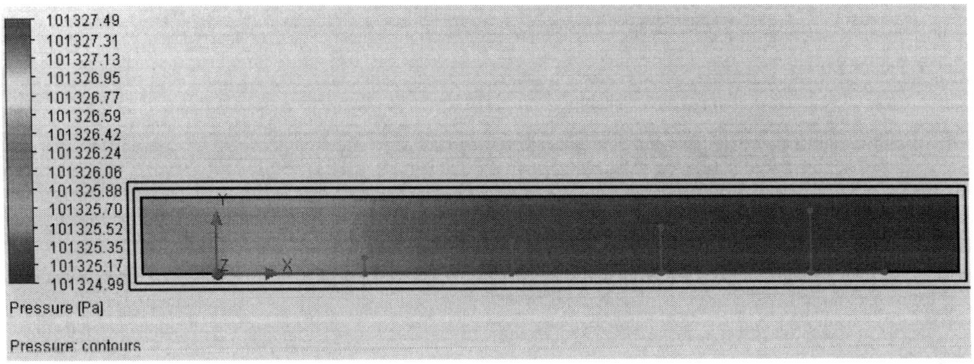

Figure 2.23a) Pressure distribution along the flat plate

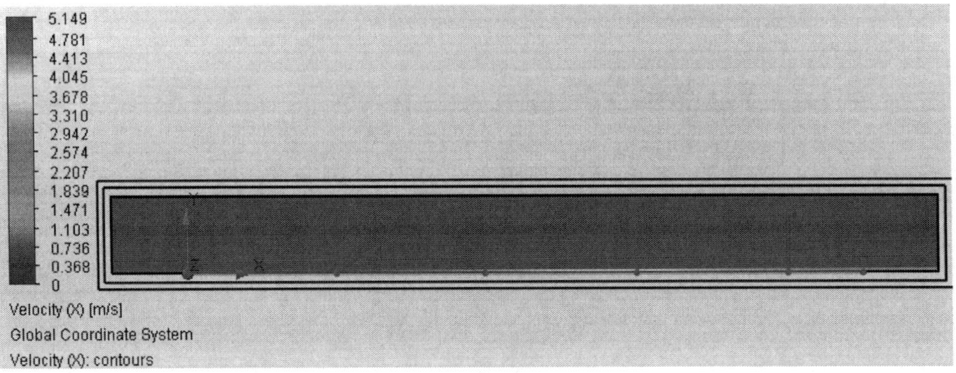

Figure 2.23b) X – Component of Velocity distribution on the flat plate

Figure 2.23c) Close up view of the velocity boundary layer

Using XY Plots with Templates

24. Place the file **"graph 2.24c)"** on the desktop. This file and the other exercise files are available for download at www.sdcpublications.com/downloads/978-1-58503-934-0/

Click on the **FeatureManager design tree**. Click on the sketch **x = 0.2, 0.4, 0.6, 0.8 m**.

Click on the **Flow Simulation analysis tree** tab. Right click **XY Plot** and select **Insert….** Check the **Velocity (X)** box. Open the **Resolution** portion of the **XY Plot** window and slide the **Geometry Resolution** as far as it goes to the right. Click on the **Evenly Distribute Output Points** button and increase the number of points to **500**. Open the **Options** portion and check the **Display boundary layer** box. Select the **"Excel Workbook (*.xlsx)"** from the drop down menu. Click **Export to Excel** to create the **XY Plot** window. An **Excel** file will open with a graph of the velocity in the boundary layer at different streamwise positions.

Double click on the **graph 2.24c)** file to open the file. Click on **Enable Content** if you get a **Security Warning** that **Macros** have been disabled. If **Developer** is not available in the menu of the **Excel** file, you will need to do the following: Select **File>>Options** from the menu and click on the **Customize Ribbon** on the left hand side. Check the **Developer** box on the right hand side under **Main Tabs**. Click **OK** to exit the **Excel Options** window.

Click on the **Developer** tab in the **Excel** menu for the **graph 2.24c)** file and select **Visual Basic** on the left hand side to open the editor. Click on the plus sign next to **VBAProject (XY Plot 1.xlsx)** and click on the plus sign next to **Microsoft Excel Objects**. Right click on **Sheet2 (Plot Data)** and select **View Object**.

Select **Module1** in the **Modules** folder under **VBAProject (graph 2.24c).xlsm)**. Select **Run>>Run Macro** from the menu of the **MVB for Applications** window. Click on the **Run** button in the **Macros** window. Figure 2.24c) will become available in **Excel** showing the streamwise velocity component ***u (m/s)*** versus wall normal coordinate ***y (m)***. Close the **XY Plot** window and the **graph 2.24c)** window in **Excel**. Exit the **XY Plot** window in **SOLIDWORKS Flow Simulation** and rename the inserted xy-plot in the **Flow Simulation analysis tree** to **Laminar Velocity Boundary Layer**.

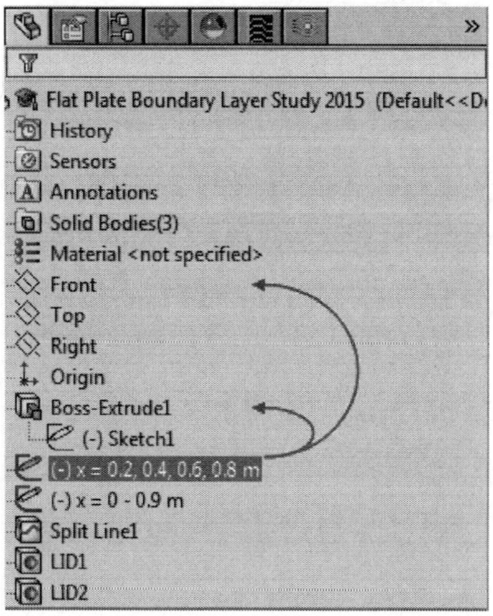

Figure 2.24a) Sketch for the XY Plot

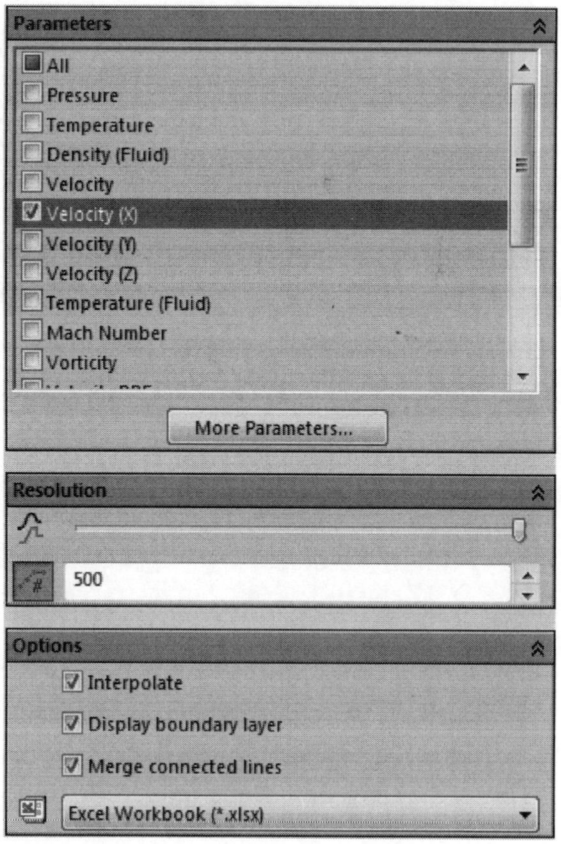

Figure 2.24b) Settings for the XY Plot

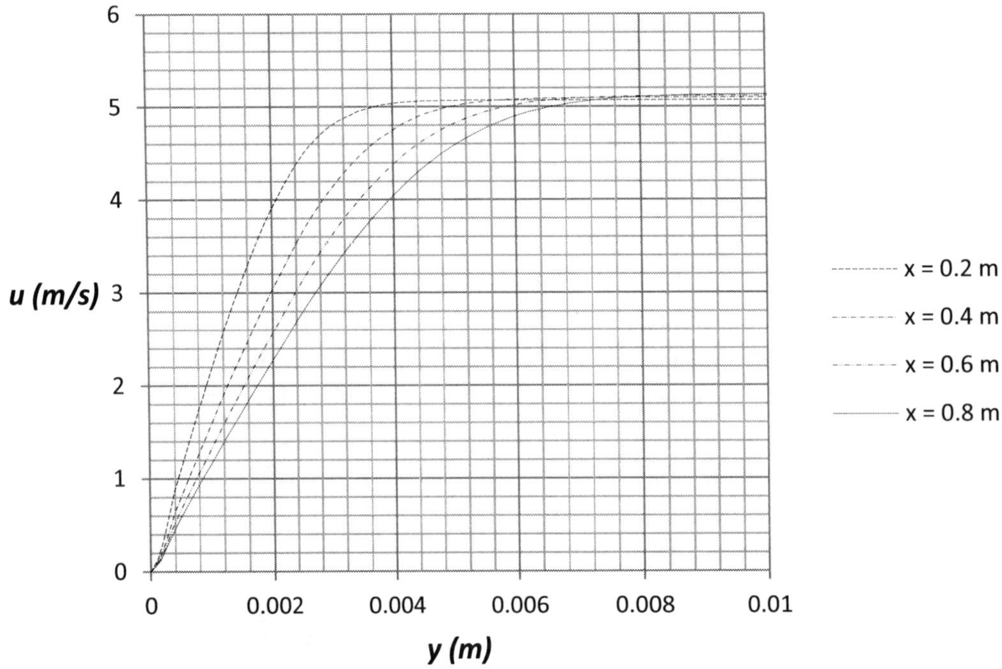

Figure 2.24c) Boundary layer velocity profiles on a flat plate at different streamwise positions

Comparison of Flow Simulation Results with Theory and Empirical Data

25. We now want to compare this velocity profile with the theoretical Blasius velocity profile for laminar flow on a flat plate. First, we have to normalize the steamwise X velocity component with the free stream velocity. Secondly, we have to transform the wall normal coordinate into the similarity coordinate for comparison with the Blasius profile. The similarity coordinate is described by

$$\eta = y\sqrt{\frac{U}{\upsilon x}} \tag{2.1}$$

where y (m) is the wall normal coordinate, U (m/s) is the free stream velocity, x (m) is the distance from the leading edge and υ is the kinematic viscosity of the fluid.

26. Place the file **"graph 2.25a)"** on the desktop. Repeat step **24** to plot Figure 2.25a). Rename the xy-plot to **Comparison with Blasius Profile**.

We see in figure 2.25a) that all profiles at different streamwise positions collapse on the same Blasius curve when we use the boundary layer similarity coordinate.

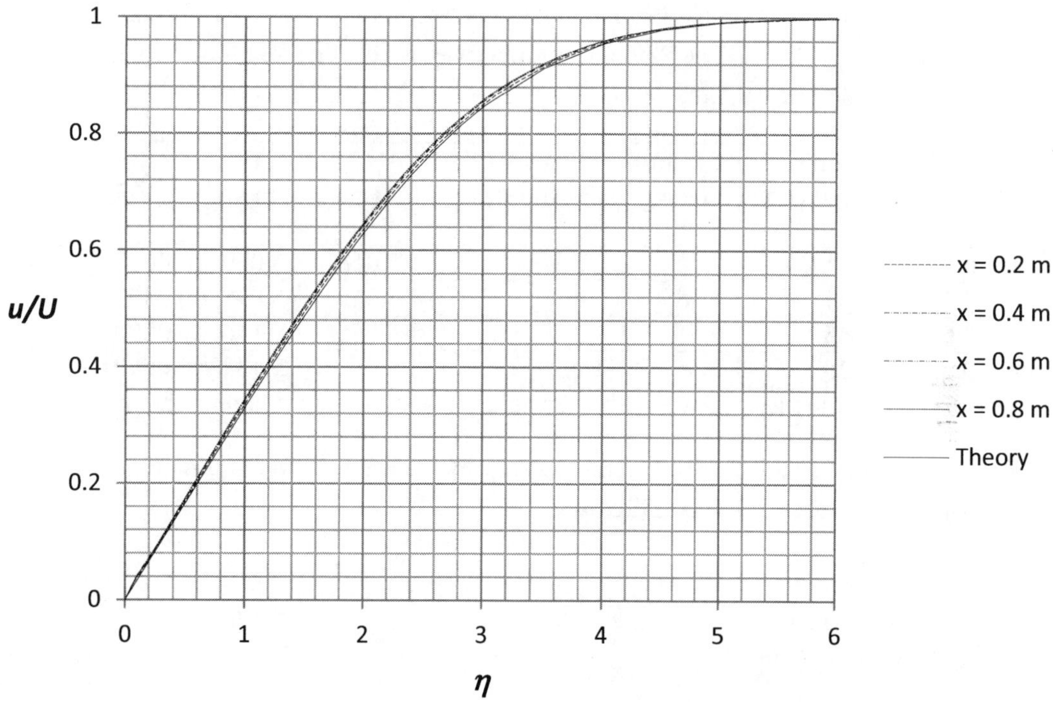

Figure 2.25a) Velocity profiles in comparison with the theoretical Blasius profile (full line)

The Reynolds number for the flow on a flat plate is defined as

$$Re_x = \frac{Ux}{\nu} \tag{2.2}$$

The boundary layer thickness δ is defined as the distance from the wall to the location where the velocity in the boundary layer has reached 99% of the free stream value. The theoretical expression for the thickness of the laminar boundary layer is given by

$$\delta = \frac{4.91x}{\sqrt{Re_x}} \tag{2.3}$$

, and the thickness of the turbulent boundary layer

$$\delta = \frac{0.16x}{{Re_x}^{1/7}} \tag{2.4}$$

From the data of figure 2.24c) we can see that the thickness of the laminar boundary layer is close to 3.80 mm at Re_x = 66,875 corresponding to x = 0.2 m. The free stream velocity at x = 0.2 m is U = 5.069 m/s (see figure 2.22c) for list of goals in solver window) and 99% of this value is U_δ =

5.018 m/s. The boundary layer thickness δ = 3.80 mm from Flow Simulation was found by finding the y position corresponding to the U_δ velocity. This value for δ at x = 0.2 m, and corresponding values further downstream at different x locations are available in the Plot Data for Figure 2.25a). The different values of the boundary layer thickness can be compared with values obtained using equation (3). In table 2.1 comparisons are shown between boundary layer thickness from Flow Simulation and theory corresponding to the four different Reynolds numbers shown in figure 2.24c). The Reynolds number varies between Re_x = 66,875 at x = 0.2 m and Re_x = 270,886 at x = 0.8 m.

x (m)	δ (mm) Simulation	δ (mm) Theory	Percent (%) Difference	U_δ (m/s)	U (m/s)	$\nu\ (\frac{m^2}{s})$	Re_x
0.2	3.81	3.80	0.3	5.018	5.069	0.00001516	66,875
0.4	5.33	5.36	0.5	5.045	5.095	0.00001516	134,444
0.6	6.45	6.55	1.5	5.065	5.116	0.00001516	202,479
0.8	7.38	7.55	2.2	5.082	5.133	0.00001516	270,886

Table 2.1 Comparison between Flow Simulation and theory for laminar boundary layer thickness

27. Place the file **"graph 2.25b)"** on the desktop. Repeat step **24** to plot Figure 2.25b). Rename the xy-plot to **Boundary Layer Thickness**.

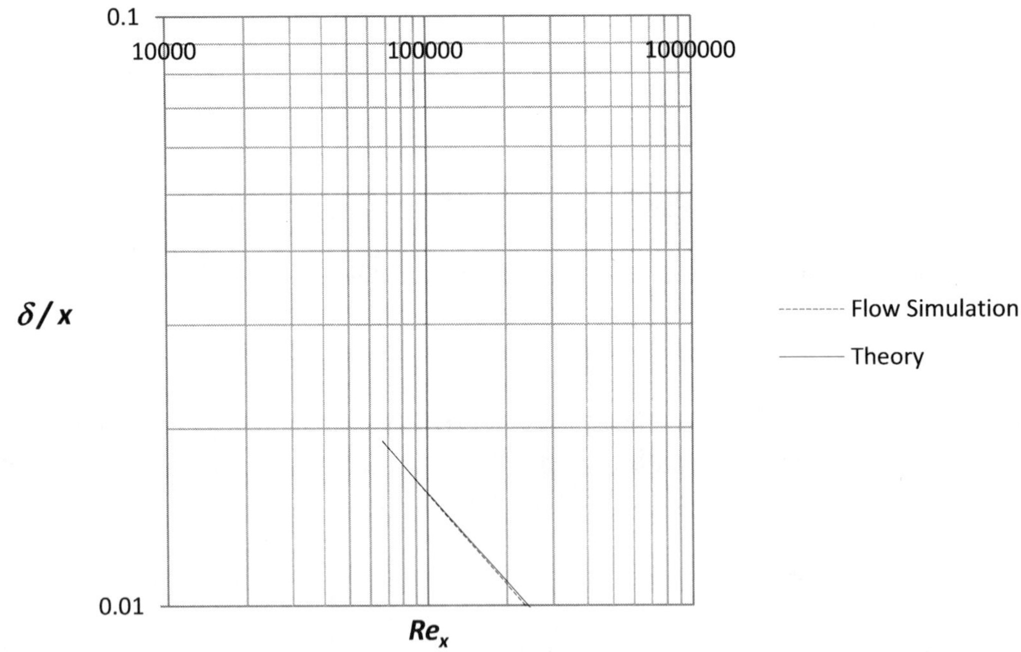

Figure 2.25b) Comparison between Flow Simulation and theory on boundary layer thickness

The displacement thickness is defined as the distance that a streamline outside of the boundary layer is deflected by the boundary layer and is given by the following integral

$$\delta^* = \int_0^\infty (1 - \frac{u}{U}) dy \tag{2.5}$$

The theoretical expression for the displacement thickness of the laminar boundary layer is given by

$$\frac{\delta^*}{x} = \frac{1.72}{\sqrt{Re_x}} \tag{2.6}$$

and the displacement thickness of the turbulent boundary layer

$$\frac{\delta^*}{x} = \frac{0.02}{{Re_x}^{1/7}} \tag{2.7}$$

x (m)	δ^* (mm) Simulation	δ^* (mm) Theory	Percent (%) Difference	Re_x
0.2	1.3342	1.3302	0.3	66,875
0.4	1.8411	1.8764	1.9	134,444
0.6	2.2365	2.2935	2.5	202,479
0.8	2.5657	2.6438	3.0	270,886

Table 2.2 Comparison between Flow Simulation and theory for laminar displacement thickness

Place the file **"graph 2.25c)"** on the desktop. Repeat step **24** to plot Figure 2.25c). Rename the xy-plot to **Displacement Thickness**.

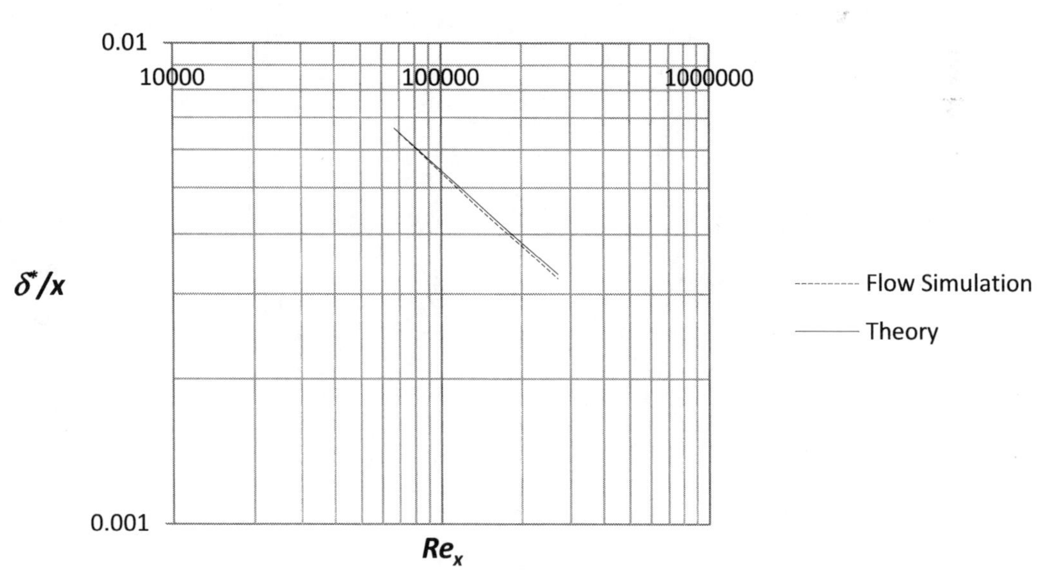

Figure 2.25c) Comparison between Flow Simulation and theory on displacement thickness

The momentum thickness is related to the loss of momentum flux caused by the boundary layer. The momentum thickness is defined by an integral similar to the one for displacement thickness

$$\theta = \int_0^\infty \frac{u}{U}(1 - \frac{u}{U})dy \quad (2.8)$$

The theoretical expression for the momentum thickness of the laminar boundary layer is given by

$$\frac{\theta}{x} = \frac{0.664}{\sqrt{Re_x}} \quad (2.9)$$

and the momentum thickness of the turbulent boundary layer

$$\frac{\theta}{x} = \frac{0.016}{Re_x^{1/7}} \quad (2.10)$$

x (m)	θ (mm) Simulation	θ (mm) Theory	Percent (%) Difference	Re_x
0.2	0.5096	0.5135	0.8	66,875
0.4	0.7080	0.7244	2.3	134,444
0.6	0.8661	0.8854	2.2	202,479
0.8	0.9970	1.0207	2.3	270,886

Table 2.3 Comparison between Flow Simulation and theory for laminar momentum thickness

Place the file **"graph 2.25d)"** on the desktop. Repeat step **24** to plot Figure 2.25d). Rename the xy-plot to **Momentum Thickness**.

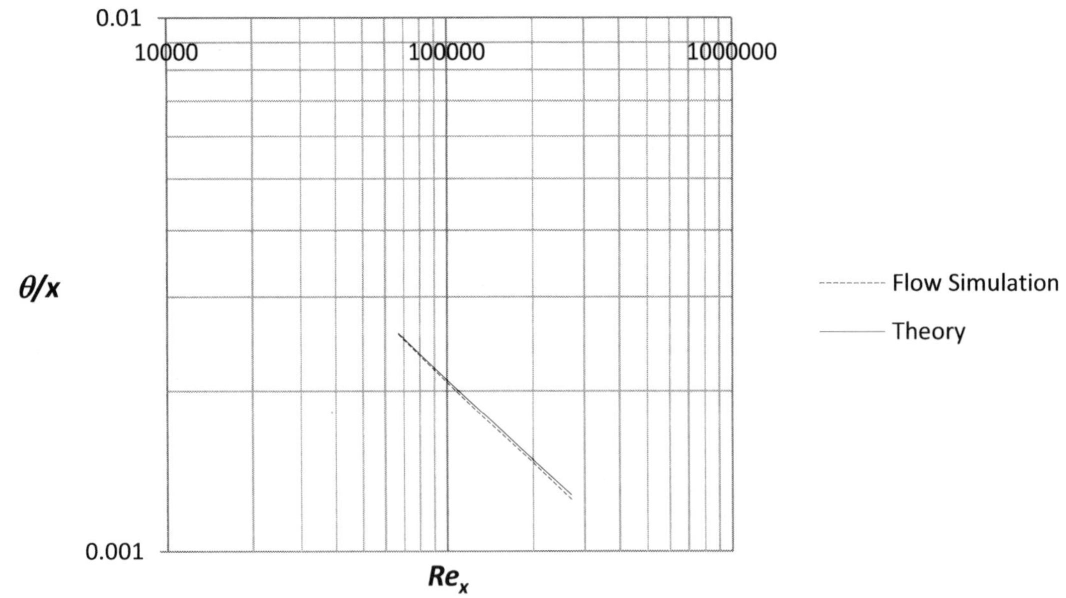

Figure 2.25d) Comparison between Flow Simulation and theory on momentum thickness

Finally, we have the shape factor that is defined as the ratio of the displacement thickness and the momentum thickness.

$$H = \frac{\delta^*}{\theta} \tag{2.11}$$

The theoretical value of the shape factor is $H = 2.59$ for the laminar boundary layer and $H = 1.25$ for the turbulent boundary layer.

x (m)	H Simulation	H Theory	Percent (%) Difference	Re_x
0.2	2.6181	2.59	1.1	66,875
0.4	2.6004	2.59	0.4	134,444
0.6	2.5823	2.59	0.3	202,479
0.8	2.5734	2.59	0.7	270,886

Table 2.4 Comparison between Flow Simulation and theory for laminar shape factor

28. We now want to study how the local friction coefficient varies along the plate. It is defined as the local wall shear stress divided by the dynamic pressure:

$$C_{f,x} = \frac{\tau_w}{\frac{1}{2}\rho U^2} \tag{2.12}$$

The theoretical local friction coefficient for laminar flow is given by

$$C_{f,x} = \frac{0.664}{\sqrt{Re_x}} \qquad Re_x < 5 \cdot 10^5 \tag{2.13}$$

and for turbulent flow

$$C_{f,x} = \frac{0.027}{{Re_x}^{1/7}} \qquad 5 \cdot 10^5 \leq Re_x \leq 10^7 \tag{2.14}$$

Place the file **"graph 2.26"** on the desktop. Repeat step **24** but this time choose the sketch **x = 0 – 0.9 m**, uncheck the box for **Velocity (X)** and check the box for **Shear Stress**. Use the file **"graph 2.26"** to create Figure 2.26. Rename the xy-plot to **Local Friction Coefficient**. Figure 2.26 shows the local friction coefficient versus the Reynolds number compared with theoretical values for laminar boundary layer flow.

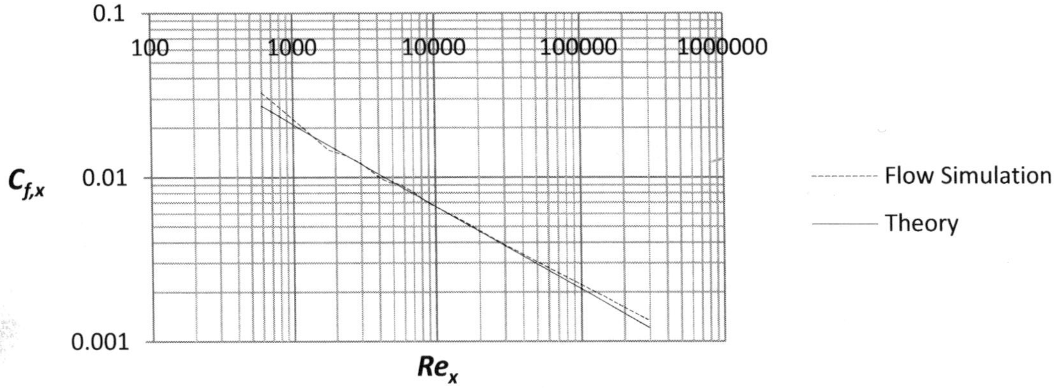

Figure 2.26 Local friction coefficient as a function of the Reynolds number

The average friction coefficient over the whole plate C_f is not a function of the surface roughness for the laminar boundary layer but a function of the Reynolds number based on the length of the plate Re_L; see figure E3 in Exercise 8 at the end of this chapter. This friction coefficient can be determined in Flow Simulation by using the final value of the global goal, the X-component of the Shear Force F_f [see figure 2.22c)], and dividing it by the dynamic pressure times the area A in the X-Z plane of the computational domain related to the flat plate.

$$C_f = \frac{F_f}{\frac{1}{2}\rho U^2 A} = \frac{0.0001475N}{\frac{1}{2} \cdot 1.204kg/m^3 \cdot 5^2 m^2/s^2 \cdot 1m \cdot 0.004m} = 0.00245 \qquad (2.15)$$

$$Re_L = \frac{UL}{\nu} = \frac{5m/s \cdot 1m}{1.516 \cdot 10^{-5} m^2/s} = 3.3 \cdot 10^5 \qquad (16)$$

The average friction coefficient from Flow Simulation can be compared with the theoretical value for laminar boundary layers

$$C_f = \frac{1.328}{\sqrt{Re_L}} = 0.002312 \qquad Re_L < 5 \cdot 10^5 \qquad (2.17)$$

This is a difference of 6 %. For turbulent boundary layers the corresponding expression is

$$C_f = \frac{0.0315}{{Re_L}^{1/7}} \qquad 5 \cdot 10^5 \le Re_L \le 10^7 \qquad (2.18)$$

If the boundary layer is laminar on one part of the plate and turbulent on the remaining part, the average friction coefficient is determined by

$$C_f = \frac{0.0315}{{Re_L}^{1/7}} - \frac{1}{Re_L}\left(0.0315{Re_{cr}}^{\frac{6}{7}} - 1.328\sqrt{Re_{cr}}\right) \qquad (2.19)$$

where Re_{cr} is the critical Reynolds number for laminar to turbulent transition.

Cloning of the Project

29. In the next step, we will clone the project. Select **Tools>>Flow Simulation>>Project>>Clone Project…**. Enter the Project Name "**Flat Plate Boundary Layer Study Using Water**." Select **Create New Configuration** and exit the **Clone Project** window. Next, change the fluid to water in order to get higher Reynolds numbers. Start by selecting **Tools>>Flow Simulation>>General Settings…** from the SOLIDWORKS menu. Click on **Fluids** in the **Navigator** portion and click on the **Remove** button. Select **Water** from the **Liquids** and **Add** it as the **Project Fluid**. Change the **Flow type** to **Laminar and Turbulent**; see figure 2.27d). Click on the **OK** button to close the **General Setting** window.

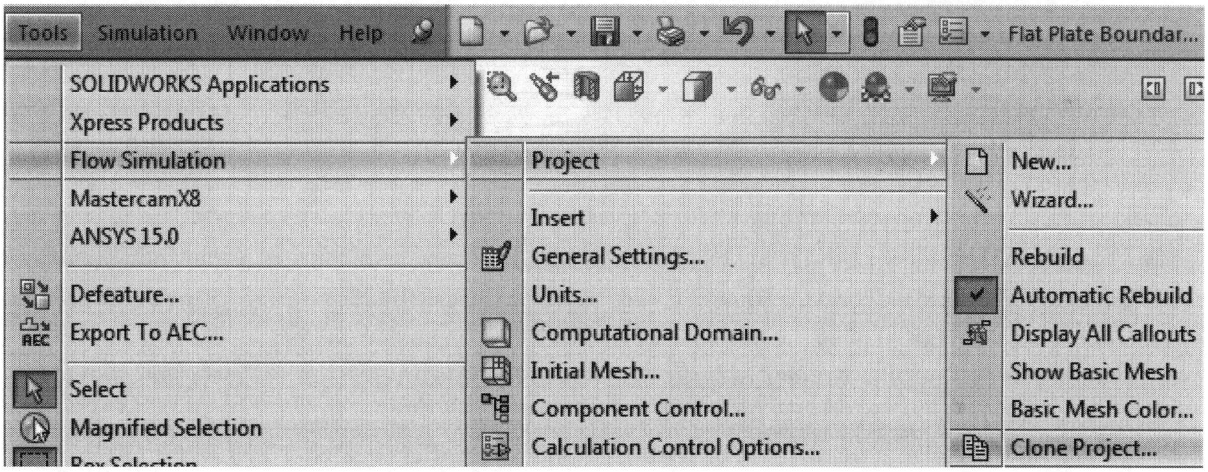

Figure 2.27a) Cloning the project

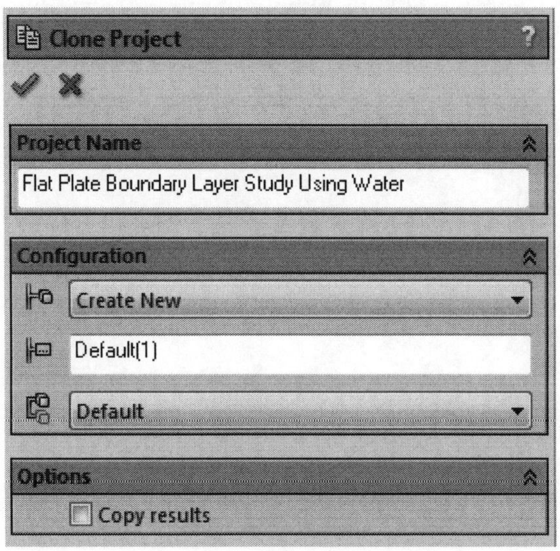

Figure 2.27b) Creating a new project

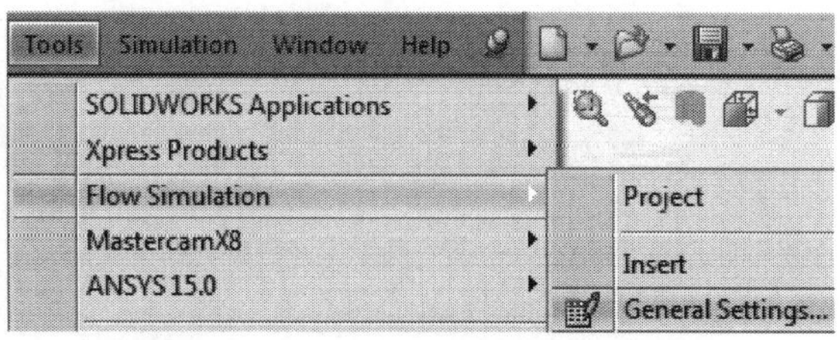

Figure 2.27c) Selection of general settings

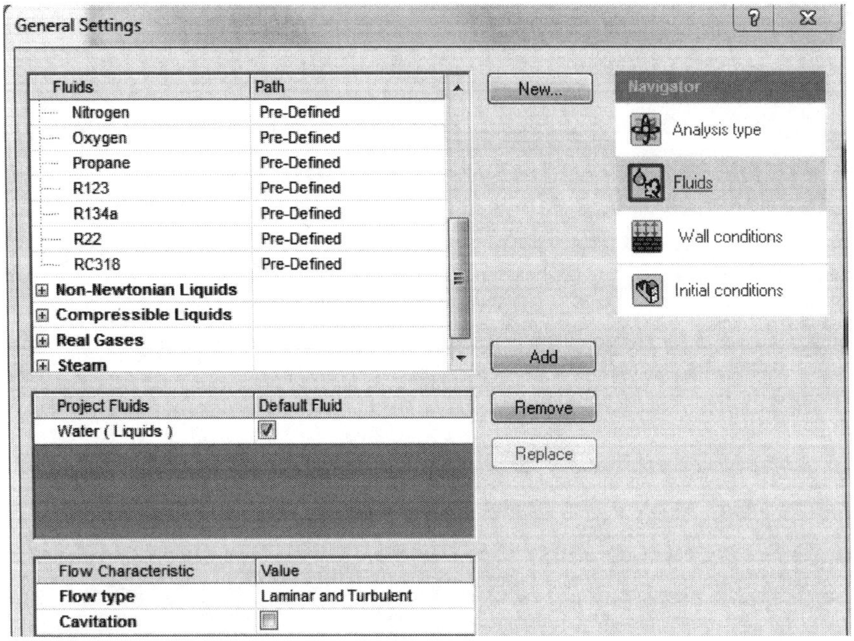

Figure 2.27d) Selection of fluid and flow type

30. Select **Tools>>Flow Simulation>>Computational Domain…** Set the size of the computational domain to the values shown in figure 2.28a). Click on the **OK** button to exit. Select **Tools>>Flow Simulation>>Initial Mesh…** from the SOLIDWORKS menu and change the **Number of cells per X:** to **400** and the **Number of Cells per Y:** to **200**. Also, in the **Control intervals** portion of the window, change the **Ratio** for **X1** to **-5** and the **Ratio** for **Y1** to **-100**. This is done to increase the number of cells close to the wall where the velocity gradient is high. Click on the **OK** button to exit. Select **Tools>>Flow Simulation>>Calculation Control Options…** from the SOLIDWORKS menu. Change the **Maximum travels value** to **5** by first changing to **Manual** from the drop down menu. Travel is a unit characterizing the duration of the calculation. Click on the **OK** button to exit.

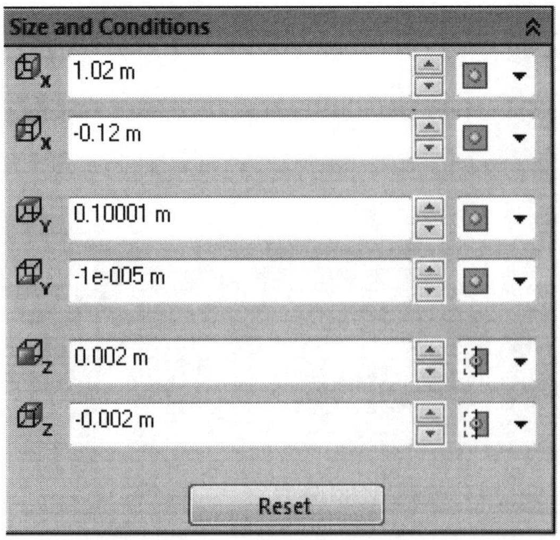

Figure 2.28a) Setting the size of the computational domain

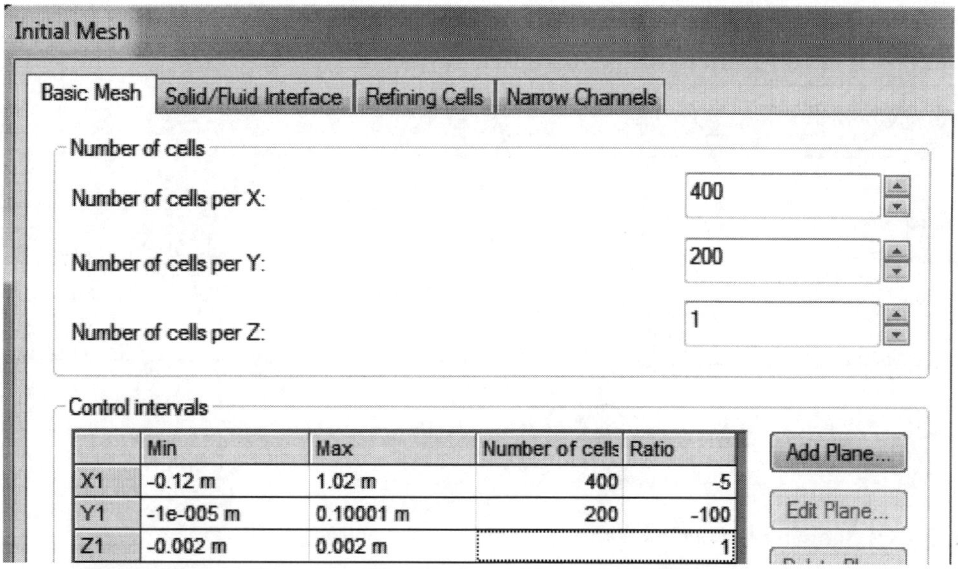

Figure 2.28b) Increasing the number of cells and the distribution of cells

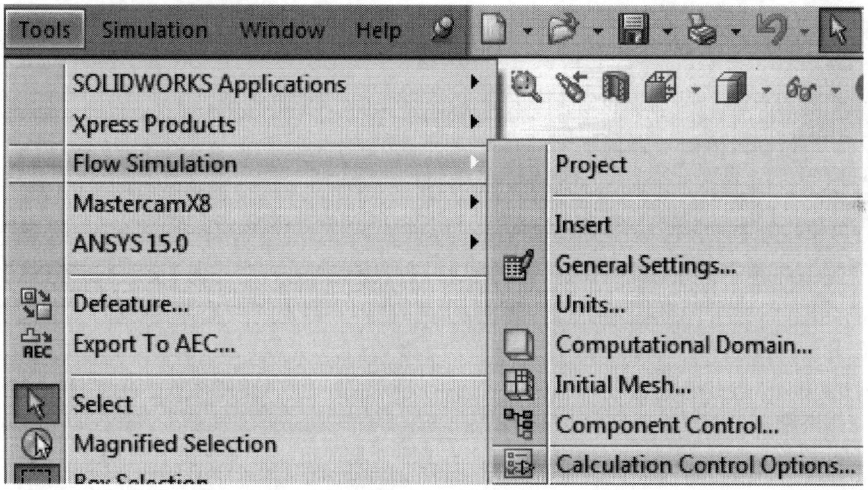

Figure 2.28c) Calculation control options

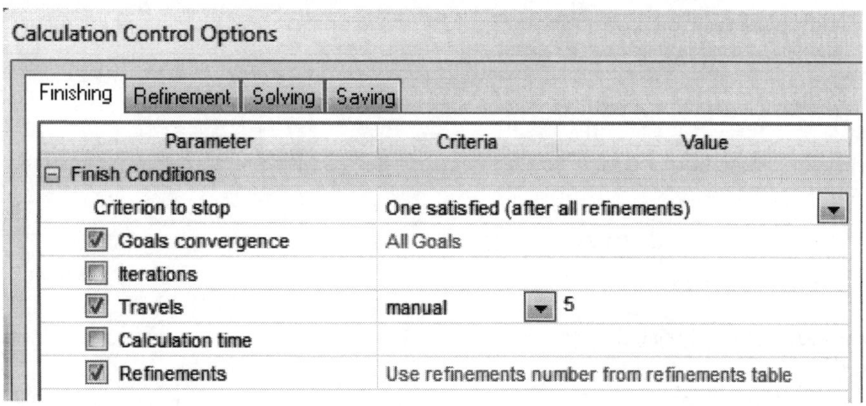

Figure 2.28d) Setting maximum travels

Select **Tools>>Flow Simulation>>Project>>Show Basic Mesh** from the SOLIDWORKS menu. We can see in figure 2.28f) that the density of the mesh is much higher close to the flat plate at the bottom wall as compared to the region further away from the wall.

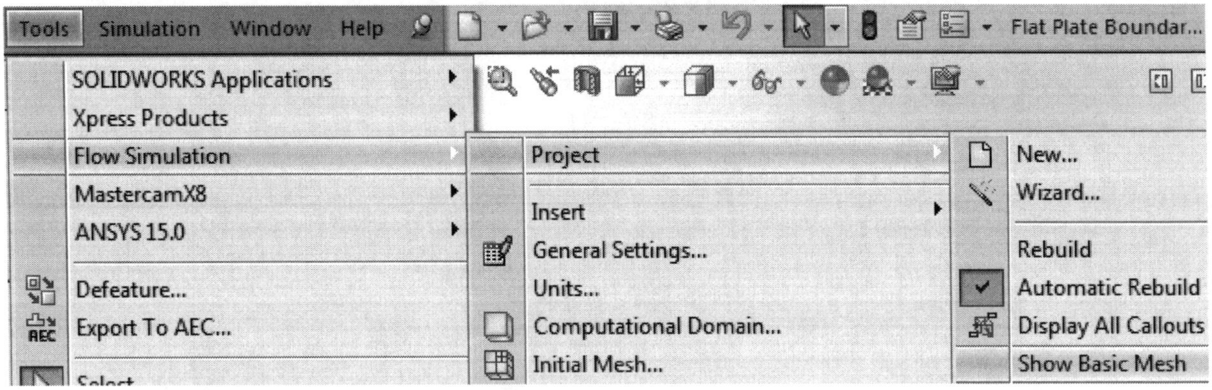

Figure 2.28e) Showing the basic mesh

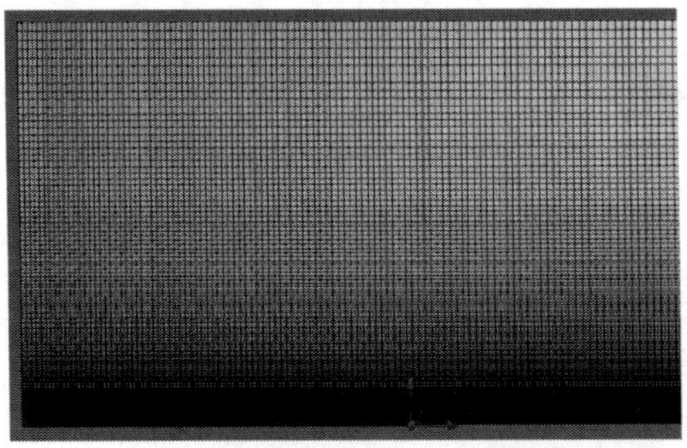

Figure 2.28f) Mesh distribution in the X-Y plane

31. Right click the **Inlet Velocity Boundary Condition** in the **Flow Simulation analysis tree** and select **Edit Definition…**. Open the **Boundary Layer** section and select **Laminar Boundary Layer**. Click **OK** to exit the **Boundary Condition** window. Right click the **Reynolds number at x = 0.2 m** goal and select **Edit Definition…**. Change the viscosity value in the **Expression** to **1.004E-6**. Click on the **OK** button to exit. Change the other three equation goals in the same way. Select **Tools>>Flow Simulation>>Solve>>Run** to start calculations. Click on the **Run** button in the **Run** window.

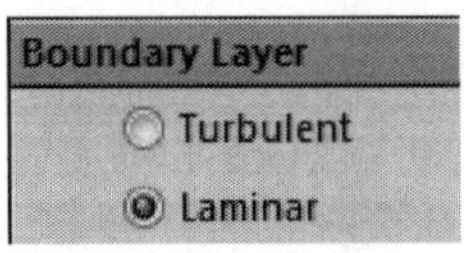

Figure 2.29a) Selecting a laminar boundary layer

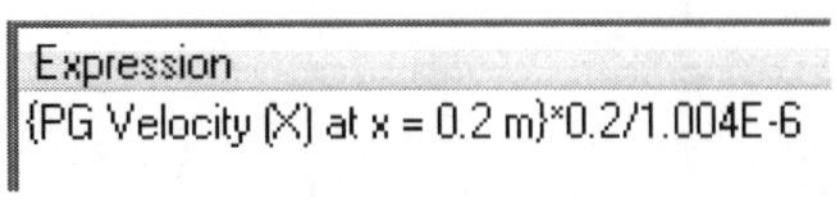

Figure 2.29b) Modifying the equation goals

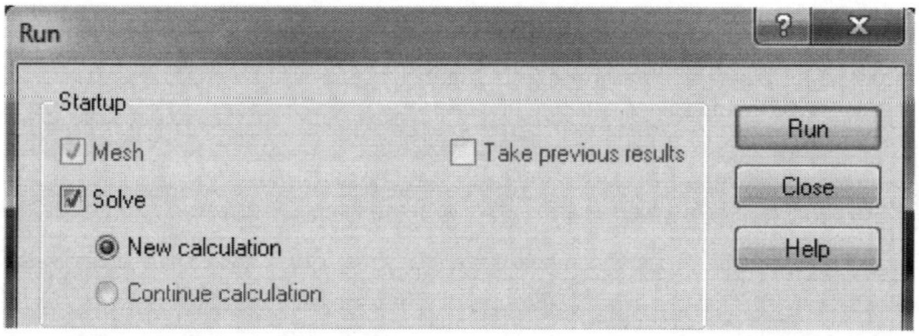

Figure 2.29c) Creation of mesh and starting a new calculation

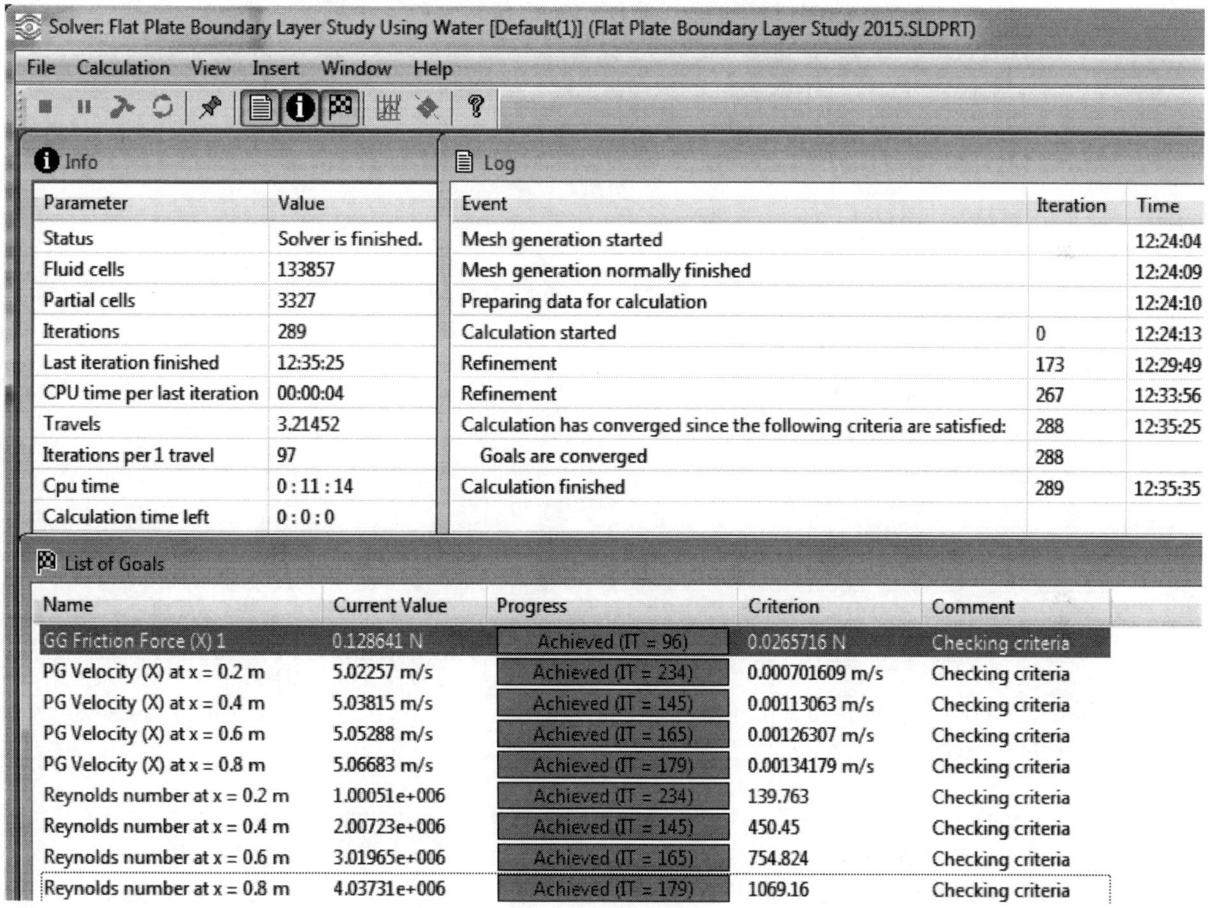

Parameter	Value
Status	Solver is finished.
Fluid cells	133857
Partial cells	3327
Iterations	289
Last iteration finished	12:35:25
CPU time per last iteration	00:00:04
Travels	3.21452
Iterations per 1 travel	97
Cpu time	0 : 11 : 14
Calculation time left	0 : 0 : 0

Event	Iteration	Time
Mesh generation started		12:24:04
Mesh generation normally finished		12:24:09
Preparing data for calculation		12:24:10
Calculation started	0	12:24:13
Refinement	173	12:29:49
Refinement	267	12:33:56
Calculation has converged since the following criteria are satisfied:	288	12:35:25
Goals are converged	288	
Calculation finished	289	12:35:35

Name	Current Value	Progress	Criterion	Comment
GG Friction Force (X) 1	0.128641 N	Achieved (IT = 96)	0.0265716 N	Checking criteria
PG Velocity (X) at x = 0.2 m	5.02257 m/s	Achieved (IT = 234)	0.000701609 m/s	Checking criteria
PG Velocity (X) at x = 0.4 m	5.03815 m/s	Achieved (IT = 145)	0.00113063 m/s	Checking criteria
PG Velocity (X) at x = 0.6 m	5.05288 m/s	Achieved (IT = 165)	0.00126307 m/s	Checking criteria
PG Velocity (X) at x = 0.8 m	5.06683 m/s	Achieved (IT = 179)	0.00134179 m/s	Checking criteria
Reynolds number at x = 0.2 m	1.00051e+006	Achieved (IT = 234)	139.763	Checking criteria
Reynolds number at x = 0.4 m	2.00723e+006	Achieved (IT = 145)	450.45	Checking criteria
Reynolds number at x = 0.6 m	3.01965e+006	Achieved (IT = 165)	754.824	Checking criteria
Reynolds number at x = 0.8 m	4.03731e+006	Achieved (IT = 179)	1069.16	Checking criteria

Figure 2.29d) Solver window and goals table for calculations of turbulent boundary layer

32. Place the file **"graph 2.30a)"** on the desktop. Repeat step **24** and choose the sketch **x = 0.2, 0.4, 0.6, 0.8 m** and check the box for **Velocity (X)**. Rename the xy-plot to **Turbulent Velocity Boundary Layer**. An Excel file will open with a graph of the streamwise velocity component versus the wall normal coordinate; see figure 2.30a). We see that the boundary layer thickness is much higher than the corresponding laminar flow case. This is related to higher Reynolds number at the same streamwise positions as in the laminar case. The higher Reynolds numbers are due to the selection of water as the fluid instead of air that has a much higher value of kinematic viscosity than water.

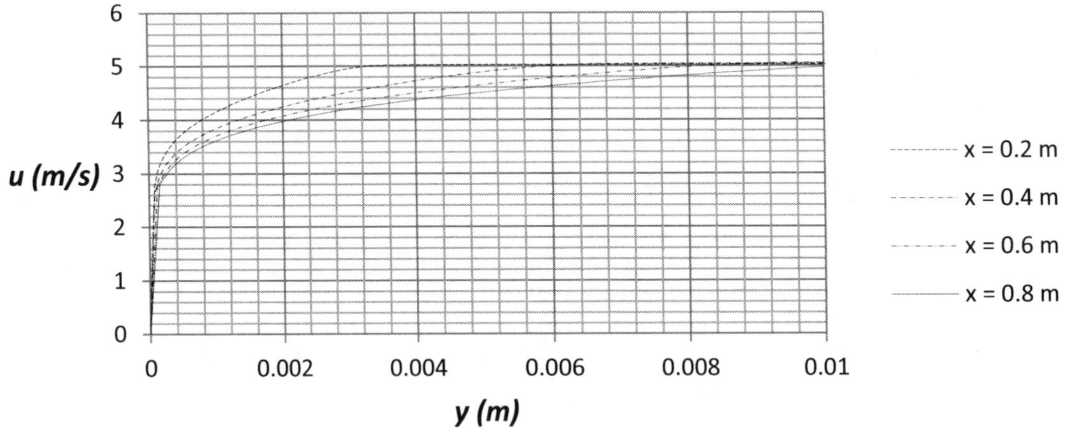

Figure 2.30a) Flow Simulation comparison between turbulent boundary layers at $Re_x = 10^6 - 4.04 \cdot 10^6$

As an example, the turbulent boundary layer thickness from figure 2.30a) is 3.55 mm at x = 0.2 m which can be compared with a value of 4.44 mm from equation (4); see table 2.5.

	δ (mm) Simulation	δ (mm) Empirical	Percent (%) Difference	U (m/s)	$\nu\ (\frac{m^2}{s})$	Re_x
x = 0.2 m	3.165	4.45	29	5.023	0.000001004	1,000,510
x = 0.4 m	5.59	8.05	31	5.038	0.000001004	2,007,230
x = 0.6 m	8.01	11.39	30	5.053	0.000001004	3,019,650
x = 0.8 m	10.37	14.57	29	5.067	0.000001004	4,037,310

Table 2.5 Comparison between Flow Simulation and empirical results for turbulent boundary layer thickness

Place the file **"graph 2.30b)"** on the desktop. Repeat step **24** and choose the sketch **x = 0.2, 0.4, 0.6, 0.8 m** and check the box for **Velocity (X)**. Rename the xy-plot to **Turbulent Boundary Layer Thickness**. An Excel file will open with a graph of the boundary layer thickness versus the Reynolds number; see figure 2.30b).

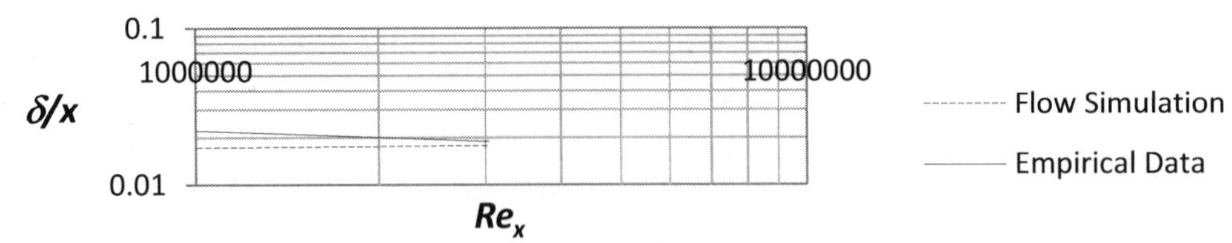

Figure 2.30b) Boundary layer thickness for turbulent boundary layers at $Re_x = 10^6 - 4.04 \cdot 10^6$

33. Place the file **"graph 2.31"** on the desktop. Repeat step **24** and choose the sketch **x = 0.2, 0.4, 0.6, 0.8 m** and check the box for **Velocity (X)**. Rename the xy-plot to **Comparison with One-Sixth Power Law**. An Excel file will open with Figure 2.31. In figure 2.31 we compare the results from Flow Simulation with the turbulent profile for $n = 6$. The power –law turbulent profiles suggested by Prandtl are given by

$$\frac{u}{U} = \left(\frac{y}{\delta}\right)^{1/n} \qquad (2.20)$$

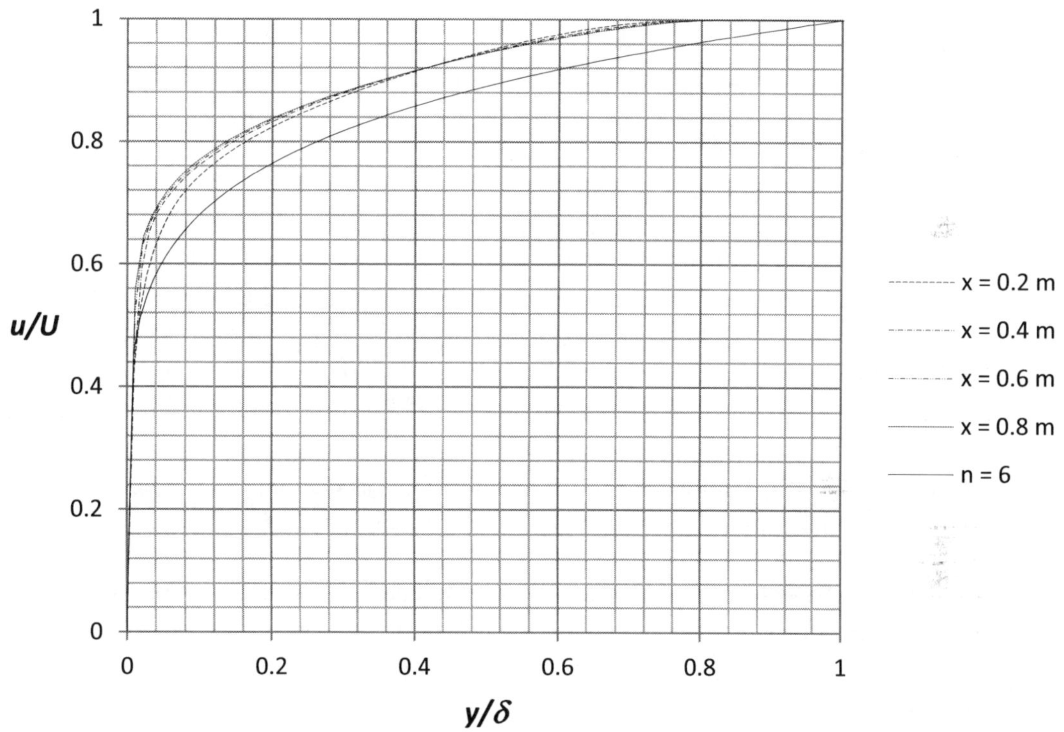

Figure 2.31 The same profiles as in figure 2.30a) compared with one-sixth power law for turbulent profile

34. Place the file **"graph 2.32"** on the desktop. Repeat step **24** and choose the sketch **x = 0 – 0.9 m**, uncheck the box for **Velocity (X)** and check the box for **Shear Stress**. Rename the xy-plot to **Local Friction Coefficient for Laminar and Turbulent Boundary Layer**. An Excel file will open with figure 2.32. Figure 2.32 is showing the Flow Simulation is able to capture the local friction coefficient in the laminar region in the Reynolds number range 10,000 – 200,000. At Re = 200,000 there is an abrupt increase in the friction coefficient caused by laminar to turbulent transition. In the turbulent region the friction coefficient is decreasing again, but the local friction coefficient from Flow Simulation is significantly lower than empirical data.

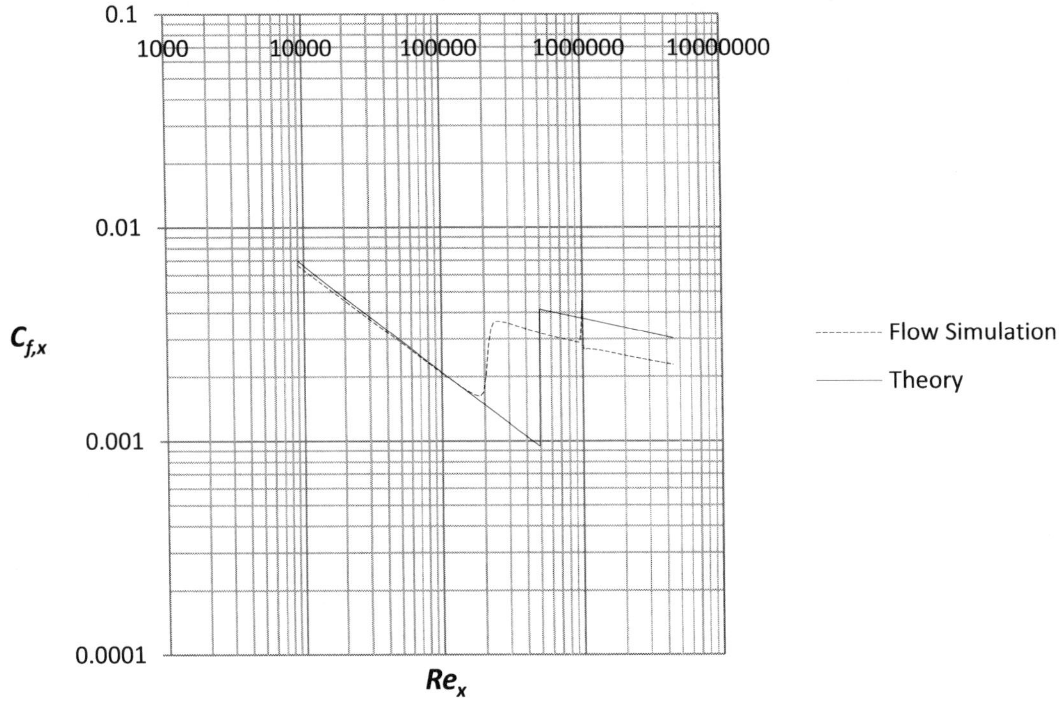

Figure 2.32 A comparison between Flow Simulation (dashed line) and theoretical laminar and empirical turbulent friction coefficients

The average friction coefficient over the whole plate C_f is a function of the surface roughness for the turbulent boundary layer and also a function of the Reynolds number based on the length of the plate Re_L; see figure E3 in Exercise 8. This friction coefficient can be determined in Flow Simulation by using the final value of the global goal, the X-component of the Shear Force F_f and dividing it by the dynamic pressure times the area A in the X-Z plane of the computational domain related to the flat plate. See figure 2.28a) for the size of the computational domain.

$$C_f = \frac{F_f}{\frac{1}{2}\rho U^2 A} = \frac{0.1286N}{\frac{1}{2}\cdot 998kg/m^3 \cdot 5^2 m^2/s^2 \cdot 1m \cdot 0.004m} = 0.00258 \tag{2.21}$$

$$Re_L = \frac{UL}{\nu} = \frac{5m/s \cdot 1m}{1.004 \cdot 10^{-6} m^2/s} = 4.98 \cdot 10^6 \tag{2.22}$$

The variation and final values of the goal can be found in the solver window during or after calculation by clicking on the associated flag; see figures 2.33 and 2.29d).

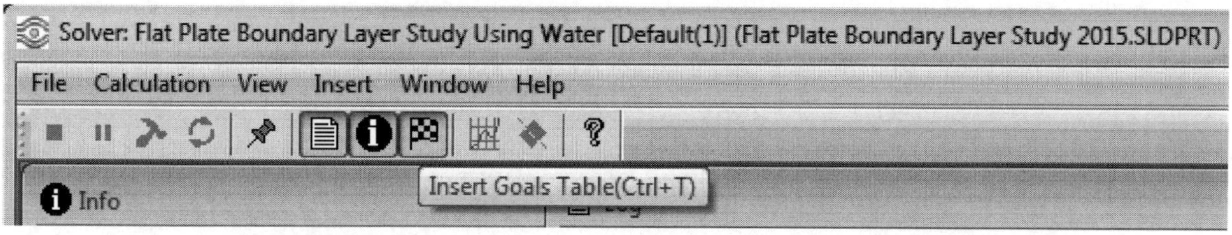

Figure 2.33 Obtaining the current value of the global goal

For comparison with Flow Simulation results we use equation (19) with Re_{cr} = 200,000

$$C_f = \frac{0.0315}{{Re_L}^{1/7}} - \frac{1}{Re_L}\left(0.0315{Re_{cr}}^{\frac{6}{7}} - 1.328\sqrt{Re_{cr}}\right) = 0.00338 \quad (2.23)$$

This is a difference of 24%.

References

[1] Çengel, Y. A., and Cimbala J.M., Fluid Mechanics Fundamentals and Applications, 1st Edition, McGraw-Hill, 2006.

[2] Fransson, J. H. M., Leading Edge Design Process Using a Commercial Flow Solver, Experiments in Fluids 37, 929 – 932, 2004.

[3] Schlichting, H., and Gersten, K., Boundary Layer Theory, 8th Revised and Enlarged Edition, Springer, 2001.

[4] SOLIDWORKS Flow Simulation 2015 Technical Reference.

[5] White, F. M., Fluid Mechanics, 4th Edition, McGraw-Hill, 1999.

Exercises

2.1 Change the number of cells per X and Y—see figure 2.16b)—for the laminar boundary layer, and plot graphs of the boundary layer thickness, displacement thickness, momentum thickness and local friction coefficient versus Reynolds number for different combinations of cells per X and Y. Compare with theoretical results.

2.2 Choose one Reynolds number and one value of number of cells per X for the laminar boundary layer and plot the variation in boundary layer thickness, displacement thickness and momentum thickness versus number of cells per Y. Compare with theoretical results.

2.3 Choose one Reynolds number and one value of number of cells per Y for the laminar boundary layer and plot the variation in boundary layer thickness, displacement thickness and momentum thickness versus number of cells per X. Compare with theoretical results.

2.4 Import the file "Leading Edge of Flat Plate." Study the air flow around the leading edge at 5 m/s free stream velocity and determine the laminar velocity boundary layer at different locations on the upper side of the leading edge and compare with the Blasius solution. Also, compare the local friction coefficient with figure 2.26. Use different values of the initial mesh to see how it affects the results.

Figure E1. Leading edge of asymmetric flat plate; see Fransson (2004)

2.5 Modify the geometry of the flow region used in this chapter by changing the slope of the upper ideal wall so that it is not parallel with the lower flat plate. By doing this you get a streamwise pressure gradient in the flow. Use air at 5 m/s and compare your laminar boundary layer velocity profiles for both accelerating and decelerating free stream flow with profiles without a streamwise pressure gradient.

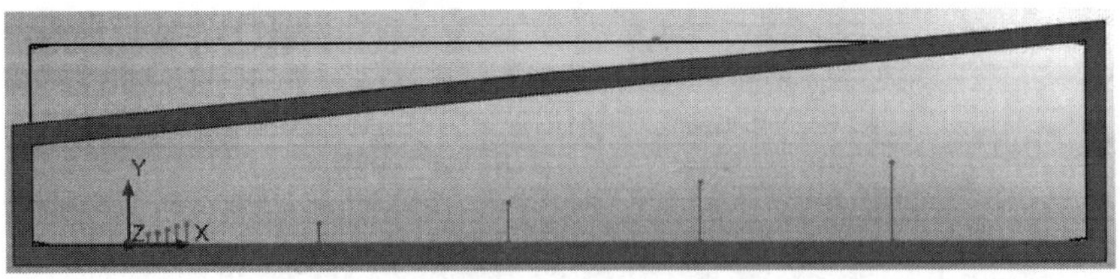

Figure E2. Example of geometry for a decelerating outer free stream flow

2.6 Determine the displacement thickness, momentum thickness and shape factor for the turbulent boundary layers in figure 2.30a), and determine the percent differences as compared with empirical data.

2.7 Change the distribution of cells using different values of the ratios in the X and Y directions see figure 2.28b) for the turbulent boundary layer and plot graphs of the boundary layer thickness, displacement thickness, momentum thickness and local friction coefficient versus Reynolds number for different combinations of ratios. Compare with theoretical results.

2.8 Use different fluids, surface roughness, free stream velocities and length of the computational domain to compare the average friction coefficient over the entire flat plate with figure E3.

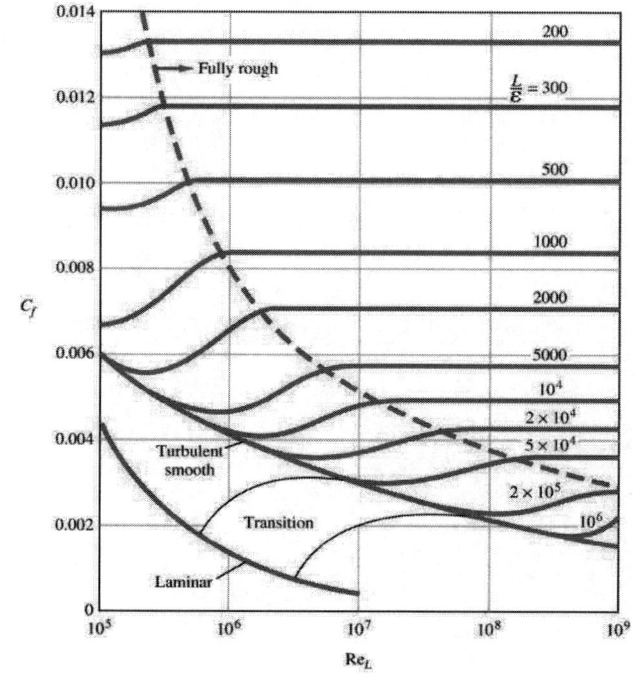

Figure E3 Average friction coefficient for flow over smooth and rough flat plates, White (1999)

Notes:

Chapter 3 Analysis of the Flow past a Sphere and a Cylinder

Objectives

- Creating the sphere and cylinder needed for the SOLIDWORKS Flow Simulation
- Setting up Flow Simulation projects for external flow
- Running the calculations
- Using XY-Plots, Cut Plots and Animation to visualize the resulting flow fields
- Study values of surface parameters
- Cloning of the project
- Run time-dependent calculations to determine the vortex shedding frequency and the Strouhal number for the cylinder
- Compare with empirical results

Problem Description

In this chapter, we will use Flow Simulation to study the three-dimensional flow of air past a sphere with a diameter of 50 mm at different Reynolds numbers and compare with empirical results for the drag coefficient. The second part of this chapter covers the two-dimensional flow around a cylinder, and we will determine the Strouhal number related to vortex shedding from the cylinder. We will start by creating the sphere needed for this simulation; see figure 3.0a).

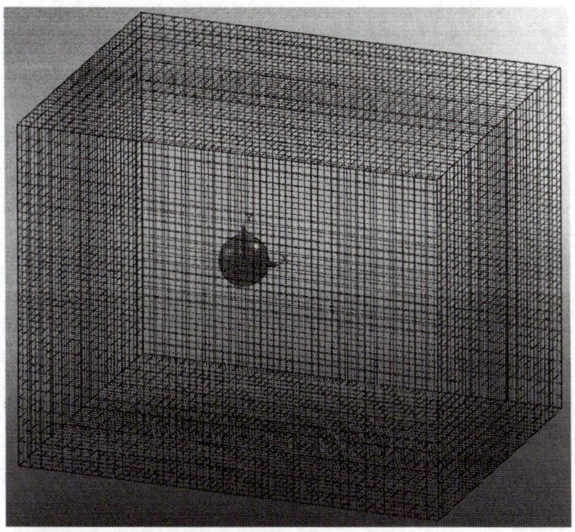

Figure 3.1 Sphere with 3D mesh

Figure 3.2 Cylinder with 2D initial mesh

Creating the SOLIDWORKS Part for the Sphere

In this exercise we will analyze the flow around a sphere. First, we have to create a model of the sphere in SOLIDWORKS and export the part to Flow Simulation. Follow these steps to create a solid model of a sphere with 50mm diameter and perform a 3D simulation of the flow field.

1. Start SOLIDWORKS and create a **New Document**.

Select **File>>New…** from the SOLIDWORKS menu.

Figure 3.3 Creating a new document in SOLIDWORKS

2. Select **Part** in **New SOLIDWORKS Document** window and click on the **OK** button.

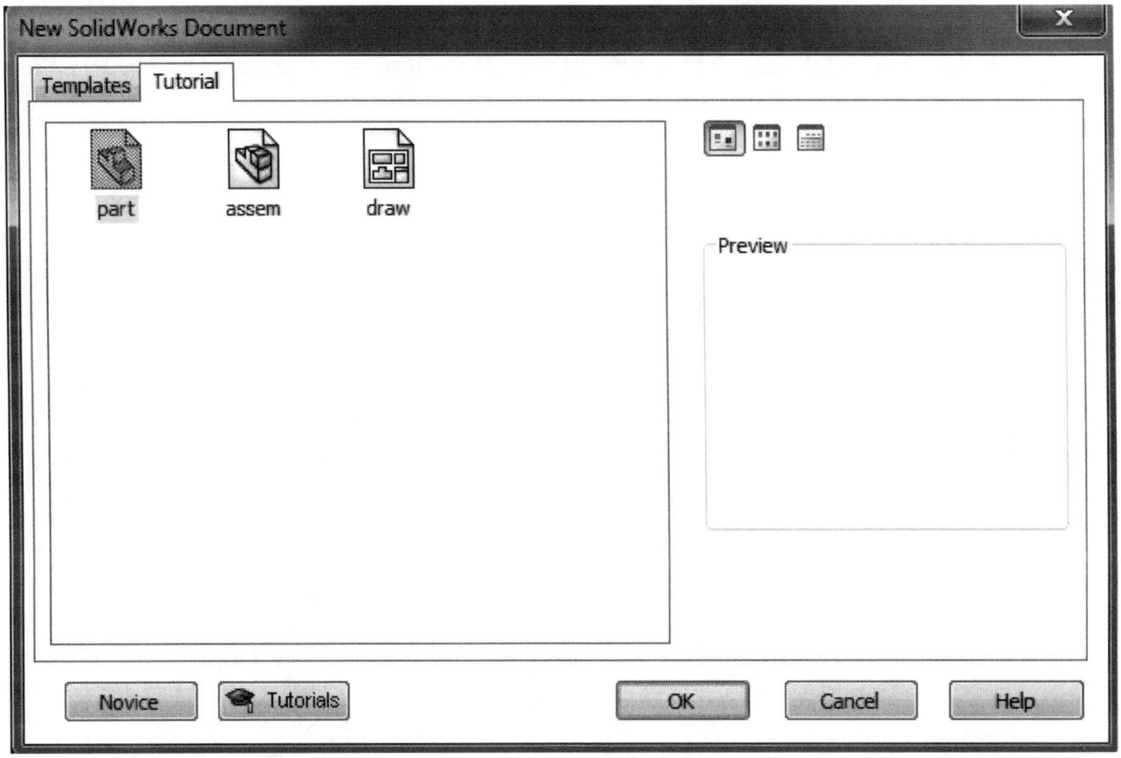

Figure 3.4 New SOLIDWORKS document selection window

In order to make the sphere we will sketch a half circle in the Front Plane and revolve it. We start this process by making a new sketch.

3. Click on the **Front Plane** to select the plane of the sketch.

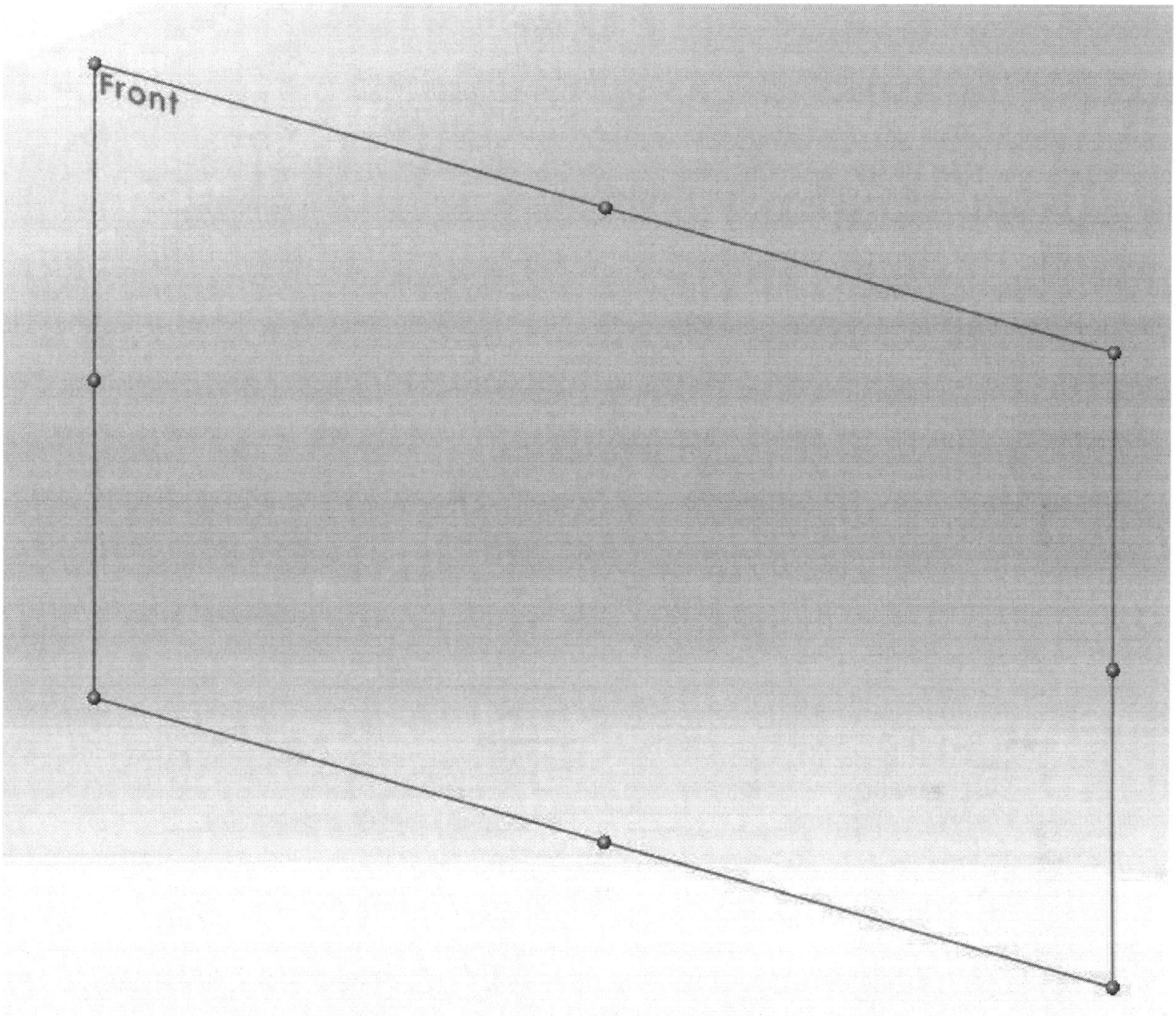

Figure 3.5 Selection of front plane for the sketch

We start sketching by drawing a vertical symmetry line in the sketch plane. This centerline will be used to create the sphere as a revolved feature.

4. Select **Line>>Centerline...**

Figure 3.6 Selection of the centerline sketch tool

5. Next, draw the vertical centerline in the sketch window. Start above the vertical coordinate axis and make sure that you get the blue dashed helpline; see figure 3.7a). Click and draw the line downward through the origin and end the line approximately the same distance below the origin; see figure 3.7b). Right click anywhere in the graphics window and click on **Select**. You have now finished the vertical centerline.

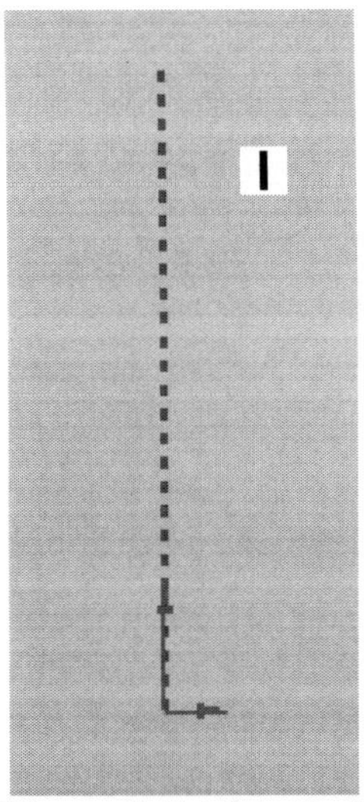
Figure 3.7a) Vertical dashed helpline

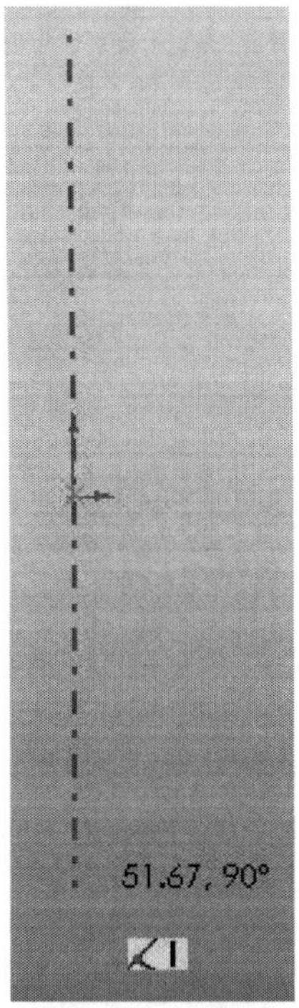

Figure 3.7b) Drawing a vertical centerline

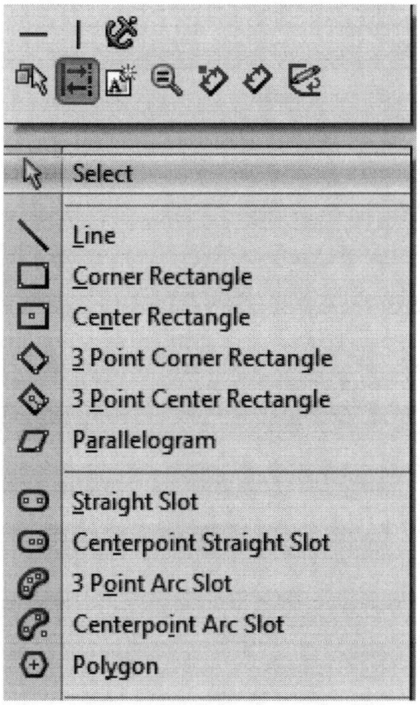

Figure 3.7c) Clicking on select

6. Select the **Centerpoint Arc** and draw the half circle. First, click on the origin. You should see a red filled circle indicating that you are at the origin; see figure 3.8b). Next, click on the centerline above the origin and draw the half circle, and click on the centerline once again but this time below the origin. Right click anywhere in the graphics window and click on **Select**. Select **Tools>>Options** from the SOLIDWORKS menu and click on the **Document Properties** tab. Click on **<u>Units</u>** and select **MMGS** (millimeter, gram, second) as Unit system.

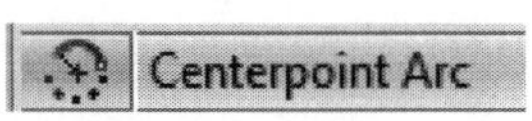

Figure 3.8a) Selecting centerline arc

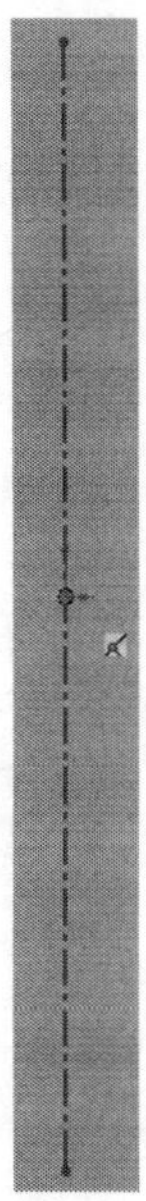
Figure 3.8b) Starting at the origin…

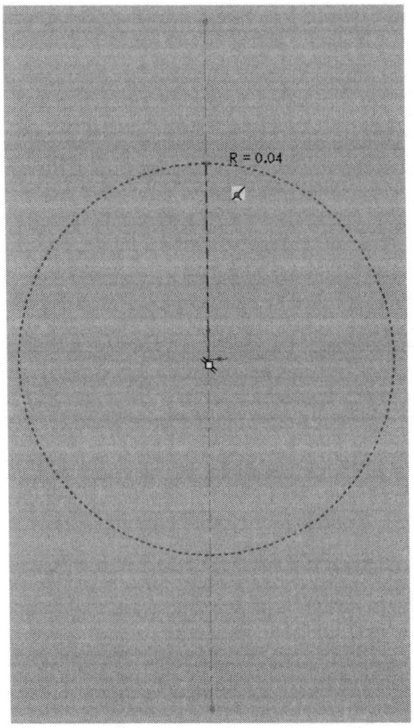

Figure 3.8c) And then above the origin…

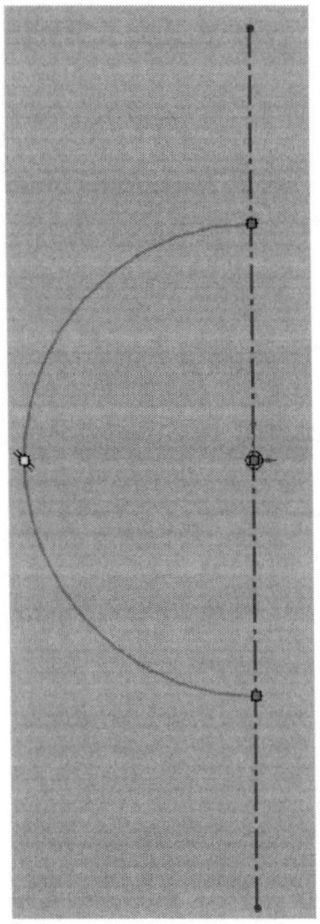

Figure 3.8d) Finished half circle

7. Next, select the **Smart Dimension** tool

Figure 3.9 Selecting the Smart Dimension tool

8. Create a radius of 25.00 mm for the half-circle by clicking on the half-circle twice, and enter the numerical value in the **Modify** window. Save the value and exit the dialog.

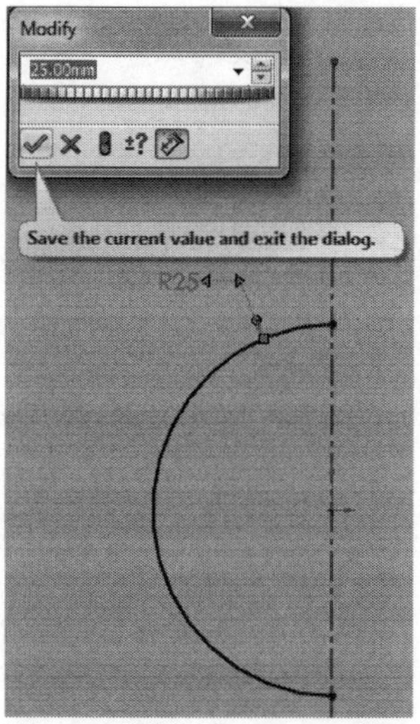

Figure 3.10 Enter a radius of 25.00 mm for the half-circle

The next step is to make the sphere by using the revolve feature in SOLIDWORKS.

9. Select the **Revolved Boss/Base** icon.

Figure 3.11a) Selection of the Revolved Boss-Base feature

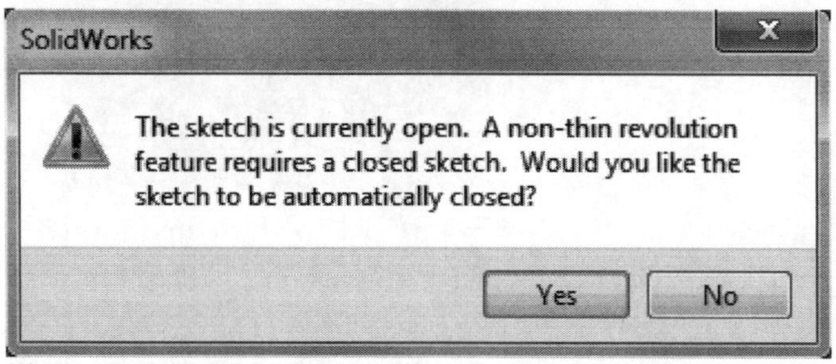

Figure 3.11b) SOLIDWORKS message window

You will get a message that the sketch is currently open and a question if you would like the sketch to be automatically closed. Choose the **Yes** button.

10. Use the default **Revolve Parameters**: Line 1, Blind Direction and 360 degrees.
Click on the OK button with the following green symbol to exit the **Revolve** window.

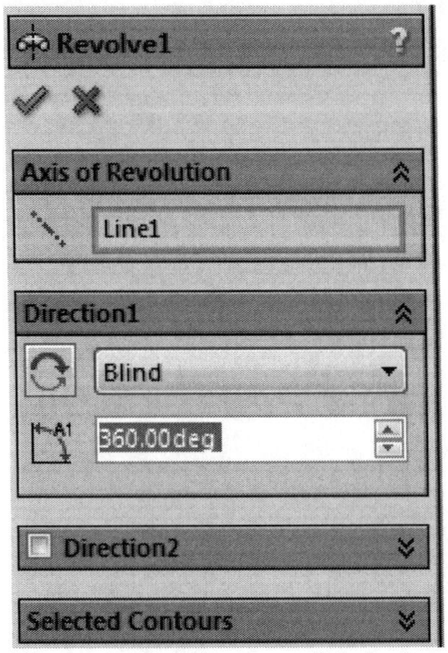

Figure 3.12 Selection of default revolve parameters

11. Move the cursor to the **File** menu and select **Save As...**
Enter **Sphere** as File name and click on the **Save** button.

Figure 3.13a) Save the solid model

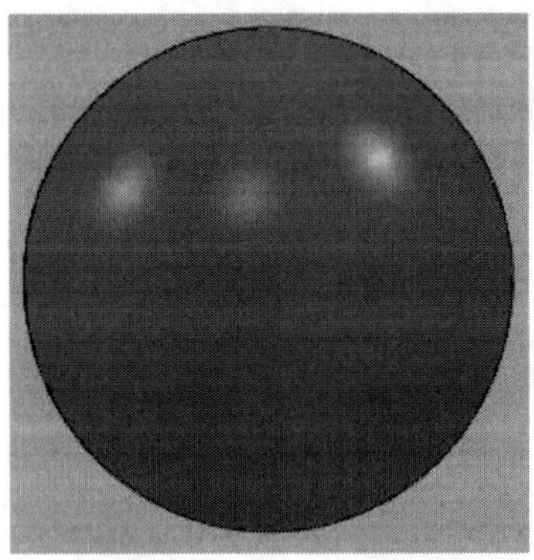

Figure 3.13b) Finished model

12. Select **Tools>>Add-Ins…**from the menu and check the **SOLIDWORKS Flow Simulation 2015** box.

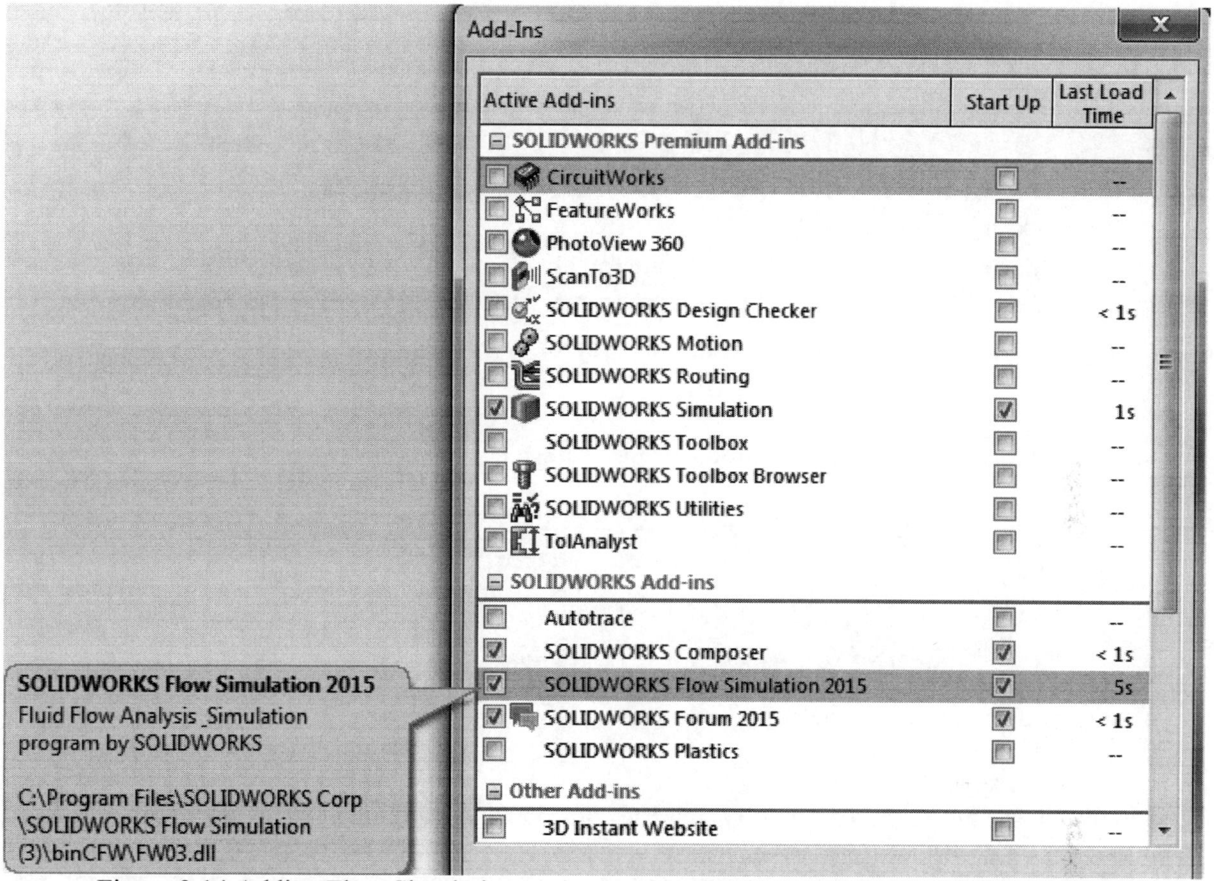

Figure 3.14 Adding Flow Simulation to the SOLIDWORKS menu

Setting up the Flow Simulation Project for the Sphere

13. We create a project by selecting **Tools>>Flow Simulation>>Project>>Wizard…** from the menu.

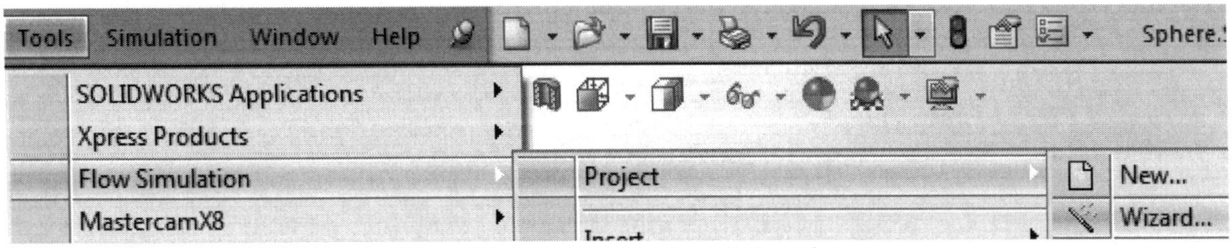

Figure 3.15 Using the Flow Simulation Project Wizard

14. Enter Project Name: "**Flow around a Sphere**." Push the **Next>** button.

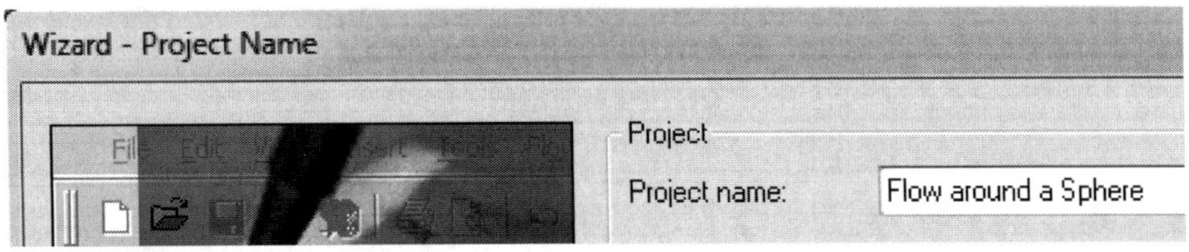

Figure 3.16 Wizard for the project name

15. We choose the **SI (m-kg-s)** unit system and click on the **Next>** button again.

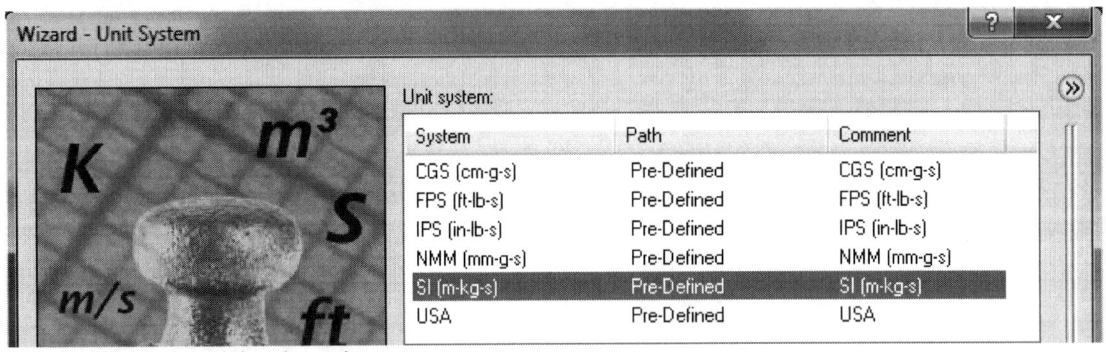

Figure 3.17 Wizard for the unit system

16. Check the **External** option for **Analysis type** and click the **Next>** button

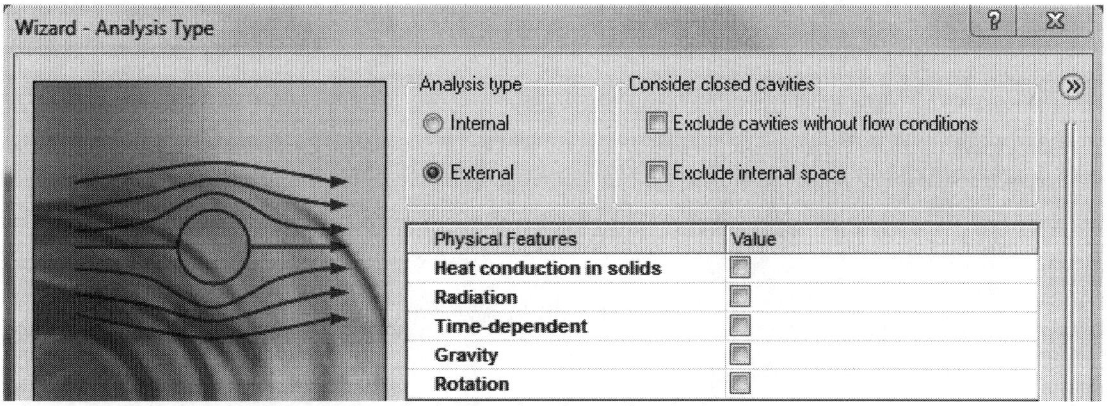

Figure 3.18 General settings of analysis type in Flow Simulation

17. Choose **Air** as the **Default Project Fluid** by clicking on the plus sign next to the **Gases** and selecting **Air**. Next, select the **Add** button. Click on the **Next>** button.

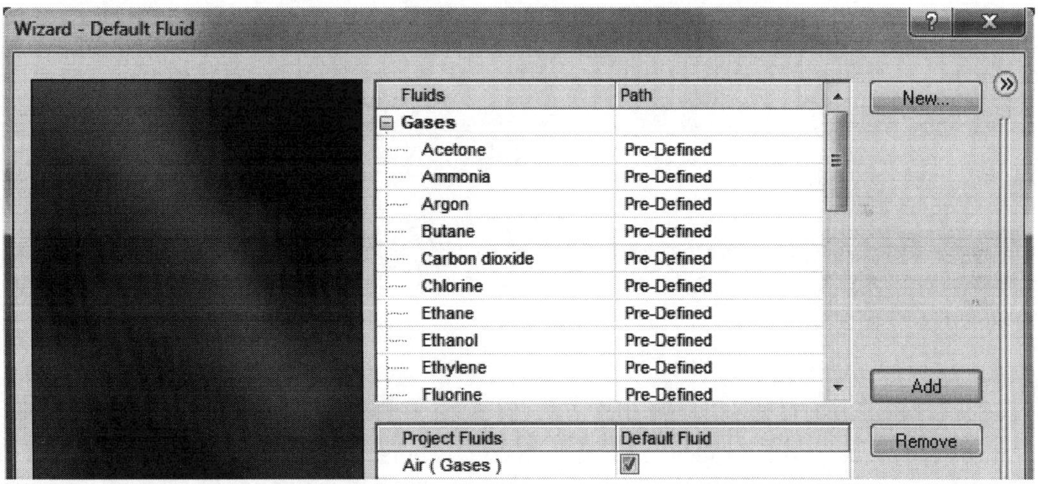

Figure 3.19 Selection of project fluid

The next part of the wizard is about **Wall Conditions**. We will use an **Adiabatic wall** for the sphere and use zero roughness on the surface of the same sphere. Next, we get the **Initial and Ambient Conditions** in the Wizard.

18. Click on the **Next>** button.

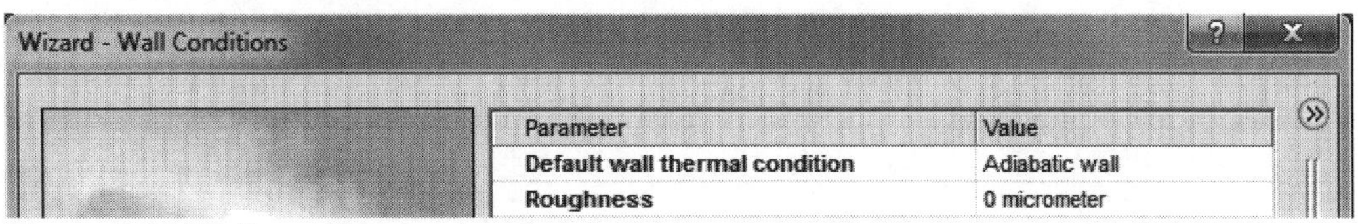

Figure 3.20 Wall conditions wizard

19. Enter **0.003 m/s** as the **Velocity in X-direction** and push the **Next>** button.

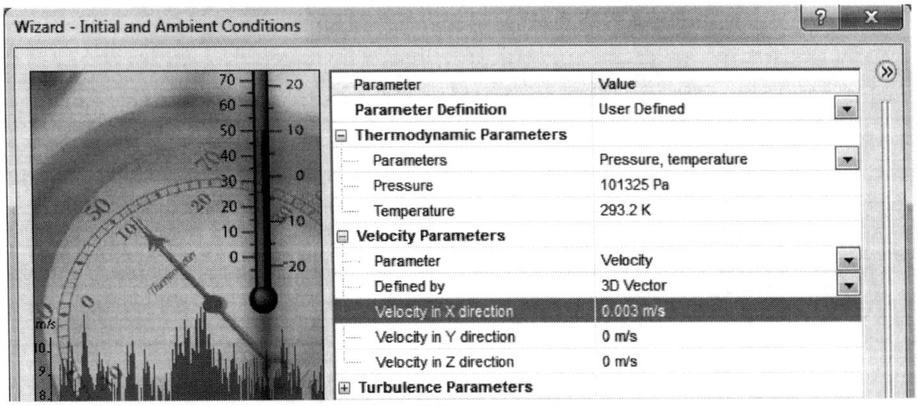

Figure 3.21 Initial and ambient conditions wizard

20. Slide the **Result resolution** to **4.** Push the **Finish** button in **Wizard - Results and Geometry Resolution** window. Right click anywhere in the graphics window and select **Zoom In/Out** to see computational domain surrounding the sphere. Select **Tools>>Flow Simulation>>Project>>Show Basic Mesh** to see the mesh surrounding the sphere; see figure 3.1.

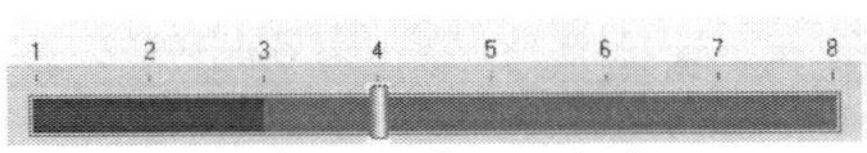

Figure 3.22a) Result resolution

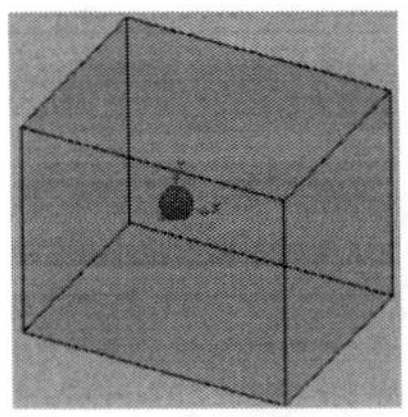

Figure 3.22b) Computational box around the sphere

Inserting Global Goal for Calculations

21. We create global goals for the project by selecting **Tools>>Flow Simulation>>Insert>>Global Goals…** from the SOLIDWORKS menu and check the box for **Force (X)**. Exit the global goals by clicking on OK . Right click on **Goals** in the **Flow Simulation analysis tree** and select **Insert Equation Goal**. Select **GG Force (X) 1** from the **Flow Simulation analysis tree**. Enter the expression for the equation goal as shown in figure 3.23e). Select **Dimensionless LMA** from the **Dimensionality** drop down menu. Exit the **Equation Goal** window. Rename the equation goal in the **Flow Simulation analysis tree** to **Drag Coefficient**.

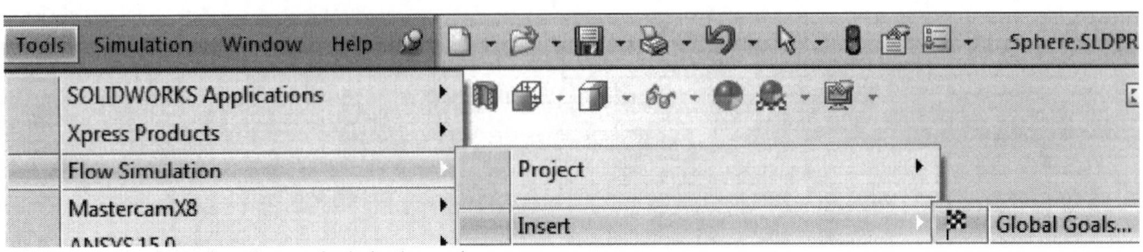

Figure 3.23a) Selection of global goals

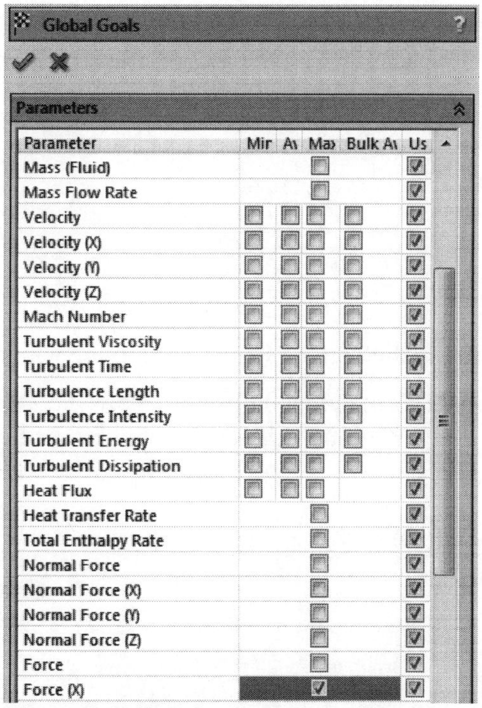

Figure 3.23b) Selection of X - Component of Force as global goal

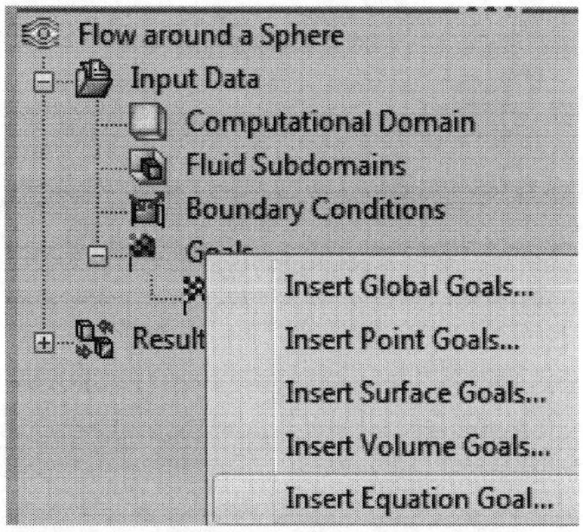

Figure 3.23c) Inserting equation goal

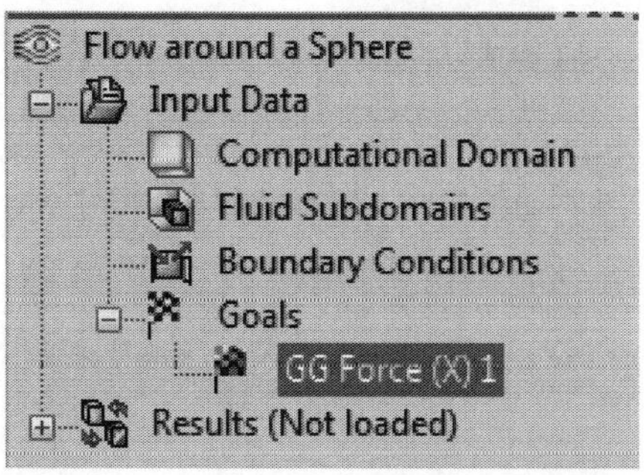

Figure 3.23d) Selection of X - Component of Force for the equation goal

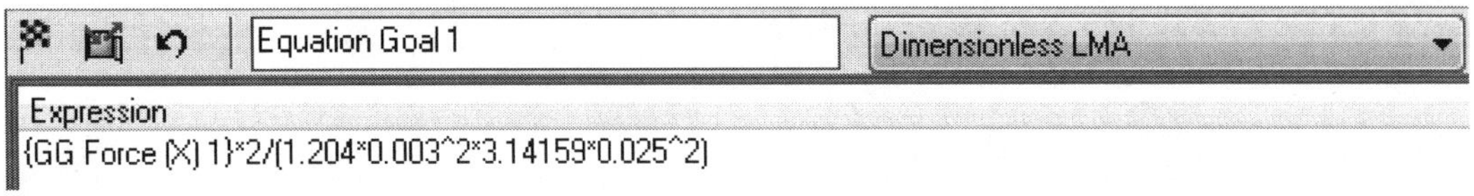

Figure 3.23e) Expression for equation goal

Running the Calculations

22. Choose **Tools>>Flow Simulation>>Solve>>Run…** Click on the **Run** button in the window that appears. Click on the goals flag to **Insert Goals Table** in the **Solver** window. You will now have the output window shown in figure 3.24a). The CPU time will depend on the speed of your computer and the amount of memory.

Select **Tools>>Flow Simulation>>Results>>Load/Unload**. Repeat this step once again.

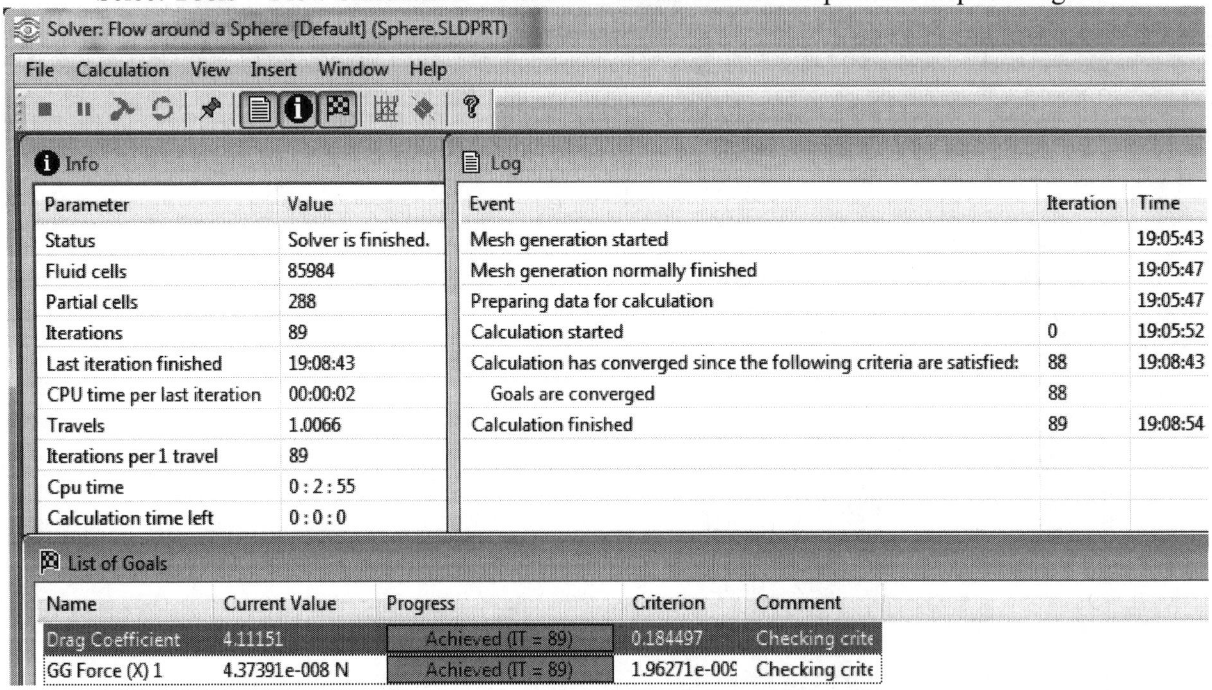

Figure 3.24a) Solver window for simulation of the flow around a sphere

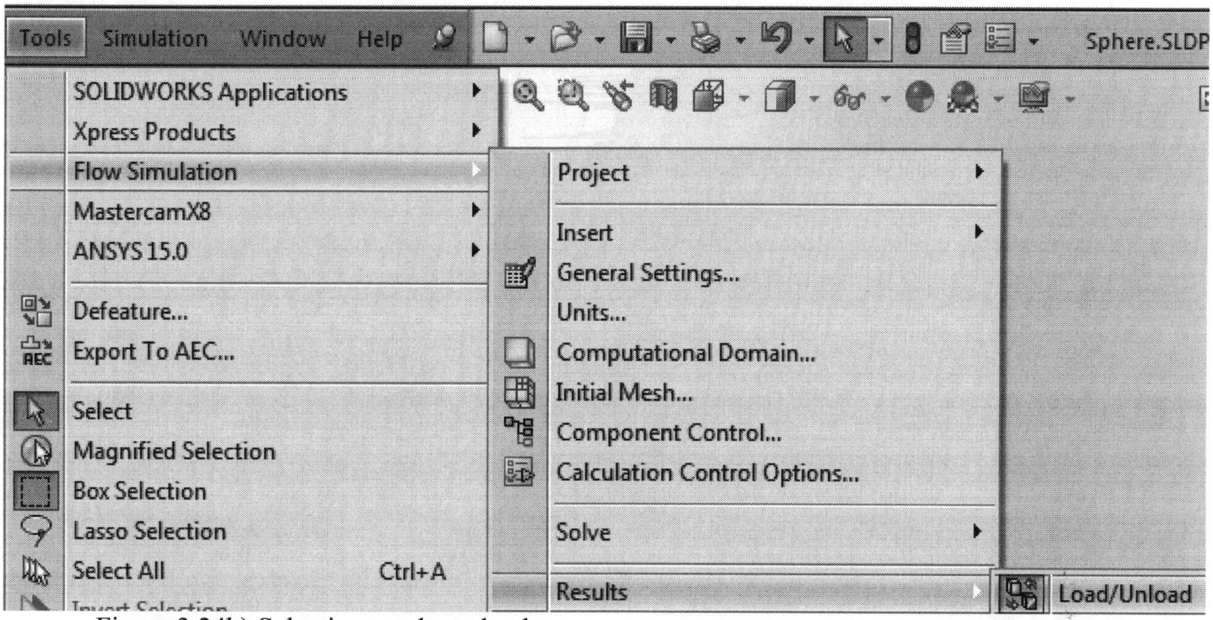

Figure 3.24b) Selecting results to load

Using Cut Plots

23. Select the **Flow Simulation analysis tree**

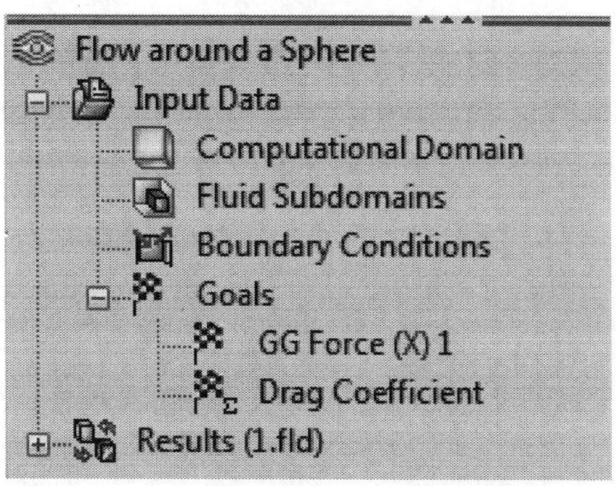

Figure 3.25 Selecting the Flow Simulation analysis tree

24. Right click on the **Cut Plots** in the Results folder of the **Flow Simulation analysis tree** and select **Insert…** Click on the **Vectors** button in the **Display** section. Choose **Velocity** from the **Contours** section drop down menu. Slide **Number of Levels** to **255**. Exit the **Cut Plot** window. Hide the mesh and rename **Cut Plot 1** to **Velocity around Sphere**. Select **Tools>>Flow Simulation>>Results>>Display>>Lighting** from the SOLIDWORKS menu.

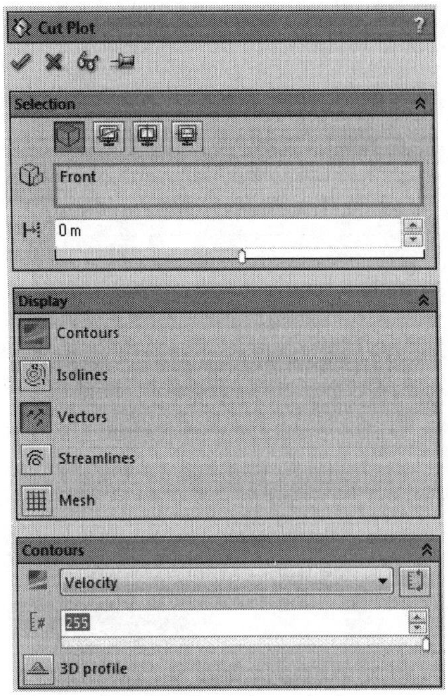

Figure 3.26a) Cut Plot window

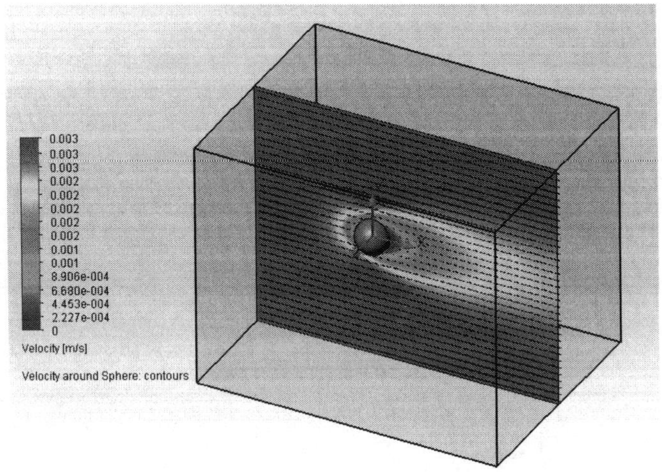

Figure 3.26b) Velocity distribution around sphere

Inserting Surface Parameters

25. Right-click on **Surface Parameters** in the **Flow Simulation analysis tree** and select **Insert....** Click on the **FeatureManager design tree** and select the **Revolve1** feature. Check the **All** box in the **Parameters** window. Push the **Export to Excel** button in the **Surface Parameters** window. An Excel file is generated with local and integral parameters.

Integral Parameters

Integral Parameter	Value	X-component	Y-component	Z-component	Surface Area [m^2]
Heat Transfer Rate [W]	0				0.007728067
Normal Force [N]	1.77205E-08	1.77204E-08	5.85867E-11	5.28636E-11	0.007728067
Friction Force [N]	2.60188E-08	2.60187E-08	3.78994E-11	3.55091E-11	0.007728067
Force [N]	4.37393E-08	4.37391E-08	9.6486E-11	8.83726E-11	0.007728067
Torque [N*m]	5.13239E-12	1.21791E-14	3.72545E-12	-3.5302E-12	0.007728067
Surface Area [m^2]	0.007728067	-6.77626E-20	4.91279E-20	9.48677E-20	0.007728067
Torque of Normal Force [N*m]	4.18803E-13	2.09091E-14	3.50606E-13	-2.2811E-13	0.007728067
Torque of Friction Force [N*m]	4.7216E-12	-8.73007E-15	3.37485E-12	-3.30209E-12	0.007728067
Uniformity Index [ ]	1				0.007728067
Area (Fluid) [m^2]	0.007853982				0.007853982

Figure 3.27a) Integral surface parameters

Local Parameters

Local Parameter	Minimum	Maximum	Average	Surface Area [m^2]
Pressure [Pa]	101325	101325	101325	0.007728067
Density (Fluid) [kg/m^3]	1.203705624	1.203705624	1.203705624	0.007728067
Velocity [m/s]	0	0	0	0.007728067
Velocity (X) [m/s]	0	0	0	0.007728067
Velocity (Y) [m/s]	0	0	0	0.007728067
Velocity (Z) [m/s]	0	0	0	0.007728067
Mach Number [ ]	0	0	0	0.007728067
Heat Transfer Coefficient [W/m^2/K]	0	0	0	0.007728067
Shear Stress [Pa]	8.95989E-08	6.48473E-06	3.91919E-06	0.007728067
Surface Heat Flux [W/m^2]	0	0	0	0.007728067
Temperature (Fluid) [K]	293.2	293.2	293.2	0.007728067
Relative Pressure [Pa]	-1.00269E-05	1.24441E-05	-8.95747E-07	0.007728067

Figure 3.27b) Local surface parameters

If we look at the Force related to the Integral parameters we see that the drag force is $D = 4.37391\text{E-}08$ N for the X-component. This value can also be found in the **List of Goals** in figure 3.24a). Exit the **Surface Parameters** window.

Theory

The drag coefficient can be determined from the following formula

$$C_D = \frac{D}{\frac{1}{2}\rho U^2 A} = \frac{4.37265\text{E-}08}{\frac{1}{2}\cdot 1.204\cdot 0.003^2\cdot \pi \cdot 0.025^2} = 4.112 \qquad (3.1)$$

, where $\rho\ (kg/m^3)$ is the free-stream density, *U (m/s)* is the free-stream velocity and *A* (m^2) is the frontal area of the sphere. The Reynolds number is determined by

$$\mathrm{Re} = \frac{Ud\rho}{\mu} = \frac{0.003\cdot 0.05\cdot 1.204}{1.825\cdot 10^{-5}} = 9.9 \qquad (3.2)$$

where $\mu\ (kg/ms)$ is the dynamic viscosity of air in the free-stream and *d* is the diameter of the sphere. The drag coefficient can be compared with the following curve-fit from experimental data

$$C_{D,Experiment} = \frac{24}{\mathrm{Re}} + \frac{6}{1+\sqrt{\mathrm{Re}}} + 0.4 = 4.273 \qquad 0 \le \mathrm{Re} \le 200{,}000 \qquad (3.3)$$

, and we see that the difference in the Flow Simulation result is only 3.8 %.

Cloning of the Project

26. We now want to run the computations for different Reynolds numbers. Select **Tools>>Flow Simulation>>Project>>Clone Project…** from the SOLIDWORKS drop down menu. Create a new project with a different configuration name than the first project; see figure 3.28b).
Exit the **Clone Project** window.

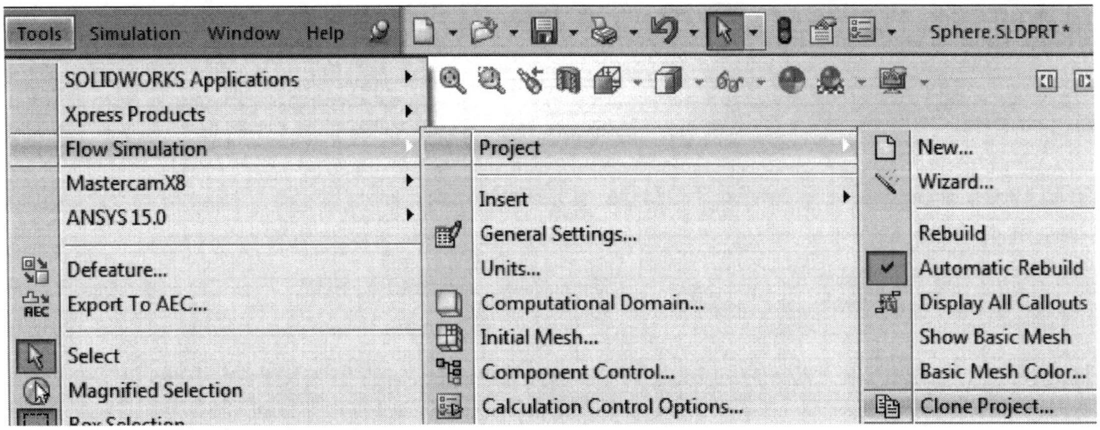

Figure 3.28a) Cloning of a project

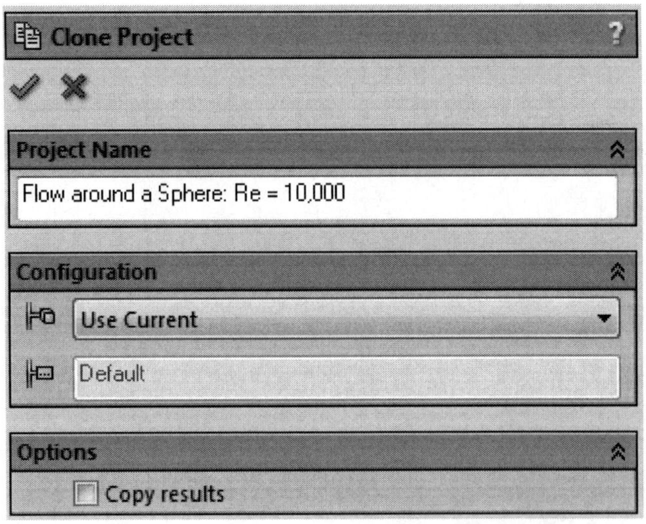

Figure 3.28b) Entering the name of the cloned project

Time-Dependent Calculations

27. Select **Tools>>Flow Simulation>>General Settings…** Check the box for Time-dependent flow under **Physical Features** for this higher Reynolds number. The flow past a sphere is time dependent for *Re* above 200.

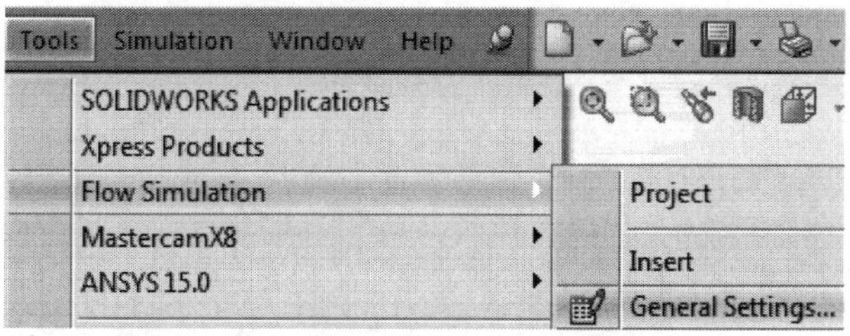

Figure 3.29a) Selecting General Settings

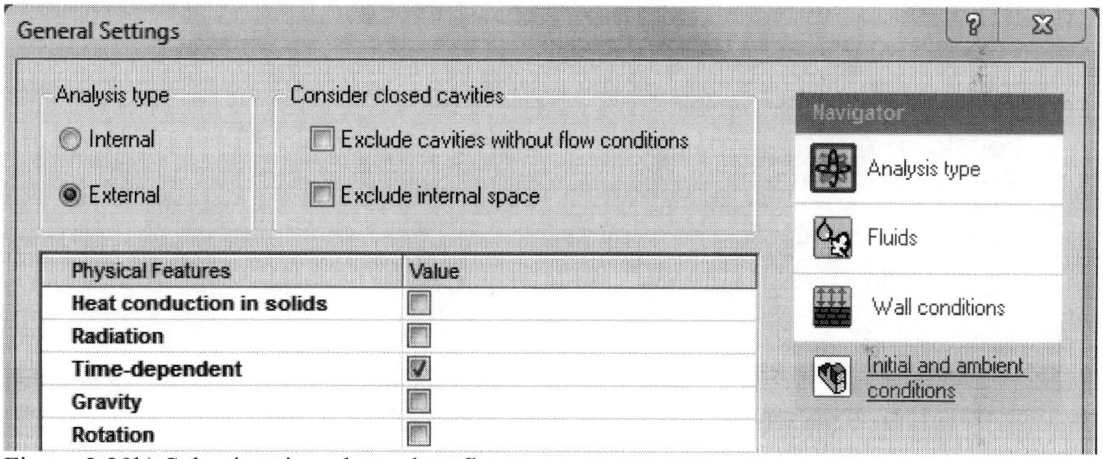

Figure 3.29b) Selecting time-dependent flow

28. Select **Initial and ambient conditions** in the **Navigator** and enter the **Velocity in X direction** to **3 m/s**. Click on the **OK** button to exit the **General Settings** window.
Right click on the **Drag Coefficient Goal** in the **Flow Simulation analysis tree** and select **Edit Definition....** Change the velocity in the **Expression** to 3 m/s; see figure 3.30b). Exit the **Equation Goal** window. You are now ready to run the calculations for this higher Reynolds number. Cloning of the project can be repeated, and results from a number of runs at different Reynolds numbers are shown in Table 3.1. You can use **Tools>>Flow Simulation>>Solve>>Batch Run** to start a batch run for the different Reynolds numbers.

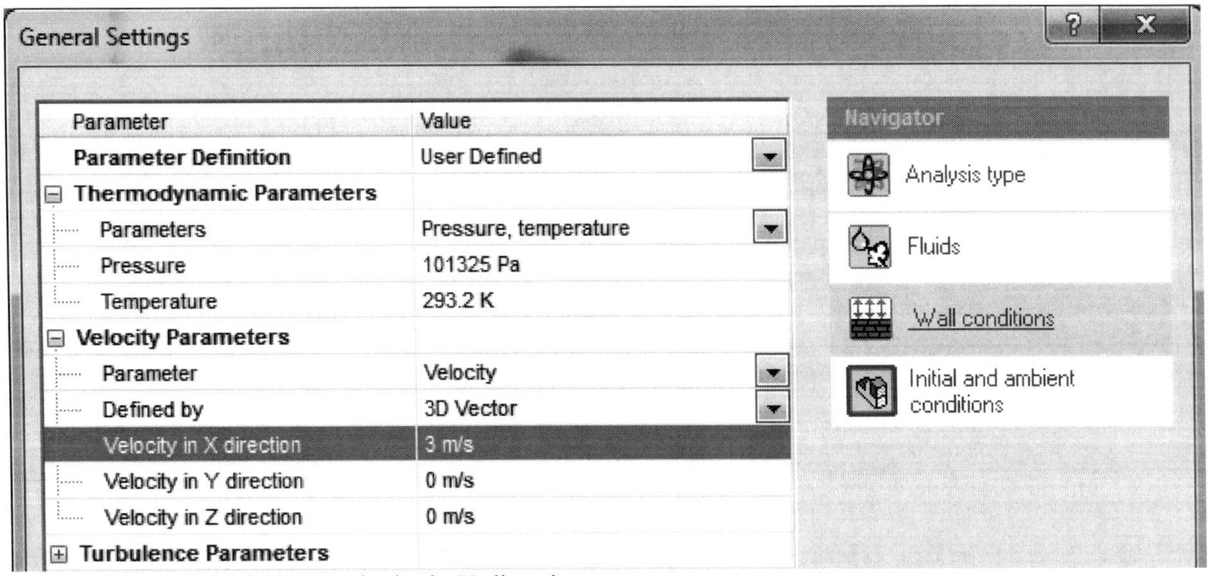

Figure 3.30a) Enter velocity in X direction

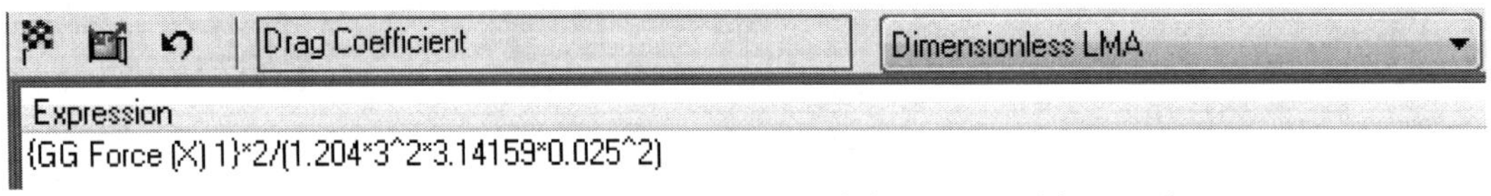

Figure 3.30b) Expression for equation goal for the higher Reynolds number

29. The following table shows a comparison of the computations and experiments at different Reynolds numbers including the percent difference for the drag coefficient:

U (m/s)	Re	$C_{D,Simulation}$	$C_{D,Experiment}$	Difference (%)
0.00003	0.1	218	248	12
0.0003	1.0	25.9	27.7	6.5
0.003	9.9	4.112	4.273	3.8
0.03	99.0	0.959	1.191	20
0.3	989	0.306	0.609	50
3.0	9,894	0.172	0.462	63
30	98,940	0.122	0.419	71

Table 3.1 Comparison of drag coefficient for a sphere at various Reynolds numbers

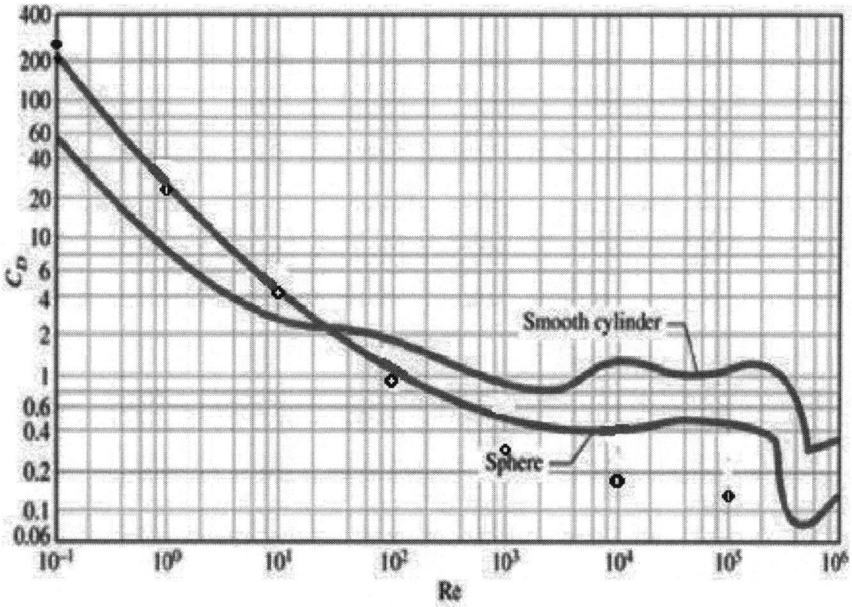

Figure 3.31 Comparison of experimental drag coefficient for a sphere and a smooth cylinder. The black circles represent results from Flow Simulations for a sphere.

We see that the Flow Simulation results follow the general trend of experimental results as the Reynolds number is increasing. A finer initial mesh and several levels of refinement are required in order to get results closer to experiments at higher Reynolds numbers. You have now completed your simulation of the flow around a sphere.

Creating the SOLIDWORKS Part for the Cylinder

30. Select **File>>New…** from the SOLIDWORKS menu. Select a new **Part** and click on the **OK** button. Select **Insert>>Sketch** from the SOLIDWORKS menu. Click on the **Front Plane** in the **FeatureManager design tree** to select the plane of the sketch. Select Front view from the **View Orientation** drop down menu in the graphics window. Select the **Circle** sketch tool from **Tools>>Sketch Entities** in the SOLIDWORKS menu.

Figure 3.32a) Creating a new SOLIDWORKS document

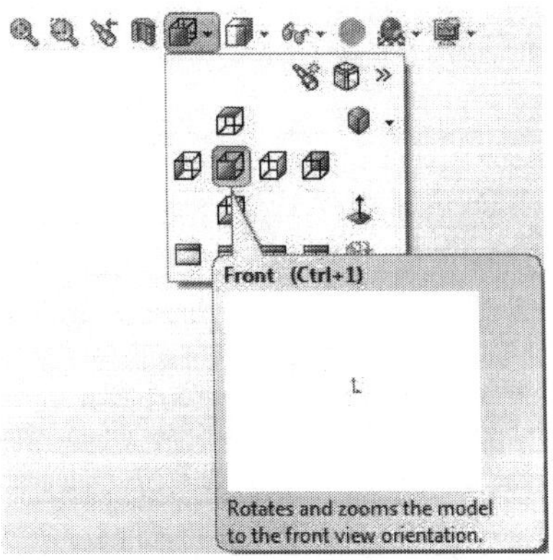

Figure 3.32b) Front view orientation

31. Draw a circle with a radius of **25.00 mm**. Close the **Circle** dialog box. Select **Insert>>Boss/Base>>Extrude** from the SOLIDWORKS menu. Check the **Direction 2** box and exit the **Extrude** dialog box. Select **File>>Save As** and enter the name "**Cylinder 2015**" as the name for the SOLIDWORKS part.

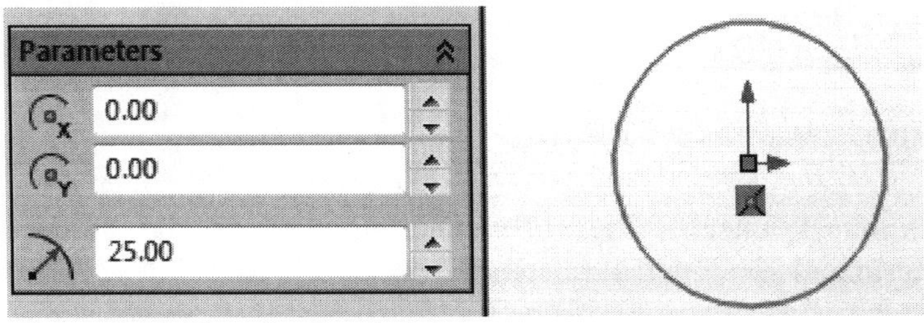

Figure 3.33 Sketch of a circle

Setting up the Flow Simulation Project for the Cylinder

32. We create a project by selecting **Tools>>Flow Simulation>>Project>>Wizard...** from the menu. Enter "**Flow around a Cylinder**" as project name. Push the **Next>** button. We choose the **SI (m-kg-s)** unit system and click on the **Next>** button again.

In the next step we check **External** as analysis type, check the box for **Time-dependent** flow and then click on the **Next>** button. The **Default Fluid Wizard** will now appear. We are going to add air as the **Project Fluid**. Start by clicking on the plus sign next to the **Gases** in the **Fluids** column. Scroll down the different gases and select **Air**. Next, click on the **Add** button so that air will appear as the **Default Fluid**. Click on the **Next>** button.

The next part of the wizard is about **Wall Conditions**. We will use an **Adiabatic wall** for the cylinder and use zero surface roughness. Next, we get the **Initial and Ambient Conditions** in the Wizard. We set the **Velocity in X-direction** to **0.06 m/s** and click on the **Next>** button.

Slide the **Result resolution** to **8.** Push the **Finish** button in **Wizard - Results and Geometry Resolution** window. Right click anywhere in the graphics window and select **Zoom In/Out** to see the computational domain surrounding the cylinder.

Select **Tools>>Flow Simulation>>Project>>Show Basic Mesh** to see the mesh surrounding the cylinder.

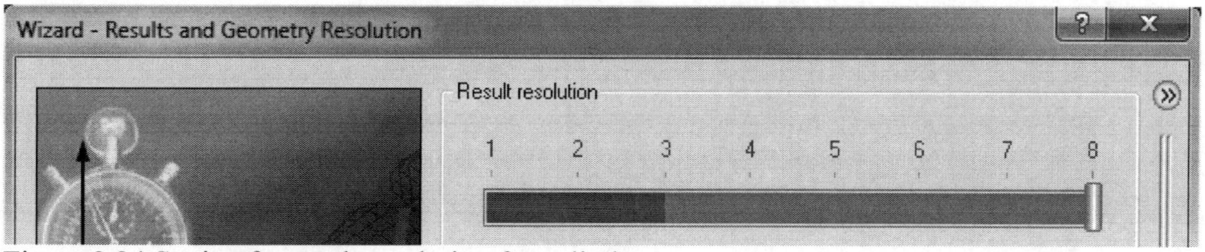

Figure 3.34 Setting for result resolution for cylinder

Inserting Global Goals for Calculations and Selecting 2D Flow

33. We create global goals for the project by selecting **Tools>>Flow Simulation>>Insert>>Global Goals…** from the SOLIDWORKS menu and check the boxes for **Force (X)** and **Force (Y)**. Exit the global goals.

Select **Tools>>Flow Simulation>>Insert>>Equation Goal…** from the menu and select **GG Force (X) 1** from the **Flow Simulation analysis tree**. Enter the expression for the equation goal as shown in figure 3.35a). Select **Dimensionless LMA** from the **Dimensionality** drop down menu. Exit the **Equation Goal** window. Rename the equation goal in the Flow Simulation analysis tree to **Drag Coefficient**. Repeat this step and create an equation goal for the lift coefficient; see figure 3.35b).

Select **Tools>>Flow Simulation>>Computational Domain…** from the SOLIDWORKS menu. Select **2D Simulation** and **XY plane**; see figure 3.35c). Exit the **Computational Domain** window.

Select **Tools>>Flow Simulation>>Initial Mesh…** from the SOLIDWORKS menu. Uncheck the **Automatic settings** box at the bottom of the **Initial Mesh** window. Set the **Number of cells per X:** to **25** and the **Number of cells per Y:** to **24**. Click on the **OK** button.

Select **Tools>>Flow Simulation>>Calculation Control Options…** from the SOLIDWORKS menu. Set **Maximum physical time** to **200 s**. Click on the **OK** button.

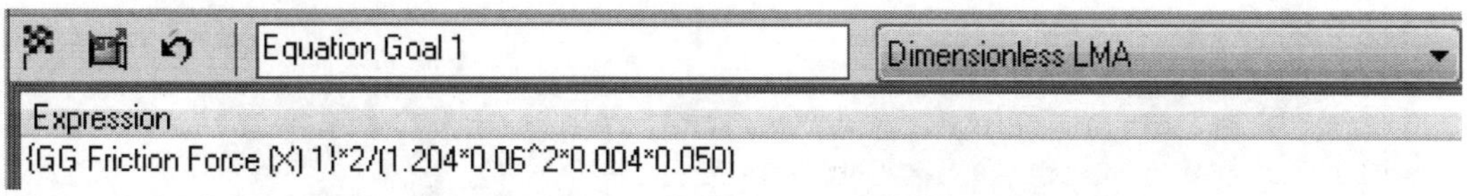

Figure 3.35a) Expression for equation goal for drag coefficient

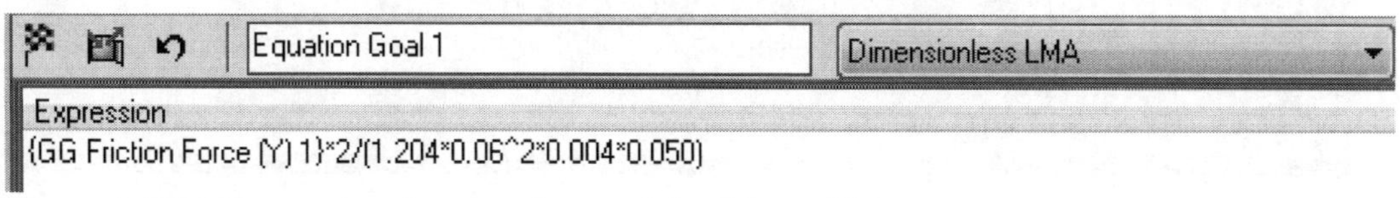

Figure 3.35b) Expression for equation goal for lift coefficient

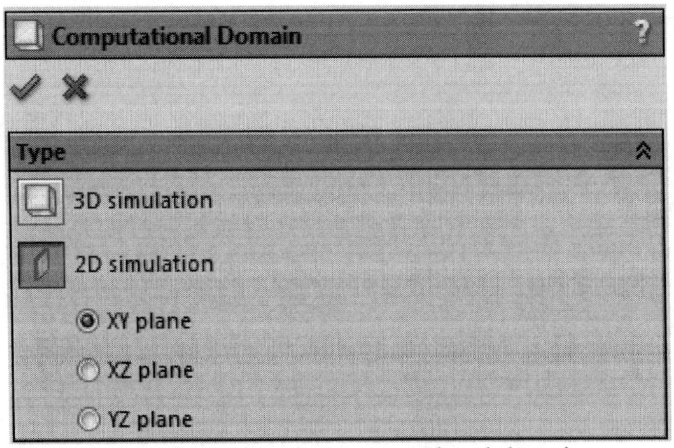

Figure 3.35c) Selecting the computational domain

Tabular Saving

34. We would like to save the calculations at different instants in time so that we can capture the vortex shedding motion. You start by selecting **Tools>>Flow Simulation>>Calculation Control Options…** from the SOLIDWORKS menu. Select the **Saving** tab and check the **Parameter Full Results** box next to **Periodic**. Set the **Start Value** to iteration number **516** and the **Period Value** to **1**; see figure 3.36. Click on the **OK** buttons to exit the **Table** and **Calculation Control Options** windows.

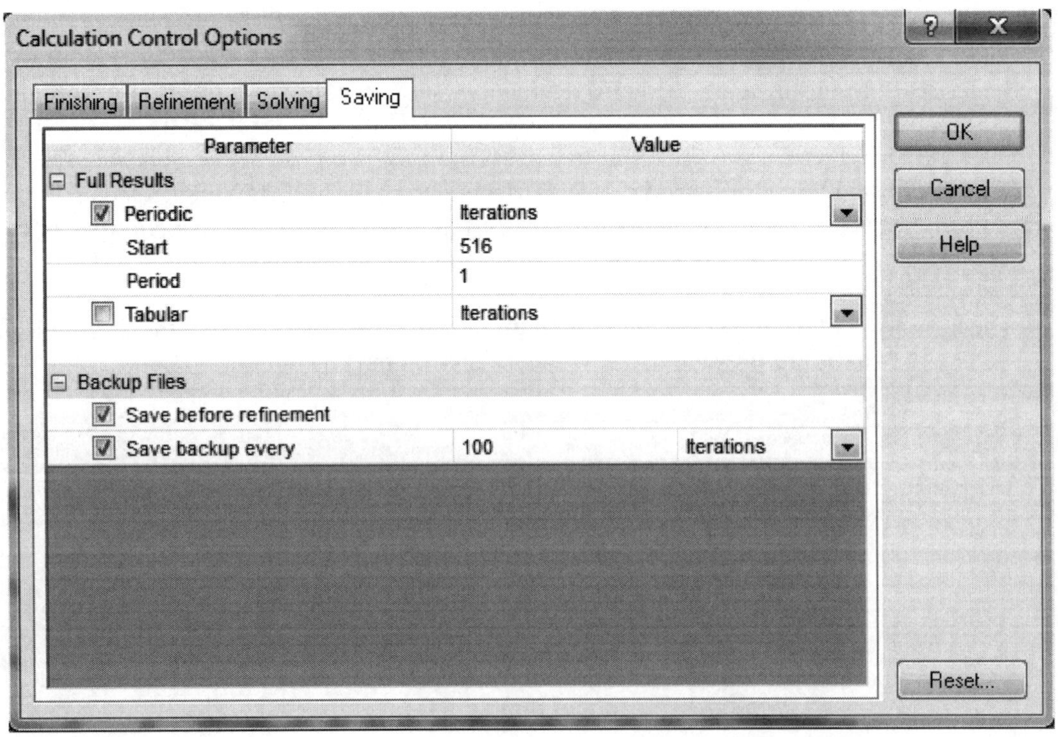

Figure 3.36 Calculation control options

Running Calculations for the Cylinder

35. Choose **Tools>>Flow Simulation>>Solve>>Run…** Click on the **Run** button in the window that appears. Click on the goals flag to **Insert Goals Table** in the **Solver** window. Click on **Insert Goals Plot** in the **Solver** window. Select **Lift Coefficient** as goal. Click on the **OK** button. Right click in the goals plot. Select **Physical time** from **X-axis units**. Slide the **Plot length** to the middle in between **min** and **max**; see figure 3.37a). Click on the **OK** button.

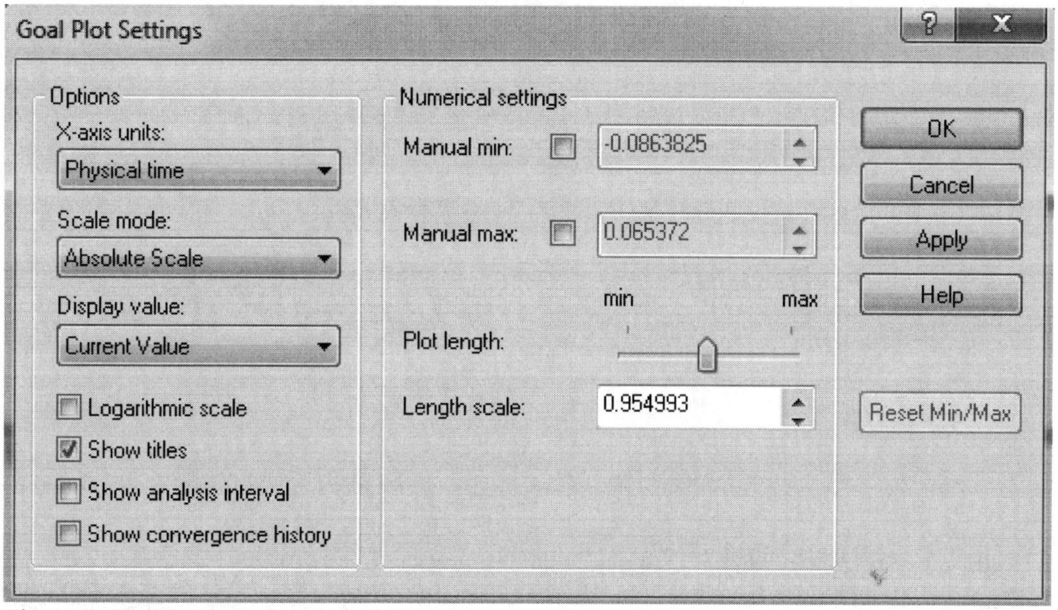

Figure 3.37a) Settings for goal plot

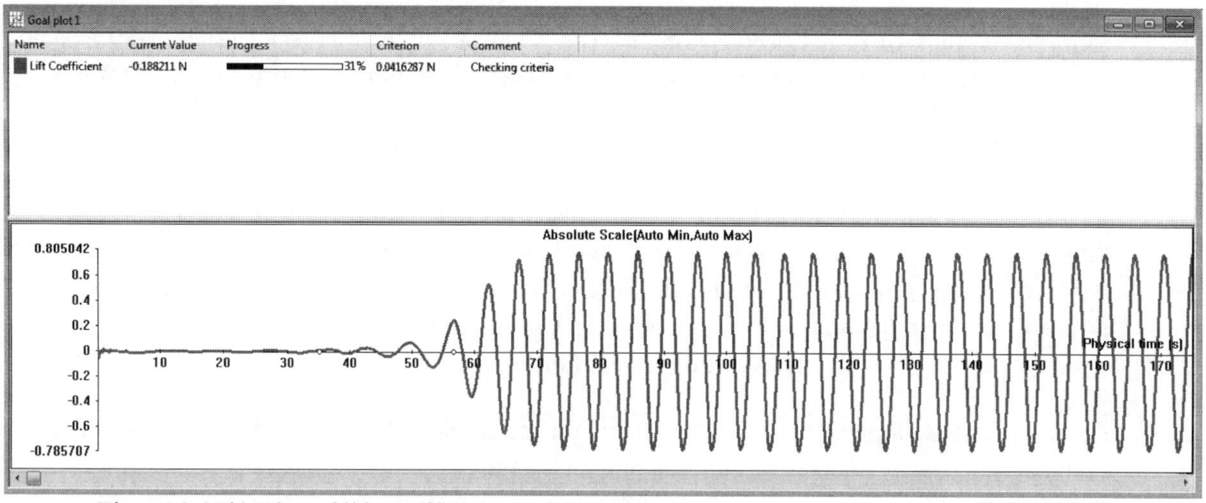

Figure 3.37b) Plot of lift coefficient variation over time

Using Excel for Frequency Analysis

36. We are now interested in determining the frequency of the time signal in figure 3.37b). In order to use FFT (Fast Fourier Transform) calculations in Excel 2010 we have to add the analysis tool packages. Select **File>>Options** from the menu in Excel. Click on the **Add-Ins** button in the Excel Options window. Select **Excel Add-Ins** from the Manage: drop down menu and click on the **Go…** button. Check the boxes for **Analysis ToolPak** and **Analysis ToolPak – VBA**. Click on the **OK** button. You will now install the add-ins. Place the files **"graph 3.39b)"** and **"graph 3.39c)"** on the desktop. These files and the other exercise files are available for download at http://www.sdcpublications.com/downloads/978-1-58503-934-0/

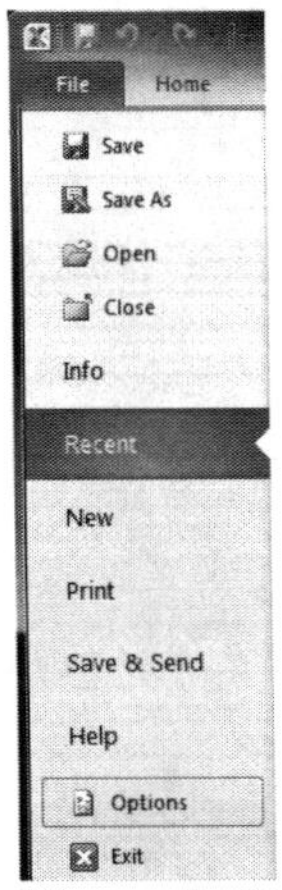

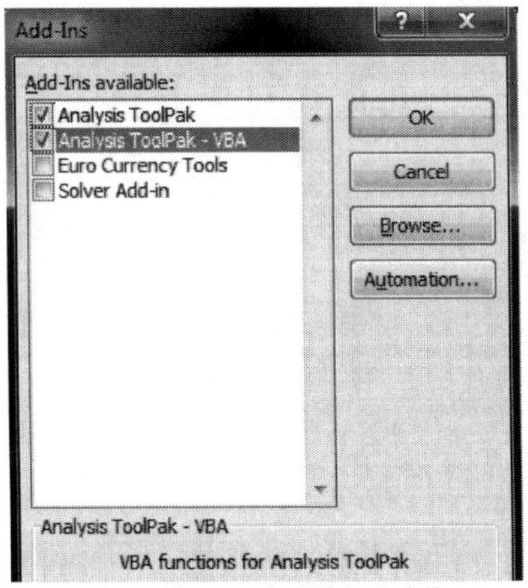

Figure 3.38a) Using Excel 2010 to add analysis   Figure 3.38b) Adding analysis tools

Inserting XY Plots

37. Right click and select **Insert…** on **Goal Plots** in the **Results** section of the **Flow Simulation analysis tree**. Check the box for **Lift Coefficient**; see figure 3.39a). Select **Physical time** from the **Abscissa** drop down menu. Select **Excel Workbook (*.xlsx)** from the **Options** drop down menu. Click on the **Export to Excel** button. An Excel file will open with a summary sheet, a lift coefficient sheet, and a plot data sheet.

    Double click on the **graph 3.39b)** file to open the file. Click on **Enable Content** if you get a **Security Warning** that **Macros** have been disabled. If **Developer** is not available in the menu of the **Excel** file, you will need to do the following: Select **File>>Options** from the menu and click on the **Customize Ribbon** on the left hand side. Check the **Developer** box on the right hand side under **Main Tabs**. Click **OK** to exit the **Excel Options** window.

    Click on the **Developer** tab in the **Excel** menu for the **graph 3.39b)** file and select **Visual Basic** on the left hand side to open the editor. Click on the plus sign next to **VBAProject (Goal Plot 1.xlsx)** and click on the plus sign next to **Microsoft Excel Objects**. Right click on **Sheet3 (Plot Data)** and select **View Object**.

    Select **Module2** in the **Modules** folder under **VBAProject (graph 3.39b).xlsm)**. Select **Run>>Run Macro** from the menu of the **MVB for Applications** window. Click on the **Run** button in the **Macros** window. Figure 3.39b) will become available in **Excel** showing the regular oscillation of the time signal for the lift coefficient. We see that the amplitude and period of the time signal is constant in the region from 70s – 200s; compare with 3.37b). Close the **Goal Plot** window and the **graph 3.39b)** window in **Excel**. Exit the **XY Plot** window in **SOLIDWORKS Flow Simulation**.

38. Repeat step **37**, but this time use the **graph 3.39c)** file to plot the amplitude versus frequency of the power spectrum from the FFT analysis of the time signal; see figure 3.39c). The spectrum is a result of using Fourier analysis on the time signal. We see that there is a clear peak in amplitude at a frequency between 0.2 Hz and 0.3 Hz. A more exact value of the frequency can be found from plot data to be 0.2374 Hz.

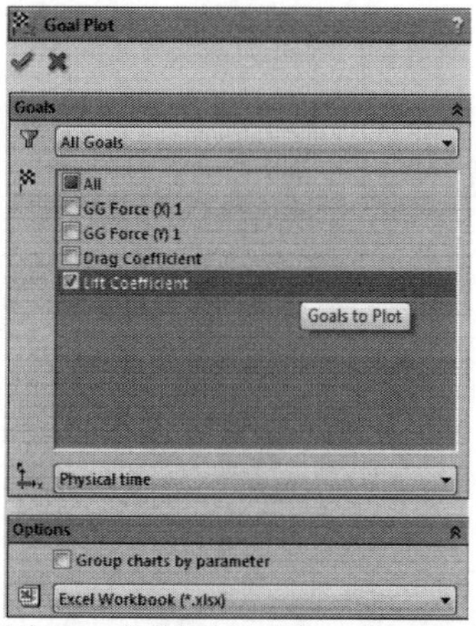

Figure 3.39a) Setting for goals plot

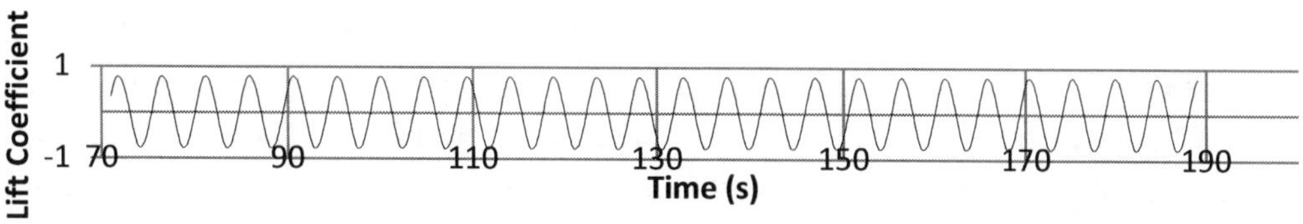

Figure 3.39b) Time signal of the lift coefficient in the region T = 70 – 190 s

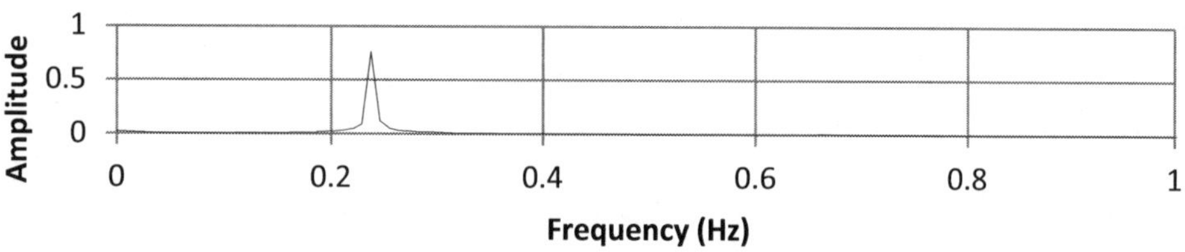

Figure 3.39c) Waveform in the frequency domain

Strouhal number

The Strouhal number S is one of the many non-dimensional numbers used in fluid mechanics and based on the oscillation frequency of fluid flows. In this case the Strouhal number is based on the vortex shedding frequency f and can be defined as

$$S = \frac{fd}{U} = \frac{0.2375\ \text{Hz} \cdot 0.050m}{0.06m/s} = 0.1979 \tag{3.4}$$

The Reynolds number for the flow around a cylinder that we have been studying is

$$\text{Re} = \frac{Ud\rho}{\mu} = \frac{0.06 \cdot 0.050 \cdot 1.204}{1.825 \cdot 10^{-5}} = 198 \tag{3.5}$$

This value of the Strouhal number from Flow Simulation can be compared with DNS (Direct Numerical Simulations) results of Henderson (1997). See also Williamson and Brown (1998).

$$S = 0.2698 - \frac{1.0272}{\sqrt{\text{Re}}} = 0.1968 \tag{3.6}$$

The difference is only 0.6%.

Inserting Cut Plots

39. We now want to plot the X-velocity component and vorticity at the different instants that we tabulated in step **34**. Select **Tools>>Flow Simulation>>Results>>Load from File...** from the SOLIDWORKS menu. Open the file **r_000518 .fld**. Right click on **Cut Plots** in the **Flow Simulation analysis tree** and select **Insert...** and select **Velocity (X)** from the **Contours** section. Slide the **Number of Levels** to **255**. Exit the cut plot dialog. Select front view from the view orientation drop down menu in the graphics window. Change the name of Cut Plot 1 to **Velocity (X) at Iteration = 518**. Insert one more cut plot and plot the vorticity. Change the name of the cut plot to **Vorticity at Iteration = 518**. Load the remaining four files **r_000527.fld**, **r_000537.fld**, **r_000546.fld** and **r_000556 .fld**. Plot Velocity (X) and Vorticity for each file; see figures 3.40a) and 3.40b).

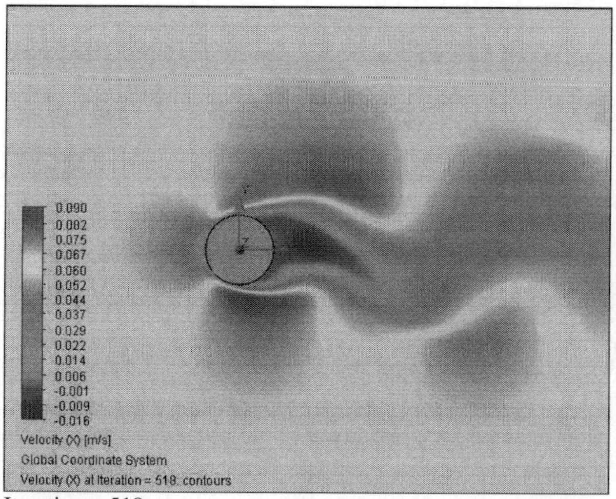

Iteration = 518

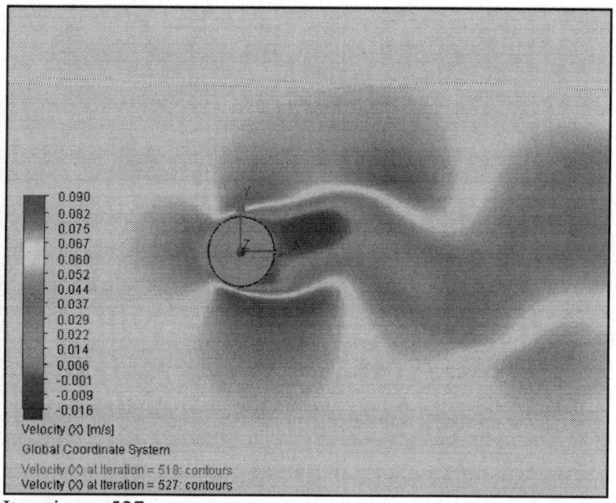

Iteration = 527

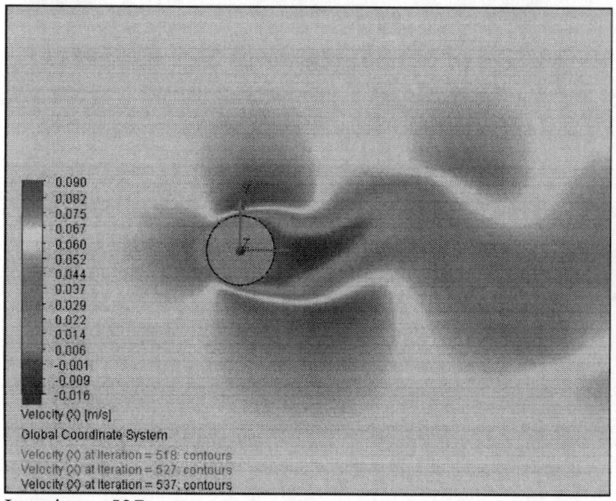

Iteration = 537

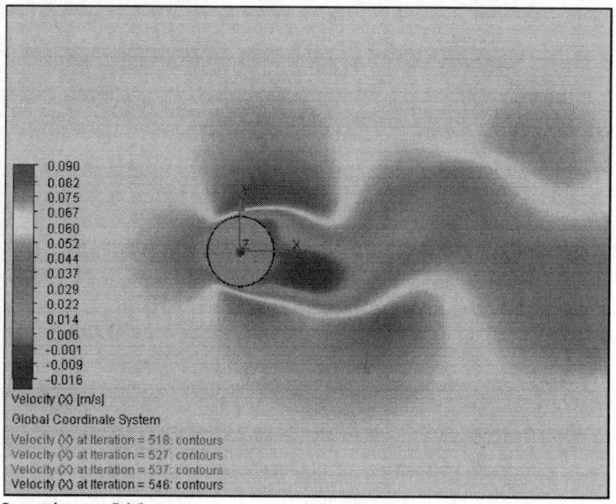

Iteration = 546

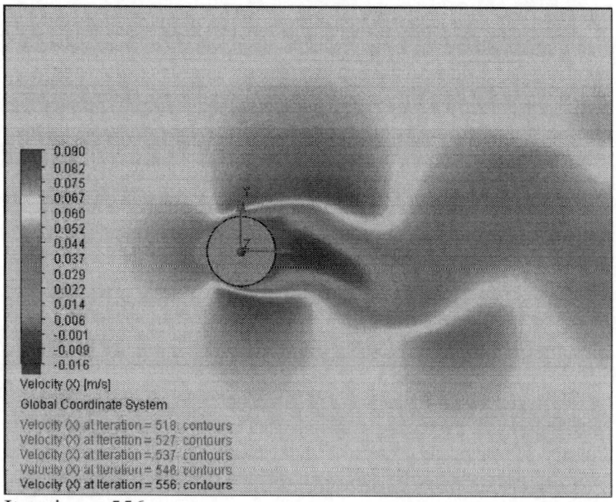

Iteration = 556

Figure 3.40a) Velocity (X) during a period of vortex shedding

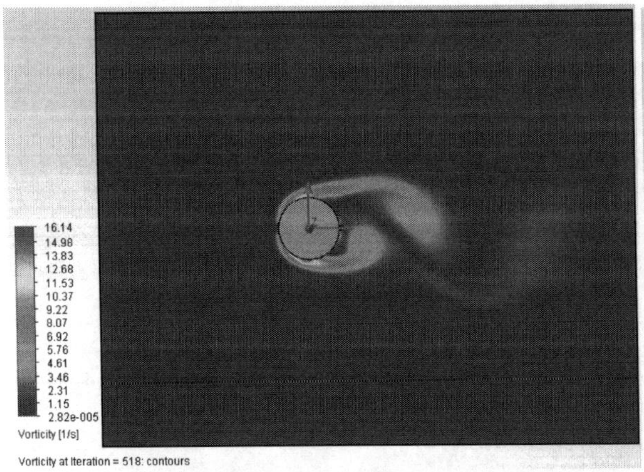

Iteration = 518

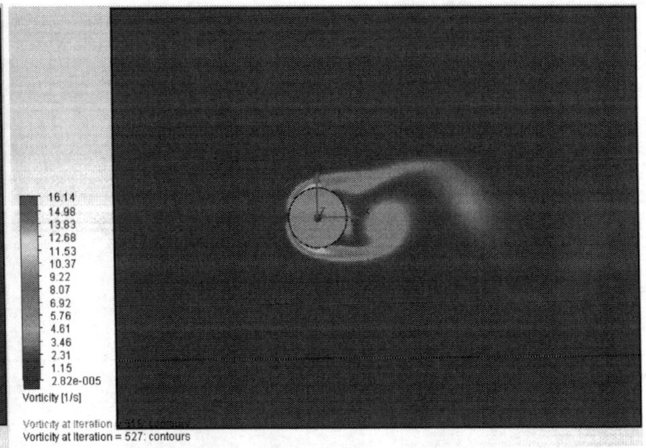

Iteration = 527

Iteration = 537

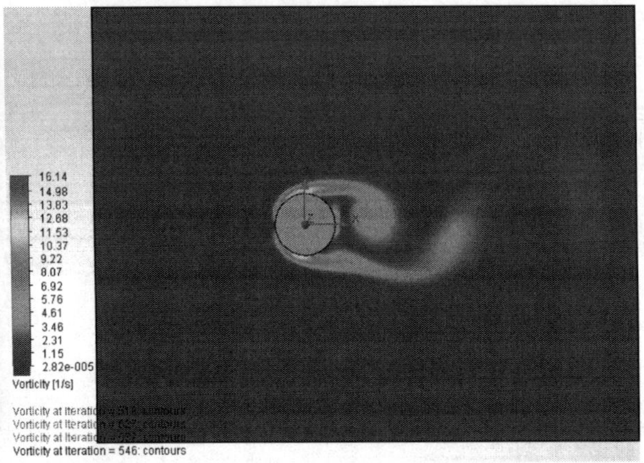

Iteration = 546

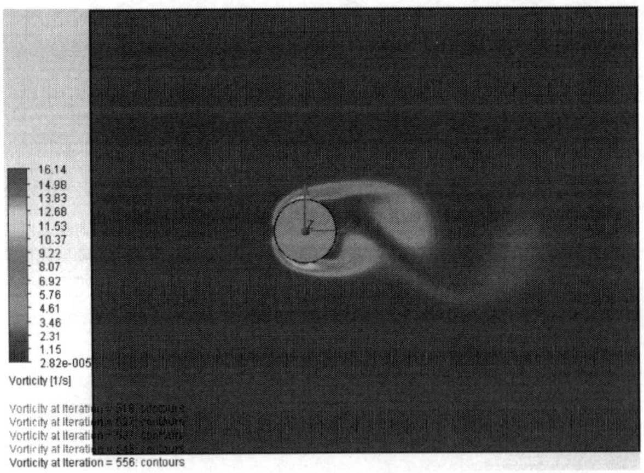

Iteration = 556

Figure 3.40b) Vorticity during a period of vortex shedding

Animating the Cut Plots

40. We now want to animate the cut plots of vorticity. Start by selecting **Tools>>Flow Simulation>>Results>>Load/Unload**. Repeat this step one more time.

Right click on the cut plot named **Vorticity at Iteration** = **518** and select **Animation….** Click on the **Expand** button to expand the animation controls section; see figure 3.41a). Click on the control point for **Animation 1** at 00:10 and drag it towards 00:00; see figure 3.41b). Select the animation wizard; see figure 3.41c). Set the animation time to **4.68 s** and click on the **Next>** button. Click on the **Next>** button in the following window. Check the **Scenario** animation type and click on the **Next>** button. Select **Uniform distribution** and **Physical time** for **Units**. Set **Start from: 0 s** and **Finish at: 200 s**. Click on the **Next>** button and click on the **Finish** button to exit the animation wizard. Click on the right control point for vorticity located close to 0 s and drag it to 4.8 s; see figure 3.41d). Click on the  **Play** button to start the animation.

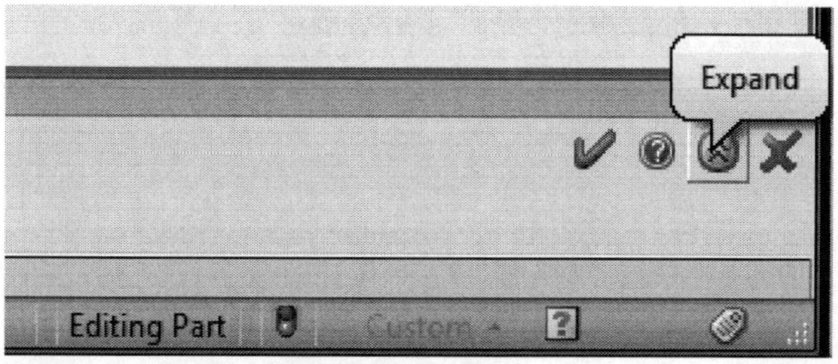

Figure 3.41a) Animation controls

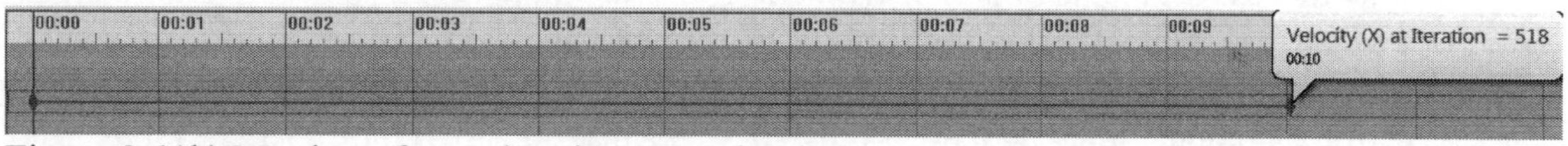

Figure 3.41b) Moving of an animation control point

Figure 3.41c) Animation wizard

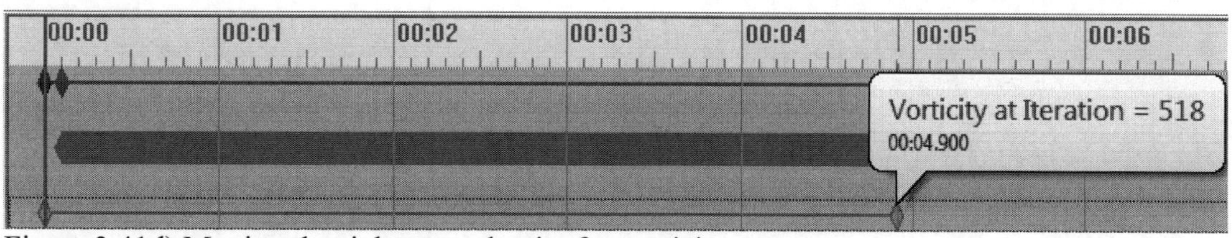

Figure 3.41d) Moving the right control point for vorticity

References

[1] Çengel, Y. A., and Cimbala, J.M., Fluid Mechanics: Fundamentals and Applications, McGraw-Hill, 2006.

[2] Henderson, R., Nonlinear dynamics and pattern formation in turbulent wake transition, *J. of Fluid Mech.*, **352**, (65-112), 1997.

[3] SOLIDWORKS Flow Simulation 2015 Technical Reference.

[4] SOLIDWORKS Flow Simulation 2015 Tutorial.

[5] White, F. M., Viscous Fluid Flow, McGraw-Hill, 1991.

[6] Williamson, C. H. K., and Brown G.L., A series in $1/\sqrt{Re}$ to represent the Strouhal-Reynolds number relationship of the cylinder wake, *Journal of Fluids and Structures*, **12**, (1073 – 1085), 1998.

Exercises

3.1 Run the steady calculations for the flow over a 25 mm radius sphere for Re = 9.9, 99 and use different levels of initial mesh: 1, 2, 3, 4 and 5. Plot the drag coefficient versus mesh level using Excel. Include both SOLIDWORKS Flow Simulation results and empirical data in the same plot. Fill out Table 3.2. Determine the percent difference variation as compared with the experimental values $C_{D,Sphere\ Experiment}$ = 4.273 and 1.191, respectively. Use the following size of the computational domain: Xmin: -0.175, Xmax: 0.275, Ymin: -0.175, Ymax: 0.175, Zmin: -0.175, Zmax: 0.175

$$Percent\ Difference = \left| \frac{C_{D,Sphere\ Simulation} - C_{D,Sphere\ Experiment}}{C_{D,Sphere\ Experiment}} \right| * 100\%$$

Discuss your results.

Initial Mesh	U (m/s)	Re	$C_{D,\ Simulation}$	$C_{D,\ Experiment}$	Difference (%)
1		9.9		4.273	
2		9.9		4.273	
3		9.9		4.273	
4		9.9		4.273	
5		9.9		4.273	
1		99		1.191	
2		99		1.191	
3		99		1.191	
4		99		1.191	
5		99		1.191	

Table 3.2 Comparison of drag coefficient for a sphere at various initial mesh and Reynolds numbers

3.2 Run the steady calculations for the flow around a 25 mm radius sphere for Re = 9.9 for an initial mesh level of 4 and use different sizes a) – d) of the computational domain. Plot the drag coefficient versus length of computational domain. Include flow simulations and empirical data in the same plot.

a) Xmin: -0.05, Xmax: 0.05, Ymin: -0.05, Ymax: 0.05, Zmin: -0.05, Zmax: 0.05
b) Xmin: -0.1, Xmax: 0.1, Ymin: -0.1, Ymax: 0.1, Zmin: -0.1, Zmax: 0.1
c) Xmin: -0.15, Xmax: 0.15, Ymin: -0.15, Ymax: 0.15, Zmin: -0.15, Zmax: 0.15
d) Xmin: -0.2, Xmax: 0.2, Ymin: -0.2, Ymax: 0.2, Zmin: -0.2, Zmax: 0.2
e) Xmin: -0.25, Xmax: 0.25, Ymin: -0.25, Ymax: 0.25, Zmin: -0.25, Zmax: 0.25

How does the drag coefficient vary with the size of the computational domain? Determine percent difference variation as compared with empirical results. Discuss your results.

Comp. Domain Length	U (m/s)	Re	$C_{D,\ Simulation}$	$C_{D,\ Experiment}$	Difference (%)
0.1		9.9		4.273	
0.2		9.9		4.273	
0.3		9.9		4.273	
0.4		9.9		4.273	
0.5		9.9		4.273	

Table 3.3 Comparison of drag coefficient for a sphere at various computational domain lengths.

3.3 Use SOLIDWORKS Flow Simulation to determine the drag coefficient for a cylinder with a radius of 25 mm. Use 2D-plane, XY-plane flow boundary condition for the calculations at Re = 0.1, 1, 10, 100, 1000, 10000, 100000 (initial mesh level of 6) and compare with experimental results using the following curve-fit formula:

$$C_{D,CylinderExperiment} = 1 + \frac{10}{\mathrm{Re}^{2/3}} \qquad 0 \leq \mathrm{Re} \leq 250{,}000$$

Determine the percentage difference from experiments in Table 3.3 for the different Reynolds numbers. Use the following size of the computational domain:
Xmin: -0.175, Xmax: 0.275, Ymin: -0.175, Ymax: 0.175, Zmin: -0.002, Zmax: 0.002

$$Percent\ Difference = \left| \frac{C_{D,Cylinder\ Simulation} - C_{D,Cylinder\ Experiment}}{C_{D,Cylinder\ Experiment}} \right| * 100\%$$

Plot drag coefficient versus Reynolds number for flow simulation results and empirical data in the same graph. Use time dependent calculation for Re ≥ 50. Discuss your results.

U (m/s)	Re	$C_{D,Simulation}$	$C_{D,Experiment}$	Difference (%)
	0.1			
	1			
	10			
	100			
	1,000			
	10,000			
	100,000			

Table 3.4 Comparison of drag coefficient for a cylinder at various Reynolds numbers

Notes:

Chapter 4 Analysis of the Flow past an Airfoil

Objectives

- Creating the wing section needed for the SOLIDWORKS Flow Simulation
- Inserting a curve through given coordinates
- Setting up a Flow Simulation project for external flow
- Inserting global goals and equation goal
- Running the calculations
- Using Cut Plots to visualize the resulting flow field
- Creating a custom visualization parameter
- Cloning of the project
- Create a batch run
- Compare with experimental results

Problem Description

In this exercise we will analyze the flow around a Selig/Donovan SD 2030 airfoil section. We will study the flow at a Reynolds number *Re* = 100,000 and determine the lift coefficient versus the angle of attack and compare with experimental data. First, we have to create a model of the airfoil in SOLIDWORKS and export the part to Flow Simulation. The chord length of the airfoil is 305 mm and the thickness is 26.1 mm. Follow the different steps in this chapter to create a solid model of the airfoil (see figure 4.0), and perform a 2D plane Flow Simulation of the flow field.

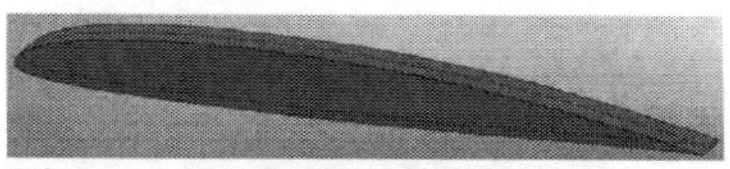

Figure 4.0 SOLIDWORKS model of Selig/Donovan SD 2030 airfoil section

Creating the SOLIDWORKS Part

1. Start SOLIDWORKS and create a New Part. Select the **Front** view from the drop down menu in the graphics window. Select **Tools>>Options…** from the SOLIDWORKS menu. Click on the Document Properties tab and select **Units**. Select **MMGS** as your **Unit system**.

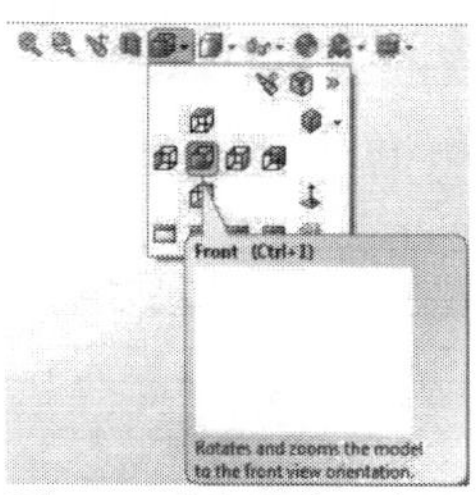

Figure 4.1 Selection of front view

2. Select **Insert>>Curve>>Curve Through XYZ Points…**

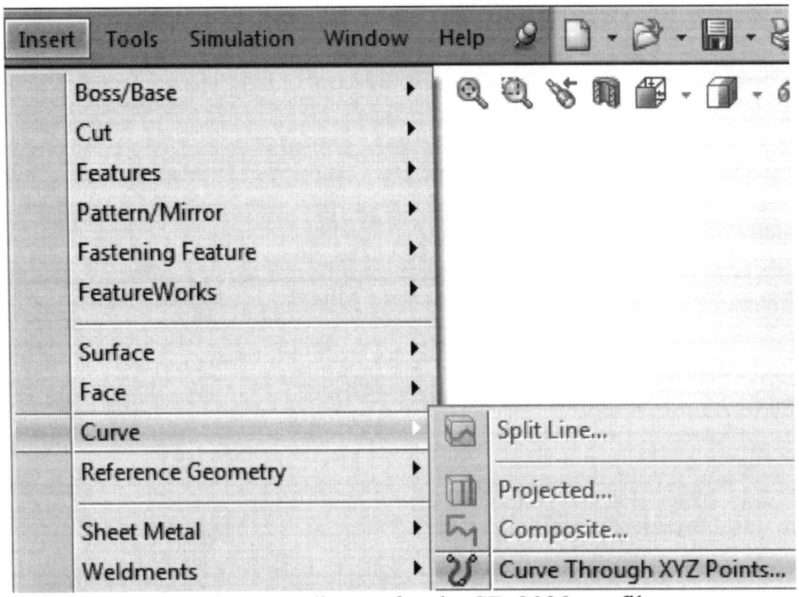

Figure 4.2 Importing coordinates for the SD 2030 profile

3. In the **Curve File** window you select **Browse** and open the file **SD2030.sldcrv** that can be downloaded from the **sdcpublications.com** website. The Curve File window appears with the X and Y coordinates shown for the airfoil. Click **OK**. Right click in the graphics window and **Zoom/Pan/Rotate>>Zoom to Fit.**

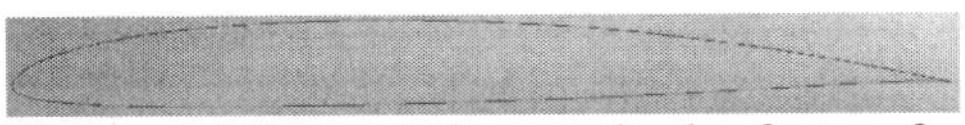

Figure 4.3 Imported curve in the form of an airfoil

4. Next, we select the **Front Plane** in the **FeatureManager design tree** and click on the **Extruded Boss/Base** feature.

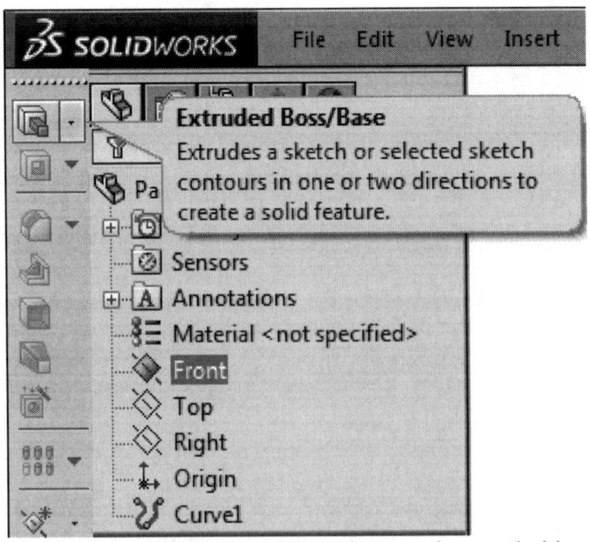

Figure 4.4 Selection of front plane and extruded boss/base feature

5. Click on **Curve1** in the **FeatureManager design tree** and select **Tools>>Sketch Tools>>Convert Entities** from the SOLIDWORKS menu.

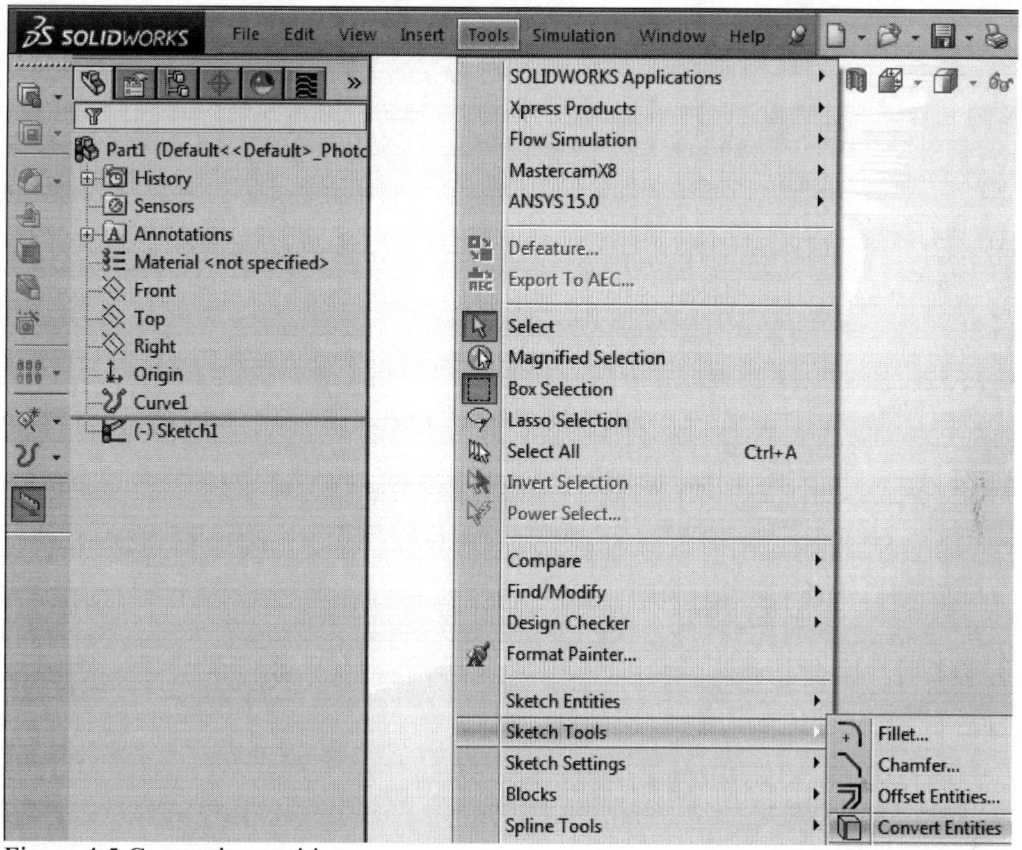

Figure 4.5 Converting entities

6. Select **Extruded Boss/Base** once again.

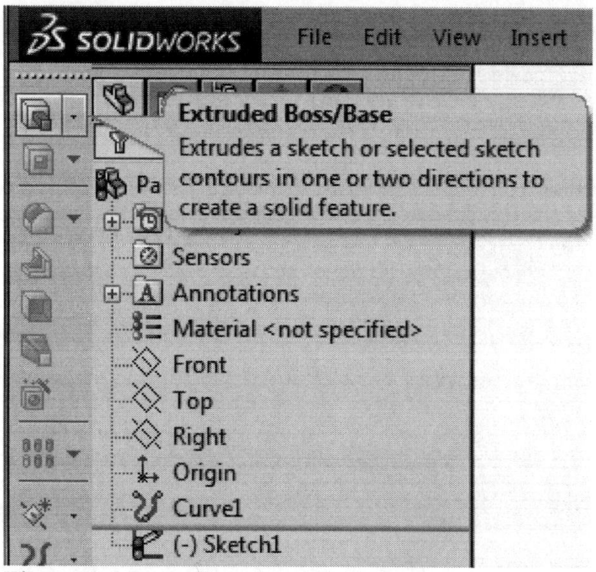

Figure 4.6 Extruding the airfoil sketch

7. Check the box for **Direction 2** and click on the **OK** button.

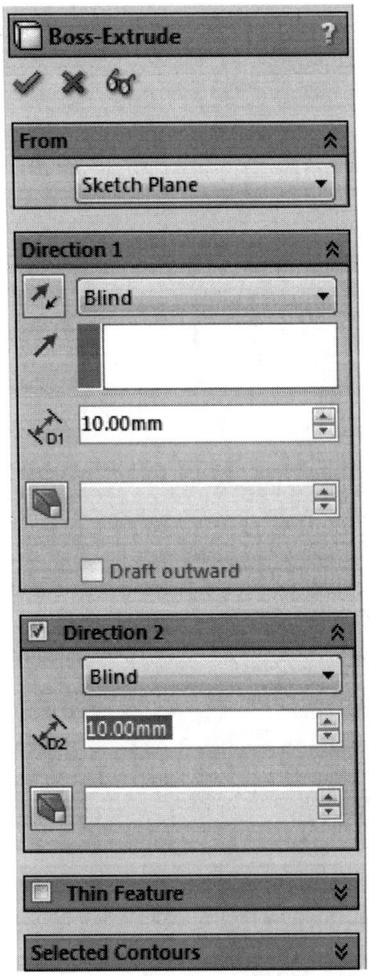

Figure 4.7 Entering the direction of the extrusion

8. Select the **Front** view from the drop down menu in the graphics window.
Right click in the graphics window and select **Zoom/Pan/Rotate>>Zoom to Fit**. Save your airfoil as **SD 2030**.

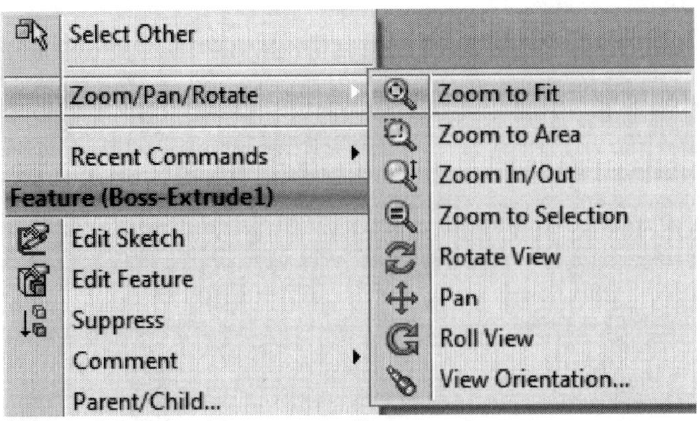

Figure 4.8 Selecting zoom to fit

9. Click on the plus sign next to the **Boss-Extrude1** symbol in the **FeatureManager design tree** and rename the sketch to **Airfoil Sketch** and the extrusion to **Extruded Airfoil Sketch**. You have now finished your SD 2030 section. Save the part.

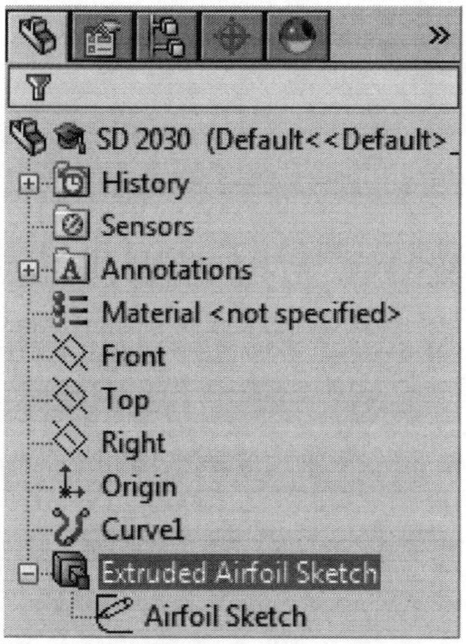

Figure 4.9 Rename the extrusion

Setting up the Flow Simulation Project

10. If Flow Simulation is not available in the SOLIDWORKS menu, select **Tools>>Add Ins...** and check the corresponding **SOLIDWORKS Flow Simulation** box. We will now create a Flow Simulation project by selecting **Tools>>Flow Simulation>>Project>>Wizard...** from the menu. Enter Project name **SD 2030 Airfoil AoA = 0**. Click on the **Next>** button.

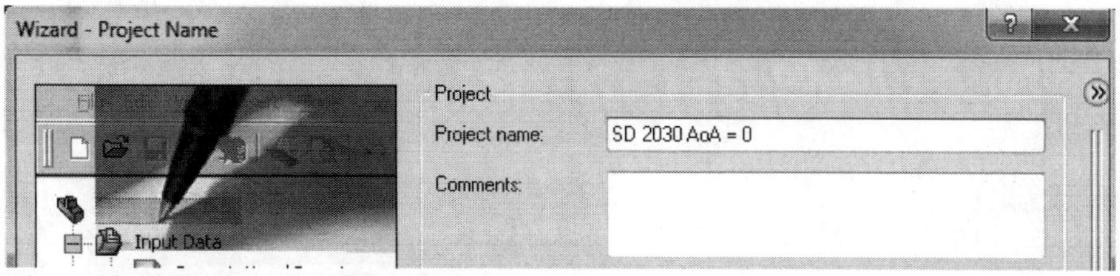

Figure 4.10 Project configuration wizard

11. Choose **SI Unit system** and click on the **Next>** button.

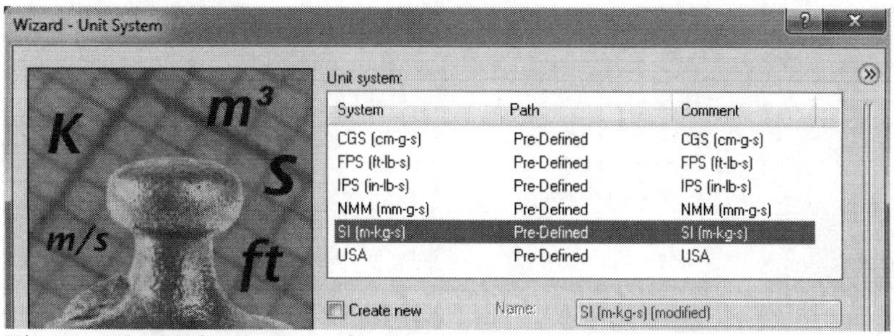

Figure 4.11 Unit system wizard

12. Check the **External Analysis type** box and click the **Next>** button.

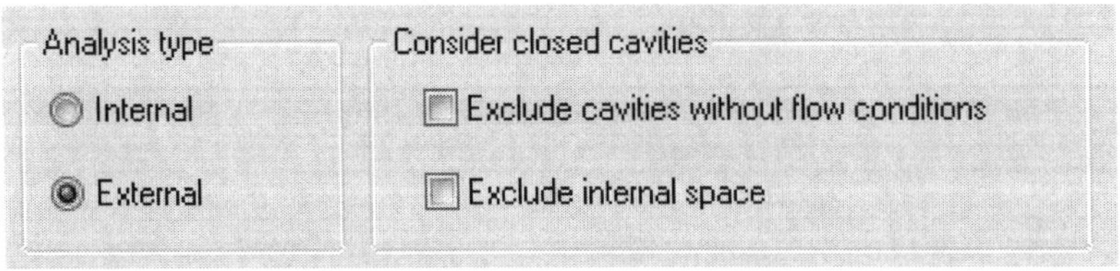

Figure 4.12 Analysis type

13. Choose **Air** from the gases in the **Fluids** window and push the **Add** button. Air will now appear as the **Default Project Fluid**. Click on the **Next>** button.

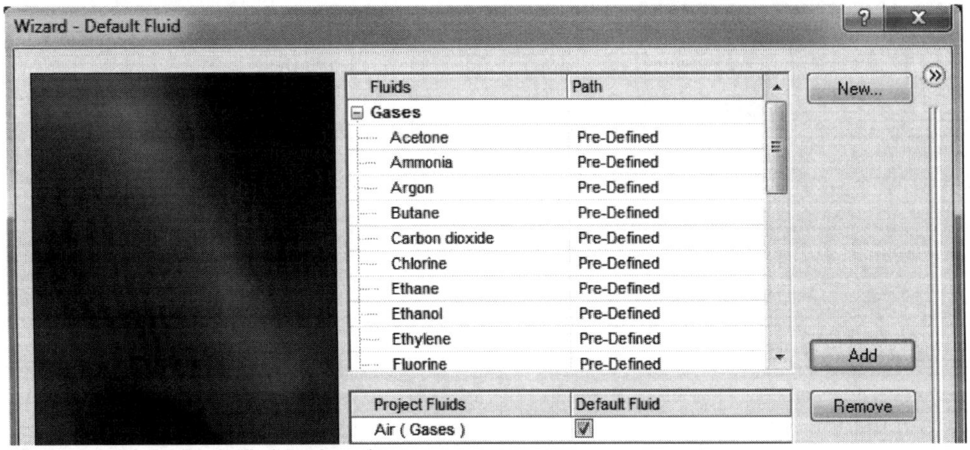

Figure 4.13 Default fluid wizard

14. In the next step we will leave the default value of the surface roughness as **Wall Condition** and click on the **Next>** button. Enter **4.9 m/s** as the **Velocity in X direction** and **0.12%** as **Turbulence intensity** from the **Turbulence Parameters** section. Click on the **Next>** button. Slide the **Result resolution** to **6** in the **Results and Geometry Resolution** window and push the **Finish** button.

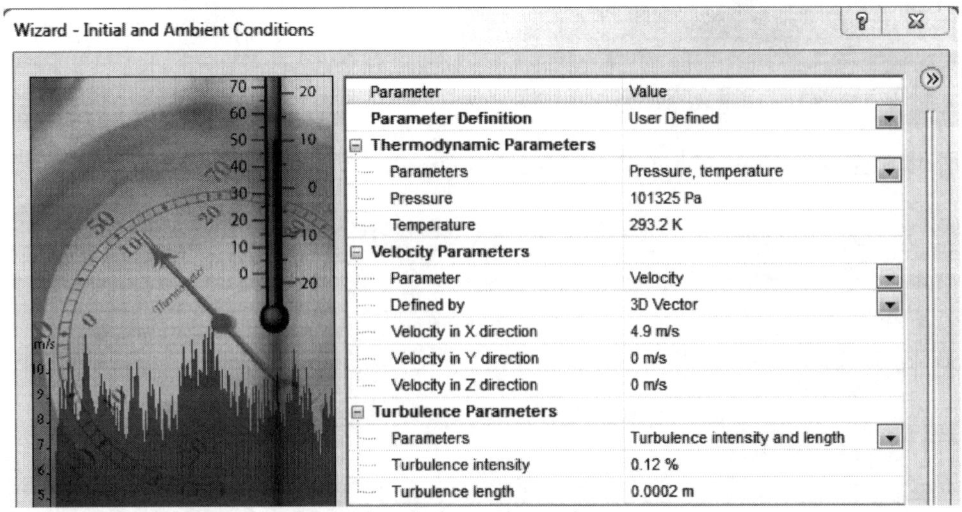

Figure 4.14 Adding velocity and turbulence intensity

15. Select **Tools>>Flow Simulation>>Computational Domain…** from the menu. Select **2D simulation** and **XY plane** from the **Type** section. Close the **Computational Domain** window.

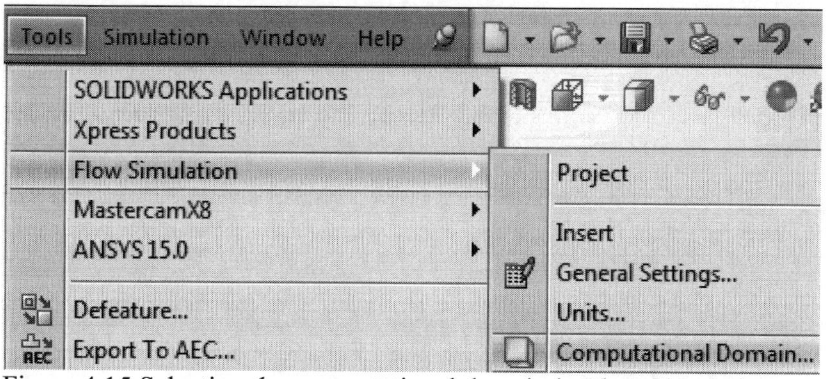

Figure 4.15 Selecting the computational domain in Flow Simulation

<u>**Inserting Global Goals for Calculations**</u>

16. Click on the **Flow Simulation analysis tree** tab and open the **Input Data** folder by clicking on the plus sign next to it. Right click on **Goals** and select **Insert Global Goals…**. Check the box for **Force (Y)** and click on the **OK** button to exit the **Global Goals** window.

.

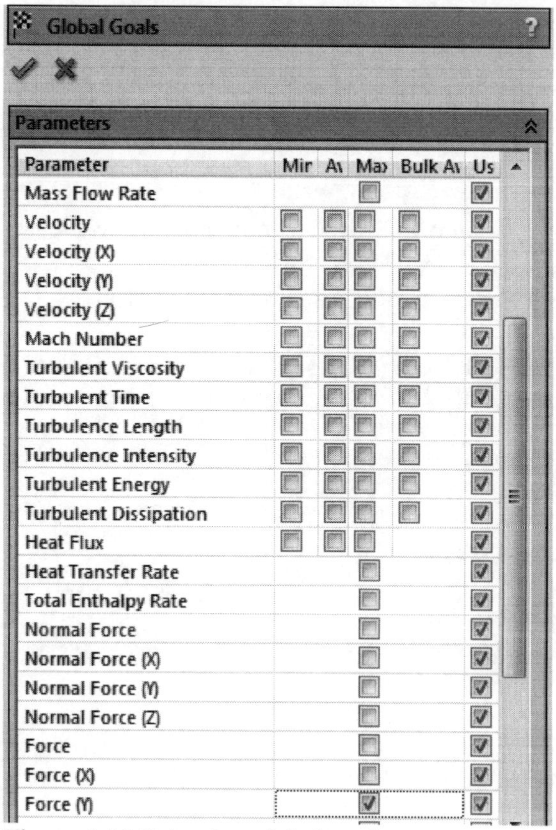

Figure 4.16 Selecting global goal

Inserting Equation Goal for Calculations

17. Right-click on **Goals** under **Input Data** in the **Flow Simulation analysis tree** and select **Insert Equation Goal….** Enter the expression for the lift coefficient by clicking on the **GG Force (Y) 1** goal under **Goals** in the **Flow Simulation analysis tree**. Complete the expression as shown in figure 4.17b). Select **Dimensionless LMA** from the **Dimensionality:** drop down menu. Exit the **Equation Goal** window. Rename the equation goal to **Lift Coefficient** in the **Flow Simulation analysis tree**.

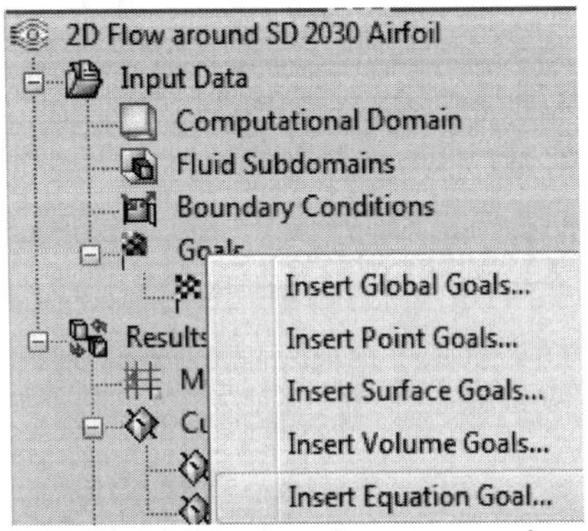

Figure 4.17a) Inserting an equation goal

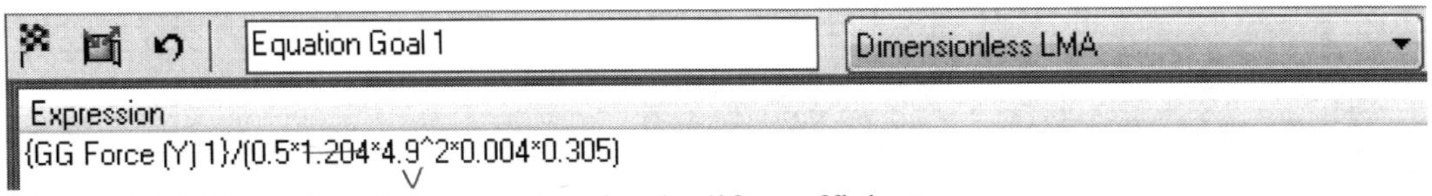

Figure 4.17b) Entering the expression for the lift coefficient

18. Right click in the graphics window and select **Zoom In/Out** and zoom out until you can see the whole computational domain around the airfoil. Select **Tools>>Flow Simulation>>Project>>Show Basic Mesh** to display the mesh around the airfoil.

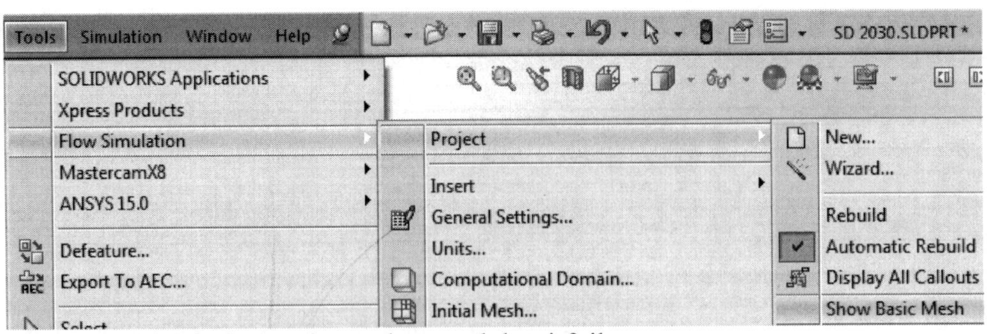

Figure 4.18a) Displaying the mesh around the airfoil

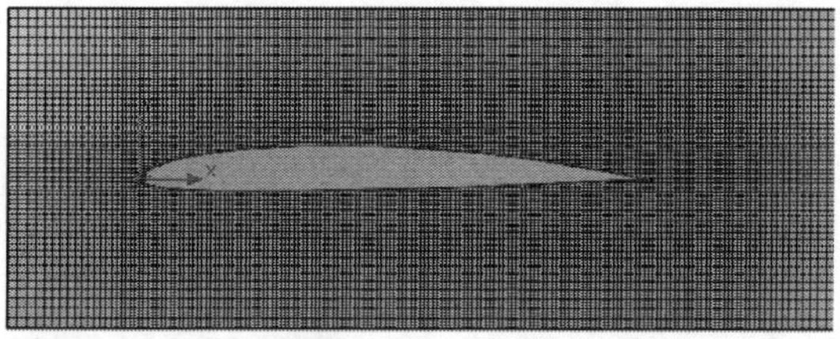

Figure 4.18b) Mesh around the airfoil

Running the Calculations

19. Select **Tools>>Flow Simulation>>Solve>>Run**. Push the **Run** button in the Run window.

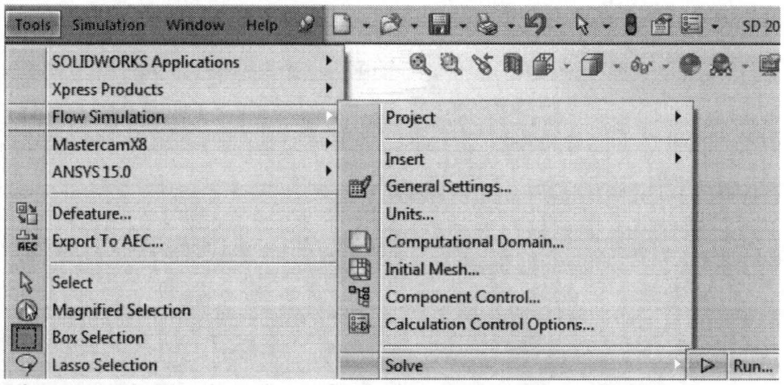

Figure 4.19 Starting the calculations of the flow field

20. Select **Insert Goal Plot…** from the menu of the **Solver**. Select **Lift Coefficient** as **Goal**. Select **Insert Preview…** from the menu to insert plots of **Velocity (X)** including the grid and **Pressure** as isolines.

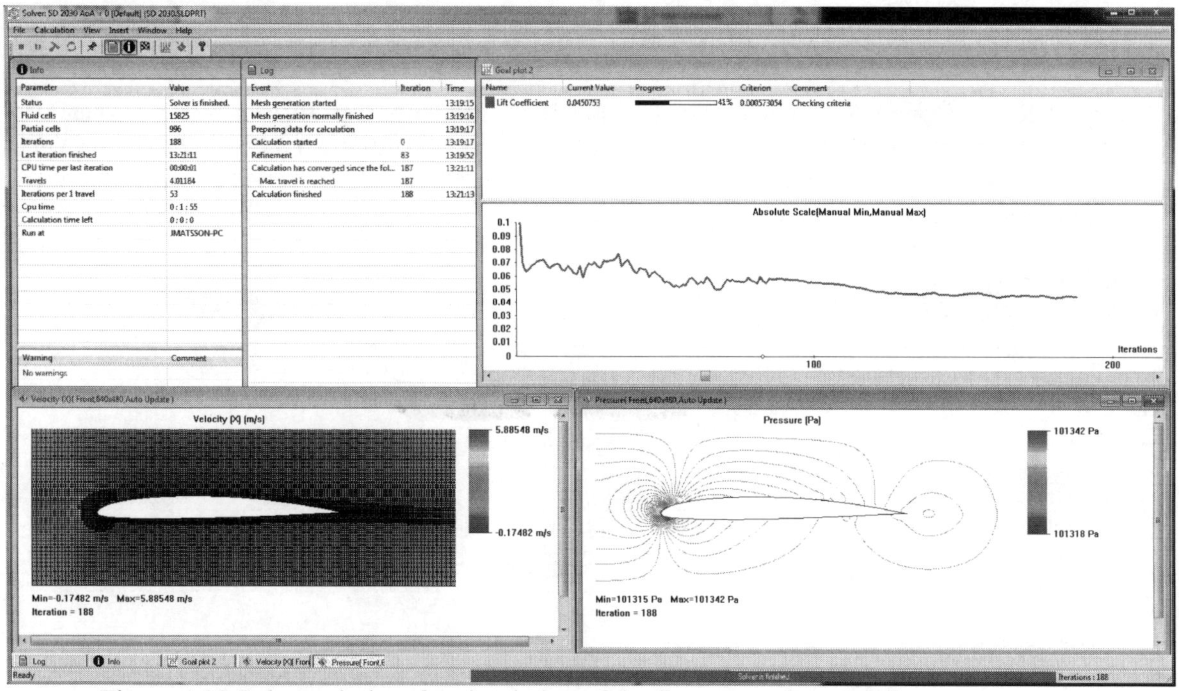

Figure 4.20 Solver window for simulation of the flow around an airfoil

Using Cut Plots

21. Select the **Flow Simulation** tab connected to the **Flow Simulation analysis tree**.

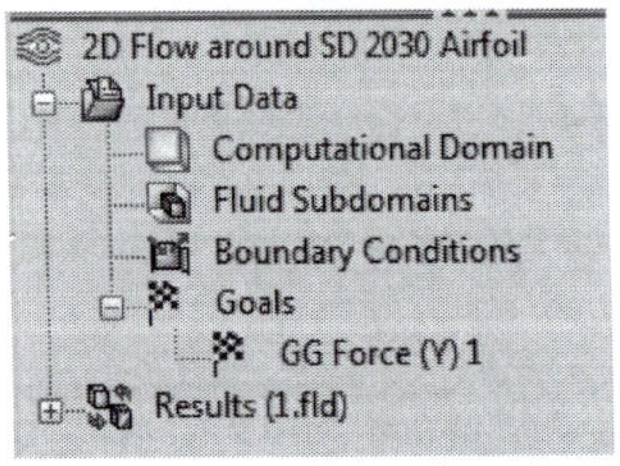

Figure 4.21 Selecting the Flow Simulation analysis tree

22. Hide the mesh around the airfoil. Right-click on the **Cut Plots** in the **Flow Simulation analysis tree** and select **Insert…**. Slide the **Number of Levels** in the **Contours** section to **255** and exit the cut plot window. Select **Tools>>Flow Simulation>>Results>>Display>>Lighting**. Rename the **Cut Plot** in the **Flow Simulation analysis tree** to **Pressure**.

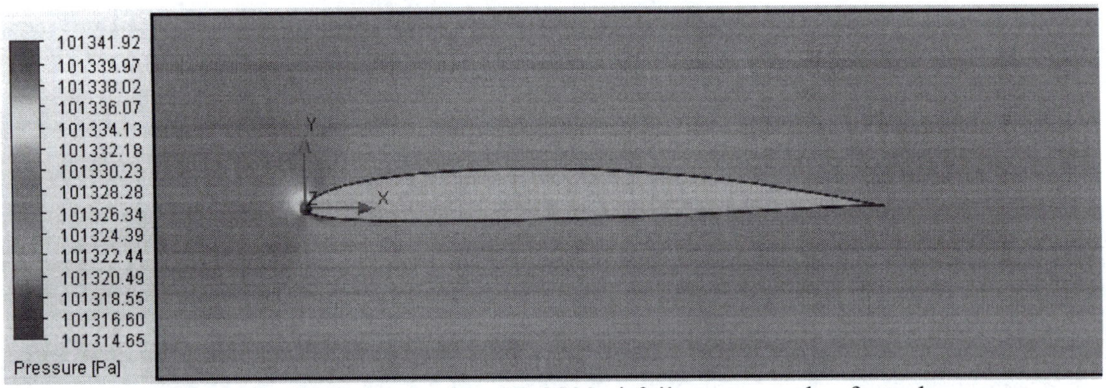

Figure 4.22 Pressure distribution around an SD 2030 airfoil at zero angle of attack

23. Right-click on **Surface Parameters** in the **Flow Simulation analysis tree** and select **Insert…**. Click on the **FeatureManager design tree** and select the **Extruded Airfoil Sketch**. Select **All Parameters** and push the **Export to Excel** button in the **Surface Parameters** window. An Excel file is generated with local and integral parameters.

Integral Parameters

Integral Parameter	Value	X-component	Y-component	Z-component	Surface Area [m^2]
Heat Transfer Rate [W]	0				0.002462848
Normal Force [N]	0.000791638	9.23766E-05	0.00078623	0	0.002462848
Friction Force [N]	0.000161648	0.000161418	8.62407E-06	-4.2617E-21	0.002462848
Force [N]	0.000834389	0.000253795	0.000794854	-4.2617E-21	0.002462848
Torque [N*m]	0.000222321	4.10785E-16	4.84297E-14	0.000222321	0.002462848
Surface Area [m^2]	0.002462848	-1.65171E-20	-6.81862E-20	0	0.002462848
Torque of Normal Force [N*m]	0.000223024	-9.26442E-23	2.48154E-23	0.000223024	0.002462848
Torque of Friction Force [N*m]	7.03231E-07	4.10785E-16	4.84297E-14	-7.03231E-07	0.002462848
Uniformity Index [ ]	1				0.002462848
Area (Fluid) [m^2]	0.002475686				0.002475686

Figure 4.23 Integral Surface Parameters

Theory

If we look at the Force related to the Integral parameters we see that the lift force is $L =$ 0.000794854 N for the Y-component and the drag force is $D =$ 0.000253795 N for the X-component. The lift and drag coefficients can be determined from

$$C_L = \frac{L}{\frac{1}{2}\rho U^2 bc} = \frac{0.000794854}{\frac{1}{2}\cdot 1.204 \cdot 4.9^2 \cdot 0.004 \cdot 0.305} = 0.045 \quad (4.1)$$

$$C_D = \frac{D}{\frac{1}{2}\rho U^2 bc} = \frac{0.00023008}{\frac{1}{2}\cdot 1.204 \cdot 4.9^2 \cdot 0.004 \cdot 0.305} = 0.014 \quad (4.2)$$

where $\rho\ (kg/m^3)$ is the free-stream density, *U (m/s)* is the free-stream velocity, *b (m)* is the airfoil wing span, and *c(m)* is the chord length of the airfoil. The value for *b* used is the difference between Z max and Z min in the computational domain.

The lift coefficient has been determined using Flow Simulation at zero angle of attack and at a Reynolds number determined by

$$\text{Re} = \frac{Uc\rho}{\mu} = \frac{4.9 \cdot 0.305 \cdot 1.204}{1.8 \cdot 10^{-5}} = 100{,}000 \quad (4.3)$$

, where $\mu\ (kg/ms)$ is the dynamic viscosity of air in the free-stream.

Next, we want to plot the pressure distribution on the airfoil expressed in dimensionless form by the pressure coefficient

$$C_p = \frac{p_i - p}{\frac{1}{2}\rho U^2} \quad (4.4)$$

, where $p_i\ (Pa)$ is the surface pressure at location *i* and *p (Pa)* is the pressure in the free-stream.

Creating a Custom Visualization Parameter

24. Select **Tools>>Flow Simulation>>Tools>>Engineering Database…** from the menu

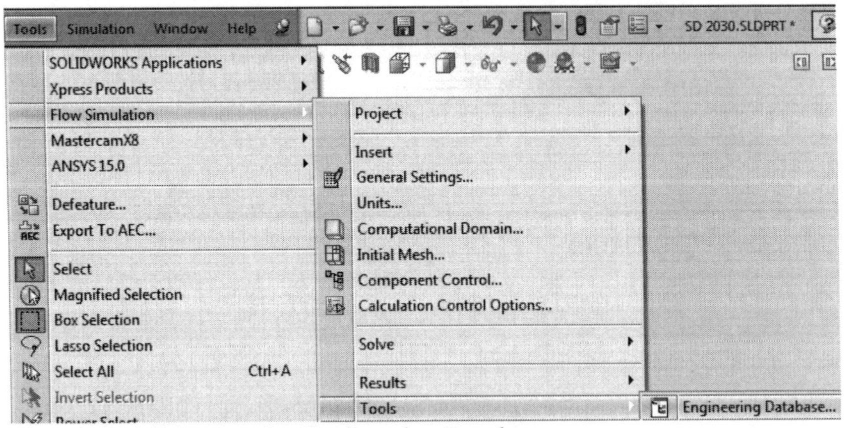

Figure 4.24 Selecting the Engineering Database

25. In the **Database tree** expand the **Custom Visualization Parameters** item, right-click the **User Defined** item and select **New Item**.

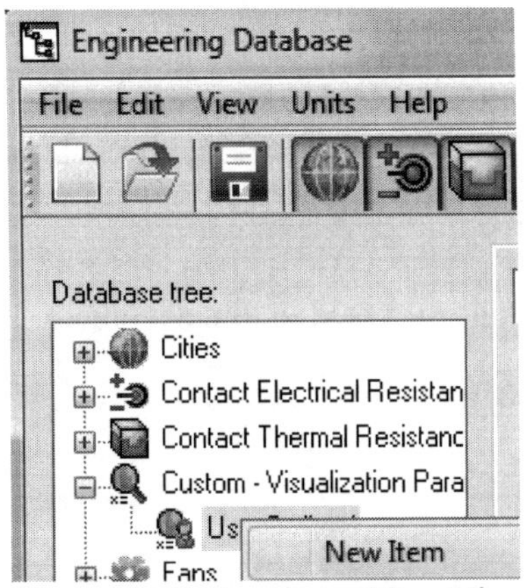

Figure 4.25 Creating a New Visualization Parameter

26. Under the **Item properties** tab type the parameter's **Name** as **Pressure Coefficient**

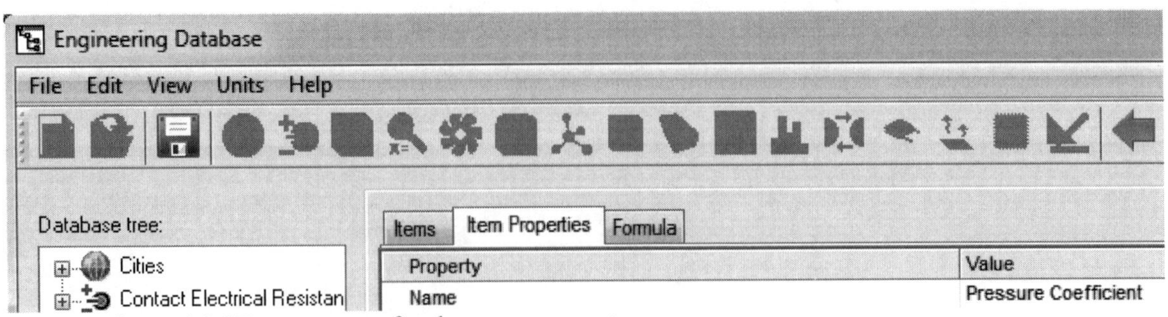

Figure 4.26 Enter a name for the new parameter

27. In the **Formula** row click on **…** and specify the parameter definition through the **Visualization parameters** drop down menu where you select **Pressure.** The formula that you enter will be the following: ({Pressure}-101324)/(0.5*1.204*4.9^2). Select **File, Save** from the **Engineering Database** menu and exit the engineering database window.

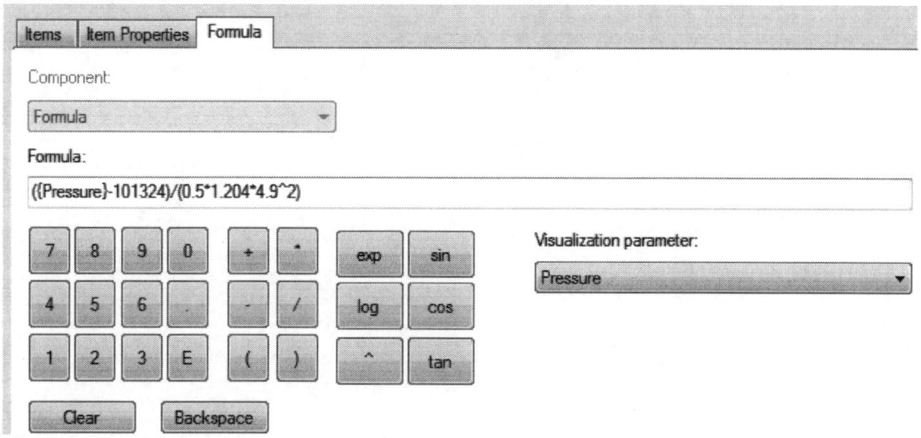

Figure 4.27 Entering a formula for the new parameter

28. Right-click on the **XY Plots** and select **Insert…** from the **Flow Simulation analysis tree**. Click on the **FeatureManager design tree** tab and select the **Airfoil Sketch** under the **Extruded Airfoil Sketch**.

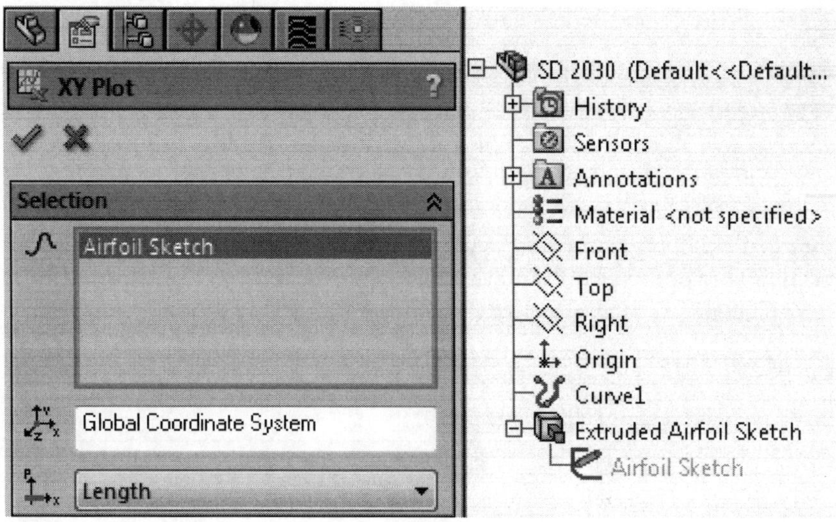

Figure 4.28 Selecting airfoil sketch for XY Plot

29. Click on **More Parameters…** and check the box for **Pressure Coefficient** under **Custom**.

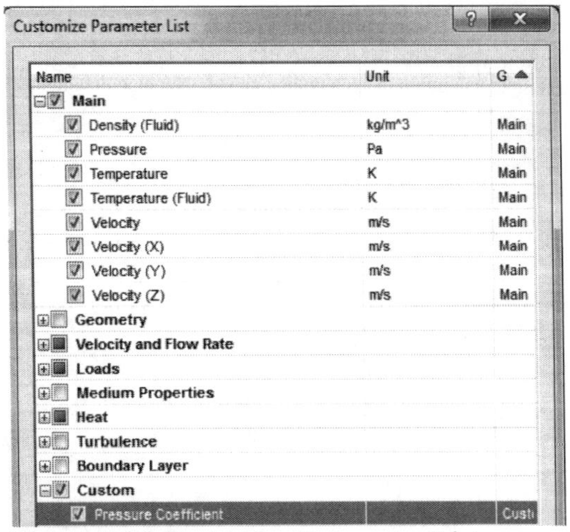

Figure 4.29 Customize Parameter List

30. Next, check **Pressure Coefficient** in the **Parameter** list of the **XY Plot window** and choose **Sketch X** for the **Abscissa** in the same window. Open the **Options** portion of the **XY Plot** window and select **Excel Workbook (*.xlsx)** from the drop down menu.

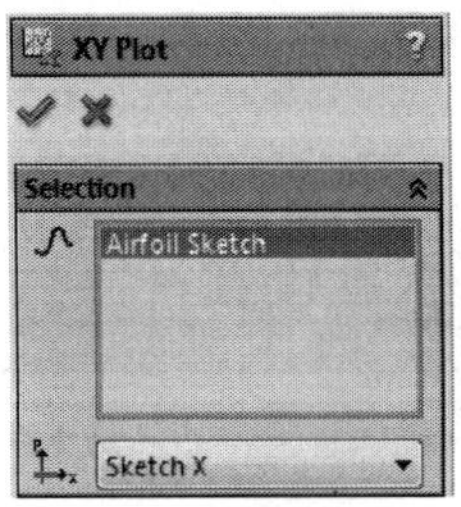

Figure 4.30 Selecting Sketch X for the abscissa.

31. Click on the **Export to Excel** button and an Excel graph will be generated showing the variation of the pressure coefficient over the airfoil. Rename the **XY Plot** in the **Flow Simulation analysis tree** to **Pressure Coefficient**.

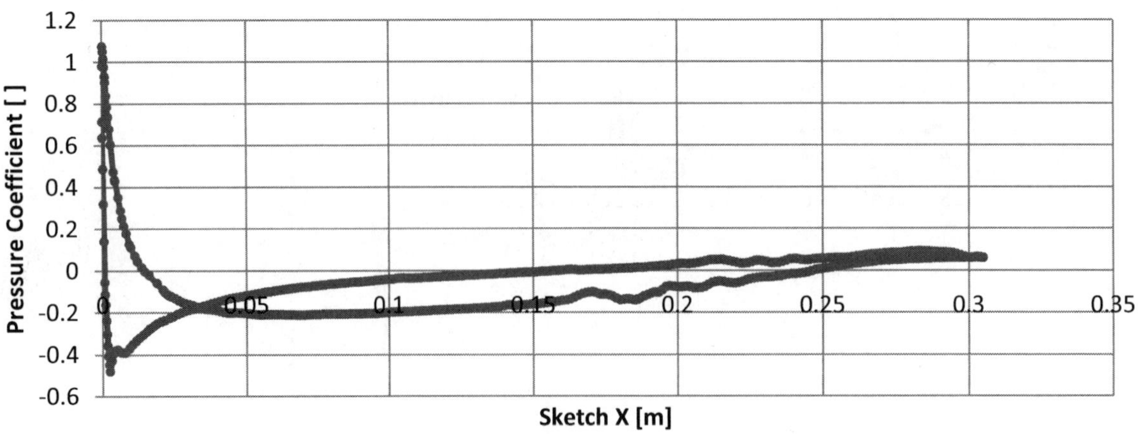

Figure 4.31 Variation of pressure coefficient on SD 2030 airfoil at zero angle of attack

32. Insert a new **Cut Plot** in the **Flow Simulation analysis tree**. Choose **Velocity** from the **Parameter Settings** drop down menu in the **Contours** section. Exit the **Cut Plot** window to display the velocity field over the airfoil. Rename the **Cut Plot** to **Velocity**. Right click on the **Pressure Cut Plot** in the **Flow Simulation analysis tree** and select **Hide** to show the **Velocity Cut Plot**.

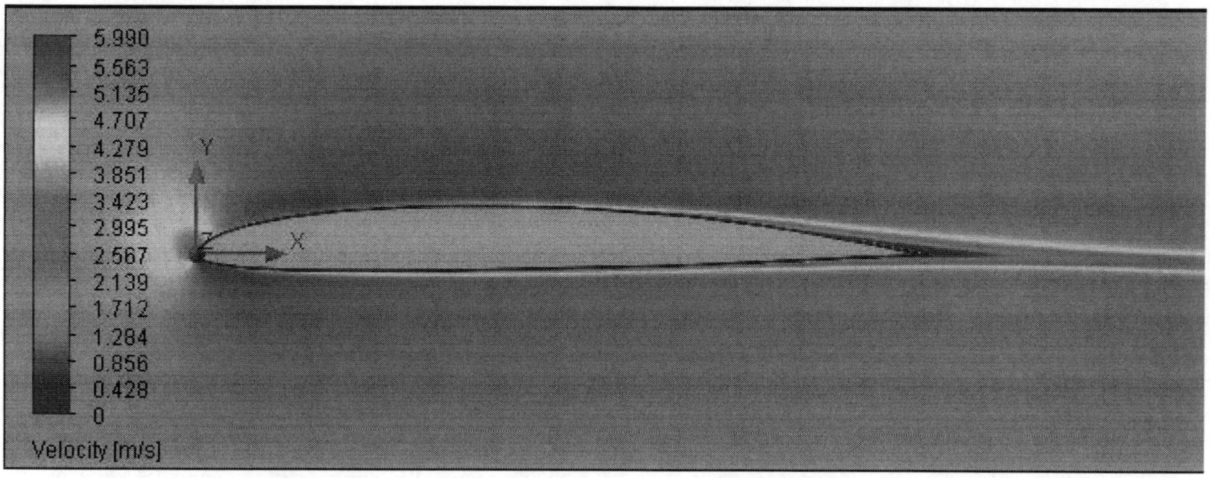

Figure 4.32 Velocity field around the SD 2030 airfoil at zero angle of attack

Cloning of the Project

33. Select **Tools>>Flow Simulation>>Project>>Clone Project…**. Create a cloned project with the name "**SD 2030 AoA = 2 degrees**." Exit the **Clone Project** window.

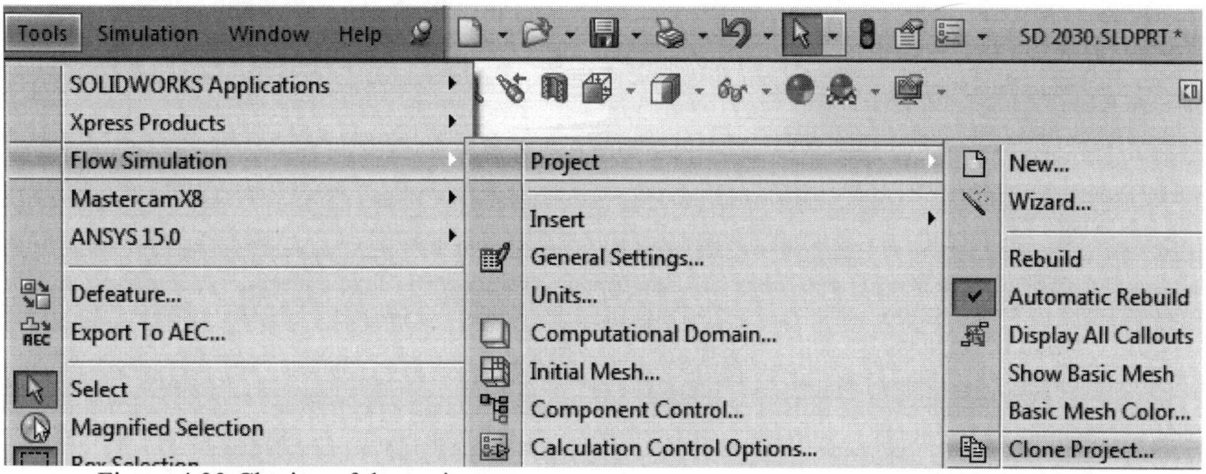

Figure 4.33 Cloning of the project

34. Select **Tools>>Flow Simulation>>General Settings**. Click on **Initial and ambient conditions** in the **Navigator**. Enter **4.897 m/s** as **Velocity in X-direction** and **0.171 m/s** as **Velocity in Y-direction** corresponding to an angle of attack of 2°. Click on the **OK** button to exit the window. Repeat steps **33** and **34** five more times and change the angles of attack and corresponding velocity components as shown in table 4.1.

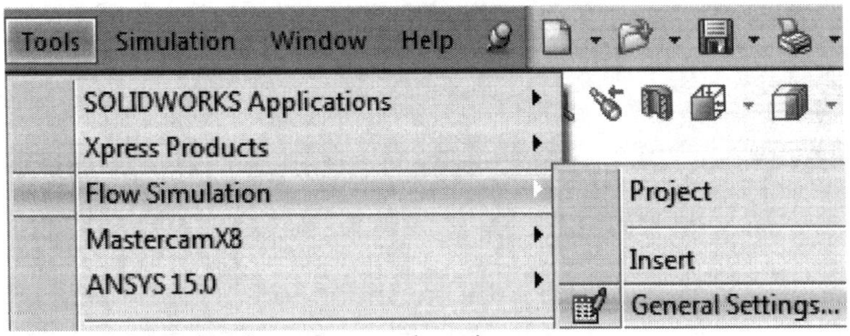

Figure 4.34 Selection of general settings

Angle of Attack	X – Velocity (m/s)	Y – Velocity (m/s)
0°	4.9000	0.0000
2°	4.8970	0.1710
4°	4.8881	0.3418
6°	4.8732	0.5122
8°	4.8523	0.6819
10°	4.8256	0.8509
12°	4.7929	1.0188

Table 4.1 Velocity component for different angles of attack

Creating a Batch Run

35. Select **Tools>>Flow Simulation>>Solve>>Batch Run…**. Make sure to check all boxes as shown in figure 4.35b). Set maximum simultaneous run at this computer to 2. Click on the **Run** button to start the calculations.

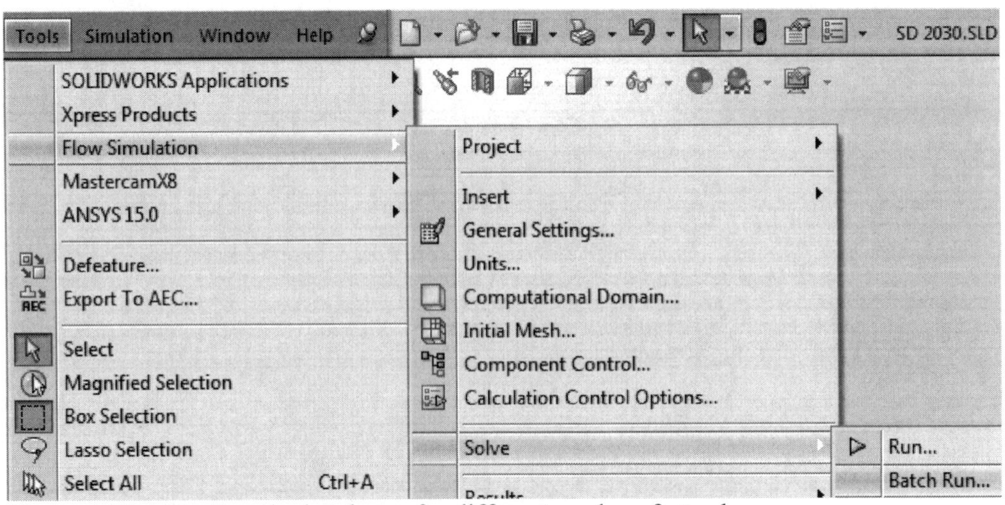

Figure 4.35a) Starting the batch run for different angles of attack

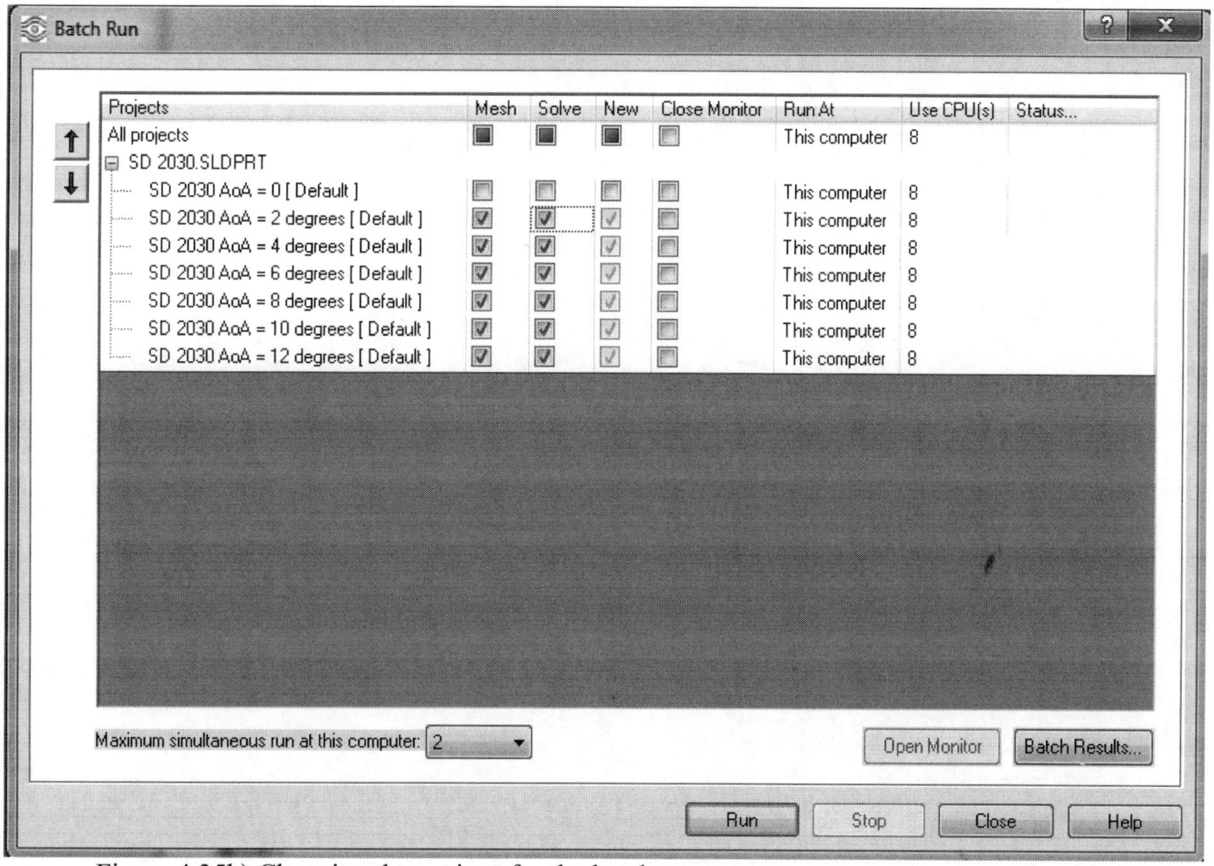

Figure 4.35b) Changing the settings for the batch run

Angle of Attack Simulation	Lift Coefficient Simulation	Angle of Attack Experiment	Lift Coefficient Experiment
0°	0.045	0.11°	0.122
2°	0.348	1.14°	0.231
4°	0.636	2.17°	0.403
6°	0.916	3.17°	0.574
8°	1.256	4.26°	0.693
10°	1.588	5.29°	0.784
12°	1.588	6.32°	0.873
		7.33°	0.945
		8.34°	1
		9.36°	1.051
		10.34°	1.09
		11.39°	1.105

Table 4.2 Lift coefficient for different angles of attack, experimental results from Selig and McGranaham (2004), *Re* = 100,000

The figure below shows a comparison of experimental results and Flow Simulation calculations for Re = 100,000. It is seen that the Flow Simulation values for the lift coefficient are lower than the corresponding values from experiments.

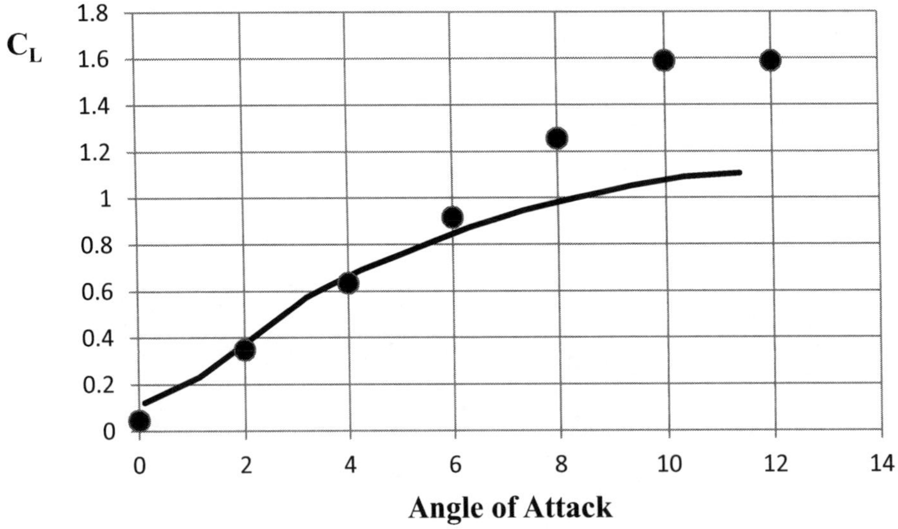

Figure 4.35c) Comparison of experiments (line) with Flow Simulation results (filled circles)

Reference

[1] Selig M.S. and McGranaham B., Wind Tunnel Aerodynamics Tests of Six Airfoils for Use on Small Wind Turbines, NREL/SR-500-34515, National Renewable Energy Laboratory, May 2004.

Exercises

4.1 Run the calculations for the flow over a SD 2030 airfoil for Re = 200,000 and use different levels of initial mesh. Plot the lift coefficient versus mesh level and study the percent difference variation as compared with the experimental values. Discuss your results.

Angle of Attack	Lift Coefficient
0.15	0.252
1.17	0.391
2.23	0.499
3.21	0.593
4.22	0.690
5.26	0.784
6.30	0.869
7.34	0.945
8.35	1.012
9.34	1.070
10.37	1.112
11.38	1.138

Table E1 Experimental values of lift coefficient for SD 2030 and Re = 200,000, from Selig and McGranaham (2004)

4.2 Run the calculations for the flow over a SD 2030 airfoil for *Re* = 500,000 for an initial mesh level of 6 and use different sizes of the computational domain:

a) Xmin: -0.2 m, Xmax: 0.4 m, Ymin: -0.2 m, Ymax: 0.2 m
b) Xmin: -0.4 m, Xmax: 0.6 m, Ymin: -0.4 m, Ymax: 0.4 m
c) Xmin: -1 m, Xmax: 2 m, Ymin: -1 m, Ymax: 1 m

How does the lift coefficient vary with the size of the computational domain?
Compare your results with the following experimental results as shown in table E2. Include solver windows and goal values for each case. Discuss your results.

Angle of Attack Experiment	**Lift Coefficient Experiment**
0.20	0.291
1.16	0.410
2.23	0.525
3.24	0.628
4.28	0.725
5.28	0.814
6.30	0.909
7.34	0.993
8.36	1.012
9.34	1.068
10.42	1.176
11.4	1.199

Table E2 Experimental values of lift coefficient for SD 2030 and *Re* = 500,000, from Selig and McGranaham (2004)

Notes:

Chapter 5 Rayleigh-Bénard Convection and Taylor-Couette Flow

Objectives

- Creating the SOLIDWORKS models needed for Flow Simulations
- Setting up Flow Simulation projects for internal flows
- Creating lids for boundary conditions and setting up boundary conditions
- Use of gravity as a physical feature and running the calculations
- Using cut plots and surface plots to visualize the resulting flow field
- Compare results with linear stability theory

Problem Description

In this chapter we will study roll cell instabilities in two simple geometries. We will start by looking closer at the flow caused by natural convection between a hot bottom wall and an upper colder wall; see figure 5.0a). This flow case is known as Rayleigh-Bénard convection. We will use water as the fluid, and only a very small temperature difference is required to get the primary instability in this flow. The lower hot wall will be set to 295 K and the upper cold wall to 293 K. The depth of the fluid layer is 4.793 mm and the inner diameter of the enclosure is 100 mm. The second flow case that will be studied in this chapter is Taylor-Couette flow (the flow between two vertical and rotating cylinders); see figure 5.0b). In this chapter, we will rotate the inner cylinder at 5 rad/s and keep the outer cylinder stationary. The inner and outer cylinders have radii of 30 mm and 35 mm, respectively, and the height of the cylinders is 100 mm. A centrifugal instability will cause the appearance of counter-rotating vortices at low rotation speed of the inner cylinder. For both flow cases, comparisons will be made with linear stability theory.

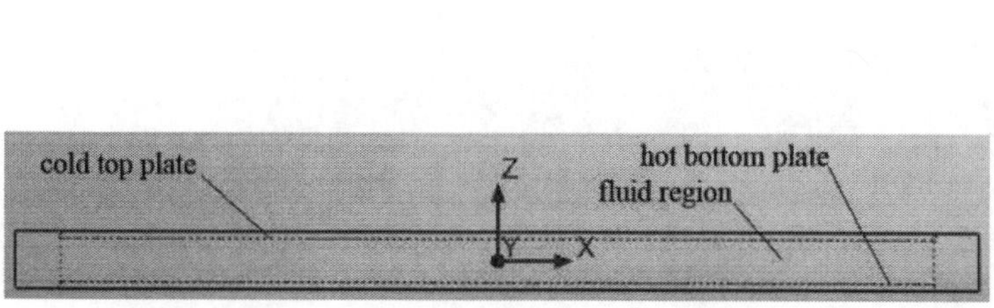

Figure 5.0a) Model of Rayleigh-Bénard convection cell

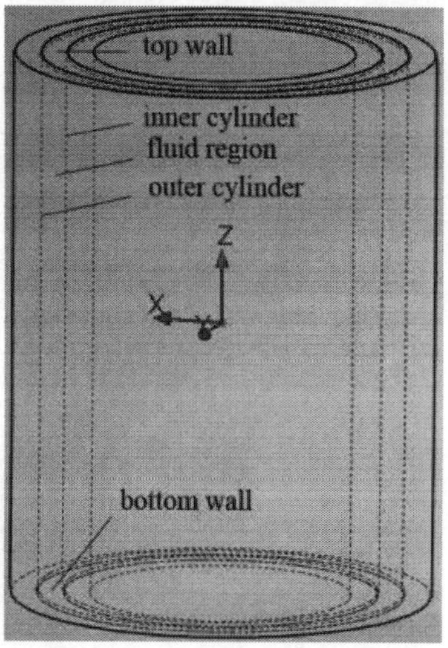

Figure 5.0b) Taylor-Couette cell

Creating the SOLIDWORKS Part for Rayleigh-Bénard Convection

1. Start SOLIDWORKS and create a New Part. Select **Tools>>Options…** from the SOLIDWORKS menu. Click on the Document Properties tab and select **Units**. Select **MMGS** as your **Unit system**. Select the **Front** view from the **View Orientation** drop down menu in the graphics window and click on the **Front Plane** in the **FeatureManager design tree**. Next, select the **Circle** sketch tool.

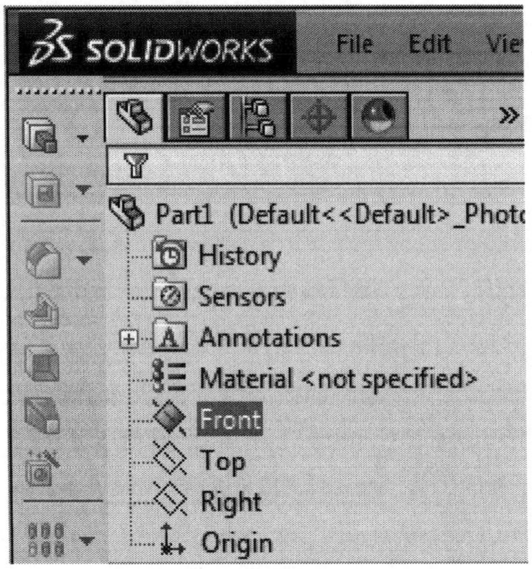

Figure 5.1a) Front Plane

Figure 5.1b) Selection of the **Circle** sketch tool

2. Click on the origin in the graphics window and create a circle. Enter 50 mm for the radius of the circle in the **Parameters** box. Close the dialog box.

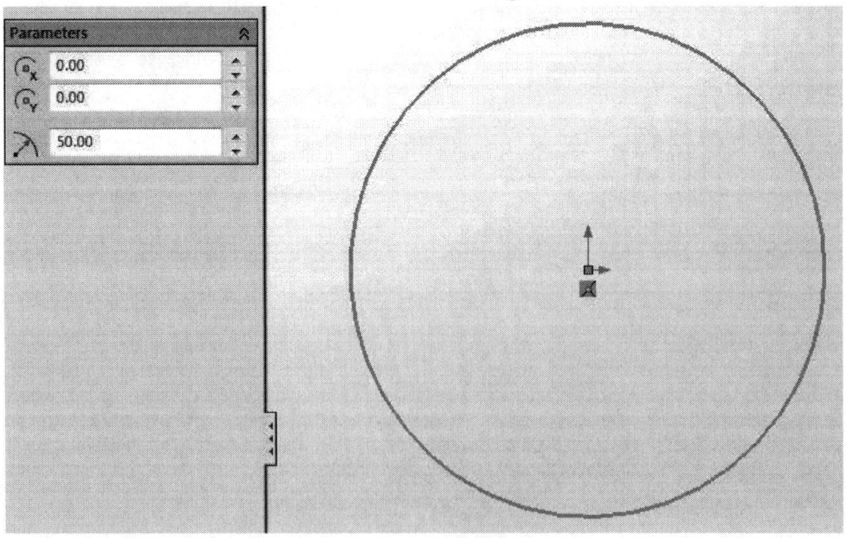

Figure 5.2 Drawing of a circle with 50 mm radius

3. Draw another larger circle concentric with the first circle and enter 55 mm for the radius. Close the dialog box.

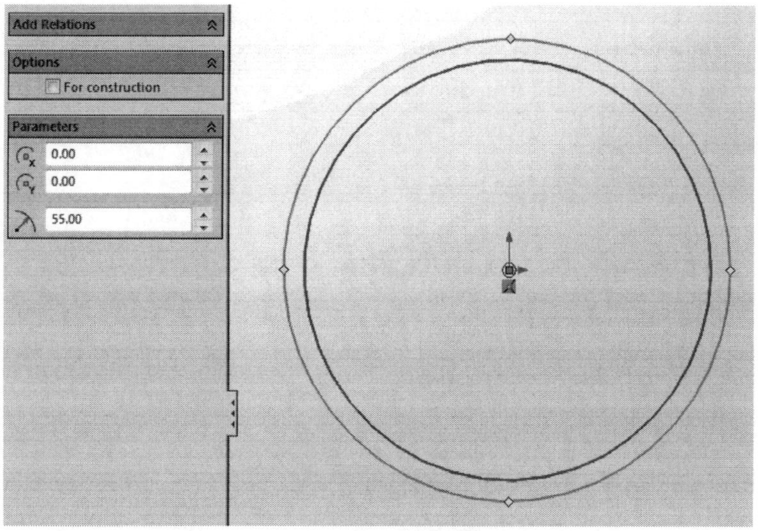

Figure 5.3 Drawing of a second circle with 55 mm radius

4. Next, make an extrusion by selecting **Extruded Boss/Base**. Enter 3.175mm in **Direction 1** and the same depth in **Direction 2**. Close the dialog box. Save the part with the name **Rayleigh-Benard Cell**.

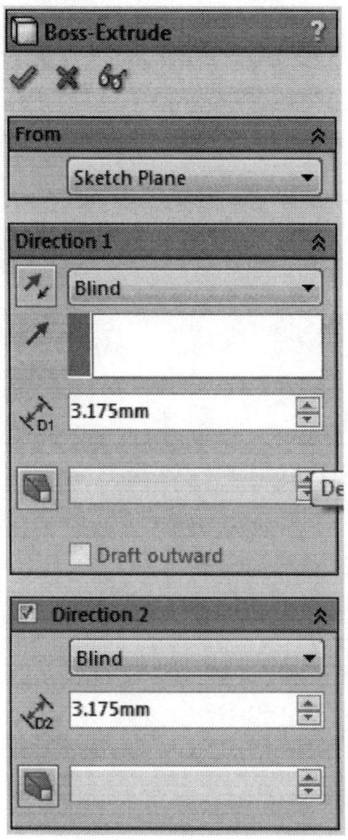

Figure 5.4a) Entering depth

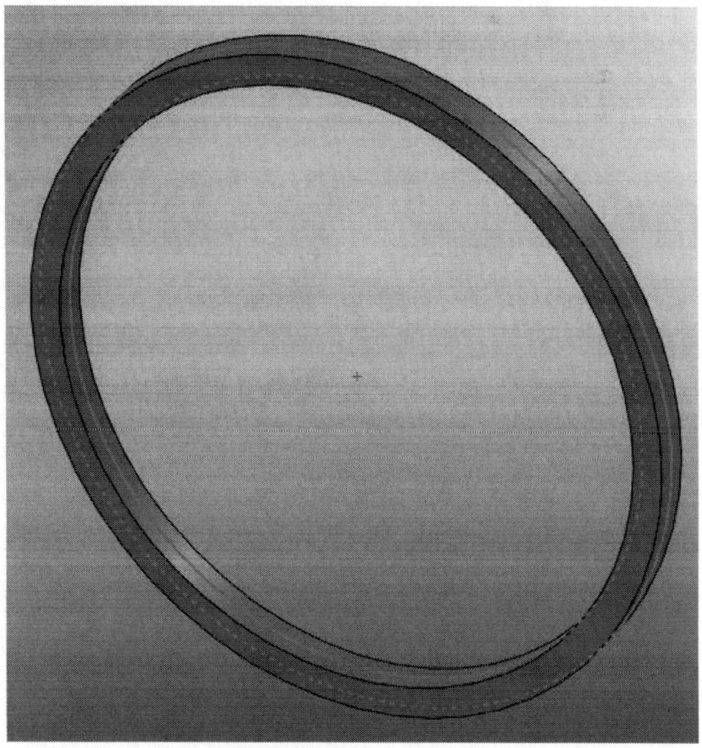

Figure 5.4b) Extruded ring

Setting up the Flow Simulation Project for Rayleigh-Bénard Convection

5. If Flow Simulation is not available in the SOLIDWORKS menu, select **Tools>>Add Ins…** and check the corresponding **SOLIDWORKS Flow Simulation** box. Start the **Flow Simulation Wizard** by selecting **Tools>>Flow Simulation>>Project>>Wizard** from the SOLIDWORKS menu.

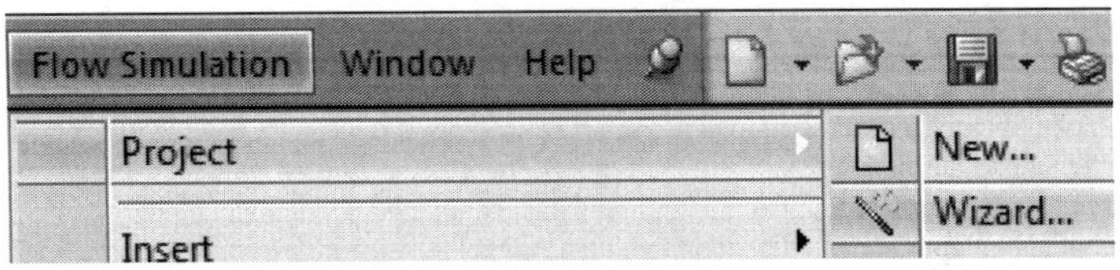

Figure 5.5 Starting the Flow Simulation Project Wizard

6. Enter Project name: **Convection in Rayleigh-Benard Cell**.

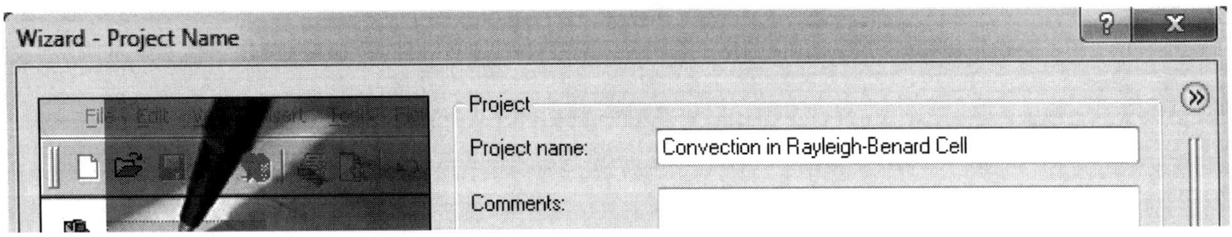

Figure 5.6 Entering configuration name

7. Select the SI unit system

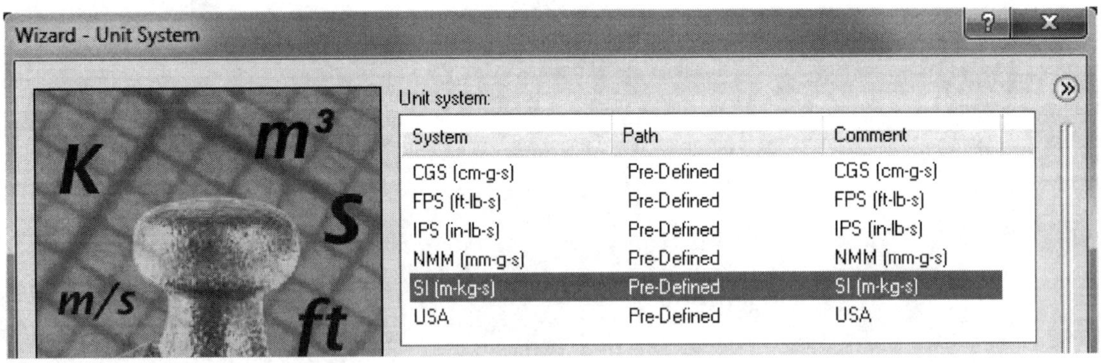

Figure 5.7 Selection of unit system

8. Select the default **Internal Analysis type** and enter **-9.81 m/s^2** as **Gravity** for the **Z component** in **Physical Features**.

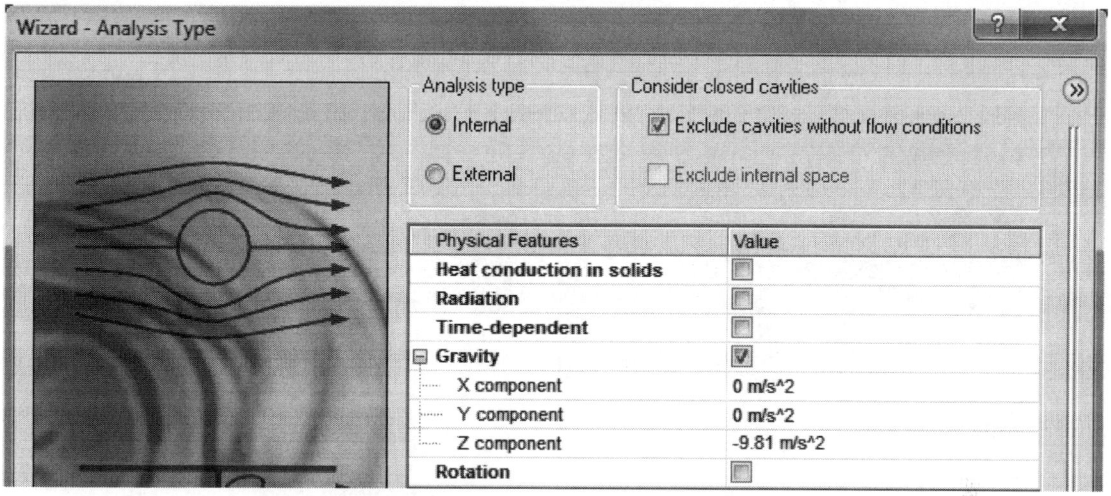

Figure 5.8 Enter gravity as physical feature

9. Add **Water** as the default **Project Fluid** by selecting it from **Liquids**. Choose default values for **Wall Conditions, Initial Conditions** and **Results and Geometry Resolution**.

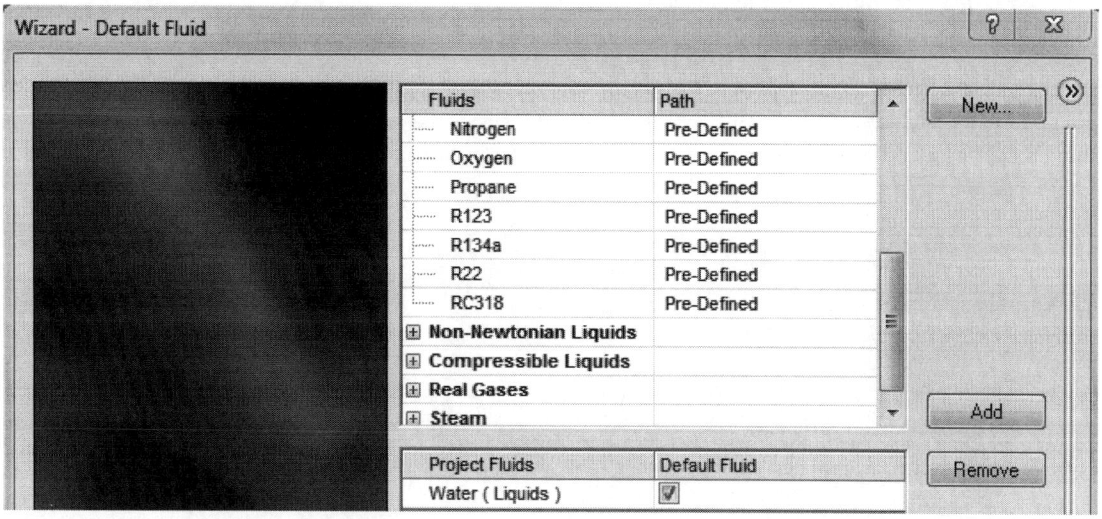

Figure 5.9 Adding the default fluid

You will get a fluid volume recognition failure message. Answer **Yes** to this question and create a lid on each side of the model as described in the next section.

Creating Lids

10. Next, we will add a lid on each side of the ring to create an enclosure. Click on one of the two plane surfaces of the ring. Note that the thickness of the lid is close to 0.7785 mm. This means that the final thickness of the fluid layer will be 4.793 mm. Click **OK** and answer "**Yes**" to the questions whether you want to reset the computational domain, mesh setting, and fluid volume recognition failure message that appears in the graphics window.

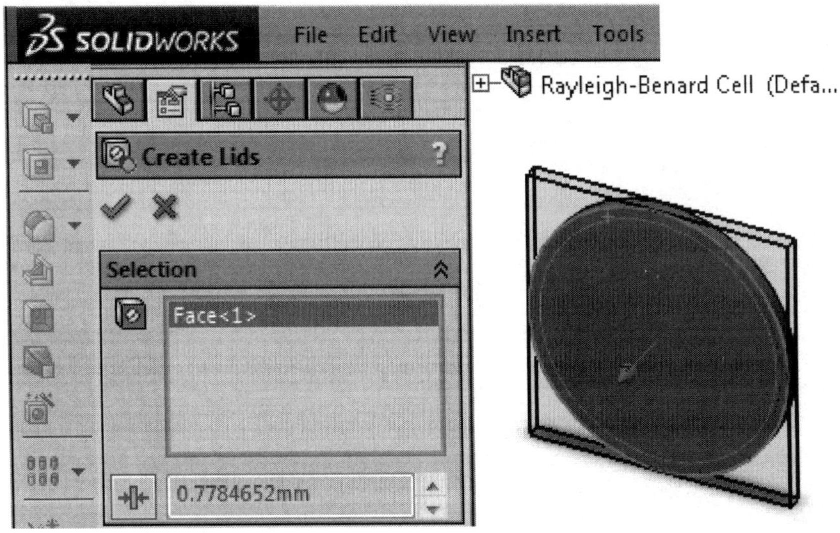

Figure 5.10 Selecting the surface

11. Next, right click in the graphics window and select **Rotate View**. Rotate the ring with a lid. Select the other plane surface of the ring and create the second lid with the same thickness as the first lid. Answer "**Yes**" when asked to reset the computational domain and mesh settings. Select **Hidden Lines Visible** from the **Display Style** drop down menu in the graphics window.

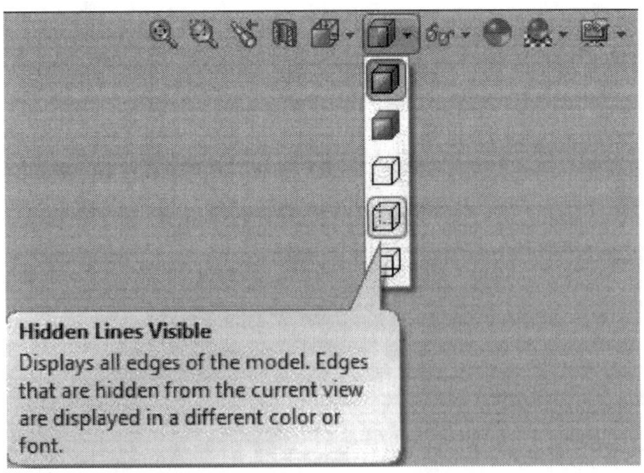

Figure 5.11 Making hidden lines visible

Inserting Boundary Conditions for Rayleigh-Bénard Convection

12. Click on the **Flow Simulation analysis tree** tab and click on the plus sign next to the **Input Data** folder. Right click on **Boundary Conditions** and select **Insert Boundary Condition…**

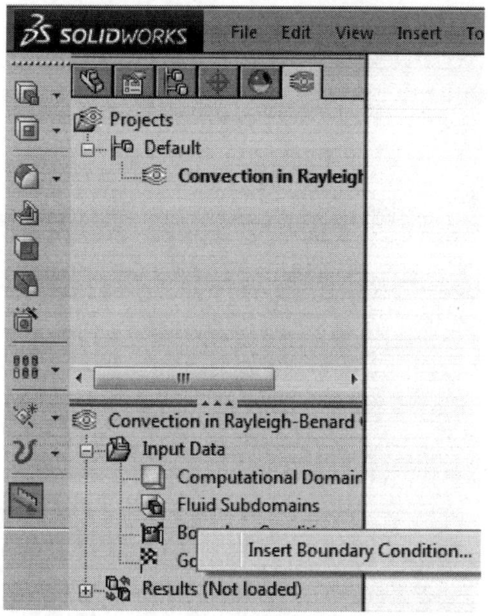

Figure 5.12 Selecting boundary conditions

13. Right click in the graphics window and select **Zoom/Pan/Rotate>>Rotate View**. Rotate the enclosure so that it has the same view as in figure 5.13a), right click and click on **Rotate View**. Move the cursor over the top lid, right-click again and click on **Select Other**. Select the face for the inner upper surface of the enclosure. Select the **Wall** button and select **Real Wall** boundary condition. Set the value of **293 K** for the wall temperature in the **Wall Parameters** window. Click **OK** to finish the first boundary condition. Rename the boundary condition from **Real Wall 1** to **Top Wall**.

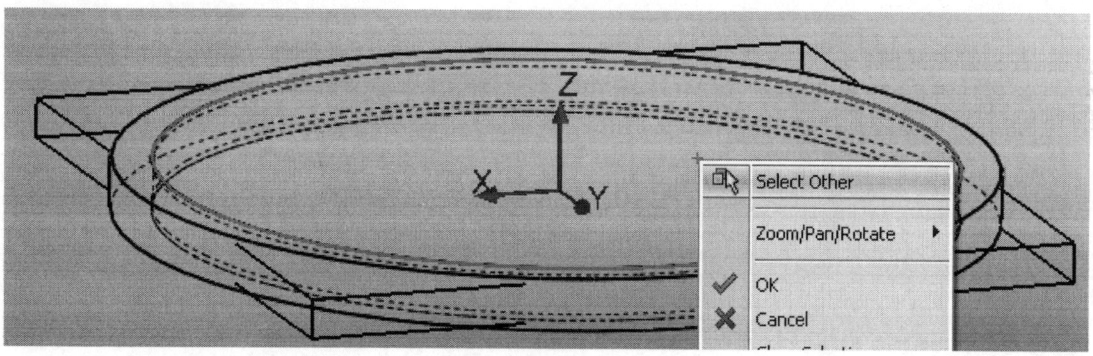

Figure 5.13a) View of enclosure for upper boundary condition

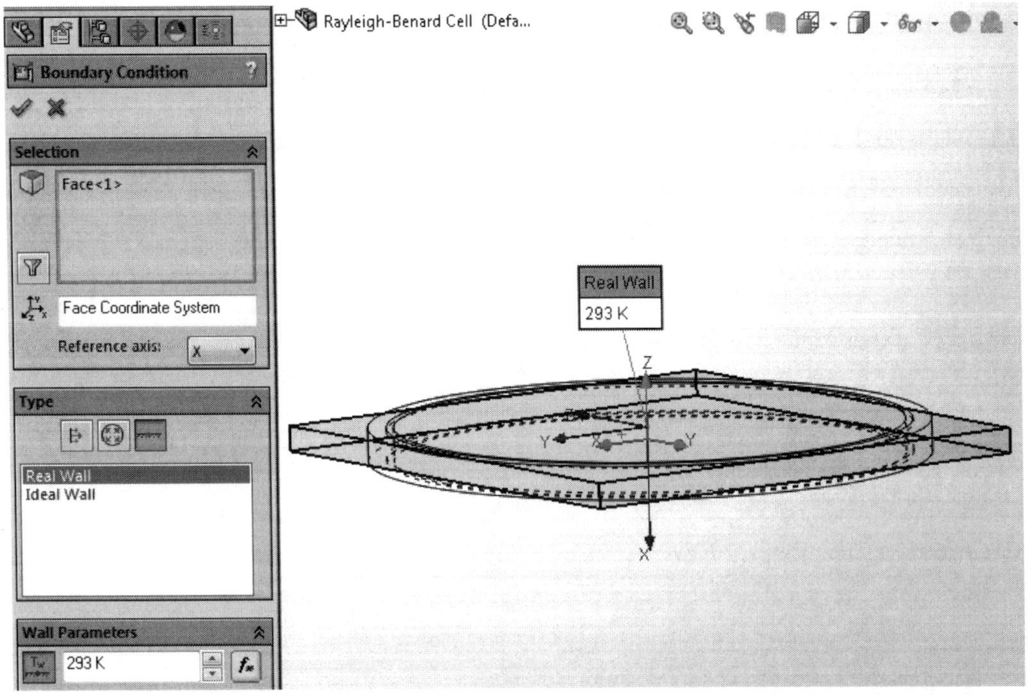

Figure 5.13b) Selection of boundary condition for upper surface

14. Repeat steps **12** and **13** but select the inner lower surface and enter **295 K** as wall temperature. Rename the boundary condition from **Real Wall 2** to **Bottom Wall**.

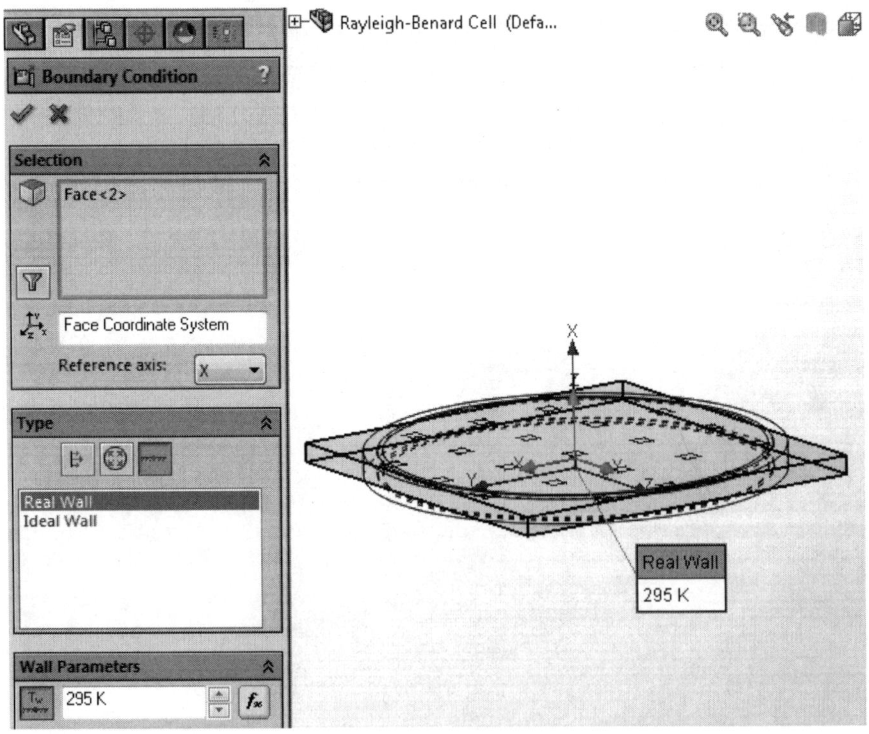

Figure 5.14 Selection of boundary condition for lower surface

15. Repeat steps **12** and **13** one more time and select the remaining inner cylindrical surface and enter **293 K** as wall temperature. Rename the boundary condition from **Real Wall 3** to **Side Wall**. Select **Bottom** view from the **View Orientation** drop down menu in the graphics window. Right click on **Boundary Conditions** and select **Display Callouts** to label all boundary conditions.

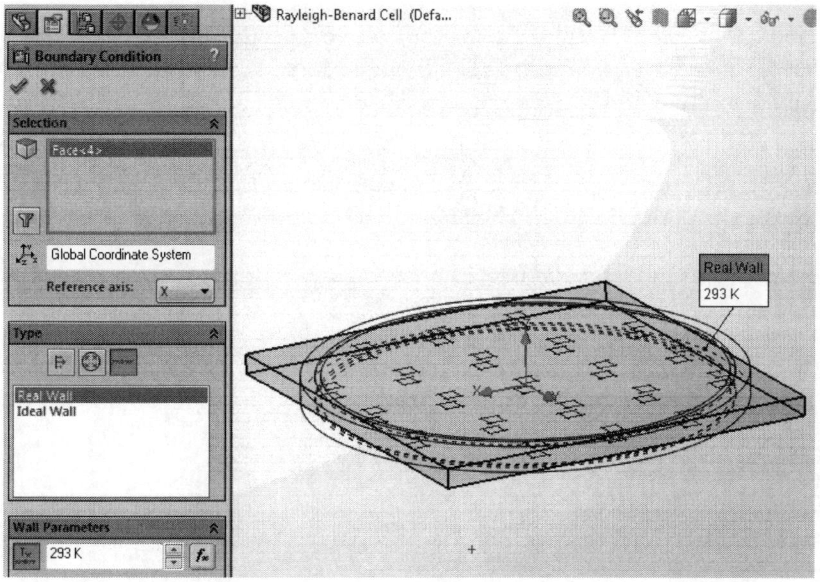

Figure 5.15a) Selection of boundary condition for cylindrical surface

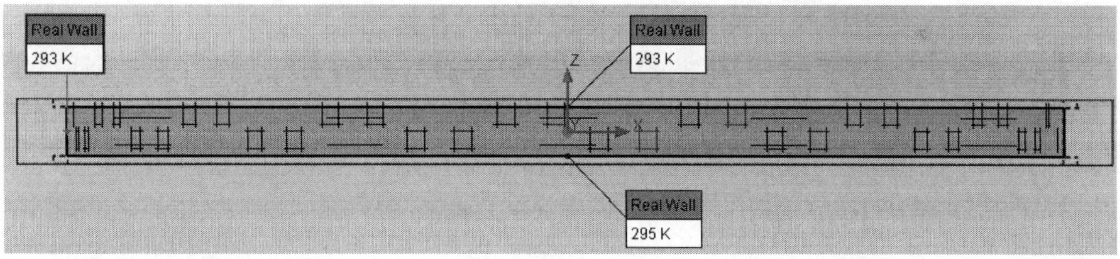

Figure 5.15b) Three real wall boundary conditions for the Rayleigh-Benard Convection Cell

Setting up 2D Flow

16. Choose **Tools>>Flow Simulation>>Computational Domain….** Select **2D simulation** and **XZ-Plane Flow**. Exit the **Computational Domain** window.

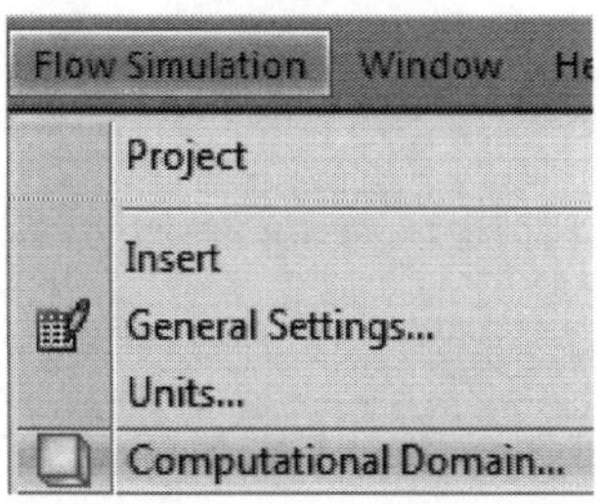

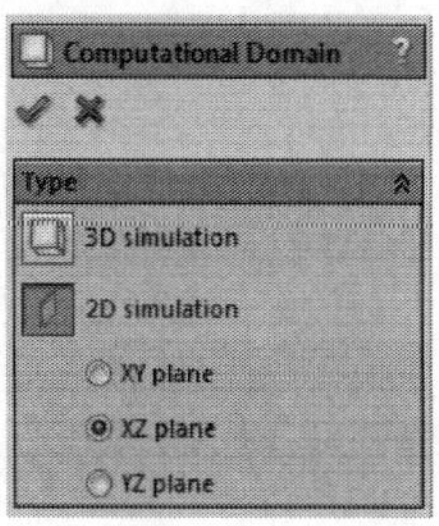

Figure 5.16a) Modifying the computational domain Figure 5.16b) Selecting XZ-Plane Flow

Inserting Global Goal for Rayleigh-Bénard Convection

17. Right click on **Goals** in the **Flow Simulation analysis tree** and select **Insert Global Goals…** Check the boxes for **Min, Av** and **Max Temperature (Fluid)** and **Min, Av** and **Max Velocity (Z)**.

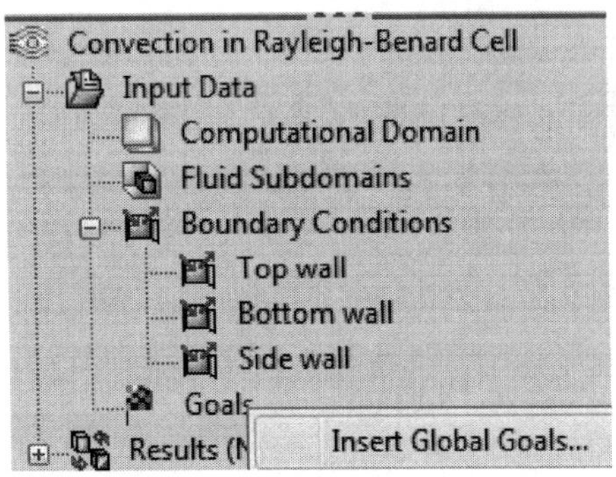

Figure 5.17a) Inserting global goals

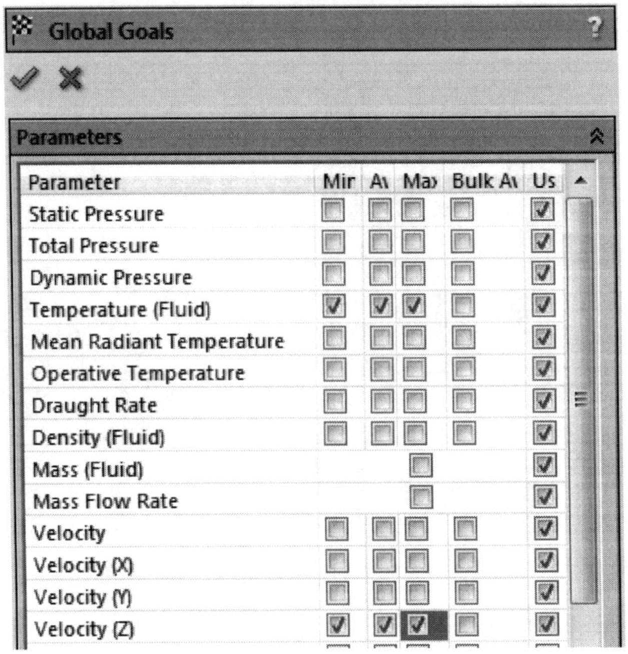

Figure 5.17b) Temperature and velocity as goals

Running the Calculations

18. Select **Tools>>Flow Simulation>>Solve>>Run**. Push the **Run** button in the window that appears.

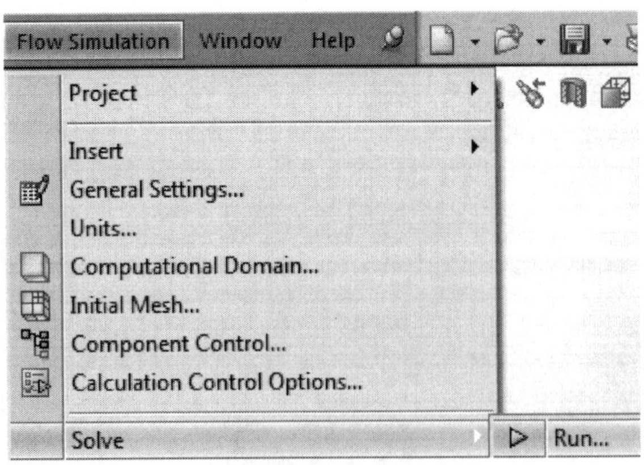

Figure 5.18 Starting the calculation of temperature and flow fields

19. Insert the goals table by clicking on the flag in the **Solver** as shown in figure 5.19a).

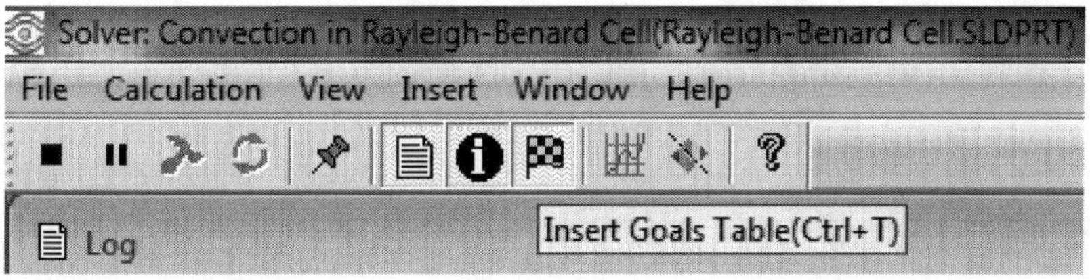

Figure 5.19a) Inserting goals

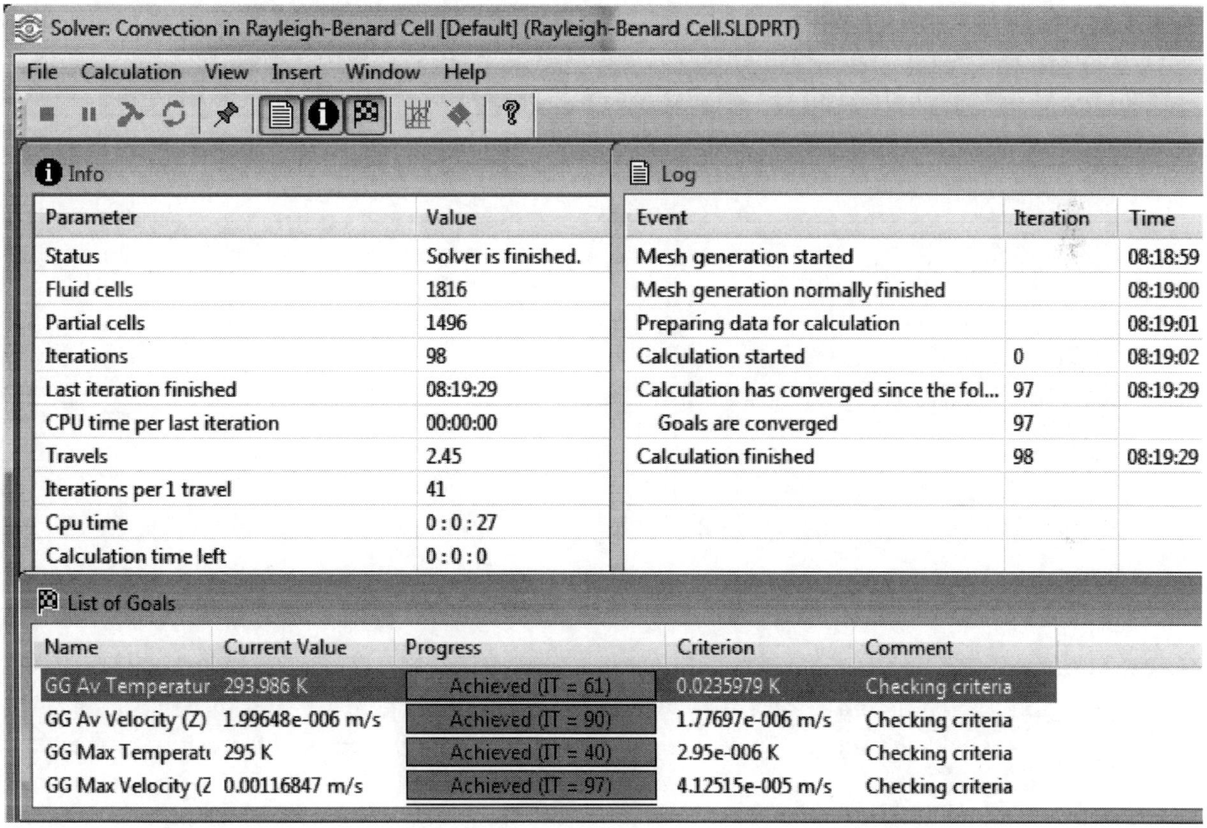

Figure 5.19b) Solver window

Inserting Cut Plots

20. Right click on **Cut Plots** in the **Flow Simulation analysis tree** and select **Insert….** Select the **Top Plane** from the **FeatureManager design tree**. Slide the **Number of Levels** setting to **255** in the **Contours** section and select **Temperature** from the **Parameters** drop down menu. Click **OK** to exit the **Cut Plot**. Rename **Cut Plot 1** and name it **Temperature**.

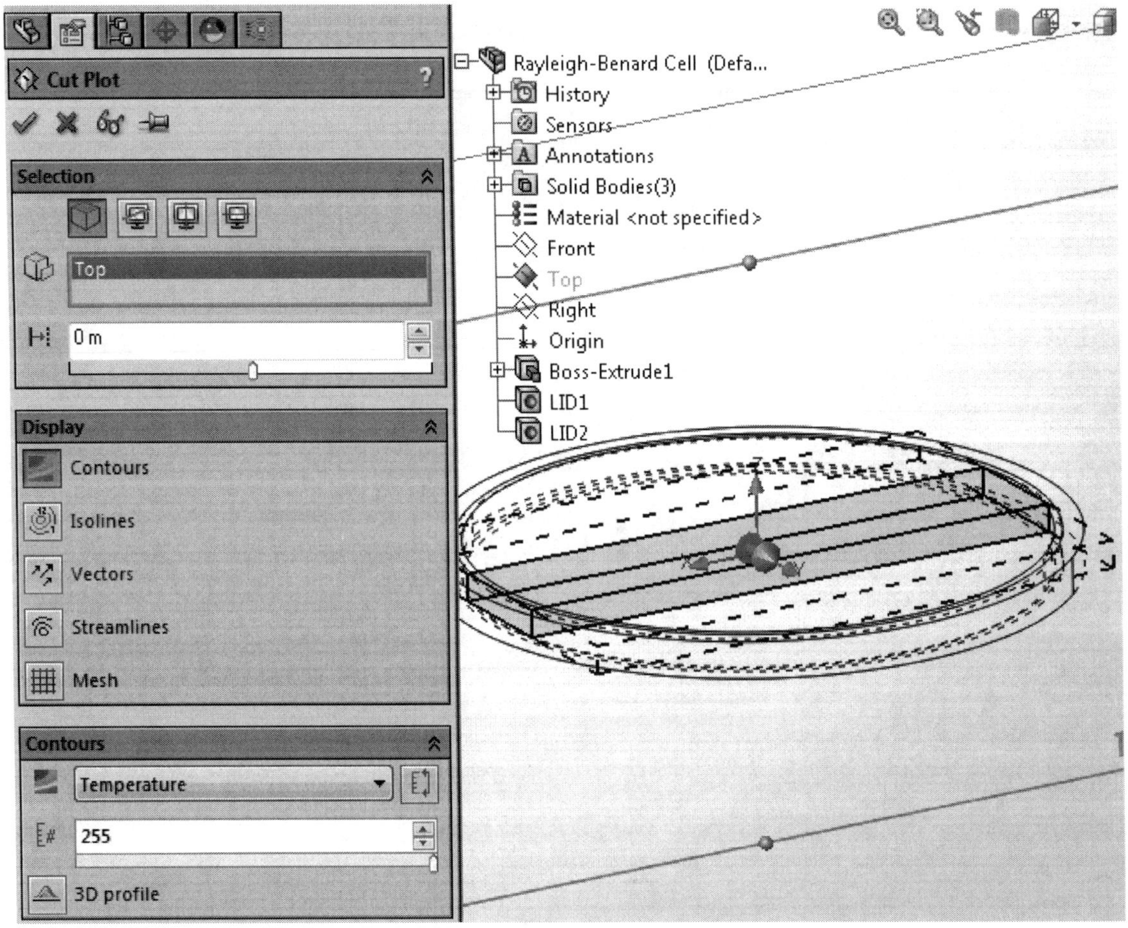

Figure 5.20 Selection of top plane for cut plot

21. Select **Bottom** view from the **View Orientation** drop down menu in the graphics window. Select **Flow Simulation>>Results>>Display>>Lighting**. In figure 5.21c) is the temperature field shown with the hot bottom wall and the colder upper wall. Plumes of hot water are seen rising from the hot wall.

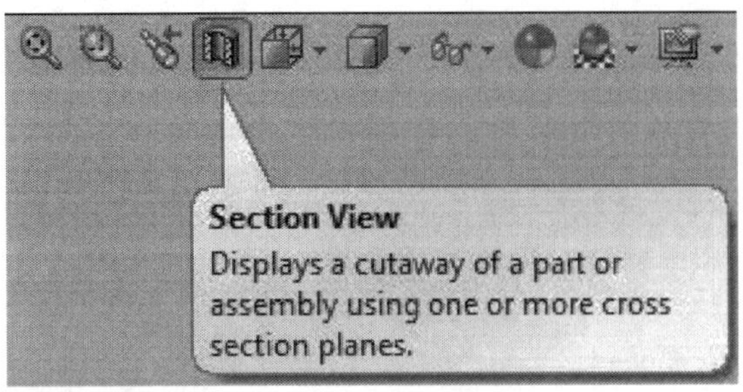

Figure 5.21a) Creating a section view

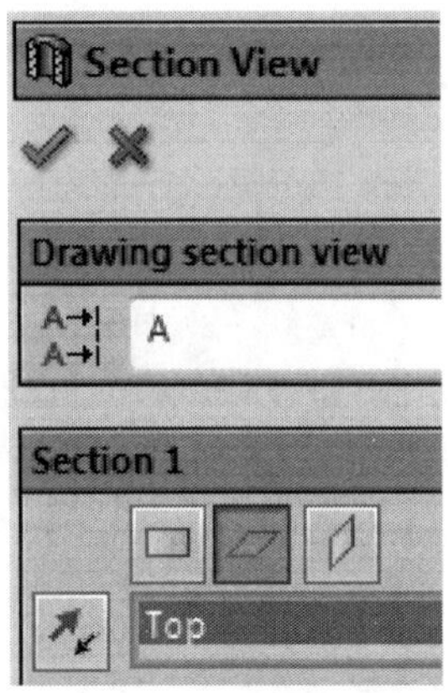

Figure 5.21b) Selection of top plane

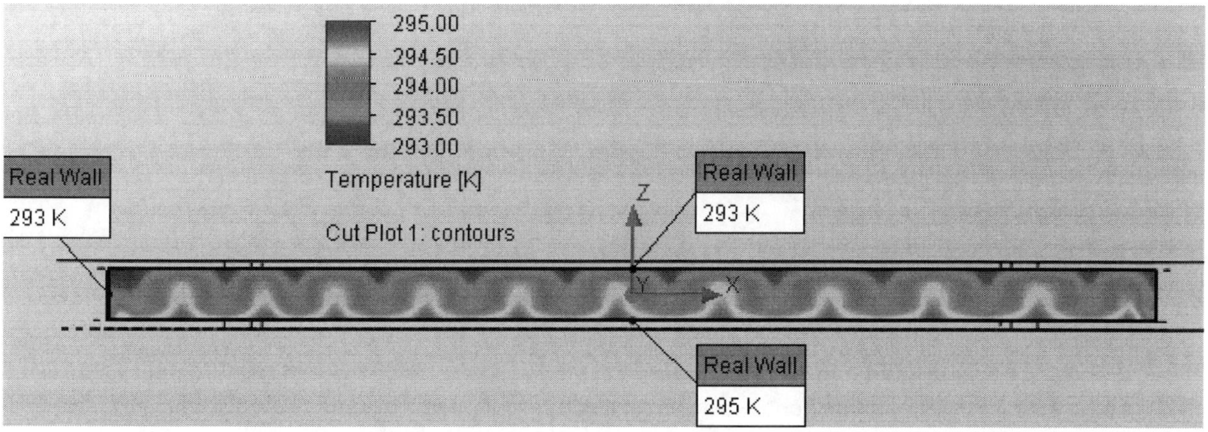

Figure 5.21c) Temperature field in Rayleigh-Bénard cell

22. Repeat step **20** and select the **Top Plane** in the **Selection** section of the **Cut Plot** window. Select **Velocity (Z)** from the **Parameters** drop down menu in the **Contours** section. Also, click on the **Vectors** button in the **Cut Plot** settings and exit the **Cut Plot** window. Right-click on the **Temperature Cut Plot** and **Hide** it. You can see alternating regions of positive and negative z-velocity indicate the presence of counter-rotating vortices in the cell. The counter-rotating motion of the vortices is shown by the vectors.

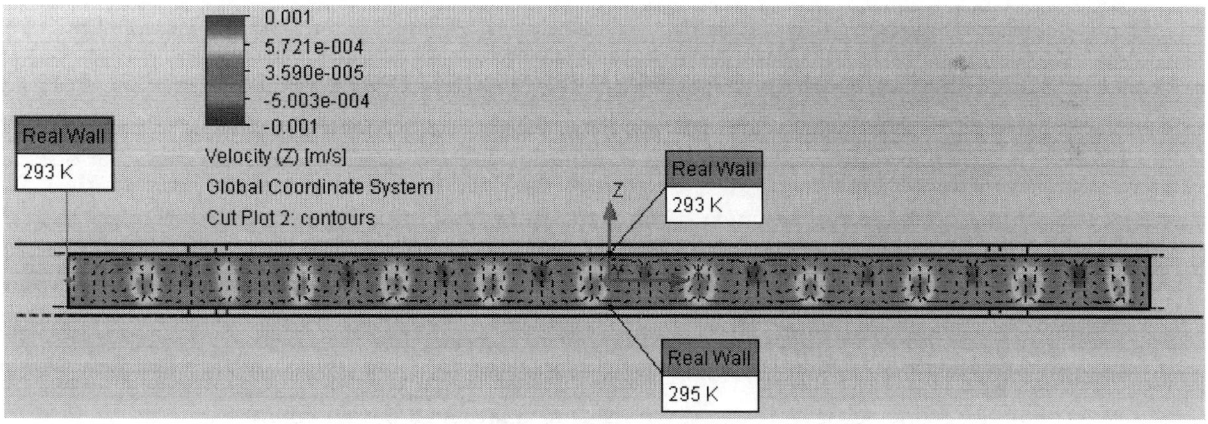

Figurc 5.22a) Velocity (Z) field in Rayleigh-Benard cell

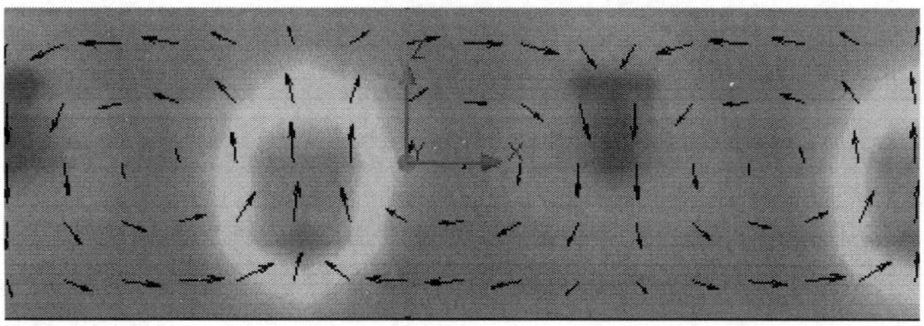

Figure 5.22b) Enlargement of cell region

Comparison with Neutral Stability Theory

23. The instability of the flow between two parallel plates heated from below is governed by the so called Rayleigh number *Ra*.

$$Ra = \frac{g\beta(T_1 - T_2)L_c^3}{\nu^2} Pr \qquad (5.1)$$

where g is acceleration due to gravity, β is the coefficient of volume expansion, T_1 and T_2 are the temperatures of the hot and cold surfaces respectively, L_c is the distance between the surfaces (fluid layer thickness). Pr is the Prandtl number and ν is the kinematic viscosity of the fluid. Below the critical $Ra_{crit} = 1715$ for a rigid upper surface, the flow is stable but convective currents will develop above this Rayleigh number. For the case of a free upper surface, the theory predicts a lower critical Rayleigh number. Unfortunately, Flow Simulation is not able to model free surface boundary conditions. The non-dimensional wave number α of this instability is determined by

$$\alpha = \frac{2\pi L_c}{\lambda} \qquad (5.2)$$

where λ is the wave length of the instability. The critical wave numbers are $\alpha_{crit} = 3.12, 2.68$ for rigid and free surface boundary conditions, respectively. From figure 5.22b) the wave number can be determined to be

$$\alpha = \frac{2\pi \cdot 0.004793}{0.00909} = 3.31 \qquad (5.3)$$

The Rayleigh number in the Flow Simulation is

$$Ra = \frac{9.81*0.000195*2*0.004793\char`^3}{10\char`^(-12)} * 6.84 = 2881 \qquad (5.4)$$

The neutral stability curve can be given to the first approximation; see figure 5.23.

$$Ra = \frac{(\pi^2+\alpha^2)^3}{\alpha^2\left\{1-16\alpha\pi^2 cosh^2(\frac{\alpha}{2})/[(\pi^2+\alpha^2)^2(sinh\alpha+\alpha)]\right\}} \qquad (5.5)$$

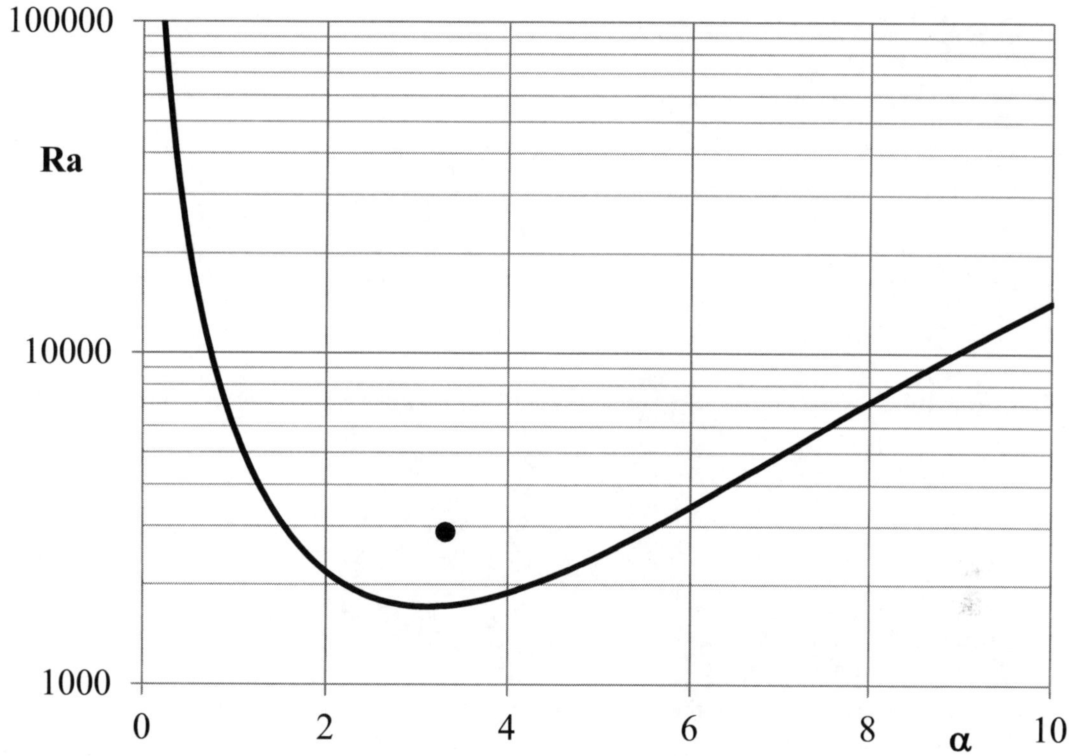

Figure 5.23 Neutral stability curve for Rayleigh-Bénard convection. The filled circle represents result from Flow Simulation.

Creating the SOLIDWORKS Part for Taylor-Couette Flow

The second flow case that we will run in this chapter is Taylor-Couette flow, the flow between rotating cylinders. In this case, we will have an inner rotating cylinder and a stationary outer cylinder. We start by creating the part using SOLIDWORKS.

24. Start by repeating steps **1 – 3** from the beginning of this chapter. Start SOLIDWORKS and create a New Part. Select **Tools>>Options…** from the SOLIDWORKS menu. Click on the Document Properties tab and select **Units**. Select **MMGS** as your **Unit system**. Select the **Front** view from the **View Orientation** drop down menu in the graphics window and click on the **Front Plane** in the **FeatureManager design tree**. Next, select the **Circle** sketch tool. Click on the origin in the graphics window and create a circle. Enter **25 mm** for the radius of the circle in the **Parameters** box. Close the dialog box. Draw another larger circle concentric with the first circle and enter **30 mm** for the radius. Close the dialog box.

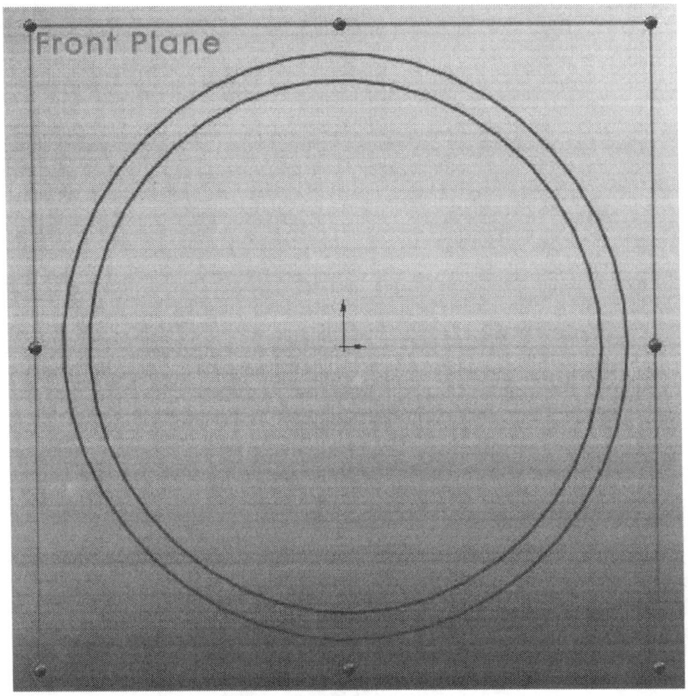

Figure 5.24 Two circles for the inner cylinder

25. The two circles for the outer cylinder are drawn in the next step. The radii for these two circles are **35 mm** and **40 mm**.

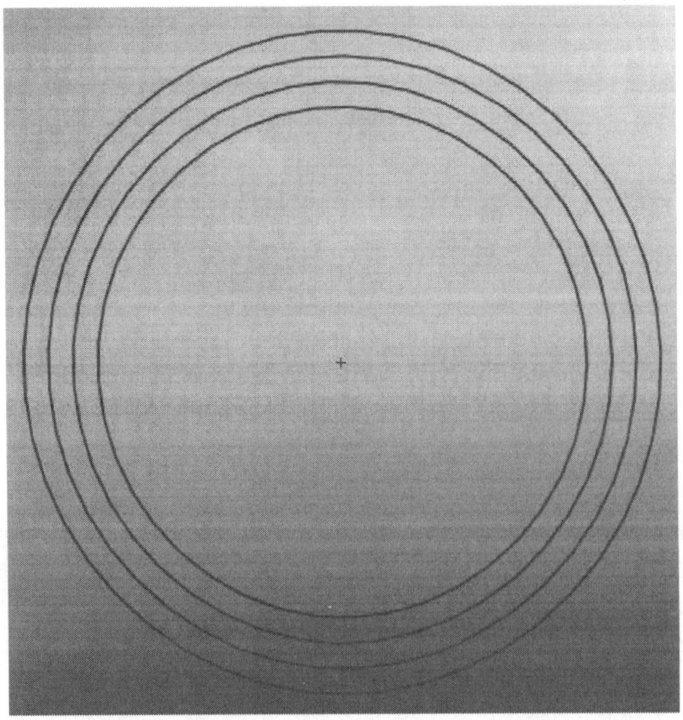

Figure 5.25 Adding two more circles for the outer cylinder.

26. Click on **Sketch 1** in the **FeatureManager design tree** followed by the selection of **Extruded Boss/Base**. Select the inner sketch region for extrusion and enter a depth of 50 mm in both **Direction 1** and **Direction 2**. Click on OK. Repeat this step and extrude the outer sketch region to the same depth in both directions. Save the part with the name **Taylor-Couette Cell**.

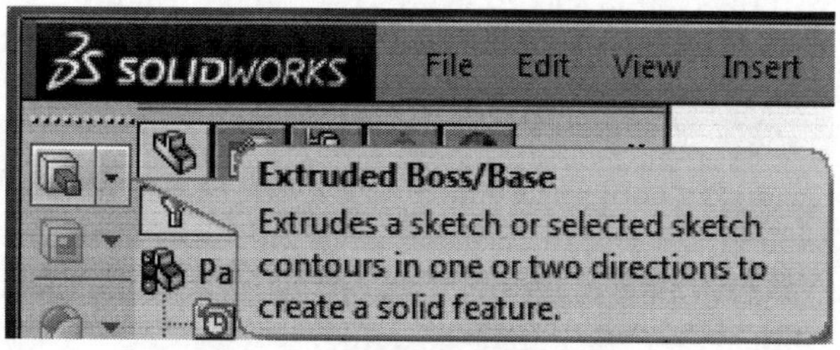

Figure 5.26a) Selection of Sketch 1 for extrusion.

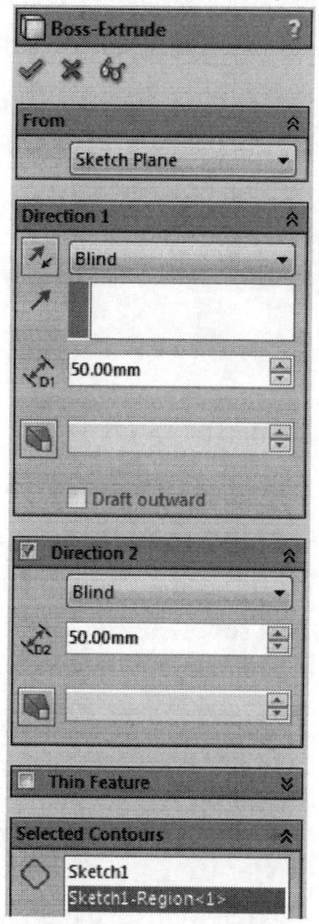

Figure 5.26b) Entering depth of extrusion

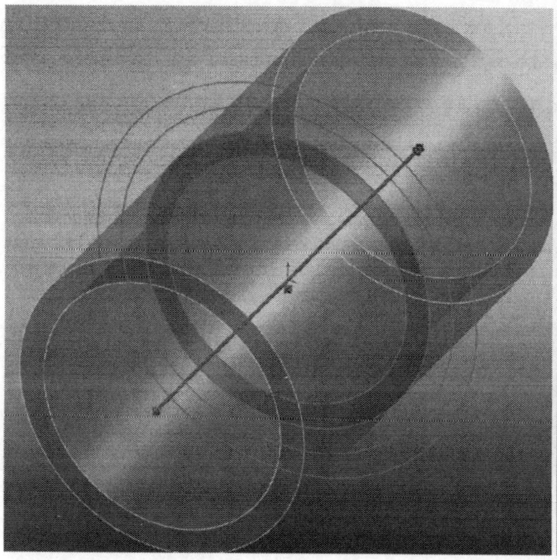

Figure 5.26c) Inner sketch region

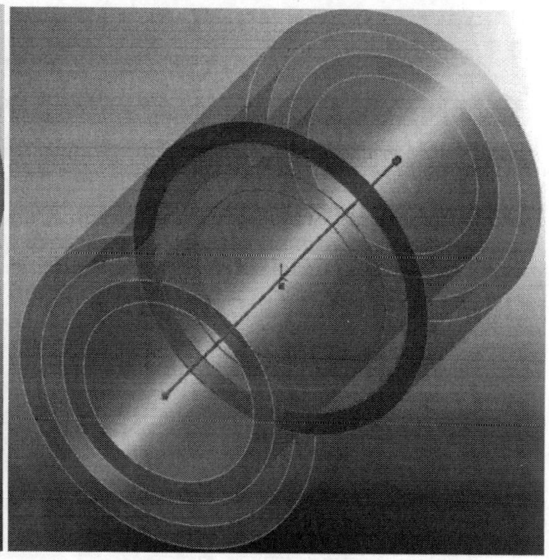

Figure 5.26d) Outer sketch region

Setting up the Flow Simulation Project for Taylor-Couette Flow

27. If Flow Simulation is not available in the SOLIDWORKS menu, select **Tools>>Add Ins…** and check the corresponding **SOLIDWORKS Flow Simulation** box. Start the Flow Simulation Wizard by selecting **Tools>>Flow Simulation>>Project>>Wizard**. Enter Project name **Instabilities in Taylor-Couette Flow**.

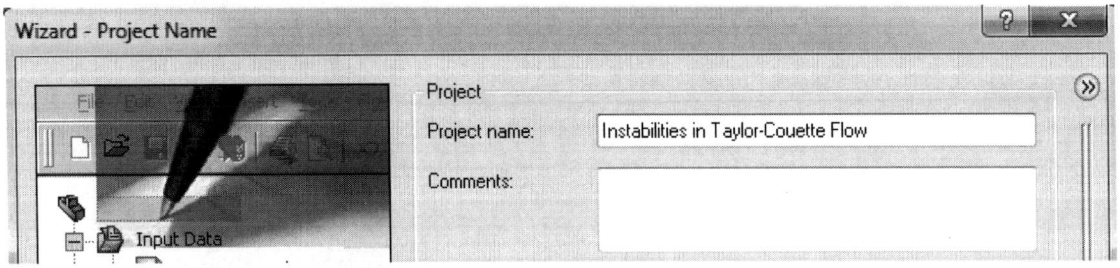

Figure 5.27 Create a new project name

28. Select the **SI unit system** in the next step followed by selection of the default **Internal Analysis type**. Add **Water** as the **Project Fluid** and use default values of wall conditions and initial conditions, and set the initial mesh to **5** in the results and geometry resolution window. You will get a fluid volume recognition failure message. Answer **Yes** to this question and create a lid on each side of the model. Select the outer ring as the face for the lid and click OK. Answer **Yes** to the questions whether you want to reset the computational domain, mesh settings, and open the Create Lids tool. Next, right click in the graphics window and select **Rotate View**. Rotate the Taylor-Couette model around. Select the outer ring and create the second lid. Answer "**Yes**" when asked to reset the computational domain and mesh settings.

Select **Tools>>Flow Simulation>>Initial Mesh** from the SOLIDWORKS menu. Uncheck the box for **Automatic settings**. Set the number of cells in all three directions X, Y and Z to **30**. Click on the **OK** button to exit the **Initial Mesh** window. Select **Tools>>Flow Simulation>>Calculation Control Options…** from the SOLIDWORKS menu. Click on the **Refinement** tab and select **level = 1** for the **Value** of the **Refinement Parameter**. Click on the **OK** button to exit the **Calculation Control Options** window.

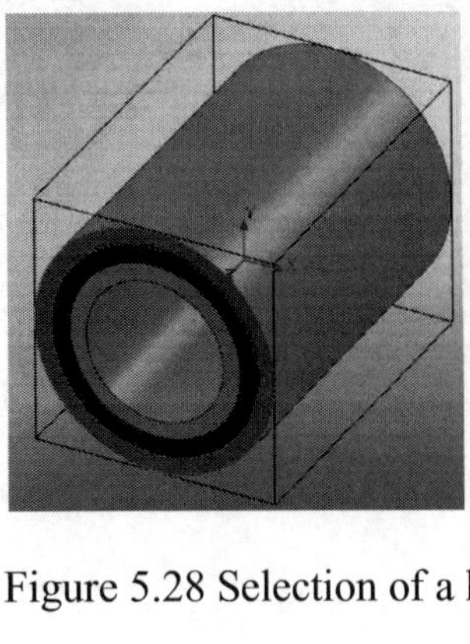

Figure 5.28 Selection of a lid for the Taylor-Couette cell

29. Select **Hidden Lines Visible** from the **Display Type** drop down menu in the graphics window and **Isometric** view from the **View Orientation** drop down menu.

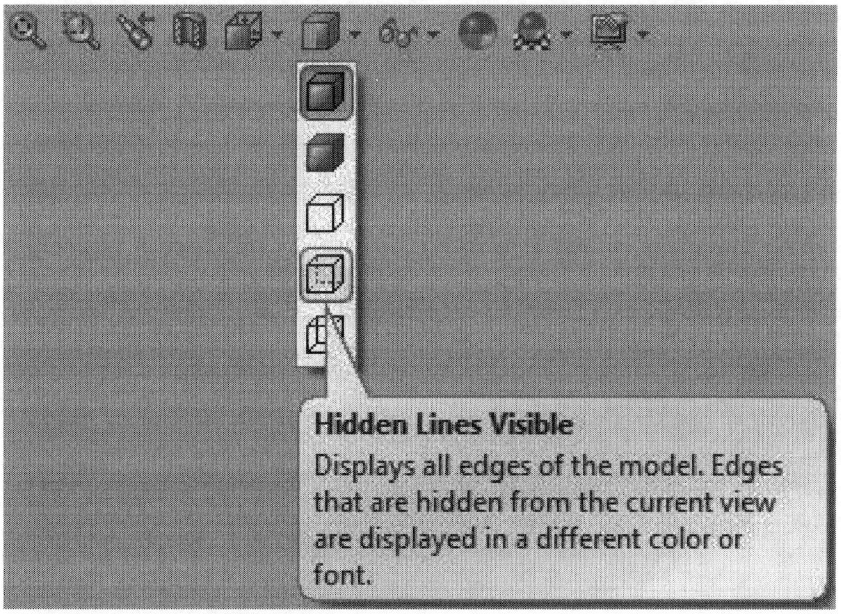

Figure 5.29a) Showing hidden lines

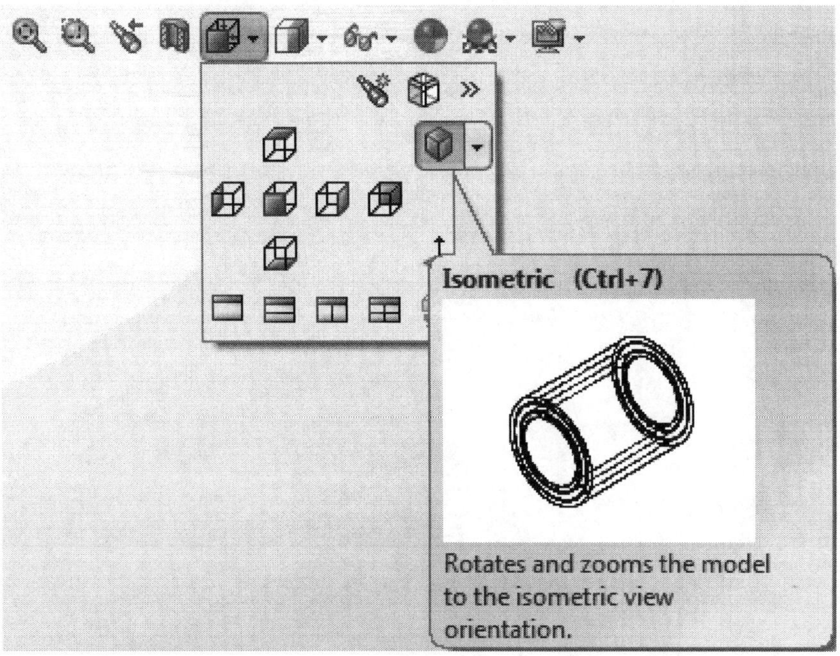

Figure 5.29b) Selection of isometric view

Inserting Boundary Conditions for Taylor-Couette Cell

30. Click on the **Flow Simulation analysis tree** tab and click on the plus sign next to the **Input Data** folder. Right click on **Boundary Conditions** and select **Insert Boundary Condition…** Move the cursor over the cylinders, right click and select **Select Other**. Select the face for the inner cylindrical surface of the flow domain; see figures 5.30 and 5.0b). Select the **Real Wall** boundary condition, check the box for **Wall Motion** and set the value of **1.5 rad/s** for the angular velocity in the **Z Axis direction** in the **Wall Motion** window; see figure 5.30. Click OK ✓ to finish the boundary condition. Rename the boundary condition in the Flow Simulation analysis tree to **Inner Cylinder**. Insert another boundary condition for the outer cylinder wall, select the **Real Wall** boundary condition without wall motion and name the boundary condition **Outer Cylinder**.

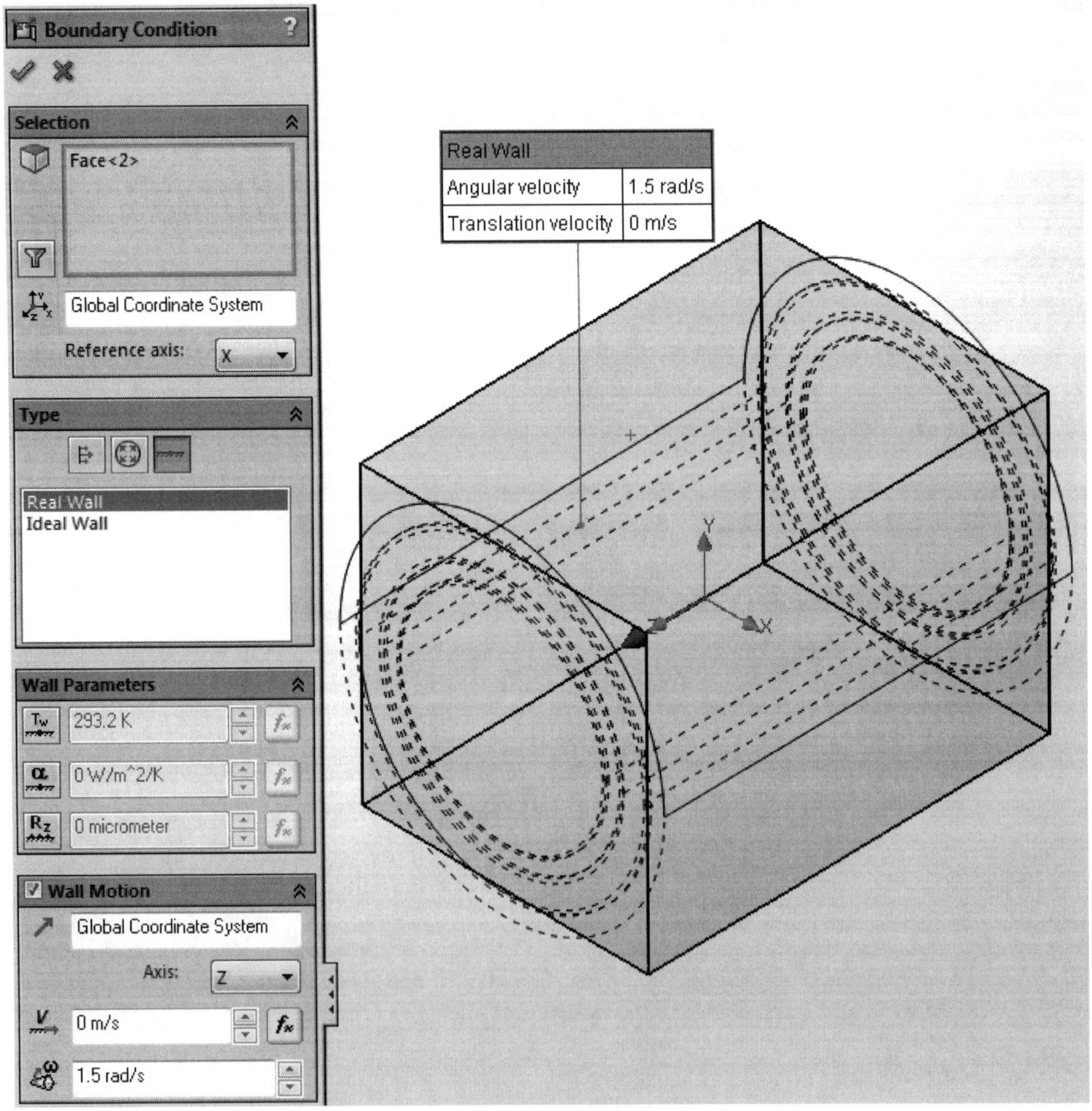

Figure 5.30 Selection of boundary condition for rotating inner cylinder.

Inserting Global Goal and Running the Calculations for Taylor-Couette Flow

31. Right click on **Goals** in the **Flow Simulation analysis tree** and select **Insert Global Goals…**

Check the boxes for **Min**, **Av** and **Max Velocity** and exit the window. Select **Tools>>Flow Simulation>>Solve>>Run**. Push the **Run** button in the window that appears.

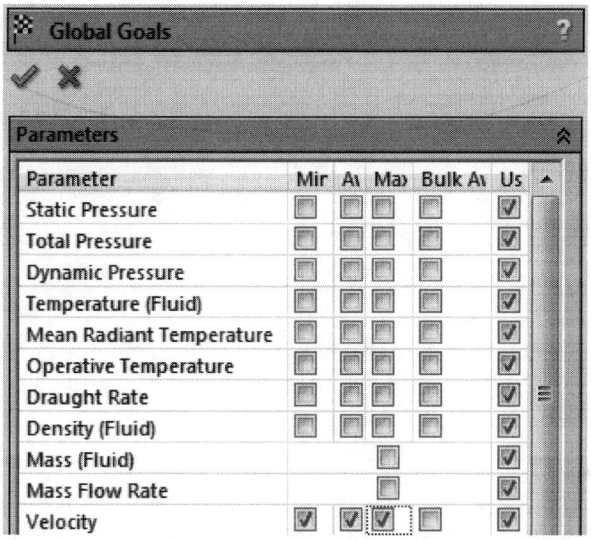

Figure 5.31a) Selecting velocity as global goal

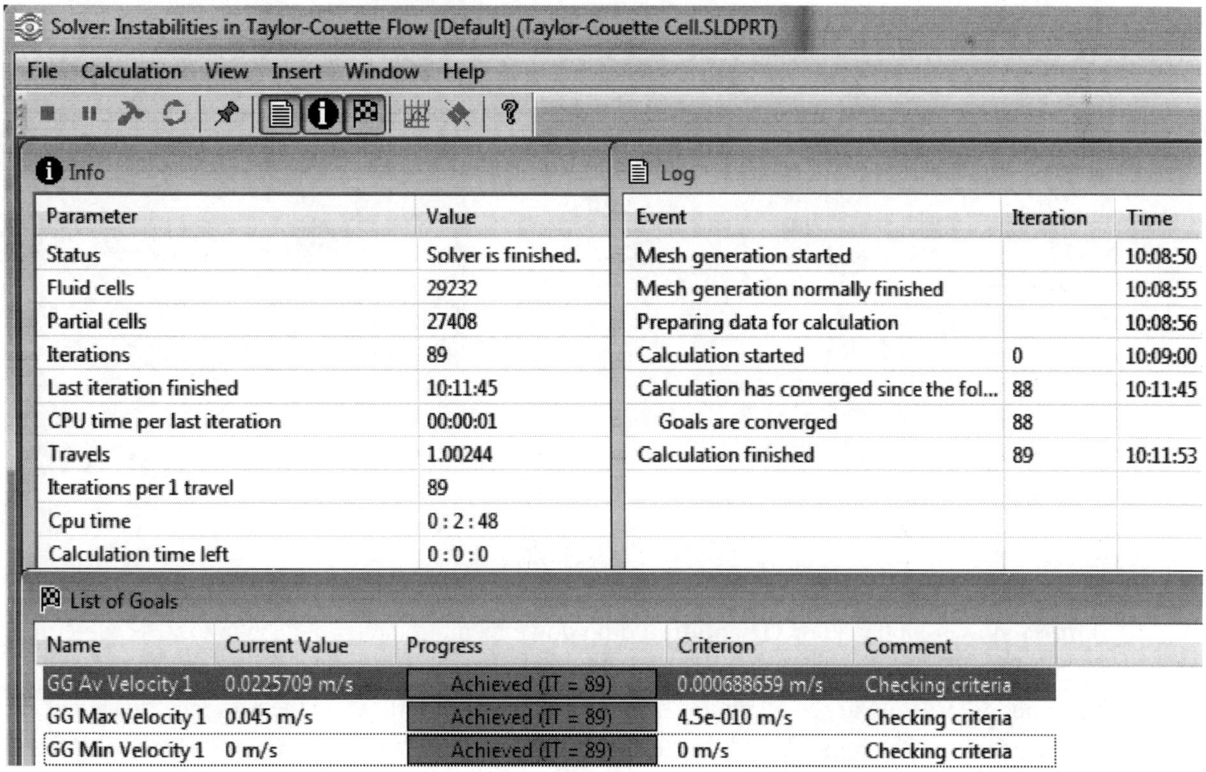

Figure 5.31b) Solver window for calculations of Taylor-Couette flow

Inserting Surface Plots

32. Right click on **Surface Plots** in the **Flow Simulation analysis tree** and select **Insert…**. Select the face of the rotating cylinder by selecting the Inner Cylinder Boundary Condition. Expand **Options** and check the **Offset** box. Select **Velocity (Z)** from the **Parameter** drop down menu in the **Contours** section. Slide the **Number of Levels** to **255** and exit the **Surface Plot** window.

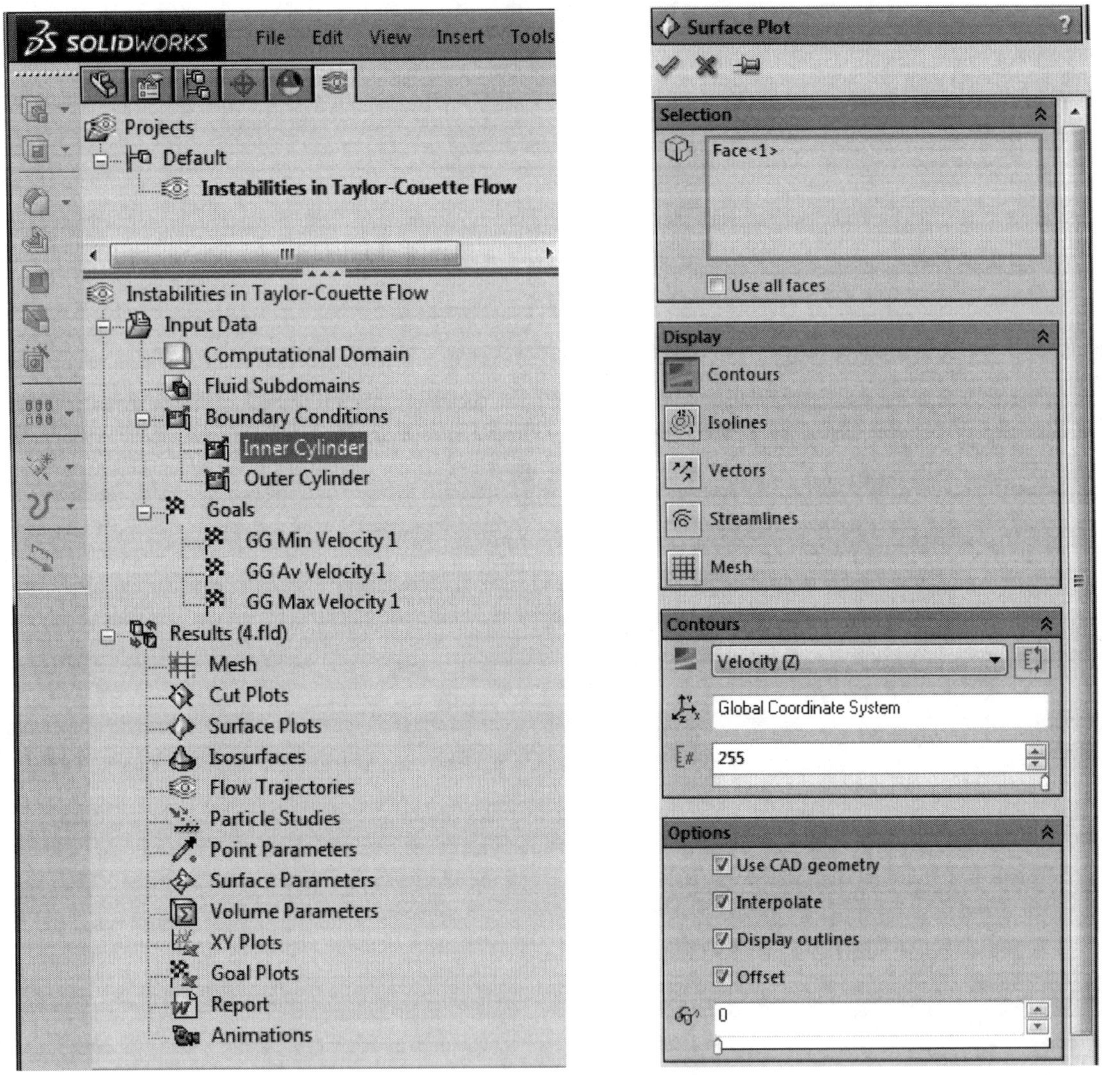

Figure 5.32 Surface plot settings.

33. Select **Flow Simulation>>Results>>Display>>Lighting** from the SOLIDWORKS menu. Select **Bottom** view from the **View Orientation** drop down menu in the graphics window. Rename the surface plot to **Velocity (Z)**. The velocity field is shown in figure 5.33a). Alternating bands of high and low velocity are shown in the spanwise *Z* direction indicating the presence of Taylor vortices. It should be remembered that the surface plot is not on the rotating cylinder but offset in the radial direction towards the outer cylinder. Insert another surface plot for the circumferential velocity and name it **Circumferential Velocity**. The velocity field is shown in figure 5.33b).

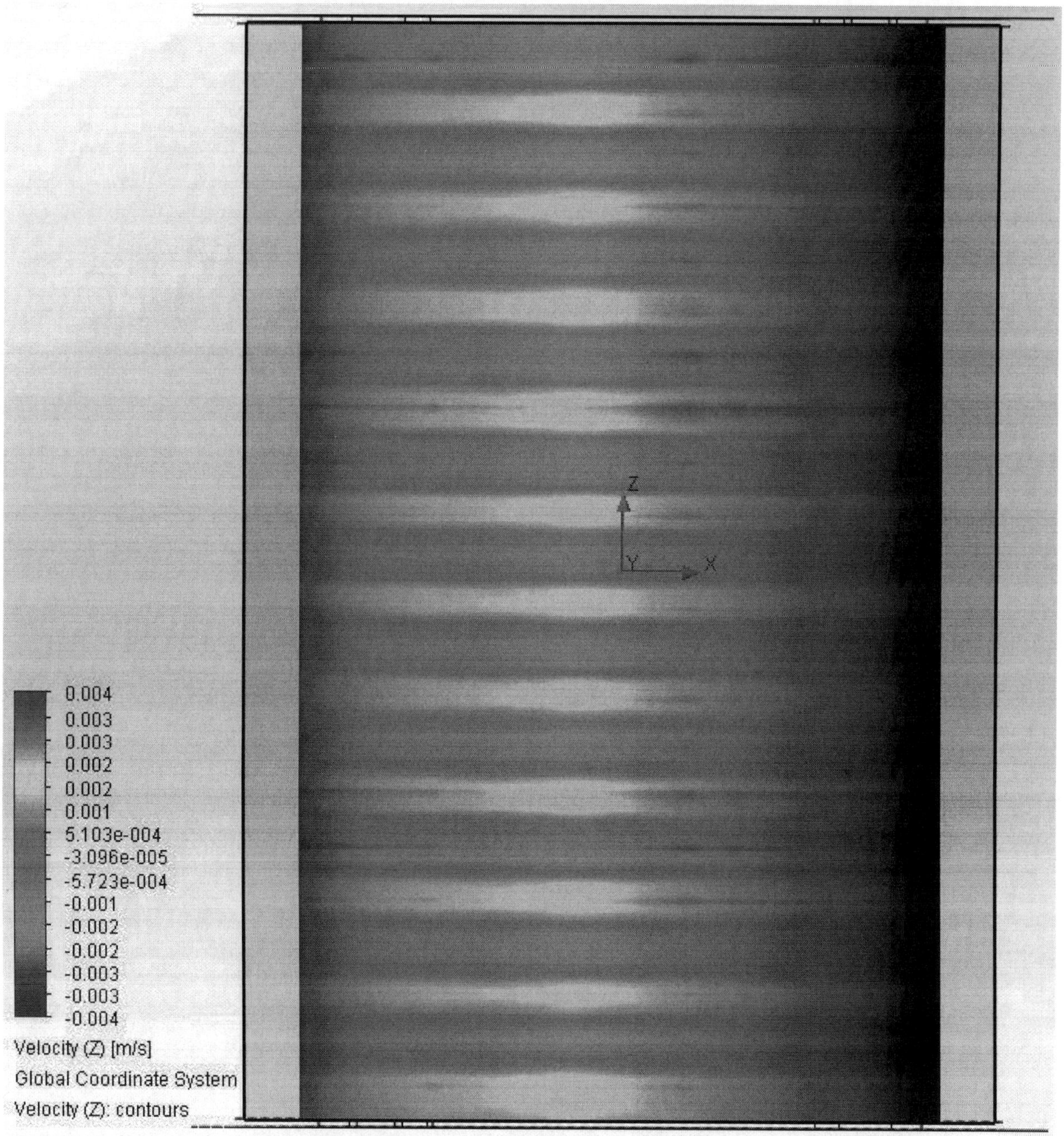

Figure 5.33a) Surface plot for Taylor-Couette flow: Velocity (Z)

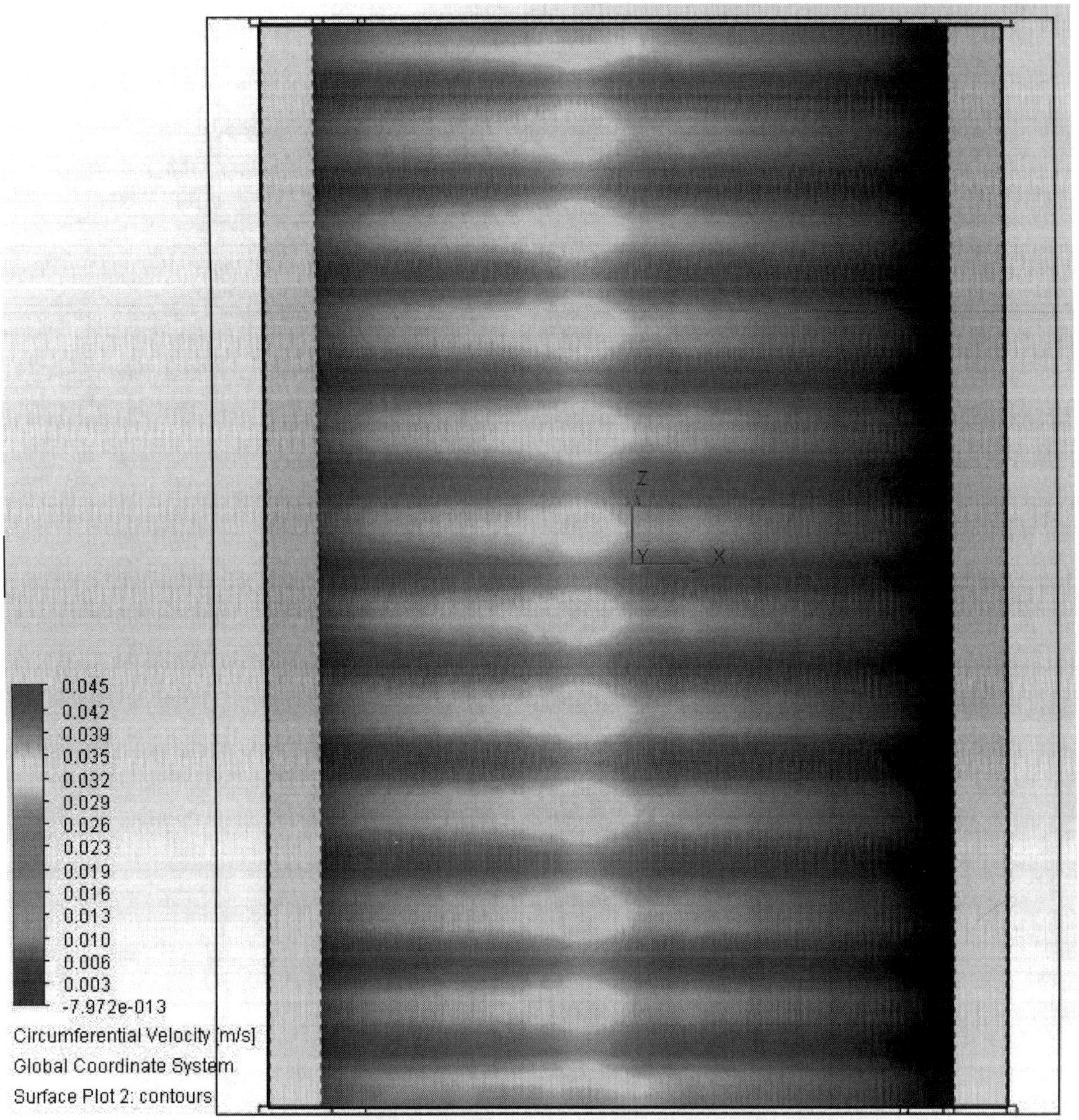

Figure 5.33b) Surface plot for Taylor-Couette flow: Circumferential Velocity

Comparison with Neutral Stability Theory

34. The instability of the flow between two vertical rotating cylinders is governed by the so called Taylor number *Ta*.

$$Ta = \frac{4\Omega_i^2 d^4}{\nu^2} \tag{5.6}$$

where Ω_i is the rotation rate of the inner cylinder, d is the distance between the cylinders and ν is the kinematic viscosity of the fluid. Below the critical $Ta_{crit} = 3430$ for a non-rotating outer cylinder, the flow is stable but instabilities will develop above this Taylor number. The non-dimensional wave number α of this instability is determined by

$$\alpha = \frac{2\pi d}{\lambda} \tag{5.7}$$

where λ is the wave length of the instability. The critical wave numbers is $\alpha_{crit} = 3.12$ in the narrow gap limit: $\eta \rightarrow 1$. The radius ratio is defined as $\eta = r_i/r_o$ where r_i and r_o is the radius of the inner and outer cylinder, respectively. From figures 5.33d), the wave number can be determined to be

$$\alpha = \frac{2\pi \cdot 0.005}{0.00894} = 3.51 \tag{5.8}$$

The Taylor number in the calculations is

$$Ta = \frac{4 \cdot 1.5^2 \cdot 0.005^4}{(1.004 \cdot 10^{-6})^2} = 5580 \tag{5.9}$$

The neutral stability curve can be given to the first approximation; see figure 5.34.

$$Ta = \frac{2(\pi^2+\alpha^2)^3}{(1+\mu)\alpha^2\left\{1-16\alpha\pi^2 cosh^2(\frac{\alpha}{2})/[(\pi^2+\alpha^2)^2(sinh\alpha+\alpha)]\right\}} \tag{5.10}$$

where $\mu = \Omega_o/\Omega_i$ and Ω_o is the rotation rate of the outer cylinder.

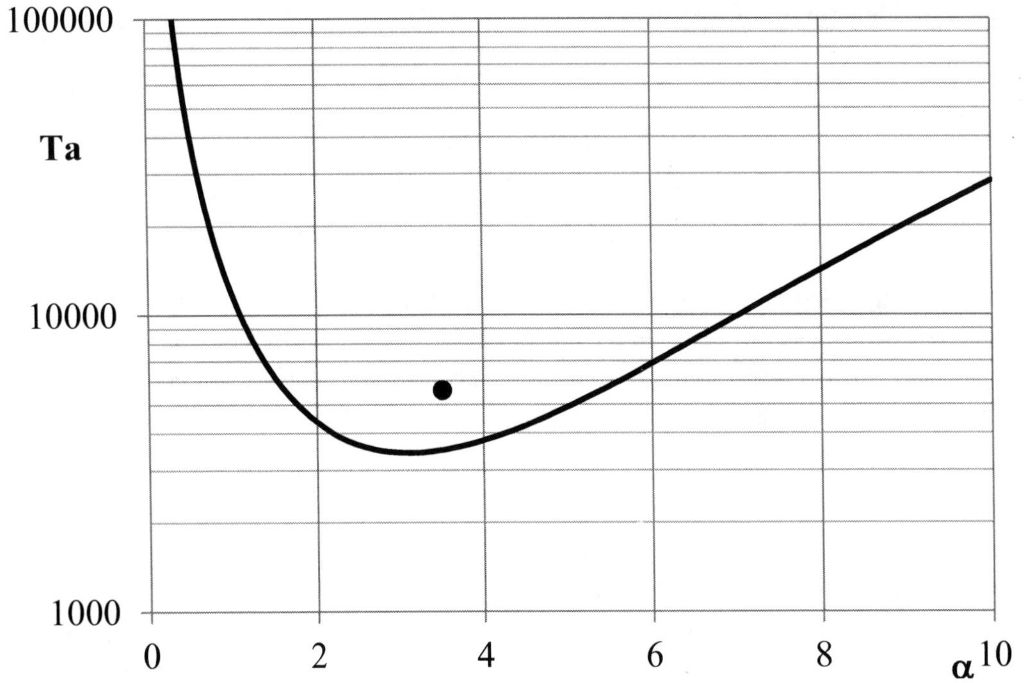

Figure 5.34 Neutral stability curve for Taylor-Couette flow with a stationary outer cylinder, $\mu = 0$. The filled circle represents result from Flow Simulation. The radius ratio $\eta = 6/7$ in the Flow Simulation calculations and $\eta = 1$ for the stability curve.

References

[1] Chandrasekhar, S., Hydrodynamic and Hydromagnetic Stability, Dover, 1981.

[2] Koschmieder, E.L., Benard Cells and Taylor Vortices, Cambridge, 1993.

Exercises

5.1 Run the calculations for the flow in the Taylor-Couette apparatus with only the inner cylinder rotating $\mu = 0$ for Taylor numbers $Ta = 10000$, 20000 and 30000 and compare the spanwise wave numbers with the one determined in this chapter for $Ta = 5580$. Include your results in figure 5.34 for comparison with the neutral stability curve.

5.2 Run the calculations for the flow in the Taylor-Couette apparatus with both cylinders rotating $\mu = 1$ and for Taylor numbers $Ta = 3000$, 5000 and 10000 and determine the spanwise wave numbers. Include your results in a graph and compare with the neutral stability curve corresponding to $\mu = -1/2$; see equation 10.

5.3 Run the calculations for the flow in a Rayleigh-Bénard cell for Rayleigh numbers $Ra = 5000$, 10000 and 20000 and compare the wave numbers with the one determined in this chapter for $Ra = 2953$. Include your results in figure 5.23 for comparison with the neutral stability curve.

Chapter 6 Pipe Flow

Objectives

- Creating the SOLIDWORKS model of the pipe needed
- Setting up Flow Simulation projects for internal flows
- Creating a fluid with a certain value of dynamic viscosity
- Creating lids for boundary conditions
- Setting up boundary conditions
- Running the calculations
- Using cut plots and XY plots to visualize the resulting flow field
- Compare results with theory and empirical data

Problem Description

In this chapter, we will use Flow Simulation to study flows in pipes and compare with the theoretical solutions and empirical data. First, we will model the laminar flow with a mean velocity of 0.5 m/s corresponding to a Reynolds number *Re* = 100 for a 5 m long pipe with an inner diameter of 200 mm. Next, we will consider turbulent flow in the same pipe extended to a length of 10 m and a higher Reynolds number *Re* = 100,000. We start by creating the part needed for this simulation.

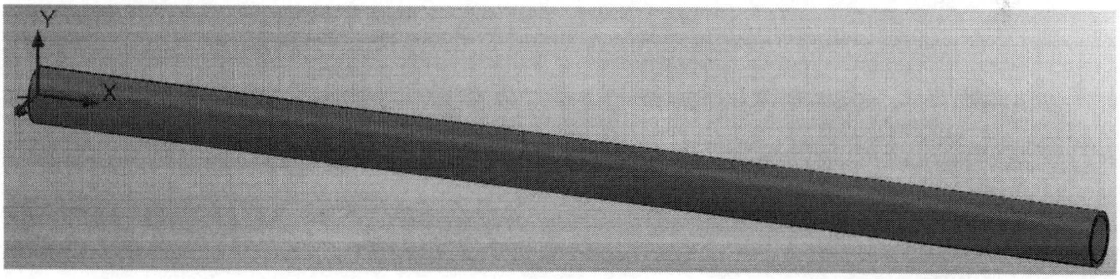

Figure 6.0 SOLIDWORKS model of pipe section

Creating the SOLIDWORKS Part

1. Start by creating a new part in SOLIDWORKS: select **File>>New** and click on the **OK** button in the **New SOLIDWORKS Document** window. Select **Tools>>Options...** from the SOLIDWORKS menu. Click on the Document Properties tab and select **Units**. Select **MMGS** as your **Unit system**. Click on **Right Plane** in the **FeatureManager design tree** and select **Right** from the **View Orientation** drop down menu in the graphics window.

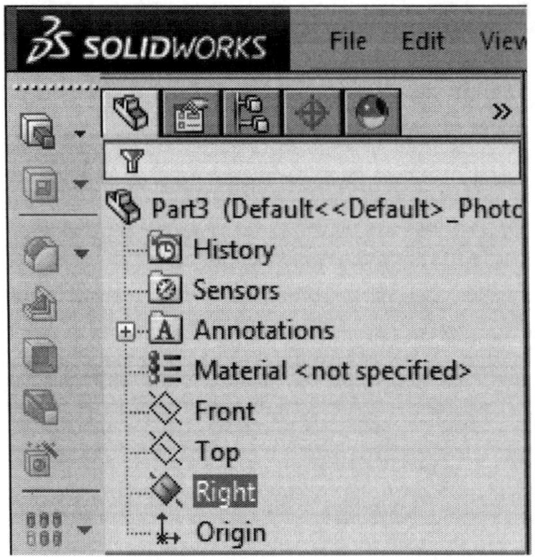

Figure 6.1a) Selection of right plane

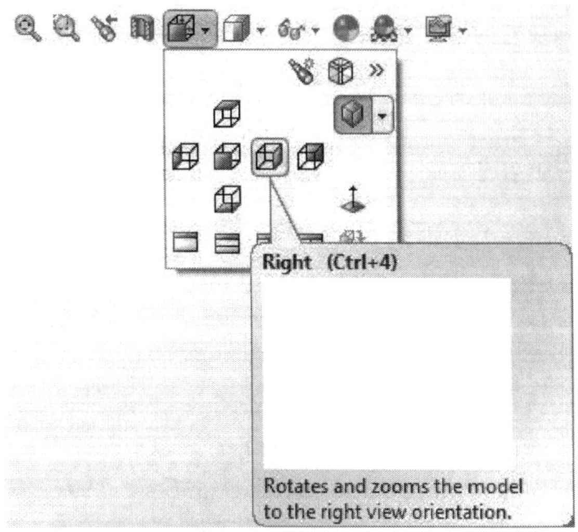

Figure 6.1b) Selection of right view

2. Click on **Circle**.

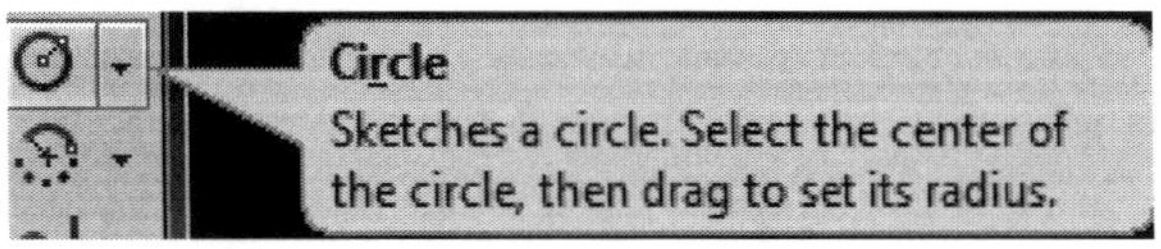

Figure 6.2 Selecting a sketch tool

3. Click on the origin in the graphics window and create a circle. Fill in the **Parameters** for the circle: **100 mm** radius. Close the **Circle** dialog box by clicking on ✓. Repeat this step and create another concentric circle with a larger radius of **120 mm**.

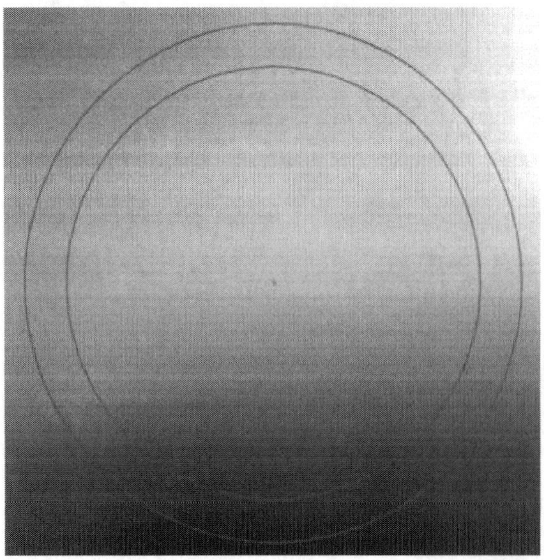

Figure 6.3 Two concentric circles with radii 100 mm and 120 mm

4. Select **Extruded Boss/Base**. Enter a **Depth D1** of **5000 mm** in **Direction 1**. Next, click **OK** to exit the **Extrude Property Manager**.

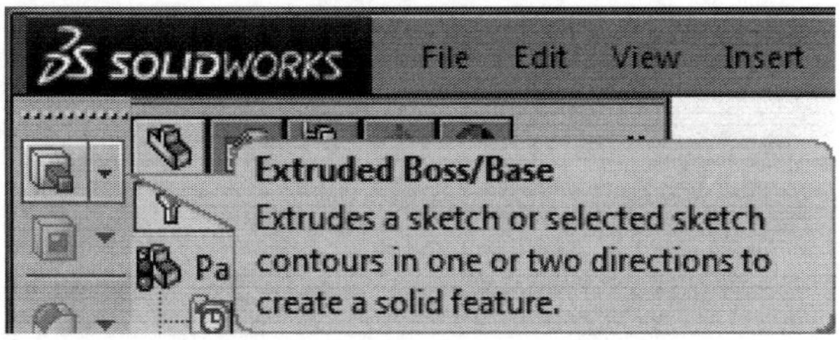

Figure 6.4a) Selection of extrusion feature

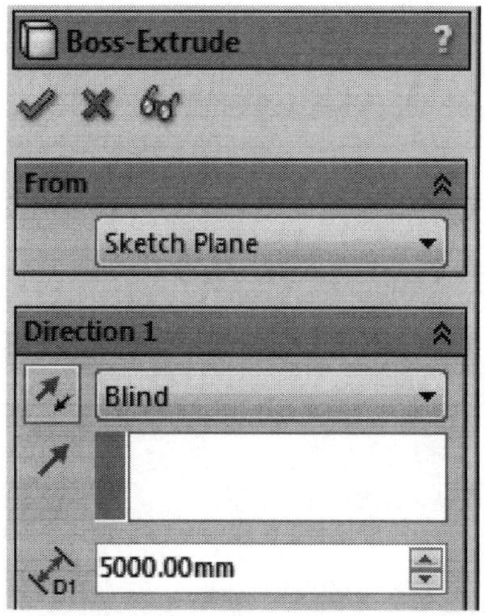

Figure 6.4b) Entering depth of extrusion

5. Select **Wireframe** from the **Display Style** drop down menu in the graphics window. Select **Front** from the **View Orientation** drop down menu in the graphics window. Click on **Front Plane** in the **FeatureManager design tree.** Right click in the graphics window and select **Zoom/Pan/Rotate>>Zoom to Area** and zoom in around the left end of the pipe.

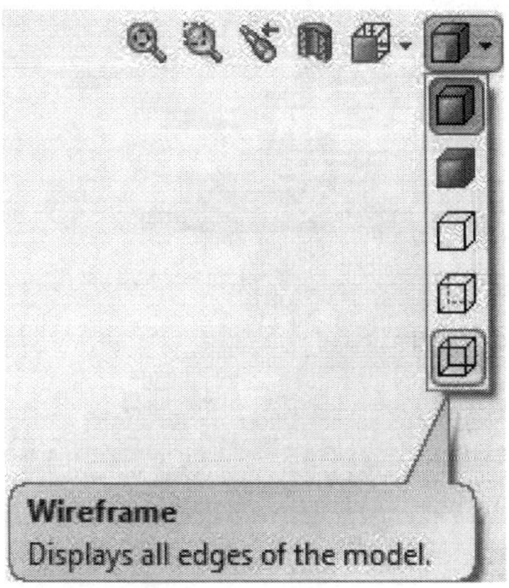

Figure 6.5a) Displaying the wireframe style

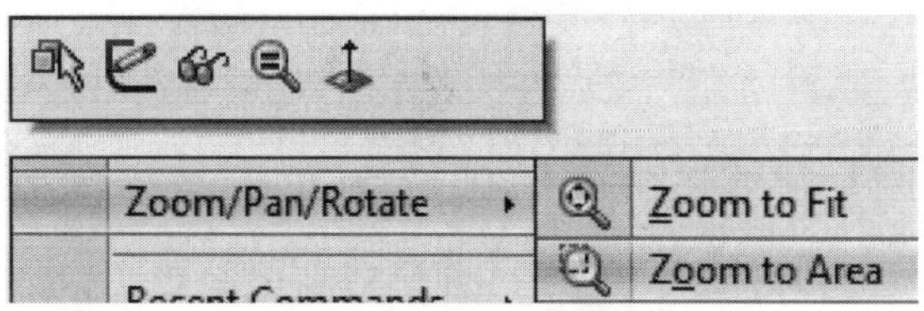

Figure 6.5b) Selection of zoom to area tool

6. Select the **Front** plane and **Line** sketch tool. Draw a vertical line in the Y-direction starting at the origin in the center of the pipe and end at the inner surface of the pipe. Right click in the graphics window and click on **Select**. Click on the new line and set the **Parameters** and **Additional Parameters** to the values shown in the figure. Close the **Line Properties** dialog .

Figure 6.6a) Selection of the line sketch tool

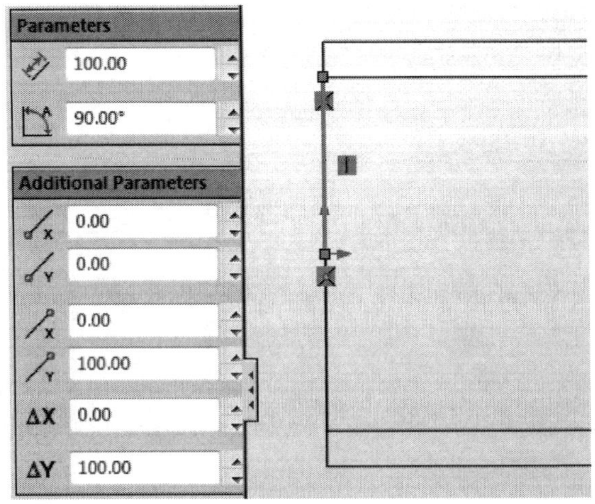

Figure 6.6b) Parameters for vertical line

7. Repeat step **6** and draw five more vertical lines with the same length and the lines positioned at *x* = 200, 400, 600, 800 and 4600 mm. These lines will be used to plot the velocity profiles at different streamwise positions along the pipe. Rename the newly created sketch in the **FeatureManager design tree** and name it **x = 0, D, 2D, 3D, 4D, 23D**; see figure 6.7a). Rebuild the part; see figure 6.7b).

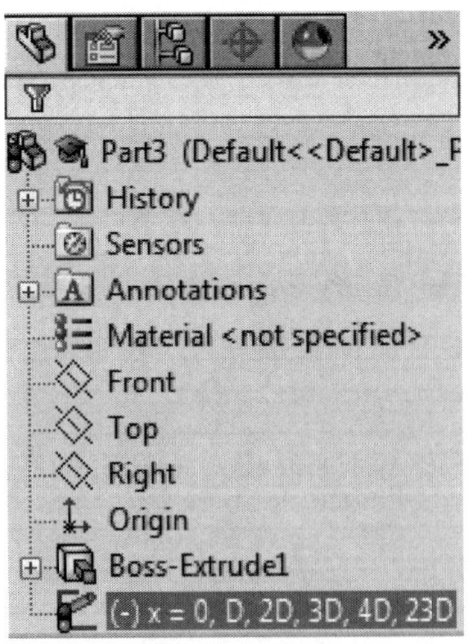

Figure 6.7a) Renaming the sketch for pipe flow

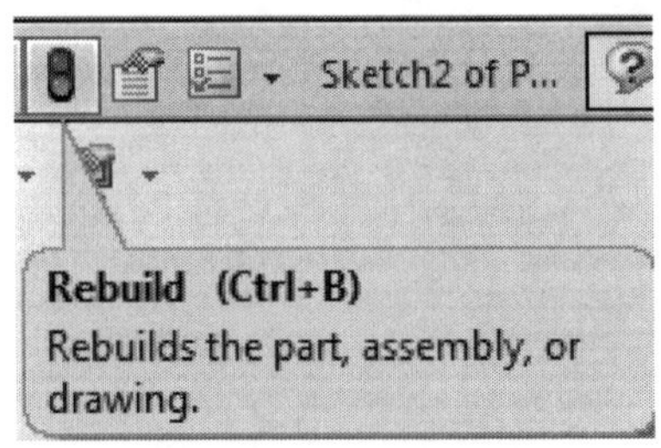

Figure 6.7b) Rebuilding the part

8. Create a new sketch by clicking on **Front Plane** in the **FeatureManager design tree** and selecting **Insert>>Sketch** from the menu. Draw a **4600 mm** long horizontal line in the x-direction starting at the origin of the pipe. Rebuild the part. Rename the sketch in the **FeatureManager design tree** and call it **x = 0 – 4.6 m (centerline)**. Repeat this step but draw the line along the wall of the pipe and name the sketch **x = 0 – 4.6 m (wall)**. Save the SOLIDWORKS part with the following name: **Pipe Flow**.

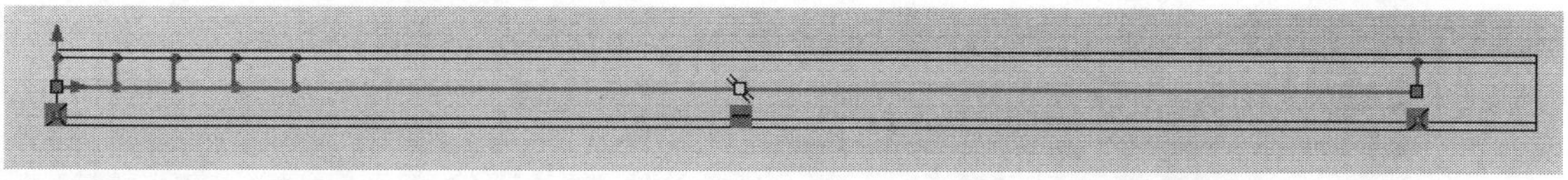

Figure 6.8a) Adding a line in the x-direction along the centerline of the pipe

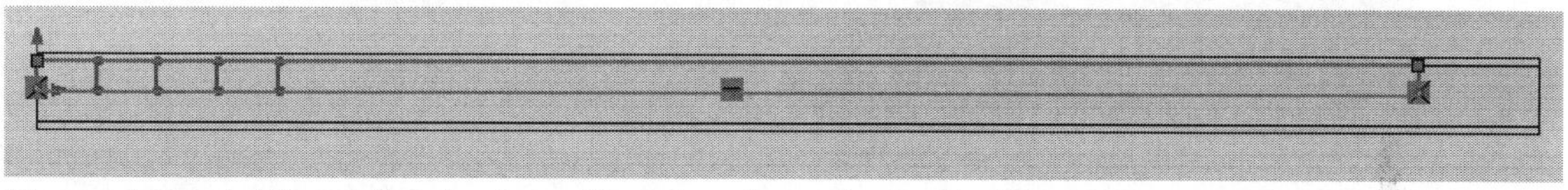

Figure 6.8b) Adding a line in the x-direction along the wall of the pipe

Setting up the Flow Simulation Project

9. If Flow Simulation is not available in the menu, you have to add it from SOLIDWORKS menu: **Tools>>Add Ins…** and check the corresponding **SOLIDWORKS Flow Simulation** box. Select **Tools>>Flow Simulation>>Project>>Wizard** from the SOLIDWORKS menu to create a new Flow Simulation project. Create a new project named "**Pipe Flow Study**." Click on the **Next >** button. Select the default **SI (m-kg-s)** unit system and click on the **Next>** button once again.

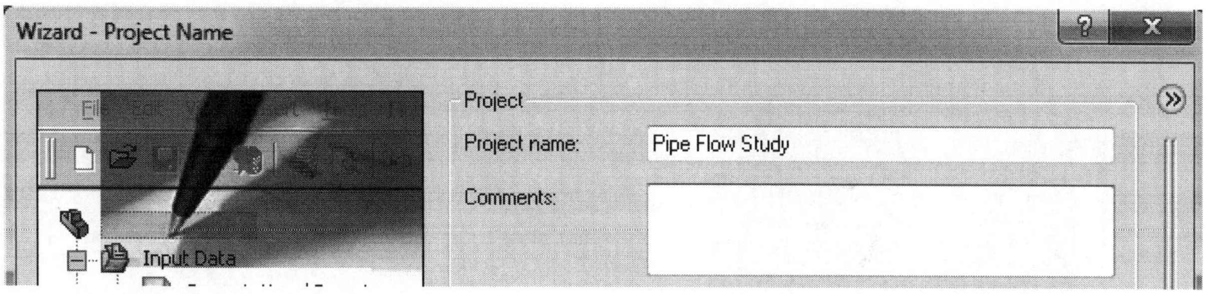

Figure 6.9 Creating a name for the project

10. Use the default **Internal Analysis type**. Click on the **Next** > button.

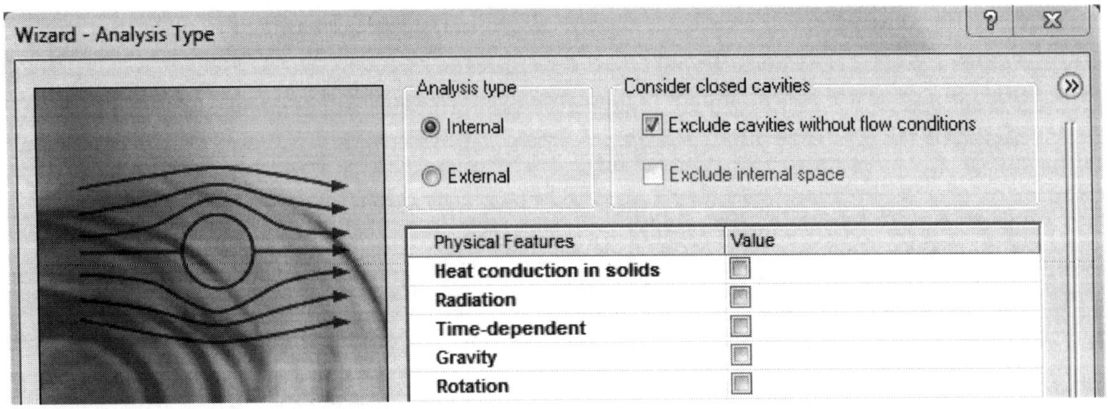

Figure 6.10 Internal analysis

11. Click on the **New…** button in the **Default Fluid** window to open the **Engineering Database**. Expand **Materials** in the **Database tree** by clicking on the plus sign next to the materials folder. Expand **Gases** and click on **Pre-Defined**. Select **Air** from the list of **Pre-Defined Items**, right click and select **Copy**. Click on **User Defined Gases** in the **Database tree**, right click in the field under the **Items** tab and **Paste**. Right click on the pasted **Air** and select **Item Properties**. Change the **Dynamic viscosity** to **0.0012 Pa*s** and change the name to the one shown in figure 6.11e). Select **File>>Save** from the **Engineering Database** menu. Close the **Engineering Database** window and add the new fluid as **Project Fluid**. Select **Laminar Only** from the **Flow Type** drop down menu. Click on the **Next** > button. Use the default **Wall Conditions** and **0.5 m/s** for **Velocity in X direction** as **Initial Condition**. Slide the **Result resolution** to **8**. Click on the **Finish** button. Answer Yes to the question whether you want to open the Create Lids tool.

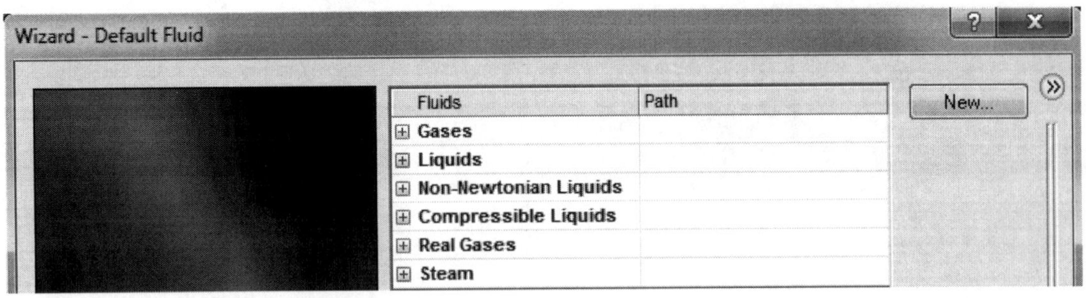

Figure 6.11a) Opening the engineering database

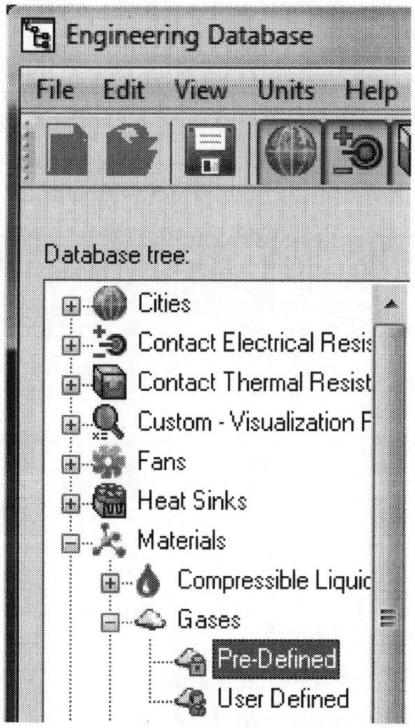

Figure 6.11b) Selecting pre-defined gases

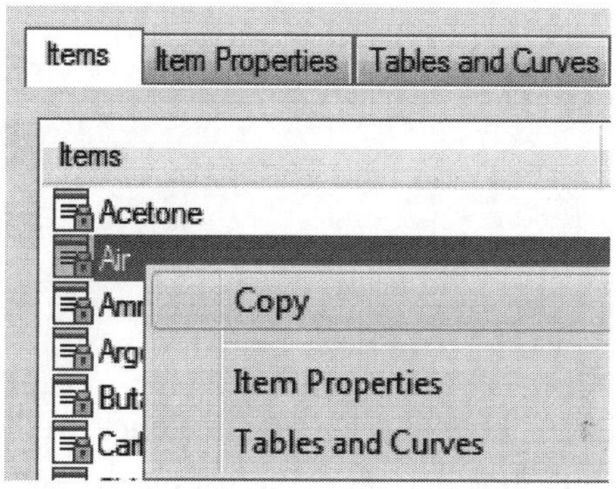

Figure 6.11c) Copying the pre-defined air

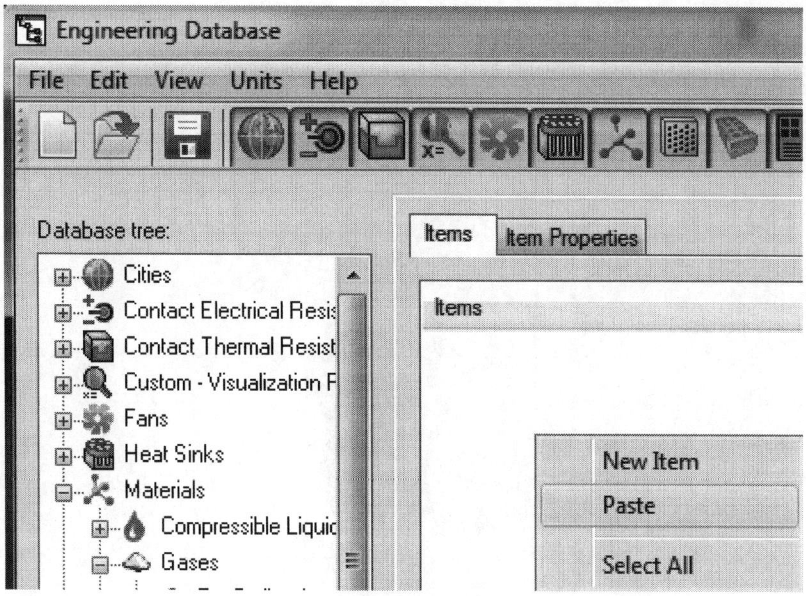

Figure 6.11d) Pasting air to user defined gases

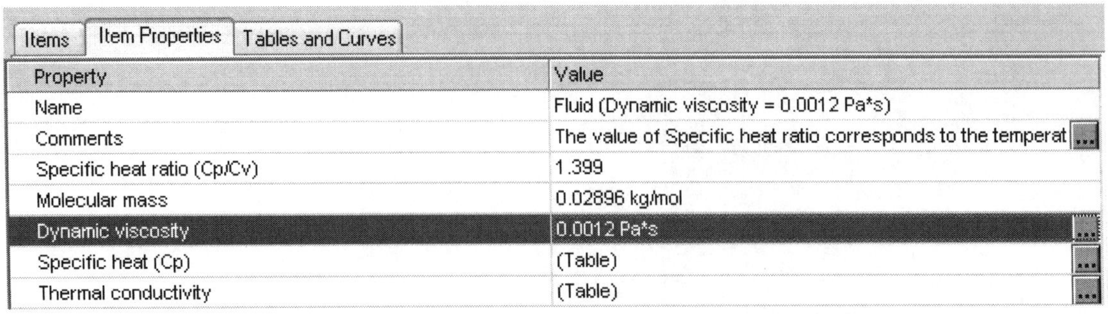

Figure 6.11e) Defining the dynamic viscosity

Creating Lids for the Pipe

12. Rotate the pipe a little bit and click on the face between the two circles. Click on the **Adjust Thickness** button and adjust the thickness of the lid to **1.00 mm**. Close the **Create Lids** dialog . Answer yes to the questions whether you want to reset the computational domain and mesh settings. Answer Yes to the question whether you want to open the Create Lids tool.

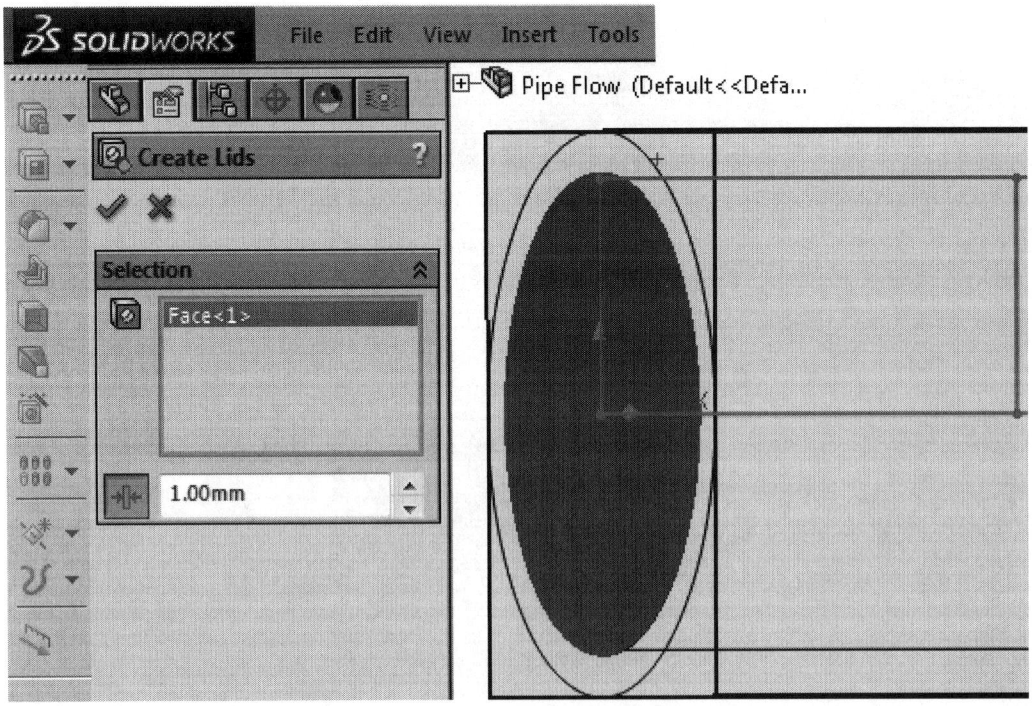

Figure 6.12 Creating a lid for the pipe

13. Repeat step **12** one more time but select the **Right** view and create a lid with the same thickness for the other end of the pipe. Answer yes to the question whether you want to reset the computational domain and also yes to the next question whether you want to reset mesh settings.

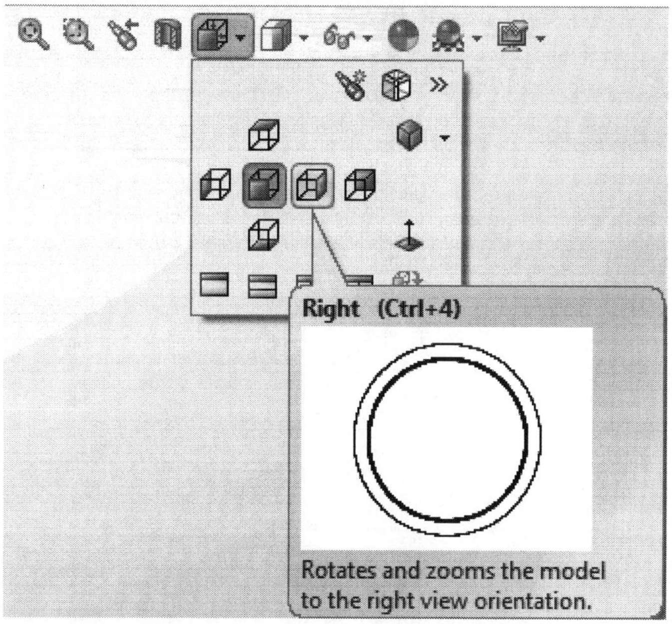

Figure 6.13 Selection of right view for the second lid

Modifying the Computational Domain and Mesh

14. Select **Tools>>Flow Simulation>>Computational Domain…**. Select **Symmetry** boundary conditions at **Y min** and **Z min**; see figure 6.14b). Set both **Y min** and **Z min** to **0 m**; see figure 6.14c). Exit the **Computational Domain** window.

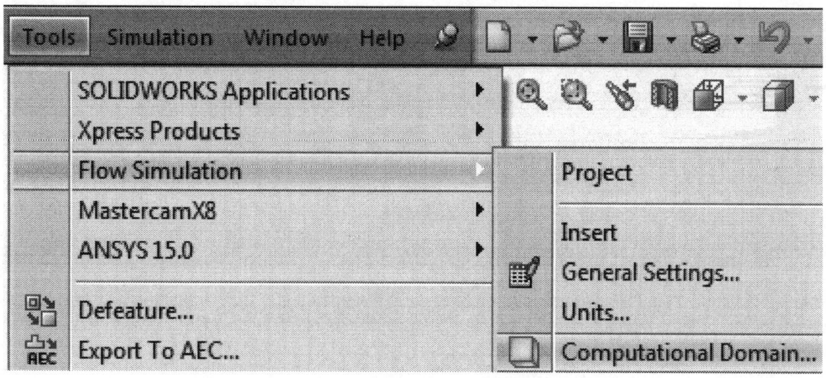

Figure 6.14a) Modifying the computational domain

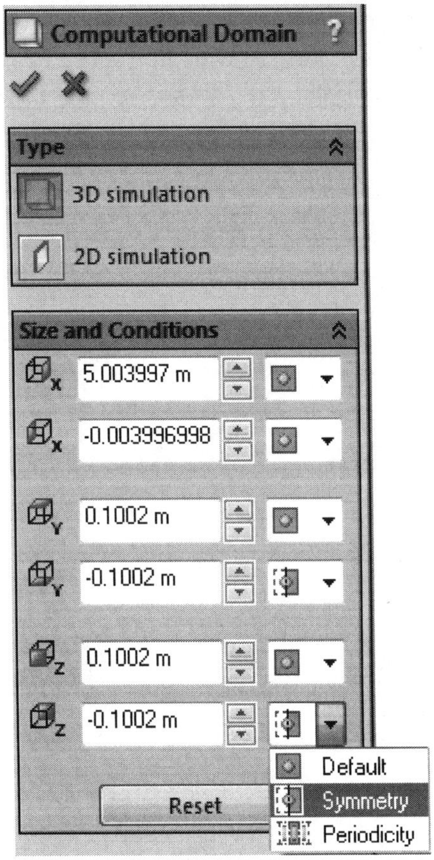

Figure 6.14b) Symmetry boundary conditions

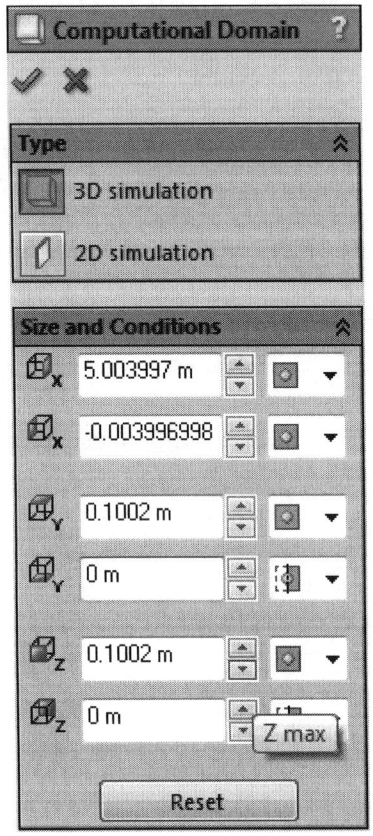

Figure 6.14c) Setting the size of the domain

15. Select **Tools>>Flow Simulation>>Initial Mesh…**. Uncheck the **Automatic setting** box at the bottom of the window. Change the **Number of cells per X:** to **100** and set both **Number of cells per Y:** and **Number of cells per Z:** to **15**. Click on the **OK** button to exit the **Initial Mesh** window.

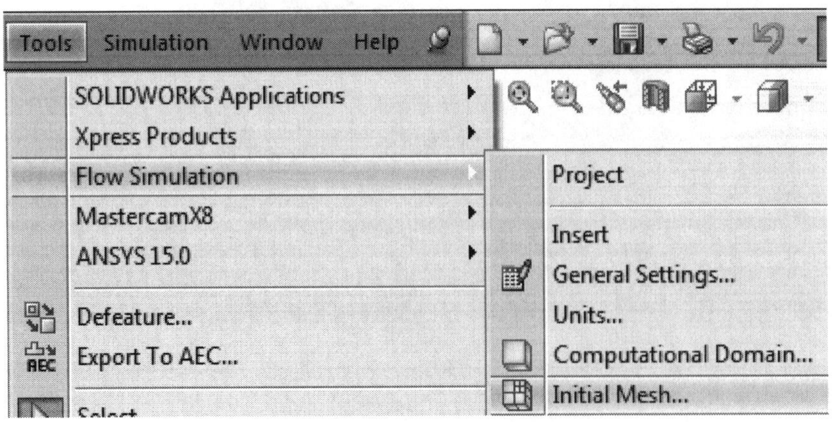

Figure 6.15a) Modifying the initial mesh

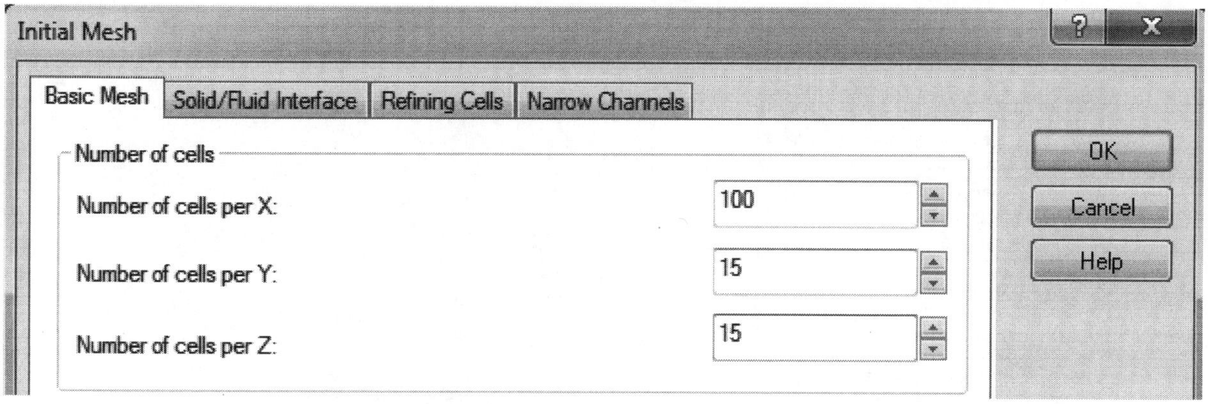

Figure 6.15b) Changing the number of cells

Inserting Boundary Conditions

16. Select the **Flow Simulation analysis tree** tab, open the **Input Data** folder by clicking on the plus sign next to it and right click on **Boundary Conditions**. Select **Insert Boundary Condition…**. Select **Front View** from the **View Orientation** drop down menu in the graphics window. Right click in the graphics window and select **Zoom/Pan/Rotate>>Zoom to Area**. Zoom in on the left end of the pipe, right click in the graphics window and select **Zoom/Pan/Rotate>>Rotate View**. Click and drag the mouse so that the inner surface of the inflow boundary is visible. Right click and unselect **Rotate View**. Right click one more time with the cursor arrow over the inflow region and click on **Select Other**. Select the surface of the inflow boundary; see figure 6.16c). Select **Inlet Velocity** in the **Type** portion of the **Boundary Condition** window and set the velocity to **0.5 m/s** in the **Flow Parameters** window. Click **OK** to exit the window.

Figure 6.16a) Inserting boundary condition

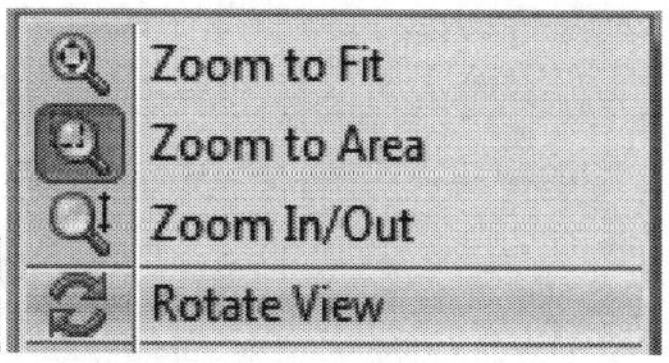

Figure 6.16b) Modifying the view

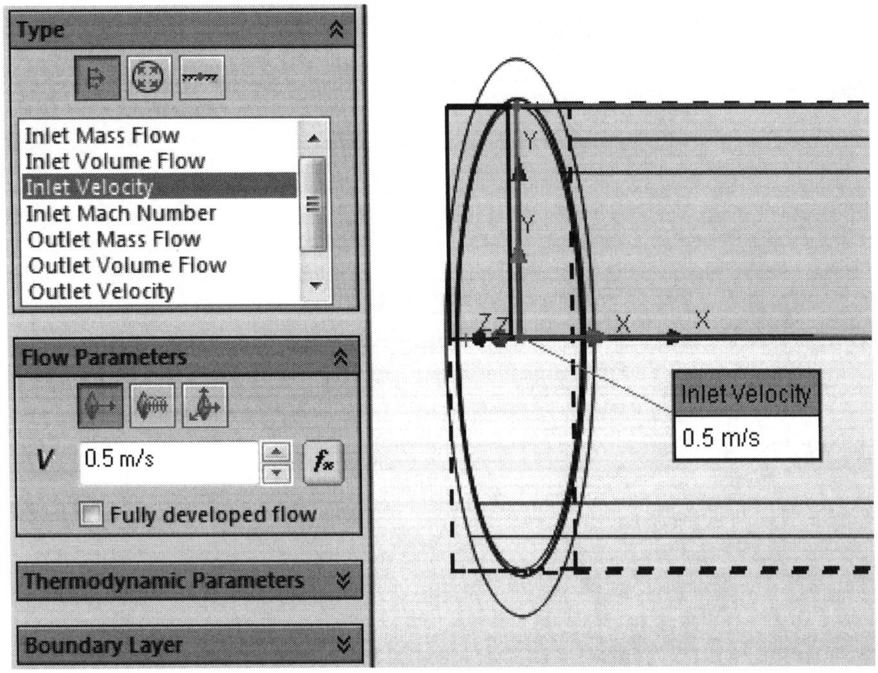

Figure 6.16c) Including a velocity boundary condition for the inflow

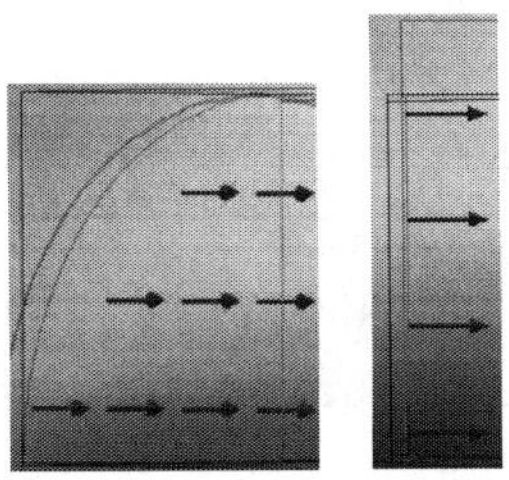

Figure 6.16d) Inlet velocity boundary condition indicated by arrows

17. Red arrows pointing in the right direction indicate the inlet velocity boundary condition; see figure 6.16d). Right click in the graphics window and select **Zoom to Fit**. Select **Front View** from the **View Orientation** drop down menu in the graphics window. Right click in the graphics window and select **Zoom to Area**. Zoom in on the right end of the pipe. Right click again in the graphics window and select **Rotate View** once again to rotate the pipe so that the inner outlet surface is visible in the graphics window. Right click and click on **Select**. Right click on **Boundary Conditions** in the **Flow Simulation analysis tree** and select **Insert Boundary Condition….** Right click one more time over the outflow region and click on **Select Other**. Select the surface of the outflow boundary; see figure 6.17a). Click on the **Pressure Openings** button in the **Type** portion of the **Boundary Condition** window and select **Static Pressure**. Click OK to exit the window. If you zoom in on the outlet boundary you will see blue arrows indicating the static pressure boundary condition; see figure 6.17b).

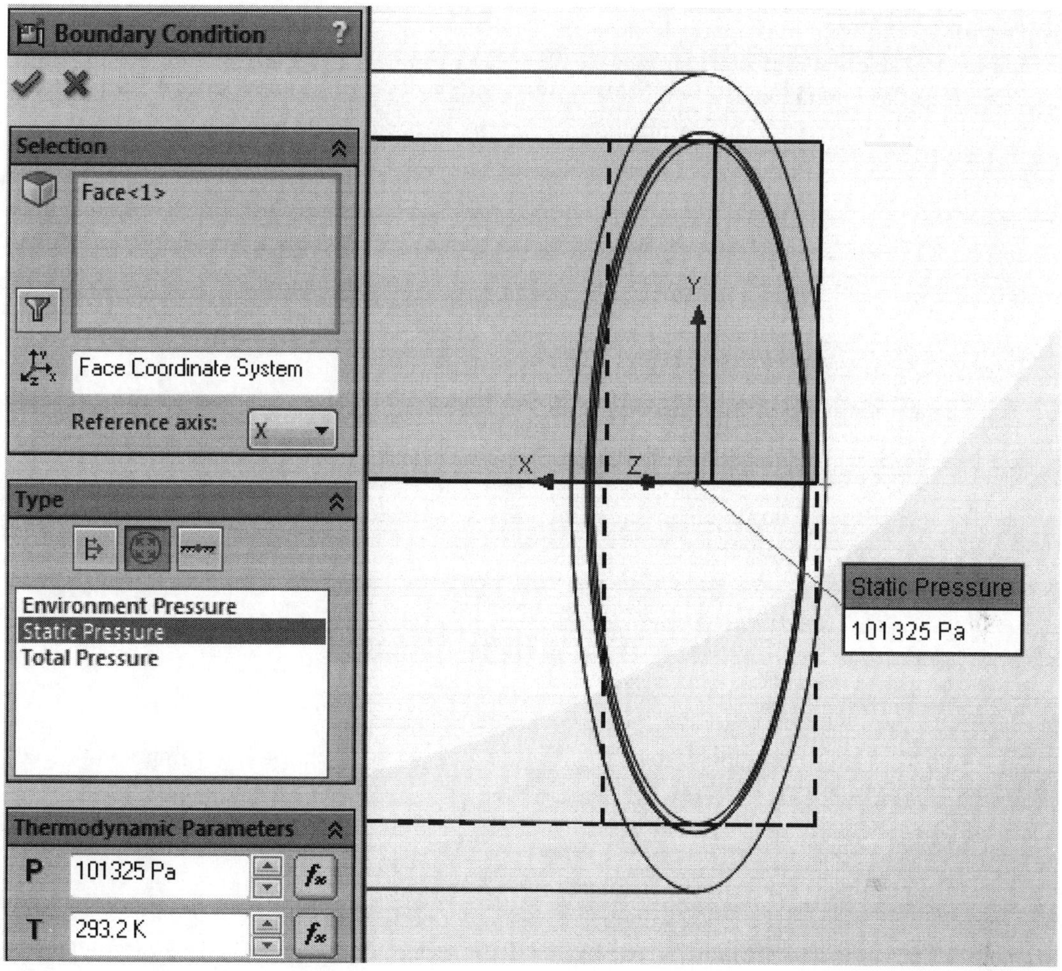

Figure 6.17a) Selection of static pressure as boundary condition at the outlet of the flow region

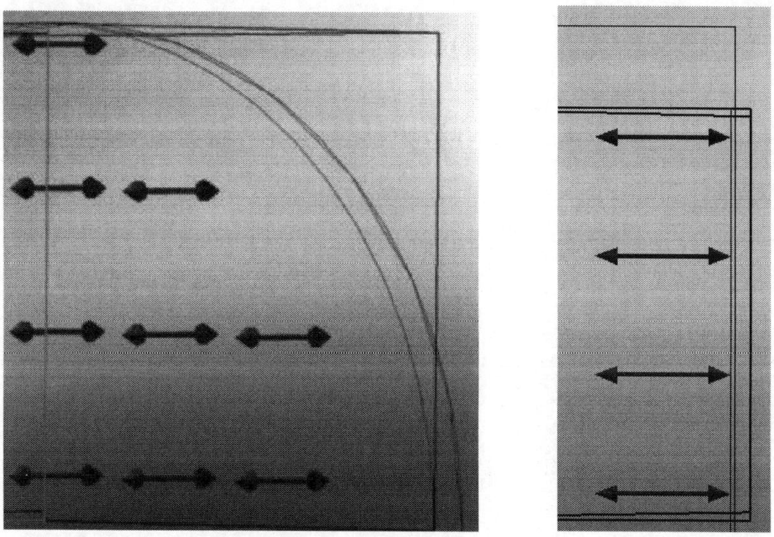

Figure 6.17b) Outlet static pressure boundary condition

Inserting a Global Goal

18. Right click on **Goals** in the **Flow Simulation analysis tree** and select **Insert Global Goals….** Select **Max Velocity (X)** as a global goal. Exit the **Global Goals** window.

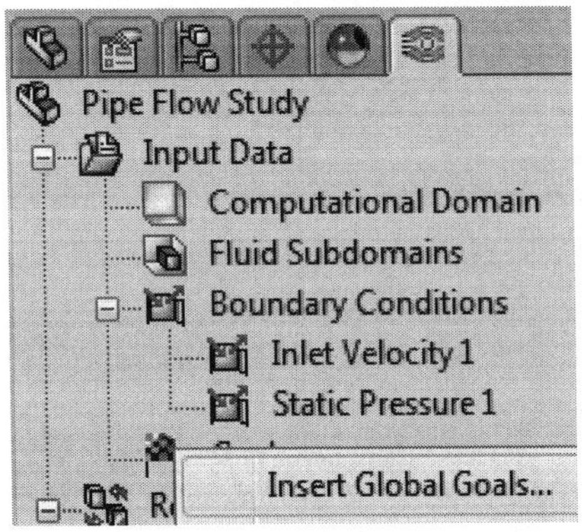

Figure 6.18a) Inserting global goals

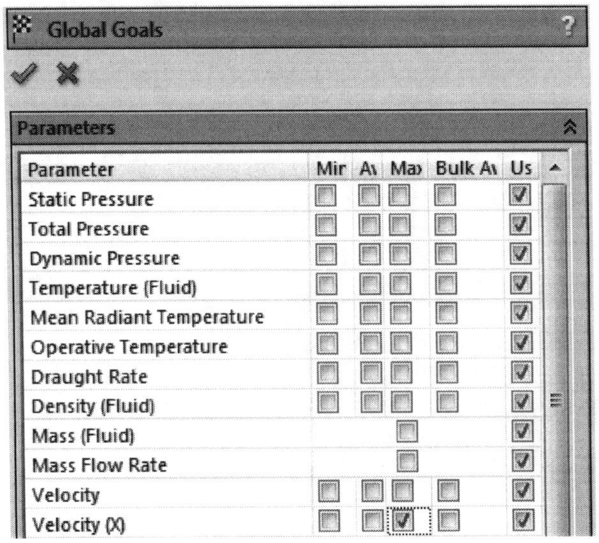

Figure 6.18b) Selection of X – component of velocity

Running the Calculations for Laminar Pipe Flow

19. Select **Tools>>Flow Simulation>>Solve>>Run** to start calculations. Click on the **Run** button in the **Run** window.

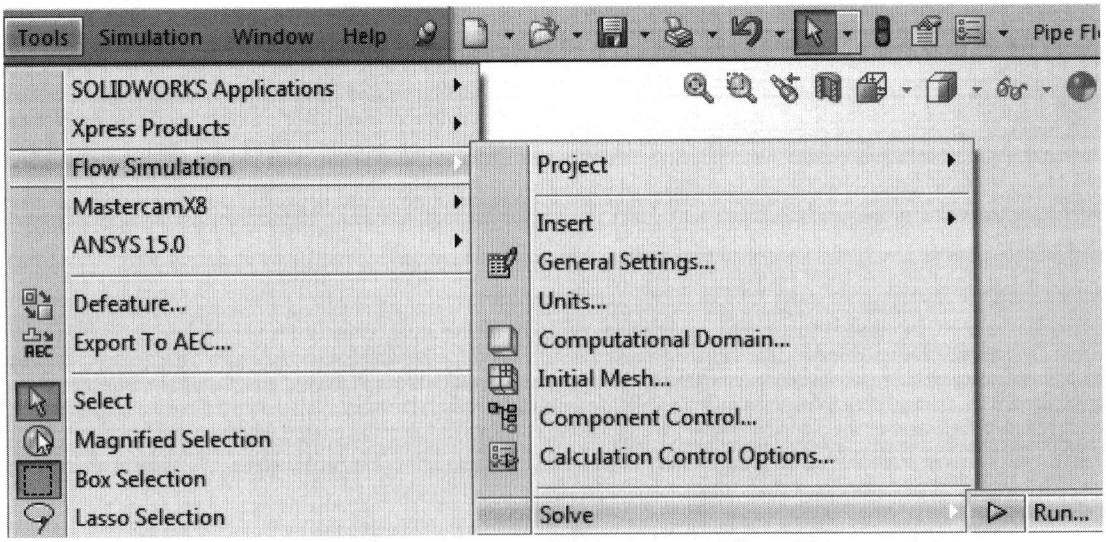

Figure 6.19a) Starting calculations

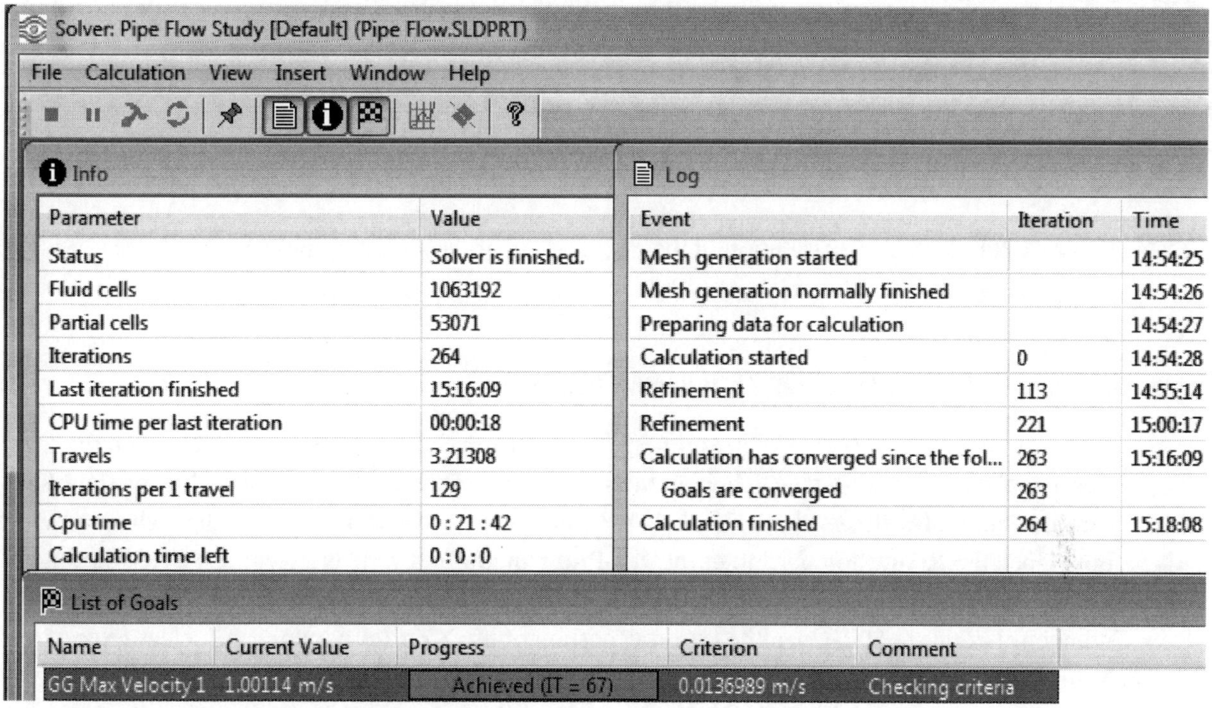

Figure 6.19b) Solver window

Inserting Cut Plots

20. Right click on Cut Plots in the **Flow Simulation analysis tree** and select **Insert…**. Select the **Front Plane** from the **FeatureManager design tree**. Slide the **Number of Levels** slide bar to **255** in the **Contours** section. Click OK to exit the **Cut Plot** window. Rename the cut plot to **Pressure**. Select **Tools>>Flow Simulation>>Results>>Display>>Lighting** from the SOLIDWORKS menu. Select **Front View** from the **View Orientation** drop down menu in the graphics window. Repeat this step but select **Velocity (X)** from the **Parameter** drop down menu in the **Contours** section. Rename the cut plot to **Velocity (X)**. Right-click on the Pressure Cut Plot and select Hide in order to display the Velocity (X) Cut Plot. Figure 6.20a) shows the pressure gradient along the length of the pipe. Figure 6.20b) is showing the velocity distribution in the pipe.

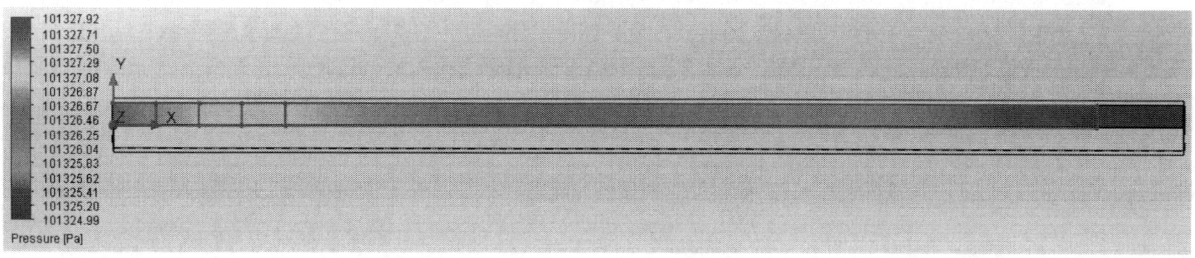

Figure 6.20a) Pressure distribution along the straight pipe

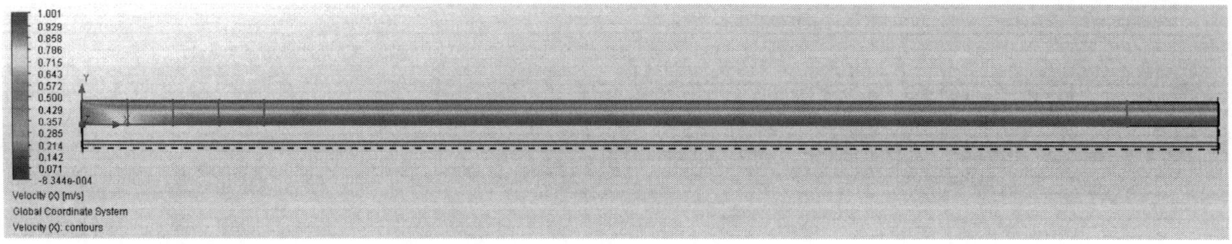

Figure 6.20b) Velocity distribution in the inlet section of the straight pipe

Inserting XY Plots for Laminar Pipe Flow using Templates

21. Place the files "**graph 6.21c)**," "**graph 6.22**,“ and "**graph 6.23**" on the desktop. Click on the **FeatureManager design tree**. Click on the sketch **x = 0, D, 2D, 3D, 4D, 23D**. Click on the **Flow Simulation analysis tree** tab. Right click **XY Plot** and select **Insert…**. Check the **Velocity (X)** box. Open the **Resolution** portion of the **XY Plot** window and slide the **Geometry Resolution** as far as it goes to the right. Click on the **Evenly Distribute Output Points** button and increase the number of points to **500**. Open the **Options** portion of the **XY Plot** window and select **Excel Workbook (*.xlsx)** from the drop down menu. Click **Export to Excel** to generate an Excel file that will open a graph of the velocity in the pipe at different streamwise positions.

Double click on the **graph 6.21c)** file to open the file. Click on **Enable Content** if you get a **Security Warning** that **Macros** have been disabled. If **Developer** is not available in the menu of the **Excel** file, you will need to do the following: Select **File>>Options** from the menu and click on the **Customize Ribbon** on the left hand side. Check the **Developer** box on the right hand side under **Main Tabs**. Click **OK** to exit the **Excel Options** window.

Click on the **Developer** tab in the **Excel** menu for the **graph 6.21c)** file and select **Visual Basic** on the left hand side to open the editor. Click on the plus sign next to **VBAProject (XY Plot 1.xlsx)** and click on the plus sign next to **Microsoft Excel Objects**. Right click on **Sheet2 (Plot Data)** and select **View Object**.

Select **Macro** in the **Modules** folder under **VBAProject (graph 6.21c).xlsm)**. Select **Run>>Run Macro** from the menu of the **MVB for Applications** window. Click on the **Run** button in the **Macros** window. **Figure 6.21c)** will become available in **Excel** showing the streamwise velocity component ***u (m/s)*** versus wall normal coordinate ***y (m)***. Close the **XY Plot** window and the **graph 6.21c)** window in **Excel**. Exit the **XY Plot** window in **SOLIDWORKS Flow Simulation** and rename the inserted xy-plot in the **Flow Simulation analysis tree** to **Laminar Velocity Boundary Layer**.

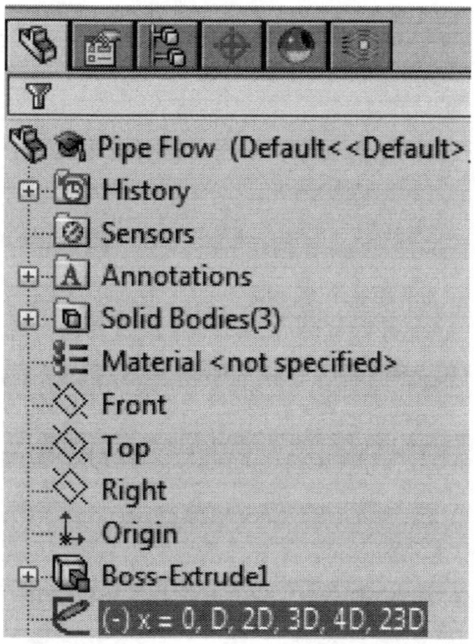

Figure 6.21a) Selecting the sketch

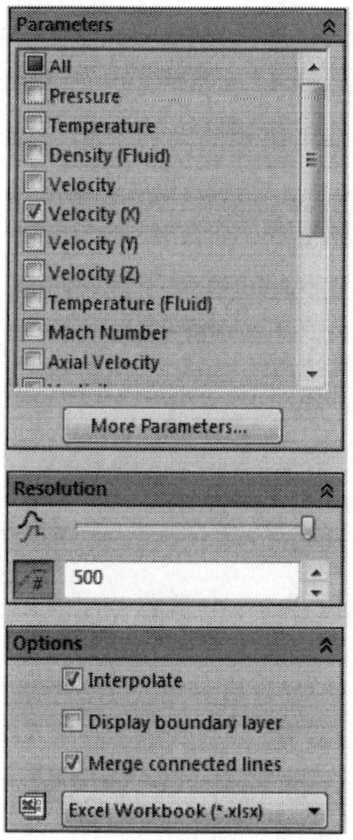

Figure 6.21b) Different settings for the XY Plot

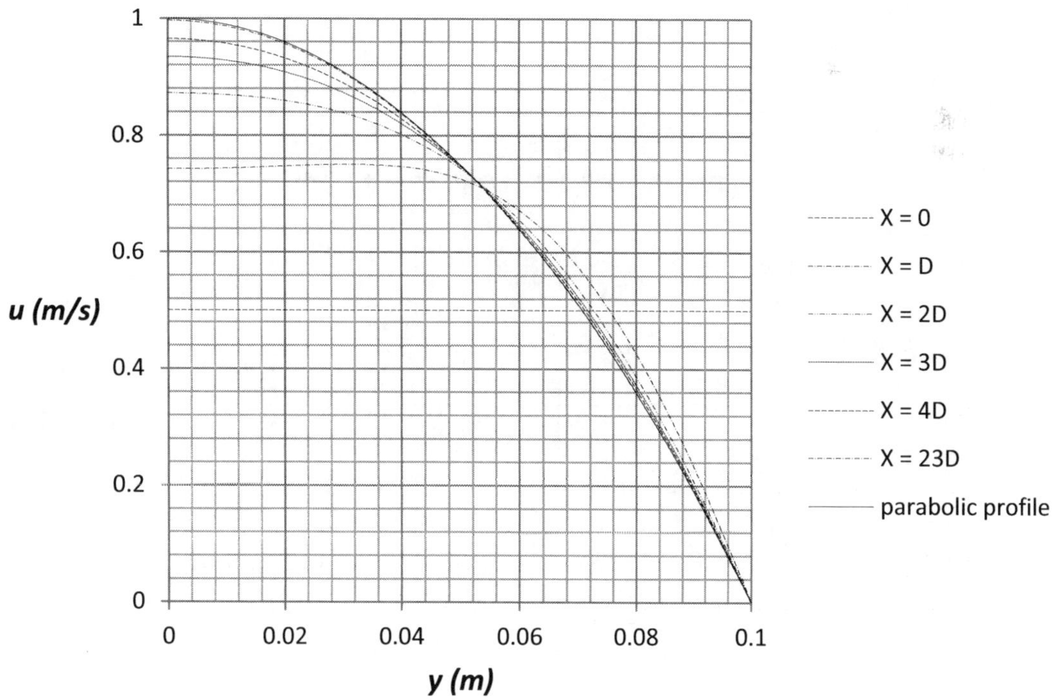

Figure 6.21c) Straight pipe velocity profiles at different streamwise positions; full line represents theoretical parabolic velocity profile and the Reynolds number is *Re* = 100

In figure 6.21c) the different velocity profiles are compared with the theoretical Hagen-Poiseuille velocity profile for laminar flow in a straight pipe:

$$u_{laminar} = U_{max}(1 - (\frac{2y}{D})^2) \qquad (6.1)$$

where y (m) is the radial coordinate, u (m/s) is the velocity in the X-direction, and D (m) is the inner diameter of the pipe. We see in figure 6.21c) that the profiles at different streamwise positions further away from the inlet get closer to the fully developed theoretical profile. The theoretical ratio between maximum velocity U_{max} (m/s) and mean velocity U_m (m/s) for fully developed laminar pipe flow is

$$(\frac{U_{max}}{U_m})_{laminar} = 2 \qquad (6.2)$$

22. Repeat step **21** but this time choose the sketch **x = 0 – 4.6 m (centerline)** and use the file "**graph 6.22.**" This results in figure 6.22 that shows the streamwise development of the centerline velocity. It takes approximately 10 pipe diameters for the flow to become fully developed. Rename the inserted xy-plot in the **Flow Simulation analysis tree** to **X-Velocity Along Centerline**.

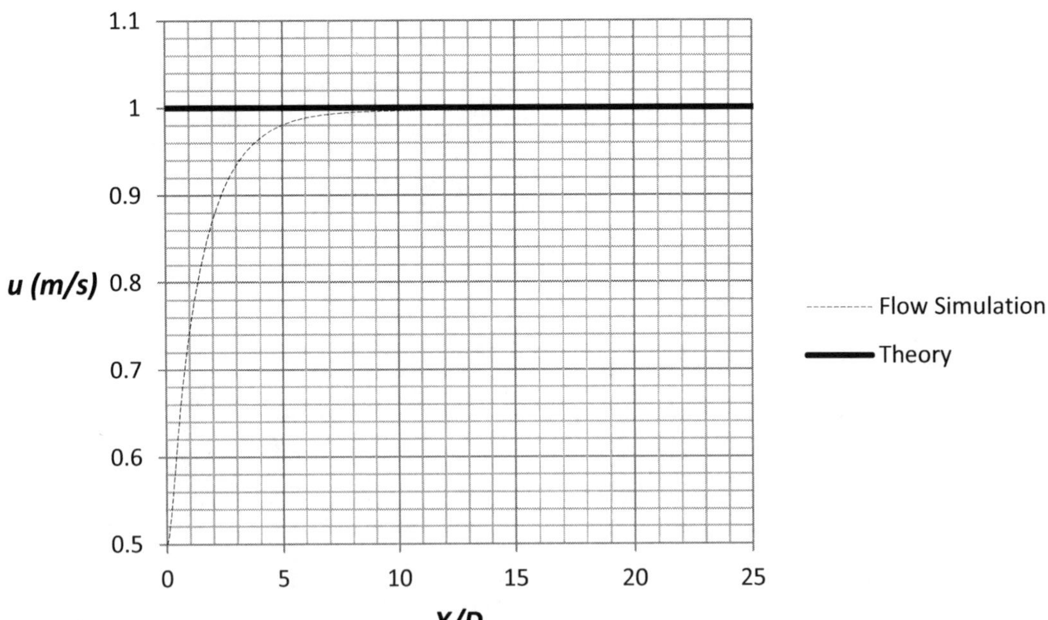

Figure 6.22 X-velocity along the centerline of the pipe at Re = 100; full line is showing theoretical value for fully developed flow

Theory for Laminar Pipe Flow

The Reynolds number for the flow in a straight pipe is defined as

$$Re = \frac{U_m D}{\nu} \tag{6.3}$$

where ν is the kinematic viscosity of the fluid. The hydrodynamic entry length L_h (m) is the distance between the pipe entrance and the location where the flow is fully developed. The entry length is approximately given by the following expression for laminar flow in a pipe:

$$\frac{L_{h,laminar}}{D} = 0.05Re \tag{6.4}$$

In our case, $D = 0.2$ m and $Re = 100$ gives an entry length of 1 m. If we define the entry length as the distance from the entrance to where the streamwise velocity maximum is within 2% of the fully developed value, Flow Simulation results in figure 6.22 give a value of 0.9915 m, only a 0.85 % difference from theoretical results.

We now want to study pressure loss and how the friction factor varies along the pipe. The pressure loss is defined by

$$\Delta P = f \frac{L}{D} \frac{\rho U_m^2}{2}$$

where L (m) is the length of the pipe and ρ (kg/m^3) is the density of the fluid. The Darcy-Weisbach friction factor f is defined as:

$$f = \frac{8\tau_w}{\rho U_m^2} \tag{6.5}$$

where τ_w (Pa) is the wall shear stress. The Fanning friction factor is defined as:

$$C_f = \frac{\tau_w}{\frac{1}{2}\rho U_m^2} = \frac{f}{4} \tag{6.6}$$

For laminar flow in a circular pipe it can be shown that

$$C_{f,laminar} = \frac{16}{Re} \tag{6.7}$$

23. Repeat step **21** once again but this time choose the sketch **x = 0 – 4.6 m (wall)** and check the box for **Shear Stress**. Use the file **"graph 6.23."** An Excel file will open with a graph of the Fanning friction factor versus the *X/D*–coordinate in comparison with theoretical values for laminar pipe flow; see figure 6.23. Rename the inserted xy-plot in the **Flow Simulation analysis tree** to **Fanning Friction Factor**.

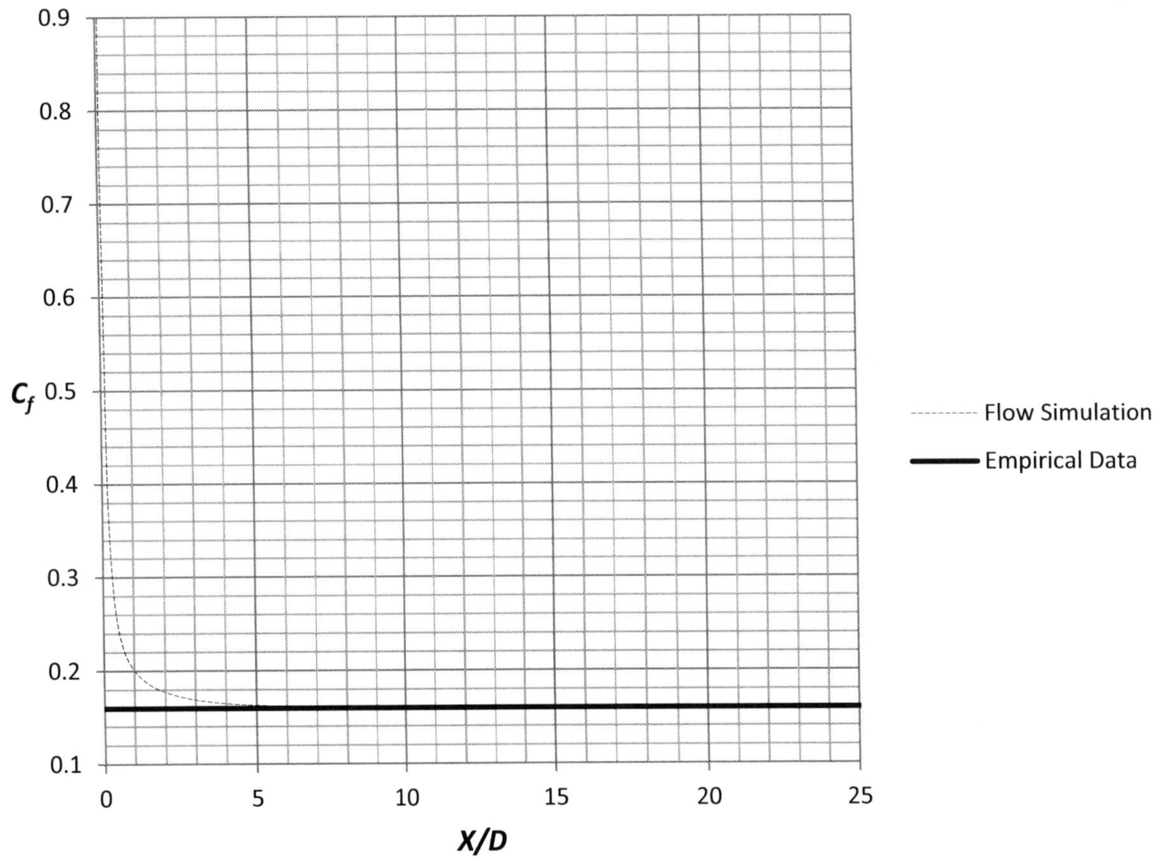

Figure 6.23 Fanning friction factor as a function of the streamwise coordinate at $Re = 100$; full line is showing theoretical value for fully developed flow

Running Calculations for Turbulent Pipe Flow

24. In the next step, we will study turbulent pipe flow. Open the file **Turbulent Pipe Flow 2015**. Select **Tools>>Flow Simulation>>Solve>>Run** to start calculations. Check the **Mesh** box and select **New Calculation**. Click on the **Run** button in the **Run** window.

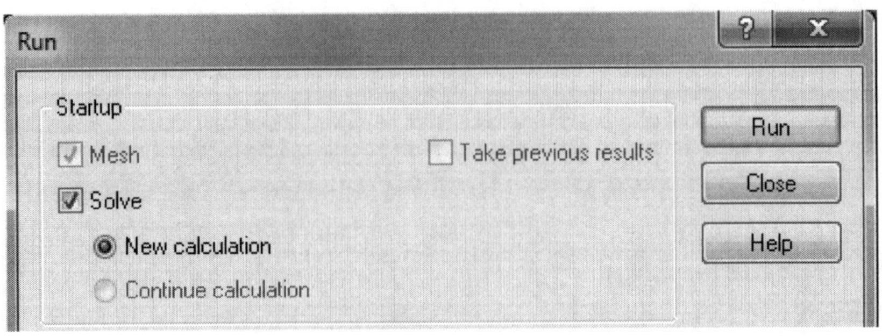

Figure 6.24a) Creation of mesh and starting a new calculation for turbulent pipe flow

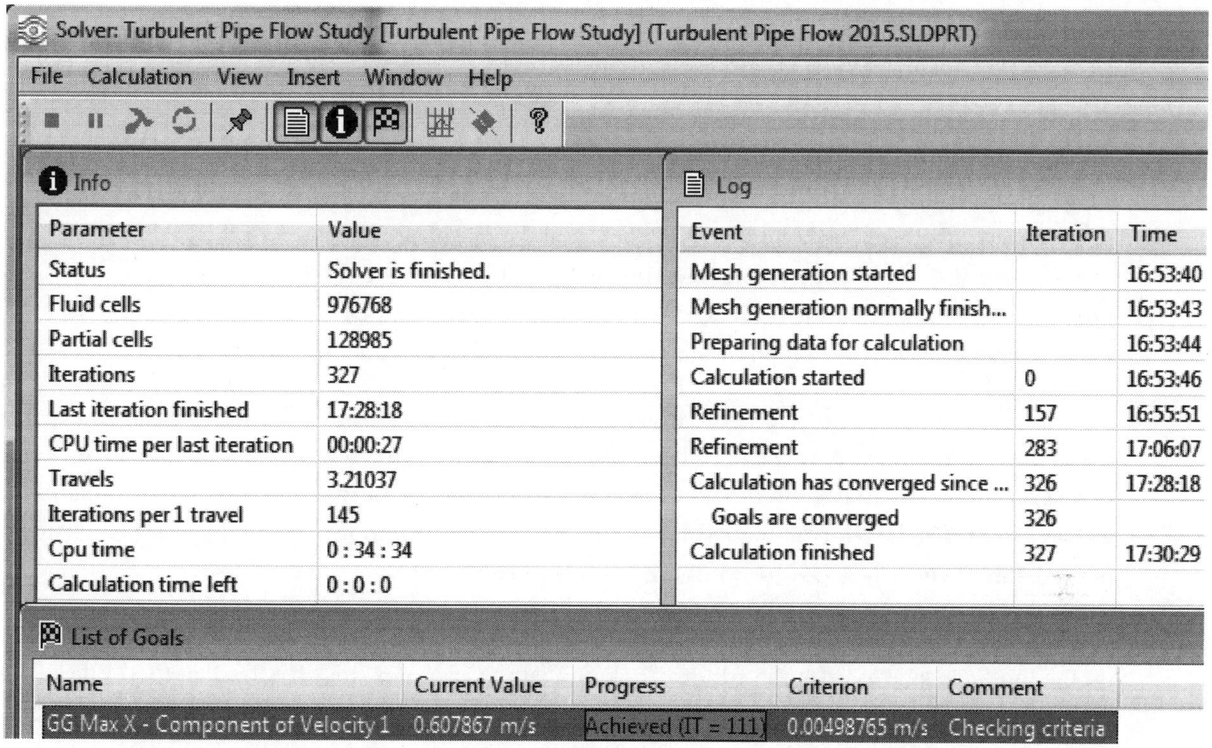

Figure 6.24b) Solver window for turbulent pipe flow calculations

Theory for Turbulent Pipe Flow

25. An approximate relation for the Darcy-Weisbach friction factor as a function of Reynolds number for turbulent pipe flow is given by Blasius:

$$f_{turbulent} = \frac{0.316}{Re^{1/4}} \qquad 4000 < Re < 10^5 \tag{6.8}$$

and the Fanning friction factor

$$C_{f,turbulent} = \frac{0.079}{Re^{1/4}} \qquad 4000 < Re < 10^5 \tag{6.9}$$

The pressure drop is given by

$$\Delta P_{turbulent} = 0.158 L \rho^{3/4} \mu^{1/4} U_m^{7/4} / D^{5/4} \tag{6.10}$$

where μ is the dynamic viscosity of the fluid. A formula can also be obtained relating max velocity to mean velocity for fully developed turbulent pipe flow:

$$\left(\frac{U_{max}}{U_m}\right)_{turbulent} = 1 + 2.66\sqrt{C_{f,turbulent}} \tag{6.11}$$

Inserting XY Plots for Turbulent Pipe Flow using Templates

Place the files "**graph 6.25a)**," "**graph 6.25b)**," "**graph 6.25c)**" and "**graph 6.25d)**" on the desktop. Click on the **FeatureManager design tree**. Click on the sketch **x = 0 – 10 m (centerline)**. Click on the **Flow Simulation analysis tree** tab. Right click **XY Plot** and select **Insert…**. Check the **Velocity (X)** box. Open the **Resolution** portion of the **XY Plot** window and slide the **Geometry Resolution** as far as it goes to the right. Select **Excel Workbook (*.xlsx)** from the drop down menu under **Options**. Click on **Export to Excel**. An Excel file will open with a graph of the velocity along the centerline of the pipe.

Double click on the **graph 6.25a)** file to open the file. Click on **Enable Content** if you get a **Security Warning** that **Macros** have been disabled. If **Developer** is not available in the menu of the **Excel** file, you will need to do the following: Select **File>>Options** from the menu and click on the **Customize Ribbon** on the left hand side. Check the **Developer** box on the right hand side under **Main Tabs**. Click **OK** to exit the **Excel Options** window.

Click on the **Developer** tab in the **Excel** menu for the **graph 6.25a)** file and select **Visual Basic** on the left hand side to open the editor. Click on the plus sign next to **VBAProject (XY Plot 1.xlsx)** and click on the plus sign next to **Microsoft Excel Objects**. Right click on **Sheet2 (Plot Data)** and select **View Object**.

Select **Macro** in the **Modules** folder under **VBAProject (graph 6.25a)).xlsm)**. Select **Run>>Run Macro** from the menu of the **MVB for Applications** window. Click on the **Run** button in the **Macros** window. **Figure 6.25a)** will become available in **Excel** showing the streamwise velocity component ***u (m/s)*** versus streamwise coordinate ***X/D***. Close the **XY Plot** window and the **graph 6.25a)** window in **Excel**. Exit the **XY Plot** window in **SOLIDWORKS Flow Simulation** and rename the inserted xy-plot in the **Flow Simulation analysis tree** to **Figure 6.25a)**.

Figure 6.25a) is showing the X-velocity along the centerline including a comparison between turbulent pipe flow and the empirical value for fully developed flow. The centerline velocity from Flow Simulation has an overshoot before attaining a level lower than the value given from empirical data. It is clearly seen that Flow Simulation is under predicting the fully developed maximum velocity.

The Fanning friction factor is shown in figure 6.25b). Repeat the steps above to get this graph. Select the sketch **x = 0 – 10 m (wall)** and check the **Shear Stress** box. Select the file **"graph 6.25b)."** An Excel file will open with a graph of the friction coefficient along the wall of the pipe; see figure 6.25b). The Fanning factor from Flow Simulation is slightly higher than the empirical.

Repeat the steps above once again. Select the sketch **x = 45D**. Check the **Velocity (X)** box. Click on the **Evenly Distribute Output Points** button and increase the number of points to **500**. Select the file **"graph 6.25c)."** In figure 6.25c) is the fully developed velocity profile from Flow Simulation compared with the power-law profile for $n = 8$.

$$u_{turbulent} = U_{max}(1 - \frac{y}{0.1})^{1/n} \tag{6.12}$$

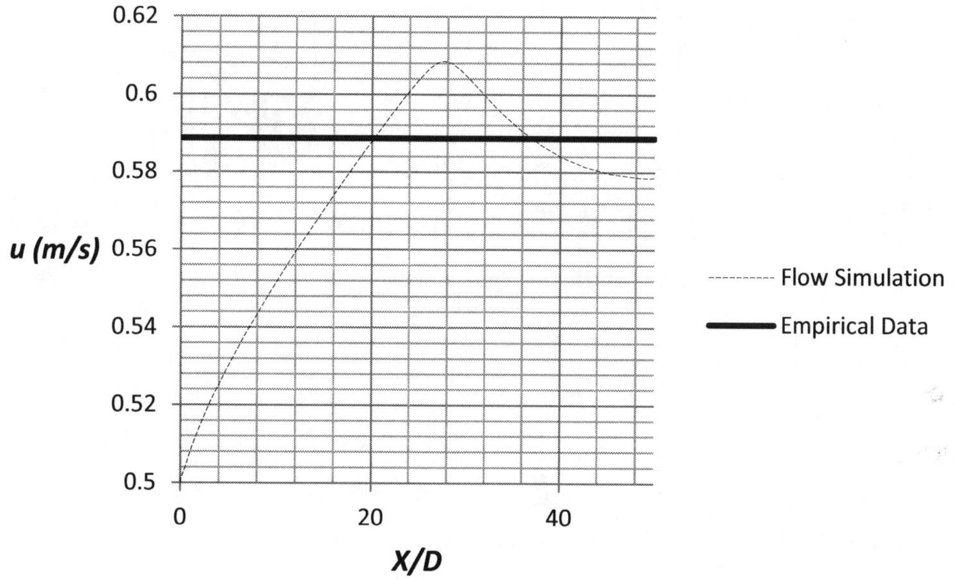

Figure 6.25a) X-velocity along the centerline of the pipe at Re = 100000; full line is showing empirical value for fully developed turbulent pipe flow

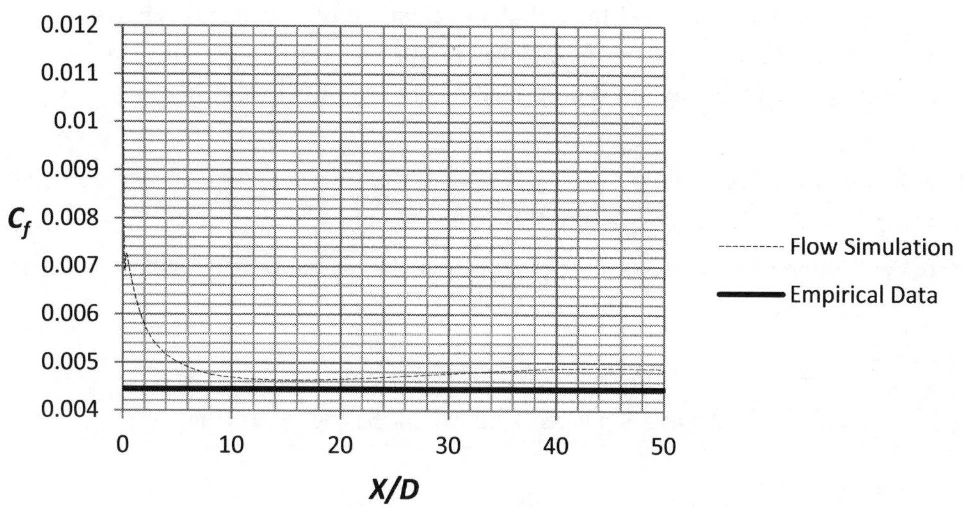

Figure 6.25b) Fanning friction factor as a function of the streamwise coordinate at Re = 100000; full line is showing empirical value for fully developed turbulent pipe flow

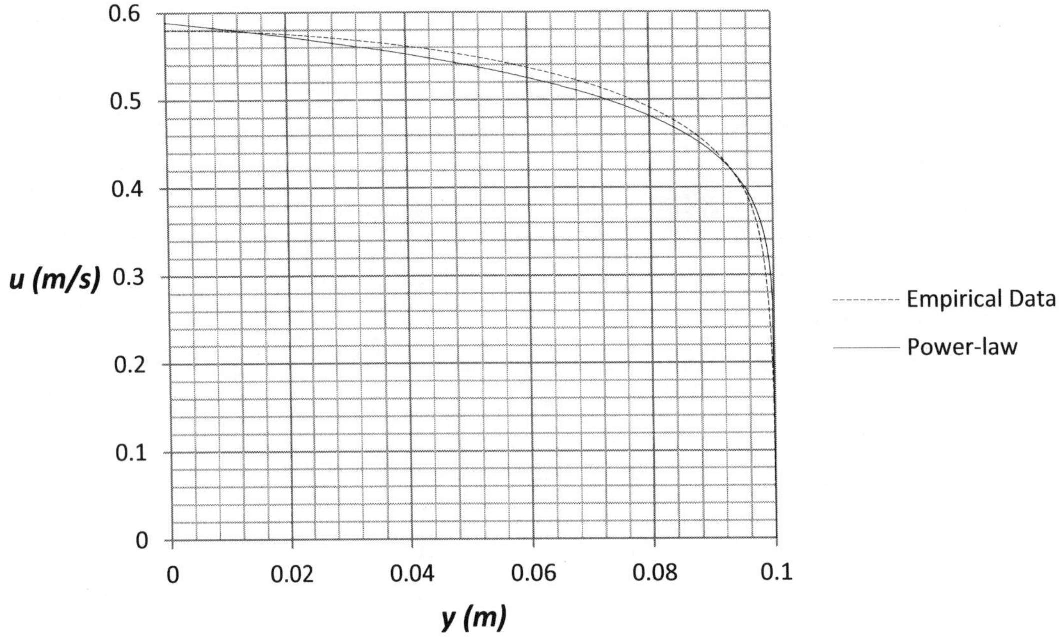

Figure 6.25c) Fully developed straight pipe turbulent velocity profile (dashed line) at *X/D* = 45, *Re* = 100000, compared with power-law velocity profile for *n* = 8

There are four different layers of the turbulent velocity profile: viscous sublayer, buffer layer, overlap layer and turbulent layer. If we start with the viscous sublayer located closest to the wall, the velocity profile in this region is described by the law of the wall:

$$u^+ = \frac{u}{u_*} = \frac{(\frac{D}{2}-y)u_*}{\nu} = y^+ \tag{6.13}$$

where the friction velocity $u_* = \sqrt{\tau_w/\rho}$. The thickness of the viscous sublayer is

$$\delta = \frac{5\nu}{u_*} \tag{6.14}$$

The velocity profile in the overlap layer is known as the logarithmic law

$$u^+ = 2.5 ln y^+ + 5.0 \tag{6.15}$$

and the profile in the outer turbulent layer is called the velocity defect law.

$$\frac{U_{max}-u}{u_*} = 2.5 ln \frac{D}{D-2y} \tag{6.16}$$

Click on the **FeatureManager design tree**. Click on the sketch **x = 45D**. Click on the **Flow Simulation analysis tree** tab. Right click **XY Plot** and select **Insert….** Check the **Velocity (X)** box. Open the **Resolution** portion of the **XY Plot** window and slide the **Geometry Resolution** as far as it goes to the right. Click on the **Evenly Distribute Output Points** button and increase the number of points to **10000**. Select **Excel Workbook (*.xlsx)** from the drop down menu under **Options**. Click on **Export to Excel**. Repeat the steps as outlined on page 6-22 and use file "**graph 6.25d)**" to create **Figure 6.25d)**. In figure 6.25d) it is seen that result from Flow Simulation is over predicting the velocity in the viscous sublayer close to the wall.

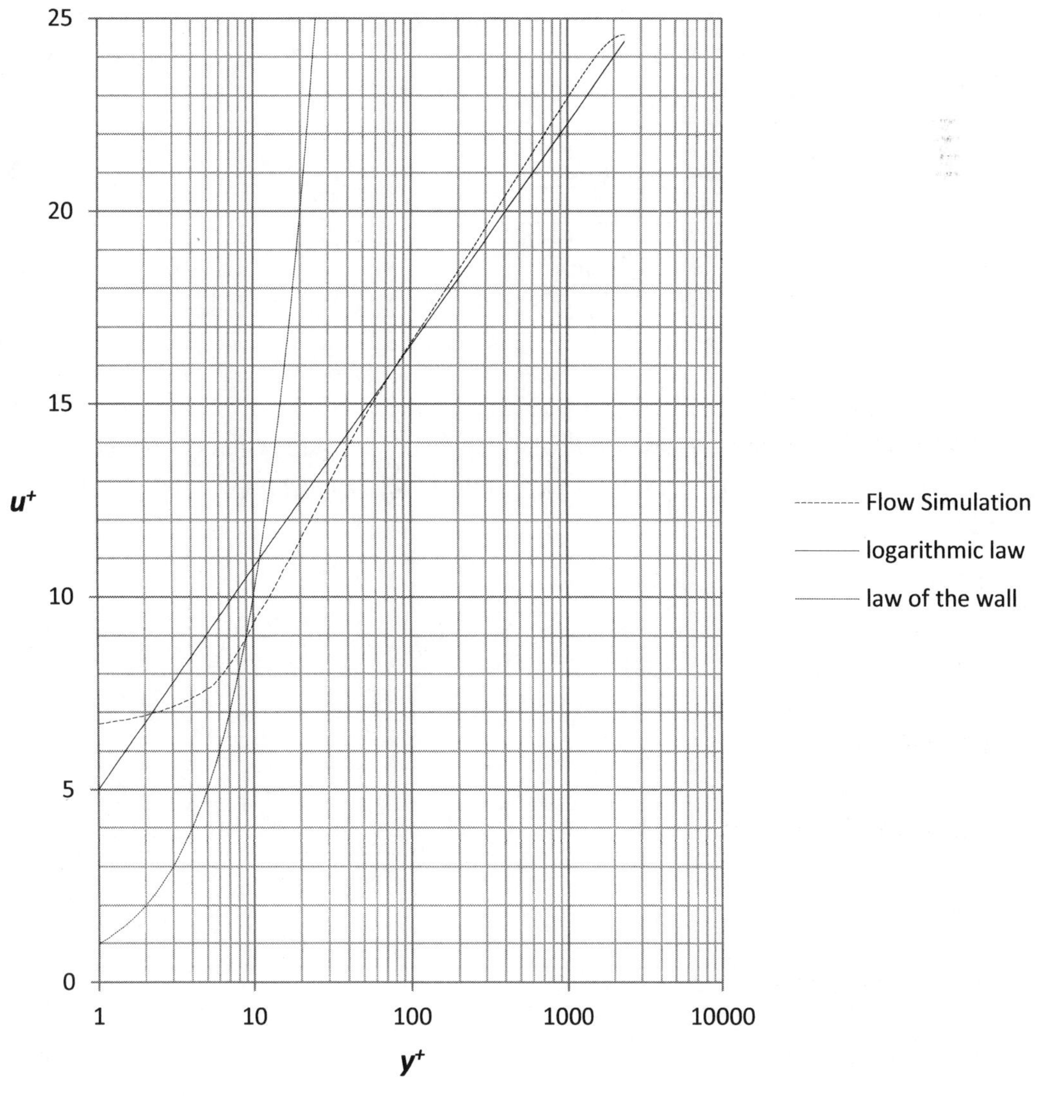

Figure 6.25d) Comparison of Flow Simulation, law of the wall and logarithmic law for fully developed turbulent flow in a pipe at *X/D = 45* and *Re* = 100000

References

[1] SOLIDWORKS Flow Simulation 2015 Technical Reference.

[2] White, F. M., Fluid Mechanics, 4th Edition, McGraw-Hill, 1999.

Exercises

6.1 Run the laminar flow case for *Re* = 300, 500 and compare X-velocity and friction factor with *Re* = 100 as shown in figures 6.21c), 6.22 and 6.23, respectively. Discuss your results.

6.2 Run the laminar flow case for *Re* = 100 and change the number of cells in the *X*, *Y*, and *Z* directions to see how it affects the results for X-velocity and friction factor. Discuss differences in results. Use the following number of cells:

X	Y	Z
33	5	5
67	10	10
100	15	15
133	20	20
167	25	25

6.3 Run the turbulent flow case for *Re* = 100000 and change the number of cells in the *X*, *Y*, and *Z* directions to see how it affects the results. Discuss and compare the results.

Chapter 7 Flow across a Tube Bank

Objectives

- Creating the SOLIDWORKS model of the tube bank
- Setting up Flow Simulation projects for external flow
- Inserting boundary condition
- Running the calculations
- Using cut plots and XY plots to visualize the resulting flow field
- Compare results with theory and empirical data

Problem Description

In this chapter, we will use Flow Simulation to study the two-dimensional flow across a tube bank. We will use a total of twelve 20 mm diameter cylinders in an in-line arrangement. The cylinders will have a temperature of 373.2 K and the free stream velocity of the air will be 4 m/s. The temperature and velocity fields will be shown inside the tube bank and the development of both temperature and velocity profiles after the tube bank. The exit temperature of the fluid from Flow Simulation calculations will be compared with theoretical and empirical results.

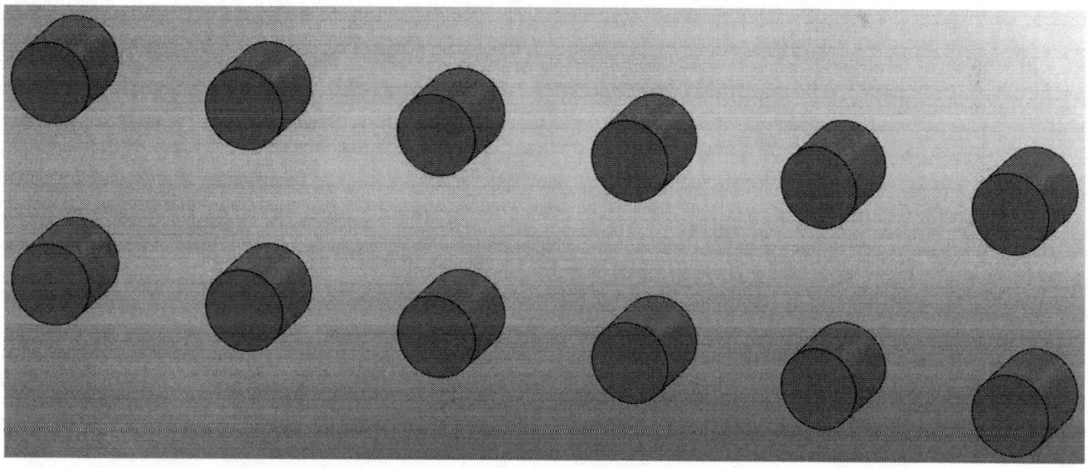

Figure 7.0 SOLIDWORKS model of in-line tube bank

Creating the SOLIDWORKS Part

1. Start by creating a new part in SOLIDWORKS: select **File>>New** and click on the **OK** button in the **New SOLIDWORKS Document** window. Select **Tools>>Options…** from the SOLIDWORKS menu. Click on the Document Properties tab and select **Units**. Select **MMGS** as your **Unit system**. Click on **Front Plane** in the **FeatureManager design tree** and select **Front** from the **View Orientation** drop down menu in the graphics window.

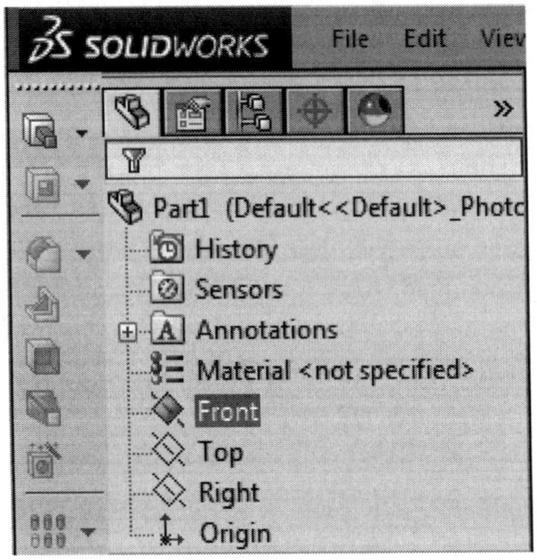

Figure 7.1a) Selection of front plane

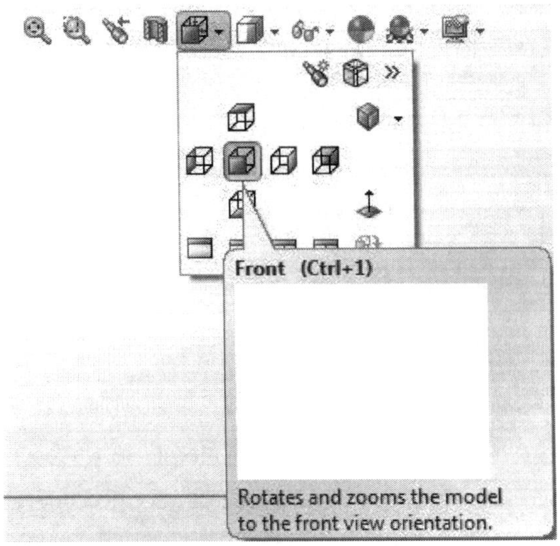

Figure 7.1b) Selection of front view

2. Click on **Circle**.

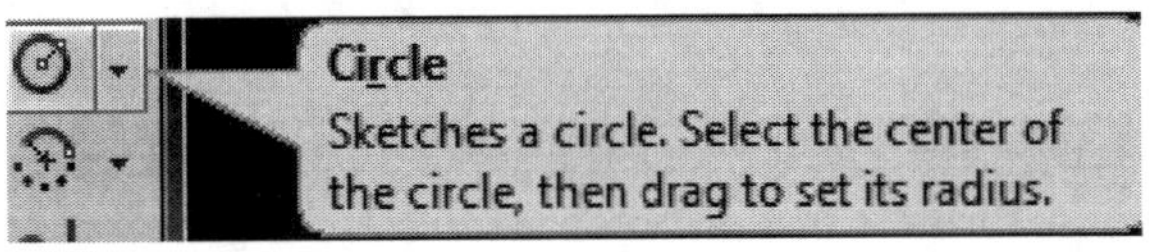

Figure 7.2 Selecting a sketch tool

3. Click at the origin in the graphics window and create a circle with a radius of 10 mm. Fill in the **Parameters** for the circle as shown in figure 7.3. Close the **Circle** dialog box by clicking on ✔.

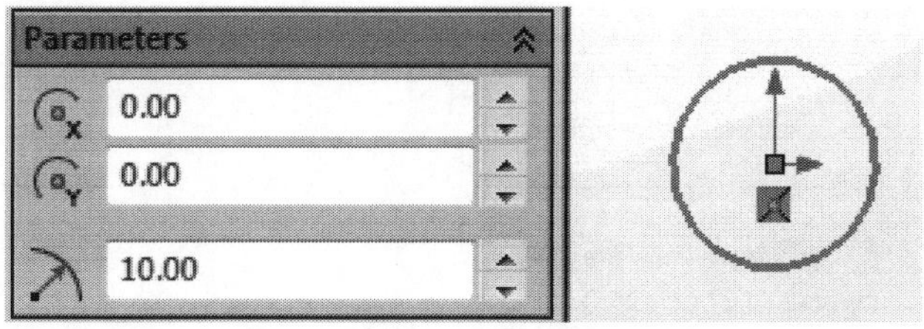

Figure 7.3 A circle with a radius of 10 mm

4. Create five more circles with the same radii and their centers located at (X,Y) = (50,0), (100,0), (150,0), (200,0) and (250,0). Next, create another line of six more identical circles with their centers at (X,Y) = (0,50), (50,50), (100,50), (150,50), (200,50) and (250,50). All dimensions in millimeter.

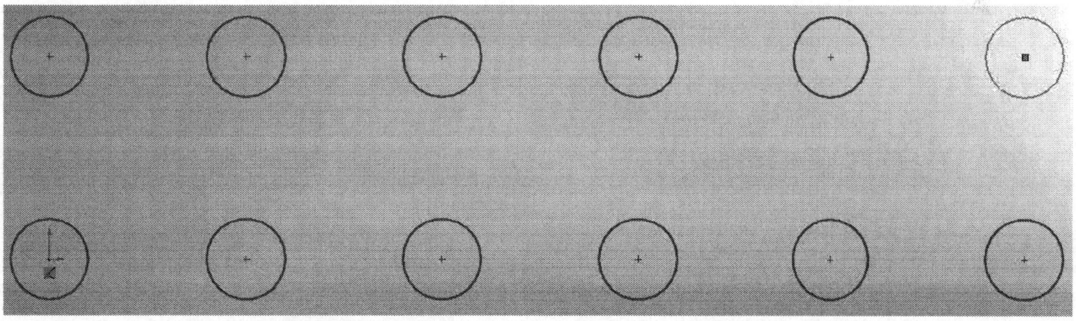
Figure 7.4 Sketch of in-line tube bank with six rows of cylinders

5. Select the **Extruded Boss/Base**. Click on **Direction 2** check box and click OK ✔ to exit the **Extrude** dialog box. Select **File>>Save As…** and save the part with the name **In-Line Tube Bank**.

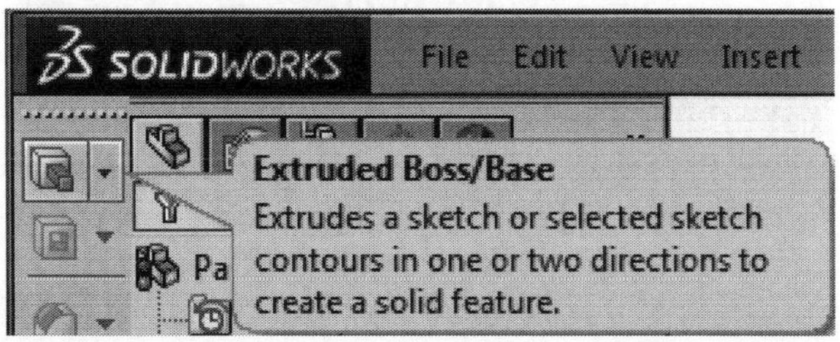

Figure 7.5a) Selection of extruded boss/base feature

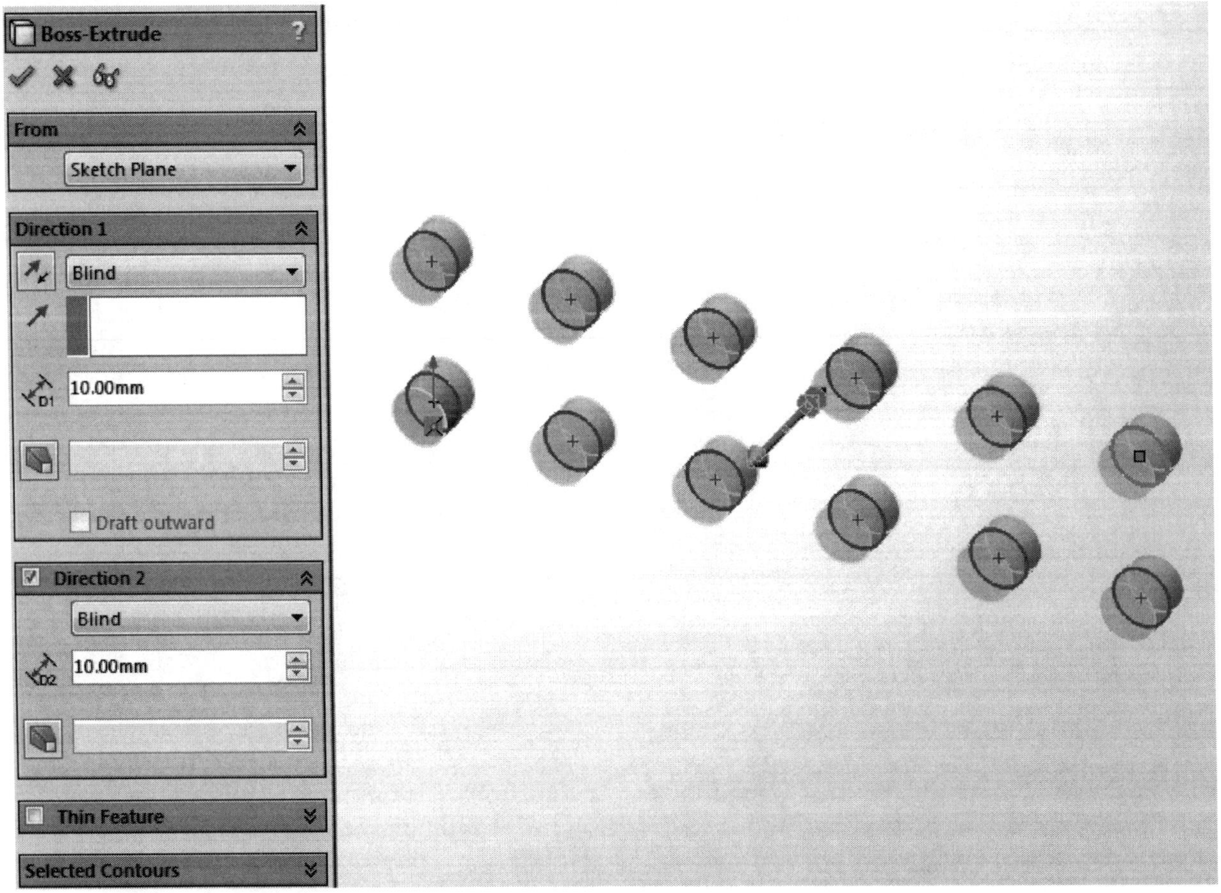

Figure 7.5b) Extruding the sketch

Setting up the Flow Simulation Project

6. If Flow Simulation is not available in the menu, you have to add it from the SOLIDWORKS menu: **Tools>>Add Ins…** and check the corresponding **SOLIDWORKS Flow Simulation** box. Select **Tools>>Flow Simulation>>Project>>Wizard** to create a new Flow Simulation project. Create a new project named "**In-Line Tube Bank Study**." Click on the **Next** > button. Select the default **SI (m-kg-s)** unit system and click on the **Next>** button once again.

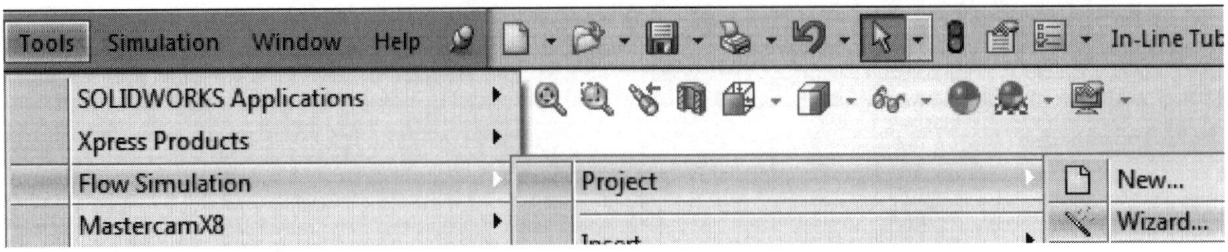

Figure 7.6a) Starting a new Flow Simulation project

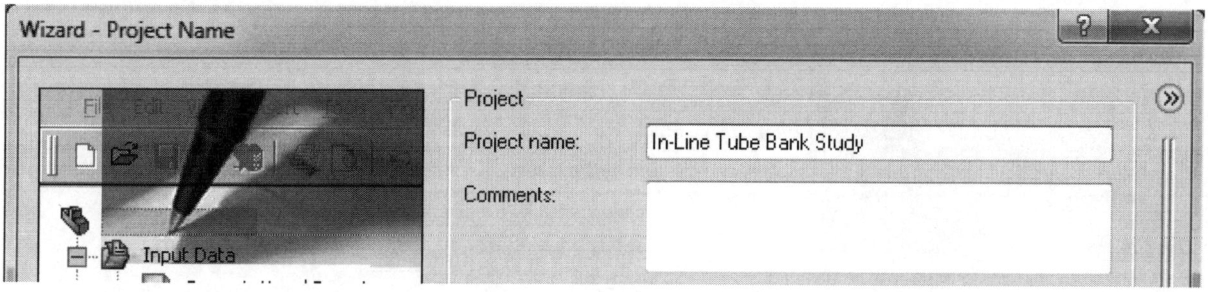

Figure 7.6b) Creating a name for the project

7. Use the **External Analysis type**. Click on the **Next** > button.

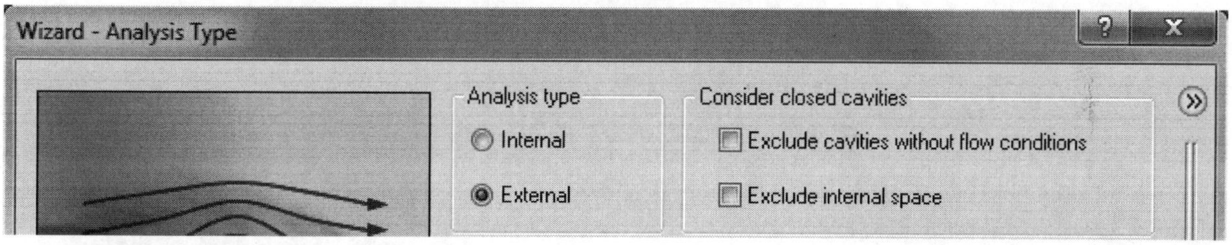

Figure 7.7 External analysis type

8. Add **Air** from **Gases** as the **Project Fluid**. Click on the **Next** > button. Use the default **Wall Conditions**. Click on the **Next** > button. Set the **Velocity in X-direction** to **4 m/s**. Click on the **Next** > button. Use the **Result resolution** at level **3**. Click on the **Finish** button.

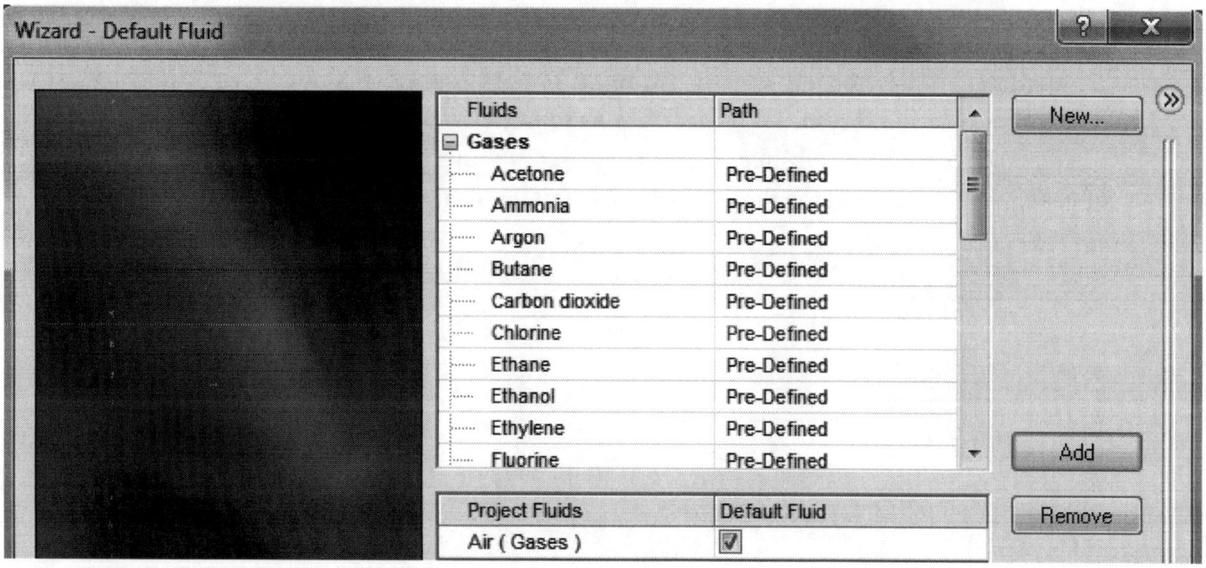

Figure 7.8a) Adding air as the project fluid

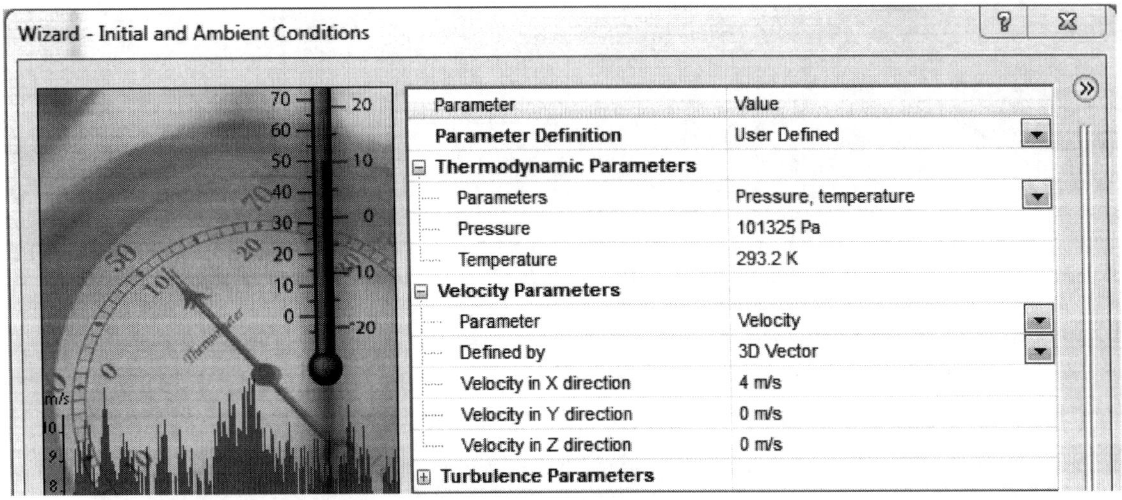

Figure 7.8b) Setting the velocity in the X-direction

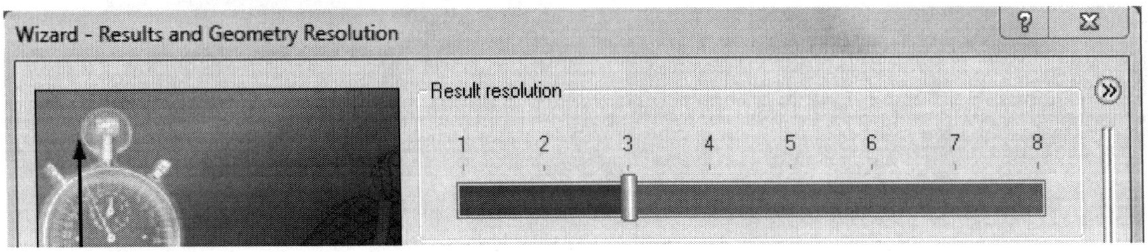

Figure 7.8c) Setting the result resolution

Modifying the Computational Domain and Mesh

9. Select **Tools>>Flow Simulation>>Computational Domain….** Select **2D simulation** and **XY plane** from the **Type** section. Exit the **Computational Domain** window. Select **Tools>>Flow Simulation>>Initial Mesh….** Uncheck the **Automatic setting** box at the bottom of the window. Change the **Number of cells per X:** to **198** and set **Number of cells per Y:** to **300** and **Number of cells per Z:** to **2**. Click on the **OK** button to exit the **Initial Mesh** window.

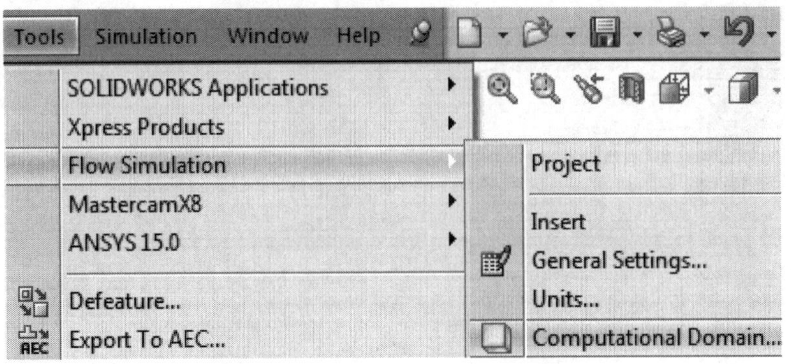

Figure 7.9a) Modifying the computational domain

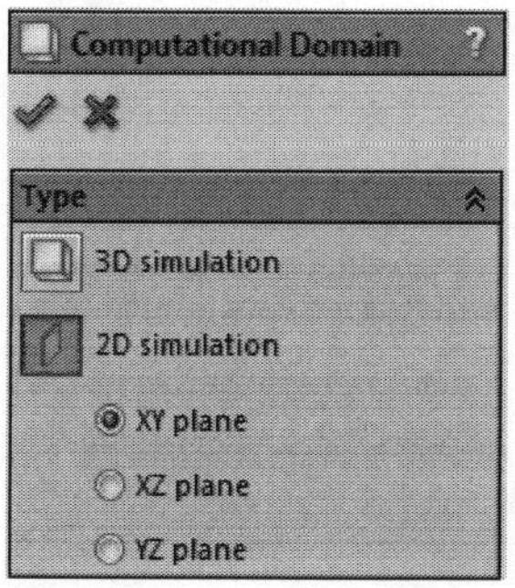

Figure 7.9b) Selecting 2D plane flow

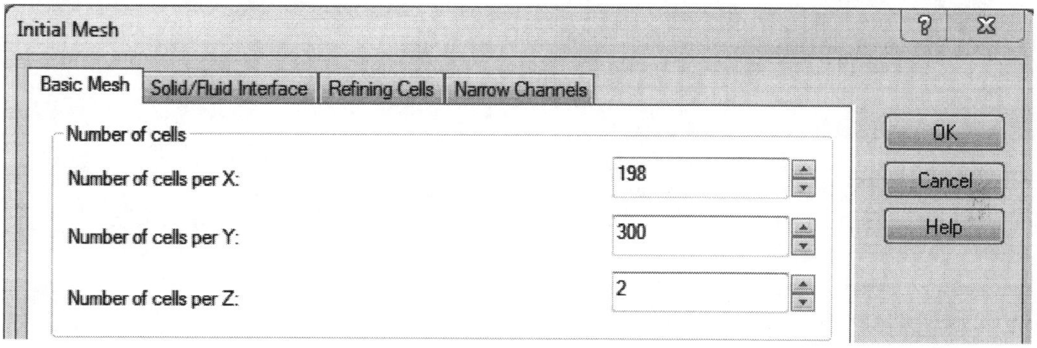

Figure 7.9c) Setting the number of cells

Inserting Boundary Conditions

10. Select **Isometric** view from the **View Orientation** drop down menu in the graphics window. Select **Tools>>Flow Simulation>>Insert>>Boundary Condition…** from the SOLIDWORKS menu. Select the twelve cylindrical surfaces. Click on the Wall button in the **Type** portion of the **Boundary Condition** window and select **Real Wall**. Adjust the **Wall Temperature** to **373.2 K** by clicking on the button and enter the numerical value in the **Wall Parameters** window. Click OK to exit the **Boundary Condition** window.

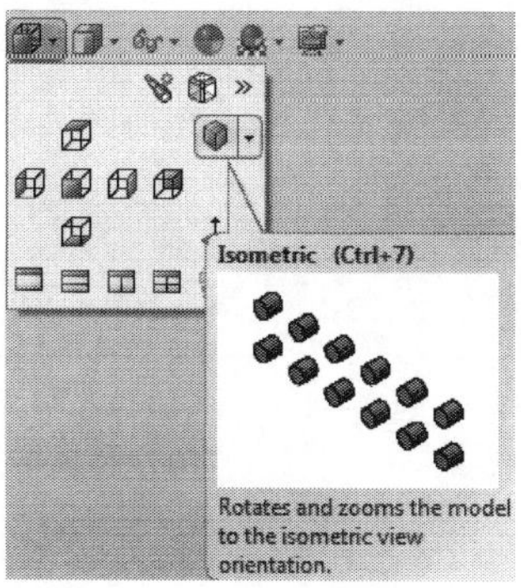

Figure 7.10a) Selecting an isometric view

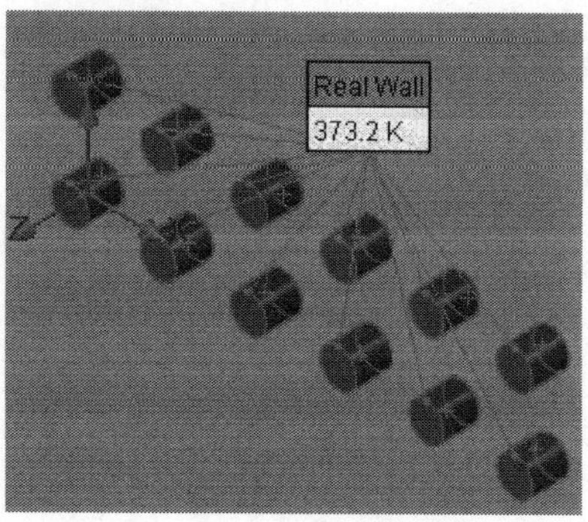

Figure 7.10b) Selection of cylindrical surfaces

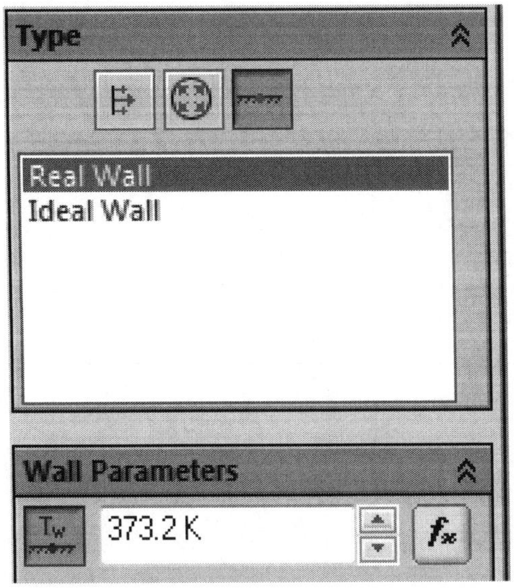

Figure 7.10c) Selecting wall temperature for in-line tube bank

Inserting Global Goals

11. Right click on **Goals** in the **Flow Simulation analysis tree** and select **Insert Global Goals….** Select **Max Velocity (X)** as a global goal. Also, select **Min**, **Av** and **Max Temperature (Fluid)** as global goals. Click OK ✔ to exit the **Global Goals** window.

Figure 7.11 Selection of X – component of velocity and temperature of fluid as global goals

Running the Calculations for Tube Bank Flow

12. Select **Tools>>Flow Simulation>>Solve>>Run** to start calculations. Click on the **Run** button in the **Run** window.

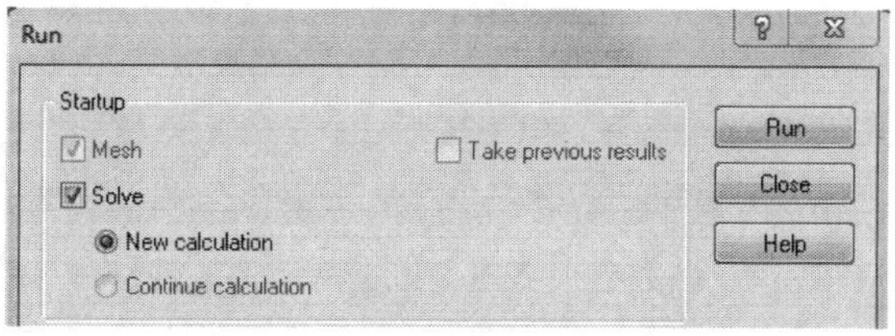

Figure 7.12a) Run window

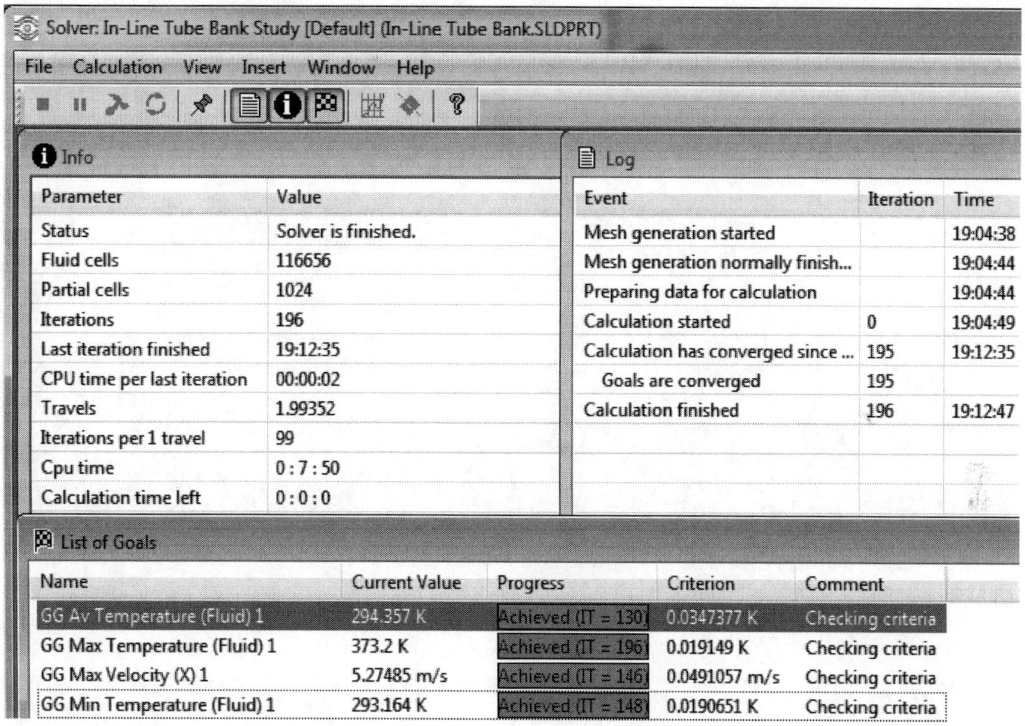

Figure 7.12b) Solver window

Inserting Cut Plots

13. Right click on Cut Plots in the **Flow Simulation analysis tree** and select **Insert...**. Select the **Front Plane** from the **FeatureManager design tree**. Slide the **Number of Levels** slide bar to **255** in the **Contours** section. Exit the **Cut Plot** window. Name the cut plot as **Pressure**. Select **Front** from the **View Orientation** drop down menu in the graphics window. Select **Tools>>Flow Simulation>>Results>>Display>>Lighting** from the SOLIDWORKS menu. Repeat this step two more times but select **Velocity (X)** and **Temperature** as parameters.

You will have to right-click on the cut plot in the FeatureManager design tree and hide it in order to display the next plot. Figure 7.13a) shows the pressure gradient along the tube bank. Figure 7.13b) is showing the velocity distribution in the same cross section and figure 7.13c) is showing the temperature distribution.

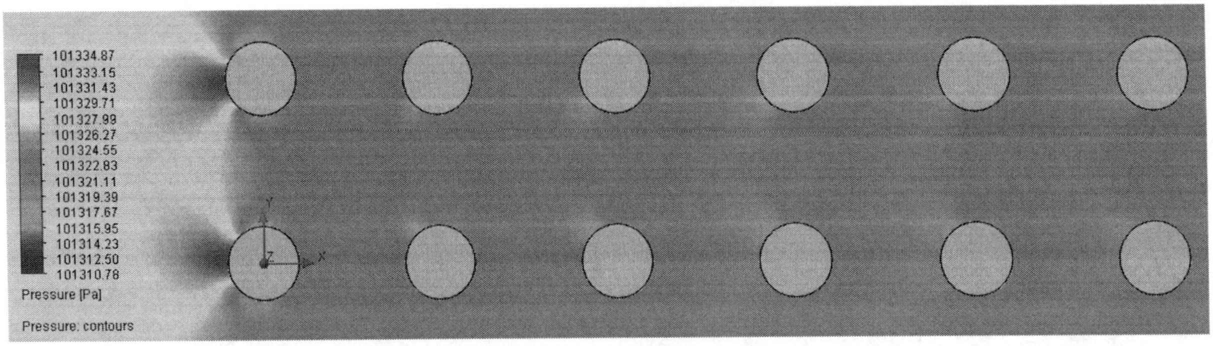

Figure 7.13a) Pressure distribution along the tube bank

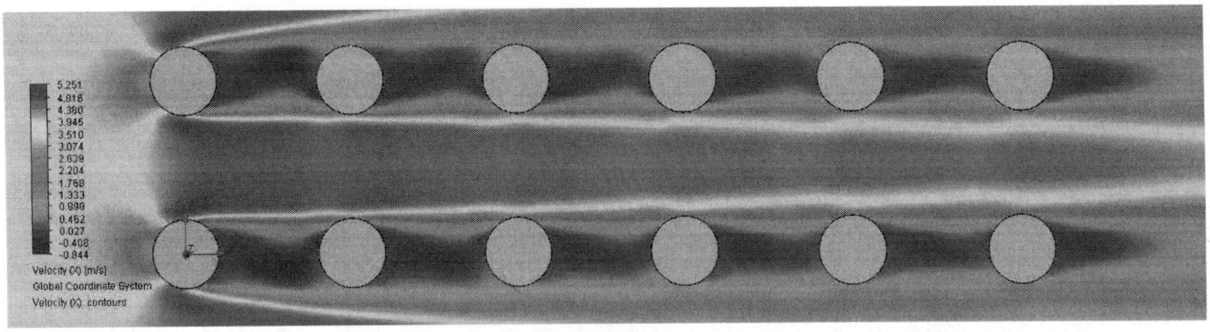

Figure 7.13b) Velocity distribution along the tube bank

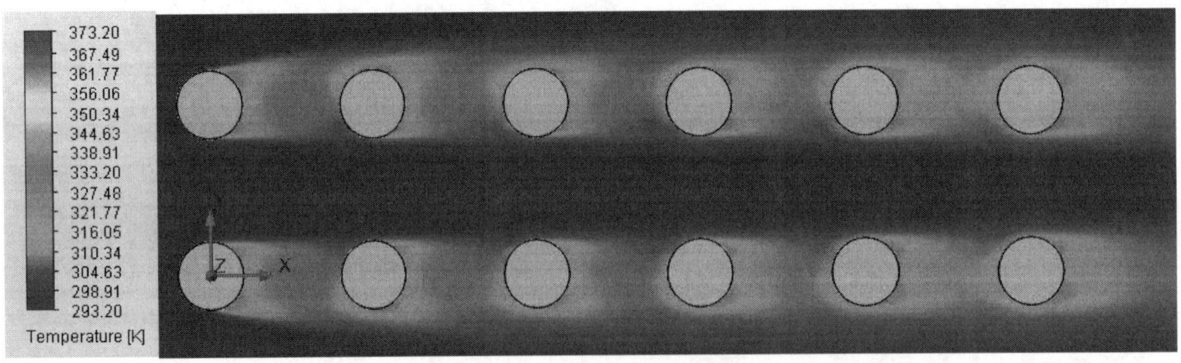

Figure 7.13c) Temperature distribution along the tube bank

Creating Sketch for XY Plots

14. Click on the **FeatureManager design tree,** select the **Front Plane** and select **Line**. Draw a 50 mm long vertical line starting at (*X,Y*) = (275 mm, 0); see figure 7.14a). Exit the **Line Properties** window and draw two more vertical lines with the same length starting at (*X,Y*) = (300 mm, 0) and (*X,Y*) = (325 mm, 0). Close the **Insert Line** window and select **Rebuild** from the SOLIDWORKS Menu. Rename the new sketch to the name **x = 275, 300, 325 mm** as shown in figure 7.14d).

Place the files "**graph 7.14f)**" and "**graph 7.14g)**" on the desktop. Click on the **Flow Simulation analysis tree** tab. Right click **XY Plot** and select **Insert…**. Check the **Temperature** box. Open the **Resolution** portion of the **XY Plot** window and slide the **Geometry Resolution** as far as it goes to the right. Open the **Options** portion of the **XY Plot** window and select **Excel Workbook (*.xlsx)** from the template drop down menu. Click on the **FeatureManager design tree** and select the sketch **x = 275, 300, 325 mm**. Click on **Export to Excel** to generate a plot.

Double click on the **graph 7.14f)** file to open the file. Click on **Enable Content** if you get a **Security Warning** that **Macros** have been disabled. If **Developer** is not available in the menu of the **Excel** file, you will need to do the following: Select **File>>Options** from the menu and click on the **Customize Ribbon** on the left hand side. Check the **Developer** box on the right hand side under **Main Tabs**. Click **OK** to exit the **Excel Options** window.

Click on the **Developer** tab in the **Excel** menu for the **graph 7.14f)** file and select **Visual Basic** on the left hand side to open the editor. Click on the plus sign next to **VBAProject (XY Plot 1.xlsx)** and click on the plus sign next to **Microsoft Excel Objects**. Right click on **Sheet2 (Plot Data)** and select **View Object**.

Select **Macro** in the **Modules** folder under **VBAProject (graph 7.14f).xlsm)**. Select **Run>>Run Macro** from the menu of the **MVB for Applications** window. Click on the **Run** button in the **Macros** window. **Figure 7.14f)** will become available in **Excel**. Close the **XY Plot** window and the **graph 7.14f)** window in **Excel**. Exit the **XY Plot** window in **SOLIDWORKS Flow Simulation** and rename the inserted xy-plot in the **Flow Simulation analysis tree** to **Temperature profiles at different streamwise positions**.

Repeat these steps once again but choose to check the **Velocity (X)** box and select the **graph figure 7.14g)** file.

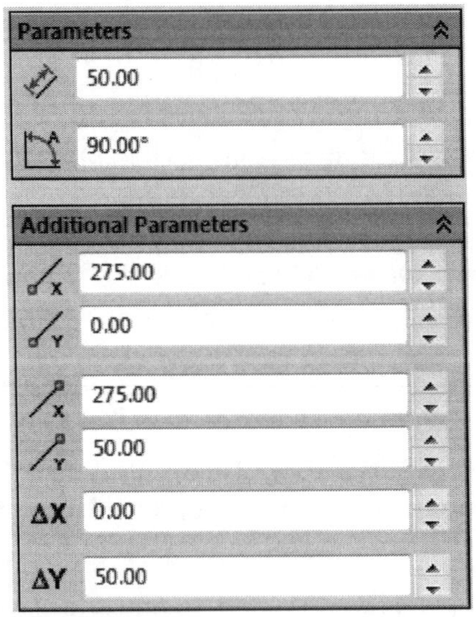

Figure 7.14a) Drawing a vertical line for the XY-plot

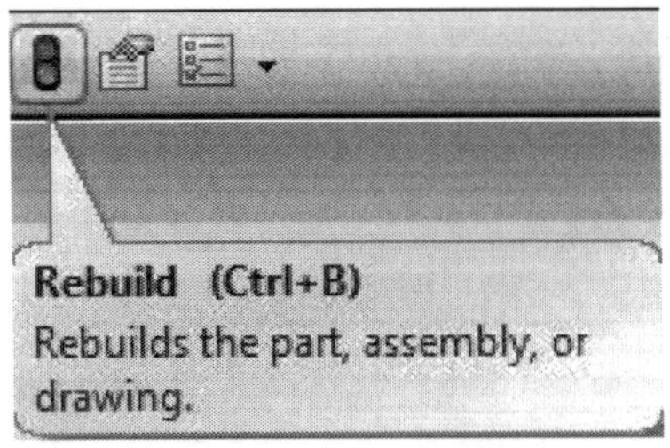

Figure 7.14b) Rebuilding the new sketch

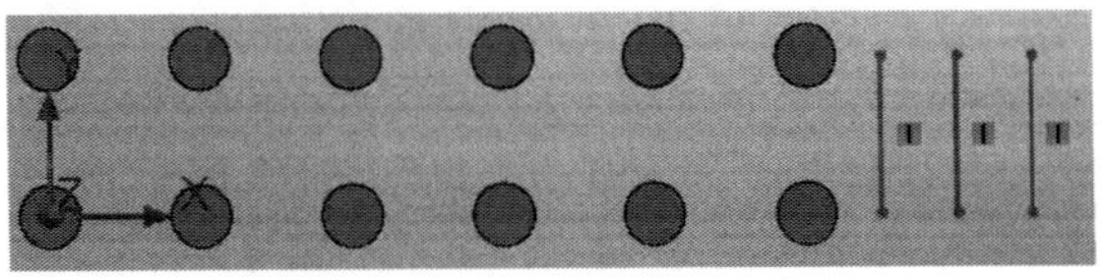

Figure 7.14c) Sketch with three lines for temperature profiles

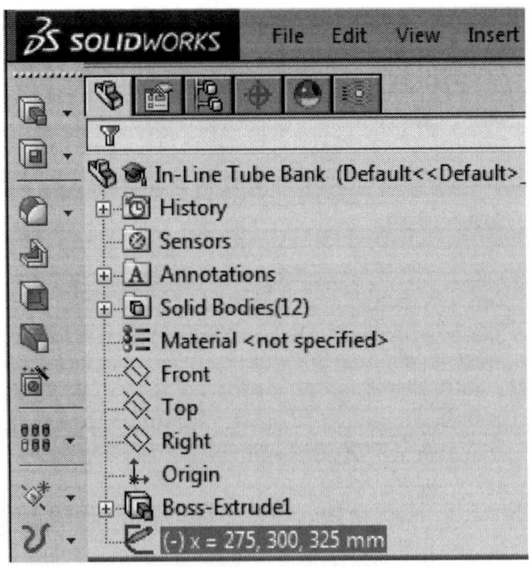

Figure 7.14d) Rename the new sketch

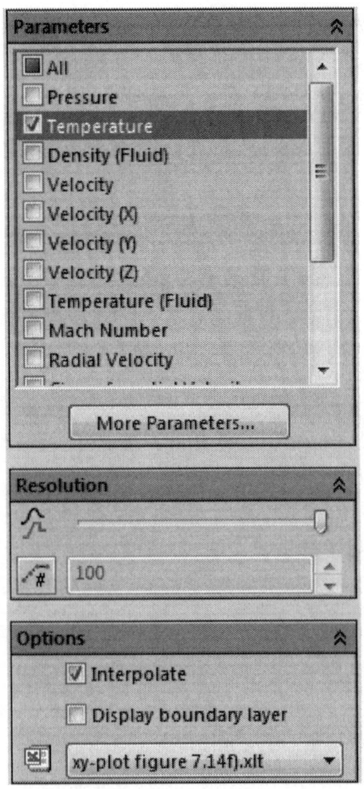

Figure 7.14e) Different settings for XY Plot

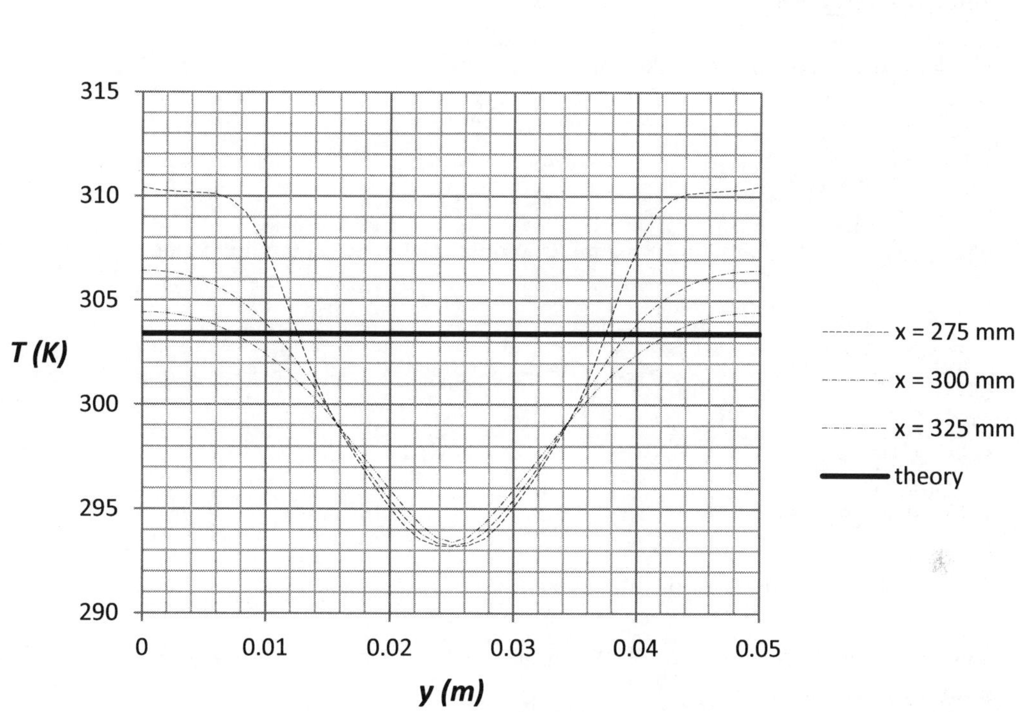

Figure 7.14f) Exit temperatures for the tube bank from Flow Simulation compared with calculations (full line)

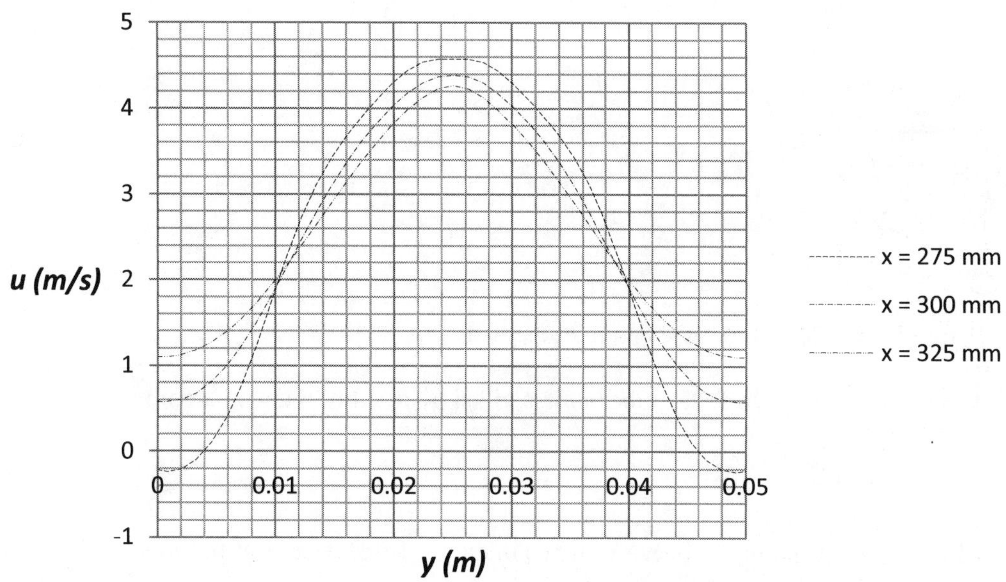

7.14g) Exit velocities for the tube bank from Flow Simulation

Theory and Empirical Data

15. The Reynolds number for a tube bank is defined based on the maximum velocity U_{max} (m/s) in the bank:

$$Re_{D,max} = \frac{U_{max}D}{\nu} \tag{7.1}$$

where D (m) is the diameter of the tubes and ν (m/s) is the kinematic viscosity of the fluid.

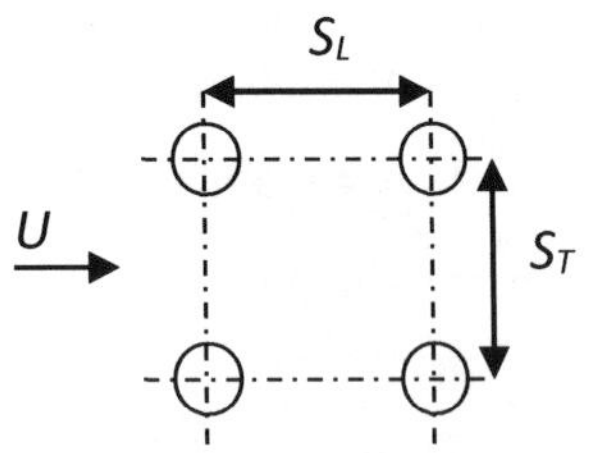

Figure 7.15a) Geometry of in-line tube bank

For the in-line tube arrangement, see figure 7.15a), the maximum velocity is related to the approach velocity U:

$$U_{max} = \frac{S_T U}{S_T - D} \tag{7.2}$$

For the staggered tube arrangement, see figure 7.15b), the maximum velocity is determined by equation (7.2) if $2A_D > A_T$. If $2A_D < A_T$, the maximum velocity is determined by

$$U_{max} = \frac{S_T U}{2(S_D - D)} \tag{7.3}$$

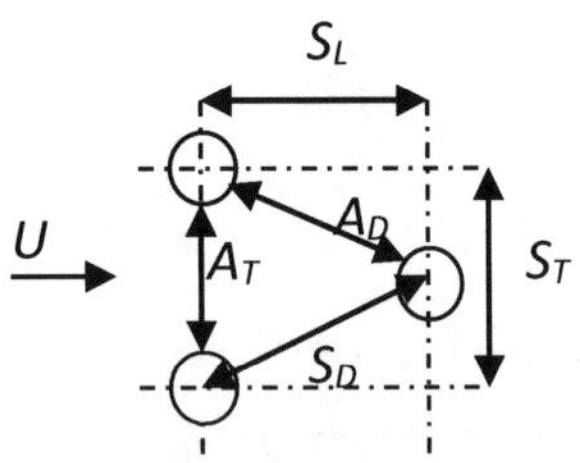

Figure 7.15b) Geometry of staggered tube bank

The pressure drop across the tube bank is given by the following equation:

$$\Delta P = \frac{N_L f \chi \rho U_{max}^2}{2} \tag{7.4}$$

where N_L is the number of rows of tubes in the flow direction, f is the friction factor, χ is a correction factor and ρ (kg/m^3) is the density of the fluid.

The friction factor for in-line and staggered tube banks can be determined from figures 7.15c) and 7.15d), respectively.

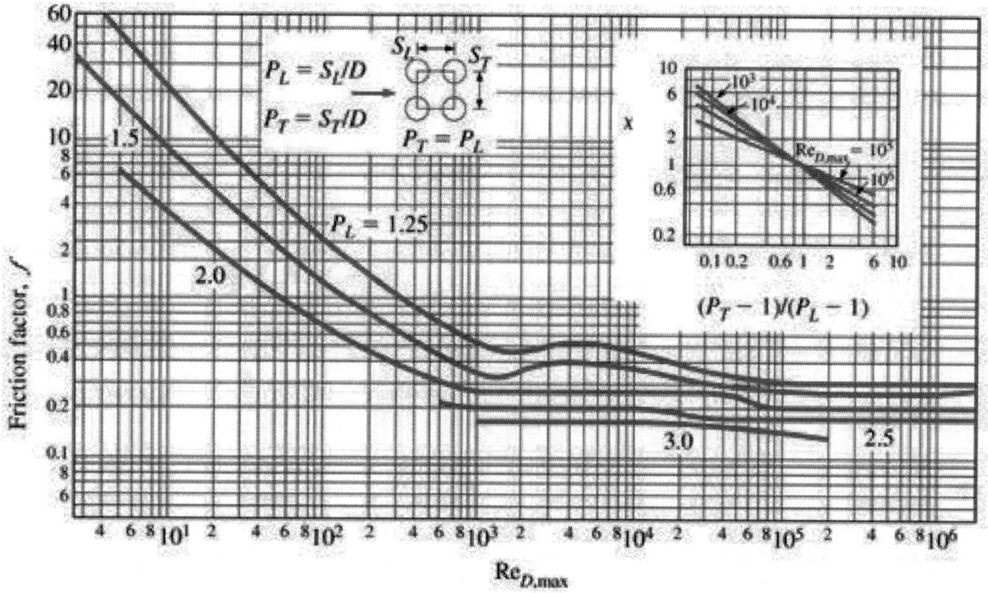

Figure 7.15c) Friction factors for in-line tube bank, from Cengel (2003)

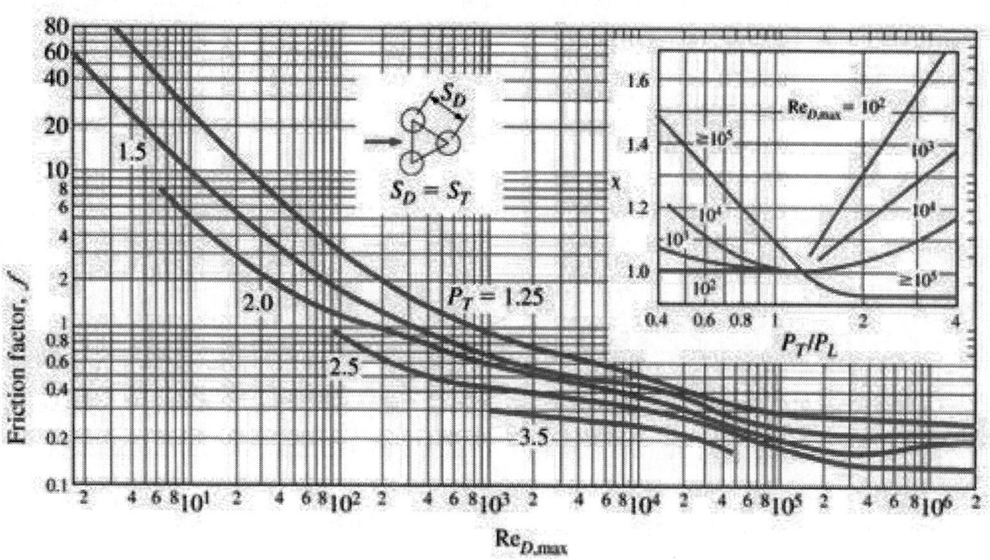

Figure 7.15d) Friction factors for staggered tube bank, from Cengel (2003)

In this case we are using a square in-line tube bank so the correction factor $\chi = 1$. The maximum velocity is

$$U_{max} = \frac{S_T U}{S_T - D} = \frac{0.050m \cdot 4m/s}{0.050m - 0.020m} = 6.67\ m/s \tag{7.5}$$

The Reynolds number can be determined based on an assumed mean temperature of 25°C based on the average of the inlet and outlet temperatures:

$$Re_{D,max} = \frac{U_{max}D}{\nu} = \frac{6.67 m/s \cdot 0.020\text{m}}{1.562 \cdot 10^{-5} m^2/s} = 8536 \quad (7.6)$$

The average Nusselt number *Nu* for six rows of in-line tubes in the flow direction

$$Nu = 0.27 F Re_{D,max}^{0.63} Pr^{0.36} (\frac{Pr}{Pr_s})^{0.25} = 0.27 \cdot 0.945 \cdot 8536^{0.63} \cdot 0.7296^{0.36} (\frac{0.7296}{0.7073})^{0.25} = 68.8$$

where *Pr* and Pr_s are the Prandtl numbers at the mean and surface temperature, respectively, and *F* is a correction factor used for $N_L < 16$ and $Re_{D,max} > 1000$.

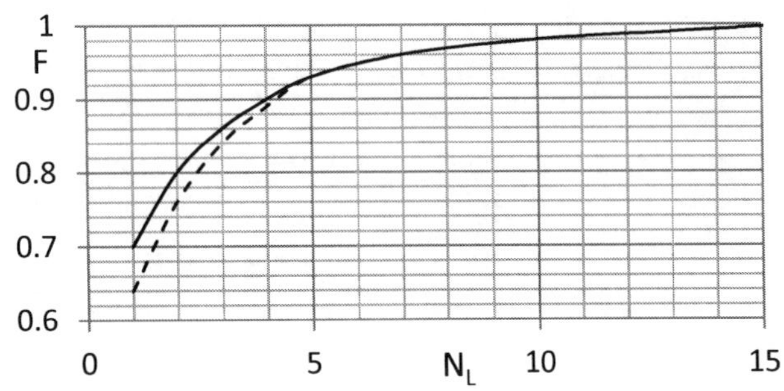

Figure 7.15e) Correction factors *F* for in-line (full line) and staggered (dashed line) tube banks

The average heat transfer coefficient *h* then becomes

$$h = \frac{kNu}{D} = \frac{0.02551 W/(m \cdot °\text{C}) \cdot 68.8}{0.02\, m} = 87.75\, W/(m^2 \cdot °\text{C}) \quad (7.7)$$

where k $(W/(m^2 \cdot °\text{C}))$ is the thermal conductivity of the fluid. The exit temperature T_e (°C) of the fluid can be determined from the inlet temperature T_i (°C) and the surface temperature T_s (°C)

$$T_e = T_s - (T_s - T_i) e^{\frac{-hN_L \pi D}{\rho U S_T C_P}} = 100°\text{C} - (100°\text{C} - 20°\text{C}) e^{\frac{-87.75 \cdot 6\pi \cdot 0.02}{1.204 \cdot 4 \cdot 0.05 \cdot 1007}} = 30.2\ °\text{C}$$

where C_P $(J/(kg \cdot °\text{C}))$ is the specific heat of the air. The average temperature as determined from Flow Simulation results, see figure 7.14f), at x = 300 mm is 30.23 °C, almost identical to the result above. Finally, the pressure drop is determined to be

$$\Delta P = \frac{N_L f \chi \rho U_{max}^2}{2} = \frac{6 \cdot 0.2 \cdot 1 \cdot 1.184 (\frac{kg}{m^3}) \cdot 6.67^2 \frac{m^2}{s}}{2} = 31.6\, Pa \quad (7.8)$$

Reference

[1] Çengel, Y. A., Heat Transfer: A Practical Approach, 2nd Edition, McGraw-Hill, 2003.

Exercises

7.1 Change the mesh resolution in the flow simulations and see how the mesh size affects the maximum velocity and temperature profiles as shown in figures 7.14f) and 7.14g). Discuss your results.

7.2 Use an in-line five rows, $N_L = 5$, tube grid for flow simulations with a rectangular arrangement $S_L = 2S_T$, see figure 7.15a), and compare exit temperatures with corresponding calculations. The diameter of each cylinder is $D = 20$ mm, $S_T = 30\ mm$, and $N_T = 2$. The coordinates for the centers of all cylinders will be $(X\ (mm), Y\ (mm))$ = (0,0), (60,0), (120,0), (180,0), (240,0), (0,30), (60,30), (120,30), (180,30), (240,30). Use air as the project fluid and the velocity in the *X*-direction is 8 m/s. For the calculation of the Reynolds number, assume a mean temperature of $T_m = 25$ °C based on the average of the inlet and outlet temperatures. The surface temperature of the cylinders is $T_s = 100$ °C and the inlet temperature is $T_i = 20$ °C. Fill out Table 7.1 and discuss your results.

D (mm)	$S_L\ (mm)$	$S_T\ (mm)$	N_L	N_T	$U\ (m/s)$	$U_{max}\ (m/s)$
20	60	30	5	2	8	
T_m (°C)	ν (m²/s)	$Re_{D,max}$	F	Pr	Pr_s	Nu
25						
k (W/m·°C)	h (W/m²·°C)	T_s (°C)	T_i (°C)	ρ (kg/m³)	C_p (J/kg·°C)	T_e (°C)
		100	20			
T_e (°C) @ X = 265mm	*% difference*	T_e (°C) @ X = 290 mm	*% difference*	T_e (°C) @ X = 315 mm	*% difference*	
P_L	P_T	f	$(P_T-1)/(P_L-1)$	χ	ΔP (Pa)	
No. of Cells per X	**No. of Cells per Y**	**No. of Cells per Z**				

Table 7.1 Data for Exercise 7.2

7.3 Use a staggered grid for flow simulations with $S_L = S_T$, see figure 7.15b), and compare exit temperature profiles with corresponding calculations as shown in this chapter for in-line arrangement. For a staggered arrangement the Nusselt number in the range of Reynolds numbers Re = 1,000 – 200,000 is given by

$$Nu = 0.35F(S_T/S_L)^{0.2}Re_{D,max}^{0.6}Pr^{0.36}\left(\frac{Pr}{Pr_s}\right)^{0.25} \quad (7.9)$$

7.4 Use a staggered grid for flow simulations with $S_L = 2S_T$, see figure 7.15b), and compare exit temperature profiles with corresponding calculations.

Notes:

Chapter 8 Heat Exchanger

Objectives

- Creating the SOLIDWORKS model of the heat exchanger
- Setting up Flow Simulation projects for internal flow
- Creating lids for the model
- Inserting boundary conditions
- Running the calculations
- Inserting surface parameters
- Using cut plots to visualize the resulting flow field
- Compare Flow Simulation results with effectiveness – NTU method

Problem Description

In this chapter, we will use SOLIDWORKS Flow Simulation to study the flow in a stainless steel parallel flow shell and tube heat exchanger. Heat transfer will occur between the hot inner tube flow and the colder outer flow in the shell. The shell has a wall thickness of 10 mm and an inner diameter of 32 mm, whereas the tube is 2 mm thick and has an outer diameter of 19 mm. The mass flow rate of water in the shell is 0.8 kg/s with an inlet temperature of 283.2 K, and the mass flow rate of water in the tube is 0.2 kg/s at an inlet temperature of 343.2 K. The temperature distributions along the shell and tube will be shown from Flow Simulation results and the temperature of the hot water at the tube outlet will be used in comparison with the effectiveness – NTU method for calculation of the effectiveness of the parallel flow shell and tube heat exchanger.

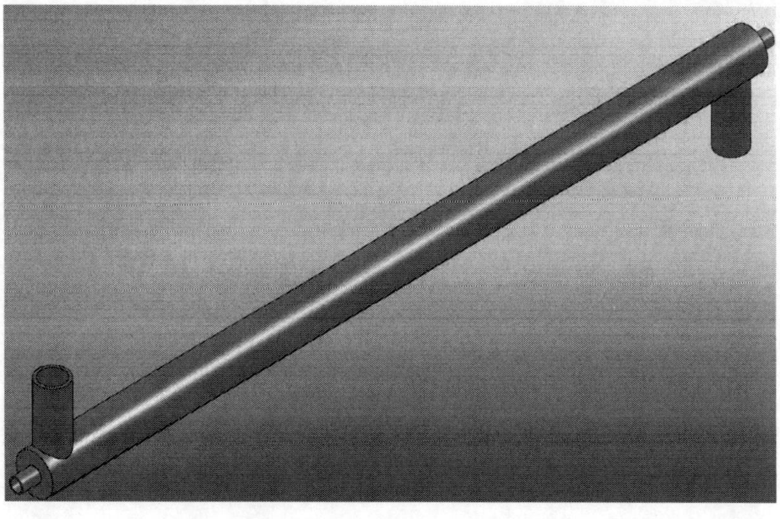

Figure 8.0 SOLIDWORKS model of shell and tube heat exchanger

Creating the SOLIDWORKS Part

1. Start by creating a new part in SOLIDWORKS: select **File>>New** and click on the **OK** button in the **New SOLIDWORKS Document** window. Select **Tools>>Options…** from the SOLIDWORKS menu. Click on the Document Properties tab and select **Units**. Select **MMGS** as your **Unit system**. Click on **Front Plane** in the **FeatureManager design tree** and select **Front** from the **View Orientation** drop down menu in the graphics window.

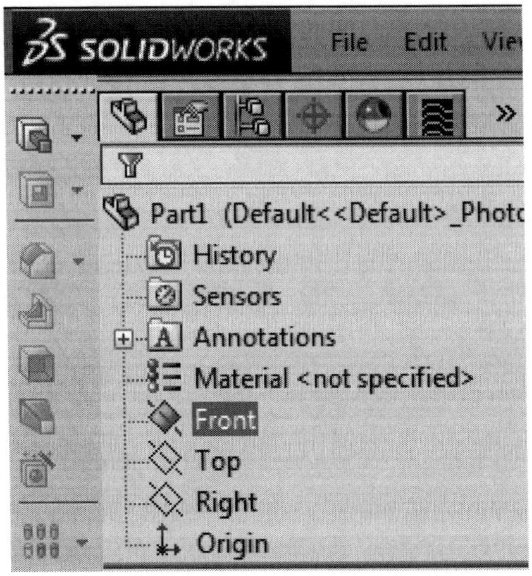

Figure 8.1a) Selection of front plane

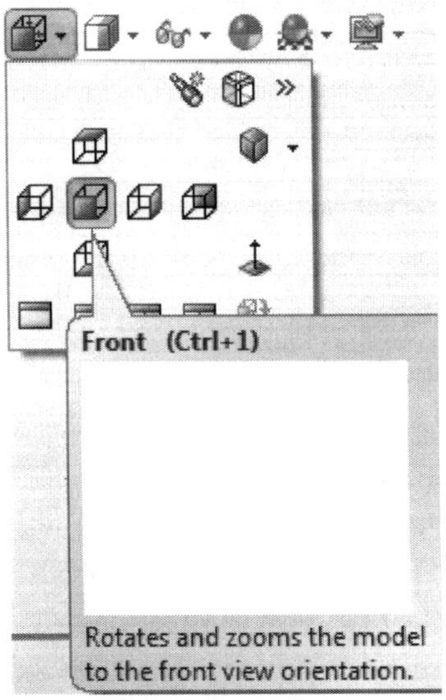

Figure 8.1b) Selection of right view

2. Click on **Circle**.

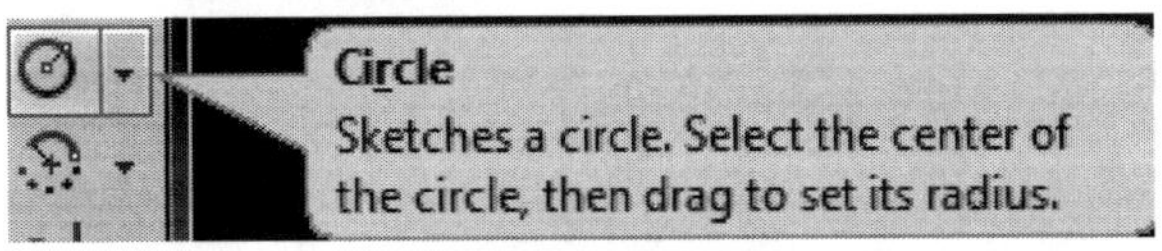

Figure 8.2 Selecting a sketch tool

3. Click at the origin in the graphics window and create a circle with a radius of 16 mm. Fill in the **Parameters** for the circle as shown in figure 8.3. Close the **Circle** dialog box by clicking on **Close Dialog** .

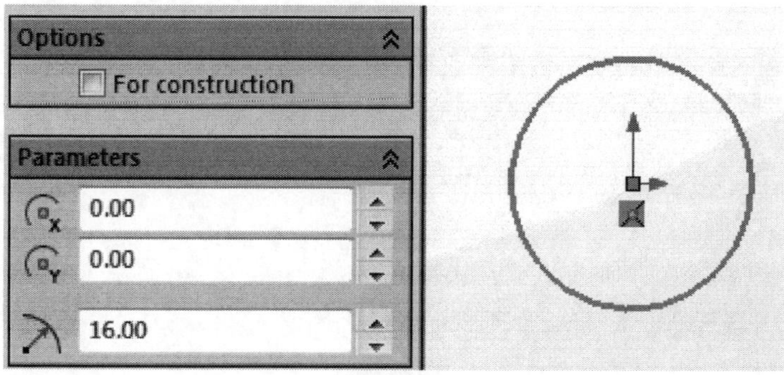

Figure 8.3 A circle with a radius of 16 mm

4. Select the **Extruded Boss/Base**. Enter **1000.00mm** for the **Depth D1** of the extrusion in **Direction 1**. Check the **Thin Feature** box and also check the **Cap ends** box. Close the **Extrude** dialog box by clicking on **OK** . Right click in the graphics window and select **Zoom/Pan/Rotate>>Zoom to Fit**. Select **Left** view from **View Orientation** in the graphics window; see figure 8.4c). Select **Top Plane** from **Featuremanager design tree**. Insert a new plane from the SOLIDWORKS menu by selecting **Insert>>Reference Geometry>>Plane**. Set the **Offset Distance** to **26.00mm** and exit the **Plane** dialog box. Select **Top** view from **View Orientation** in the graphics window; see figure 8.4g).

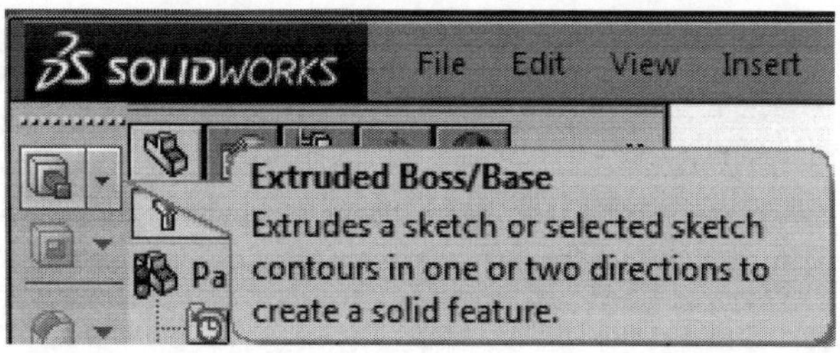

Figure 8.4a) Selection of extruded boss/base feature

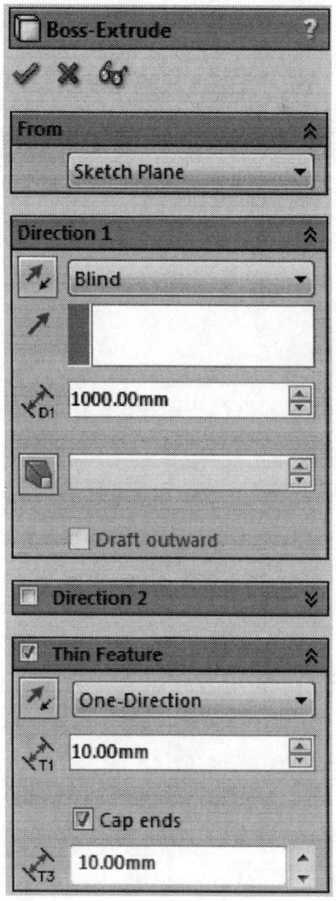

Figure 8.4b) Extruding the sketch

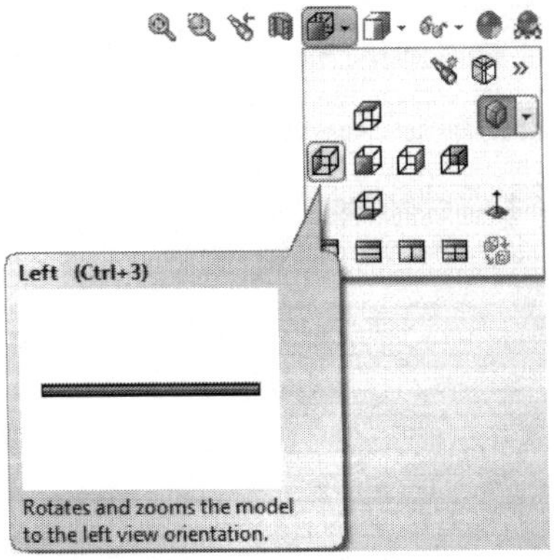

Figure 8.4c) Selecting a left view

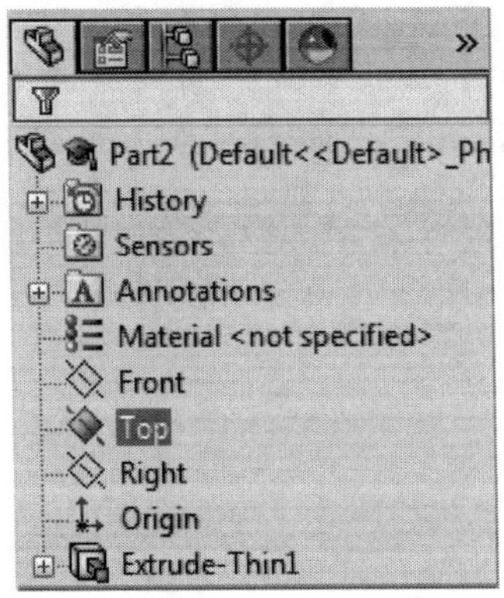

Figure 8.4d) Selecting top plane

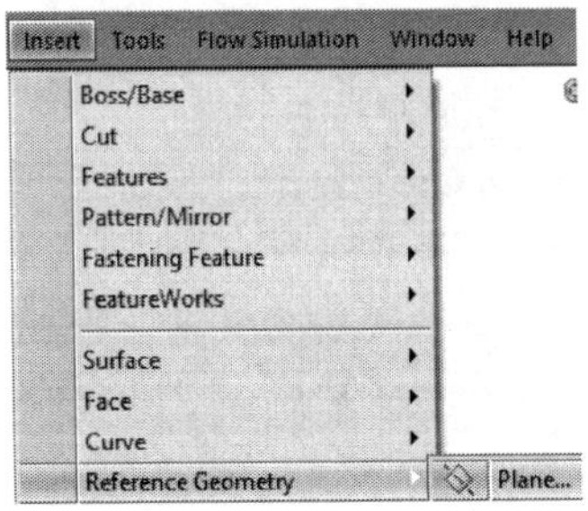

Figure 8.4e) Inserting a plane

Figure 8.4f) Setting the location of the plane

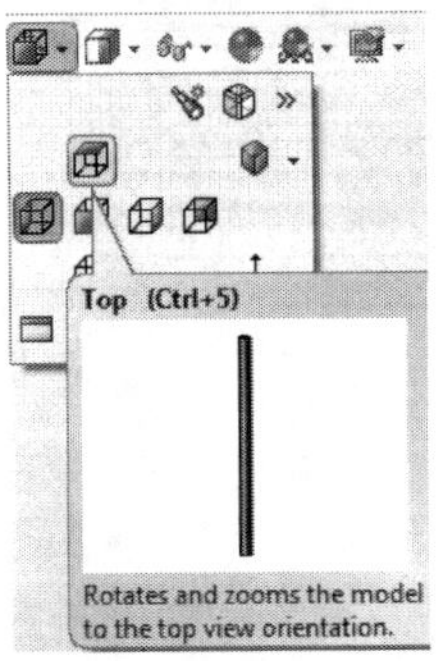

Figure 8.4g) Selecting top view

5. Right click in the graphics window and select **Zoom/Pan/Rotate>>Zoom to Area**. Select a region in the graphics window around the lower end of the tube. Click on **Plane 1** in the **Featuremanager design tree** and select **Circle**. Draw a circle with the parameters as given in figure 8.5b). Close the **Circle** dialog box by clicking on **OK** ✓. Select the **Extruded Cut**. Set the **Depth** of the cut to **26.00mm**. Close the **Extrude** dialog box by clicking on **OK** ✓.

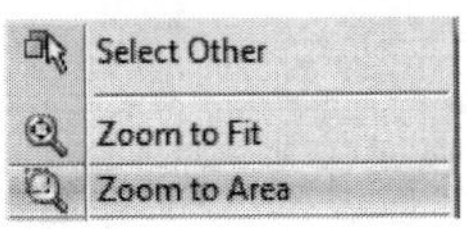

Figure 8.5a) Selecting zoom to area

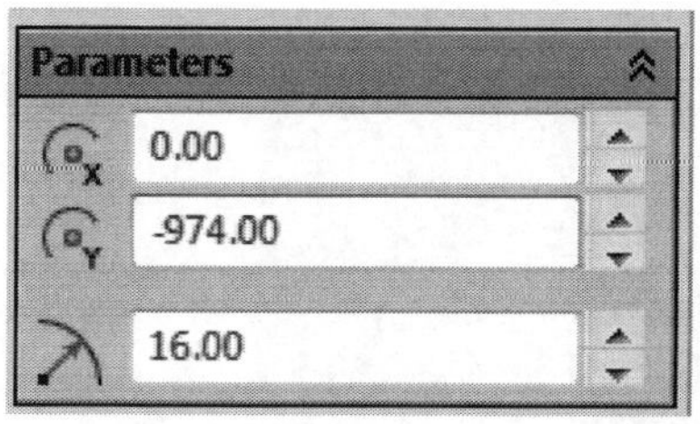

Figure 8.5b) Drawing of a circle for the extrusion.

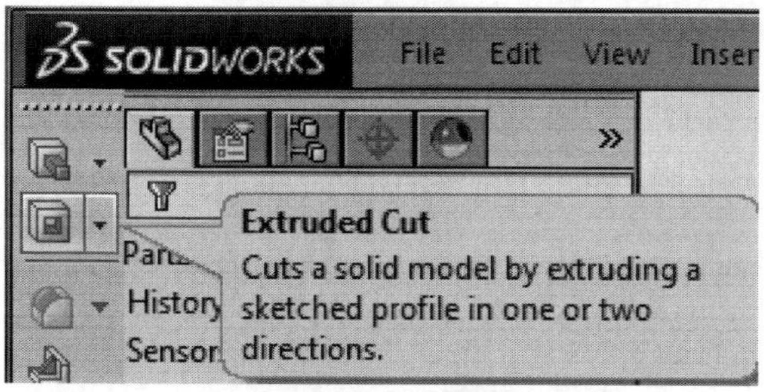

Figure 8.5c) Selecting the extruded cut tool

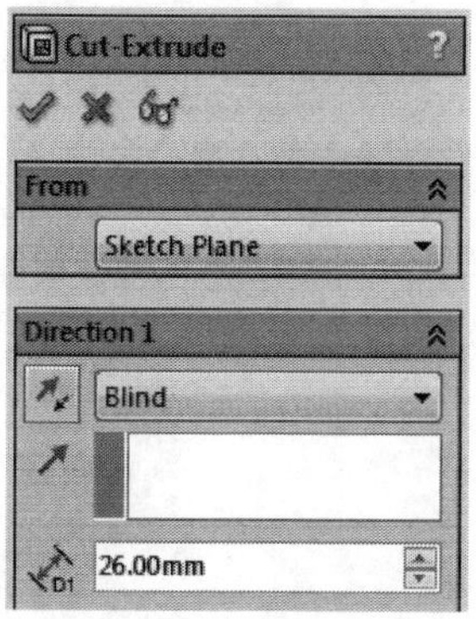

Figure 8.5d) Settings for extruded cut

6. Click on the plus sign next to **Cut-Extrude 1**, select **Sketch 2** in the **Featuremanager design tree** and click on **Extruded Boss/Base**. Set the **Depth D1** of the extrusion in **Direction 1** to **75.00mm**. Check the **Direction 2** box and enter **10.00mm** for the **Depth**. Check the **Thin Feature** box and enter **4.00mm** for the **Thickness**. Close the **Boss-Extrude** dialog box.

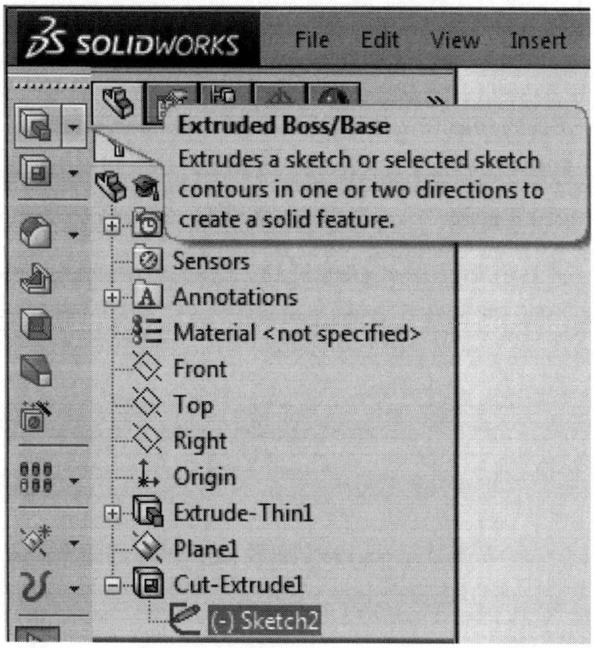

Figure 8.6a) Selecting sketch 2 and the extruded boss/base feature

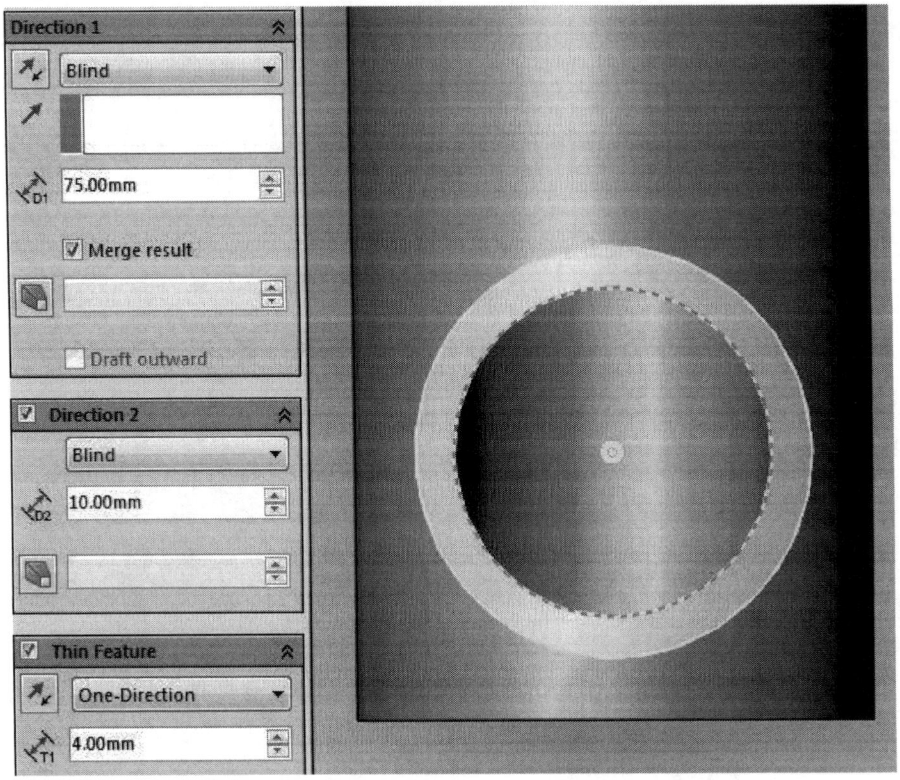

Figure 8.6b) Settings for dimensions of the extrusion from plane 1

7. Select **Left** view from **View Orientation** in the graphics window; see figure 8.4c). Select **Top Plane** from **Featuremanager design tree**. Insert a new plane from the SOLIDWORKS menu by selecting **Insert>>Reference Geometry>>Plane**. Set the **Offset Distance** to **26.00mm**, check the **Flip** box and exit the **Plane** dialog box. Select **Bottom** view from **View Orientation** in the graphics window; see figure 8.7a). Right click in the graphics window and select **Zoom/Pan/Rotate>>Zoom to Area**. Select a region in the graphics window around the lower end of the tube. Click on **Plane 2** in the **Featuremanager design tree** and select **Circle**. Draw a circle with the parameters as given in figure 8.7b). Close the **Circle** dialog box by clicking on **OK** . Select the **Extruded Cut**. Set the **Depth** of the cut to **26.00mm** and click on the **Reverse Direction** button. Close the **Extrude** dialog box by clicking on **OK** .

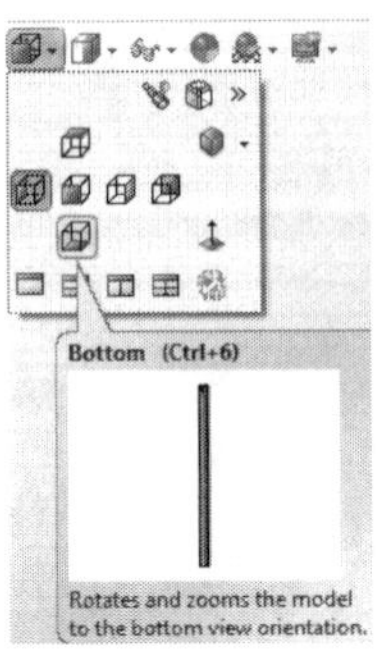

Figure 8.7a) Bottom view from view orientation

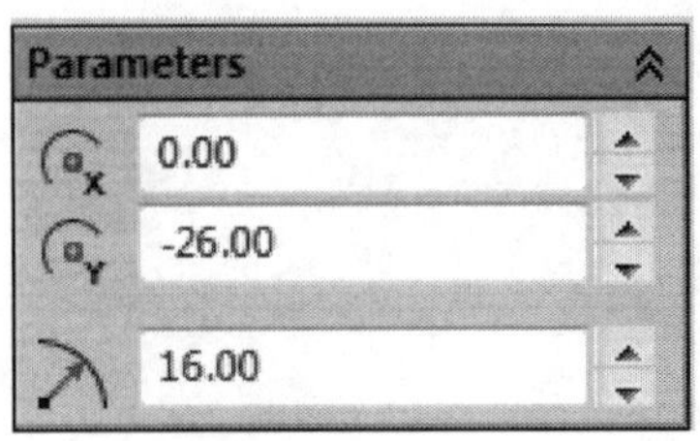

Figure 8.7b) Parameters for circle

8. Click on the plus sign next to **Cut-Extrude 2**, select **Sketch 3** in the **Featuremanager design tree** and click on **Extruded Boss/Base**. Enter **10.00mm** as the **Depth** for **Direction 1**. Check the **Direction 2** box and enter **75.00mm** for the **Depth**. Check the **Thin Feature** box and enter **4.00mm** for the **Thickness**. Close the **Boss-Extrude** dialog box by clicking on **OK** .

Figure 8.8 Extrusion from plane 2

9. Select **Back** view from **View Orientation** in the graphics window; see figure 8.9a). Select **Front Plane** from **Featuremanager design tree**. Select **Circle**. Draw a circle with the parameters as given in figure 8.9b). Close the **Circle** dialog box by clicking on **OK** . Select the **Extruded Cut**. Set the **Depth** of the cut to **1000.00mm** and click on the **Reverse Direction** button. Close the **Extrude** dialog box by clicking on **OK** .

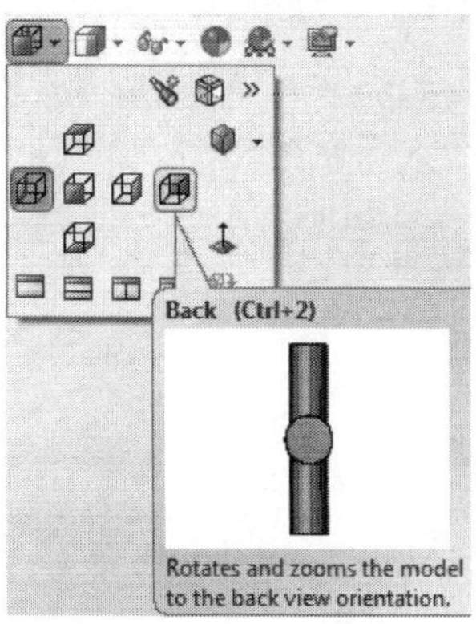

Figure 8.9a) Selection of back view

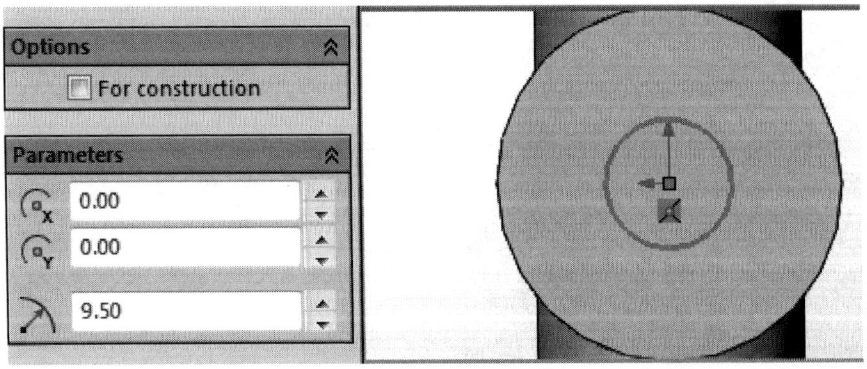

Figure 8.9b) Parameters for circle

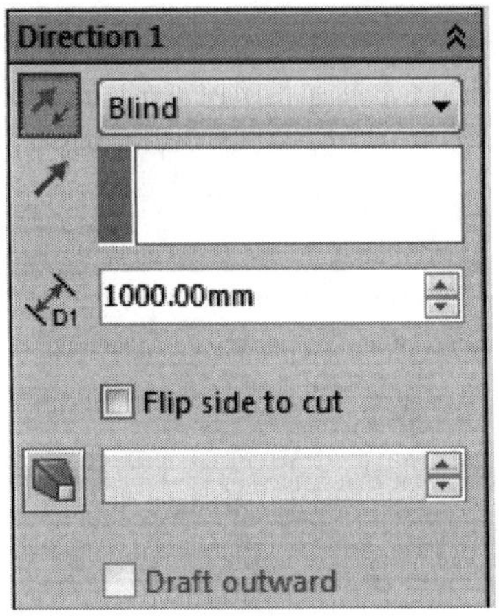

Figure 8.9c) Settings for extruded cut

10. Click on the plus sign next to **Cut-Extrude 3**, select **Sketch 4** in the **Featuremanager design tree** and click on **Extruded Boss/Base**. Enter **1026.00mm** as the **Depth** for **Direction 1**. Check the **Direction 2** box and enter **26.00mm** for the **Depth**. Check the **Thin Feature** box, click on the **Reverse Direction**  button and enter **2.00mm** for **Thickness**. Close the **Boss-Extrude** dialog box by clicking on **OK** . Right click on **Plane 1** in the **Featuremanager design tree** and select **Hide** 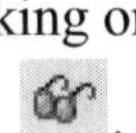. Repeat this step for **Plane 2**. Select **Left** view from **View Orientation** in the graphics window; see figure 8.4c). Save the part with the name **Heat Exchanger Shell and Tube**.

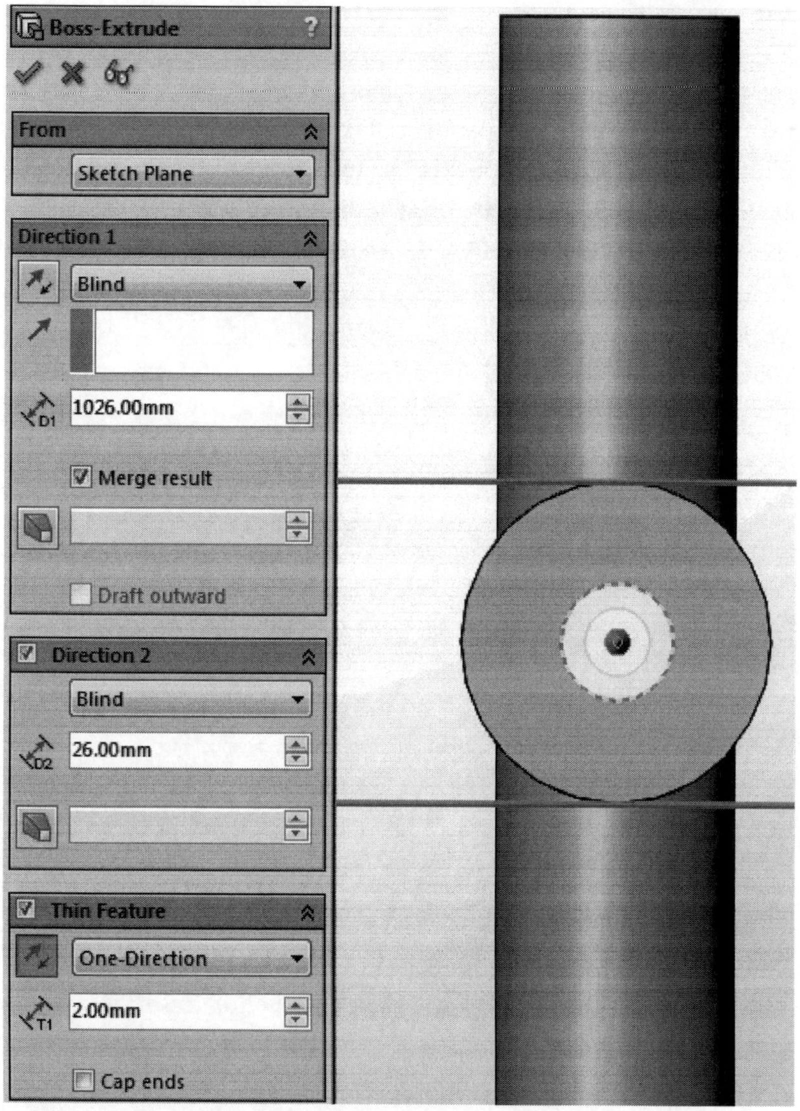

Figure 8.10a) Settings for extrusion from front plane

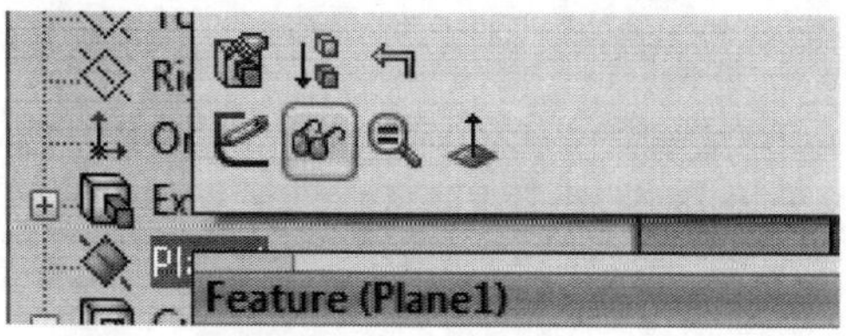

Figure 8.10b) Hiding plane 1

Figure 8.10c) Finished shell and tube heat exchanger

Setting up the Flow Simulation Project

11. If Flow Simulation is not available in the menu, you have to add it from SOLIDWORKS menu: Select **Tools>>Add Ins…** and check the corresponding **SOLIDWORKS Flow Simulation** box. Select **Tools>>Flow Simulation>>Project>>Wizard** to create a new Flow Simulation project. Create a new project named "**Shell and Tube Heat Exchanger Study**." Click on the **Next >** button. Select the default **SI (m-kg-s)** unit system and click on the **Next>** button once again.

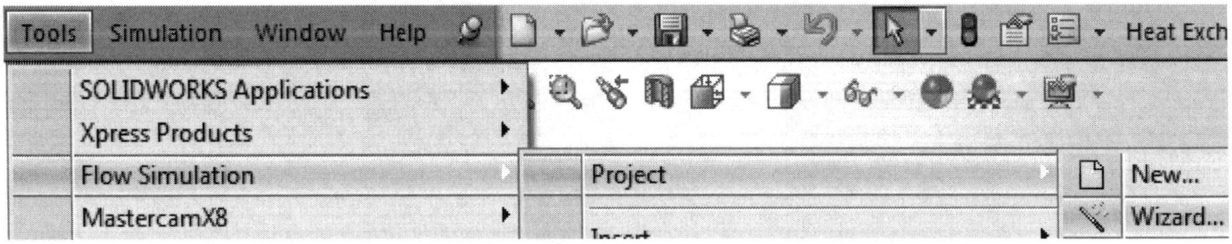

Figure 8.11a) Starting a new Flow Simulation project

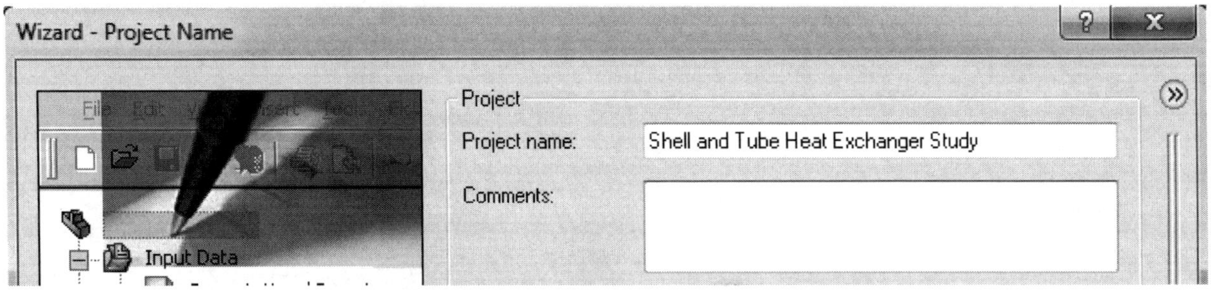

Figure 8.11b) Creating a name for the project

12. Use the default **Internal Analysis type** and check the **Heat conduction in solids** box. Click on the **Next >** button.

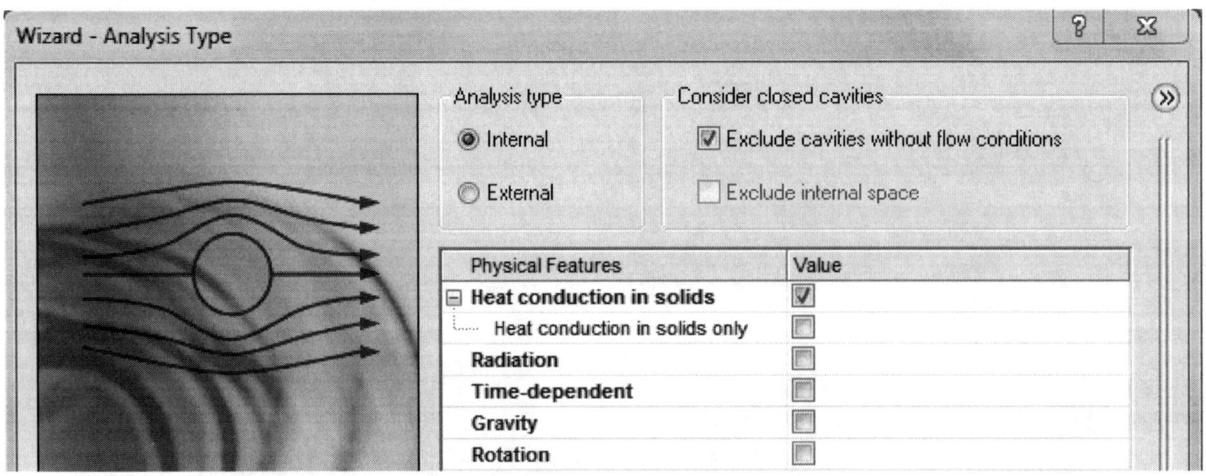

Figure 8.12 Internal analysis type with heat conduction in solids

13. Add **Water** from **Liquids** as the **Project Fluid**. Click on the **Next** > button. Select **Alloys>> Stainless Steel 321** as the **Default Solid**. Click on the **Next** > button. Use the default **Wall Conditions** and the default **Initial Conditions**. Click on the **Next** > button. Use the **Result resolution** of level **3**. Click on the **Finish** button. Answer Yes to the question whether you want to open the Create Lids tool.

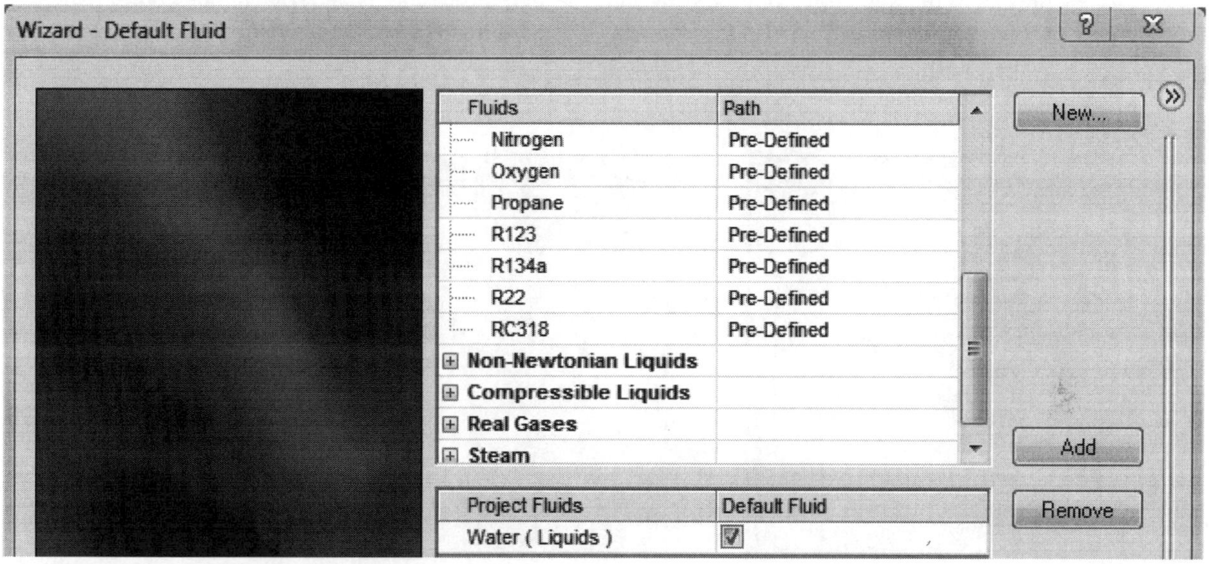

Figure 8.13a) Adding water as the project fluid

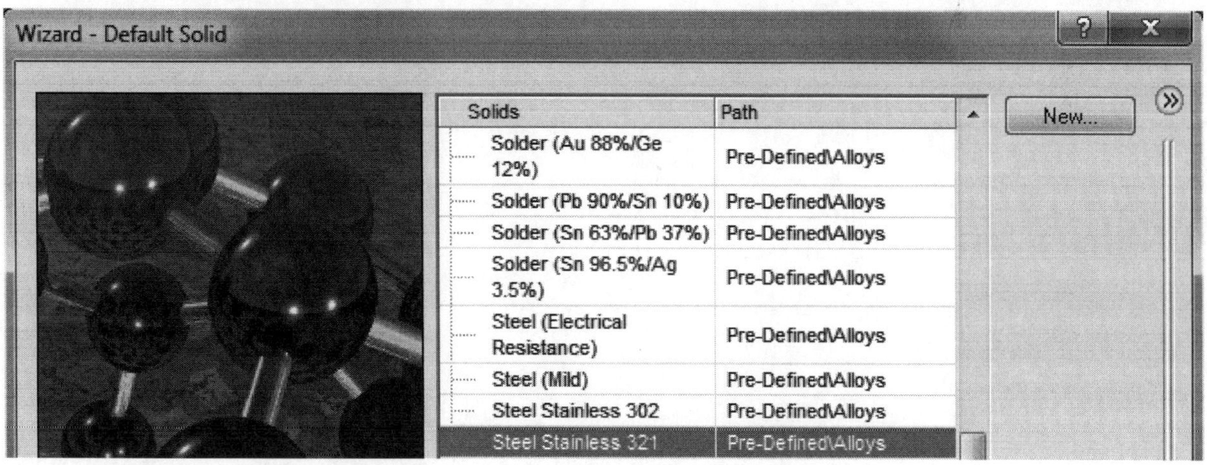

Figure 8.13b) Selecting stainless steel as the default solid

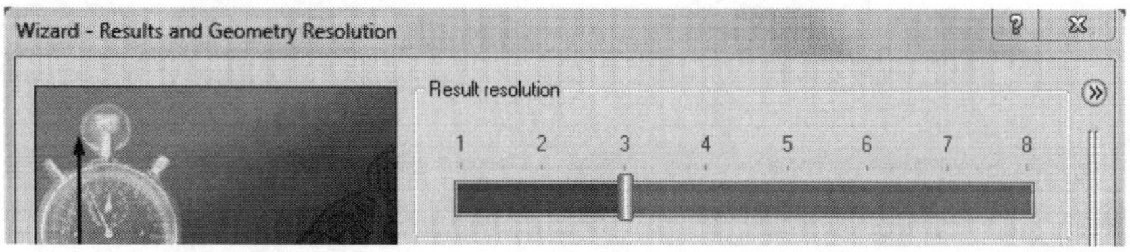

Figure 8.13c) Setting the result resolution

Creating Lids

14. Select **Back** view from **View Orientation** in the graphics window; see figure 8.9a). Select the face as shown in figure 8.14. Close the **Create Lids** dialog box by clicking on **OK** . Answer yes to the questions whether you want to reset the computational domain and mesh setting. Answer Yes to the question whether you want to open the Create Lids tool. Select **Front** view from **View Orientation** in the graphics window. Select the similar face as above and close the **Create Lids** dialog box by clicking on **OK** . Answer yes to the questions.

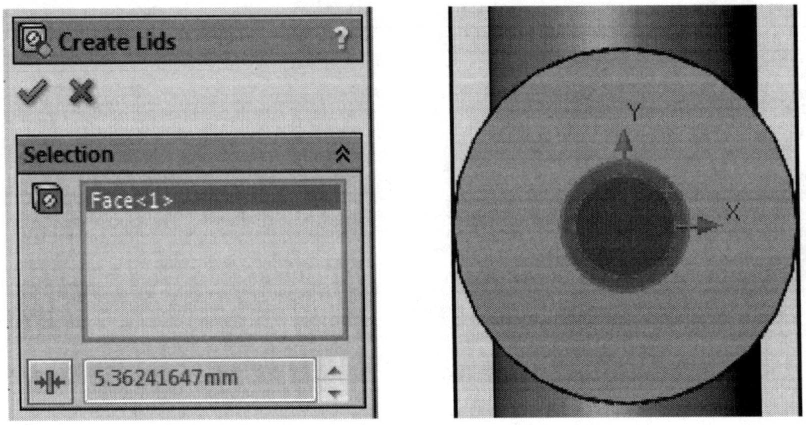

Figure 8.14 Selecting the face for the lid

15. Select **Tools>>Flow Simulation>>Tools>>Create Lids…** from the SOLIDWORKS menu. Select **Bottom** view from **View Orientation** in the graphics window. Zoom in on the bottom part of the heat exchanger and select the face as shown in figure 8.15. Close the **Create Lids** dialog box by clicking on **OK** . Answer yes to the questions whether you want to reset the computational domain and mesh setting. Select **Tools>>Flow Simulation>>Tools>>Create Lids…** from the SOLIDWORKS menu. Select **Top** view from **View Orientation** in the graphics window. Zoom in and select the similar face as shown in figure 8.15. Close the **Create Lids** dialog box by clicking on **OK** . Answer yes to the same questions as listed above.

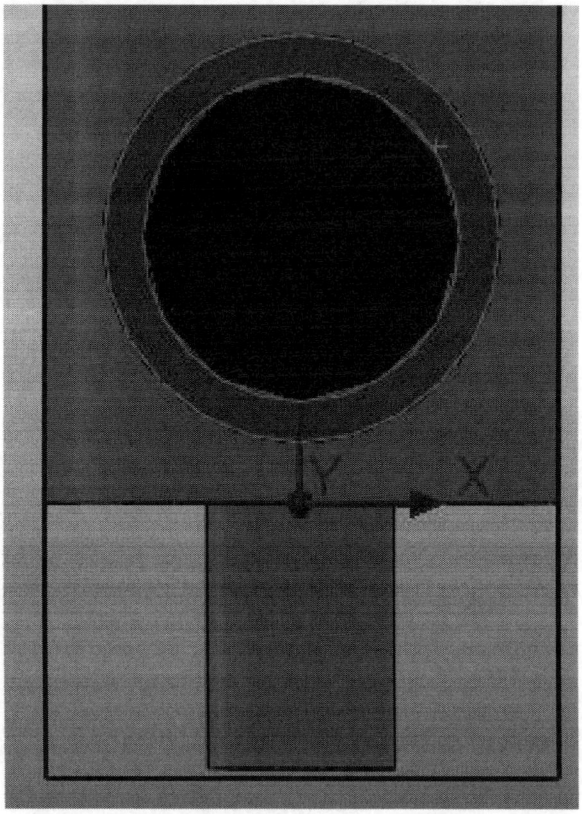

Figure 8.15 Selection of face for third lid

Inserting Boundary Conditions

16. Select **Left** view from **View Orientation** in the graphics window. Right click in the graphics window and select **Zoom/Pan/Rotate>>Rotate View**. Rotate the view and select **Zoom to Area**. Zoom in at the left end of the heat exchanger; see figure 8.16b). Click on the plus sign next to the **Input Data** folder in the **Flow Simulation analysis tree**. Right click on **Boundary Conditions** and select **Insert Boundary Condition….** Right click on the tube and select **Select Other**. Select the inner surface of the lid; see figure 8.16b). Set the inlet mass flow to **0.2 kg/s** and the **Temperature** to **343.2 K**. Click OK to exit the **Boundary Condition** window. Rename the created boundary condition in the **Flow Simulation analysis tree** to **Inlet Mass Flow for Tube**.

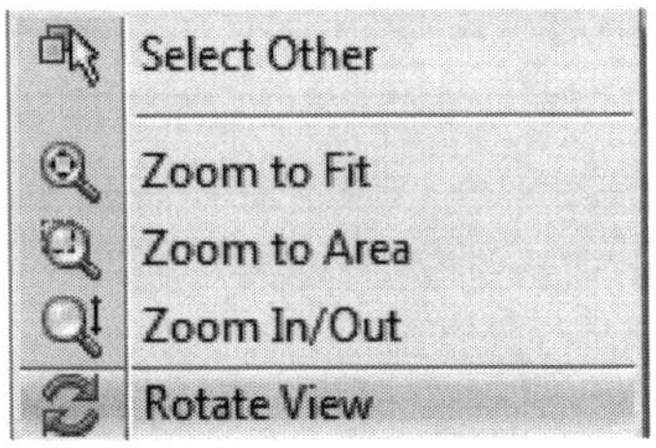

Figure 8.16a) Selection of rotate view

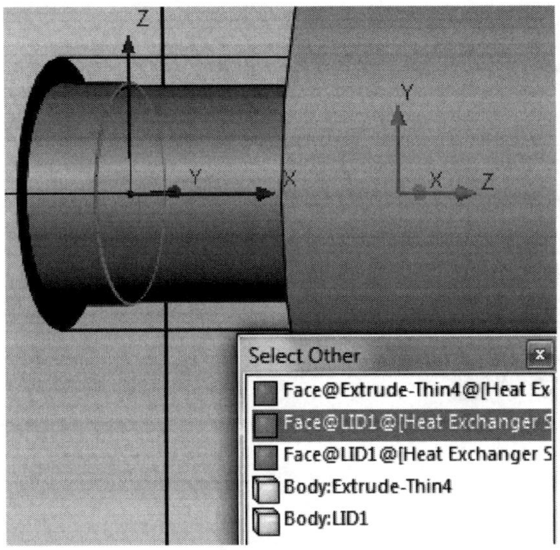

Figure 8.16b) Selecting face for tube inflow region

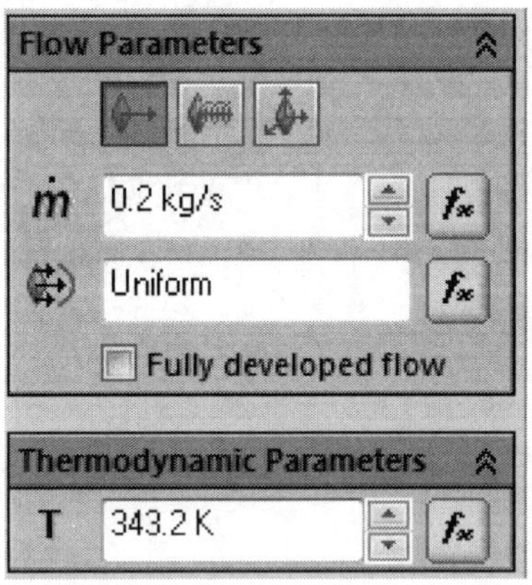

Figure 8.16c) Tube inflow parameters

17. Zoom out a little bit and rotate the view a little bit; see figure 8.17a). Right click on **Boundary Conditions** and select **Insert Boundary Condition….** Right click on the shell and select the inner surface of the shell inflow lid; see figure 8.17a). Set the inlet mass flow to **0.8 kg/s** and the **Temperature** to **283.2 K**. Click OK to exit the **Boundary Condition** window. Rename the boundary condition to **Inlet Mass Flow for Shell**.

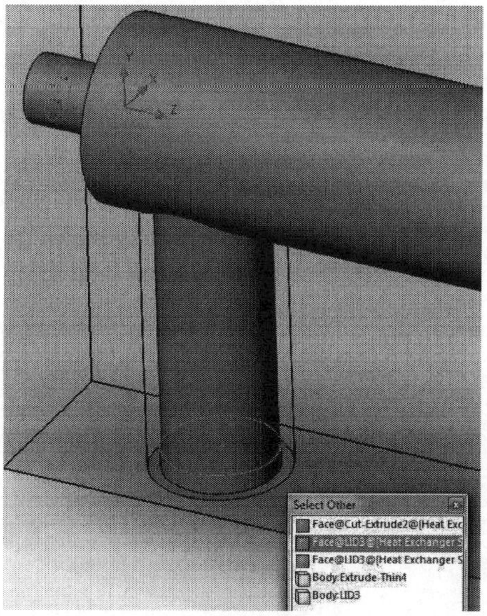

Figure 8.17a) Selecting face for shell inflow region

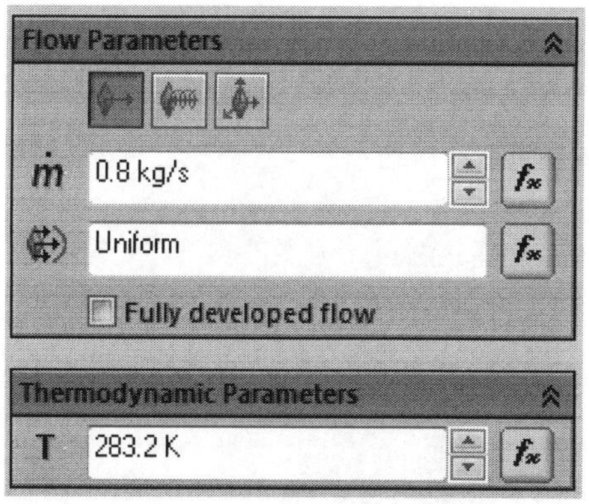

Figure 8.17b) Shell inflow parameters

18. Select **Left** view from **View Orientation** in the graphics window. Right click in the graphics window and select **Zoom/Pan/Rotate>>Rotate View**. Rotate the view and select **Zoom to Area**. Zoom in at the right end of the heat exchanger; see figure 8.18a). Right click on **Boundary Conditions** and select **Insert Boundary Condition…**. Right click on the tube outflow region and click on **Select Other**. Select the inner surface of the lid; see figure 8.18a). Click on the **Pressure Openings** button and select **Environment Pressure**. Click OK to exit the **Boundary Condition** window. Rename the boundary condition to **Environment Pressure for Tube**.

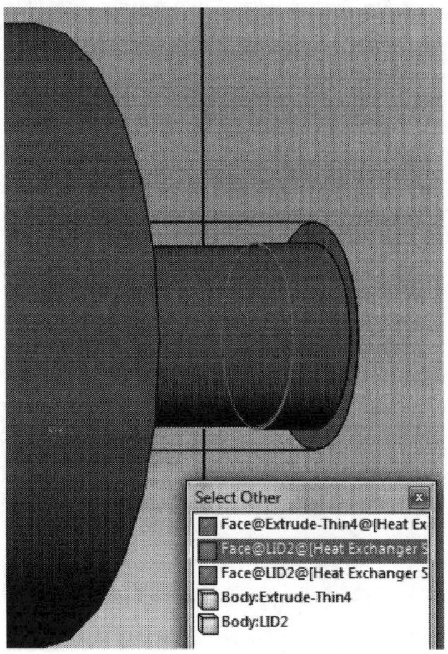

Figure 8.18a) Selecting face for tube outflow region

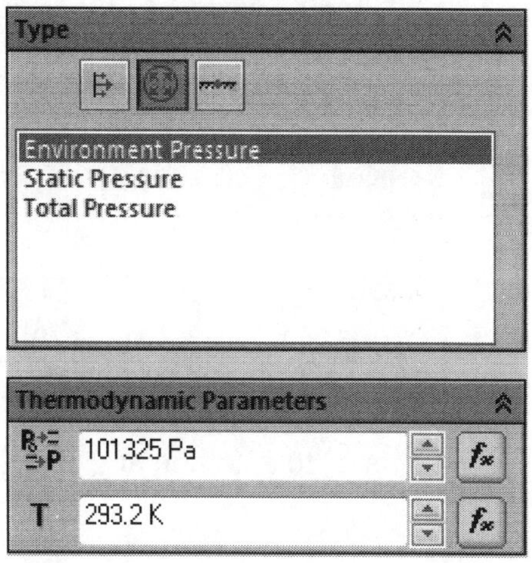

Figure 8.18b) Tube outflow parameters

19. Right click in the graphics window and select **Zoom/Pan/Rotate>>Rotate View**. Rotate the view a little bit and zoom out a little bit; see figure 8.19a). Right click on **Boundary Conditions** and select **Insert Boundary Condition….** Right click on the shell outflow region and click on **Select Other**. Select the inner surface of the lid; see figure 8.19b). Click on the **Pressure Openings** button. Select **Environment Pressure** and click OK to exit the **Boundary Condition** window. Rename the boundary condition to **Environment Pressure for Shell.**

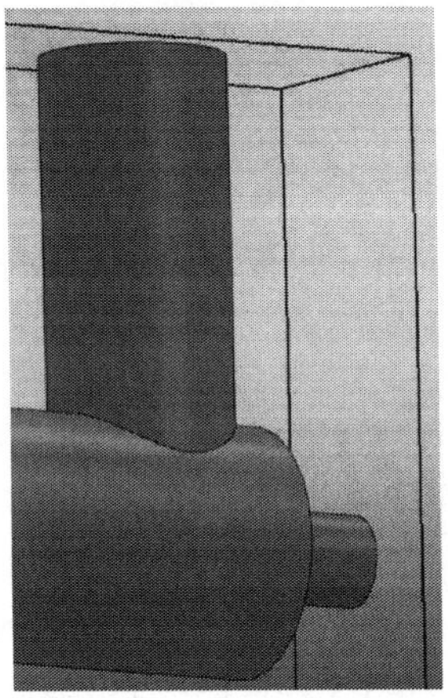

Figure 8.19a) Rotating the view

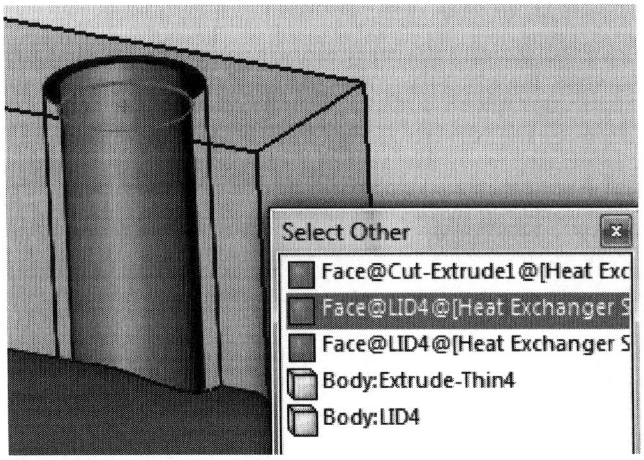

Figure 8.19b) Selecting face for shell outflow region

__Inserting Goals__

20. Right click on **Goals** in the **Flow Simulation analysis tree** and select **Insert Global Goals….** Select **Min**, **Av** and **Max Temperature (Fluid)** and **Min**, **Av** and **Max Temperature (Solid)** as global goals. Click OK to exit the **Global Goals** window.

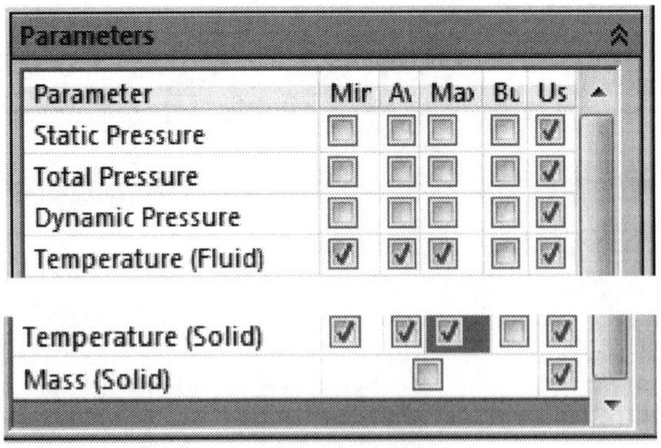

Figure 8.20 Selection of global goals

Running the Calculations for Heat Exchanger

21. Select **Tools>>Flow Simulation>>Solve>>Run** to start calculations. Click on the **Run** button in the **Run** window.

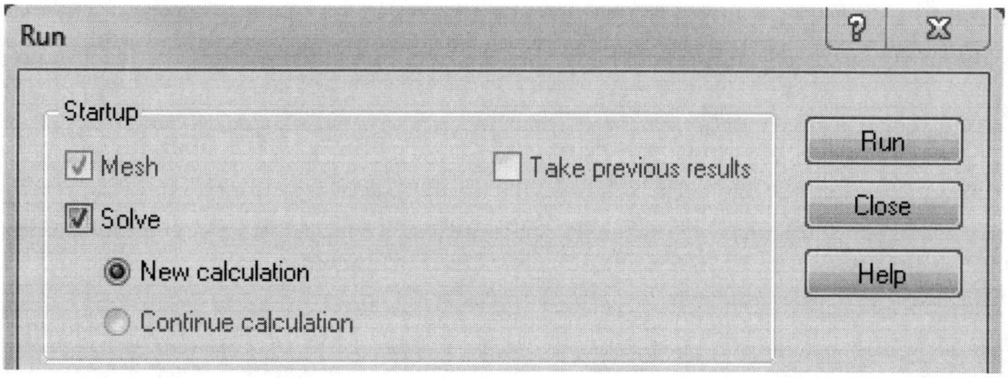

Figure 8.21a) Run window

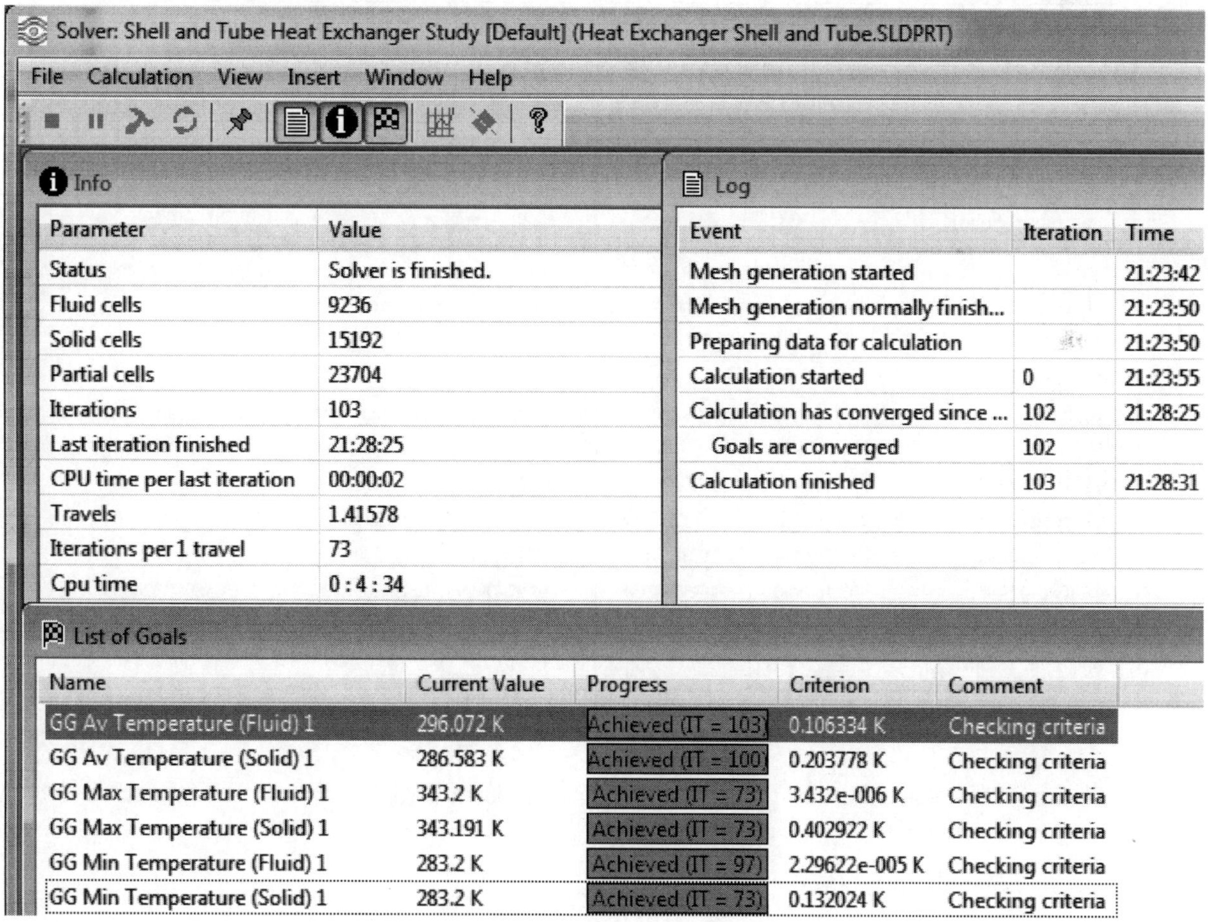

Figure 8.21b) Solver window

Inserting Surface Parameters

22. Right click on **Surface Parameters** in the **Flow Simulation analysis tree** and select **Insert…**. Select the **Environment Pressure for Tube Boundary Condition** in the **Flow Simulation analysis tree**. Check the **All Parameters** box and click on the **Export to Excel** button in the **Surface Parameters** window. Select the **Local parameters**. The minimum fluid temperature at the tube outflow region is **334.60 K** and the average value at the same outflow region is **335.885 K**. Select the **Environment Pressure for Shell Boundary Condition** in the **Flow Simulation analysis tree**. Click on the **Export to Excel** button once again in the **Surface Parameters** window. Select the **Local parameters**. The average fluid temperature at the shell outflow region is **285.314 K**. Exit the **Surface Parameters** window.

Local Parameters

Local Parameter	Minimum	Maximum	Average	Bulk Average	Surface Area [m^2]
Pressure [Pa]	101325	101325.4491	101325.2175	101325.2097	0.000169852
Density (Fluid) [kg/m^3]	981.0400371	982.1888561	981.5499227	981.5218392	0.000169852
Velocity [m/s]	0.93524861	1.331669267	1.199801237	1.208992805	0.000169852
Velocity (X) [m/s]	-0.001718364	0.00167168	-4.26506E-05	-4.37588E-05	0.000169852
Velocity (Y) [m/s]	-0.001380378	0.001371466	-6.25991E-06	-7.67382E-06	0.000169852
Velocity (Z) [m/s]	0.935248433	1.331669169	1.199800593	1.208992164	0.000169852
Temperature (Fluid) [K]	334.6023782	336.8998384	335.8845816	335.940595	0.000169852
Temperature (Solid) [K]	335.1392858	335.5654638	335.2948196		0.000169852

Figure 8.22a) Values of local parameters at the tube outflow region

Local Parameters

Local Parameter	Minimum	Maximum	Average	Bulk Average	Surface Area [m^2]
Pressure [Pa]	101316.8468	101325	101324.7792	101324.9965	0.000798804
Density (Fluid) [kg/m^3]	999.0679714	999.4395553	999.3858339	999.3822621	0.000798804
Velocity [m/s]	0.078057935	1.752587086	1.013793832	1.353866122	0.000798804
Velocity (X) [m/s]	-0.075822843	0.08478602	-2.73122E-05	-0.00023161	0.000798804
Velocity (Y) [m/s]	-0.11318801	1.752533381	0.999770979	1.350587379	0.000798804
Velocity (Z) [m/s]	-0.157539799	-0.002550653	-0.060470872	-0.058155514	0.000798804
Temperature (Fluid) [K]	284.724407	293.2	285.3142614	285.0254747	0.000798804
Temperature (Solid) [K]	284.9304885	285.3523599	285.085492		0.000798804

Figure 8.22b) Values of local parameters at the shell outflow region

Inserting Cut Plots

23. Right click on **Cut Plots** in the **Flow Simulation analysis tree** and select **Insert…**. Select the **Right Plane** from the **FeatureManager design tree**. Slide the **Number of Level** slide bar to **255** in the **Contours** section. Select **Temperature** from the **Parameter** dropdown menu. Set the **Min:** temperature to **334.60 K**. Exit the **Cut Plot** window. Rename the cut plot to **Tube Temperature**.

Select **Tools>>Flow Simulation>>Results>>Display>>Geometry** to display the cut plot. Select **Left** view from **View Orientation** in the graphics window. Repeat this step and insert another cut plot but set the minimum temperature to **283.2 K** and the maximum temperature to **285.314 K** in order to see the temperature variation of the shell; see figure 8.23b). Rename the cut plot to **Shell Temperature**. Right-click on the Tube Temperature Cut Plot in the Flow Simulation analysis tree and select Hide in order to display the shell temperature.

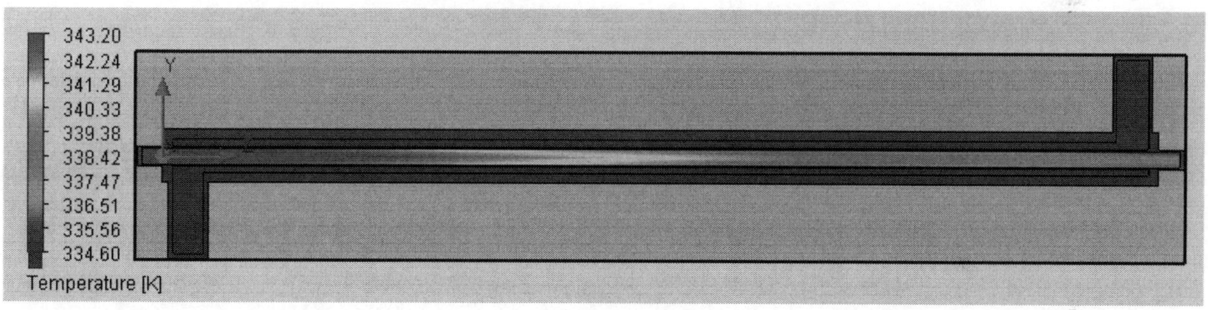

Figure 8.23a) Temperature distribution along the tube

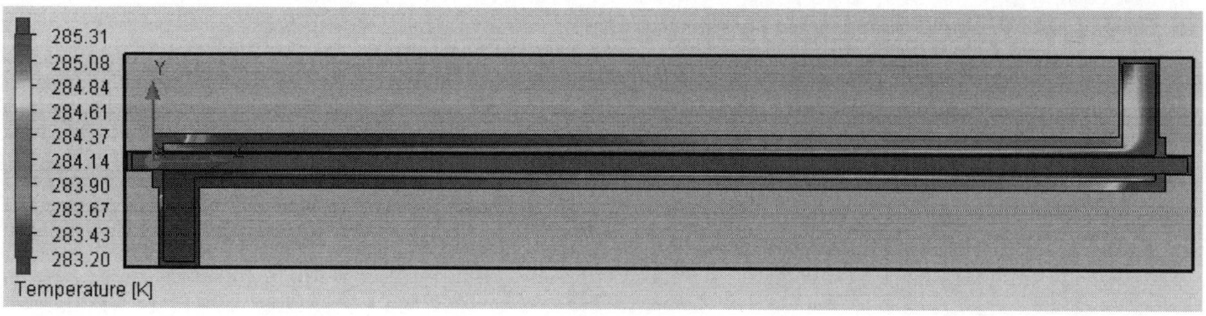

Figure 8.23b) Temperature distribution along the shell

Effectiveness – NTU Method

24. We will now use the effectiveness –NTU method for comparison of outlet temperatures with Flow Simulation results for the shell and tube heat exchanger. First, we determine the heat capacity rates of the shell and the tube fluids, respectively. The heat capacity rate of the shell C_s and tube C_t fluids are

$$C_s = \dot{m}_s C_{ps} = 0.8kg/s \cdot 4194J/(kg \cdot K) = 3355.2\ W/K \tag{8.1}$$

$$C_t = \dot{m}_t C_{pt} = 0.2kg/s \cdot 4190J/(kg \cdot K) = 838\ W/K \tag{8.2}$$

where $\dot{m}$ is the mass flow rate and C_p is the specific heat. The maximum heat transfer rate is given by

$$\dot{Q}_{max} = C_{min}(T_{max,in} - T_{min,in}) = C_t(T_{t,in} - T_{s,in}) = 838\frac{W}{K} \cdot (343.2 - 283.2)K = 50.28\ kW$$

where $T_{t,in}$ and $T_{s,in}$ are the tube and shell inflow temperatures, respectively. The heat transfer surface area is

$$A = \pi D_{it} L = \pi \cdot 0.015m \cdot 0.98m = 0.046m^2 \tag{8.3}$$

where D_{it} is the inner diameter of the tube and L is the length. The number of transfer units *NTU* is given by

$$NTU = \frac{UA}{C_{min}} \tag{8.4}$$

where U is the overall heat transfer coefficient. The mean velocities U_m in the tube is

$$U_{mt} = \frac{4\dot{m}_t}{\pi \rho_t D_{it}^2} = \frac{4 \cdot 0.2kg/s}{\pi \cdot 977.5\frac{kg}{m^3} \cdot 0.015^2 m^2} = 1.158m/s \tag{8.5}$$

where ρ_t is the density of the tube fluid. The Reynolds number Re_t for the tube flow is given by

$$Re_t = \frac{\rho_t U_{mt} D_{it}}{\mu_t} = \frac{977.5\frac{kg}{m^3} \cdot 1.158\frac{m}{s} \cdot 0.015m}{0.404 \cdot 10^{-3}\frac{kg}{m \cdot s}} = 42{,}021 \tag{8.6}$$

where μ_t is the dynamic viscosity of the tube fluid. The flow is turbulent and for smooth tubes the friction factor f can be determined from the Petukhov equation (for laminar tube flow $f = 64/Re$)

$$f = \frac{1}{(0.79 lnRe - 1.64)^2} \qquad 10^4 < Re < 10^6 \tag{8.7}$$

For the fluid in the tube the friction factor $f_t = 0.0218$. The Nusselt number *Nu* for turbulent pipe flow is a function of the friction factor, Reynolds number and Prandtl number ($Pr_t = 2.55$) according to the Gnielinski equation (for laminar smooth tube flow $Nu = 3.66$)

$$Nu = \frac{(\frac{f}{8})(Re-1000)Pr}{1+12.7\left(\frac{f}{8}\right)^{\frac{1}{2}}(Pr^{\frac{2}{3}}-1)} \qquad 3 \cdot 10^3 < Re < 5 \cdot 10^6,\ 0.5 \le Pr \le 2000 \tag{8.8}$$

For the fluid in the tube the Nusselt number $Nu_t = 181.16$. The convection heat transfer coefficient h_t for the tube flow can then be determined from

$$h_t = \frac{k_t Nu_t}{D_{it}} = \frac{0.663\frac{W}{m \cdot K} \cdot 181.16}{0.015m} = 8{,}007.13\frac{W}{m^2 \cdot K} \tag{8.9}$$

where k_t is the thermal conductivity of the tube fluid. For the shell the mean velocity

$$U_{ms} = \frac{4\dot{m}_s}{\pi \rho_s (D_{is}^2 - D_{ot}^2)} = \frac{4 \cdot 0.8kg/s}{\pi \cdot 999.7\frac{kg}{m^3} \cdot (0.032^2 m^2 - 0.019^2 m^2)} = 1.537m/s \tag{8.10}$$

where D_{is} is the inner diameter of the shell and D_{ot} is the outer diameter of the tube. The Reynolds number for the shell is given by

$$Re_s = \frac{\rho_s U_{ms}(D_{is} - D_{ot})}{\mu_s} = \frac{999.7\frac{kg}{m^3} \cdot 1.537\frac{m}{s} \cdot 0.013m}{1.307 \cdot 10^{-3}\frac{kg}{m \cdot s}} = 15{,}281 \tag{8.11}$$

This flow is also turbulent since $Re_s > 10{,}000$ and from eq. (7) we get the friction factor $f_s = 0.0280$. The Nusselt number $Nu_s = 122.57$ from eq. (8) multiplied with the Petukhov and Roizen correction factor $0.86(D_{ot}/D_{is})^{-0.16}$ for the annular shell flow using $Pr_s = 9.45$. If the flow in the annulus is laminar, the Nusselt number according to Kays and Perkins can be found for the inner surface by interpolation from Table 8.1

D_{ot}/D_{is}	Nu_s
0	---
0.05	17.46
0.10	11.56
0.25	7.37
0.50	5.74
1.00	4.86

Table 8.1 Nusselt number for fully developed laminar flow in an annulus

The convection heat transfer coefficient for the shell flow

$$h_s = \frac{k_s Nu_s}{D_{is} - D_{ot}} = \frac{0.58\frac{W}{m \cdot K} \cdot 131.09}{0.013m} = 5{,}848.74\frac{W}{m^2 \cdot K} \tag{8.12}$$

The thermal resistance R for the shell and tube heat exchanger becomes

$$R = \frac{1}{UA} = \frac{1}{\pi L}\left(\frac{1}{h_i D_{it}} + \frac{\ln\left(\frac{D_{ot}}{D_{it}}\right)}{2k_{ss}} + \frac{1}{h_o D_{ot}}\right) = 0.00817K/W \tag{8.13}$$

where $k_{ss} = 15.1\ W/(m \cdot K)$ is the thermal conductivity of stainless steel. Equation (4) can now be used to determine *NTU = 0.1426*. The capacity ratio *c* is given by

$$c = \frac{C_{min}}{C_{max}} = \frac{C_t}{C_s} = 0.25 \tag{8.14}$$

Finally, the effectiveness of a parallel-flow shell and tube heat exchanger can be determined

$$\epsilon_{parallel-flow} = \frac{1-e^{-NTU(1+c)}}{1+c} = 0.1306 \tag{8.15}$$

Using results from Flow Simulation, we get the following effectiveness

$$\epsilon = \frac{T_{max,in}-T_{max,out}}{T_{max,in}-T_{min,in}} = \frac{T_{t,in}-T_{t,out}}{T_{t,in}-T_{s,in}} = \frac{343.2K-335.852K}{343.2K-283.2K} = 0.122 \tag{8.16}$$

This is a difference of 6.2 % as compared with the effectiveness – NTU method.

Figure 8.24 is showing an effectiveness comparison between parallel-flow and counter-flow heat exchangers. We see that difference is very small for low NTU values and for low C_{min}/C_{max} values. The NTU value can be increased, for example, by increasing the length of the heat exchanger and/or decreasing the mass flow rate of the tube flow.

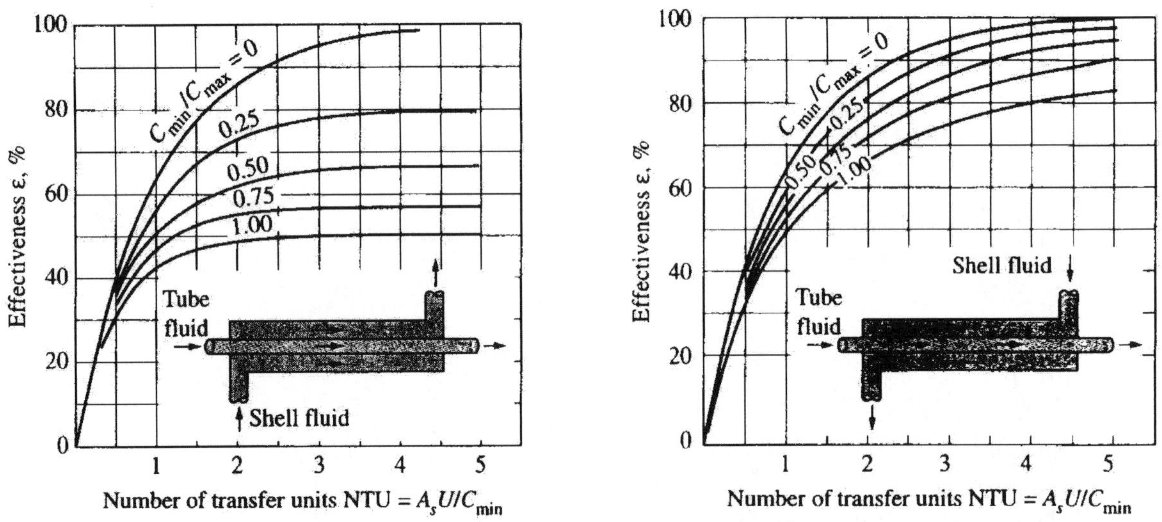

(*a*) Parallel-flow (*b*) Counter-flow

Figure 8.24 Effectiveness for parallel-flow and counter-flow heat exchangers from Cengel (2003)

References

[1] Çengel, Y. A., Heat Transfer: A Practical Approach, 2nd Edition, McGraw-Hill, 2003.

[2] SOLIDWORKS Flow Simulation 2015 Tutorial.

Exercises

8.1 Change the mesh resolution in flow simulations and see how the mesh size affects the effectiveness of the parallel-flow shell and tube heat exchanger.

8.2 Use counter-flow instead of parallel-flow for flow simulations and compare effectiveness with corresponding calculations as shown above for parallel-flow. For a counter-flow shell and tube heat exchanger the effectiveness in equation (15) is replaced by

$$\epsilon_{counter-flow} = \frac{1-e^{-NTU(1-c)}}{1-ce^{-NTU(1-c)}}$$

Discuss your results in comparison with figure 8.24. The difference in effectiveness between parallel and counter flow will be very small for this case.

8.3 Open the file Effectiveness-NTU Method for Exercise 8.3.xls. Calculations are shown related to the SOLIDWORKS model for this exercise. Open the two files SOLIDWORKS Model for Exercise 8.3 corresponding to both parallel flow and counter-flow cases. Run both cases and compare the effectiveness from SOLIDWORKS Flow Simulation results with the effectiveness-NTU method. Include cut plots of the temperature distributions for the two cases. Files can be downloaded from www.SDCpublications.com/downloads/978-1-58503-934-0.

8.4 Open the Excel file Effectiveness-NTU Method.xls. This file can be downloaded from www.SDCpublications.com/downloads/978-1-58503-934-0. Use the Excel file to design a parallel flow tube and shell heat exchanger with an effectiveness of 70%. The input data that can be varied are tube inner and outer diameter, shell inner diameter, length, tube and shell inflow temperatures, and tube and shell mass flow rates. The material that the heat exchanger is made of can also be changed. The tube and shell fluids are both water. The inflow temperatures must be in the region 273.3K $\leq T \leq$ 373.2K. Create a model of your design and determine the effectiveness using SOLIDWORKS Flow Simulation for both parallel flow and counter flow. Compare with results from the effectiveness-NTU method. Include cut plots of the temperature distributions for the two cases.

Notes:

Chapter 9 Ball Valve

Objectives

- Creating the SOLIDWORKS parts and assembly for the ball valve, housing and pipe section
- Setting up Flow Simulation projects for internal flow
- Creating lids for the assembly
- Inserting boundary conditions
- Creating surface goals
- Running the calculations
- Using cut plots to visualize the resulting flow field
- Determine hydraulic resistance for the ball valve

Problem Description

SOLIDWORKS Flow Simulation will be used to study the flow through a ball valve. The pipe has an inner diameter of 50 mm and the length of the pipe is 600 mm on each side of the ball valve. Air will be used as the fluid and the inlet velocity will be set to 10 m/s. The velocity and the pressure distribution at the ball valve will be shown and the hydraulic resistance of the valve will be determined for an opening angle of 20 degrees.

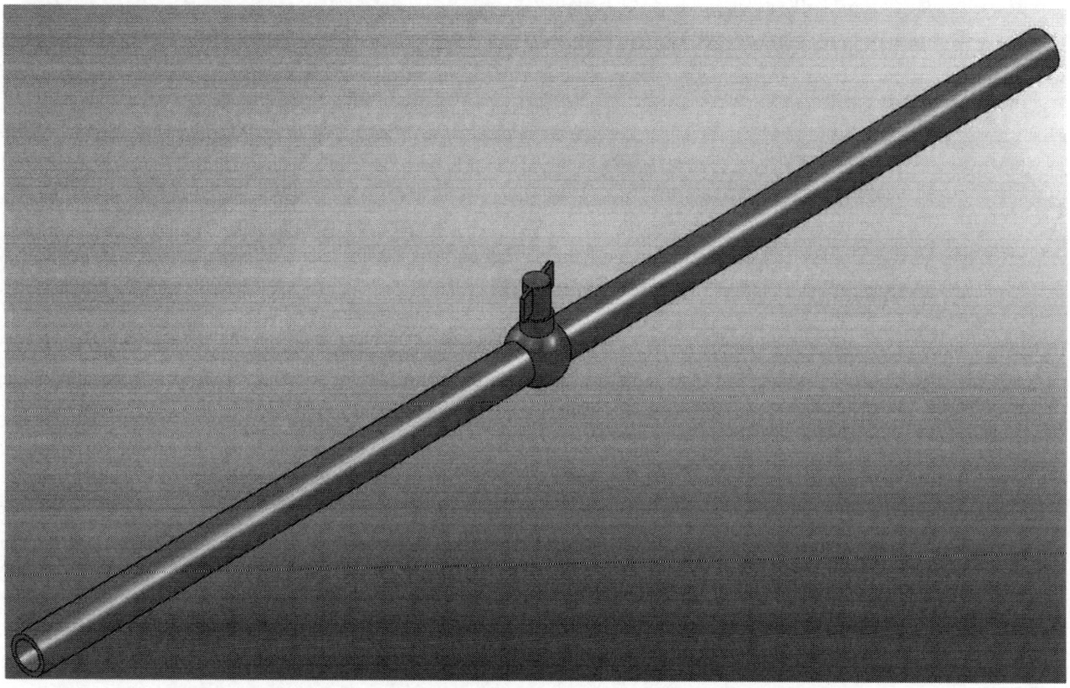

Figure 9.0 SOLIDWORKS assembly for ball valve, housing and pipe section

Creating the Ball Valve

1. Start by creating a new part in SOLIDWORKS: select **File>>New** and click on the **OK** button in the **New SOLIDWORKS Document** window. Select **Tools>>Options…** from the SOLIDWORKS menu. Click on the Document Properties tab and select **Units**. Select **MMGS** as your **Unit system**. Click on **Front Plane** in the **FeatureManager design tree** and select **Front** from the **View Orientation** drop down menu in the graphics window.

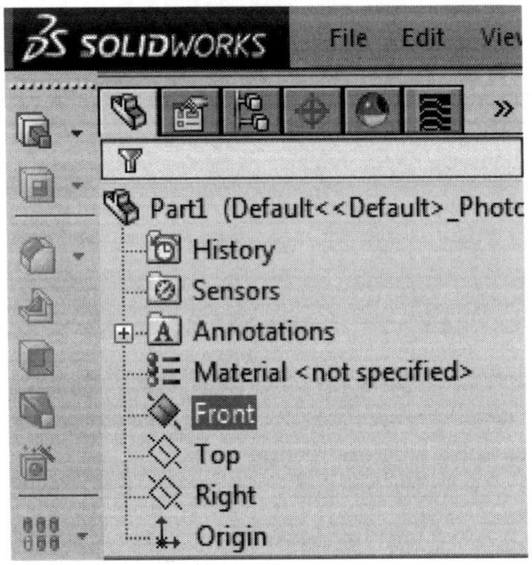

Figure 9.1a) Selection of front plane

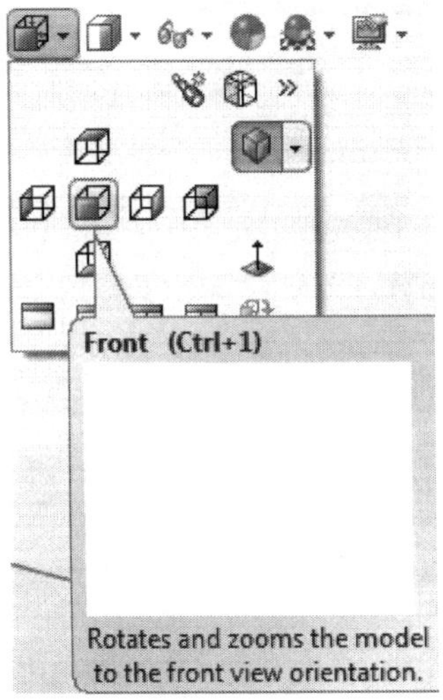

Figure 9.1b) Selection of front view

2. Click on **Centerline**. Draw a 70.00 mm long vertical centerline through the origin with Additional Parameters as shown in Fig. 9.2b). Close the **Line Properties** dialog.

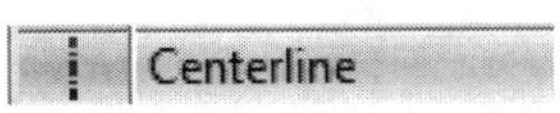

Figure 9.2a) Selecting the centerline sketch tool

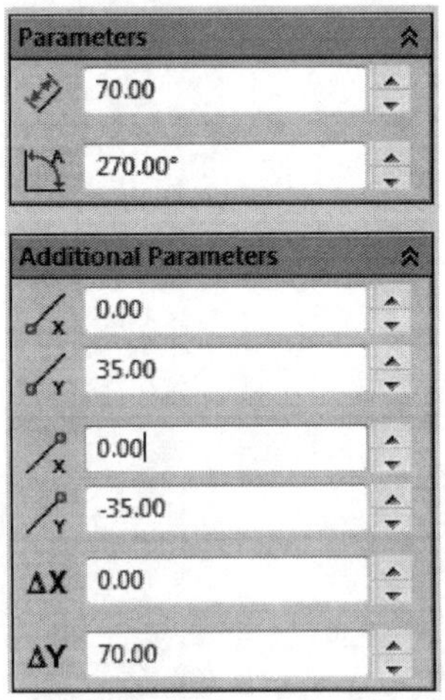

Figure 9.2b) Vertical centerline

3. Select **Centerpoint Arc**. Click at the origin in the graphics window, then click somewhere on the vertical center line above the origin and complete the half-circle by finally clicking on the vertical center line below the origin. Fill in the **Parameters** for the half-circle as shown in figure 9.3b). Close the **Arc** dialog box by clicking on .

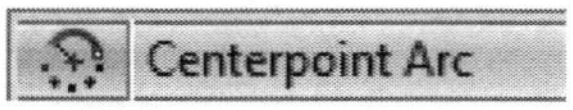

Figure 9.3a) Selecting the center point arc sketch tool

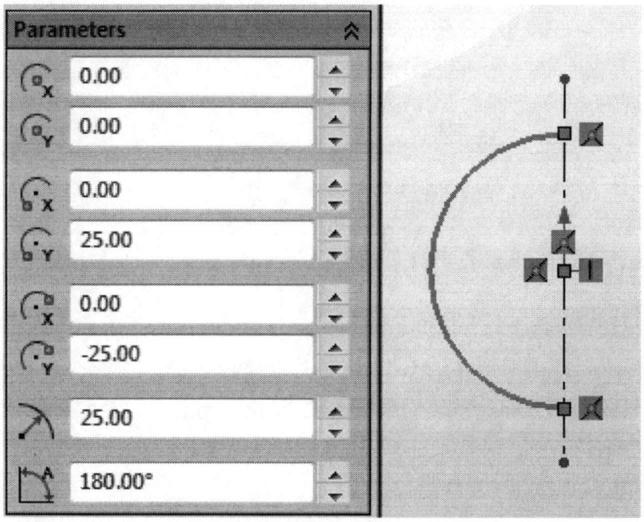

Figure 9.3b) Sketch of a half-circle

4. Select the **Revolved Boss/Base**, see figure 9.4a). Answer Yes to the question if you want the sketch to be automatically closed. Close the **Revolve** dialog box by clicking on **OK**. Right click in the graphics window and select **Zoom/Pan/Rotate>>Zoom to Fit**. Select **Front** view from **View Orientation** in the graphics window; see figure 9.1b). Select **Top Plane** from **Featuremanager design tree**. Insert a new plane from the SOLIDWORKS menu by selecting **Insert>>Reference Geometry>>Plane**. Set the **Offset Distance** to **25.00 mm** and exit the **Plane** dialog box. Select **Top** view from **View Orientation** in the graphics window; see figure 9.4e).

Figure 9.4a) Revolved boss/base feature

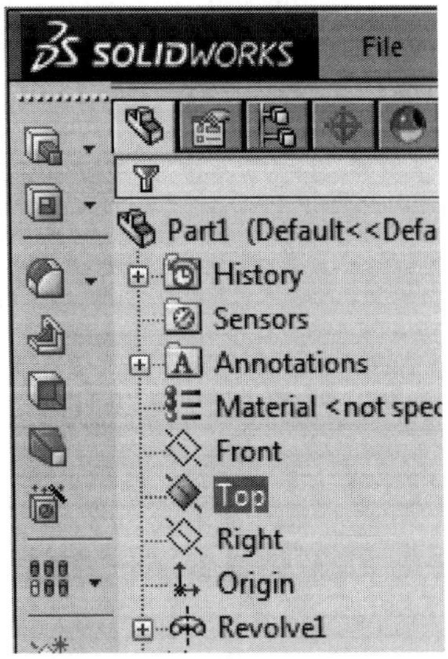

Figure 9.4b) Selecting top plane

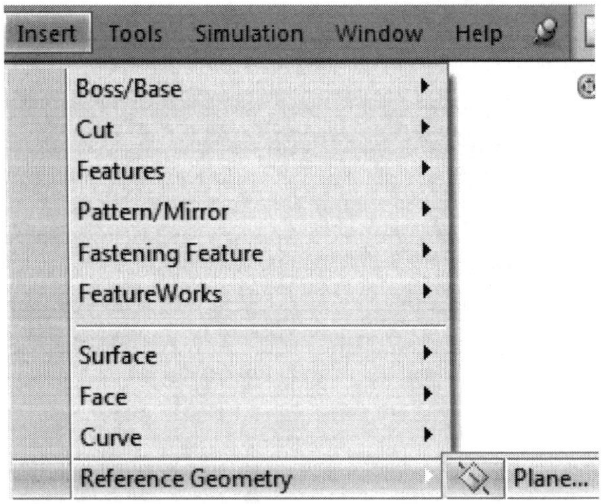

Figure 9.4c) Inserting a plane

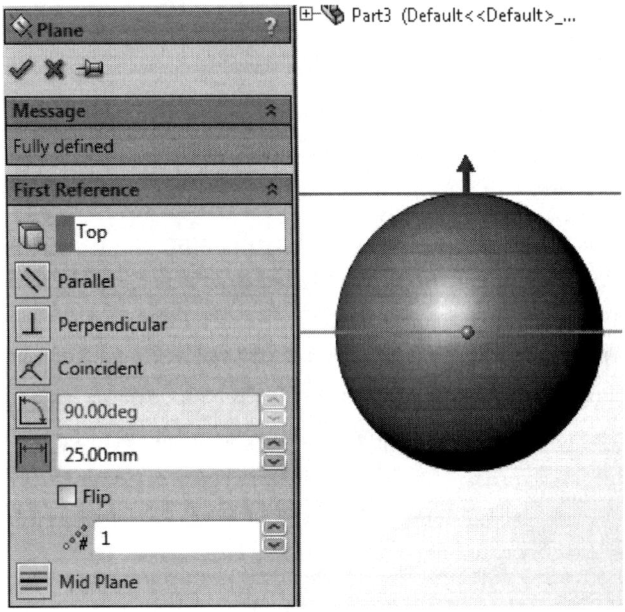

Figure 9.4d) Setting the location of the plane

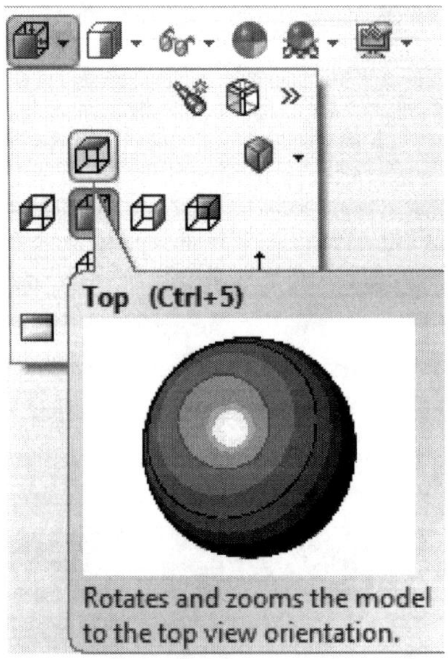

Figure 9.4e) Selecting a top view

5. Click on **Plane 1** in the **Featuremanager design tree** and select **Circle** from the **Sketch** tools. Draw a circle with the parameters as given in figure 9.5a). Close the **Circle** dialog box by clicking on **OK** . Select **Extruded Boss/Base**. Set the **Depth** of the extrusion to **50.00mm**. Check the **Direction 2** box and select **Up To Next** from the drop down menu; see figure 9.5b). Close the **Extrude** dialog box by clicking on **OK** .

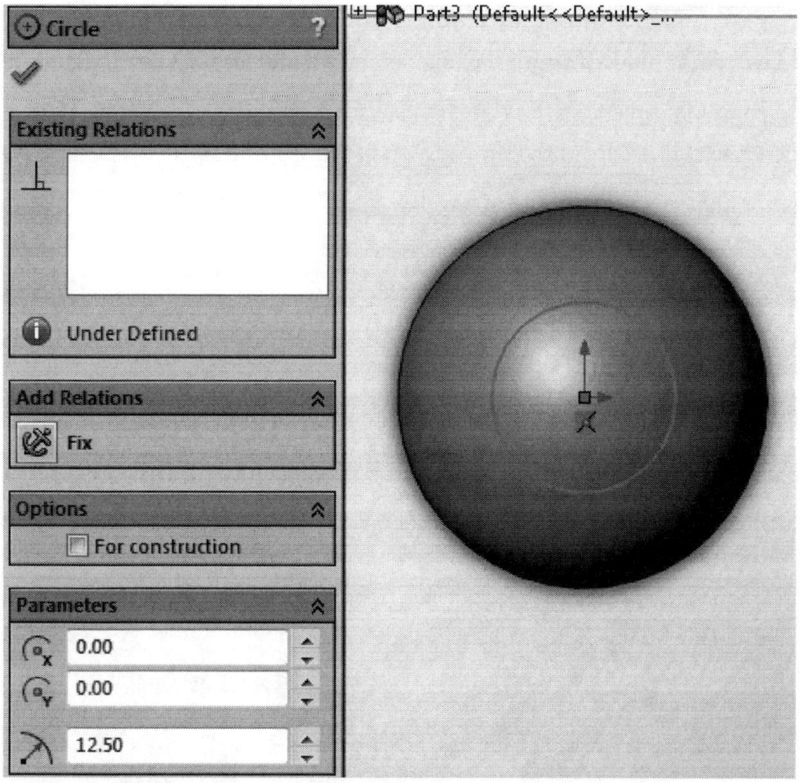

Figure 9.5a) Drawing of a circle for the extrusion

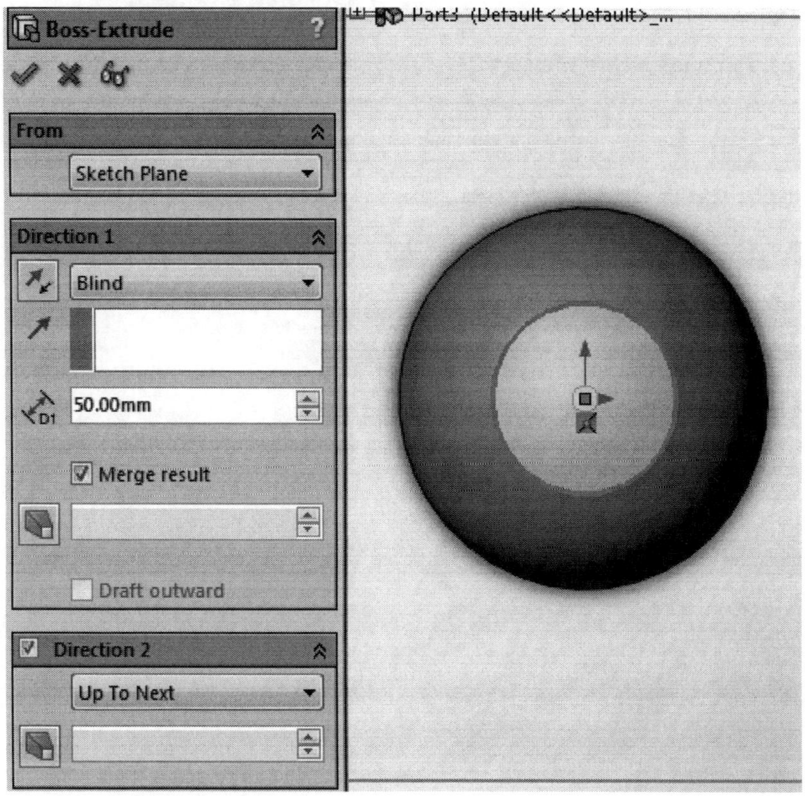

Figure 9.5b) Settings for extrusion

6. Select **Front** view from **View Orientation** in the graphics window; see figure 9.1b). Click on **Front Plane** in the **Featuremanager design tree** and select **Circle**. Draw a circle with the parameters as given in figure 9.6a). Close the **Circle** dialog box by clicking on **OK**. Select **Extruded Cut**. Select **Through All** from the drop-down menu for both directions; see figure 9.6c). Close the **Extrude** dialog box by clicking on **OK**.

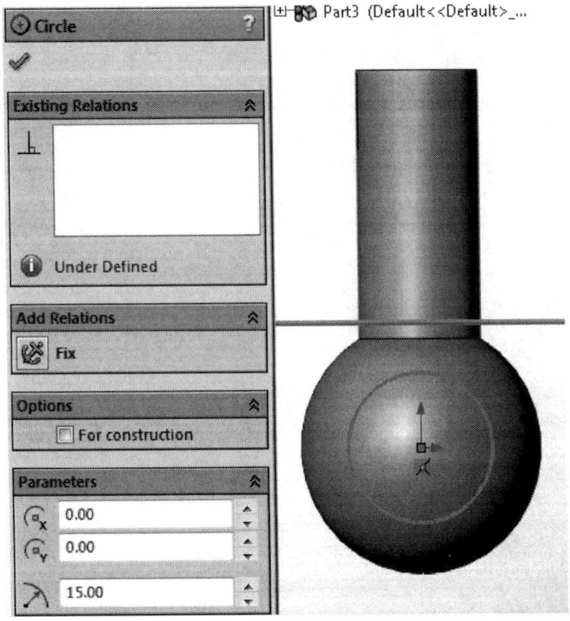

Figure 9.6a) Settings for dimensions of a circle

Figure 9.6b) Selection of extruded cut

Figure 9.6c) Settings for extruded cut

7. Click on **Front Plane** in the **Featuremanager design tree** and select **Corner Rectangle**. Draw a rectangle with the parameters as given in figure 9.7b). Close the **Rectangle** dialog box by clicking on **OK** . Select the **Extruded Boss/Base**. Set the **Depth** of the extrusion to **30.00mm** in both directions. Close the **Extrude** dialog box by clicking on **OK** . Save the part with the name "**Ball Valve 2015.**"

Figure 9.7a) Selection of corner rectangle

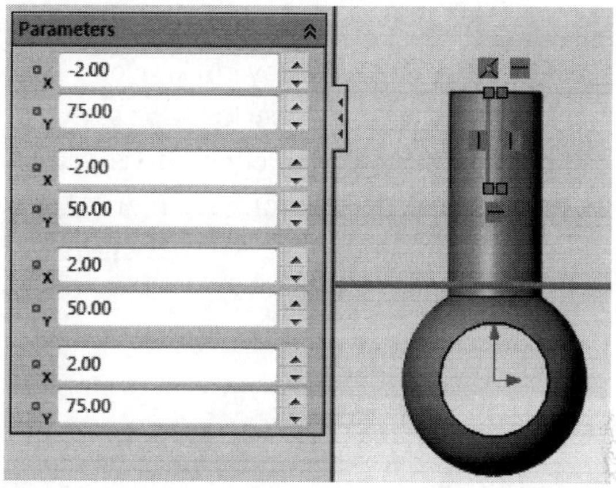

Figure 9.7b) Parameter settings for rectangle

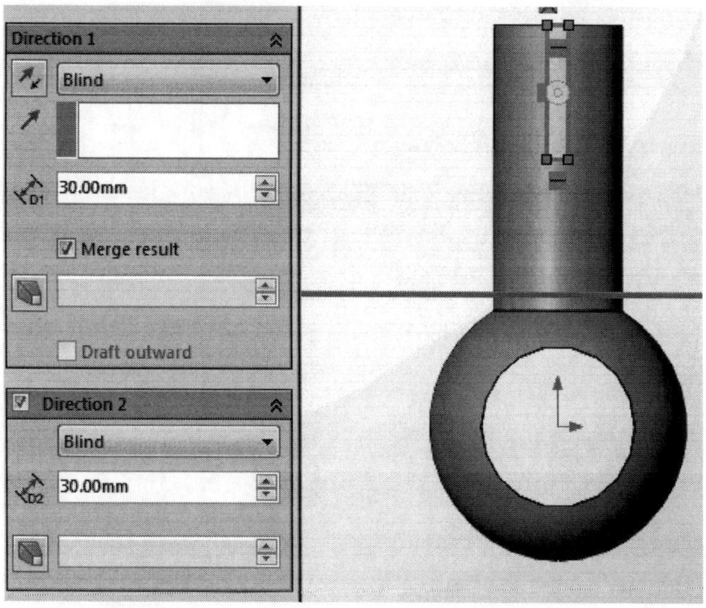

Figure 9.7c) Directions setting for extrusion

Creating the Ball Valve Housing and Pipe Sections

8. Create another part in SOLIDWORKS: select **File>>New** and click on the **OK** button in the **New SOLIDWORKS Document** window. Select **Tools>>Options...** from the SOLIDWORKS menu. Click on the Document Properties tab and select **Units**. Select **MMGS** as your **Unit system**. Click on **Front Plane** in the **FeatureManager design tree** and select **Front** from the **View Orientation** drop down menu in the graphics window; see step **1**. Repeat step **2** by

selecting the **Centerline**. Draw a 70.00 mm long vertical centerline through the origin. Close the **Line Properties** dialog box and the **Insert Line** dialog by clicking on .

Select **Centerpoint Arc**. Click at the origin in the graphics window, then click somewhere on the vertical center line below the origin and complete the arc at an angle of 150°. Set the angle to 150.00° and fill in the other **Parameters** for the arc section as shown in figure 9.8a). Close the **Arc** dialog box by clicking on . Repeat this process and create another arc section; see figure 9.8b). Next, use the **Line** sketch tool and complete the closed contour as shown in figure 9.8c). Start by completing the vertical line on the centerline. Next, draw the inner vertical line with a length of 20 mm; see figure 9.8c). Continue with the short horizontal line and close the contour with the outer vertical line. Close the **Line Properties** dialog box and the **Insert Line** dialog by clicking on .

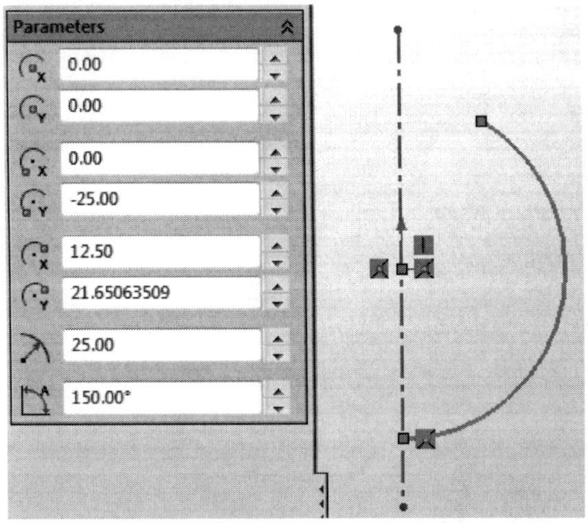

Figure 9.8a) Parameters for first arc section

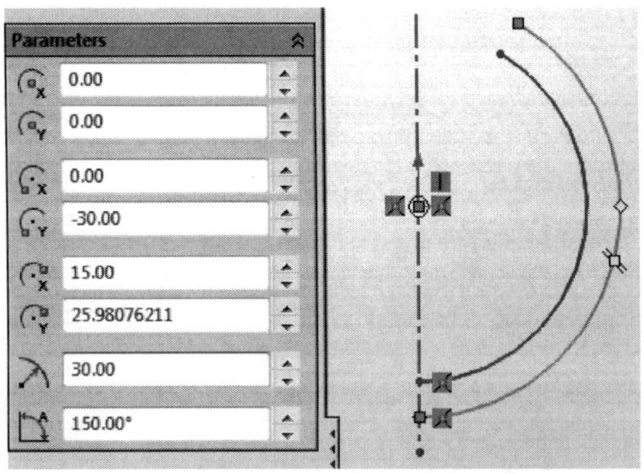

Figure 9.8b) Parameters for second arc section

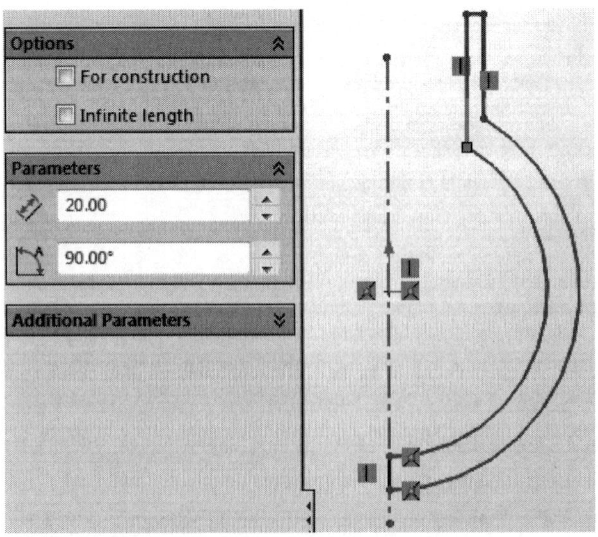

Figure 9.8c) Completed closed contour

9. Select the **Revolved Boss/Base**. Click on the vertical center line in the graphics window. Close the **Revolve** dialog box by clicking on **OK**. Right click in the graphics window and select **Zoom/Pan/Rotate>>Zoom to Fit**. Select **Front** view from **View Orientation** in the graphics window; see figure 9.1b).

Figure 9.9 Housing for the ball valve

10. Click on **Front Plane** in the **Featuremanager design tree** and select **Circle** from the **Sketch** tools. Draw a circle with **15 mm** radius; see figure 9.10a). Close the **Circle** dialog box by clicking on **OK**. Select **Extruded Cut**. Select **Through All** from the drop-down menu for both directions; see figure 9.10b). Close the **Cut-Extrude** dialog box by clicking on **OK**.

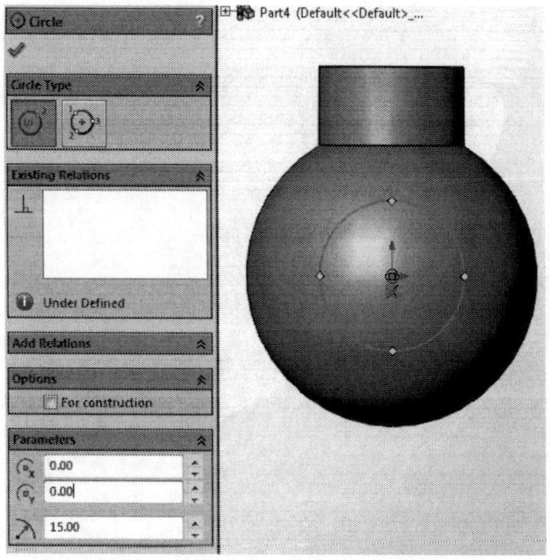

Figure 9.10a) Dimensions of the circle

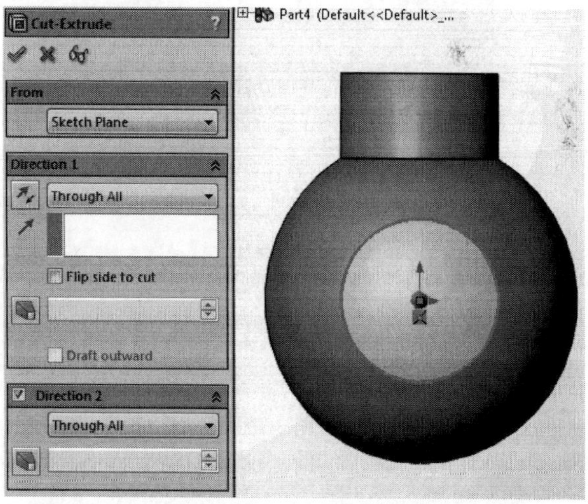

Figure 9.10b) Extrusion of ball valve housing

11. Select **Front Plane** from **Featuremanager design tree**. Insert a new plane from the SOLIDWORKS menu by selecting **Insert>>Reference Geometry>>Plane**. Set the **Offset Distance** to **30.00mm** (see figure 9.11a) and exit the **Plane** dialog box. Click on **Plane 1** in the **FeatureManager design tree** and select **Circle** from the sketch tools. Draw a circle with a radius of **15.00mm**; see figure 9.11b). Close the **Circle** dialog box by clicking on **OK**. Select the **Extruded Boss/Base**. Set the **Depth D1** for the extrusion in **Direction 1** to **600.00mm**. Check the **Direction 2** box and select **Up To Next** from the drop down menu. Check the **Thin Feature** box

and set the thickness **T1** to **5.00mm**; see figure 9.11c). Close the **Extrude** dialog box by clicking on **OK** ✔.

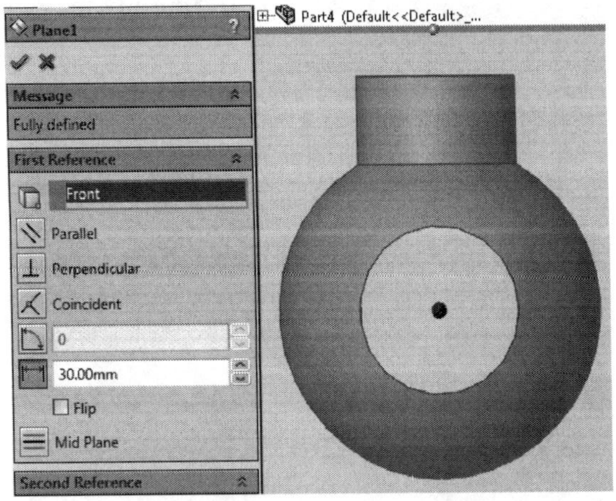

Figure 9.11a) Setting the location of the new plane

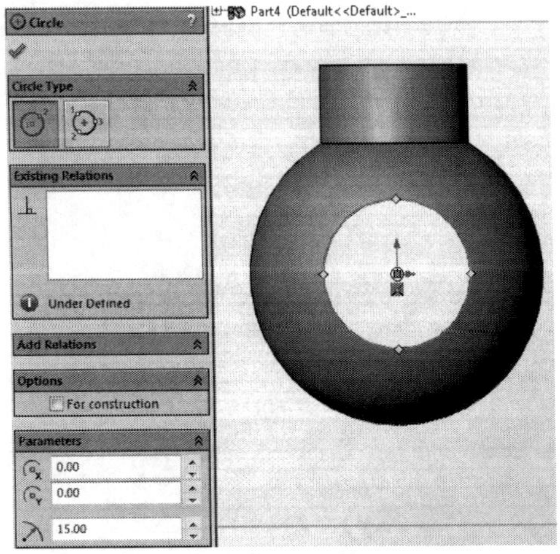

Figure 9.11b) Drawing of a circle

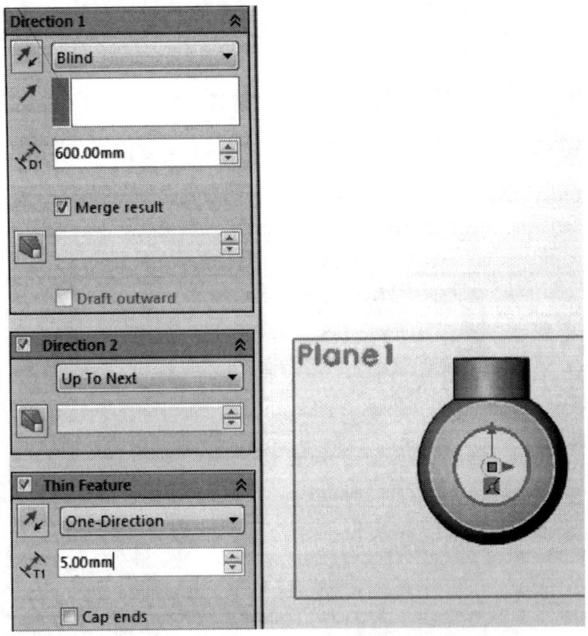

Figure 9.11c) Settings for the pipe extrusion

12. Repeat step **11** by selecting **Front Plane** from **Featuremanager design tree**. Insert a new plane from the SOLIDWORKS menu by selecting **Insert>>Reference Geometry>>Plane**. Set the **Offset Distance** to **30.00mm** and check the **Flip offset** box—see figure 9.12a), and exit the **Plane** dialog box. Click on **Plane 2** in the **FeatureManager design tree** and select **Circle** from the **Sketch** tools. Draw a circle with a radius of **15.00mm**. Close the **Circle** dialog box by clicking on **OK** ✔. Select the **Extruded Boss/Base**. Click on the **Reverse Direction** button for **Direction 1**. Check the **Thin Feature** box and set the thickness **T1** to **5.00mm**. Check the

Direction 2 box and select **Up To Next** from the drop down menu; see figure 9.12b). Close the **Extrude** dialog box by clicking on **OK** .

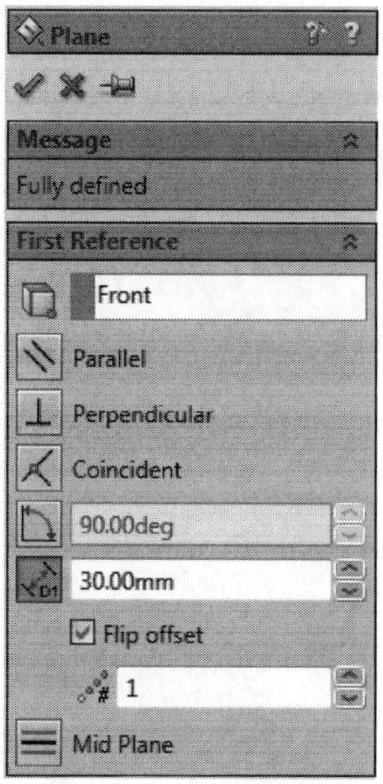

Figure 9.12a) Settings for plane

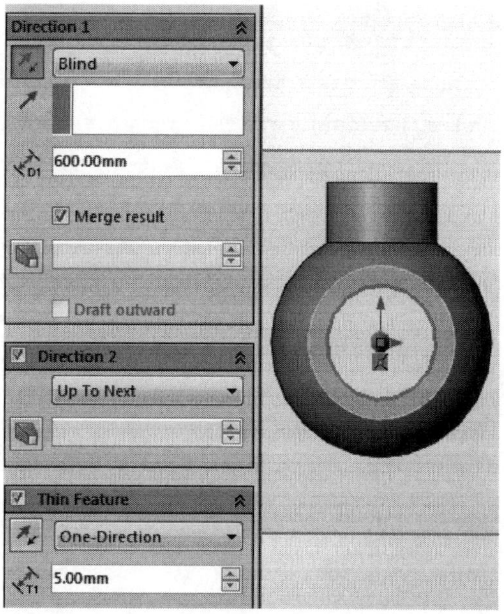

Figure 9.12b) Settings for the pipe extrusion

13. Select **Left** view from **View Orientation** in the graphics window. Right click in the graphics window and select **Zoom/Pan/Rotate>>Zoom to Fit**. Hide the two planes and save the part with the name "**Ball Valve Housing and Pipe Sections 2015**."

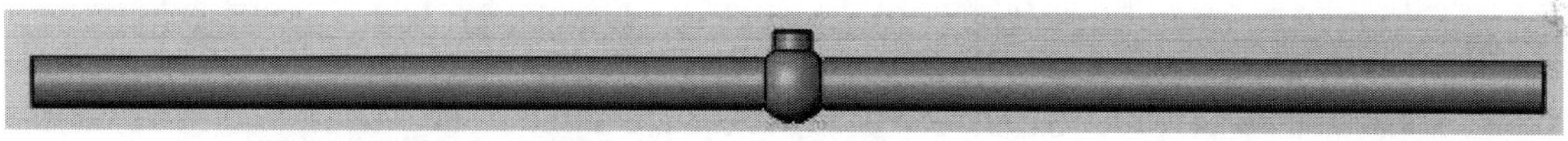

Figure 9.13 Finished ball valve housing and pipe sections

Creating the Ball Valve and Pipe Assembly

14. Create a new assembly in SOLIDWORKS: select **File>>New** and click on the **Assembly** button followed by the **OK** button in the **New SOLIDWORKS Document** window; see figure 9.14a). Click on **Front Plane** in the **FeatureManager design tree** and select **Front** from the **View Orientation** drop down menu in the graphics window. Select the **Browse...** button in the **Begin Assembly** window and open the **Ball Valve Housing and Pipe Sections 2015** part. Click in the graphics window. Select **Isometric** view from **View Orientation** in the graphics window. Select **Insert>>Component>>Existing Part/Assembly...** from the SOLIDWORKS menu. Select the **Browse...** button in the **Insert Component** window and open the **Ball Valve 2015** part. Click in the graphics window above the other part. Select **Insert>>Mate...** from the SOLIDWORKS menu. Click on the cylindrical face of the ball valve and the inner cylindrical face of the ball valve housing. Select the **Concentric** standard mate and exit the **Concentric 1** window. Exit the **Mate** window.

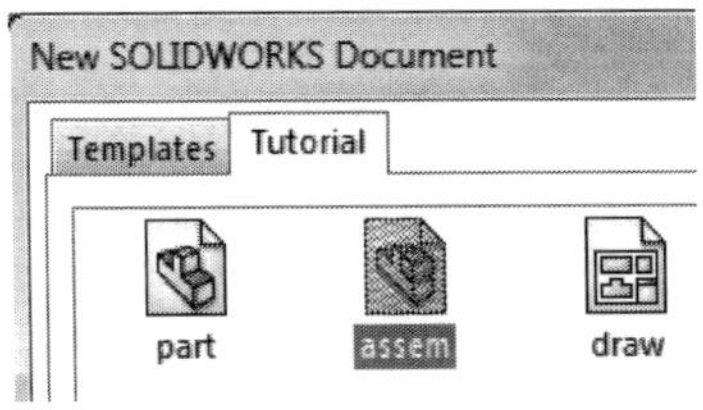

Figure 9.14a) Creating a new assembly

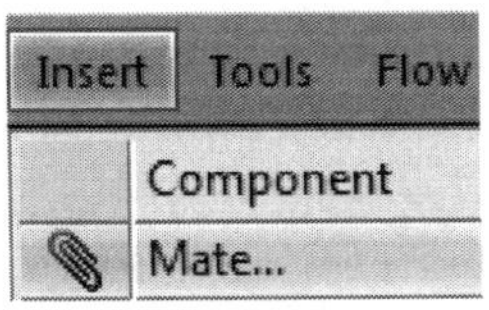

Figure 9.14b) Inserting a mate

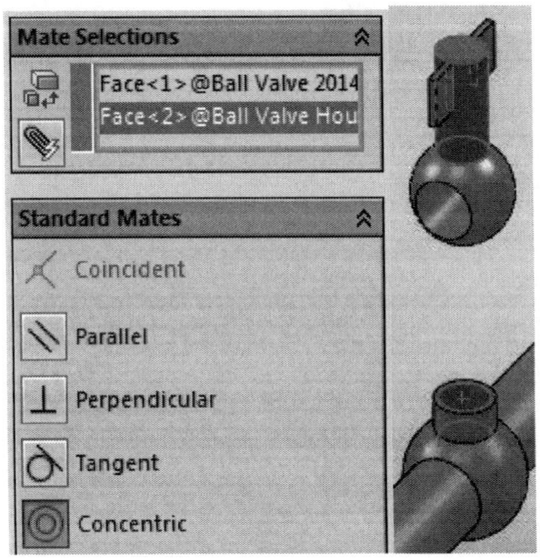

Figure 9.14c) Creating a concentric mate

15. Select **Insert>>Mate…** from the SOLIDWORKS menu. Right click in the **Mate Selections** portion of the **Mate** window and select **Clear Selections**. Select the spherical face of the ball valve and the inner spherical face of the ball valve housing by right clicking on the outer face of the housing and selecting **Select Other**; see figure 9.15a). Select the inner spherical face of the housing, select the **Concentric** standard mate and exit the **Concentric2** window. Exit the **Mate** window. You should now have figure 9.15b) in your graphics window.

Figure 9.15a) Selecting the valve housing

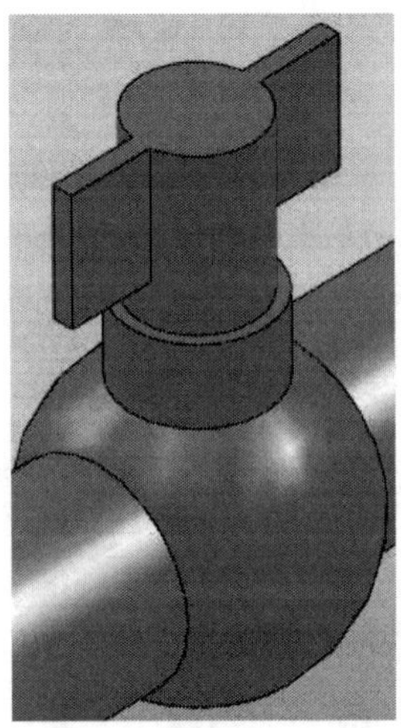

Figure 9.15b) Ball valve and housing

16. Select **Insert>>Mate…** from the SOLIDWORKS menu. Select the **Front Plane** from the ball valve housing on the fly-out assembly and also select the corresponding **Front Plane** from the ball valve. Select the  **Angle** button from **Standard Mates** and enter **20.00 deg**. Exit both the angle window and the mate window.

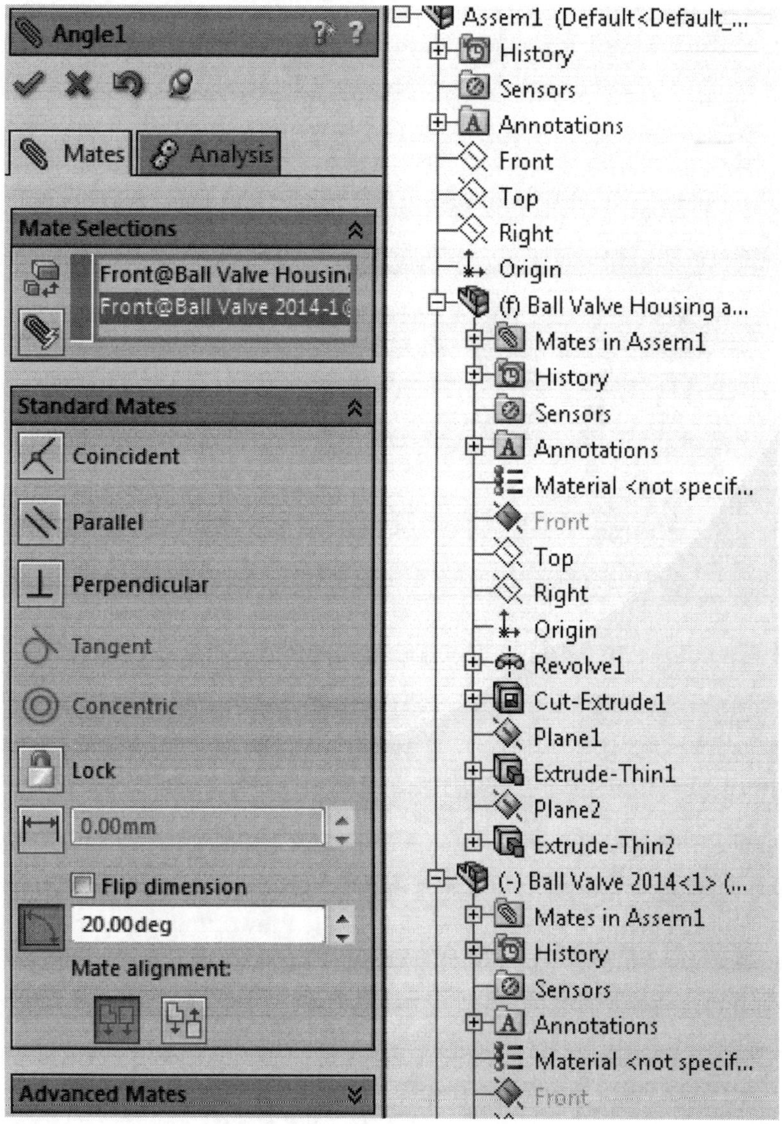

Figure 9.16) Settings for angle mate

17. Select **Front** view from **View Orientation** in the graphics window. You have now finished the ball valve assembly and in figure 9.17 you can see the partially open ball valve. Save the assembly with the name "**Ball Valve and Pipe Assembly 2015**."

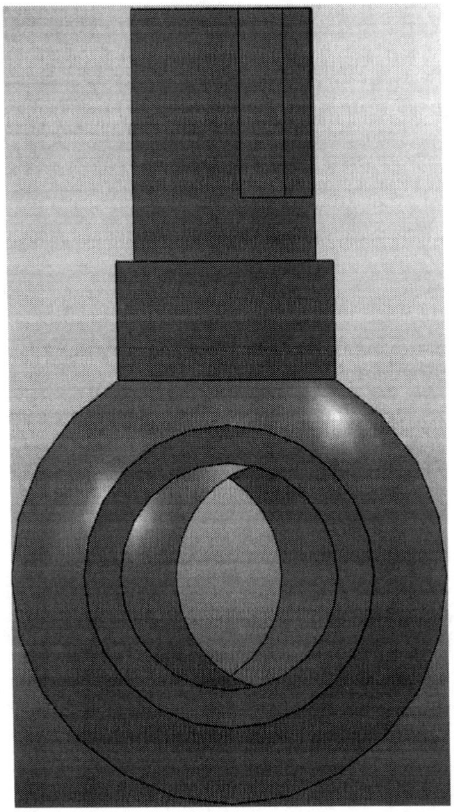

Figure 9.17 Ball valve assembly with partially open valve

Setting up the Flow Simulation Project for the Ball Valve

18. If Flow Simulation is not available in the menu, you have to add it from SOLIDWORKS menu: **Tools>>Add Ins…** and check the corresponding **SOLIDWORKS Flow Simulation** box. Select **Tools>>Flow Simulation>>Project>>Wizard** to create a new Flow Simulation project. Create a new project named "**Ball Valve Study**." Click on the **Next** > button. Select the default **SI (m-kg-s)** unit system and click on the **Next>** button once again. Use the default **Internal Analysis type**. Click on the **Next** > button.

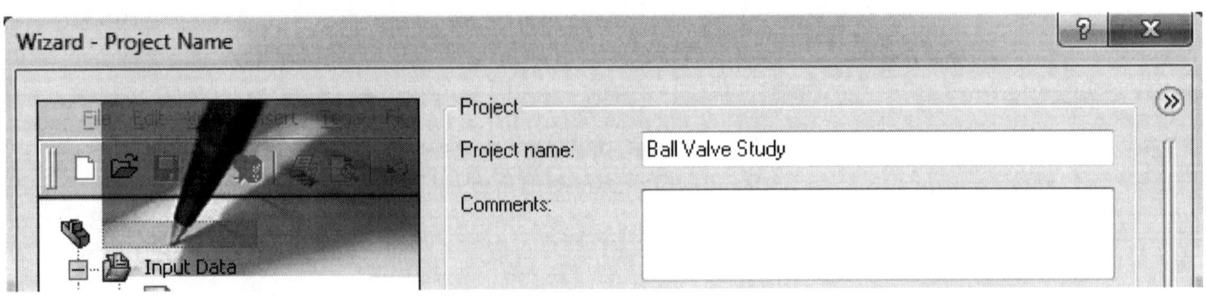

Figure 9.18 Creating a name for the project

19. Add **Air** from **Gases** as the **Project Fluid**. Click on the **Next** > button. Use the default **Wall Conditions**. Click on the **Next** > button. Use the default **Initial Conditions**. Click on the **Next** > button. Set the **Result resolution** to **6**. Click on the **Finish** button. Answer Yes to the question whether you want to open the Create Lids tool.

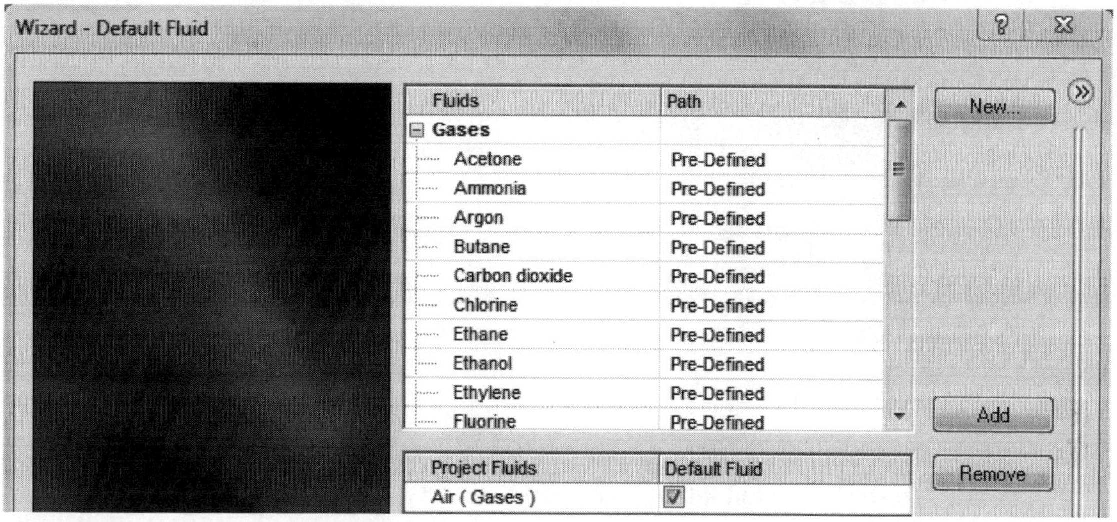

Figure 9.19a) Adding air as the project fluid

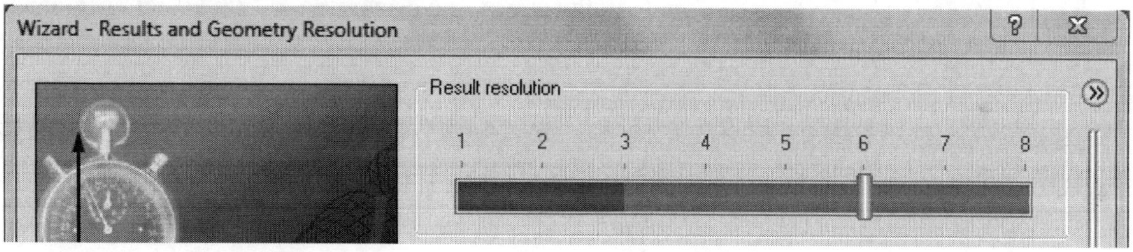

Figure 9.19b) Setting result resolution

Creating Lids and Setting the Minimum Gap Size and Number of Cells

20. Select **Front** view from **View Orientation** in the graphics window. Select the face as shown in figure 9.20. Close the **Create Lids** dialog box by clicking on **OK** . Answer yes to the questions. Select **Back** view from **View Orientation** in the graphics window. Select the similar face as described above and close the **Create Lids** dialog box by clicking on **OK** . Answer yes to the questions if you want to reset the computational domain and the mesh setting.

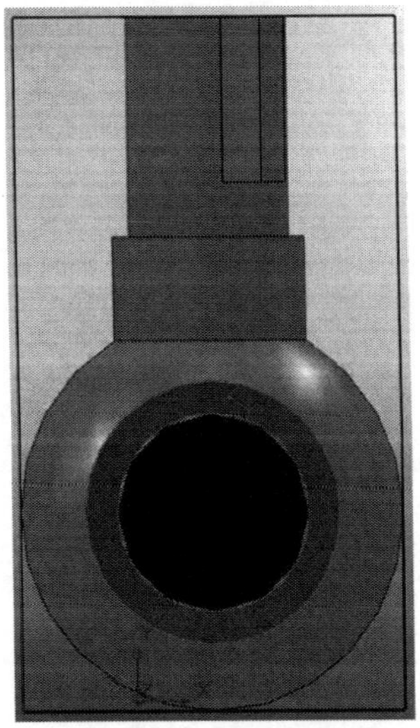

Figure 9.20 Selection of surface for lid

Select **Tools>>Flow Simulation>>Initial Mesh….** Check the box for **Manual specification of the minimum gap size**. Enter the value **0.022255 m** for **Minimum gap size**. This is the size *d* of the opening as shown in figure 9.17 for a valve angle of 20 degrees. The size of the opening can be determined from the valve angle θ, the closed valve angle $\theta_c = 73.74°$ and the diameter of the ball $D_b = 50\ mm$.

$$d = \sqrt{D_b^2 Sin^2\left(\frac{\theta_c-\theta}{2}\right) - \frac{D_b^2}{4}(Cos\left(\frac{\theta_c}{2}-\theta\right) - Cos\left(\frac{\theta_c}{2}\right))^2} \quad (9.1)$$

where $\theta_c = 2Sin^{-1}(D_p/D_b)$ and D_p = 30 mm is the inner diameter of the pipe section.

Uncheck the box for **Automatic settings** at the bottom of the **Initial Mesh** window. Set the **Number of cells per X:** to **8**, the **Number of cells per Y:** to **6** and the **Number of cells per Z:** to **236**. Click on the OK button to exit the window.

Inserting Boundary Conditions

21. Select **Left** view from **View Orientation** in the graphics window. Right-click in the graphics window and select **Zoom/Pan/Rotate>>Zoom to Area**. Zoom in on the left end of the pipe, right click in the graphics window and select **Zoom/Pan/Rotate>>Rotate View**. Rotate the view a little bit; see figure 9.21. Click on the plus sign next to the **Input Data** folder in the **Flow Simulation analysis tree**. Right click on **Boundary Conditions** and select **Insert Boundary Condition….** Right click on the end section of the pipe and select **Select Other**. Select the inner surface of the lid; see figure 9.21. Select **Inlet Velocity** in the **Type** portion of the boundary condition window. Set the inlet velocity to **10 m/s**. Click OK to exit the **Boundary Condition** window.

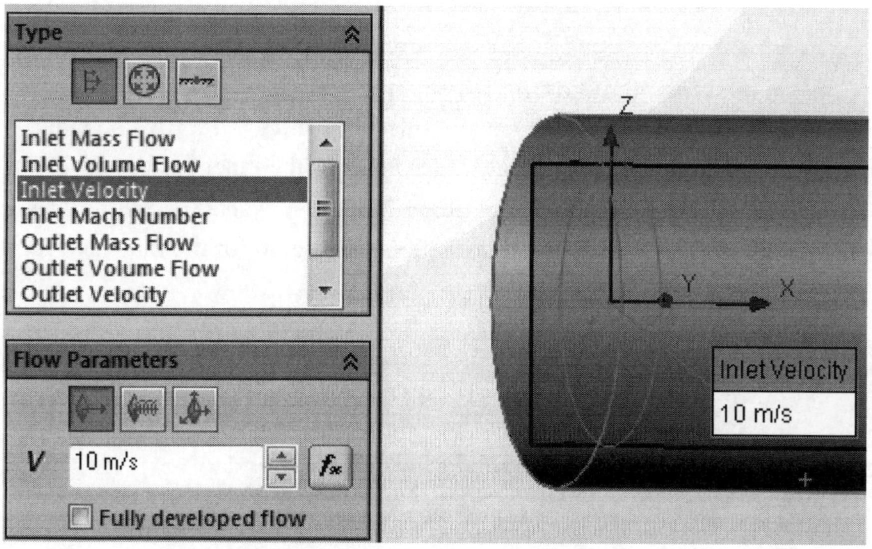

Figure 9.21 Selection of inflow boundary condition

22. Select **Left** view from **View Orientation** in the graphics window. Select **Zoom/Pan/Rotate>>Zoom to Area** and zoom in on the right end of the pipe, right click in the graphics window and select **Zoom/Pan/Rotate>>Rotate View**. Rotate the view a little bit. Right click on **Boundary Conditions** and select **Insert Boundary Condition…**. Right click on the pipe and select the inner surface of the pipe outflow lid; see figure 9.22. Select **Pressure Openings** in the **Type** portion of the **Boundary Condition** window. Select **Static Pressure**. Click OK to exit the **Boundary Condition** window.

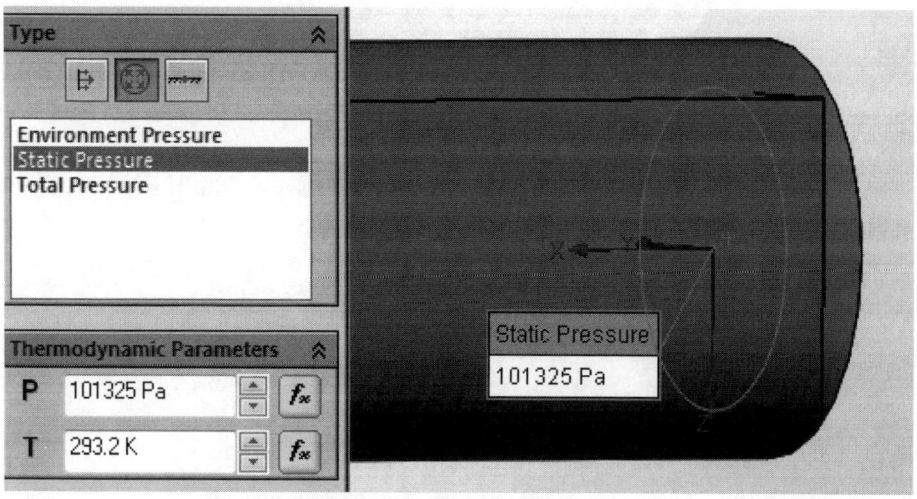

Figure 9.22 Selection of outflow boundary condition

Inserting Goals

23. Right click on **Goals** in the **Flow Simulation analysis tree** and select **Insert Surface Goals…**. Click on the **Flow Simulation analysis tree** tab and select the **Inlet Velocity 1** boundary condition. Select **Average Total Pressure** as a surface goal for the inner surface of the inflow lid. Click OK ✓ to exit the **Surface Goals** window. Repeat this step, select the **Static Pressure 1** boundary condition and insert an average total pressure surface goal for the inner surface of the outflow lid.

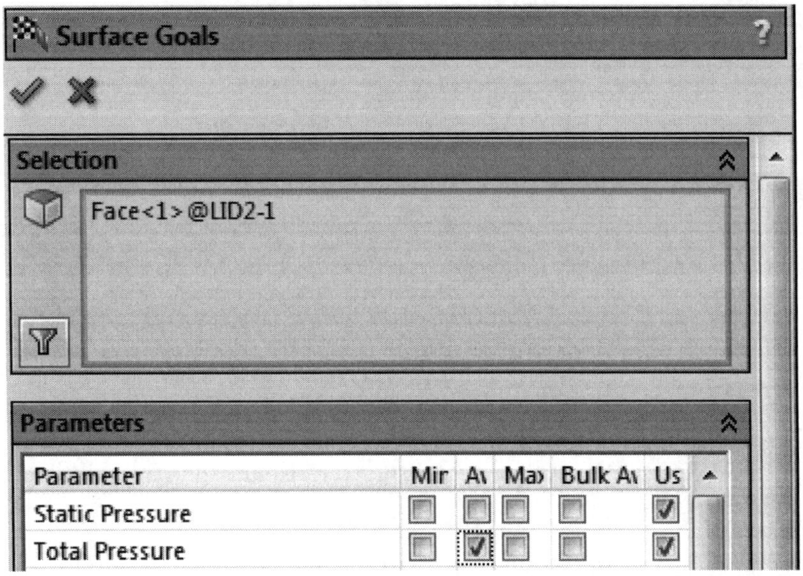

Figure 9.23 Selection of surface goal

Running the Calculations for Ball Valve

24. Select **Tools>>Flow Simulation>> Calculation Control Options…** from the SOLIDWORKS menu, click on the **Refinement** tab and disable the refinement from the **Value** drop down menu. Click on the **OK** button to exit the window. Select **Tools>>Flow Simulation>>Solve>>Run** to start calculations. Click on the **Run** button in the **Run** window.

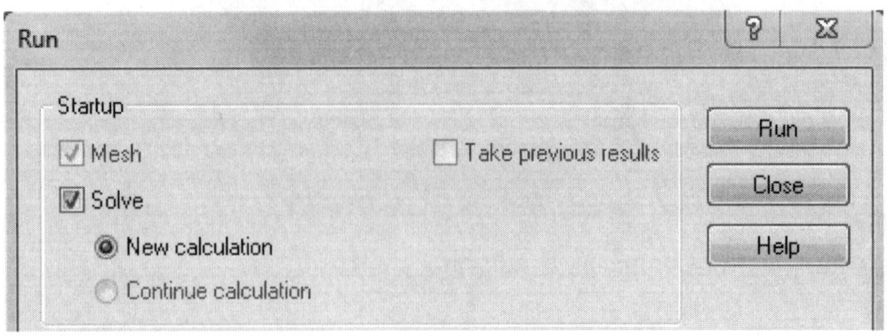

Figure 9.24a) Run window

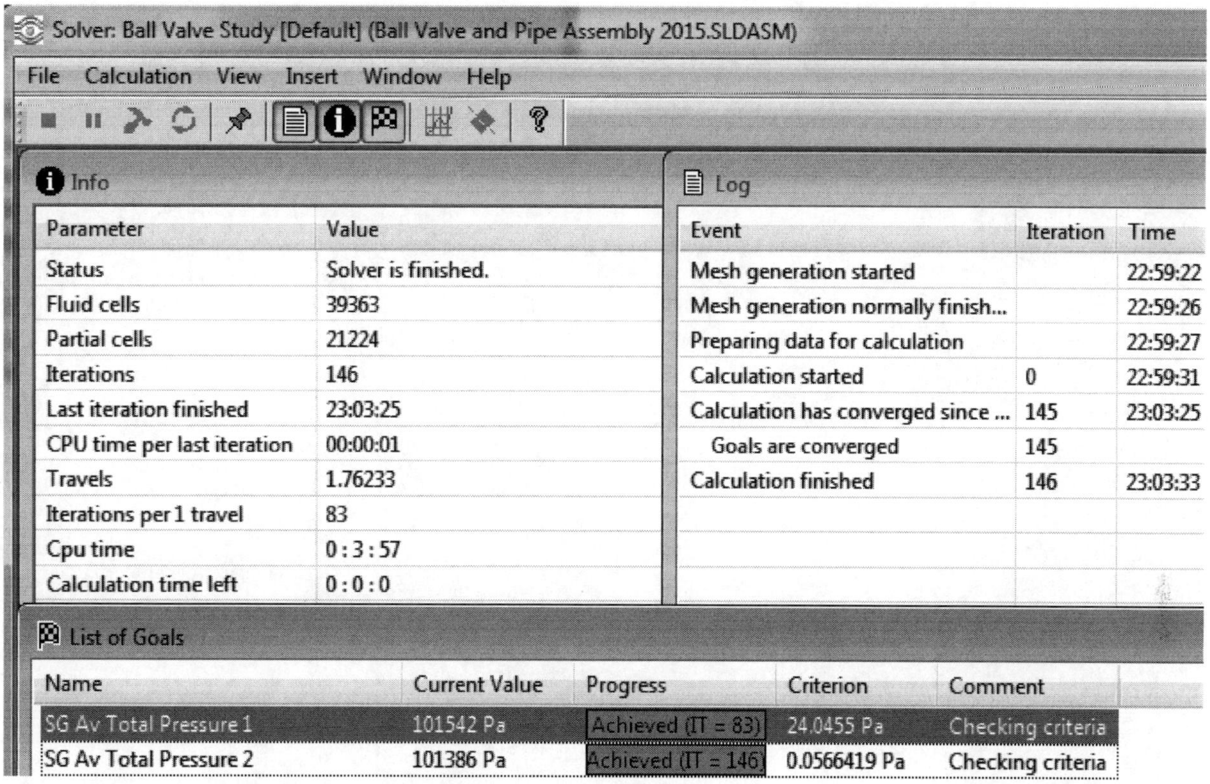

Figure 9.24b) Solver window, valve angle θ = 20 deg

Inserting Cut Plots

25. Right click on **Cut Plots** in the **Flow Simulation analysis tree** and select **Insert….** Select the **Top Plane** from the **FeatureManager design tree** for the **Ball Valve and Pipe Assembly 2015**. Click on the **Vectors** button in the **Display** portion of the **Cut Plot** window. Slide the **Number of Levels** slide bar to **255** in the **Contours** section. Select **Velocity** from the **Parameter** drop down menu. Exit the **Cut Plot** window. Rename the cut plot to **Velocity for Valve Angle = 20 deg**. Select **Tools>>Flow Simulation>>Results>>Display>>Geometry** to display the cut plot. Select **Top** view from **View Orientation** in the graphics window. We see the velocity distribution in figure 9.25a). Repeat this step but select **Pressure** instead of **Velocity**; see figure 9.25b). Rename the cut plot to **Pressure for valve angle = 20 deg**. Right-click on the velocity cut plot in the Flow Simulation analysis tree and select hide to display the pressure cut plot.

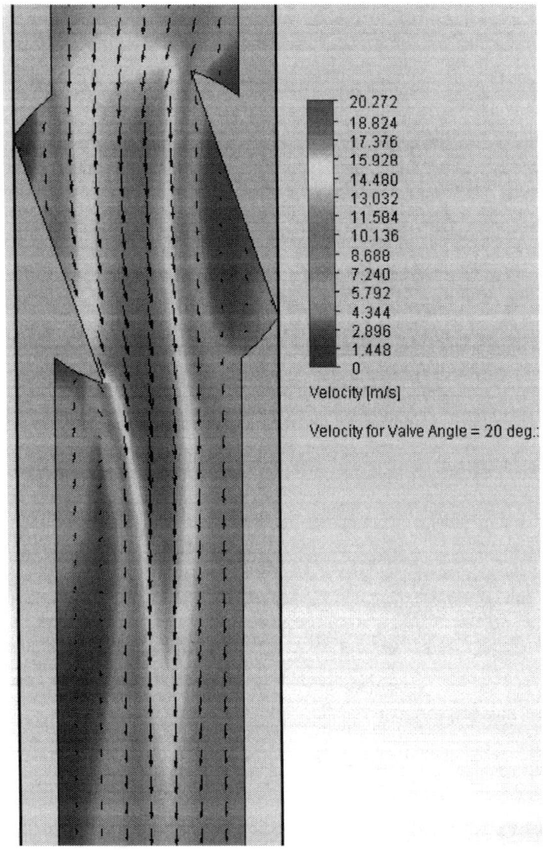

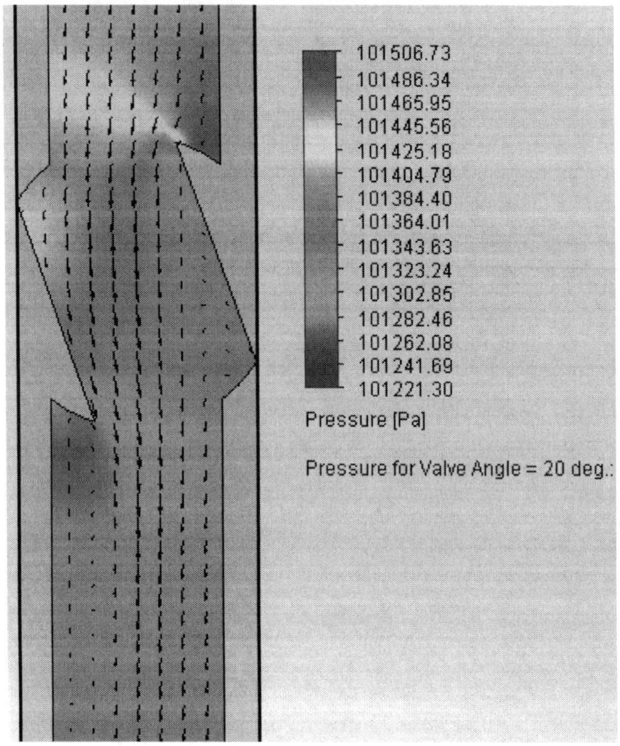

Figure 9.25a) Ball valve velocity distribution

Figure 9.25b) Ball valve pressure distribution

Determining Hydraulic Resistance

26. In the next step we want to determine the hydraulic resistance of the ball valve. In order to do this, we first have to determine the total pressure drop without the valve. Click on the plus sign next to **Mates** in the **Featuremanager Design Tree**. Right click on **Angle1** and select **Edit Feature** and set the angle θ to **0.00deg**. Exit the **Angle1** and **Mate** windows. Answer yes to the question if you want to reset the computational domain. Select **Tools>>Flow Simulation>>Initial Mesh…**. Check the box for **Automatic settings** at the bottom of the **Initial Mesh** window. Check the box for **Manual specification of the minimum gap size**. Enter the value **0.03 m** for **Minimum gap size**. This value is the inside diameter of the pipe. Click on the **OK** button to exit the **Initial Mesh** window. Select **Tools>>Flow Simulation>>Initial Mesh…** and uncheck the **Automatic settings** box. Set the **Number of cells per X** to **6**, **Number of cells per Y** to **6** and **Number of cells per Z** to **240**. Click on the **OK** button to exit.

Select **Tools>>Flow Simulation>>Solve>>Run** to start calculations. Click on the **Run** button in the **Run** window. Repeat step **25** and create a cut plot with the velocity distribution for the ball valve for zero valve angle θ; see figure 9.26c).

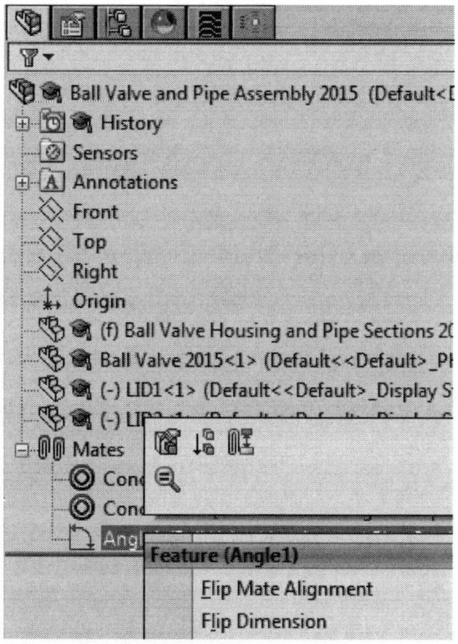

Figure 9.26a) Changing the angle of the ball valve

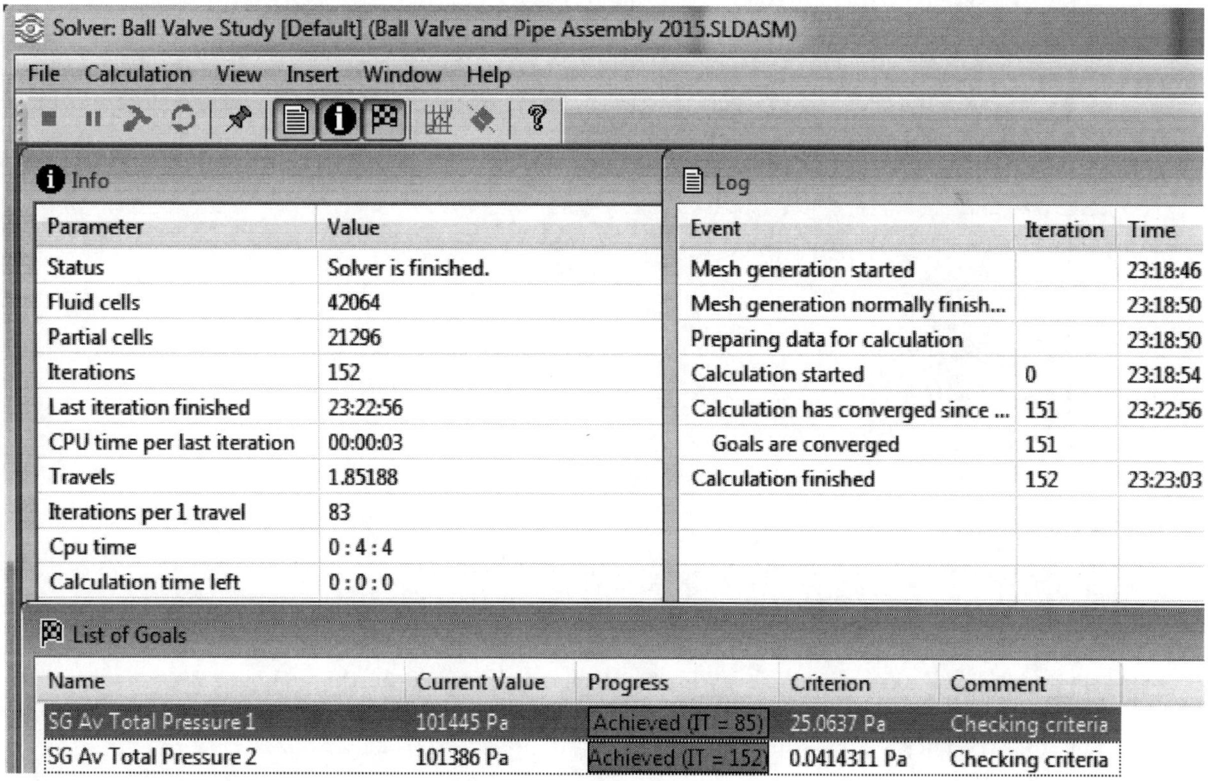

Figure 9.26b) Solver window, valve angle $\theta = 0$ deg

From figure 9.26b) in the list of goals, we see that the total pressure difference between inlet and outlet based on current values is 101,445 Pa – 101,386 Pa = 59 Pa. This value has to be subtracted from the pressure difference value that we determine from figure 9.24c). The final total pressure difference over the valve is 97 Pa for a 20 deg valve angle. We can now determine the hydraulic resistance ξ of the valve to be

$$\xi = \frac{2\Delta P}{\rho U^2} = \frac{2 \cdot 97\text{Pa}}{1.204\frac{kg}{m^3} \cdot 10^2 m^2/s^2} = 1.61 \quad (9.2)$$

where ρ is the density of air, ΔP is the difference in total pressure over the valve and U is the average velocity in the pipe.

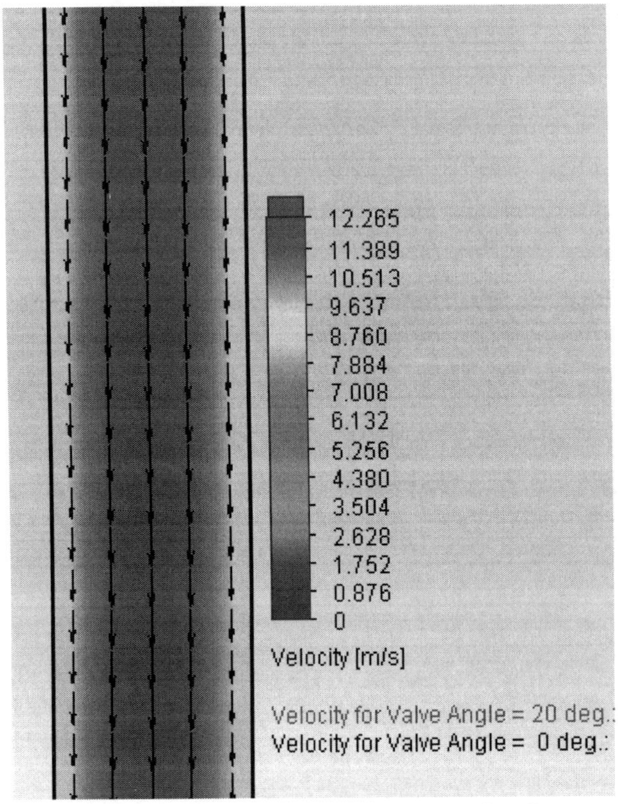

Figure 9.26c) Ball valve velocity distribution for zero valve angle

References

[1] Idelchik, I.E., Handbook for Hydraulic Resistance, Jaico Publishing House, 2005.

[2] SOLIDWORKS Flow Simulation 2015 Tutorial.

Exercises

9.1 Change the mesh resolution in the flow simulations and study how the mesh size affects the velocity and pressure distributions and the hydraulic resistance.

9.2 Set the angle θ of the ball valve to different values (0°, 10°, 20°, 30°, 40°, 50°) and compare the results with those shown in this chapter. Determine and plot the variation in hydraulic resistance with ball valve angle θ; see table below. Remember to change the minimum gap size for different ball valve angles. Use the same result resolution (6) for all calculations. Include copies of solver windows and velocity and pressure plots for each angle. Discuss results and determine the exponential equation for the variation of the hydraulic resistance with ball valve angle.

***θ* (deg.)**	***d* (m)**	***No of cells per X***	***No of cells per Y***	***No of cells per Z***	ξ
5	0.03	6	6	240	
10	0.0263	6	6	236	
20	0.022255	8	6	236	1.56
30	0.01799	8	6	236	
40	0.013635	8	6	236	
45	0.009321	8	6	236	

Table 9.1 Data for exercise 9.2

Notes:

Chapter 10 Orifice Plate and Flow Nozzle

Objectives

- Creating the SOLIDWORKS part for the orifice plate
- Setting up Flow Simulation projects for internal flow
- Inserting boundary conditions
- Creating point goals
- Running the calculations
- Using cut plots, XY plots and flow trajectories to visualize the resulting flow fields
- Determine discharge coefficients for orifice plate and flow nozzle

Problem Description

We will use Flow Simulation to study the flow through an orifice plate and a long radius flow nozzle. Obstruction flow meters are commonly in use to measure flow rates in pipes. Both the orifice and nozzle are modeled inside a pipe with an inner diameter of 50 mm and a length of 1 m. Water in the pipe flows with a mean velocity of 1 m/s corresponding to a Reynolds number *Re* = 50,000. The opening in the orifice is 20 mm in diameter. The long radius nozzle has a length of 33.6 mm and the opening is 21 mm in diameter. We will study how the centerline velocity varies along the length of the pipe for both cases and plot both pressure and velocity fields. The discharge coefficients will be determined and compared with experimental values.

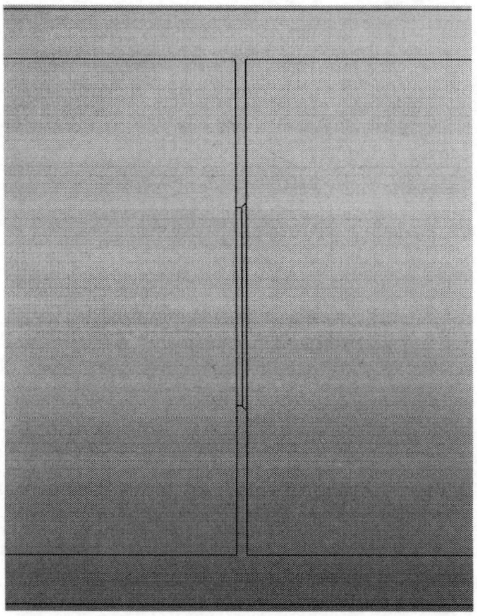

Figure 10.0a) Orifice plate

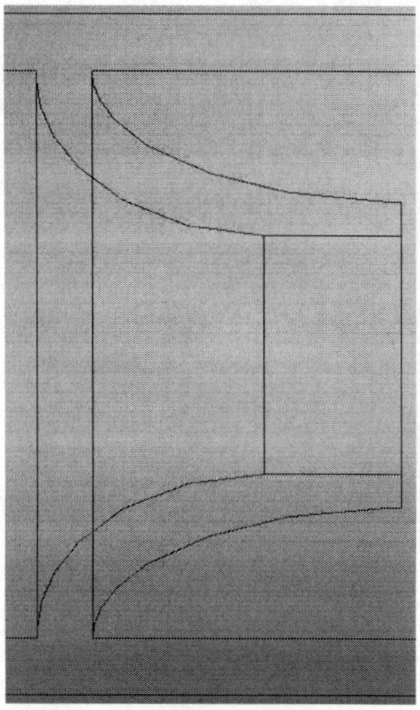

Figure 10.0b) Nozzle

Creating the Orifice Plate in a Pipe

1. Start by creating a new part in SOLIDWORKS: select **File>>New**, select **Part** and click on the **OK** button in the **New SOLIDWORKS Document** window. Select **Tools>>Options…** from the SOLIDWORKS menu. Click on the Document Properties tab and select **Units**. Select **MMGS** as your **Unit system**. Click on **Front Plane** in the **FeatureManager design tree** and select **Front** from the **View Orientation** drop down menu in the graphics window.

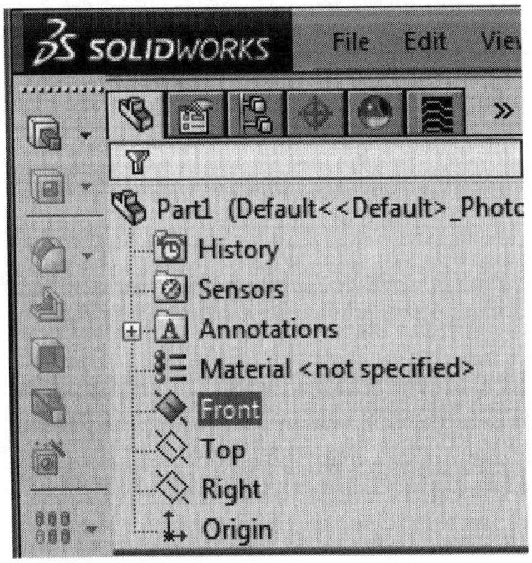

Figure 10.1a) Selection of front plane

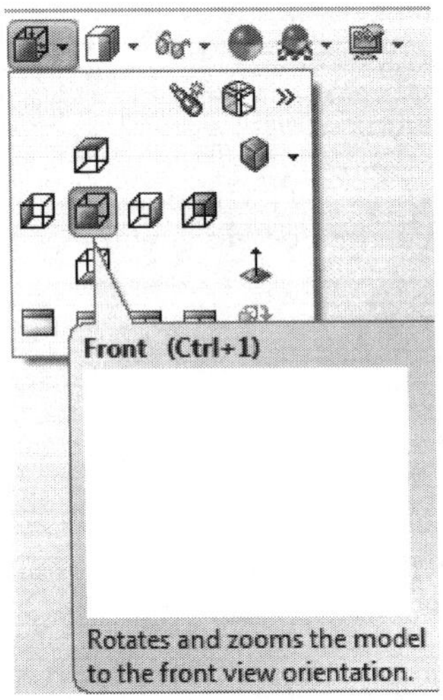

Figure 10.1b) Selection of front view

2. Click on **Circle** from the sketch tools. Draw a circle with a **25.00mm** radius. Close the **Circle** dialog box by clicking on .

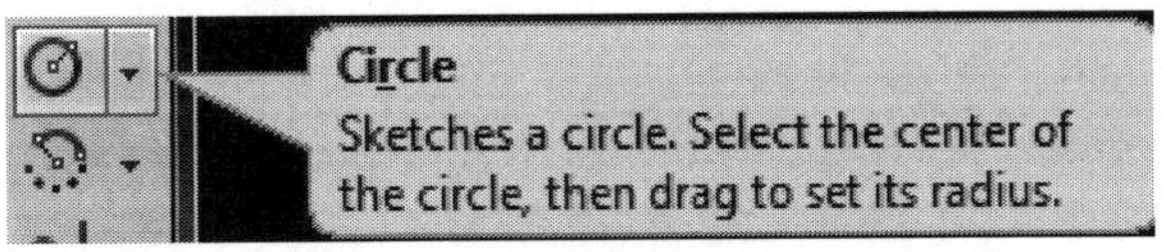

Figure 10.2a) Selecting the circle sketch tool

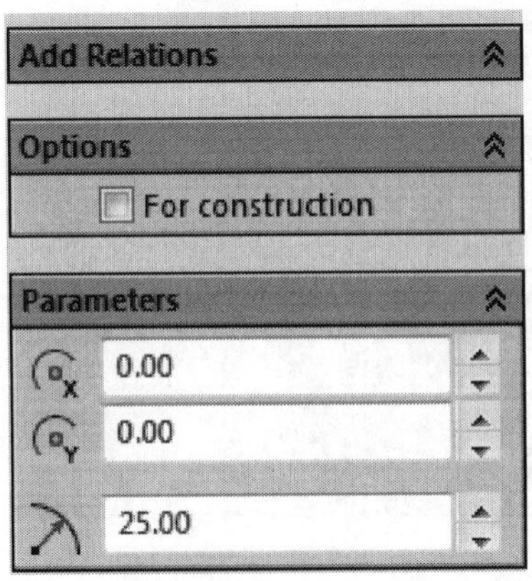

Figure 10.2b) Sketch parameters for circle

3. Select the **Extruded Boss/Base** feature. Set the **Depth** of the extrusion to **500.00mm** in both directions. Check the **Thin Feature** box and enter a **Thickness** value of **5.00mm**. Check the **Cap ends** box and enter **5.00 mm** for the thickness. Close the **Boss-Extrude** dialog box by clicking on **OK** .

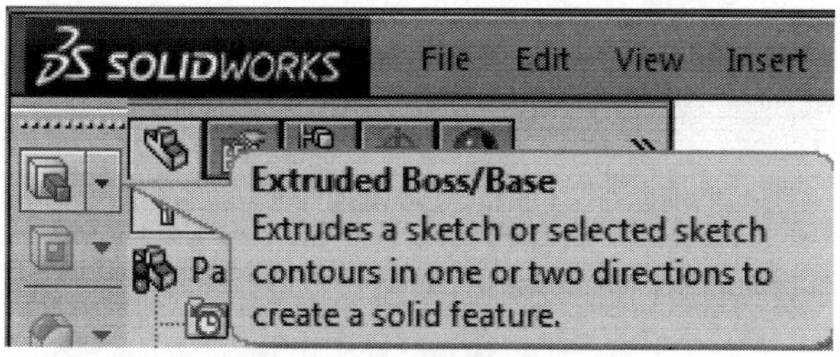

Figure 10.3a) Selecting extruded boss/base feature

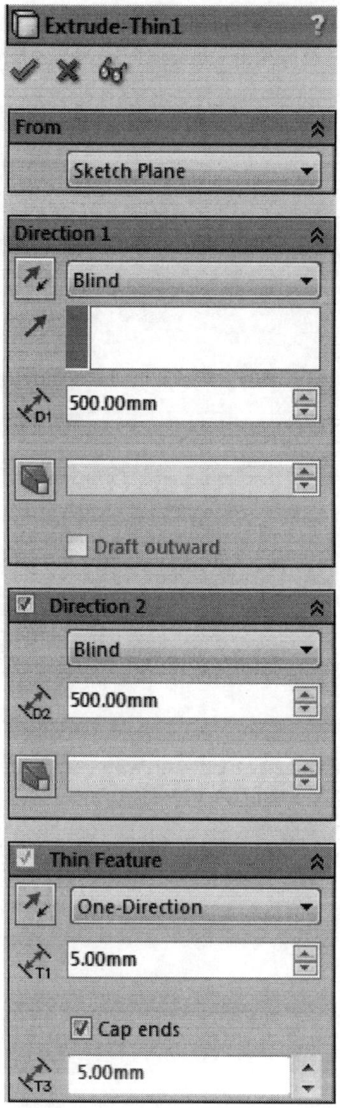

Figure 10.3b) Settings for extrusion

4. Select **Front** view from **View Orientation** in the graphics window. Click on **Front Plane** in the **Featuremanager design tree** and select **Circle** from the sketch tools. Draw a circle with a **25 mm** radius; see figure 10.4a). Close the **Circle** dialog box by clicking on **OK** . Select the **Extruded Boss/Base** feature. Set the **Depth** of the extrusion to **0.50mm** in both directions. Close the **Boss-Extrude** dialog box by clicking on **OK** .

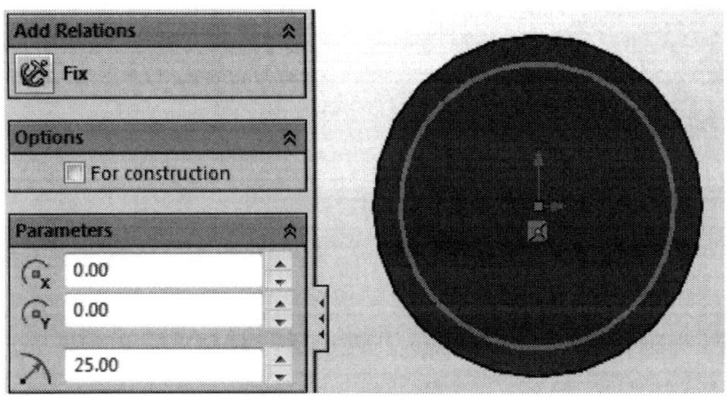

Figure 10.4a) Parameter settings for a circle

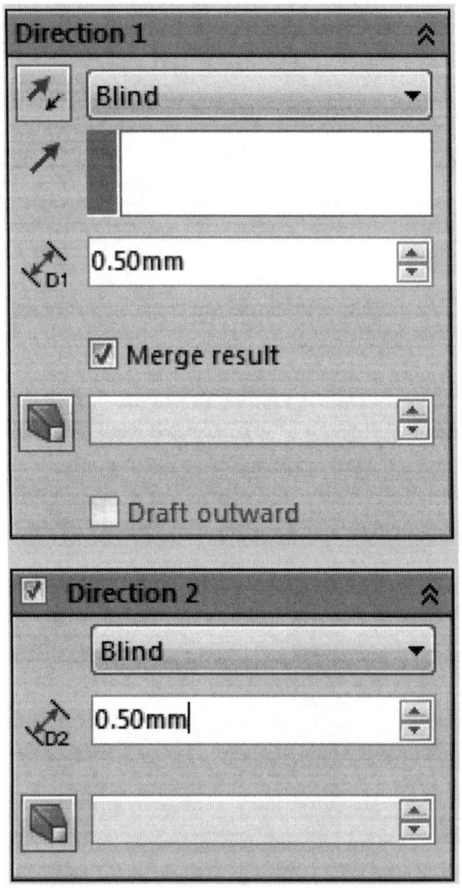

Figure 10.4b) Settings for extrusion

5. Click on **Front Plane** in the **Featuremanager design tree** and select **Circle** from the sketch tools. Draw a circle with a **10 mm** radius. Close the **Circle** dialog box by clicking on **OK** . Select the **Extruded Cut** feature. Set the **Depth** of the cut to **0.50mm** in both directions. Click on the **Draft** button for **Direction 2** and enter **45.00deg**. Check the **Draft outward** box; see figure 10.5. Exit the cut-extrude window.

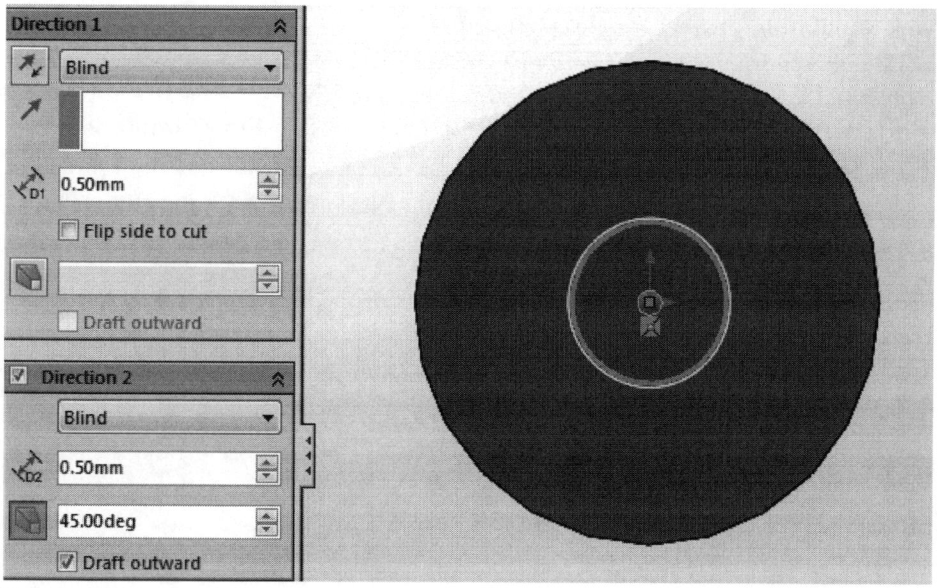

Figure 10.5 Extruded cut parameters

6. Select **Left** view from **View Orientation** in the graphics window. Select **Wireframe** display style from the drop down menu in the graphics window. Select **Zoom/Pan/Rotate>>Zoom to Area** and zoom in on the middle section of the pipe, right click in the graphics window and select **Zoom/Pan/Rotate>>Rotate View**. Rotate the view a little bit to get figure 10.6b). You have now completed your orifice plate inside a pipe. Save the part as **Orifice Plate**.

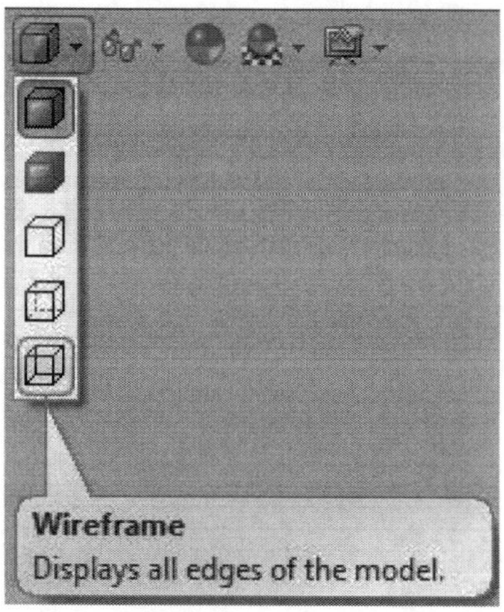

Figure 10.6a) Wireframe display style

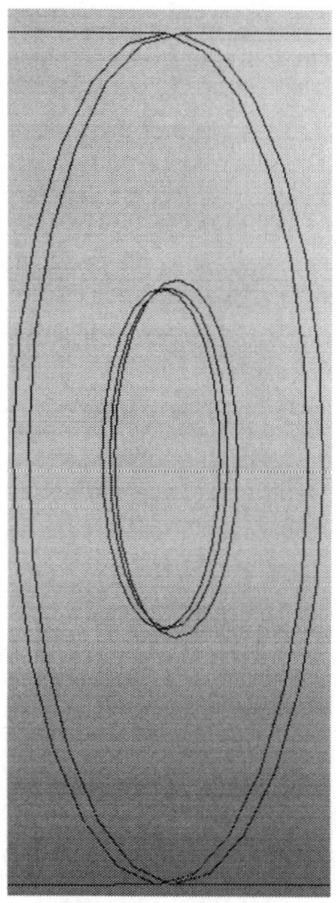

Figure 10.6b) Orifice plate

Setting up the Flow Simulation Project for the Orifice Plate

7. If Flow Simulation is not available in the menu, you have to add it from SOLIDWORKS menu: **Tools>>Add Ins…** and check the corresponding **SOLIDWORKS Flow Simulation** box. Select **Tools>>Flow Simulation>>Project>>Wizard** to create a new Flow Simulation project. Create a new project named "**Orifice Plate Study**." Click on the **Next** > button. Select the default **SI (m-kg-s)** unit system and click on the **Next>** button once again. Use the default **Internal Analysis type**. Click on the **Next** > button.

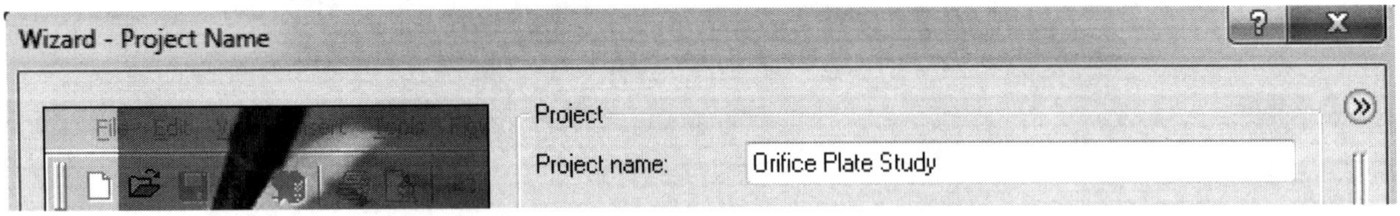

Figure 10.7 Creating a name for the project

8. Add **Water** from **Liquids** as the **Project Fluid**. Click on the **Next** > button. Use the default **Wall Conditions**. Click on the **Next** > button. Use the default **Initital Conditions**. Click on the **Next** > button. Set the **Result resolution** to **5**. Check the box **Manual specification of the minimum gap size** and set the **Minimum gap size:** to **0.02 m**. Check the box **Manual specification of the minimum wall thickness** and set **Minimum wall thickness:** to **0.001 m**. This is done in order to resolve the opening of the orifice and the thickness of the orifice plate. Click on the **Finish** button.

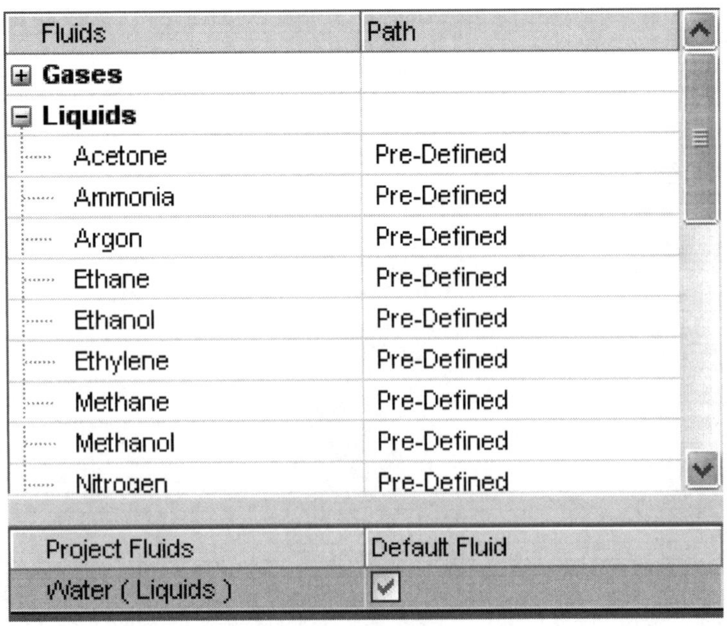

Figure 10.8a) Adding water as the project fluid

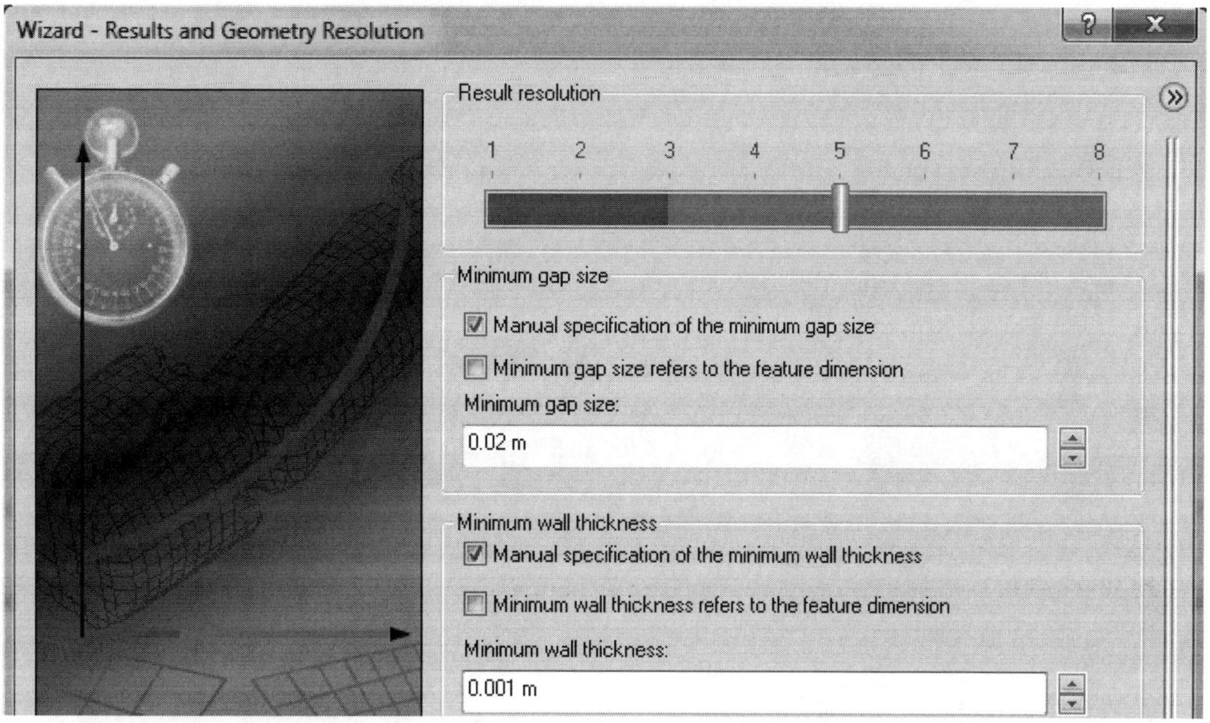

Figure 10.8b) Setting the result resolution, minimum gap size and minimum wall thickness

<u>**Inserting Boundary Conditions**</u>

9. Select **Left** view from **View Orientation** in the graphics window. Select **Zoom/Pan/Rotate>>Zoom to Area** and zoom in on the left end of the pipe, right click in the graphics window and select **Zoom/Pan/Rotate>>Rotate View**. Rotate the view a little bit; see figure 10.9a). Click on the plus sign next to the **Input Data** folder in the **Flow Simulation analysis tree**. Right click on **Computational Domain** and select **Hide**. Right click on **Boundary Conditions** and select **Insert Boundary Condition…**. Right click on the end of the pipe and select **Select Other**. Select the inner surface of the end cap. Select **Inlet Velocity** in the **Type** portion of the boundary condition window. Set the inlet velocity to **1 m/s** and check the box for **Fully developed flow**; see figure 10.9a). Click OK to exit the **Boundary Condition** window. Red arrows will appear showing the inlet velocity boundary condition; see figure 10.9b).

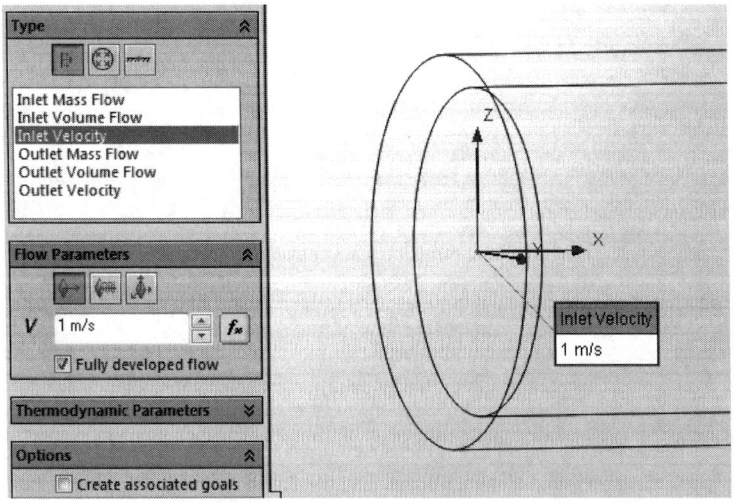

Figure 10.9a) Selection of inflow boundary condition

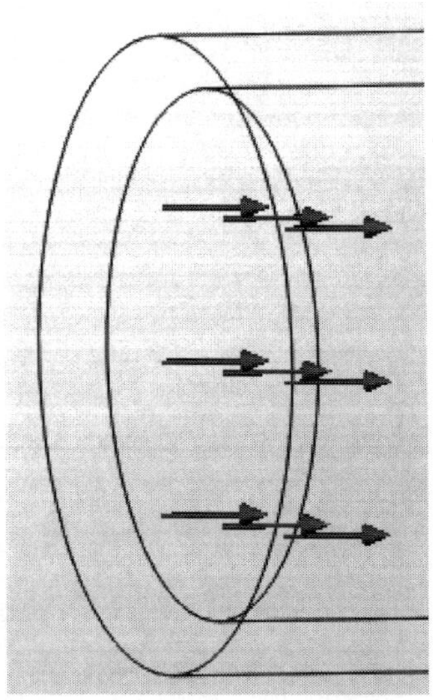

Figure 10.9b) Inlet velocity

10. Select **Left** view from **View Orientation** in the graphics window. Select **Zoom/Pan/Rotate>>Zoom to Area** and zoom in on the right end of the pipe. Right click in the graphics window and select **Zoom/Pan/Rotate>>Rotate View**. Rotate the view a little bit; see figure 10.10a). Right click on **Boundary Conditions** and select **Insert Boundary Condition…**. Right click on the end of the pipe and select **Select Other**. Select the inner surface of the pipe outflow cap. Select **Pressure Openings** in the **Type** portion of the **Boundary Condition** window. Select **Static Pressure**. Click OK to exit the **Boundary Condition** window.

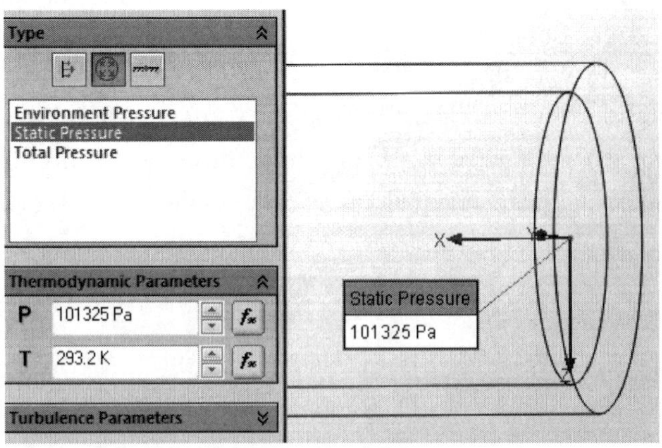

Figure 10.10a) Selection of outflow boundary condition

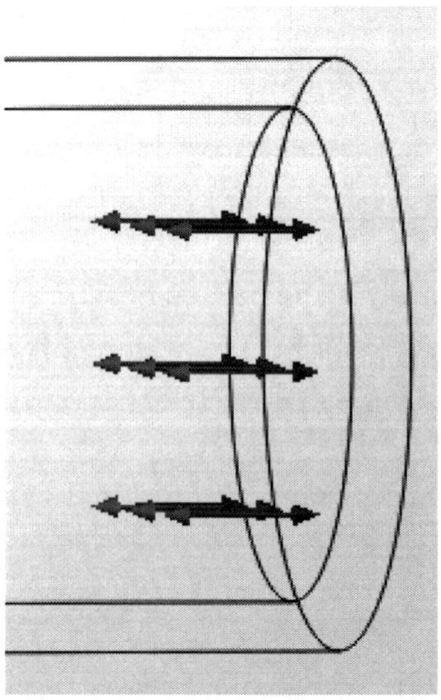

Figure 10.10b) Static pressure

Inserting Goals

11. Right click on **Goals** in the **Flow Simulation analysis tree** and select **Insert Point Goals…**.

Click on the Point Coordinates button and enter the coordinates as shown in figure 10.11a).

Check the **Static Pressure** box as a point goal for the coordinate. Click on the **Add Point** button to add this point to the table. Add another point to the table of point goals and make sure that the **Static Pressure** box is checked; see figure 10.11b). Click OK to exit the **Point Goals** window.

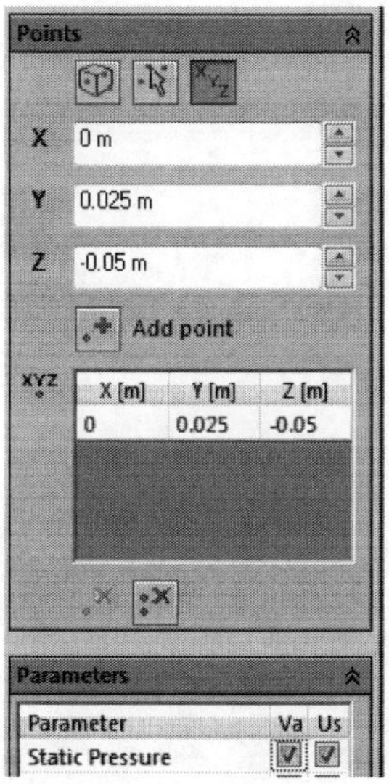

Figure 10.11a) Selection of first point

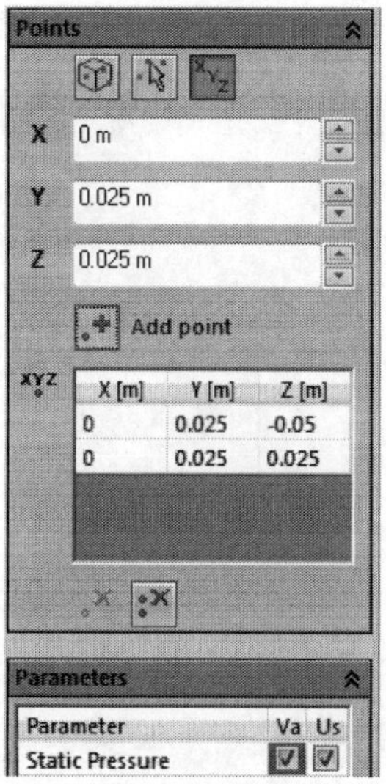

Figure 10.11b) Selection of second point

Running the Calculations for Orifice Plate

12. Select **Tools>>Flow Simulation>>Solve>>Run** to start calculations. Click on the **Run** button in the **Run** window.

Click on **Insert Goals Table** to view the static pressure goals in a table. Click on **Insert Goals Plot** to view a graph of the pressure goals. Click on the **Add All** button in the **Add/Remove Goals** window and click on the **OK** button to exit the window.

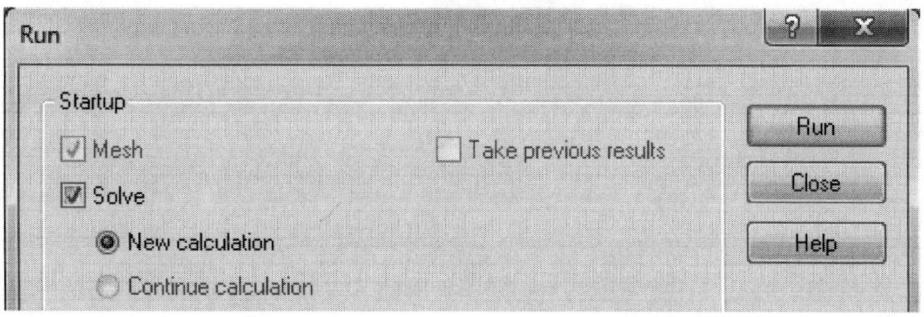

Figure 10.12a) Run window

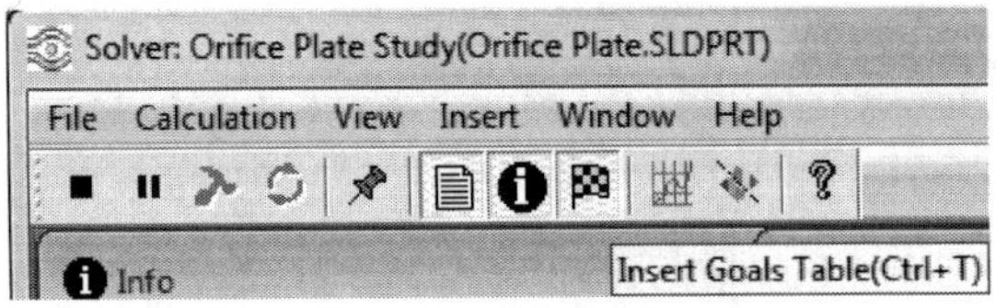

Figure 10.12b) Inserting goals table

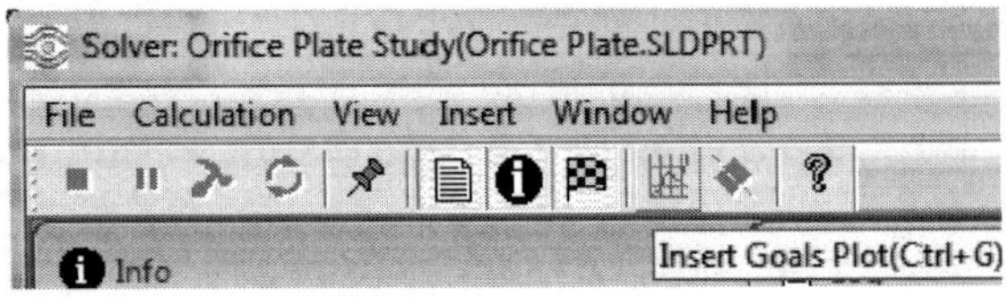

Figure 10.12c) Inserting goals plot

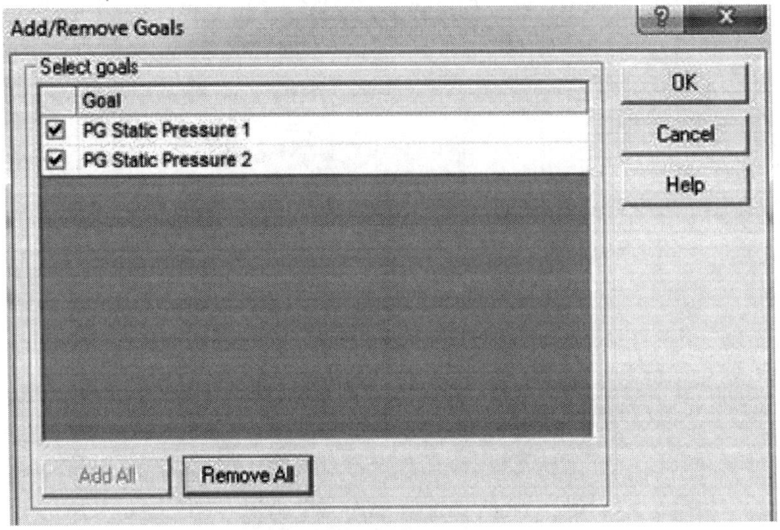

Figure 10.12d) Adding goals to the goals plot

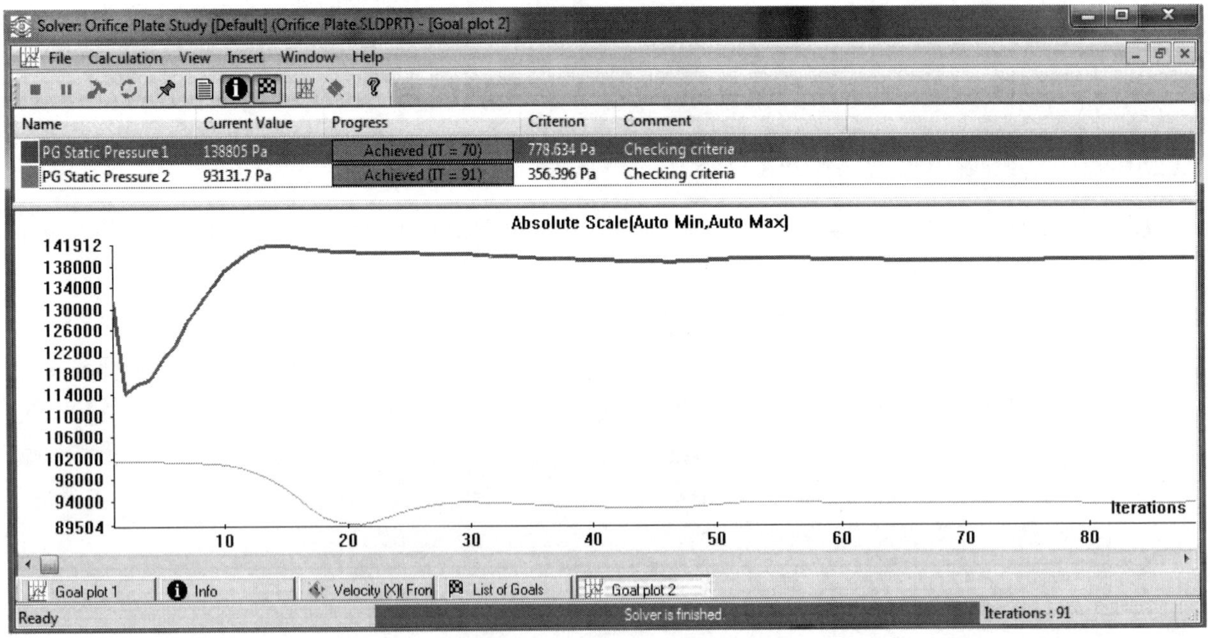

Figure 10.12e) Variation of static pressure goals before and after orifice plate

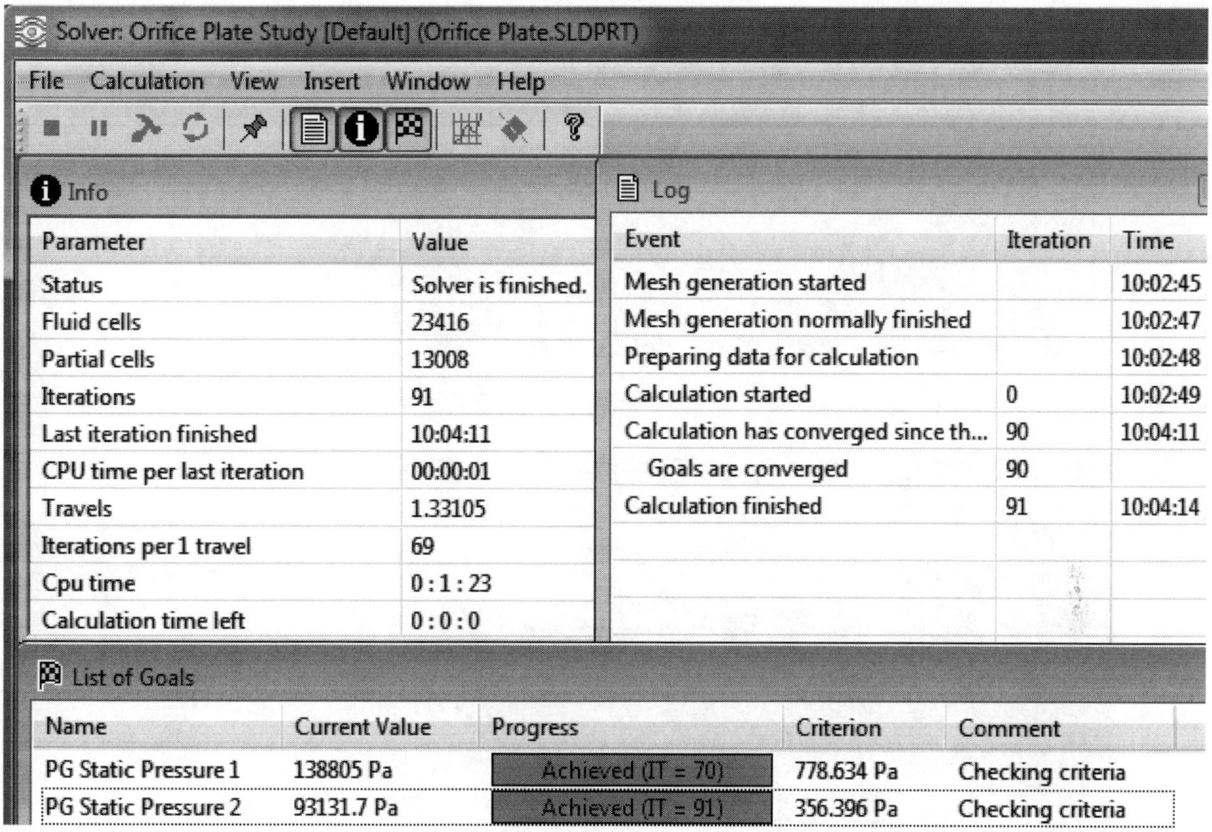

Figure 10.12f) Solver window for orifice plate flow

Inserting Cut Plots

13. Right click on **Cut Plots** in the **Flow Simulation analysis tree** and select **Insert…**. Select the **Right Plane** from the **FeatureManager design tree**. Slide the **Number of Levels:** slide bar to **255**. Select **Velocity (Z)** from the **Parameter:** dropdown menu. Click OK to exit the **Cut Plot** window. Rename the cut plot to **Velocity (Z)**.
    Select **Left** view from **View Orientation** in the graphics window; see figure 10.13b). Repeat this cut plot but select **Pressure** from the **Parameter:** dropdown menu. Click OK to exit the **Cut Plot** window; see figure 10.13c). Rename the cut plot to **Pressure**.

Figure 10.13a) Velocity (Z) distribution before and after the orifice plate

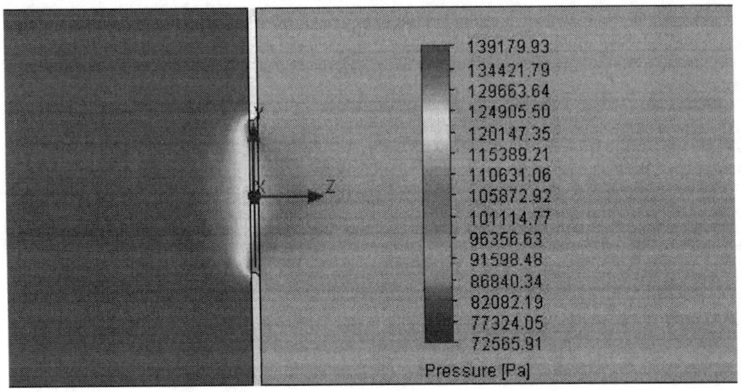

Figure 10.13b) Pressure distribution before and after the orifice plate

Determining Discharge Coefficient for Orifice Plate

14. From a mass balance and from Bernoulli equation we can derive an expression for the velocity at the orifice V_o

$$V_o = \sqrt{\frac{2\Delta P}{\rho(1-\beta^4)}} \tag{1}$$

where $\Delta P = P_1 - P_2$ is the pressure difference between the pressure P_1 before and P_2 after the orifice, ρ is the density of the fluid and $\beta = d/D$ is the ratio of the orifice diameter d and the inner pipe diameter D. Due to frictional effects and the vena contracta, we have to incorporate a correction factor known as the discharge coefficient C_d in order to determine the volume flow rate $\dot{V}$ in the pipe

$$\dot{V} = C_d A_o V_o \tag{2}$$

where A_o is the area of the orifice hole. The discharge coefficient has been experimentally determined for orifice flow meters as

$$C_d = 0.5959 + 0.0312\beta^{2.1} - 0.184\beta^8 + 91.71\frac{\beta^{2.5}}{Re^{0.75}} + 0.09A\frac{\beta^4}{1-\beta^4} - 0.0337B\beta^3 \qquad (3)$$

where the Reynolds number $Re = V_1 D/\nu$ is based on the approach velocity V_1 and kinematic viscosity ν of the fluid. The constants A and B are zero for corner taps (pipe wall taps, one on each side adjacent to the orifice plate) that have the values $A = 0.4333$ and $B = 0.47$ for pipe wall taps located the distance D upstream from the orifice and $D/2$ downstream. Equation (3) is valid in the region $10^4 < Re < 10^7$, $0.25 < \beta < 0.75$.

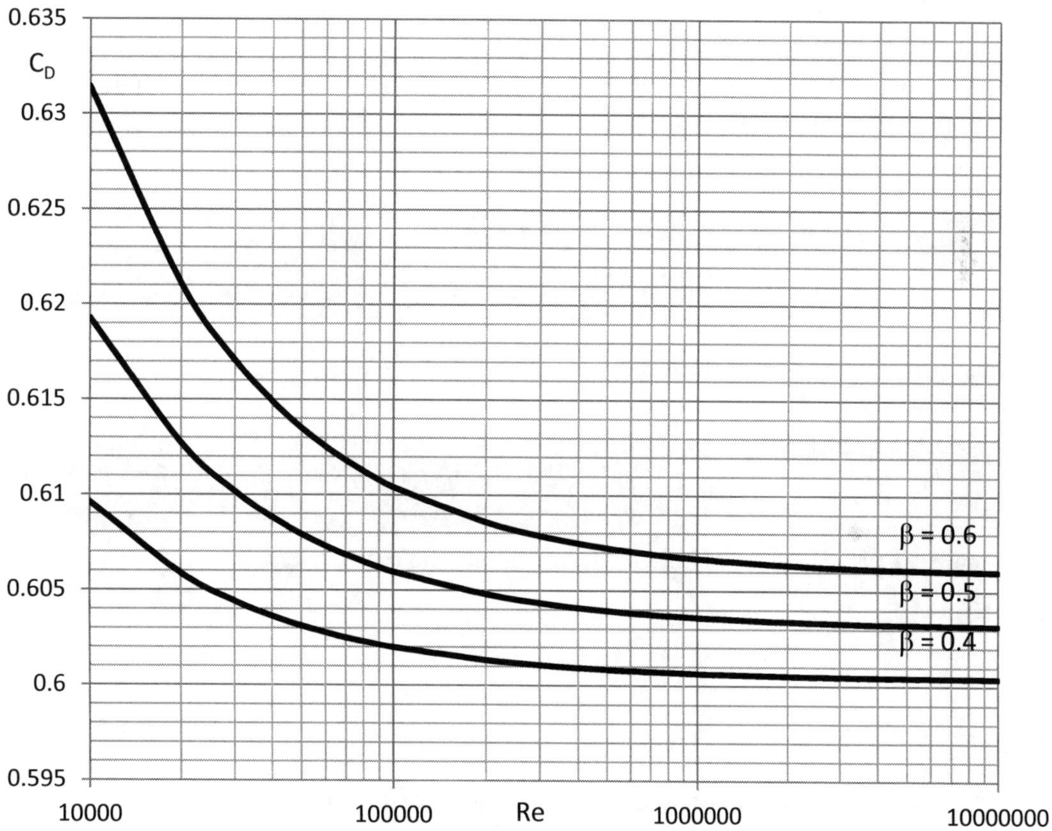

Figure 10.14a) Discharge coefficient versus Reynolds number for three different β ratios, pipe wall taps located distance D upstream and $D/2$ downstream from orifice plate

The diameter ratio $\beta = 20\text{mm}/50\text{mm} = 0.4$ in the Flow Simulation calculations and the Reynolds number is

$$Re = \frac{V_1 D}{\nu} = \frac{1m/s \cdot 0.050m}{1 \cdot 10^{-6} m^2/s} = 50{,}000 \qquad (4)$$

The pressure difference can be determined from data in figure 10.12g) as $\Delta P = 138{,}805\ Pa - 93{,}131.7 = 45{,}673.3\ Pa$. The discharge coefficient from Flow Simulation is

$$C_D = \frac{\dot{V}}{A_o V_o} = \frac{A_1 V_1}{A_o}\sqrt{\frac{\rho(1-\beta^4)}{2\Delta P}} = \frac{V_1}{\beta^2}\sqrt{\frac{\rho(1-\beta^4)}{2\Delta P}} = \frac{1m/s}{0.4^2}\sqrt{\frac{998kg/m^3(1-0.4^4)}{2\cdot 45{,}673.3\text{Pa}}} = 0.645 \qquad (5)$$

The corresponding value from experiments, equation (3), is 0.603, a 7 % difference.

We would now like to see the velocity and pressure variation along the pipe. Click on the **Featuremanager design tree** tab and select the **Right Plane**. Select **Line** from the sketch tools. Draw a horizontal **990.00 mm** long line along the pipe wall; see figure 10.14b). Exit the **Line Properties** window and the **Insert Line** window. Click on **Rebuild** from the SOLIDWORKS menu. Rename the sketch and call it "**Wall**." Repeat this step and sketch another horizontal line with the same length along the centerline of the pipe—see figure 10.14c), and name the sketch "**Centerline**."

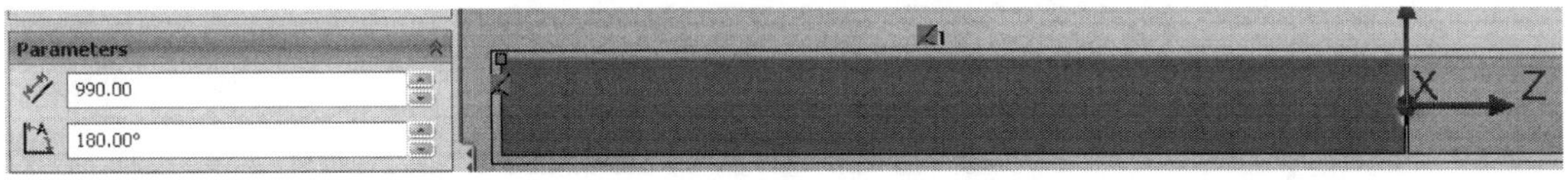

Figure 10.14b) Drawing of horizontal lines along the pipe wall

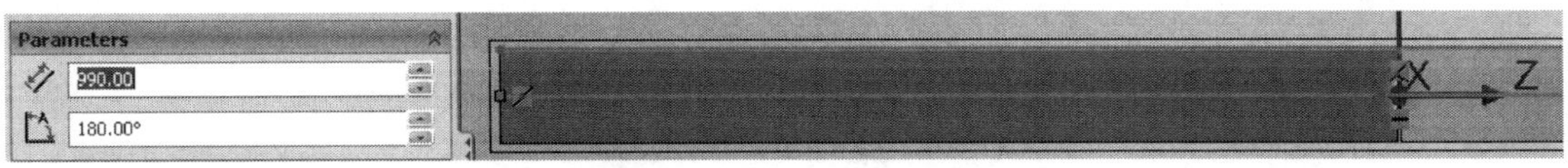

Figure 10.14c) Drawing of horizontal lines along the pipe centerline

Inserting XY Plots

Click on the **Flow Simulation analysis tree** tab and right click on **XY Plots** and select **Insert…**. Click on the **Featuremanager design tree** tab and select the sketch named "**Centerline**." Choose **Model Z** from the **Abscissa:** drop down menu. Check the **Velocity** box in the **Parameters** portion of the **XY Plot** window. Slide the **Resolution** to the maximum value and set the number of evenly distributed output points to **200**. Open the **Options** portion of the **XY Plot** window and select **Excel Workbook (*.xlsx)**; see figure 10.14d). Click on the button **Export to Excel**. An Excel file will open. The maximum velocity along the centerline is around eight times higher than the approach velocity; see figure 10.14e). Rename the XY Plot to in the Flow Simulation analysis tree to **Velocity along Centerline**. Repeat this step but select the sketch named "**Wall**" and check the box for **Pressure**. Rename the XY Plot to **Pressure along Wall**. We can see in figure 10.14f) that there is a partial recovery in pressure after the orifice.

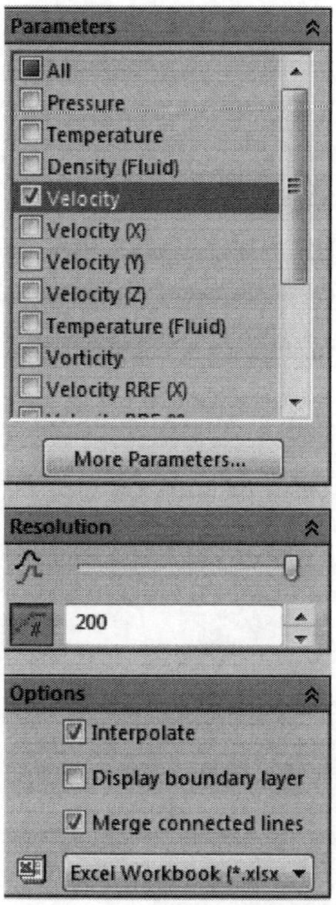

Figure 10.14d) Settings for XY plot

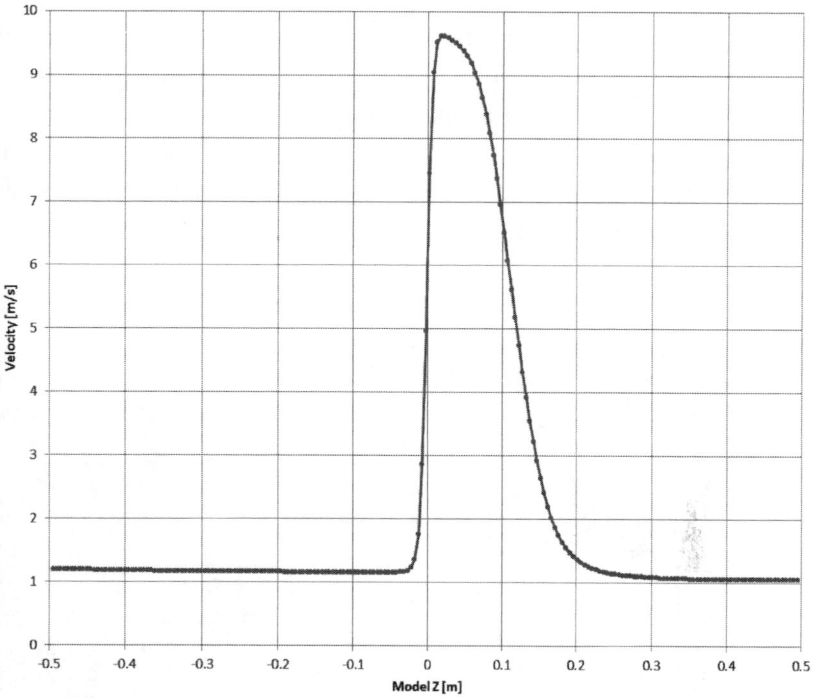

Figure 10.14e) Velocity along the centerline

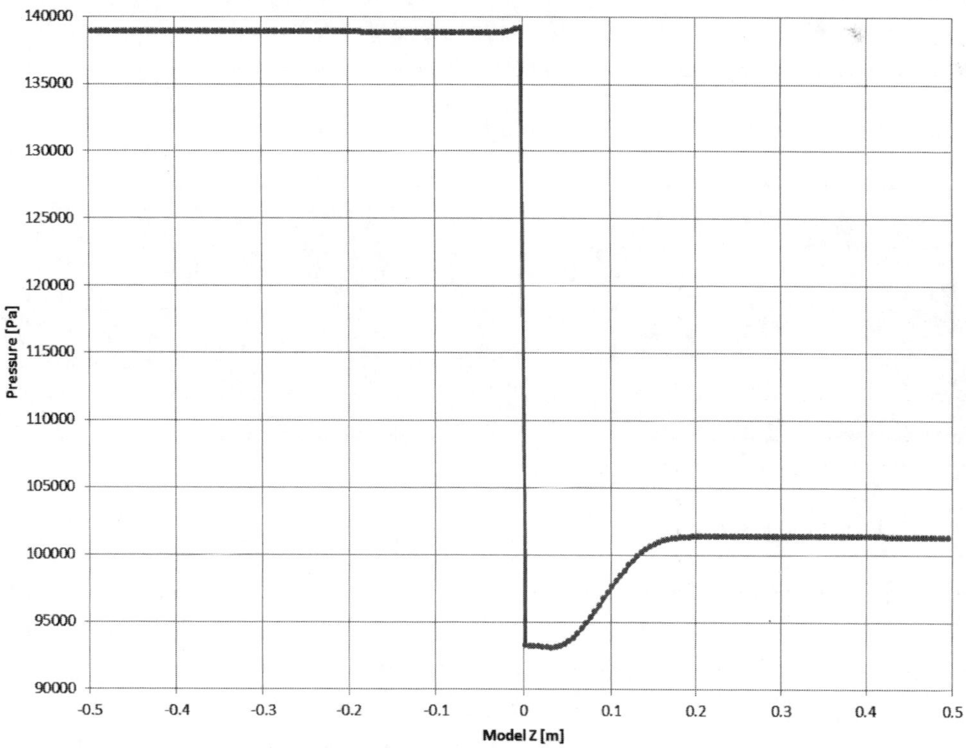

Figure 10.14f) Pressure variation along the pipe wall

Creating Sketch for XY Plots

Next, we want to see the variation of the velocity profile at different positions upstream and downstream of the orifice. Click on the **Featuremanager design tree** tab and select the **Right Plane**. Select **Line** from the **Sketch** tools. Draw vertical lines across the pipe at different model positions Z = -50, 50, 100, 150, 200 mm. These positions are corresponding to x = 50, -50, -100, -150, and -200 mm, see figure 10.14g), for the first vertical line at Z = -50 mm (x = 50 mm). Exit the **Line Properties** window when you have completed all five vertical lines; see figure 10.14h).

Click on **Rebuild** from the SOLIDWORKS menu. Name the sketch "**Velocity profiles**."

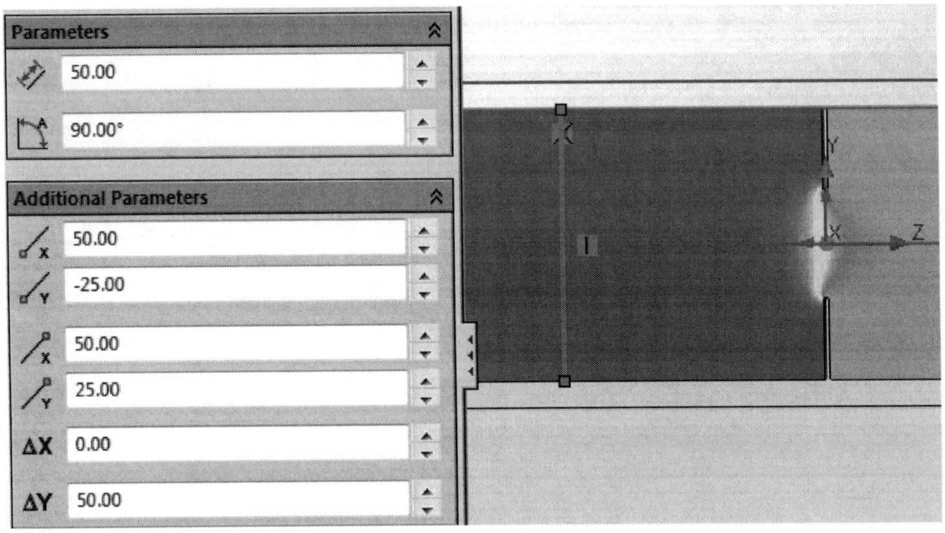

Figure 10.14g) First line across the pipe with local parameter values

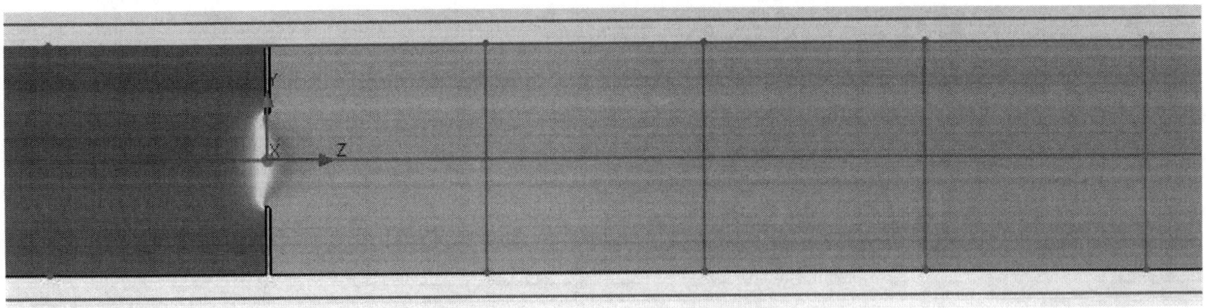

Figure 10.14h) Five lines across the pipe for velocity profiles

Click on the **Flow Simulation analysis tree** tab and right click on **XY Plots** and select **Insert….** Click on the **Featuremanager design tree** tab and select the sketch "**Velocity profiles**." Choose **Model Y** from the **Abscissa:** drop down menu. Check the **Velocity (Z)** box in the **Parameters** portion of the **XY Plot** window. Slide the **Resolution** to the maximum value and set the number of evenly distributed output points to **200**. Open the **Options** portion of the **XY Plot** window and select **Excel Workbook (*.xlsx)**. Click on the button **Export to Excel**. An Excel file will open; see figure 10.14i). Exit the **XY Plot**. Rename the XY Plot to **Velocity (Z) Profiles**.

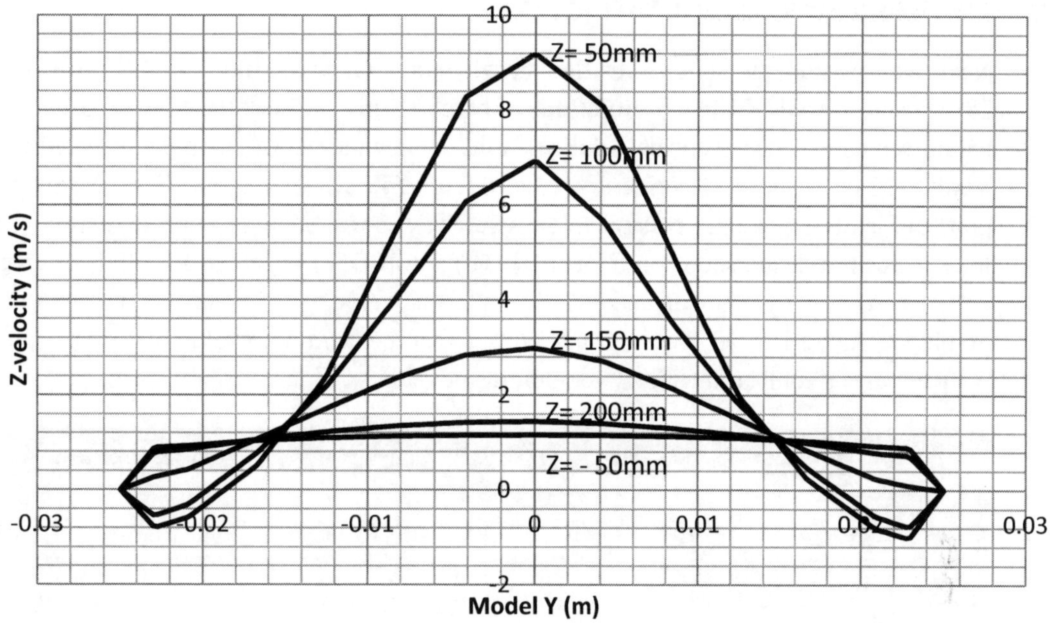

Figure 10.14i) Velocity profiles at different streamwise positions, results obtained for initial mesh level 5 and refinement of the mesh is disabled

Flow Trajectories

Flow trajectories show the streamlines of the flow and we will now insert them for the orifice plate flow. Right click on the **Pressure** cut plot in the Flow Simulation analysis tree and select **Hide**. Right click on the **Velocity (Z)** cut plot in the Flow Simulation analysis tree and select **Hide**. Right click on **Flow Trajectories** in the Flow Simulation analysis tree and select **Insert…**. Go to the FeatureManager design tree and click on the **Front Plane**. The front plane will now be listed as the **Reference** plane in the **Flow Trajectories** window. Set the **Number of Points** to **100**. Select **Lines** from the **Draw Trajectories As** drop down menu in the **Appearance** section. Select **Velocity** from the **Color by Parameter** drop down menu. Click on the **OK** button to exit the **Flow Trajectories** window.

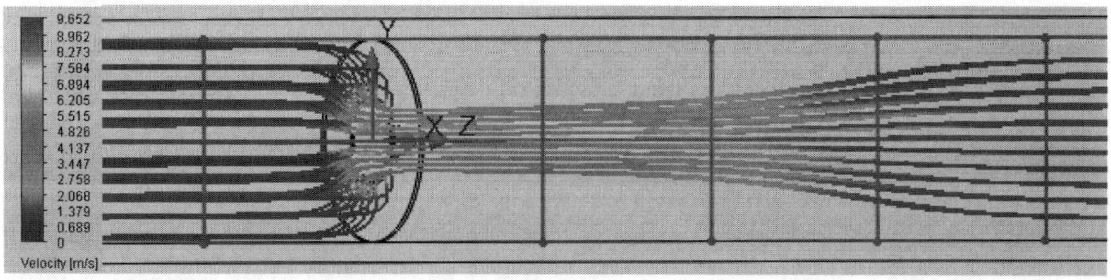

Figure 10.14j) Flow trajectories for orifice plate flow

Running the Calculations for Long Radius Nozzle

15. Next, we will study the long radius flow nozzle meter. Open the file "**Long Radius Nozzle 2015.**" Select **Tools>>Flow Simulation>>Solve>>Run….** Check the **Mesh** box in the **Run** window and also check **New calculation** in the same window. Click on the **Run** button. Select **Tools>>Flow Simulation>>Results>>Load from File….** Click on the Open button. Insert cut plots of **Velocity (Z)** and **Pressure** in the same way as was shown in step **13**. The cut plots for the long radius nozzle are shown in figures 10.15b) and 10.15c). Insert an XY-Plot of centerline velocity. Also, copy plot data and include centerline velocity for the orifice plate in the same graph; see figure 10.15e) for the result. We see that the maximum velocity is 70 % higher for the orifice plate as compared with the long radius nozzle.

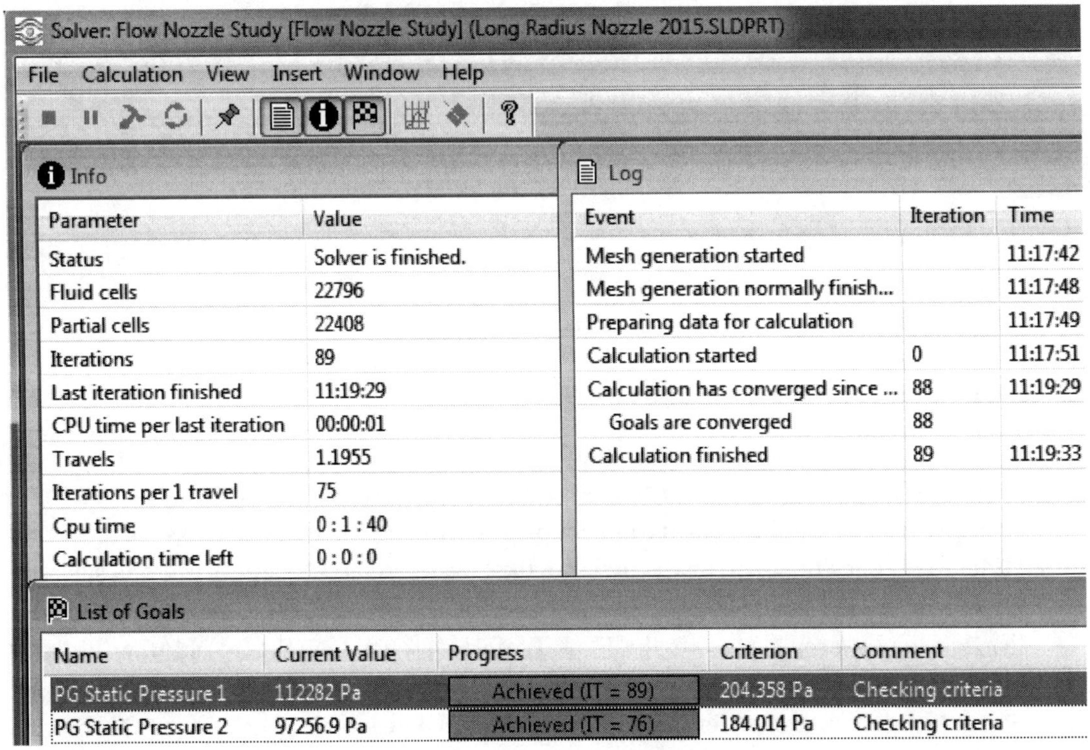

Figure 10.15a) Solver window for long radius nozzle calculation

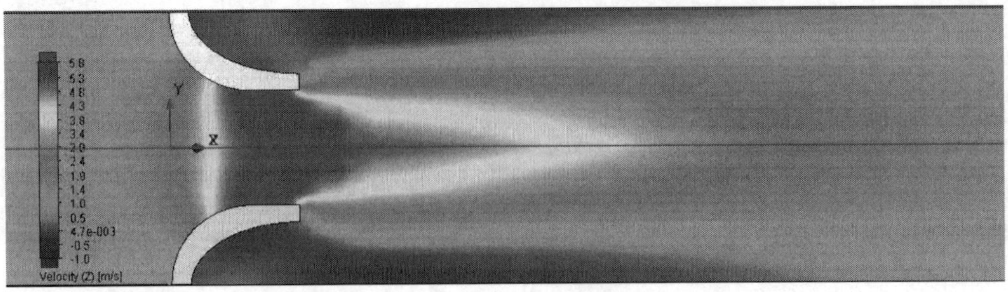

Figure 10.15b) Velocity (Z) distribution along long-radius flow nozzle

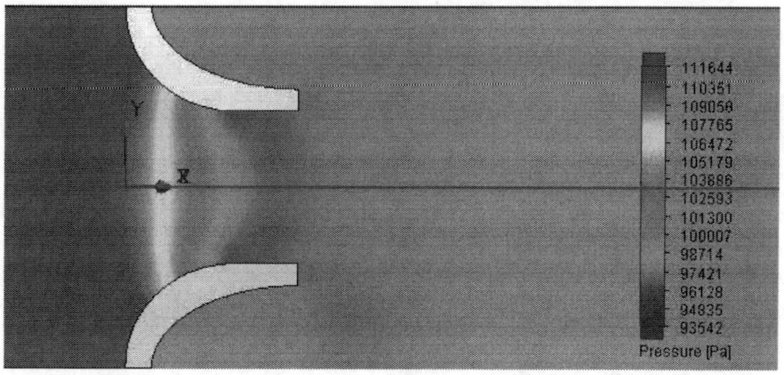

Figure 10.15c) Pressure distribution along long-radius flow nozzle

Determining Discharge Coefficient for Long Radius Nozzle

The discharge coefficient for the long radius nozzle is given by

$$C_d = 0.9975 - 6.53\sqrt{\frac{\beta}{Re}} \tag{6}$$

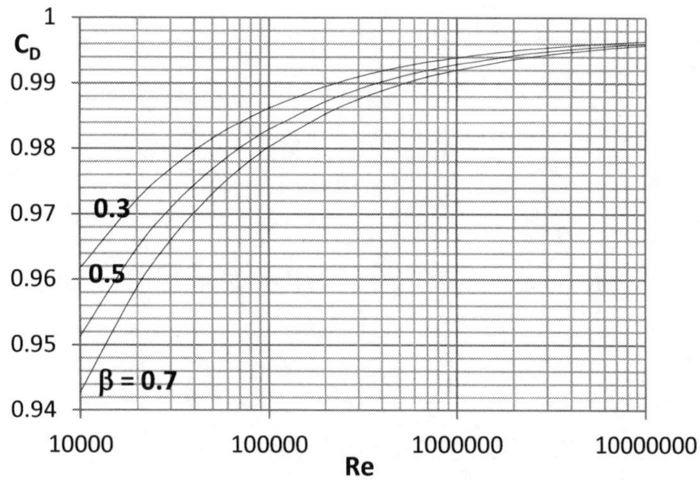

Figure 10.15d) Discharge coefficient versus Reynolds number for three different β ratios

The diameter ratio β = 21mm/50mm = 0.42 in the Flow Simulation calculations and the Reynolds *Re* number is 50,000; see equation (4). The pressure difference can be determined from data in figure 10.15a) as $\Delta P = 112{,}208\ Pa - 97{,}292.5 = 14{,}915.5\ Pa$. The discharge coefficient from Flow Simulation is

$$C_D = \frac{\dot{V}}{A_o V_o} = \frac{A_1 V_1}{A_o}\sqrt{\frac{\rho(1-\beta^4)}{2\Delta P}} = \frac{V_1}{\beta^2}\sqrt{\frac{\rho(1-\beta^4)}{2\Delta P}} = \frac{1m/s}{0.42^2}\sqrt{\frac{998kg/m^3(1-0.42^4)}{2\cdot 14{,}915.5\text{ Pa}}} = 1.021 \tag{7}$$

The corresponding value from experiments, equation (6), is 0.979, a difference of 4.3 %.

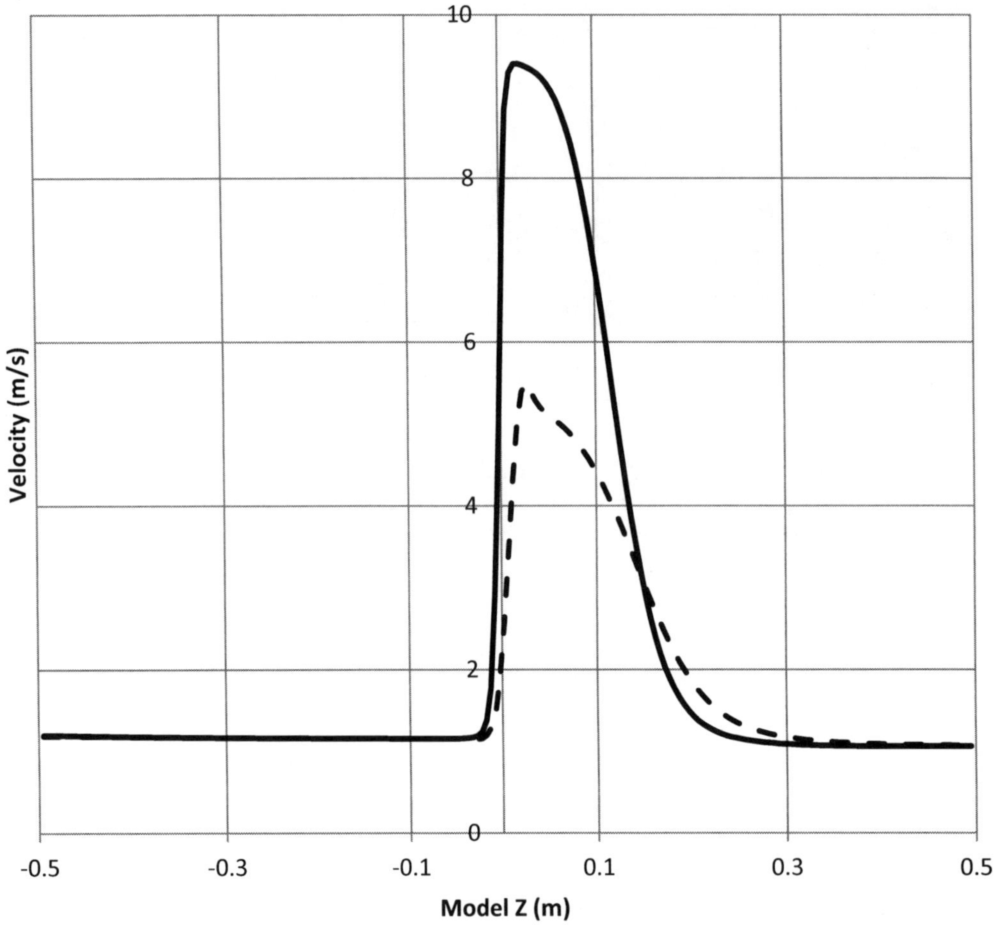

Figure 10.15e) A comparison of centerline velocity for orifice flow $\beta = 0.4$ (full line) and long-radius flow nozzle $\beta = 0.42$ (dashed line) at $Re = 50{,}000$

Reference

[1] White, F. M., Fluid Mechanics, 4th Edition, McGraw-Hill, 1999.

Exercises

1. Change the mesh resolution in flow simulations and see how the mesh size affects the discharge coefficient in comparison with experimental values for the orifice plate and long radius nozzle.

2. Determine the pressure difference between corner taps (where the orifice plate meets the pipe wall), determine the discharge coefficient using equation (5), and compare with equation (3) using values for $A = B = 0$. The thickness of the orifice is 1 mm. Use coordinates $(x,y,z) =$ (0,0.025,0.001) m and (0,0.025,-0.001) m for corner taps.

3. Use SOLIDWORKS Flow Simulation to determine the discharge coefficient for different Reynolds numbers and compare in graphs with figure 10.14a) for the orifice plate and figure 10.15d) for the long-radius nozzle. Use Re = 10,000; 25,000; 50,000, and 100,000. Plot graphs including both SOLIDWORKS and experimental data in the same graphs.

4. Use SOLIDWORKS Flow Simulation to keep the Reynolds number constant at Re = 50,000 and determine the discharge coefficient for different β ratios and compare with figure 10.14a) for the orifice plate and figure 10.15d) for the long-radius nozzle. Use β = 0.3, 0.4, 0.5, 0.6, and 0.7. Remember to change the minimum gap size for each case. Plot graphs including both SOLIDWORKS and experimental data in the same graphs.

Notes:

Chapter 11 Thermal Boundary Layer

Objectives

- Setting up a Flow Simulation project for internal flow
- Inserting boundary conditions, creating goals and running the calculations
- Using cut plots and XY plots to visualize the resulting flow field
- Compare Flow Simulation results with theoretical and empirical data

Problem Description

In this chapter, we will use Flow Simulation to study the thermal two-dimensional laminar and turbulent boundary layer flow on a flat plate and compare with the theoretical boundary layer solution and empirical results. The inlet velocity for the 1 m long plate is 5 m/s and, we will be using air as the fluid for laminar calculations and water to get a higher Reynolds number for turbulent boundary layer calculations. The temperature of the hot wall will be set to 393.2 K while the temperature of the approaching free stream is set to 293.2 K. We will determine the temperature profiles and plot the same profiles using the well-known boundary layer similarity coordinate. The variation of the local Nusselt number will also be determined.

Figure 11.0 Thermal velocity boundary layer close to horizontal wall

Setting up the Flow Simulation Project

1. Open the part named "**Thermal Boundary Layer Part 2015**."

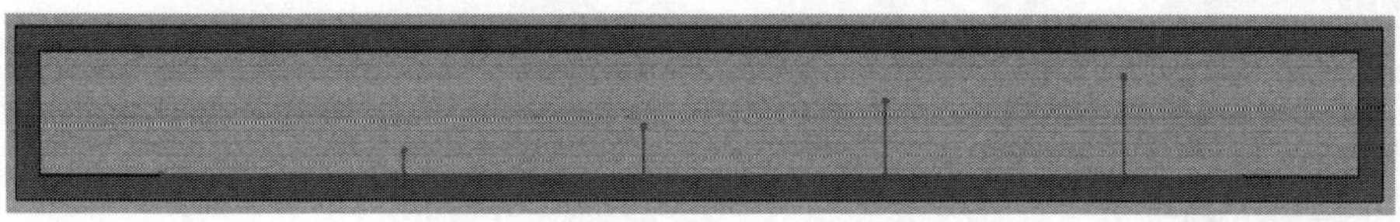

Figure 11.1 SOLIDWORKS model for thermal boundary layer

2. If Flow Simulation is not available in the menu, you have to add it from SOLIDWORKS menu: **Tools>>Add Ins…** and check the corresponding **Flow Simulation** box. Select **Tools>>Flow Simulation>>Project>>Wizard** to create a new Flow Simulation project. Create a new project named "**Thermal Boundary Layer**." Click on the **Next** > button. Select the default **SI (m-kg-s)** unit system and click on the **Next>** button once again.

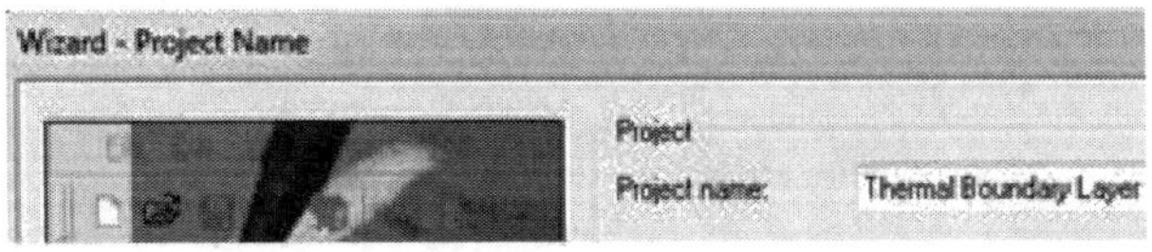

Figure 11.2 Creating a name for the project

3. Use the default **Internal Analysis type**. Click on the **Next** > button.

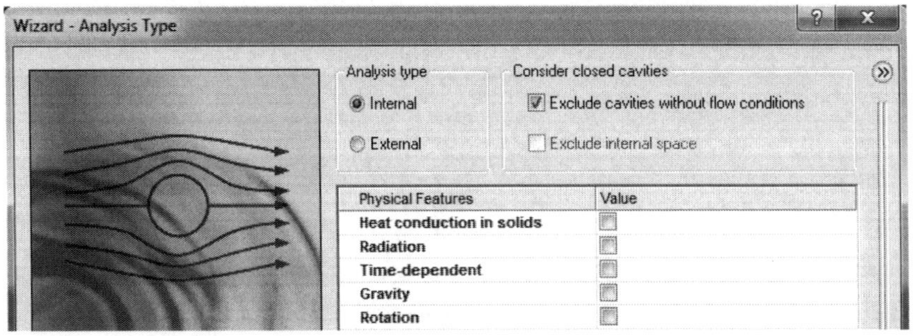

Figure 11.3 Analysis type window

4. Select **Air** from the **Gases** and add it as **Project Fluid**. Select **Laminar Only** from the **Flow Type** drop down menu. Click on the **Next** > button. Use the default **Wall Conditions** and **5 m/s** for **Velocity in X direction** as **Initial Condition**. Slide the **Result resolution** to **8**. Click on the **Finish** button. Answer Yes to the question whether you want to open the Create Lids tool. Select one open side of the model and close the Create Lids dialog box. Answer Yes to the questions whether you want to reset mesh settings and open the Create Lids tool. Turn the model around and select the other open face of the model. Close the Create Lids dialog box and answer yes to the questions whether you want to reset the computational domain and reset the mesh settings.

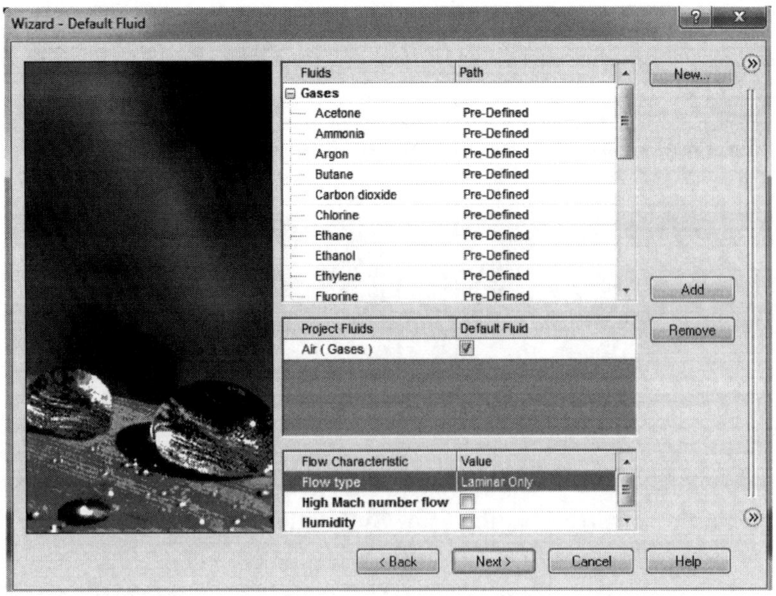

Figure 11.4 Selection of fluid for the project and flow type

5. Select **Tools>>Flow Simulation>>Computational Domain…**. Click on the **2D simulation** button and select **XY plane**. Exit the **Computational Domain** window.

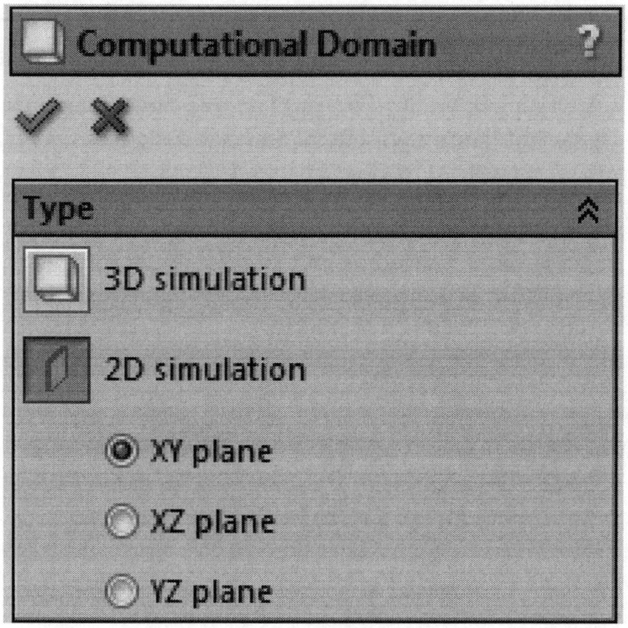

Figure 11.5 Selecting two dimensional flow condition

6. Select **Tools>>Flow Simulation>>Initial Mesh…**. Uncheck the **Automatic setting** box at the bottom of the window. Change both the **Number of cells per X:** to **300** and the **Number of cells per Y:** to **200**. Click on the **OK** button to exit the **Initial Mesh** window.

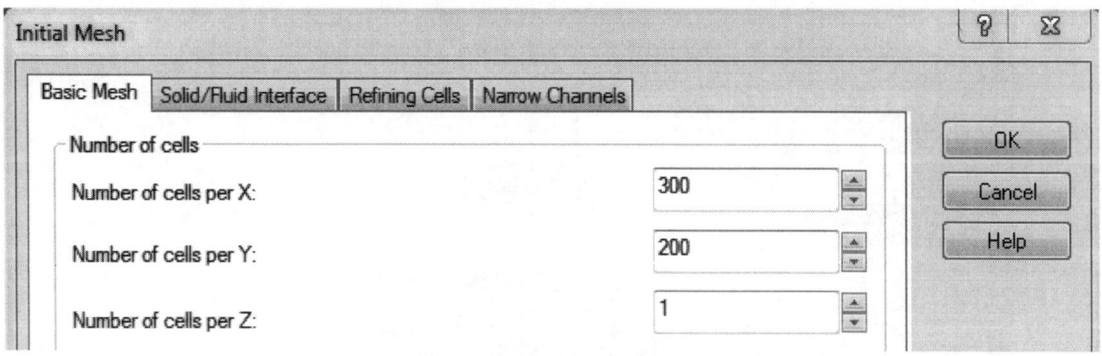

Figure 11.6 Changing the number of cells in both directions

Inserting Boundary Conditions

7. Select the **Flow Simulation analysis tree** tab, open the **Input Data** folder by clicking on the plus sign next to it and right click on **Boundary Conditions**. Select **Insert Boundary Condition….** Right click in the graphics window and select **Zoom/Pan/Rotate>>Rotate View**. Click and drag the mouse so that the left boundary is visible. Right click on the left inflow boundary surface and select Select Other. Select the inner surface of the inflow region. Select **Inlet Velocity** in the **Type** portion of the **Boundary Condition** window and set the velocity to **5 m/s** in the **Flow Parameters** window. Click **OK** to exit the window.

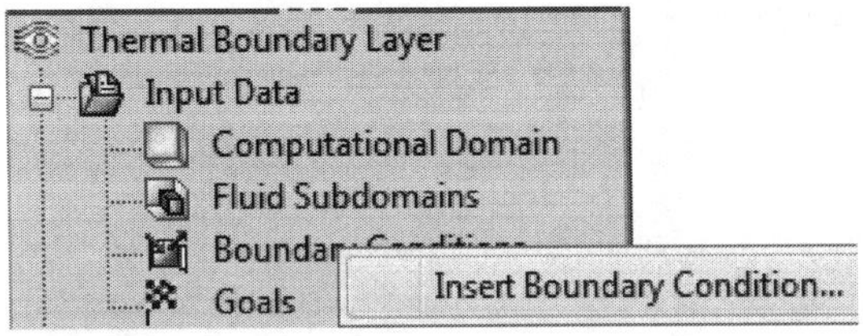

Figure 11.7a) Inserting boundary condition

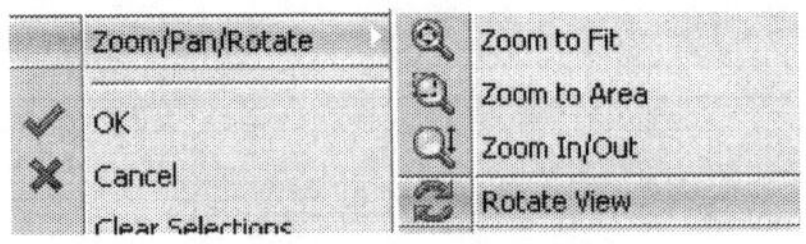

Figure 11.7b) Modifying the view

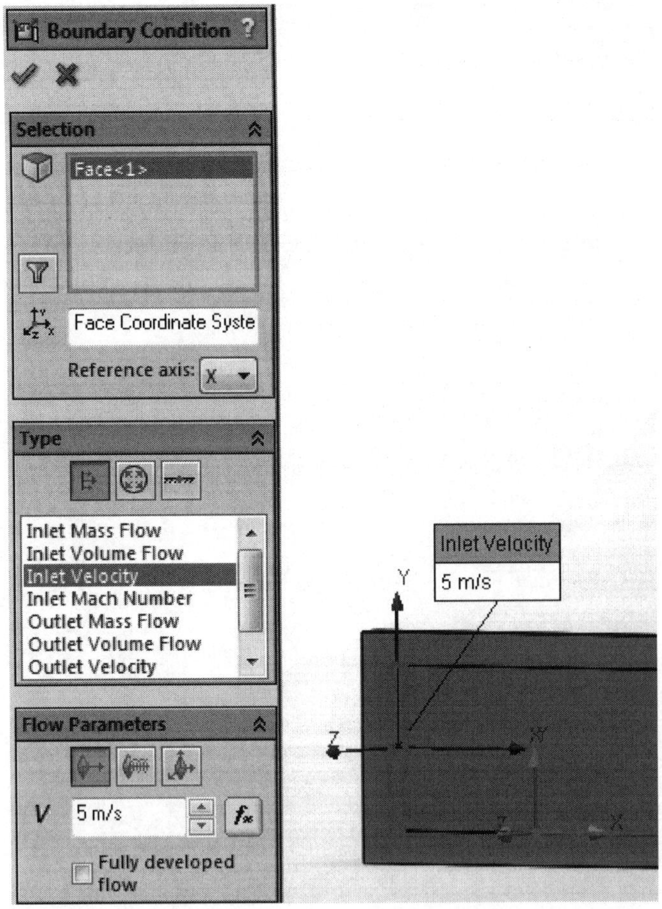

Figure 11.7c) Including a velocity boundary condition on the inflow

8. Right click again in the graphics window and select **Rotate View** once again to rotate the part so that the inner right surface is visible in the graphics window. Right click and click on **Select**. Right click on **Boundary Conditions** in the **Flow Simulation analysis tree** and select **Insert Boundary Condition…**. Right click on the outlet boundary and select Select Other. Select the outflow boundary of the model; see figure 11.8. Click on the **Pressure Openings** button in the **Type** portion of the **Boundary Condition** window and select **Static Pressure**. Click OK to exit the window.

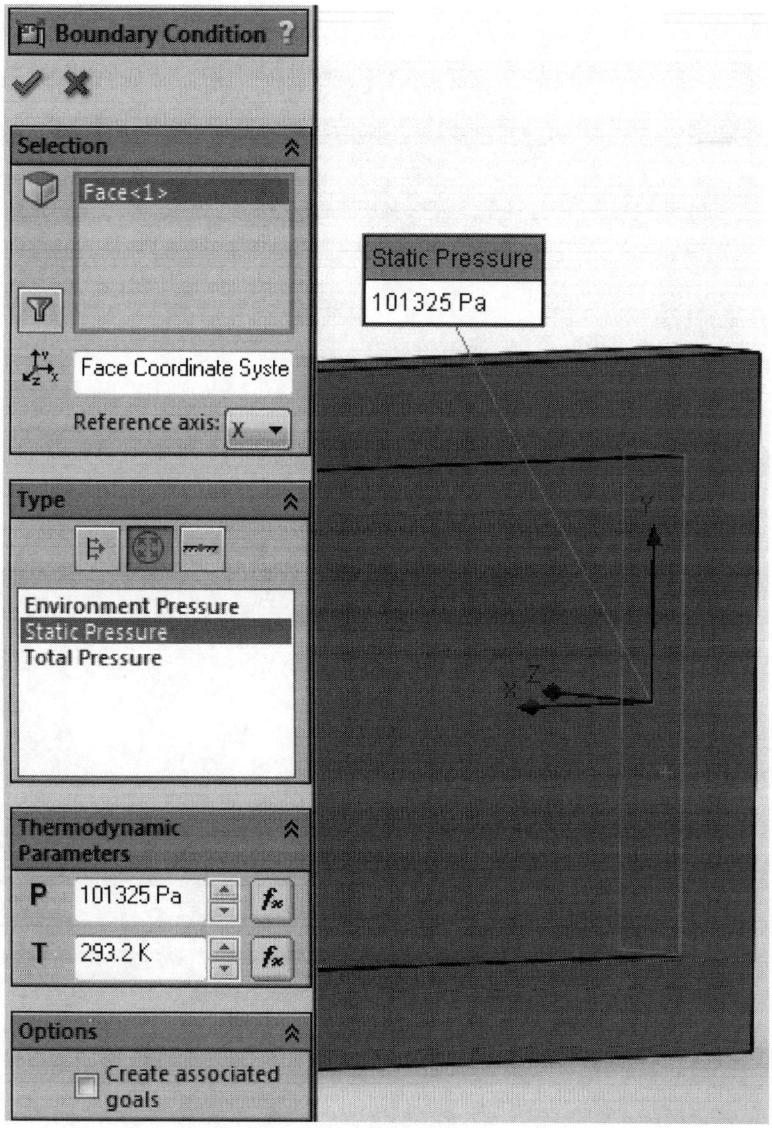

Figure 11.8 Selection of static pressure as boundary condition at the outlet of the flow region

9. Insert the following boundary conditions: Ideal Wall for the upper wall and lower wall at the inflow region; see figures 11.9a) and 11.9b). These will be adiabatic and frictionless walls.

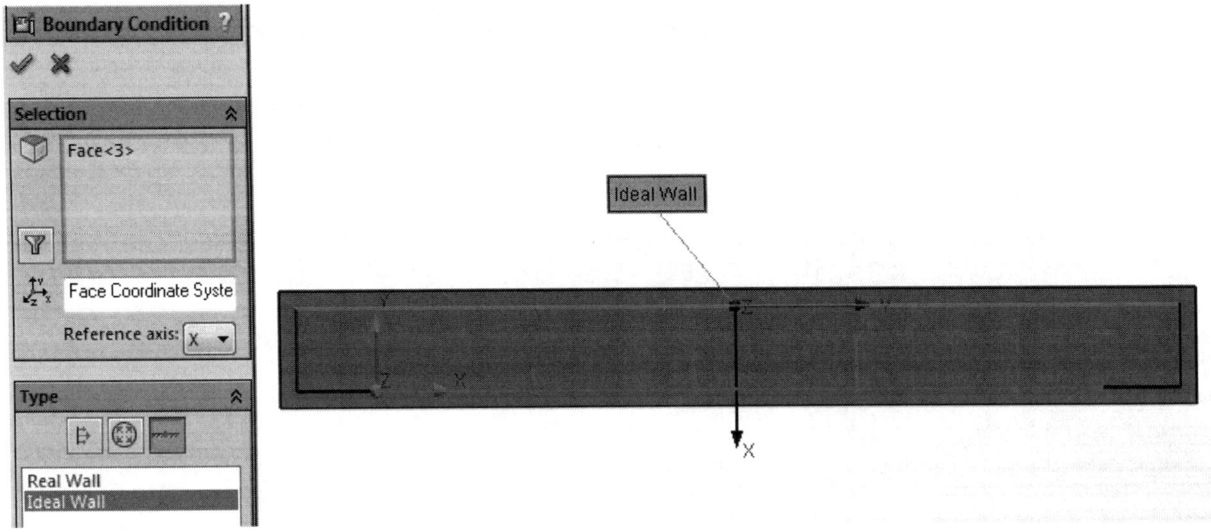

Figure 11.9a) Ideal wall boundary condition for upper wall

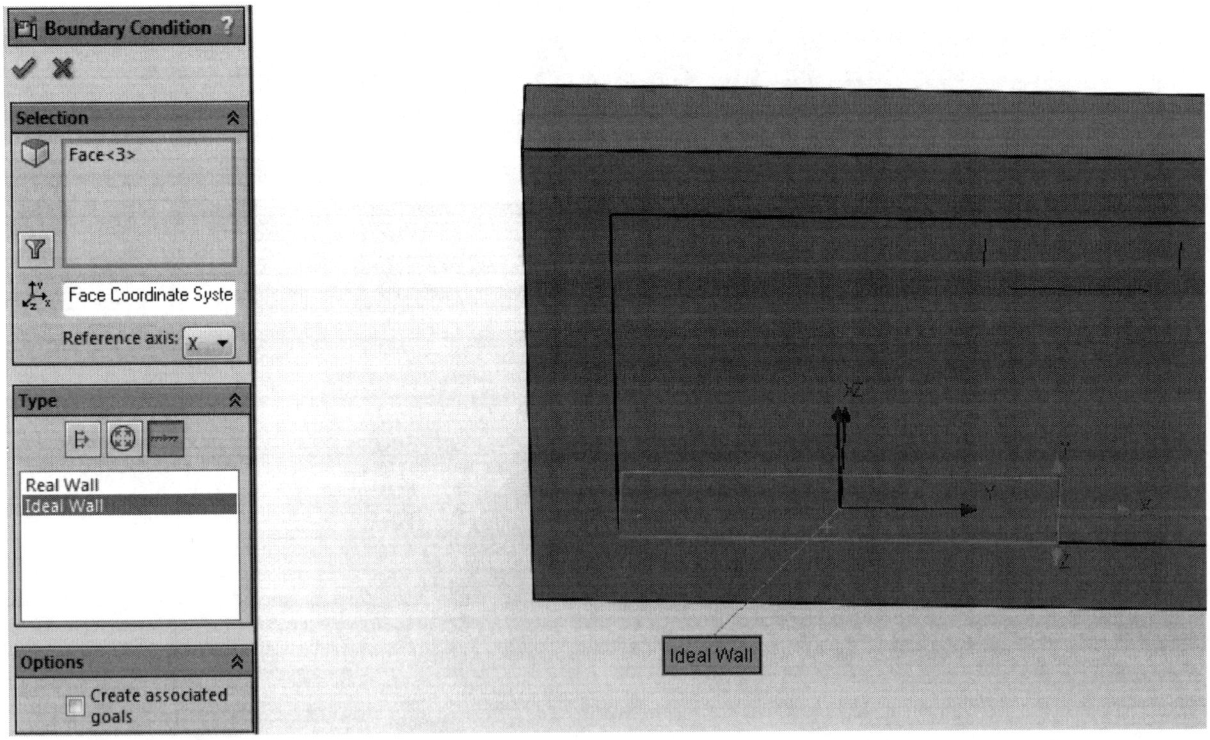

Figure 11.9b) Ideal wall boundary condition for lower wall at the inflow region

10. The last boundary condition will be in the form of a real wall. We will study the development of the thermal boundary layer on this wall. Set the temperature of the wall to **393.2 K**.

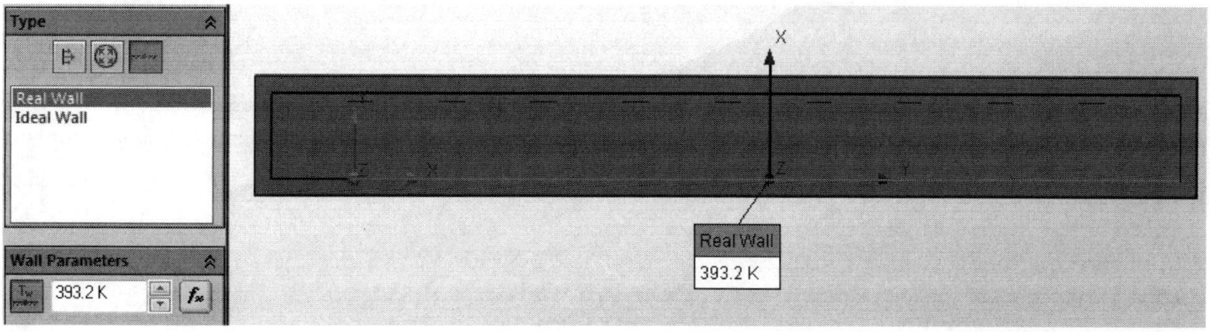

Figure 11.10 Real wall boundary condition for the flat plate

Inserting Goals

11. Right click on **Goals** in the **Flow Simulation analysis tree** and select **Insert Global Goals…**. Select **Av Temperature (Fluid)** as global goal.

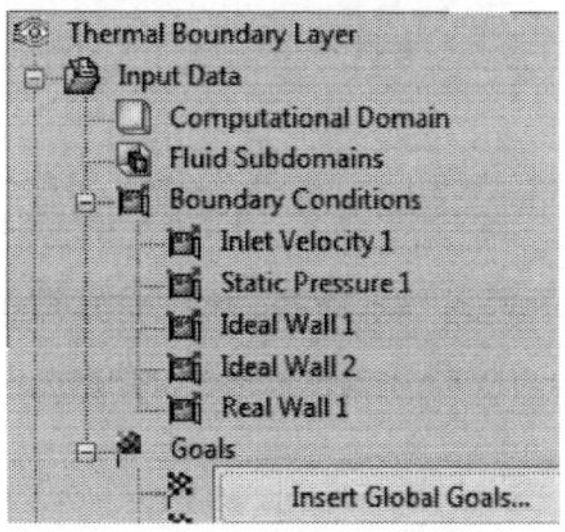

Figure 11.11 Inserting global goals

Running the Calculations for Low Reynolds Number

12. Select **Tools>>Flow Simulation>>Solve>>Run** to start calculations. Click on the **Run** button in the **Run** window.

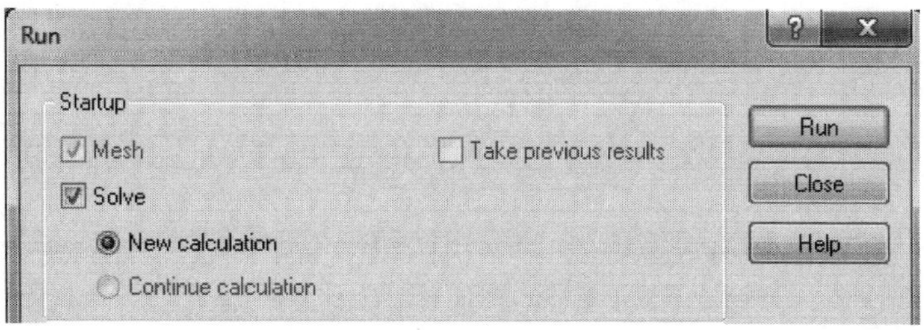

Figure 11.12a) Run window

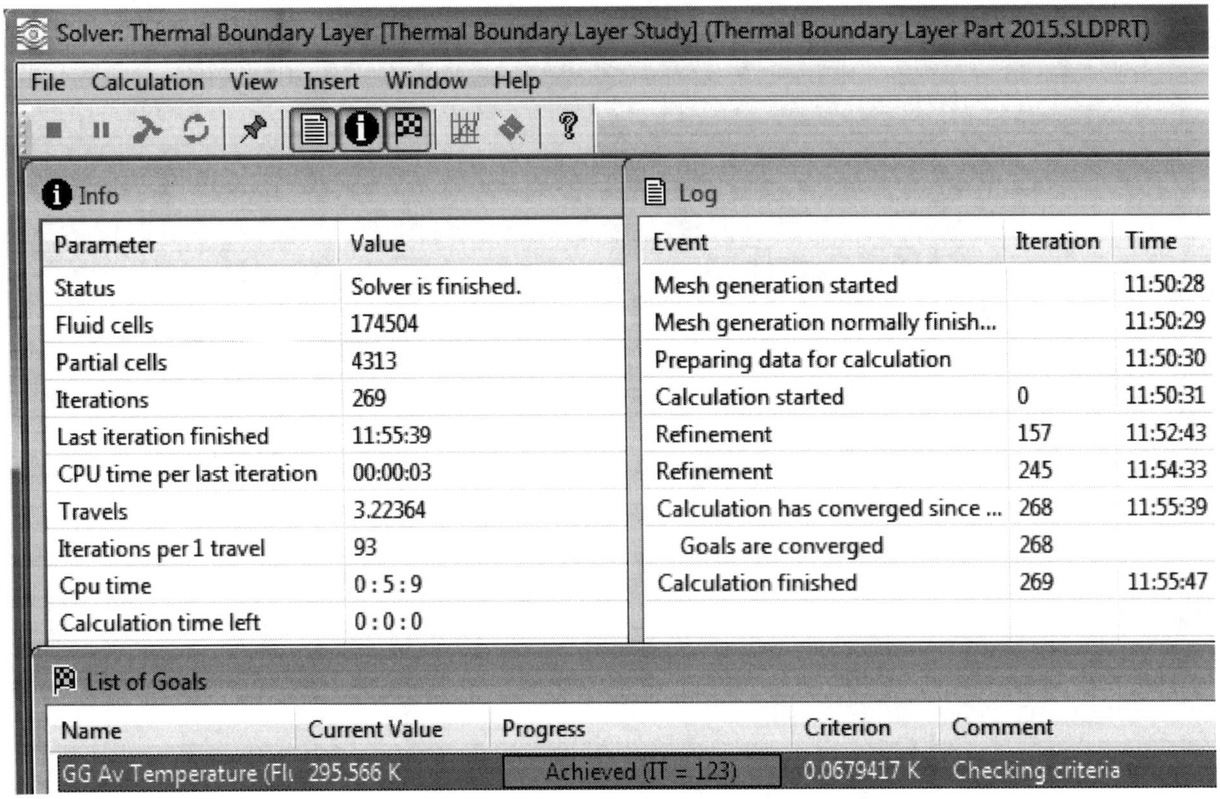

Figure 11.12b) Solver window

Inserting Cut Plots

13. Right click on Cut Plots in the **Flow Simulation analysis tree** and select **Insert…**. Select the **Front Plane** from the **FeatureManager design tree**. Slide the **Number of Levels** slide bar to **255**. Select **Temperature** from the **Parameter** drop down menu. Click OK to exit the **Cut Plot** window. Click on Section View and exit the dialog box by clicking OK. Select **Tools>>Flow Simulation>>Results>>Display>>Lighting**. Figures 11.13a) and 11.13b) show the temperature gradient close to the heated wall of the flat plate.

Figure 11.13a) Thermal boundary layer along the flat plate

Figure 11.13b) Thermal boundary layer close to the wall

Plotting Temperature Profiles using Template

14. Place the file **"graph 11.14c)"** on the desktop. Click on the **FeatureManager design tree**. Click on the sketch **x = 0.2, 0.4, 0.6, 0.8 m**. Click on the **Flow Simulation analysis tree** tab. Right click **XY Plot** and select **Insert…**. Check the **Temperature** box. Open the **Resolution** portion of the **XY Plot** window and slide the **Geometry Resolution** as far as it goes to the right. Click on the **Evenly Distribute Output Points** button and increase the number of points to **500**. Open the **Options** portion and check the **Display boundary layer** box. Select the **Excel Workbook (*.xlsx)** from the drop down menu. Click on the **Export to Excel** button. Click OK to exit the **XY Plot** window. An Excel file will open with a graph of the temperature in the boundary layer at different streamwise positions.

Double click on the **graph 11.14c)** file to open the file. Click on **Enable Content** if you get a **Security Warning** that **Macros** have been disabled. If **Developer** is not available in the menu of the **Excel** file, you will need to do the following: Select **File>>Options** from the menu and click on the **Customize Ribbon** on the left hand side. Check the **Developer** box on the right hand side under **Main Tabs**. Click **OK** to exit the **Excel Options** window.

Click on the **Developer** tab in the **Excel** menu for the **graph 11.14c)** file and select **Visual Basic** on the left hand side to open the editor. Click on the plus sign next to **VBAProject (XY Plot 1.xlsx)** and click on the plus sign next to **Microsoft Excel Objects**. Right click on **Sheet2 (Plot Data)** and select **View Object**.

Select **Macro** in the **Modules** folder under **VBAProject (graph 11.14c).xlsm)**. Select **Run>>Run Macro** from the menu of the **MVB for Applications** window. Click on the **Run** button in the **Macros** window. Figure 11.14c) will become available in **Excel** showing temperature ***T (K)*** versus wall normal coordinate ***y (m)***. Close the **XY Plot** window and the **graph 11.14c)** window in **Excel**. Exit the **XY Plot** window in **SOLIDWORKS Flow Simulation** and rename the inserted xy-plot in the **Flow Simulation analysis tree** to **Laminar Temperature Boundary Layer**.

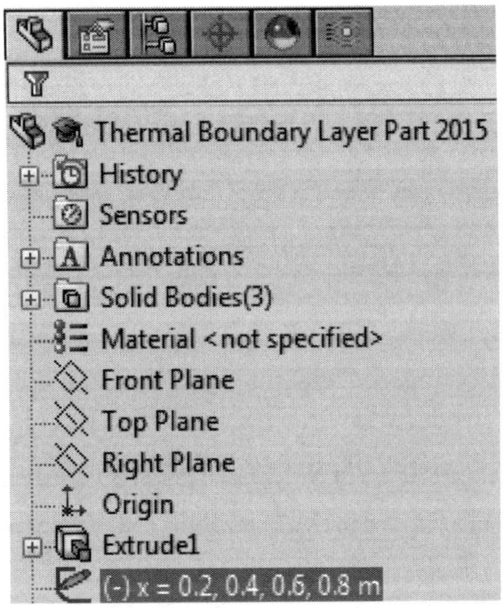

Figure 11.14a) Selecting the sketch for the XY Plot

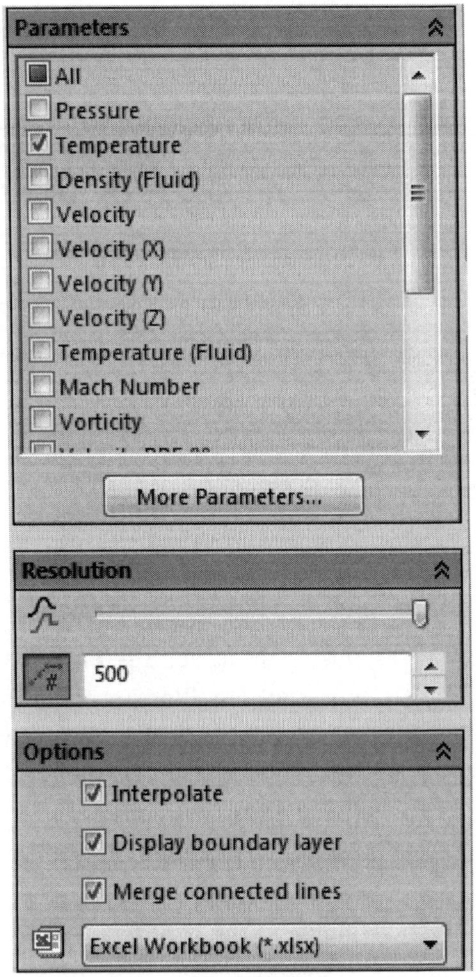

Figure 11.14b) Settings for the XY plot

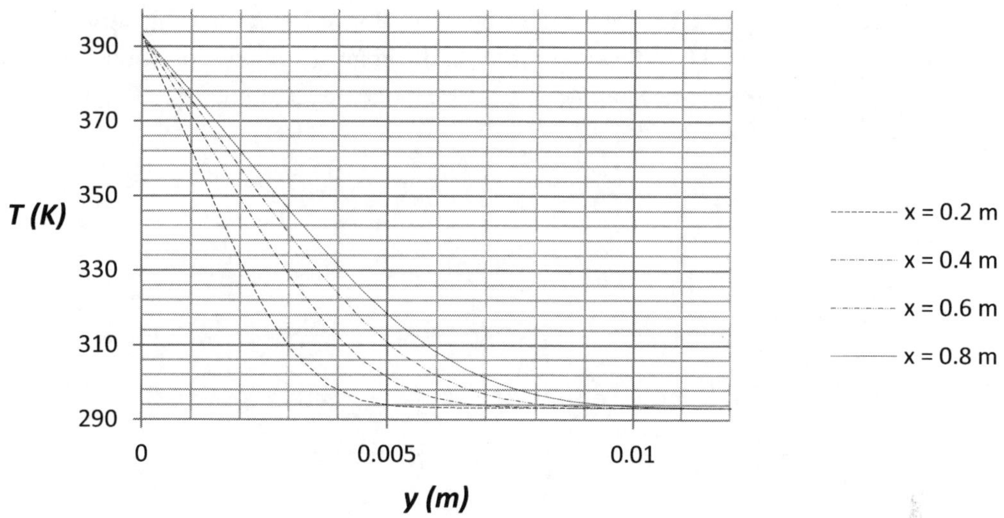

Figure 11.14c) Boundary layer temperature profiles on a flat plate at different streamwise positions

Theory

15. We now want to compare the temperature profiles with the theoretical temperature profile for laminar flow on a flat plate. First, we have to normalize the temperature T in the boundary layer

$$\Theta = \frac{T - T_\infty}{T_w - T_\infty} \tag{1}$$

where T_∞ is the temperature in the free stream and T_w is the wall temperature. We also have to transform the wall normal coordinate into the similarity coordinate for comparison with the theoretical profile. The similarity coordinate is described by

$$\eta = y\sqrt{\frac{U}{\upsilon x}} \tag{2}$$

where y (m) is the wall normal coordinate, U (m/s) is the free stream velocity, x (m) is the distance from the leading edge and υ (m^2/s) is the kinematic viscosity of the fluid. The fluid properties are evaluated at the film temperature $T_f = (T_w + T_\infty)/2$.

Plotting Non-Dimensional Temperature Profiles using Template

Place the file **"graph 11.15"** on the desktop. Repeat step **14** and select **graph 11.15** for the XY-plot. We see in figure 11.15 that all profiles at different streamwise positions approximately collapse on the same curve when we use the boundary layer similarity coordinate.

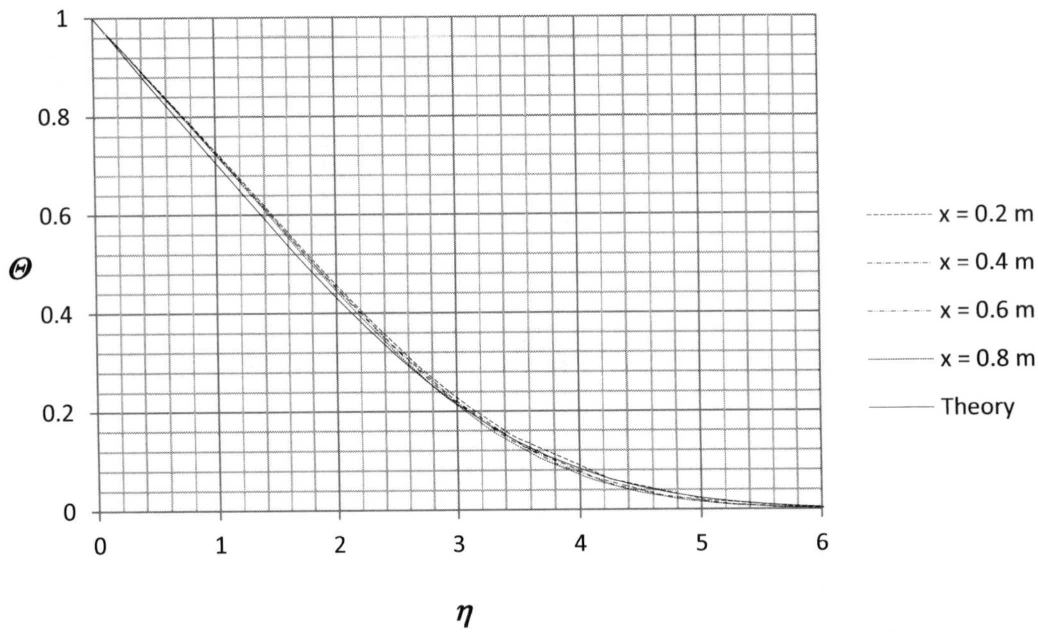

Figure 11.15 Temperature profiles in comparison with the theoretical profile (full line)

The Reynolds number for the flow on a flat plate is defined as

$$Re_x = \frac{Ux}{\nu} \tag{3}$$

The Reynolds number varies between $Re = 50{,}100$ at $x = 0.2$ m and $Re = 200{,}400$ at $x = 0.8$ m. We now want to study how the local Nusselt number varies along the plate. It is defined as the local convection coefficient h_x times the streamwise coordinate x divided by the thermal conductivity k:

$$Nu_x = \frac{h_x x}{k} \tag{4}$$

The theoretical local Nusselt number for laminar flow is given by

$$Nu_x = 0.332 Pr^{1/3} Re_x^{1/2} \qquad Pr > 0.6 \tag{5}$$

and for turbulent flow

$$Nu_x = 0.0296 Pr^{1/3} Re_x^{4/5} \qquad 5 \cdot 10^5 \leq Re_x \leq 10^7, 0.6 \leq Pr \leq 60 \tag{6}$$

Plotting Local Nusselt Number using Template

16. Place the file **"graph 11.16"** on the desktop. Repeat step **14** but this time choose the sketch **x = 0 – 0.9 m** and check the box for **Heat Transfer Coefficient**. An Excel file will open with a graph of the local Nusselt number versus the Reynolds number and compared with theoretical values for laminar thermal boundary layer flow; see figure 11.16.

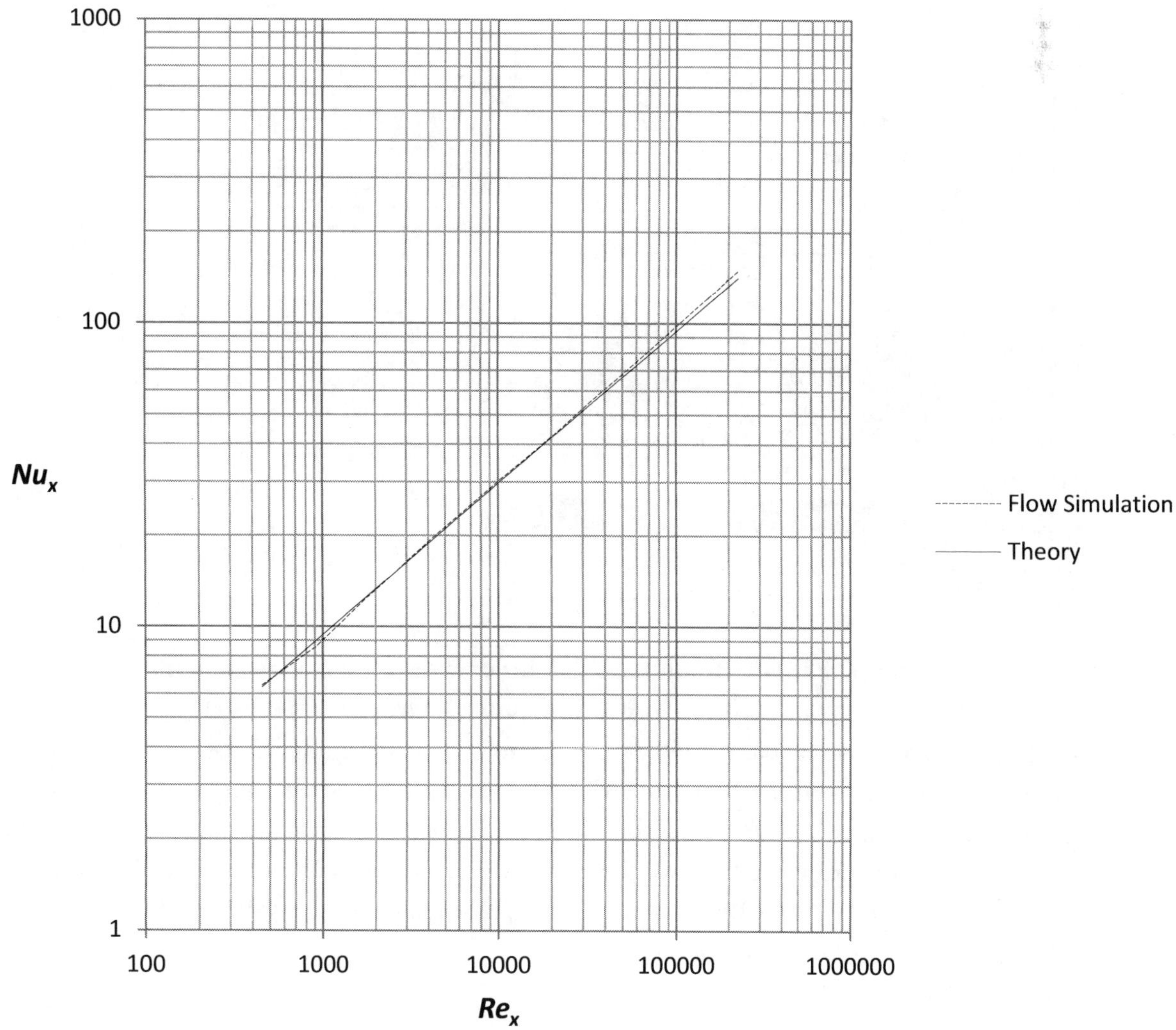

Figure 11.16 Local Nusselt number as a function of the Reynolds number

Running the Calculations at a High Reynolds Number

17. In the next step, we will change the fluid to water in order to get higher Reynolds numbers. Start by selecting **Tools>>Flow Simulation>>General Settings…** from the SOLIDWORKS menu. Click on **Fluids** in the **Navigator** portion and click on the **Remove** button. Answer **OK** to the question that appears. Select **Water** from the **Liquids** and **Add** it as the **Project Fluid**. Change the **Flow type** to **Laminar and Turbulent**; see figure 11.17. Close the **General Setting** window.

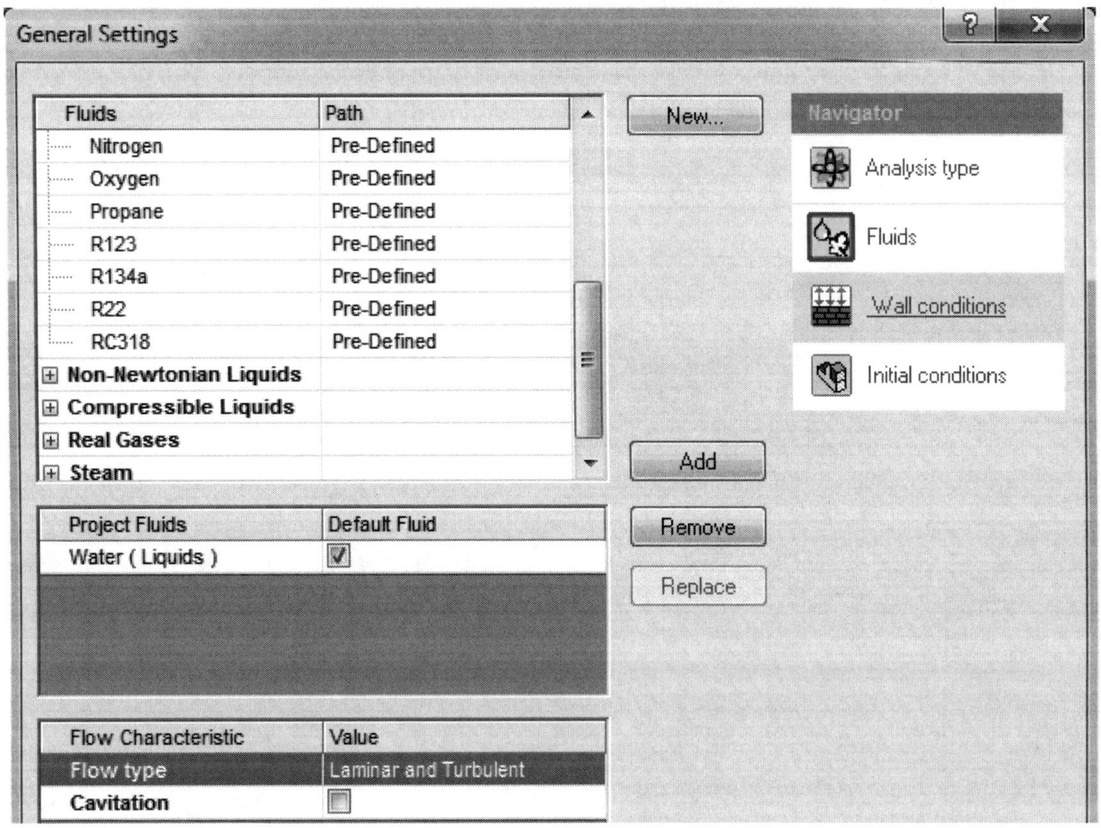

Figure 11.17 Selection of fluid and flow type

18. Right click the **Static Pressure Boundary Condition** in the **Flow Simulation analysis tree** and select **Edit Definition…**. Select **Turbulent Boundary Layer** in the **Boundary Layer** portion of the **Boundary Condition** window. Click **OK** to exit the **Boundary Condition** window. Right click the **Inlet Velocity Boundary Condition** in the **Flow Simulation analysis tree** and select **Edit Definition…**. Select **Laminar Boundary Layer**. Click **OK** to exit the **Boundary Condition** window. Right click the **Real Wall Boundary Condition** in the **Flow Simulation analysis tree** and select **Edit Definition…**. Set the temperature of the wall to **353.2 K**. Click **OK** to exit the **Boundary Condition** window.

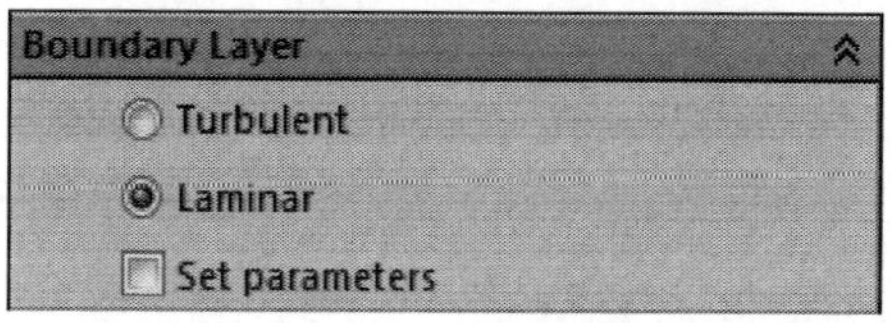

Figure 11.18 Selection of laminar boundary layer for inlet

19. Select **Tools>>Flow Simulation>>Solve>>Run** to start calculations. Check the **Create Mesh** box and select **New calculation**. Click on the **Run** button in the **Run** window.

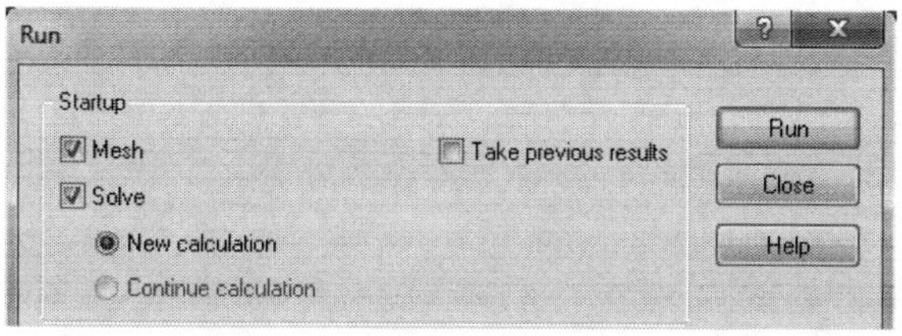

Figure 11.19a) Creation of mesh and starting a new calculation

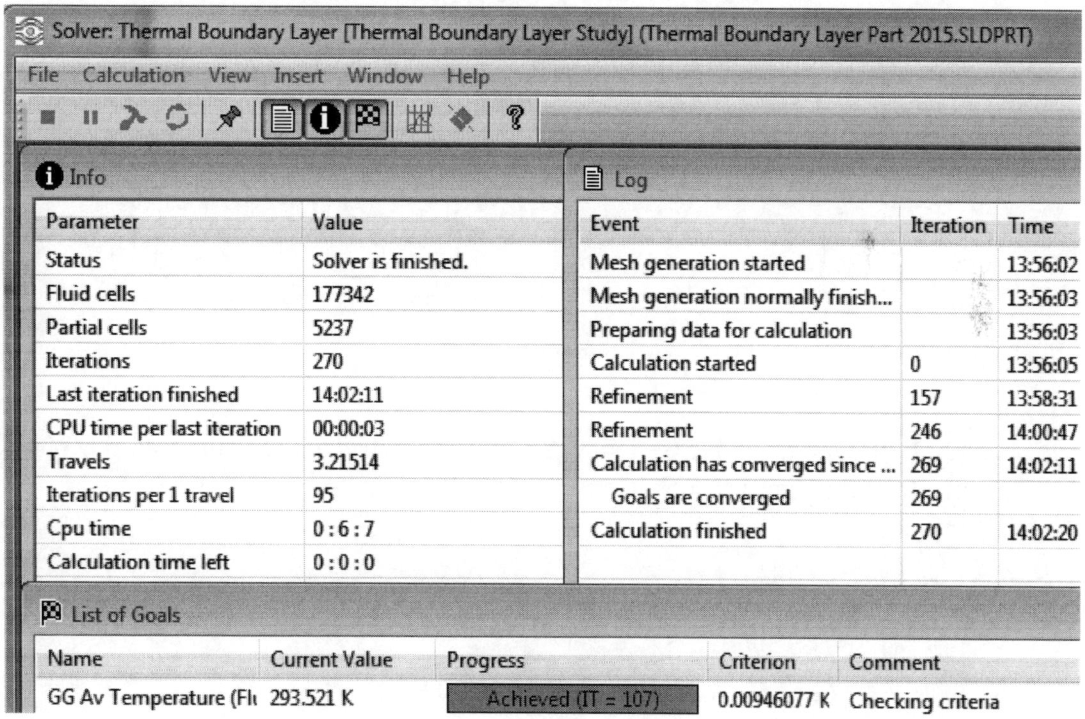

Figure 11.19b) Solver window for higher Reynolds number

20. Place the file **"graph 11.20"** on the desktop. Repeat step **16** but choose the file **"graph 11.20**." An Excel file will open with a graph of the local Nusselt number versus the Reynolds number and compared with theoretical values for laminar and turbulent thermal boundary layer flow; see figure 11.20.

Figure 11.20 is showing the Flow Simulation is able to capture the local Nusselt number in the laminar region in the Reynolds number range 40,000 – 400,000. At the critical Reynolds number Re_{cr} = 400,000 there is an abrupt increase in the Nusselt number caused by laminar to turbulent transition. In the turbulent region the Nusselt number is increasing again with a higher slope than in the laminar region.

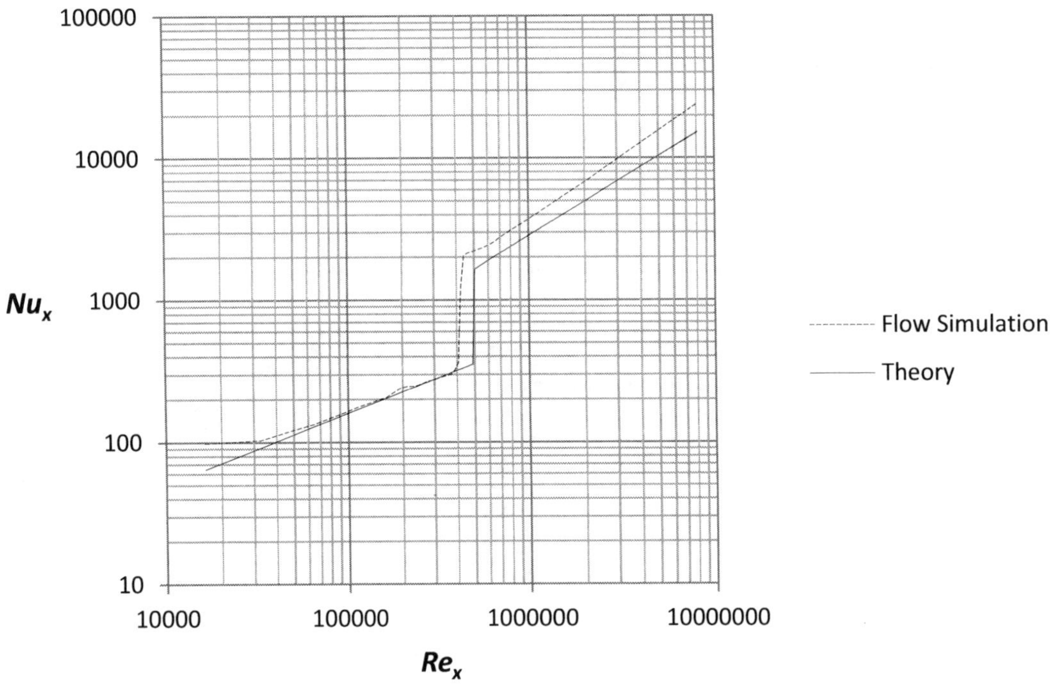

Figure 11.20 Comparison between Flow Simulation (dashed line) and theoretical laminar and empirical turbulent local Nusselt numbers

The average Nusselt number Nu over the entire length L of the plate for laminar flow is given by

$$Nu = 0.664 Pr^{1/3} Re_L^{1/2} \qquad Pr > 0.6,\ Re_L \leq 5 \cdot 10^5 \tag{7}$$

and for turbulent flow

$$Nu = 0.037 Pr^{1/3} Re_L^{4/5} \qquad 5 \cdot 10^5 \leq Re_L \leq 10^7, 0.6 \leq Pr \leq 60 \tag{8}$$

If the boundary layer is laminar on one part of the plate and turbulent on the remaining part, the average Nusselt number is determined by

$$Nu = \left[0.664\sqrt{Re_{cr}} + 0.037\left(Re_L^{4/5} - Re_{cr}^{4/5}\right)\right] Pr^{1/3} \tag{9}$$

References

[1] Çengel Y.A., Heat Transfer: A Practical Approach, 2nd Edition, 2003.

[2] Schlichting H. and Gersten K., Boundary Layer Theory, 8th Revised and Enlarged Edition, Springer, 2001.

[3] SOLIDWORKS Flow Simulation 2015 Technical Reference.

[4] White, F. M., Fluid Mechanics, 4th Edition, McGraw-Hill, 1999.

Exercise

1. Change the number of cells per X and Y, see figure 11.6b), for the laminar boundary layer and plot graphs of the local Nusselt number versus Reynolds number for different combinations of cells per X and Y. Compare with theoretical results.

2. Modify the length of the heated section so that there is an unheated starting length and the heated section starts at $x = 0.4$ m. You get a cold real wall section for the part upstream of $x = 0.4$ m with the same temperature as the free stream temperature. Use cut plots and XY-Plots for temperature profiles in Flow Simulation to study the development of the thermal boundary layer on the flat plate.

3. Modify the length of the heated section so that it ends at x = 0.6 m and you get a cold real wall section for the remaining part of the plate with the same temperature as the free stream temperature. Use cut plots and XY-Plots for temperature profiles in Flow Simulation to study the development of the thermal boundary layer after the heated section.

Notes:

Chapter 12 Free-Convection on a Vertical Plate and from a Horizontal Cylinder

Objectives

- Setting up Flow Simulation projects for external flow
- Creating goals
- Running the calculations
- Using cut plots, XY plots from templates and animations to visualize the resulting flow fields
- Compare Flow Simulation results with theoretical and empirical data

Problem Description

We will use Flow Simulation to study the thermal two-dimensional laminar flow on a vertical flat plate and compare with the theoretical boundary layer solution. We will be using air as the fluid for the flow calculations. The temperature of the vertical hot wall will be set to 296.2 K while the temperature of the surrounding air is 293.2 K. We will determine temperature and velocity profiles and plot the same profiles using similarity variables. The variation of the local Nusselt number will be determined. We will also look at free convection from a heated cylinder in air. The diameter of the cylinder is 20 mm and the temperature of the same cylinder will be set to 393.2 K.

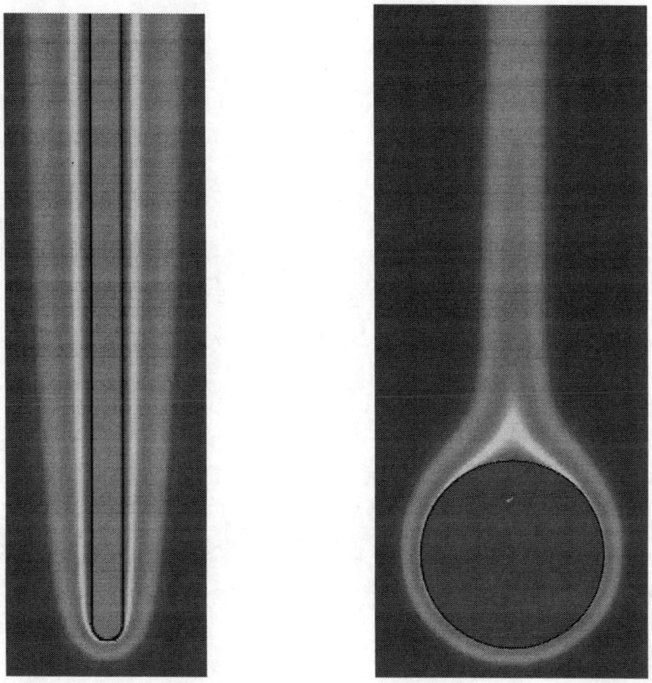

Figure 12.0 Thermal boundary layers on a vertical wall and around a horizontal cylinder

Setting up the Flow Simulation Project

1. Open the part named "**Free-Convection Boundary Layer Part 2015**."

Figure 12.1 SOLIDWORKS model for free-convection boundary layer

2. If Flow Simulation is not available in the menu, you have to add it from SOLIDWORKS menu: **Tools>>Add Ins...** and check the corresponding **SOLIDWORKS Flow Simulation** box. Select **Tools>>Flow Simulation>>Project>>Wizard** to create a new Flow Simulation project. Create a new project named "**Free-Convection Boundary Layer Study**." Click on the **Next >** button. Select the default **SI (m-kg-s)** unit system and click on the **Next>** button once again.

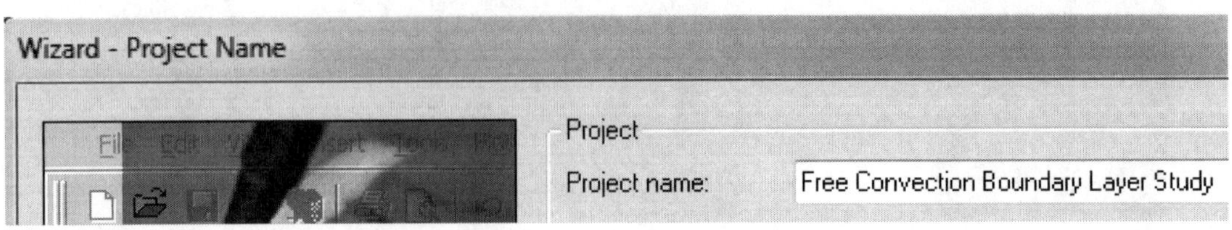

Figure 12.2 Creating a name for the project

3. Use the **External Analysis type** and check the box for **Gravity** as **Physical Feature**. Click on the **Next >** button.

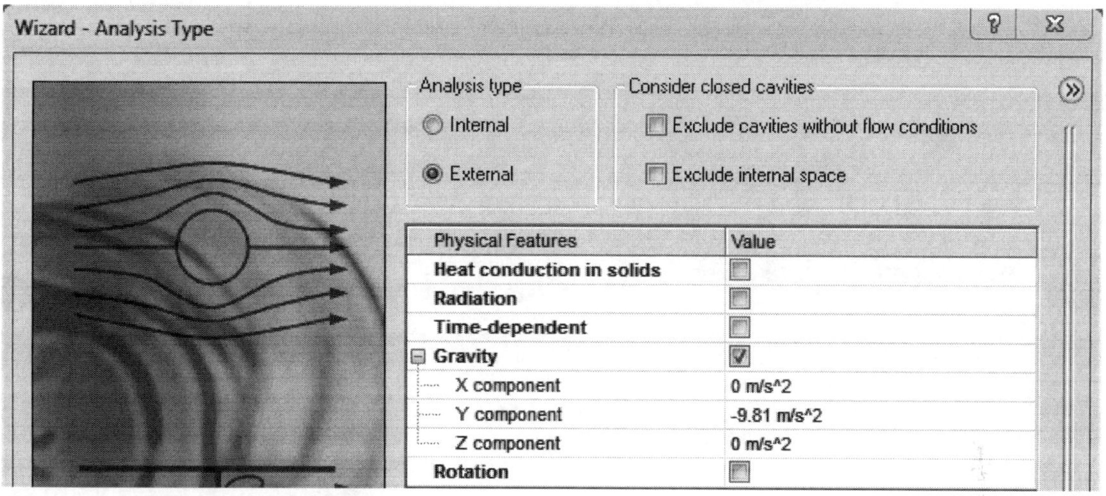

Figure 12.3 Analysis type window

4. Select **Air** from the **Gases** and add it as **Project Fluid**. Select **Laminar Only** from the **Flow Type** drop down menu. Click on the **Next >** button. Select **Wall temperature** from the **Default wall thermal condition Value** drop down menu. Set the **Wall temperature** to **296.2 K**. Click on the **Next >** button. Use default values for **Initial and Ambient Conditions**. Click on the **Next >** button. Slide the **Result resolution** to **8**. Click on the **Finish** button.

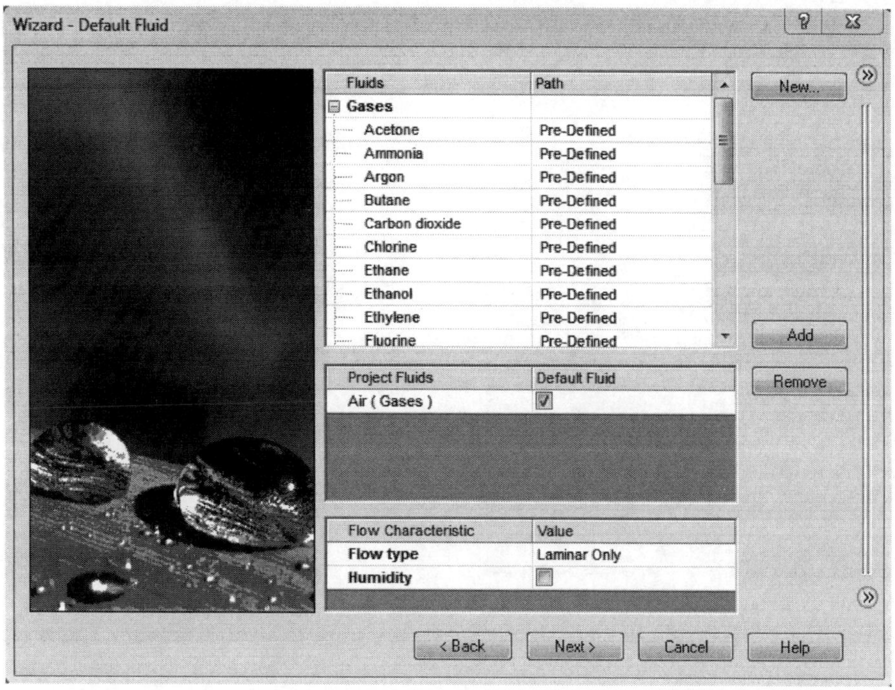

Figure 12.4a) Selection of fluid for the project and flow type

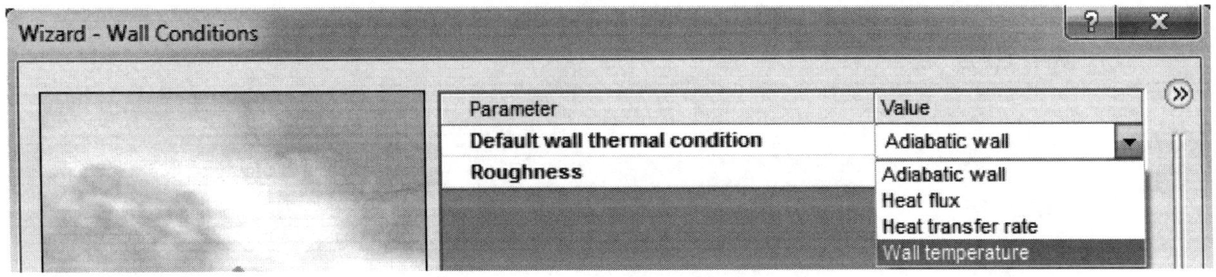

Figure 12.4b) Selection of wall temperature as thermal condition

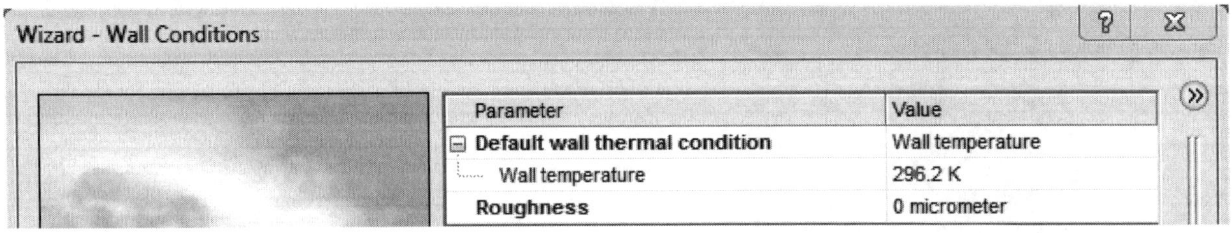

Figure 12.4c) Wall temperature setting

5. Select **Tools>>Flow Simulation>>Computational Domain…**. Click on the **2D simulation** button and select **XY plane**. Set the size of the computational domain as shown in figure 12.5b). Click on the **OK** button to exit the **Computational Domain** window.

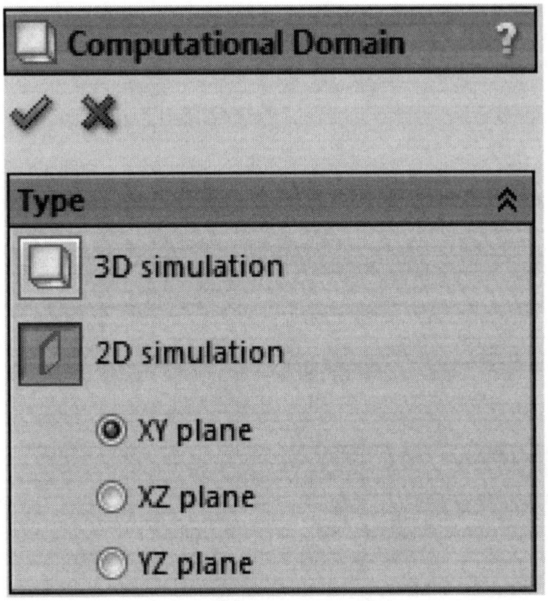

Figure 12.5a) Selecting two dimensional flow condition

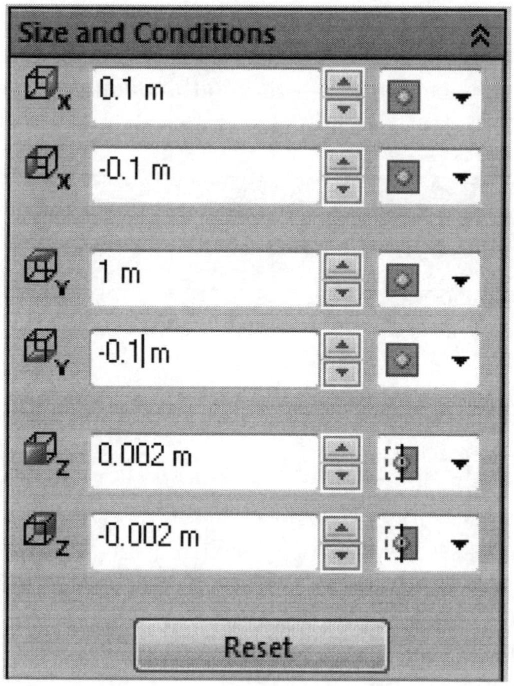

Figure 12.5b) Size of computational domain

6. Select **Tools>>Flow Simulation>>Initial Mesh…**. Uncheck the **Automatic setting** box at the bottom of the window. Change both the **Number of cells per X:** to **200** and the **Number of cells per Y:** to **196**. Click on the **OK** button to exit the **Initial Mesh** window.

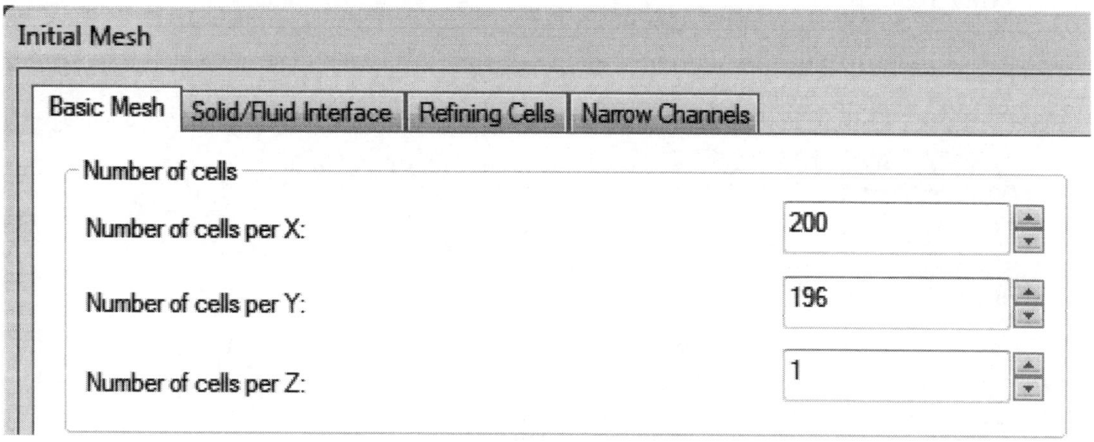

Figure 12.6 Changing the number of cells in both directions

Inserting Goals

7. Open the **Input Data** folder and right click on **Goals** in the **Flow Simulation analysis tree** and select **Insert Global Goals…**. Select global goals as shown in figure 12.7b).

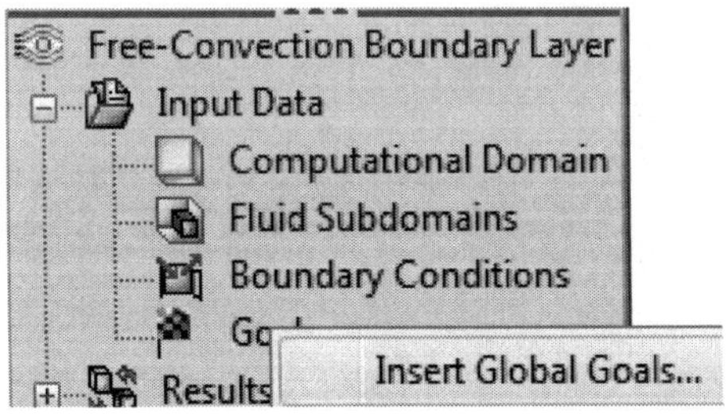

Figure 12.7a) Inserting global goals

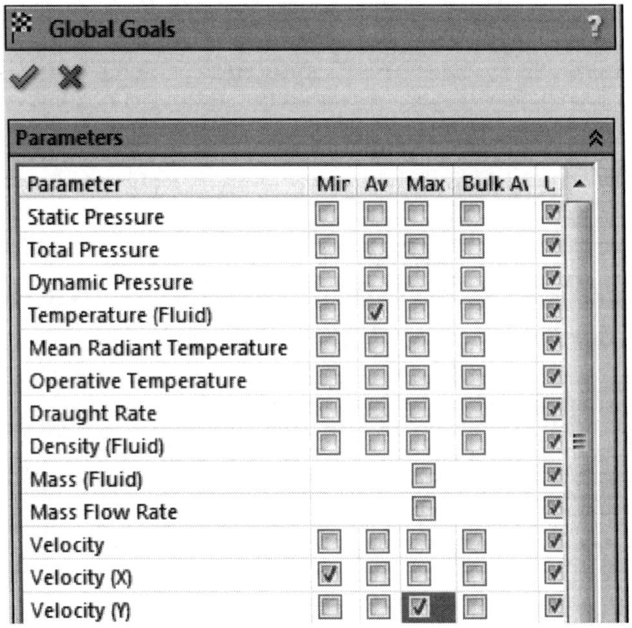

Figure 12.7b) Selection of temperature of fluid

Running Calculations

8. Select **Tools>>Flow Simulation>>Solve>>Run** to start calculations. Click on the **Run** button in the **Run** window.

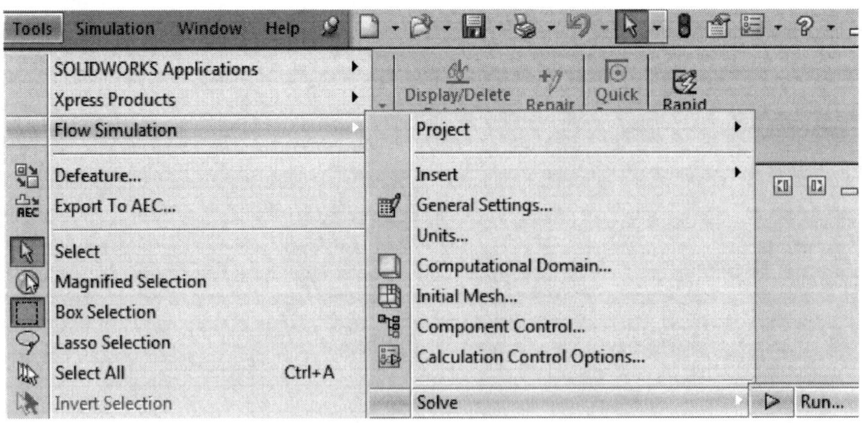

Figure 12.8a) Starting calculations

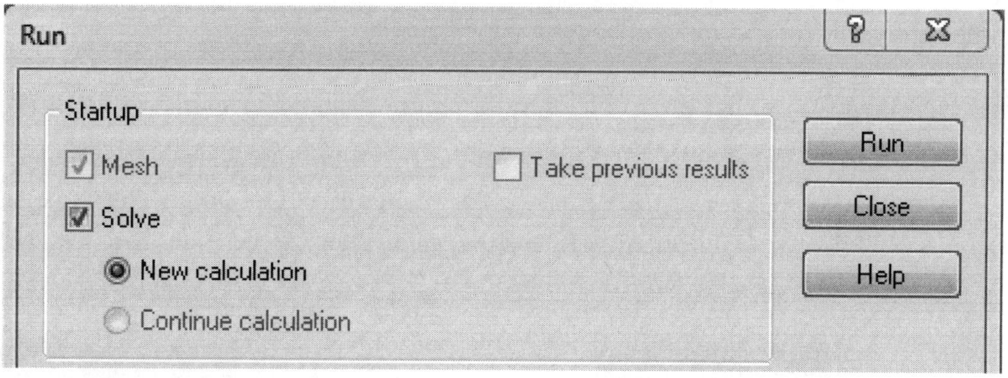

Figure 12.8b) Run window

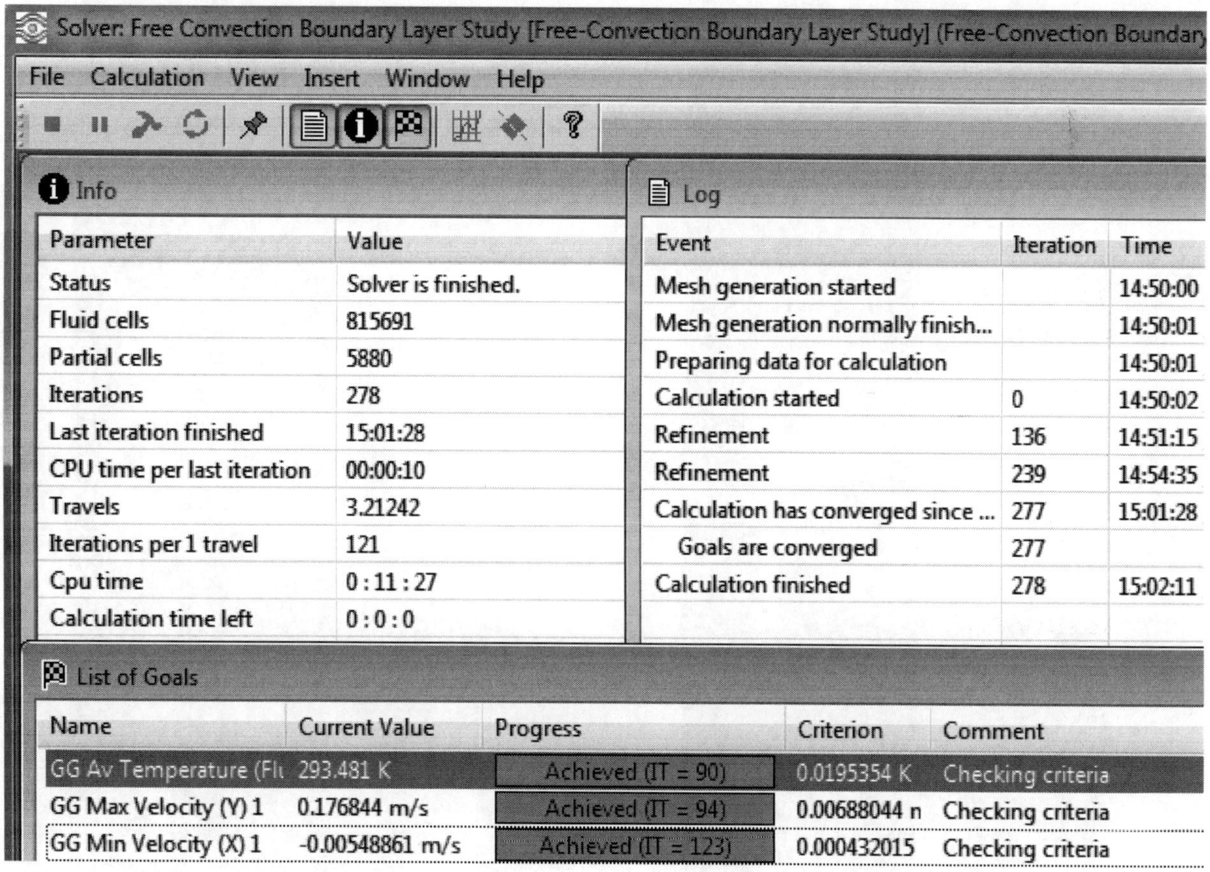

Figure 12.8c) Solver window

Inserting Cut Plots

9. Right click on Cut Plots in the **Flow Simulation analysis tree** and select **Insert…**. Select the **Front Plane** from the **FeatureManager design tree**. Slide the **Number of Levels** slide bar to **255**. Select **Temperature** from the **Parameter** drop down menu. Click OK to exit the **Cut Plot** window. Figure 12.9a) shows the temperature distribution along the vertical wall and figure 12.9b) shows the velocity distribution.

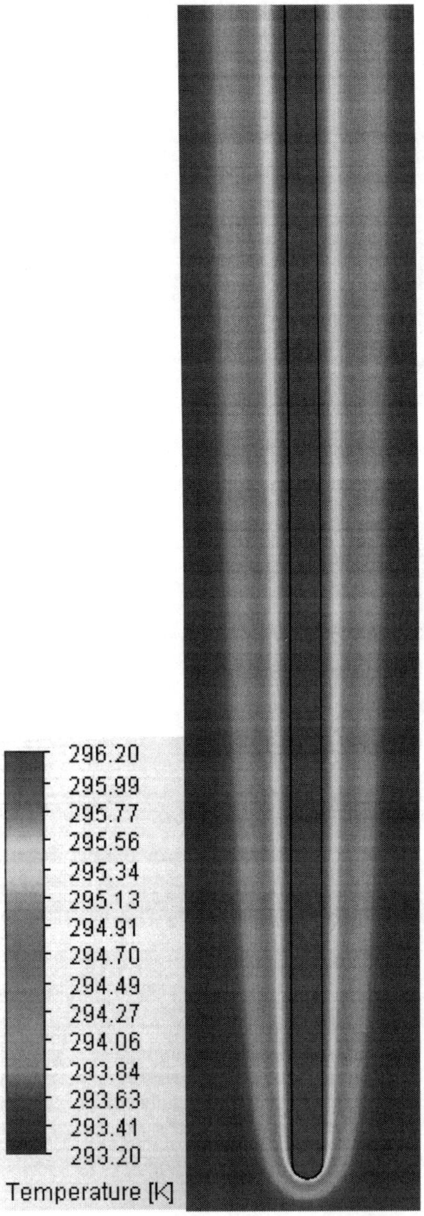

Figure 12.9a) Thermal boundary layer

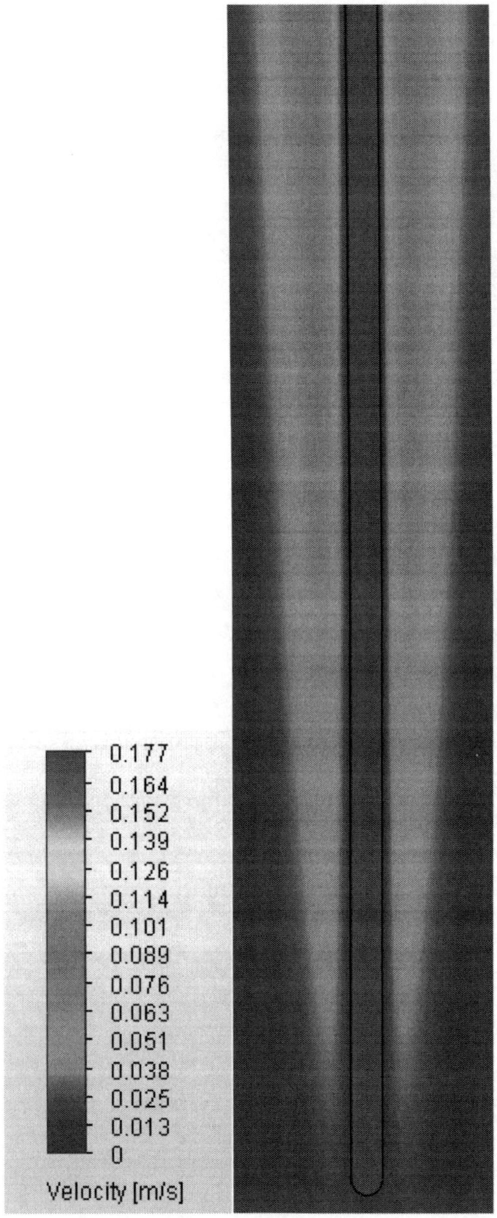

Figure 12.9b) Velocity boundary layer

Plotting Temperature and Velocity Profiles using Templates

10. Place the files "**graph 12.10c)**" and "**graph 12.10d)**" on the desktop. Click on the **FeatureManager design tree**. Click on the sketch **y = 0.2, 0.4, 0.6, 0.8 m**. Click on the **Flow Simulation analysis tree** tab. Right click **XY Plot** and select **Insert….** Check the **Temperature** box. Open the **Resolution** portion of the **XY Plot** window and slide the **Geometry Resolution** as far as it goes to the right. Click on the **Evenly Distribute Output Points** button and increase the number of points to **500**. Open the **Options** portion and check the **Display boundary layer** box. Select **Excel Workbook (*.xlsx)** from the drop down menu. Click on the **Export to Excel** button. Click OK to exit the **XY Plot** window. An Excel file will open with a graph of the temperature in the boundary layer.

Double click on the **graph 12.10c)** file to open the file. Click on **Enable Content** if you get a **Security Warning** that **Macros** have been disabled. If **Developer** is not available in the menu of the **Excel** file, you will need to do the following: Select **File>>Options** from the menu and click on the **Customize Ribbon** on the left hand side. Check the **Developer** box on the right hand side under **Main Tabs**. Click **OK** to exit the **Excel Options** window.

Click on the **Developer** tab in the **Excel** menu for the **graph 12.10c)** file and select **Visual Basic** on the left hand side to open the editor. Click on the plus sign next to **VBAProject (XY Plot 1.xlsx)** and click on the plus sign next to **Microsoft Excel Objects**. Right click on **Sheet2 (Plot Data)** and select **View Object**.

Select **Macro** in the **Modules** folder under **VBAProject (graph 12.10c).xlsm)**. Select **Run>>Run Macro** from the menu of the **MVB for Applications** window. Click on the **Run** button in the **Macros** window. Figure 12.10c) will become available in **Excel** showing temperature ***T (K)*** versus wall normal coordinate ***x (m)***. Close the **XY Plot** window and the **graph 12.10c)** window in **Excel**. Exit the **XY Plot** window in **SOLIDWORKS Flow Simulation**.

Repeat this step and select files "**graph 12.10d)**" and **Velocity (Y)** for the XY-plot; see figure 12.10d).

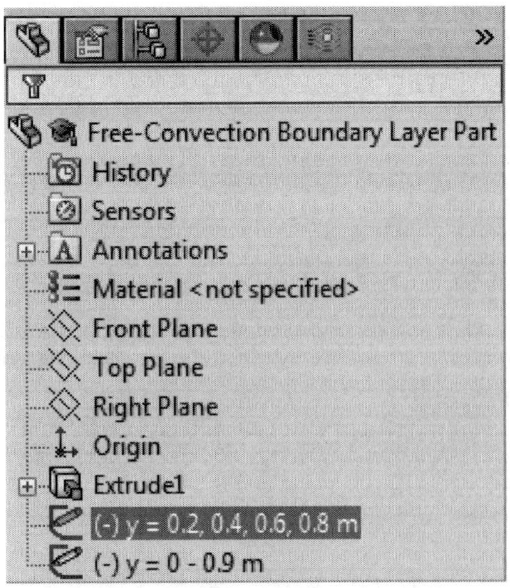

Figure 12.10a) Selecting the sketch

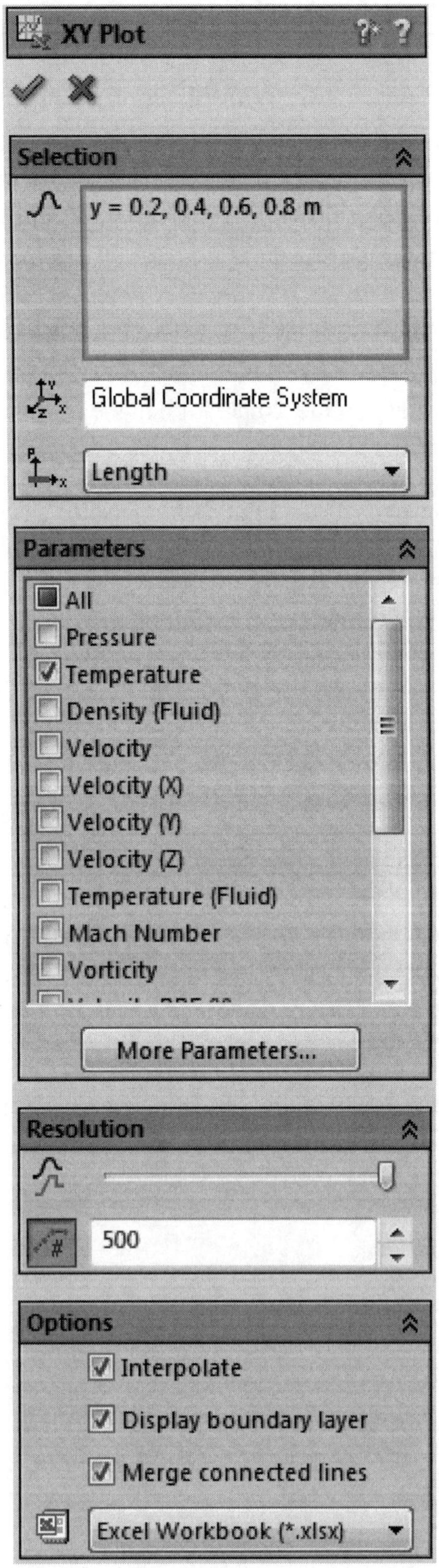

Figure 12.10b) Settings for the XY plot

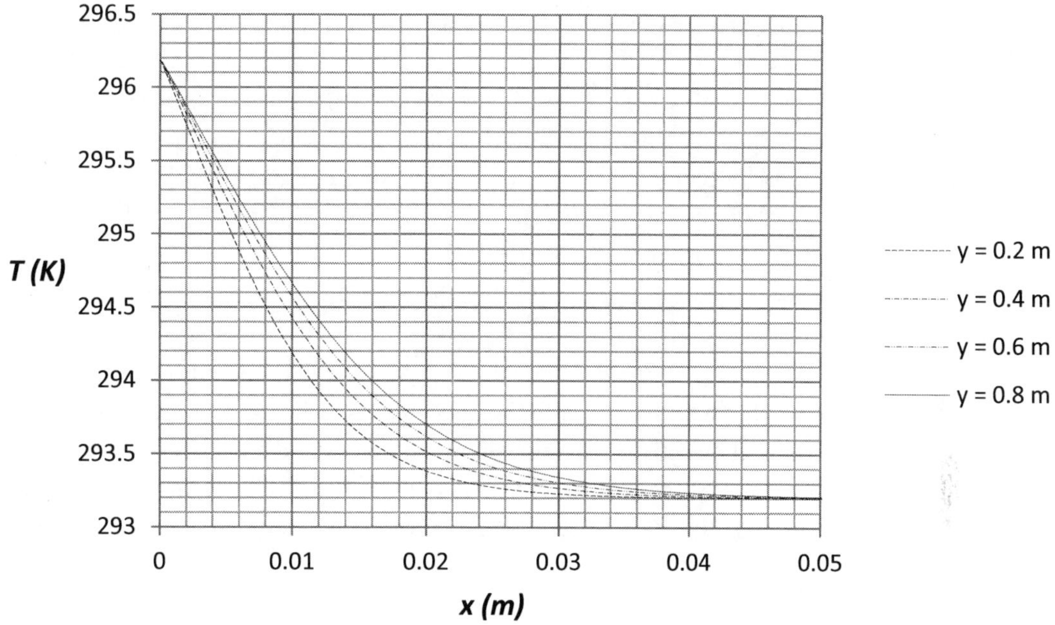

Figure 12.10c) Boundary layer temperature profiles on a vertical heated flat plate

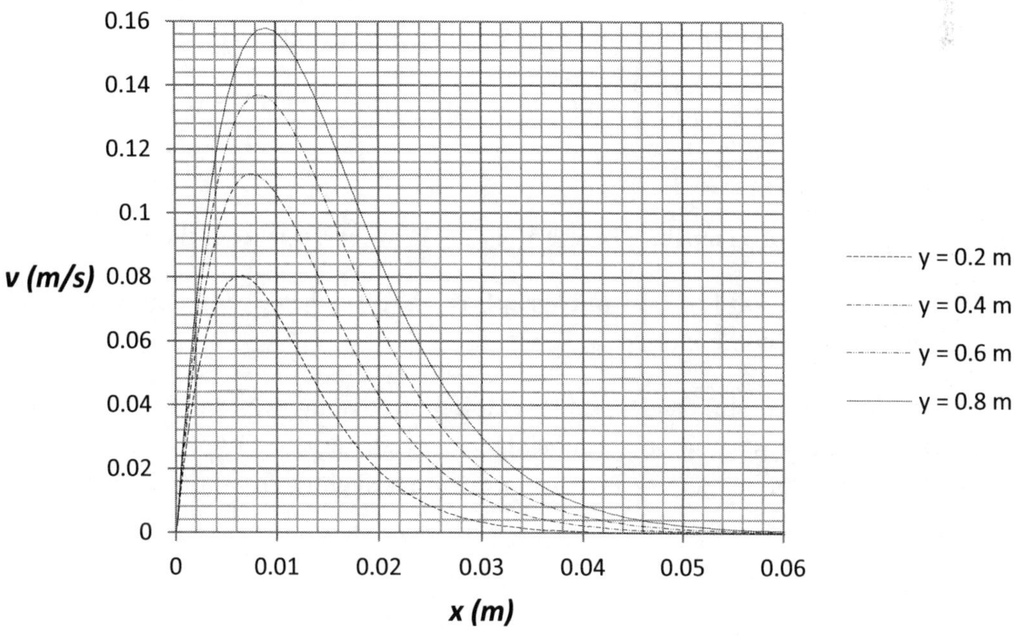

Figure 12.10d) Boundary layer velocity profiles on a vertical heated flat plate

Theory

11. We now want to compare the temperature and velocity profiles with the theoretical profiles. First, we have to normalize the temperature T in the boundary layer

$$\Theta = \frac{T - T_\infty}{T_W - T_\infty} \tag{1}$$

where T_∞ is the ambient temperature and T_W is the wall temperature. We also have to transform the wall normal coordinate into the similarity coordinate for comparison with the theoretical profile. The similarity coordinate is described by

$$\eta = \frac{x}{y} Ra^{1/4} \qquad Ra = \frac{\beta g (T_W - T_\infty) y^3}{\alpha \upsilon} \tag{2}$$

where Ra is the Rayleigh number, x is the wall normal coordinate, y is the coordinate along the vertical wall, g is acceleration due to gravity, α is the thermal diffusivity, β is the coefficient of volume expansion and υ is the kinematic viscosity of the fluid. The fluid properties are evaluated at the film temperature $T_f = (T_W + T_\infty)/2$. The theoretical velocity component v in the y direction is given by

$$\upsilon = -\frac{\alpha}{y} Ra^{1/2} f' \tag{3}$$

and there are two nonlinear coupled differential equations for f and Θ

$$4\mathrm{Pr}(f''' - \Theta) - 3ff'' + 2f'^2 = 0 \qquad 4\Theta'' - 3\Theta' f = 0 \tag{4}$$

where Pr is the Prandtl number. We have the following boundary conditions

$$f(0) = f'(0) = f'(\infty) = 0 \qquad \Theta(0) = 1, \Theta(\infty) = 0 \tag{5}$$

Plotting Non-Dimensional Temperature and Velocity Profiles using Templates

Place the files **"graph 12.11a)" and "graph 12.11b)"** on the desktop. Repeat step **10** and select the new files for the XY-plots.

We see in figure 12.11a) that all profiles at different streamwise positions approximately collapse on the same curve when we use the boundary layer similarity coordinate. For the theoretical velocity maximum in figure 12.11b) the maximum is slightly lower than Flow Simulation results.

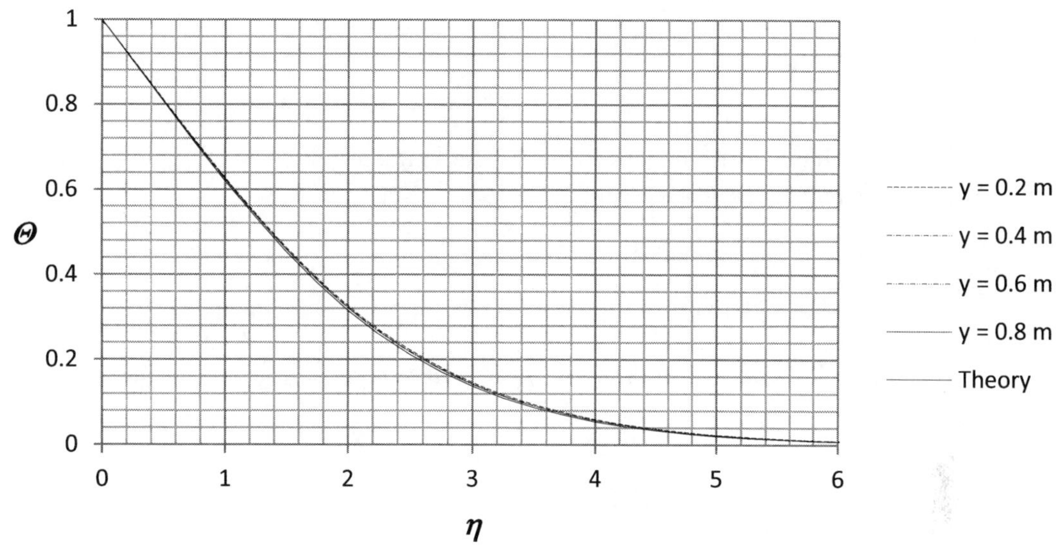

Figure 12.11a) Temperature profiles in comparison with the theoretical profile (full line)

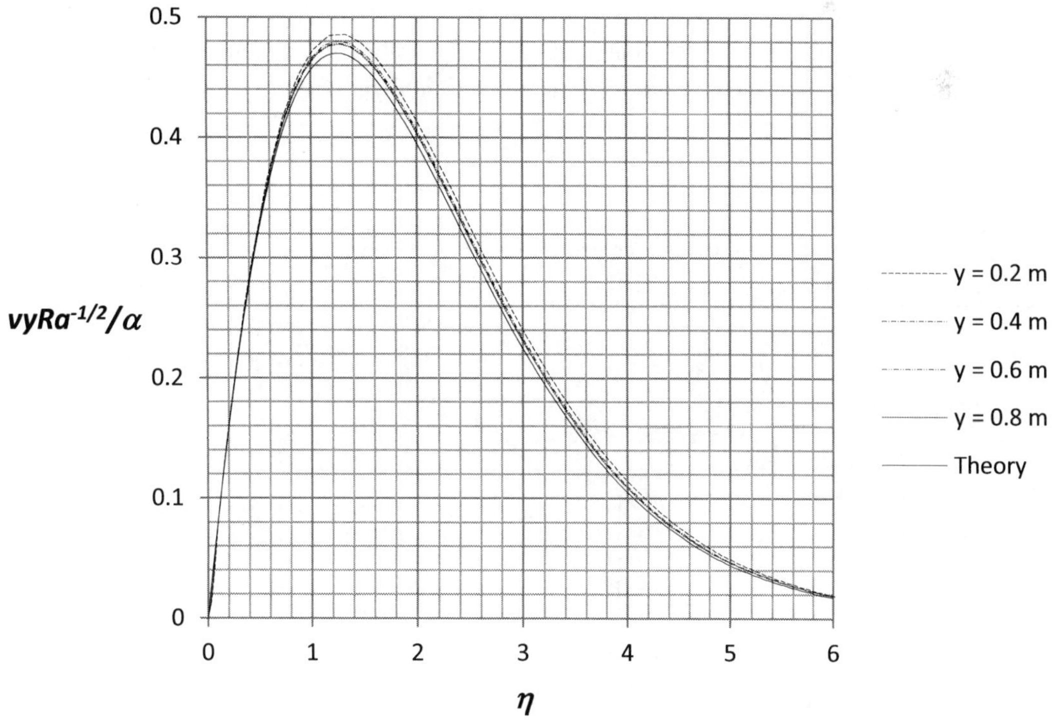

Figure 12.11b) Velocity profiles in comparison with the theoretical profile (full line)

We now want to study how the local Nusselt number varies along the vertical plate. It is defined as the local convection coefficient h_y times the vertical coordinate y divided by the thermal conductivity k:

$$Nu_y = \frac{h_y y}{k} \tag{6}$$

A curve-fit formula for local Nusselt number for laminar free-convection flow on a vertical flat wall is given by Churchill and Usagi

$$Nu_y = \frac{0.503Ra^{1/4}}{[1+\left(\frac{0.492}{\mathrm{Pr}}\right)^{\frac{9}{16}}]^{4/9}} \qquad 10^5 < Ra < 10^9 \tag{7}$$

The overall Nusselt number for free-convection flow on a vertical plate is given by Churchill and Chu

$$Nu_L^{1/2} = 0.825 + \frac{0.387Ra_L^{1/6}}{[1+\left(\frac{0.492}{\mathrm{Pr}}\right)^{\frac{9}{16}}]^{8/27}} \qquad Ra_L \leq 10^{12} \tag{8}$$

Plotting Local Nusselt Number using Template

12. Place the file **"graph 12.12"** on the desktop. Repeat step **10** but this time choose the sketch **y = 0 – 0.9 m** and check the box for **Heat Transfer Coefficient**. An Excel file will open with a graph of the local Nusselt number versus the Rayleigh number and compared with empirical curve-fit values for laminar free-convection flow on a vertical wall; see figure 12.12.

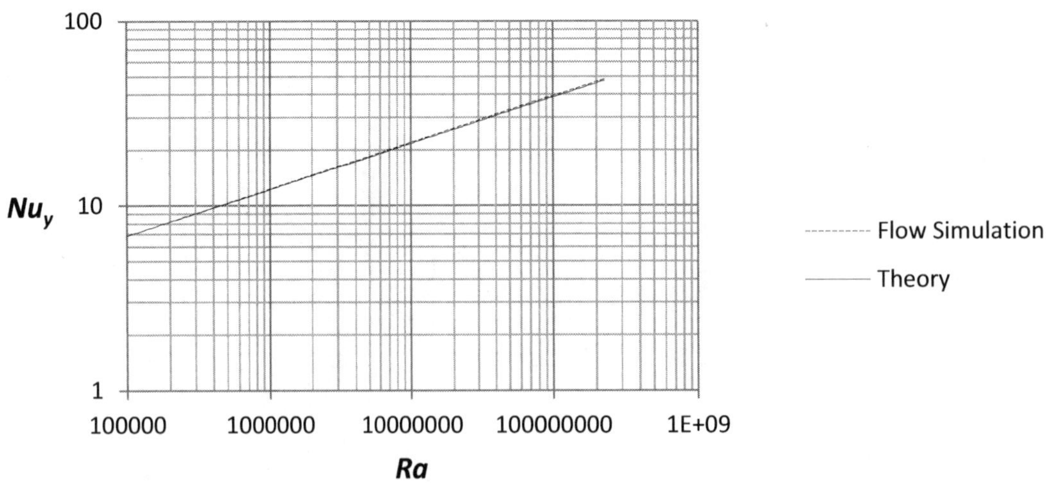

Figure 12.12 Local Nusselt number as a function of the Rayleigh number

Creating the SOLIDWORKS Part for Free Convection from a Horizontal Cylinder

13. Select **File>>New…** from the SOLIDWORKS menu. Select a new **Part** and click on the **OK** button. Select **Insert>>Sketch** from the SOLIDWORKS menu. Click on the **Front Plane** in the **FeatureManager design tree** to select the plane of the sketch. Select Front view from the **View Orientation** drop down menu in the graphics window. Select the **Circle** sketch tool from **Tools>>Sketch Entities** in the SOLIDWORKS menu.

Figure 12.13a) Creating a new SOLIDWORKS document

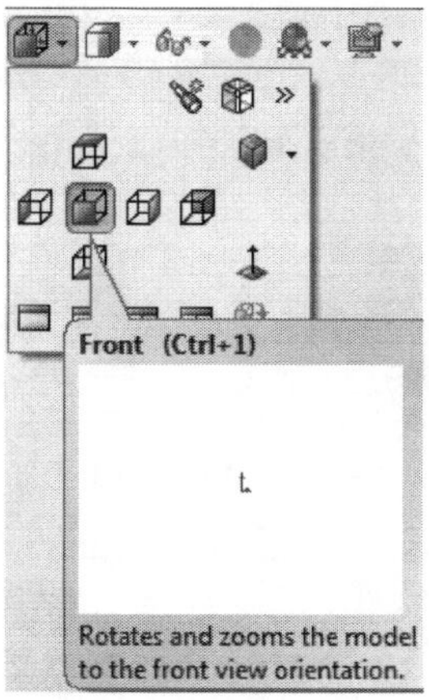

Figure 12.13b) Front view orientation

14. Draw a circle with a radius of **25.00 mm**. Close the **Circle** dialog box. Select **Insert>>Boss/Base>>Extrude** from the SOLIDWORKS menu. Check the **Direction 2** box and exit the **Extrude** dialog box. Select **File>>Save As** and enter the name "**Free Convection from Horizontal Cylinder**" as the name for the SOLIDWORKS part.

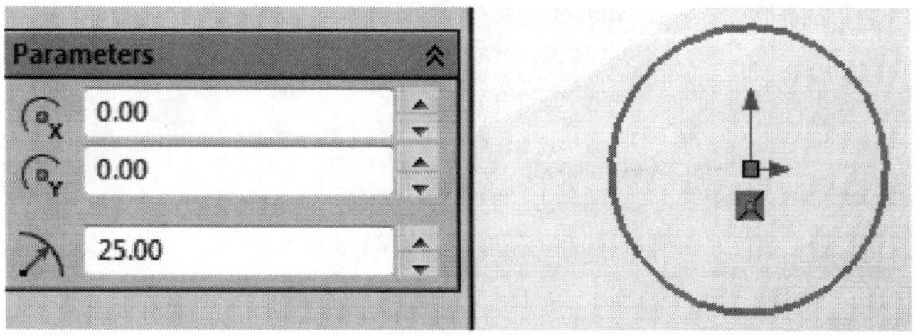

Figure 12.14 Sketch of a circle

Setting up the Flow Simulation Project for Free Convection from a Horizontal Cylinder

15. We create a project by selecting **Tools>>Flow Simulation>>Project>>Wizard…** from the menu. Create a new project and enter "**Free Convection from a Horizontal Cylinder**" as configuration name. Push the **Next>** button. We choose the **SI (m-kg-s)** unit system and click on the **Next>** button again.

In the next step we check **External** as analysis type, check the boxes for **Time-dependent** flow and **Gravity**. Click on the **Next>** button. The **Default Fluid Wizard** will now appear. We are going to add air as the **Project Fluid**. Start by clicking on the plus sign next to the **Gases** in the **Fluids** column. Scroll down the different gases and select air. Next, click on the **Add** button so that air will appear as the **Default Fluid**. Click on the **Next>** button.

The next part of the wizard is about **Wall Conditions**. We will use an **Adiabatic wall** for the cylinder and use zero surface roughness. Next, we get the **Initial and Ambient Conditions** in the Wizard. Click on the **Next>** button.

Slide the **Result resolution** to **8.** Push the **Finish** button in **Wizard - Results and Geometry Resolution** window.

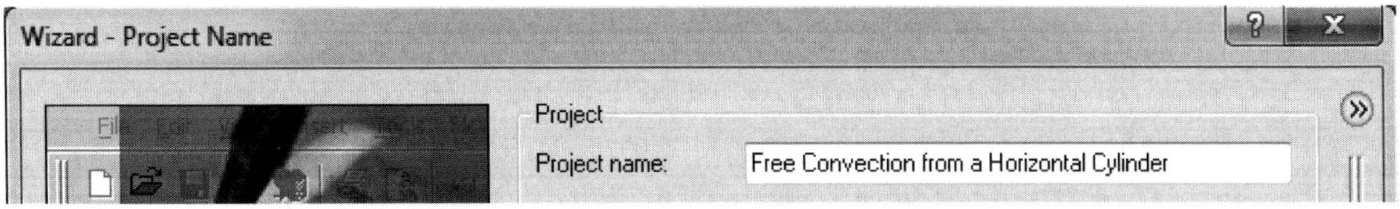

Figure 12.15a) Entering configuration name for project

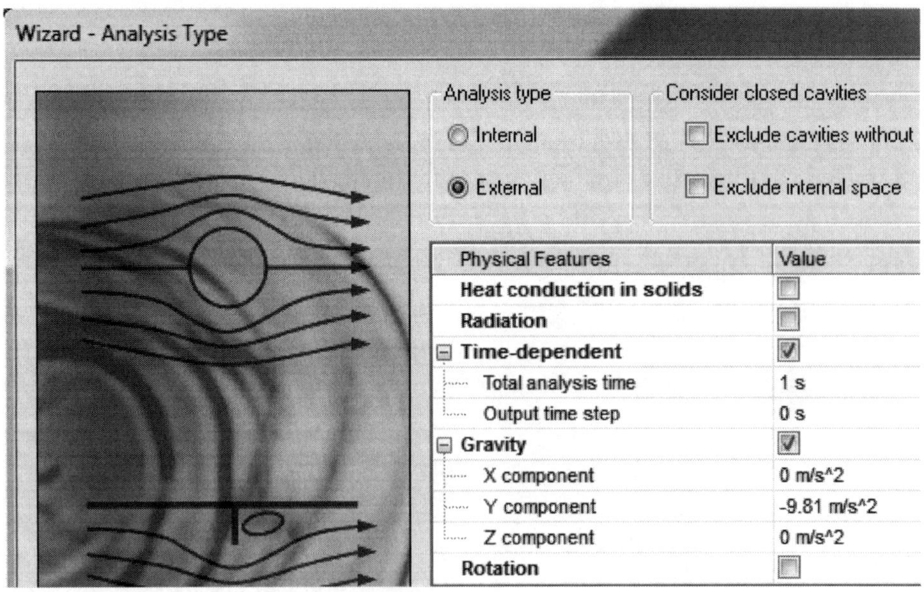

Figure 12.15b) Adding time-dependent flow and gravity to the project

Inserting Global Goal and Selecting 2D Flow for Free Convection from a Horizontal Cylinder

16. We create a global goal for the project by selecting **Tools>>Flow Simulation>>Insert>>Global Goals…** from the SOLIDWORKS menu and check the box for **Max Heat Transfer Rate**. Exit the global goals.

Select **Tools>>Flow Simulation>>Computational Domain…** from the SOLIDWORKS menu. Select **2D Simulation** and **XY plane**; see figure 12.16. Set the **Y max** to **1 m**. Click on the **OK** button to exit the **Computational Domain** window.

Select **Tools>>Flow Simulation>>Initial Mesh…** from the SOLIDWORKS menu. Uncheck the **Automatic settings** box at the bottom of the **Initial Mesh** window. Set the **Number of cells per X:** to **24** and the **Number of cells per Y:** to **20**. Click on the **OK** button.

Select **Tools>>Flow Simulation>>Calculation Control Options…** from the SOLIDWORKS menu. Set **Maximum physical time** to **45 s**. Click on the **OK** button.

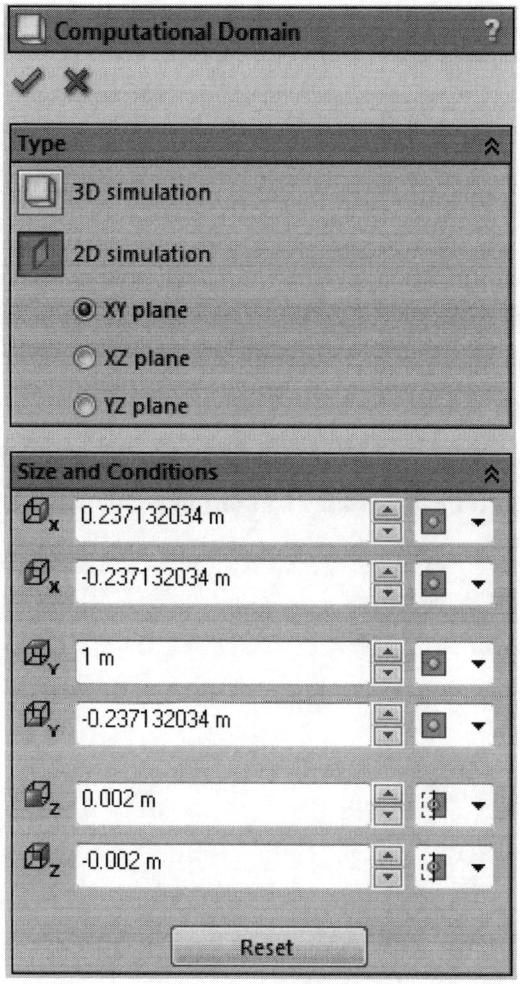

Figure 12.16 Selecting the computational domain for free convection from a horizontal cylinder

Tabular Saving for Free Convection from Horizontal Cylinder

17. Select **Tools>>Flow Simulation>>Calculation Control Options...** from the SOLIDWORKS menu. Select the **Saving** tab and check on the **Value** box next to **Periodic Saving**. Click on the plus sign next to **Periodic Saving** and set the **Start Value** to iteration number **200** and the **Period Value** to **1**; see figure 12.17. Click on the **OK** buttons to exit the **Table** and **Calculation Control Options** windows.

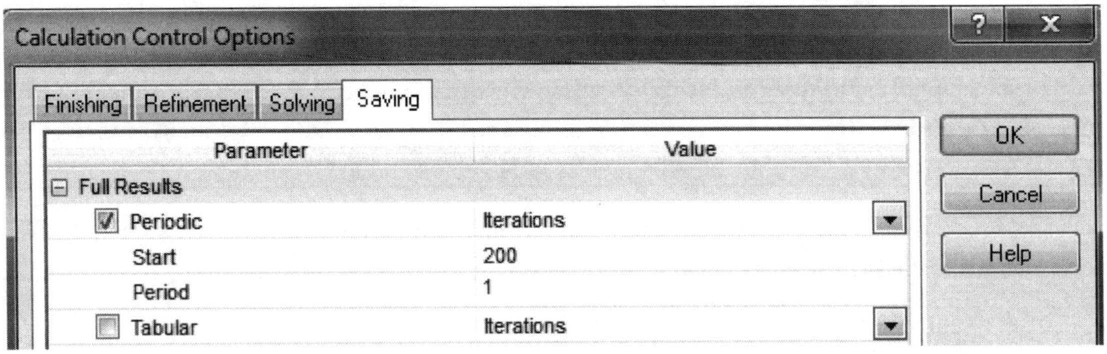

Figure 12.17 Calculation control options for free convection from a horizontal cylinder

Inserting Boundary Condition for Free Convection from Horizontal Cylinder

18. Select **Isometric** view from the **View Orientation** drop down menu in the graphics window. Select **Tools>>Flow Simulation>>Insert>>Boundary Condition...** from the SOLIDWORKS menu. Select the cylindrical surface of the cylinder. Click on the **Wall** button in the **Type** portion of the **Boundary Condition** window and select **Real Wall**. Adjust the **Wall Temperature** to **393.2 K** by clicking on the button and entering the numerical value in the **Wall Parameters** window. Click OK to exit the **Boundary Condition** window.

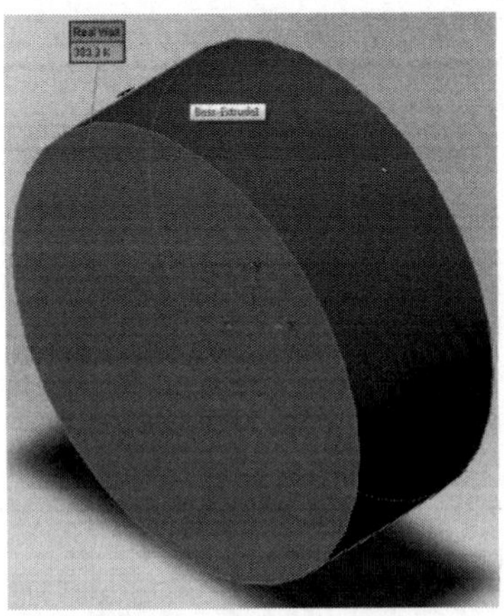

Figure 12.18 Cylindrical surface with real wall boundary condition at 393.2 K

Running Calculations for Free Convection from Horizontal Cylinder

19. Choose **Tools>>Flow Simulation>>Solve>>Run…**. Click on the **Run** button in the window that appears. Click on the goals flag to **Insert Goals Table** in the **Solver** window. Click on **Insert Goals Plot** in the **Solver** window. Click on the Add All button followed by the OK button. Right click in the goals plot. Select **Physical time** from **X-axis units**. Slide the **Plot length** to the middle in between **min** and **max**. In the Numerical settings, set Manual min to 0.3 and Manual max to 0.7. Click on the **OK** button.

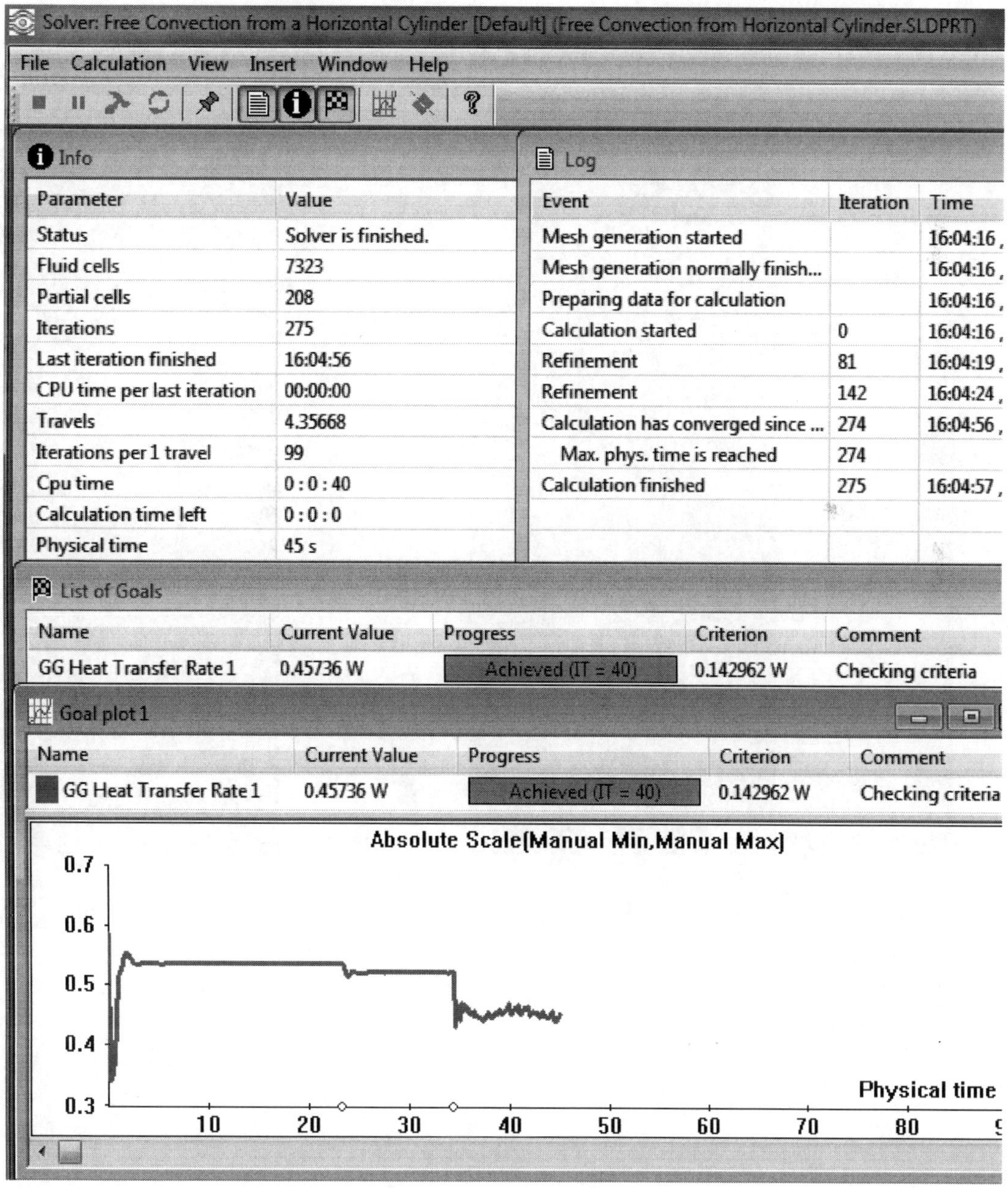

Figure 12.19a) Solver window for free convection from a horizontal cylinder

Inserting Cut Plots for Free Convection from Horizontal Cylinder

20. Select **Tools>>Flow Simulation>>Results>>Load from File...** from the SOLIDWORKS menu. Open the file **r_000270.fld**. Right click on **Cut Plots** in the **Flow Simulation analysis tree** and select **Insert...** and select **Temperature** from the **Contours** section. Slide the **Number of Levels** to **255**. Exit the cut plot dialog. Select front view from the view orientation drop down menu in the graphics window. Change the name of Cut Plot 1 to **Temperature at Iteration = 270**. Insert one more cut plot and plot the velocity. Change the name of the cut plot to **Velocity at Iteration = 270**.

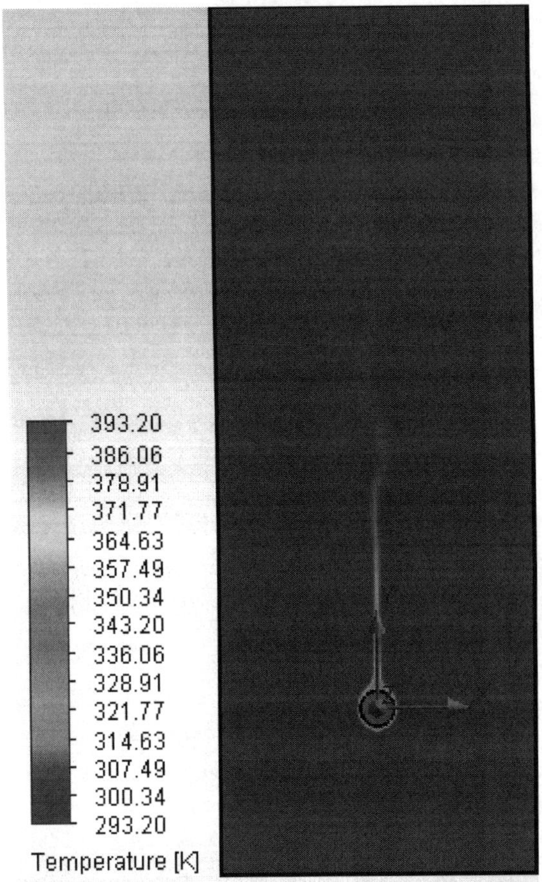

Figure 12.20a) Temperature field

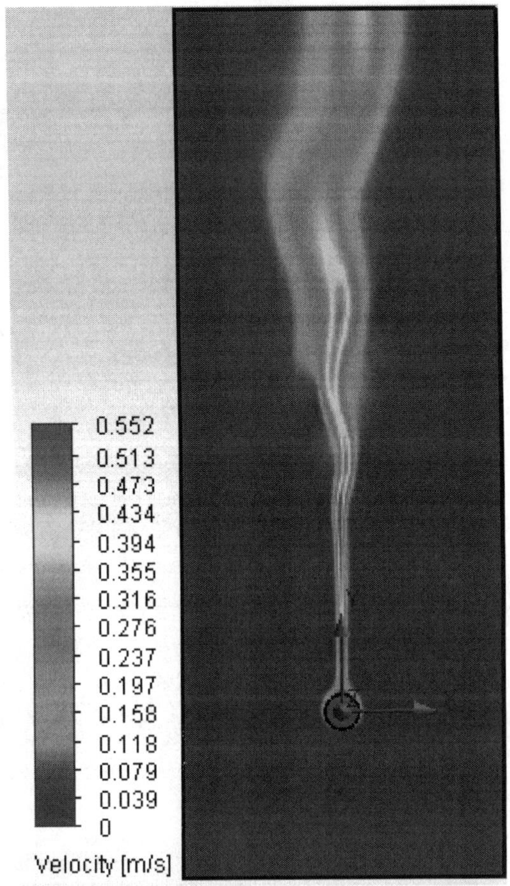

Figure 12.20b) Velocity field from cylinder

Animating the Temperature Field for Free Convection from a Horizontal Cylinder

21. We now want to animate the cut plots for the temperature field. Right click on the cut plot for temperature and select **Animation….** Click on **Expand** to expand the animation controls section; see figure 12.21a). Click on the control point for **Animation 1** at 00:10 and drag it towards 00:00; see figure 12.21b). Select the animation wizard; see figure 12.21c). Use the animation time of **1 s** and click on the **Next>** button. Click on the **Next>** button in the following window. Check the **Scenario** animation type and click on the **Next>** button. **Start from: 0 s** and **Finish at 45 s**. Click on the **Finish** button to exit the animation wizard. Click on the right control point for **Temperature** located close to 0 s and drag it to 1 s; see figure 12.14d). Click on the **Play** button to start the animation. Exit animation 1. Repeat this step and create an animation for the velocity field.

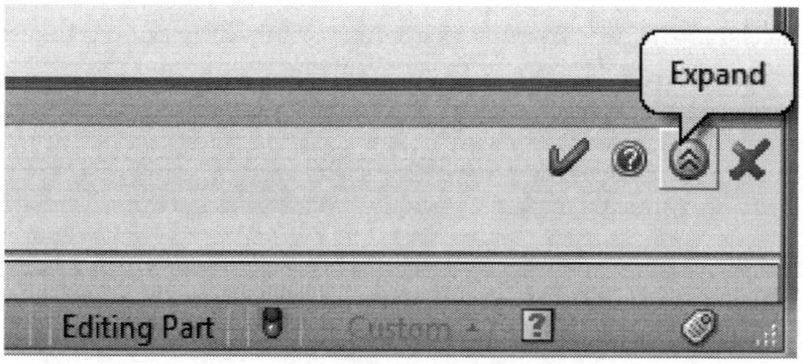

Figure 12.21a) Animation controls

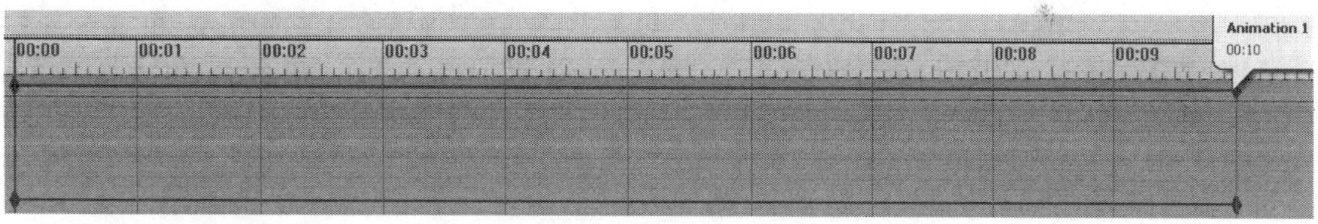

Figure 12.21b) Moving of an animation control point

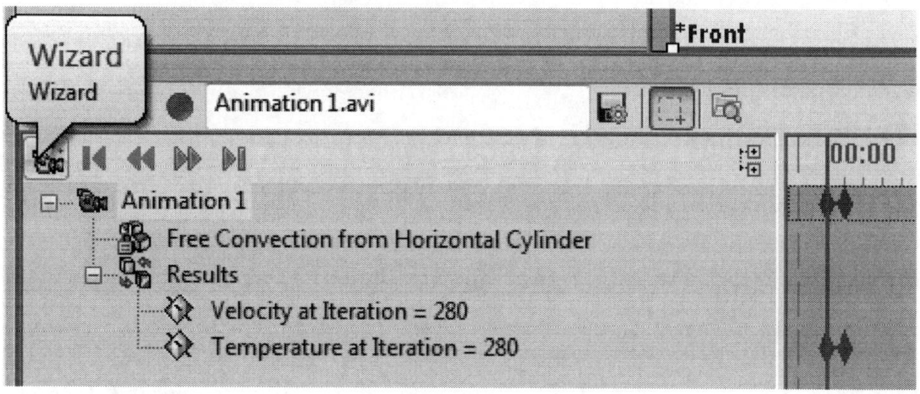

Figure 12.21c) Animation wizard

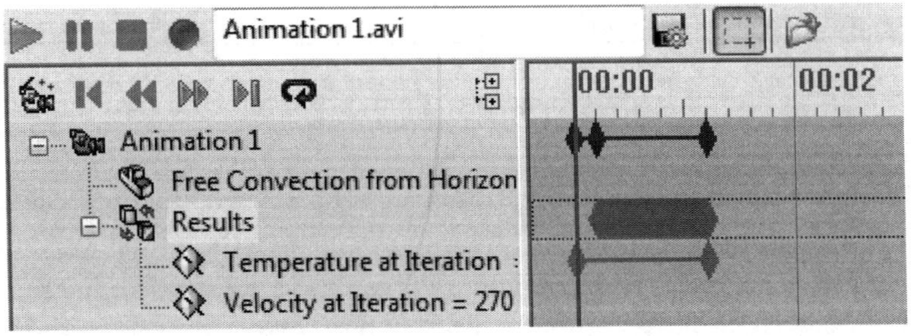

Figure 12.21d) Animation settings

References

[1] Bejan A., Convection Heat Transfer, 3rd Edition, Wiley, 2004.

[2] Sparrow E.M., Husar R.B. and Goldstein R.J., Observations and other characteristics of thermals. *J. Fluid Mech.,* **42**, 465 – 470, 1970.

[3] White F. M., Viscous Fluid Flow, 2nd Edition, McGraw-Hill, 1991.

Exercises

1. Use Flow Simulation to study two-dimensional free-convection interaction between four heated horizontal cylinders arranged in a staggered grid; see figure E1. Make cut plots and animations of the temperature and velocity fields from the cylinders. Use a cylinder diameter of 20 mm and set the surface temperature of each cylinder to 393.2 K. Use air as the fluid. Set the center distance between the horizontal cylinders to H = 30 mm and the center distance between the vertical cylinders V = 60 mm.

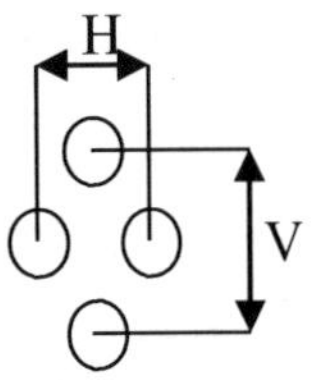

Figure E1 Geometry for staggered grid of four horizontal cylinders

2. Use Flow Simulation to study free-convection on a vertical cylinder in air with a diameter of 20 mm and a length of 1 m. Set the surface temperature to 300 K and determine temperature and velocity profiles at different locations along cylinder.

3. Use Flow Simulation to study two-dimensional, time-dependent free-convection from a horizontal flat plate; use a 1 m wide plate, but choose your own thickness of the plate. Set the temperature and roughness of the plate to different values and make cut plots and animations of the temperature and velocity fields in water to see if you can get Flow Simulation to generate intermittent rise of thermals as shown in experiments by Sparrow et al.[2]

Chapter 13 Swirling Flow in a Closed Cylindrical Container

Objectives

- Creating the SOLIDWORKS models needed for Flow Simulations
- Setting up Flow Simulation projects for internal flows
- Creating lids for boundary conditions and setting up boundary conditions
- Use of gravity as a physical feature and running the calculations
- Using cut plots and flow trajectories to visualize the resulting flow field

Problem Description

In this chapter we will study the swirling flow in a cylindrical container with a rotating lid. We will start by looking closer at the flow caused by a rotating top lid (see figure 13.0), and we will use water as the fluid.

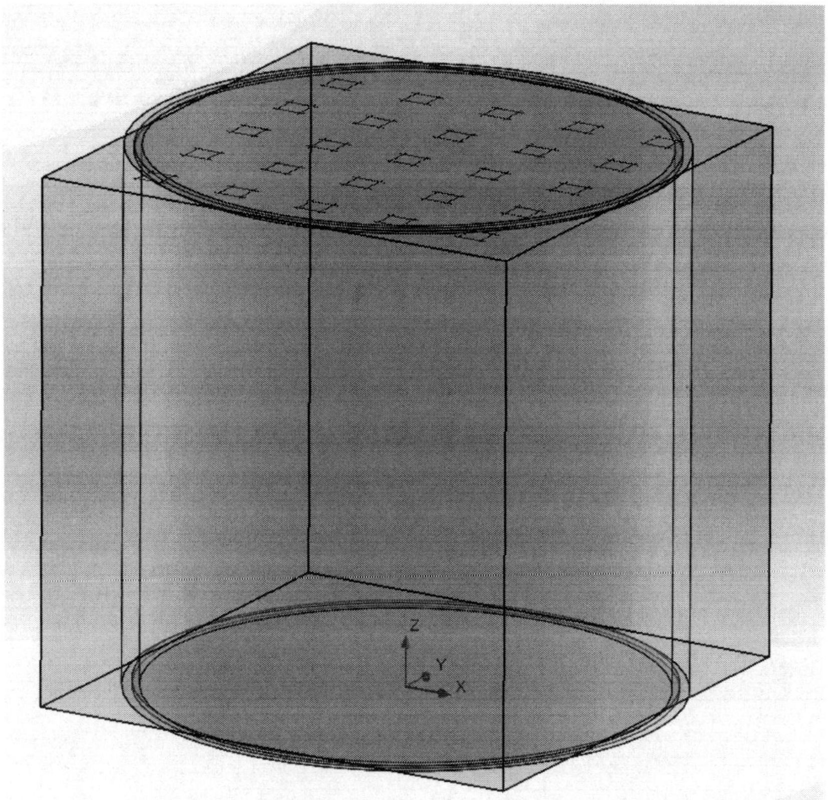

Figure 13.0 Model of Swirling Flow in a Closed Container with a Rotating Lid

Creating the SOLIDWORKS Part for Swirling Flow in a Closed Cylindrical Container

1. Start SOLIDWORKS and create a New Part. Select **Tools>>Options…** from the SOLIDWORKS menu. Click on the Document Properties tab and select **Units**. Select **MMGS** as your **Unit system**. Select the **Front** view from the **View Orientation** drop down menu in the graphics window and click on the **Front Plane** in the **FeatureManager design tree**. Next, select the **Circle** sketch tool.

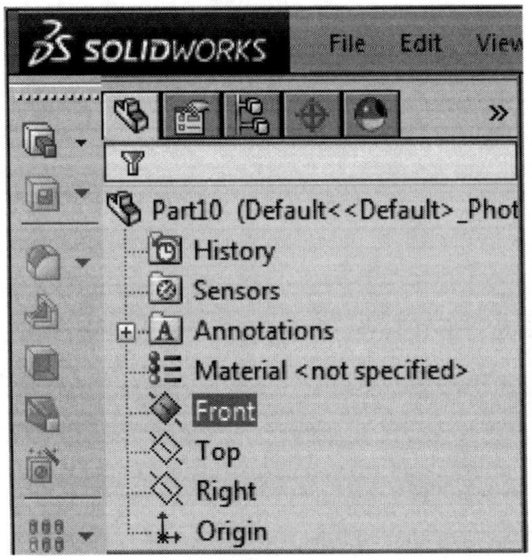

Figure 13.1a) Front Plane

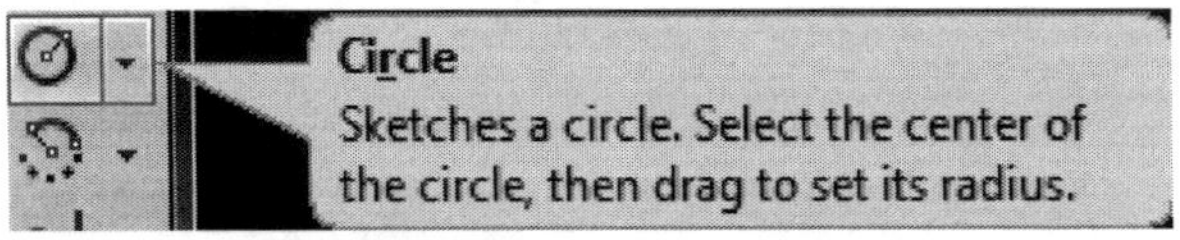

Figure 13.1b) Selection of the **Circle** sketch tool

2. Click on the origin in the graphics window and create a circle. Enter **47.5 mm** for the radius of the circle in the **Parameters** box. Close the dialog box.

Figure 13.2 Parameters for a circle with 47.5 mm radius

3. Next, make an extrusion by selecting **Extruded Boss/Base**. Enter **95 mm** in **Direction 1** and check the **Thin Feature**. Enter **3.175 mm** for the thickness. Close the dialog box. Save the part with the name **Swirling Flow in Closed Cylindrical Container**.

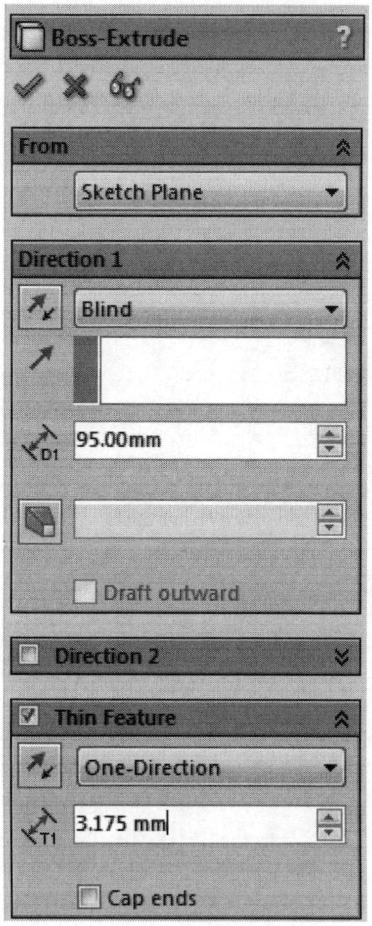

Figure 13.3a) Entering data

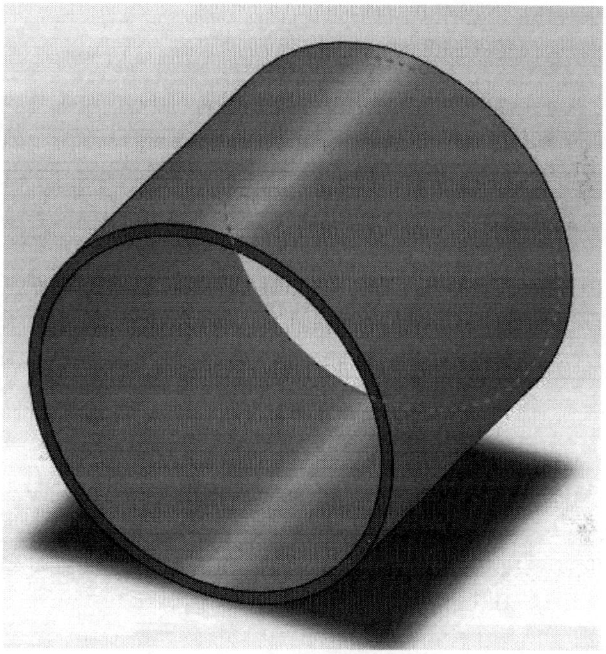

Figure 13.3b) Extruded ring

Setting up the Flow Simulation Project for Swirling Flow in a Closed Cylindrical Container

4. If Flow Simulation is not available in the SOLIDWORKS menu, select **Tools>>Add Ins…** and check the corresponding **SOLIDWORKS Flow Simulation** box. Start the **Flow Simulation Wizard** by selecting **Tools>>Flow Simulation>>Project>>Wizard** from the SOLIDWORKS menu.

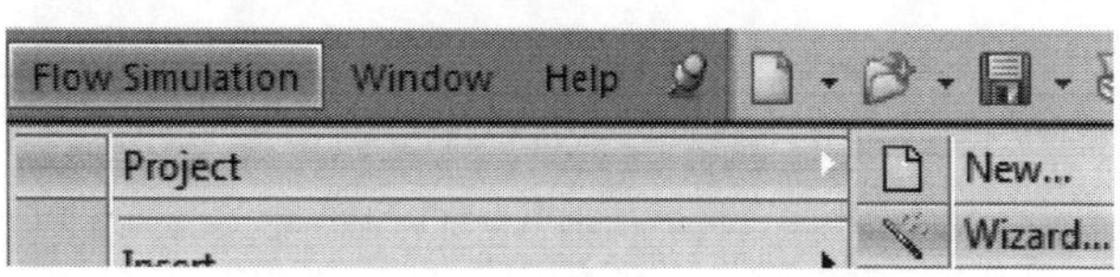

Figure 13.4 Starting the Flow Simulation Project Wizard

5. Create a new project with the following name: **Swirling Flow**.

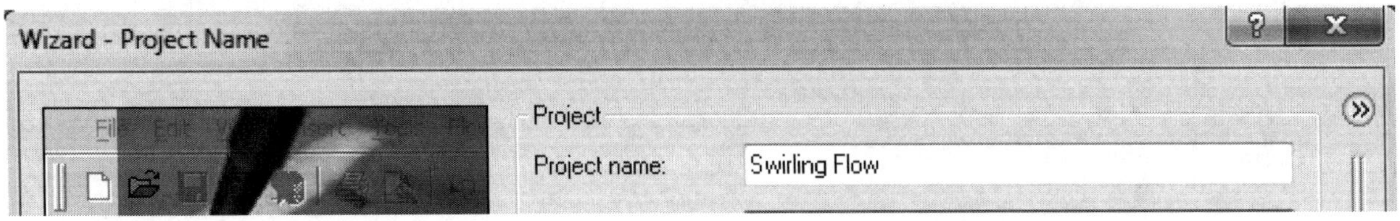

Figure 13.5 Entering configuration name

6. Select the SI unit system

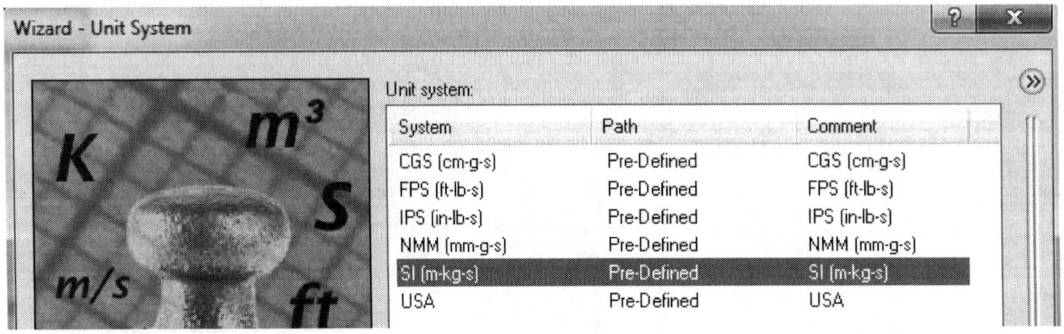

Figure 13.6 Selection of unit system

7. Select the default **Internal Analysis type** and enter **-9.81 m/s^2** as **Gravity** for the **Z component** in **Physical Features**.

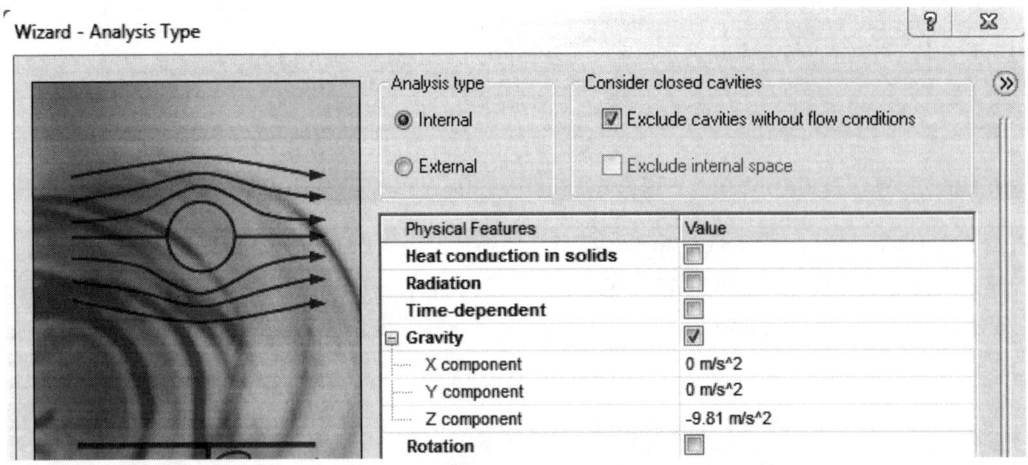

Figure 13.7 Enter gravity as physical feature

8. Add **Water** as the default **Project Fluid** by selecting it from **Liquids**. Choose default values for **Wall Conditions** and **Initial Conditions**. Slide the **Initial Mesh** to **3**. Finish the Wizard. Answer Yes to the question whether you want to open the Create Lids tool.

Figure 13.8 Adding water as the default fluid

Creating Lids

9. Next, we will add a lid on both ends of the extrusion to create an enclosure. Click on one of the two plane surfaces of the extrusion and set the thickness of the lid to **1.00 mm**. Click **OK** and answer **"Yes"** to the questions whether you want to reset the computational domain, mesh setting, and open the Create Lids tool that appears in the graphics window. Repeat this step for the other plane surface.

Select the FeatureManager Design Tree and right click on **Material** and select **Edit Material**. Select **Acrylic (Medium-high impact)** from the **Plastics** folder. Click on the **Apply** button and close the window.

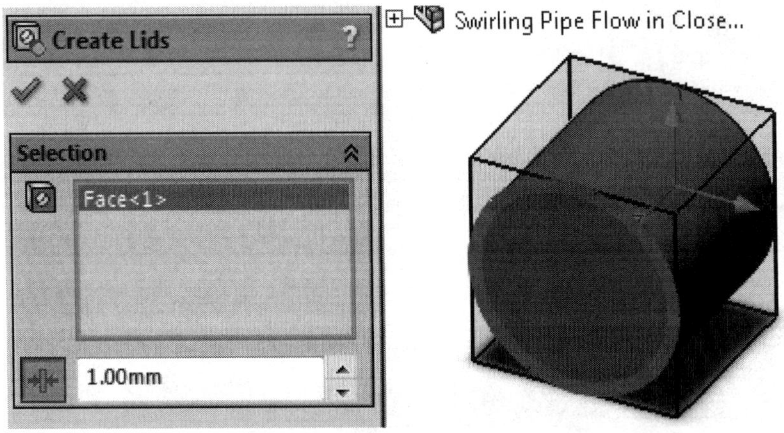

Figure 13.9 Selecting the face and thickness of the lid

Inserting Boundary Condition for Swirling Flow in a Closed Cylindrical Container

10. Click on the **Flow Simulation analysis tree** tab and click on the plus sign next to the **Input Data** folder. Right click on **Boundary Conditions** and select **Insert Boundary Condition…**

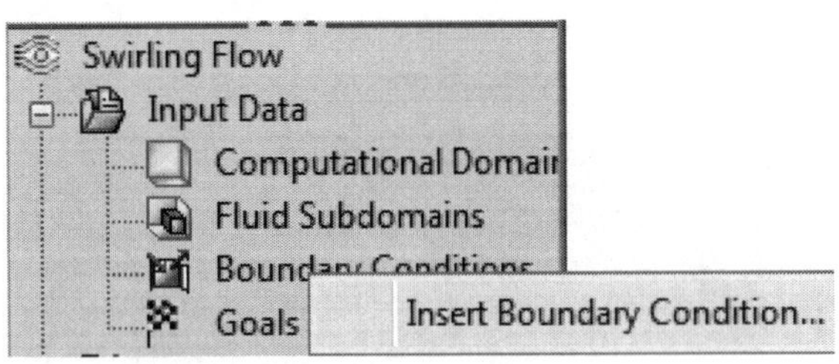

Figure 13.10 Selecting boundary conditions.

11. Select Bottom view from View Orientation. Tilt the cylinder a little bit and position the cursor over the top lid, right-click and click on **Select Other**. Select the face for the inner upper surface of the enclosure. Select the **Wall** button and select **Real Wall** boundary condition. Check the box for **Wall Motion** and set the value of **0.4449 rad/s** for angular velocity. Click **OK** to finish the boundary condition. Rename the boundary condition from **Real Wall 1** to **Rotating Top Lid**.

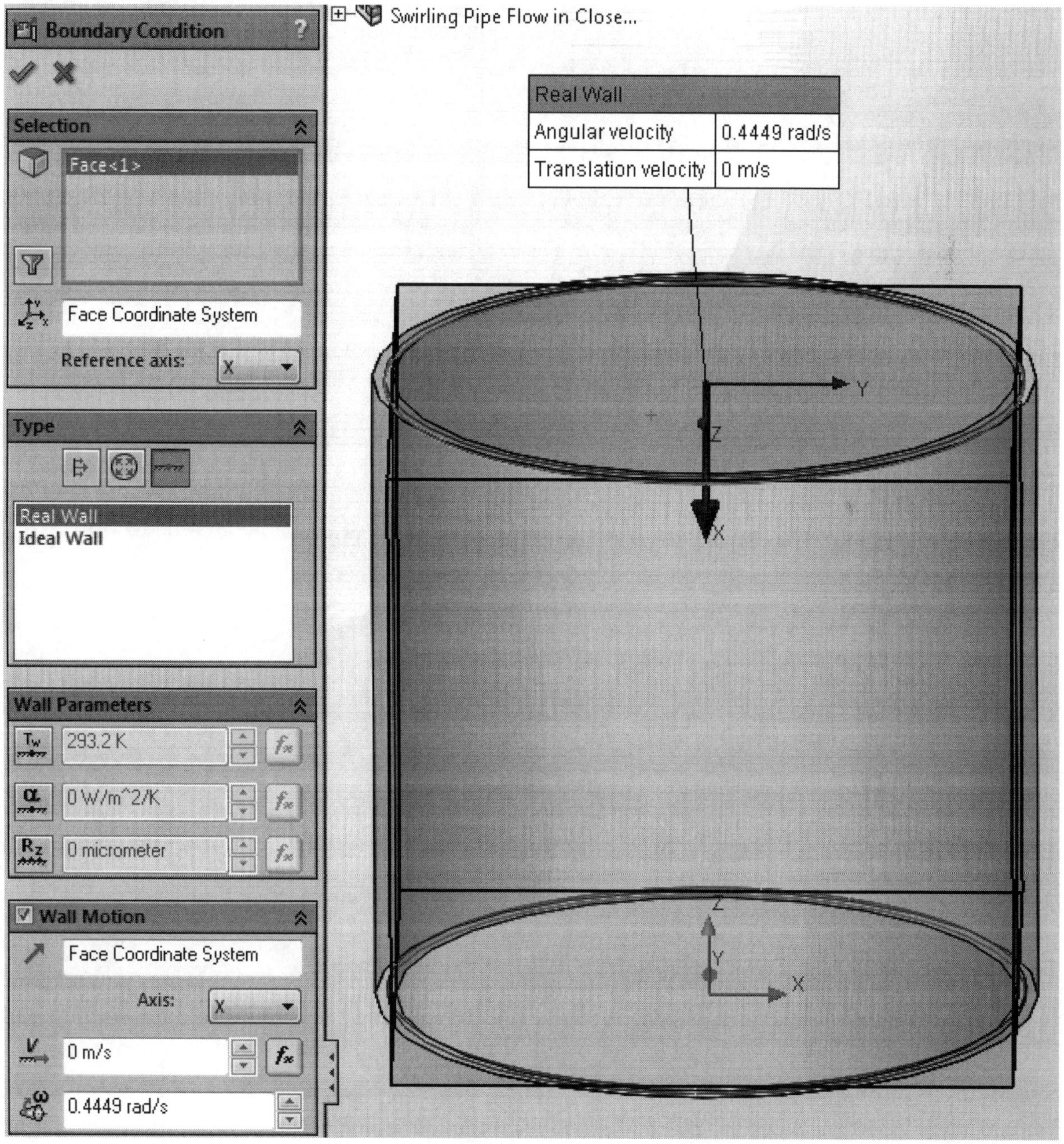

Figure 13.11 View of enclosure with upper rotating lid boundary condition

Inserting Global Goal for Swirling Flow in a Closed Cylindrical Container

12. Right click on **Goals** in the **Flow Simulation analysis tree** and select **Insert Global Goals…** Check the boxes for **Min, Av** and **Max Velocity**.

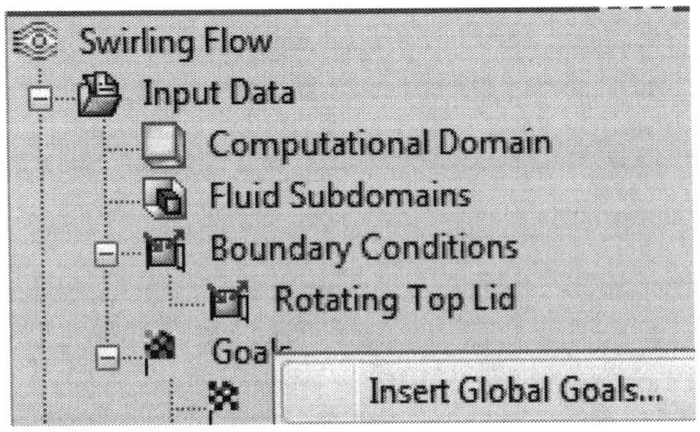

Figure 13.12a) Inserting global goals

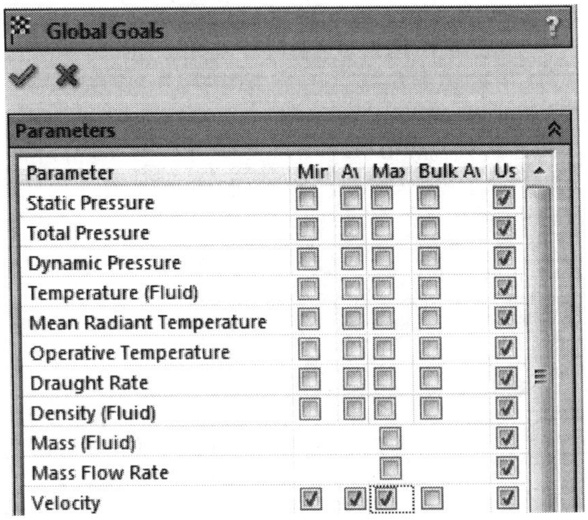

Figure 13.12b) Velocity as goals

Running the Calculations

13. Select **Tools>>Flow Simulation>>Solve>>Run**. Push the **Run** button in the window that appears.

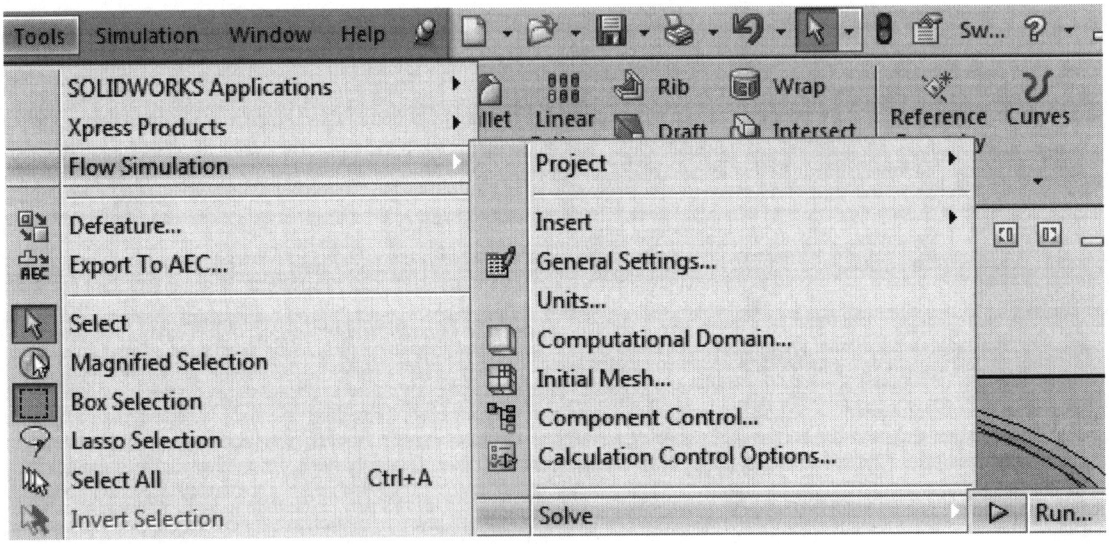

Figure 13.13 Starting the calculation of flow field

14. Insert the goals table by clicking on the flag in the **Solver** as shown in figure 13.14a).

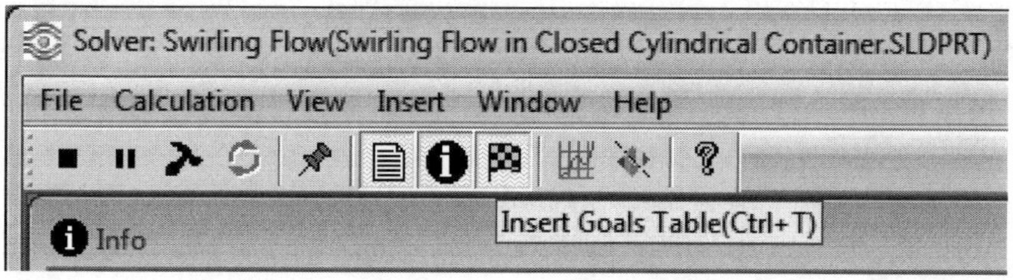

Figure 13.14a) Inserting goals

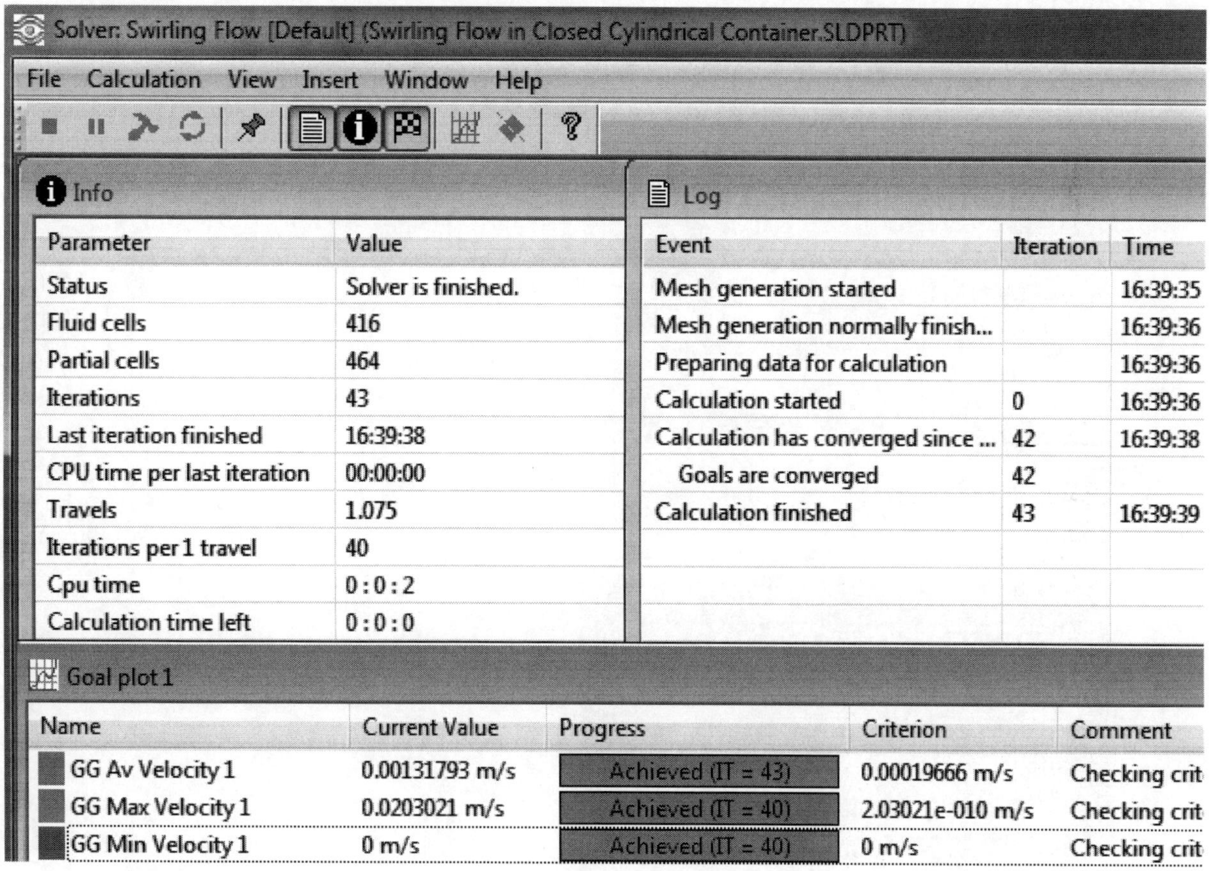

Figure 13.14b) Solver window

Inserting Flow Trajectories

15. Right click on **Flow Trajectories** in the **Flow Simulation analysis tree** and select **Insert…**. Select the **Top Plane** from the **FeatureManager design tree**. Check the **In plane** box. Select to draw trajectories as **Lines** from the drop down menu in the **Appearance** section. Select **Velocity** from the **Color by Parameter** drop down menu. Click **OK** to exit **Flow Trajectories**. Rename **Flow Trajectories 1** and name them **Streamlines**.

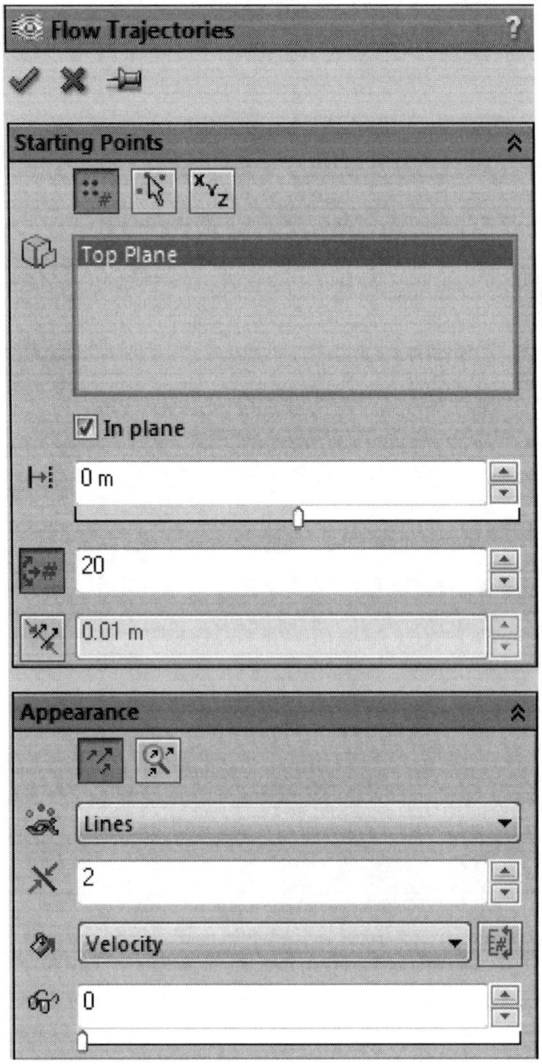

Figure 13.15a) Settings for flow trajectories

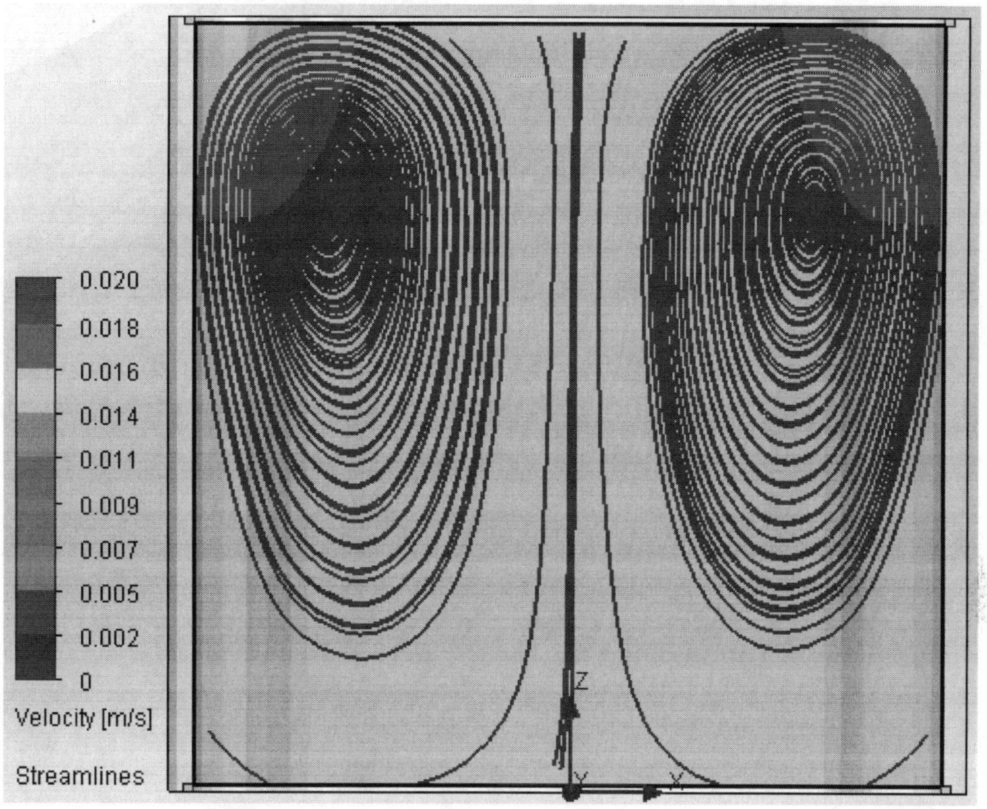

Figure 13.15b) Streamlines for *Re* = 1,000 and *H/R* = 2

In figure 13.15b) we can see the streamlines of the first breakdown structure at the Reynolds number $Re = \frac{\Omega R^2}{v} = 1{,}000$ and H/R = 2, where *Ω* is the angular velocity of the rotating top lid, *R* is the radius of the cylinder, v is the kinematic viscosity of the fluid, and *H* is the height of the cylinder. The fluid is rising in the center of the cylinder and flowing downward along the cylindrical wall.

Reference

[1] Granger R.A., Experiments in Fluid Mechanics, Holt, Rinehart and Winston, Inc., 1988.

Exercise

1. Run the flow case as described in this chapter for different Reynolds numbers and different height over radius ratios to see if you can find the second breakdown structure.

Notes:

Chapter 14 Flow past a Model Rocket

Objectives

- Creating the SOLIDWORKS model needed for Flow Simulations
- Setting up a Flow Simulation project for external flows
- Using cut plots to visualize the resulting flow field

Problem Description

In this chapter we will study the flow past a model rocket. The rocket that we will model is the Estes Firestreak SST.

Figure 14.0 SOLIDWORKS model of Estes Firestreak SST

Creating the SOLIDWORKS Parts for the Model Rocket

1. Start SOLIDWORKS and create a New Part. Select **Tools>>Options…** from the SOLIDWORKS menu. Click on the Document Properties tab and select **Units**. Select **MMGS** as your **Unit system**. Select the **Front** view from the **View Orientation** drop down menu in the graphics window and click on the **Front Plane** in the **FeatureManager design tree**. Next, select the **Circle** sketch tool.

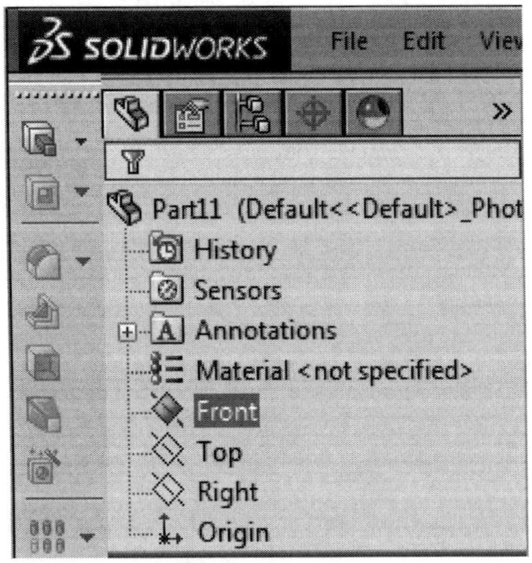

Figure 14.1a) Front Plane

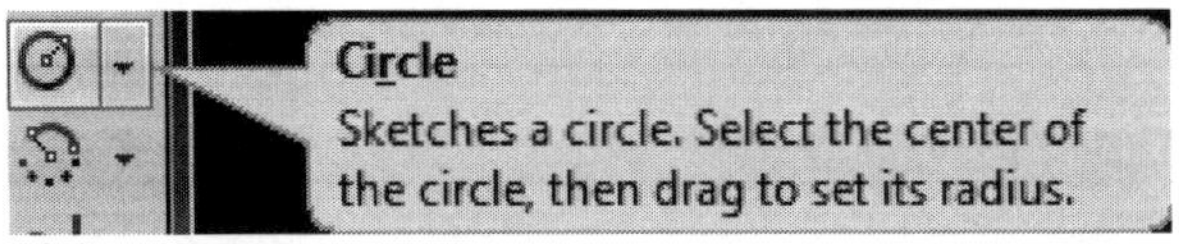

Figure 14.1b) Selection of the **Circle** sketch tool

2. Click on the origin in the graphics window and create a circle. Enter **10.85 mm** for the radius of the circle in the **Parameters** box. Close the dialog box.

Figure 14.2 Parameters for a circle with 10.85 mm radius

3. Next, make an extrusion by selecting **Extruded Boss/Base**. Enter **165 mm** in **Direction 1** and check the **Thin Feature**. Check the button for Reverse Direction and enter **4.00 mm** for the thickness. Close the dialog box. Save the part with the name **Body Tube**.

Figure 14.3a) Entering data

Figure 14.3b) Extruded hollow Body Tube

4. Create a New Part. Select **Tools>>Options…** from the SOLIDWORKS menu. Click on the Document Properties tab and select **Units**. Select **MMGS** as your **Unit system**. Select the **Front** view from the **View Orientation** drop down menu in the graphics window and click on the **Front Plane** in the **FeatureManager design tree**. Next, select the **Line** sketch tool. Draw a horizontal line from the origin to the right that is **10.85 mm** long. Next, draw a vertical line from the origin upward that is **71.5 mm** long followed by a **Spline** between the two open end points of the vertical and horizontal lines. Right click and select **Select** after you have included the spline. Click on the **Spline** and click on the orange control points of the spline in order to modify the shape of the nose cone. Drag the control points until the shape of the spline resembles the nose cone of a rocket; see Fig. 14.4d). Close the **Spline** dialog.

Figure 14.4a) Selection of the **Line**

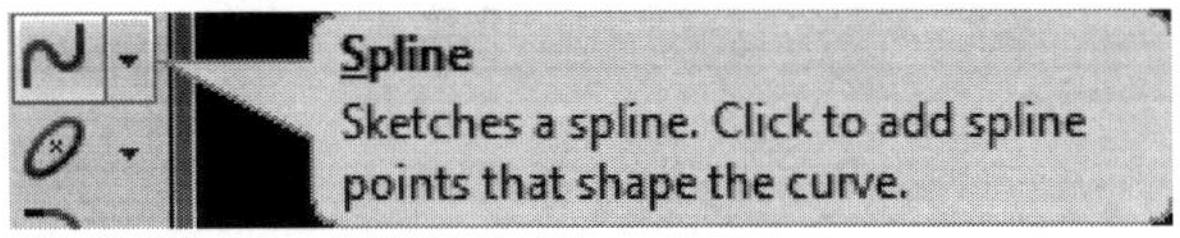

Figure 14.4b) Selection of the **Spline**

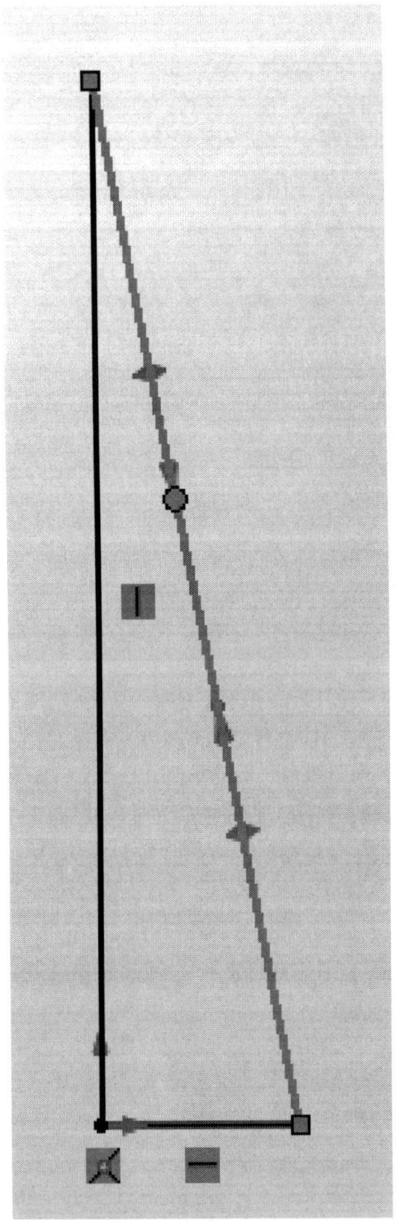

Figure 14.4c) Spline with control point

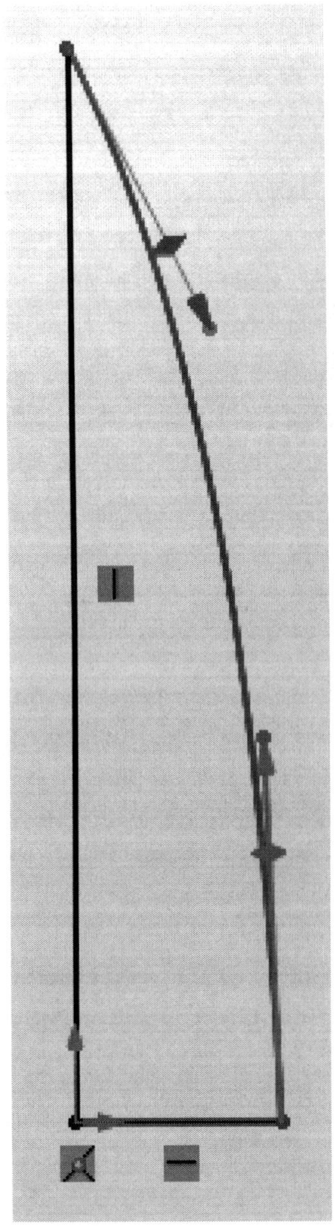

Figure 14.4d) Modified shape of spline

5. Click on the **Revolved Boss/Base** feature. Click on the vertical line in the graphics window and exit the **Revolve** dialog. Select the **Top** plane in the Featuremanager Design Tree and select **Top View** from **View Orientation** drop down menu in the graphics window. Next, select the **Circle** sketch tool. Click on the origin in the graphics window and create a circle. Enter **6.4 mm** for the radius of the circle in the **Parameters** box. Close the **Circle** dialog box. Click on **Extruded Boss/Base** feature. Select **Isometric** view from View Orientation drop down menu in the graphics window. Select  **Reverse Direction** under **Direction 1**. Enter **12.65mm** for the  Depth of the Extrusion; see Fig. 14.5e). Exit the **Boss-Extrude** dialog. Save the part with the name **Nose cone**.

Figure 14.5a) Selecting Revolved Boss/Base

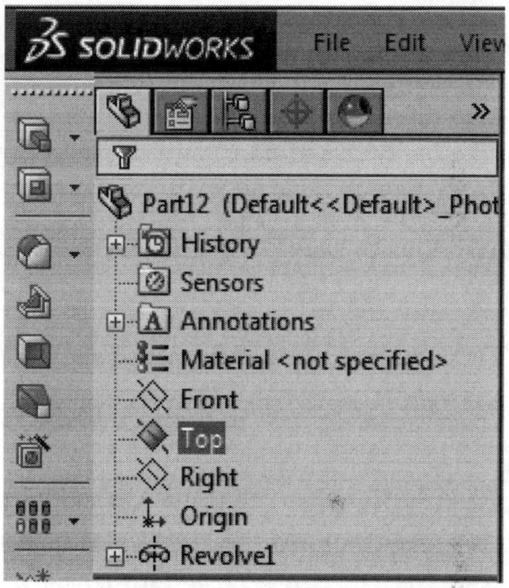

Figure 14.5b) Selecting the Top plane

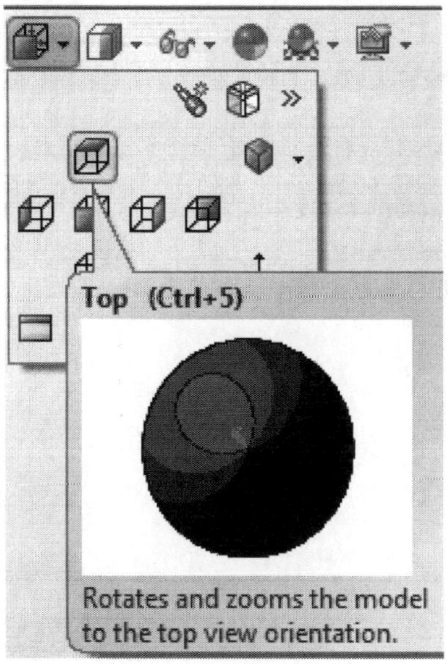

Figure 14.5c) Selecting the Top view

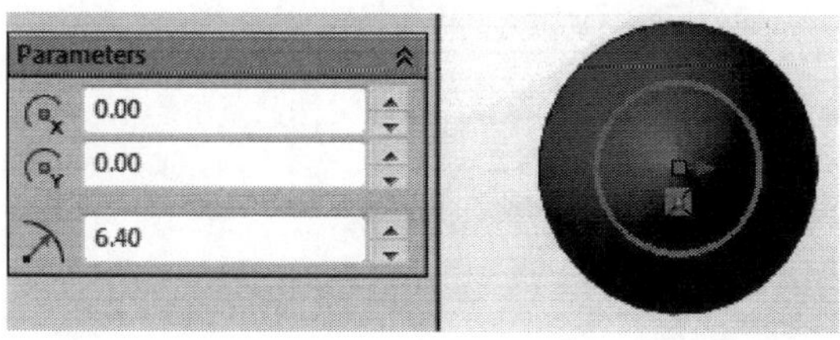

Figure 14.5d) Drawing of a circle

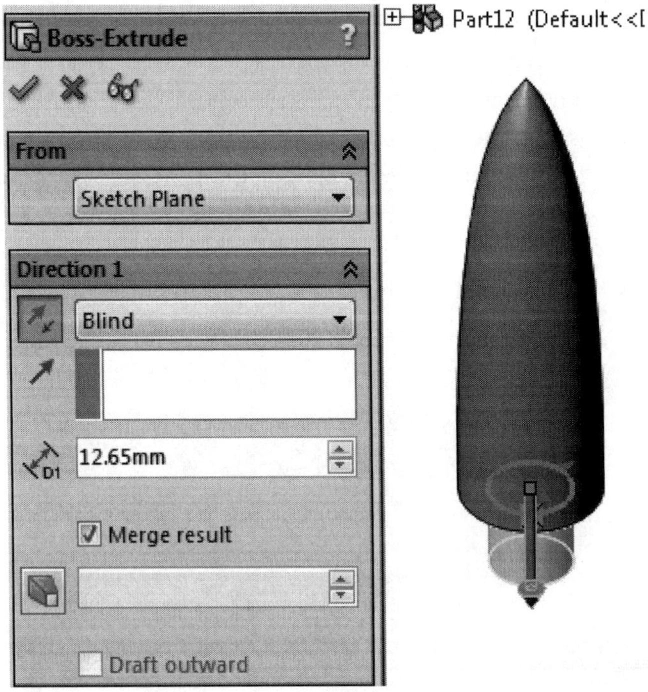

Figure 14.5e) Settings for nose cone extrusion

6. Create a New Part. Select **Tools>>Options…** from the SOLIDWORKS menu. Click on the Document Properties tab and select **Units**. Select **MMGS** as your **Unit system**. Select the **Front** view from the **View Orientation** drop down menu in the graphics window and click on the **Front Plane** in the **FeatureManager design tree**. Next, select the **Circle** sketch tool. Draw a circle from the origin with a radius of **10.85 mm**. Make an extrusion by selecting **Extruded Boss/Base**. Enter **9.50 mm** in **Direction 1**. Click on **Draft** and enter **15.60deg**. Close the dialog box. Select the **Front** plane in the **Featuremanager Design Tree**. Select the **Front** view in the **View Orientation** drop down menu in the graphics window. Draw a circle with a radius of **9 mm**. Select the **Extruded Cut** feature. Reverse the direction of the extruded cut, turn the draft on and exit the **Cut-Extrude** dialog. Save the part with the name **Engine Lock Ring**.

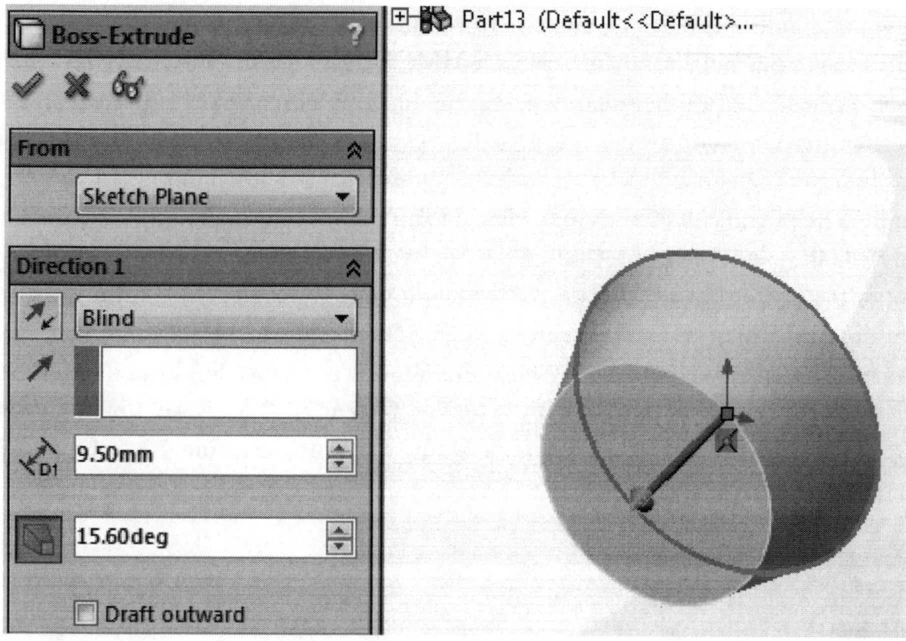

Figure 14.6a) Settings for engine lock ring extrusion

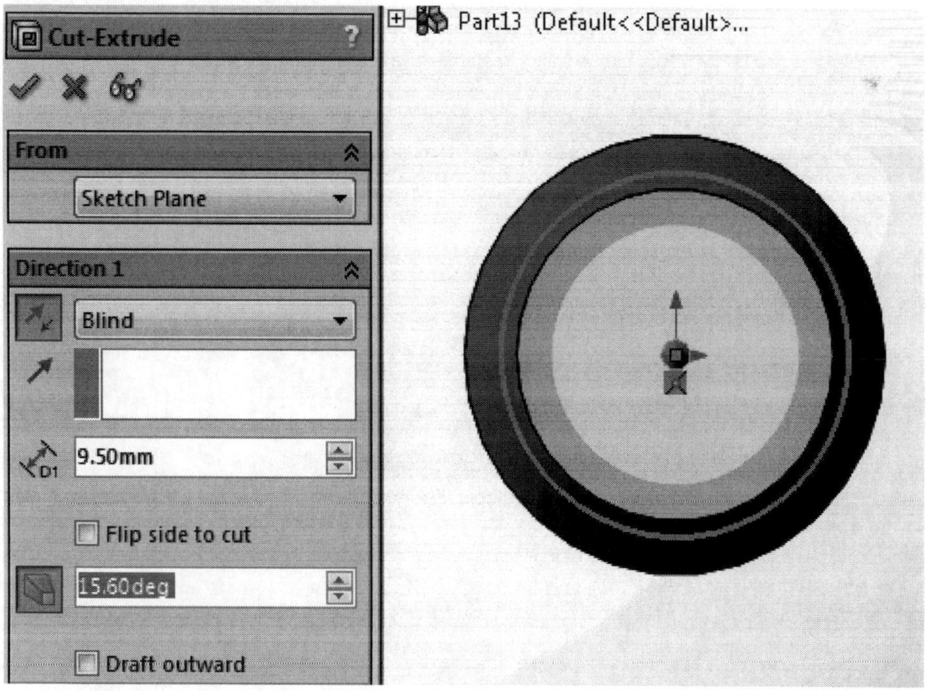

Figure 14.6b) Settings for engine lock ring cut extrude

7. Create a New Part. Select **Tools>>Options…** from the SOLIDWORKS menu. Click on the Document Properties tab and select **Units**. Select **MMGS** as your **Unit system**. Select the **Front** view from the **View Orientation** drop down menu in the graphics window and click on the **Front Plane** in the **FeatureManager design tree**. Next, select the **Line** sketch tool. Draw a **38.00 mm** long vertical line starting above the origin with the parameters as shown in Fig. 14.7a). Next, draw an inclined line that is **60.00 mm** long starting from the top endpoint of the vertical line. Set the angle to **310.00°**; see Fig. 14.7b). Continue by drawing a **10.00 mm** long vertical line from the endpoint of the inclined line. Next, draw another sloping line with a **33.00 mm** length starting from the bottom endpoint of the second vertical line. Set the angle to **160.00°**; see Fig. 14.7d). Finally, connect the two open end points with a straight line and close the **Line Properties** and **Insert Line** dialogues. Make an extrusion by selecting **Extruded Boss/Base**. Enter **0.35 mm** for the depth of the extrusion in **Direction 1** and the same depth for **Direction 2**; see Fig. 14.7e). Save the part with the name **Fin**.

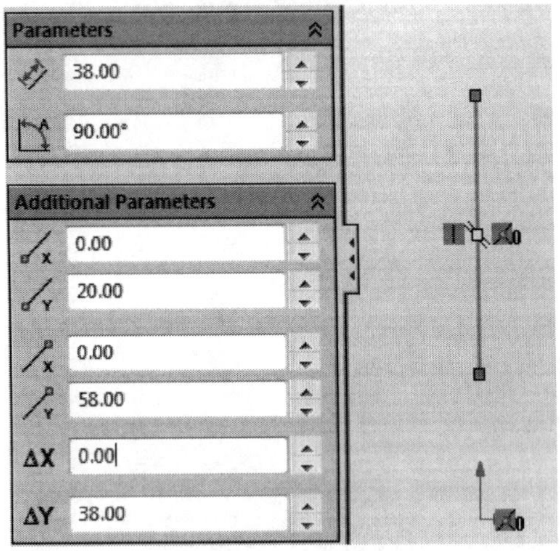

Figure 14.7a) Parameters for vertical line

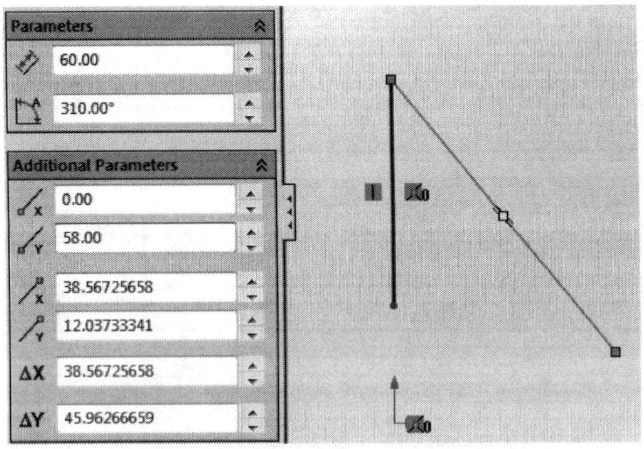

Figure 14.7b) Parameters for inclined line

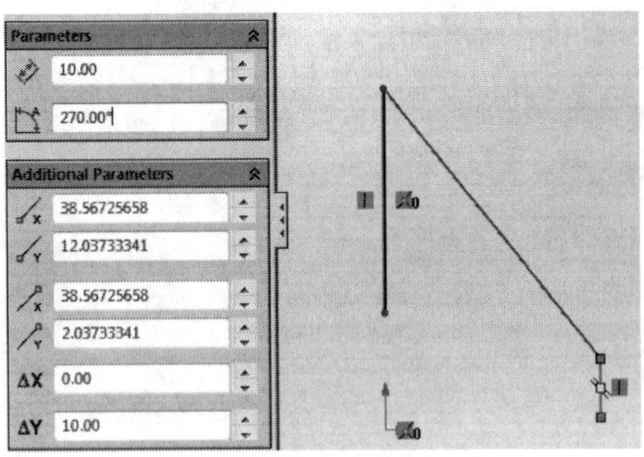

Figure 14.7c) Second vertical line

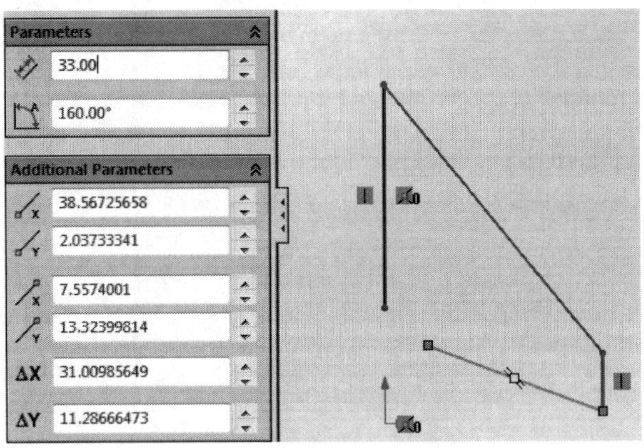

Figure 14.7d) Second sloping line

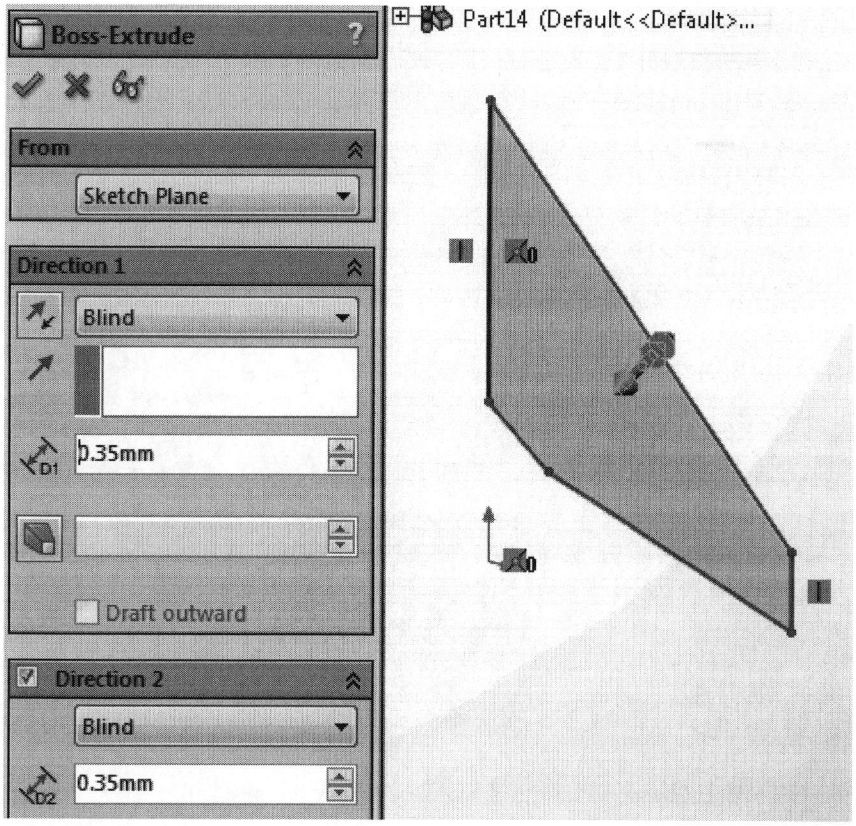

Figure 14.7e) Extrusion settings for fin

Creating the SOLIDWORKS Assembly for the Model Rocket

8. Create a New Assembly. Drag the **Body Tube** from the **Open Documents** in **Part/Assembly to Insert** and insert the **Body Tube** in the graphics window. Select **Insert>>Component>>Existing Part/Assembly…** from the menu. Drag the **Fin** from the Open Documents in **Part/Assembly to Insert** to the graphics window and insert the **Fin** beside the **Body Tube**; see Fig. 14.8b). Select **Insert>>Mate…** from the menu. Select the **Right** plane of the **Body Tube** and the **Front** plane of the **Fin** for a **Coincident1** mate; see Fig. 14.8c). Click on the OK green check mark to exit the **Coincident1** mate. Next, select the cylindrical surface of the **Body Tube** and the 38 mm long and 0.7 mm thin face of the **Fin** for a **Tangent1** mate. Set the **Mate alignment:** **Anti-Aligned** so that the **Fin** is correctly mated on the **Body Tube**; see Fig. 14.8d). Click on the OK green check mark to exit the **Tangent1** mate. Select the circular plane face at the end of the **Body Tube** and select the corresponding edge of the **Fin** for the **Coincident2** mate; see Figs. 14.8e-f). Click on the OK green check mark to exit the **Coincident2** mate. Click on the OK green check mark once again to exit the **Mate** dialog.

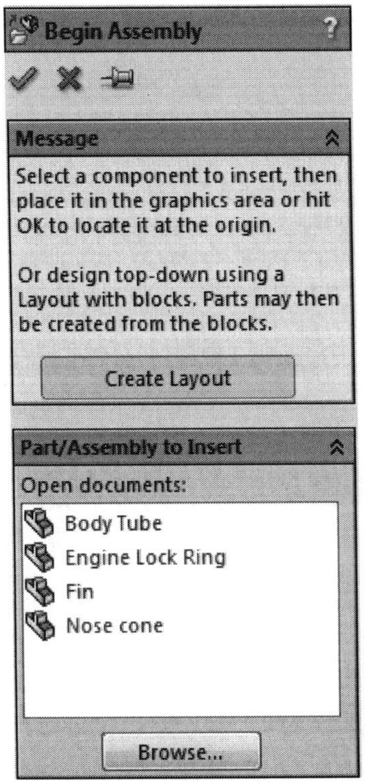

Figure 14.8a) Assembly settings Figure 14.8b) Body Tube and Fin

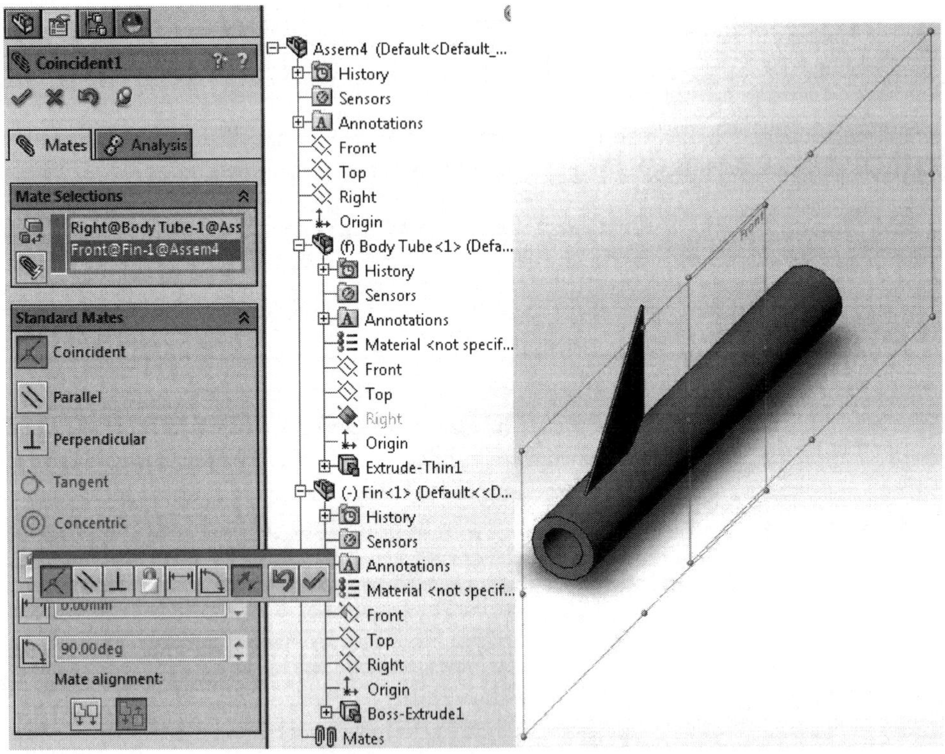

Figure 14.8c) Coincident1 mate settings for Fin and Body Tube

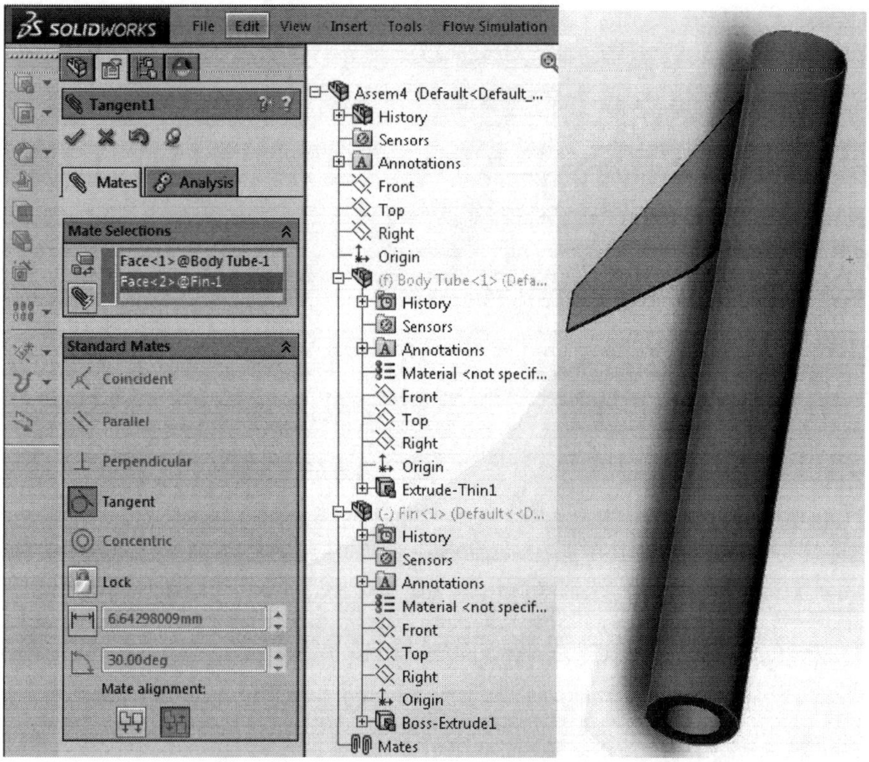

Figure 14.8d) Tangent mate settings for Fin and Body Tube

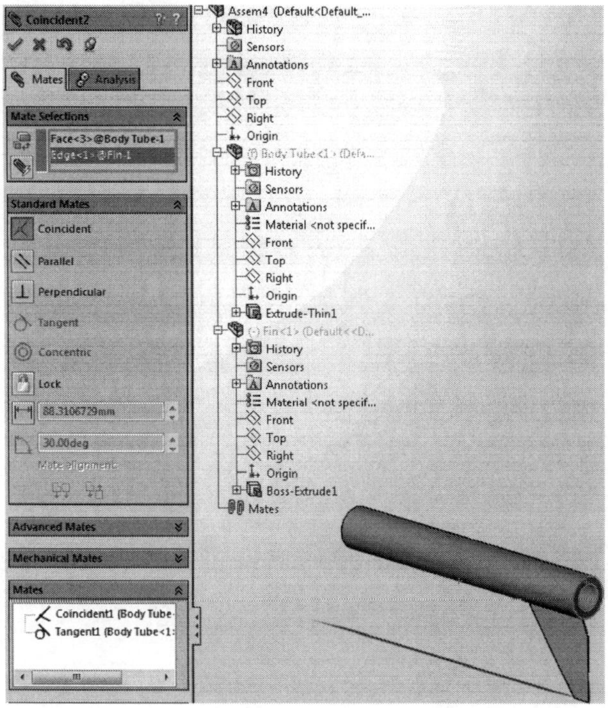

Figure 14.8e) Coincident2 mate settings for Fin and Body Tube

Figure 14.8f) Face and Line selection for Coincidence Mate

9. Select **View>>Temporary Axis** from the menu. Select **Insert>>Component Pattern…>>Circular Pattern…** from the menu. Select the Temporary Axis **as the Pattern Axis.** Set the **Number of Instances** to **4** and check the box for **Equal Spacing**. Select the **Fin** as the component to pattern. Click on the OK green check mark  to exit the **Circular Pattern** dialog. Select **View>>Temporary Axis** from the menu once again to hide the temporary axis.

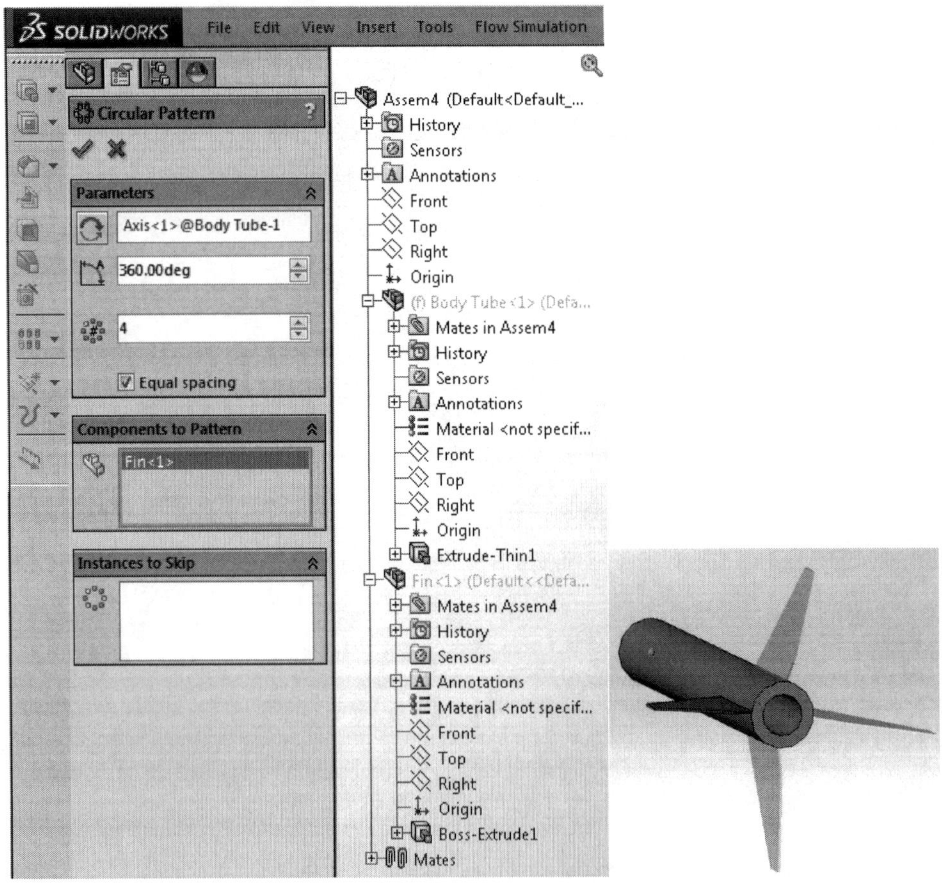

Figure 14.9a) Circular pattern settings for fins

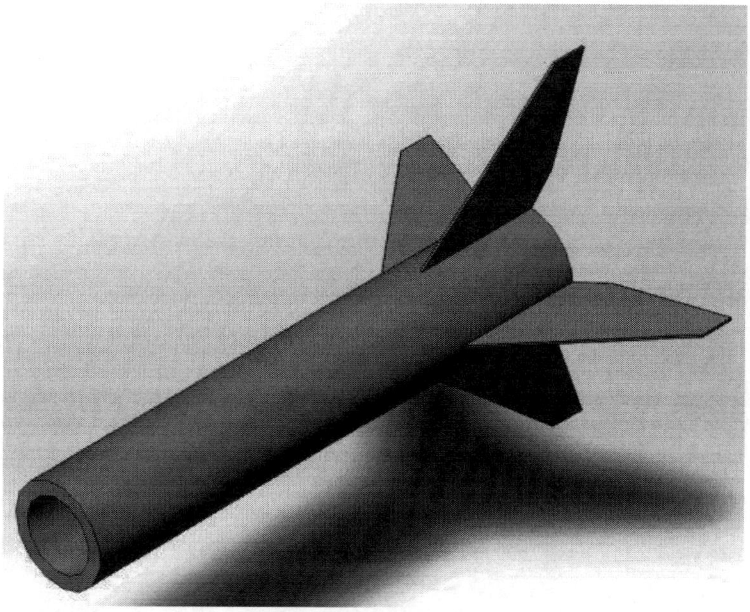

Figure 14.9b) Completed body tube with four fins assembled

10. Select **Insert>>Component>>Existing Part/Assembly…** from the menu. Drag the **Nose Cone** from the Open Documents: in **Part/Assembly to Insert** to the graphics window and insert the **Nose Cone** beside the **Body Tube** and **Fins** assembly; see Fig. 14.10a). Select **Insert>>Mate…** from the menu. Select the plane circular face of the **Nose Cone** and the corresponding face of the **Body Tube**; see Fig. 14.10b). Exit the **Coincident3** dialog. Select the circular outer edge of the **Body Tube** and the corresponding circular edge of the **Nose Cone**; see Fig. 14.10c). Exit the **Coincident4** and **Mate** dialogues.

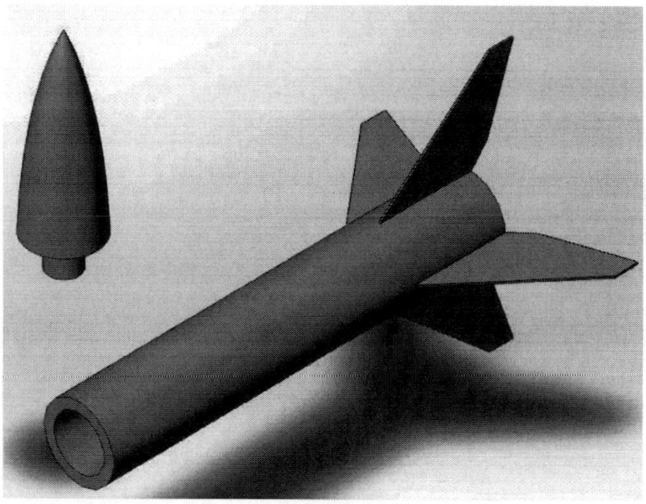

Figure 14.10a) Nose cone and the rest of the assembly

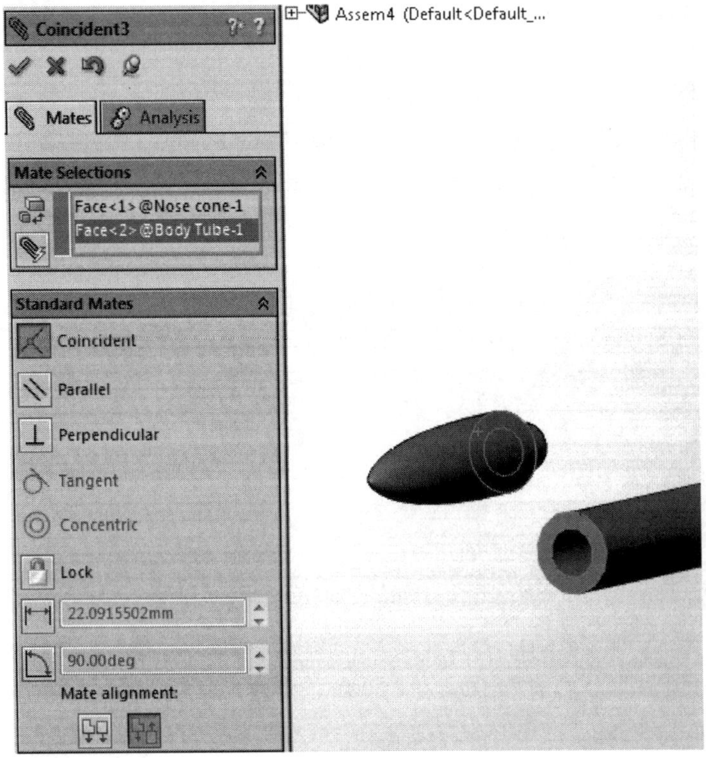

Figure 14.10b) Coincident3 mate of Nose cone and Body Tube

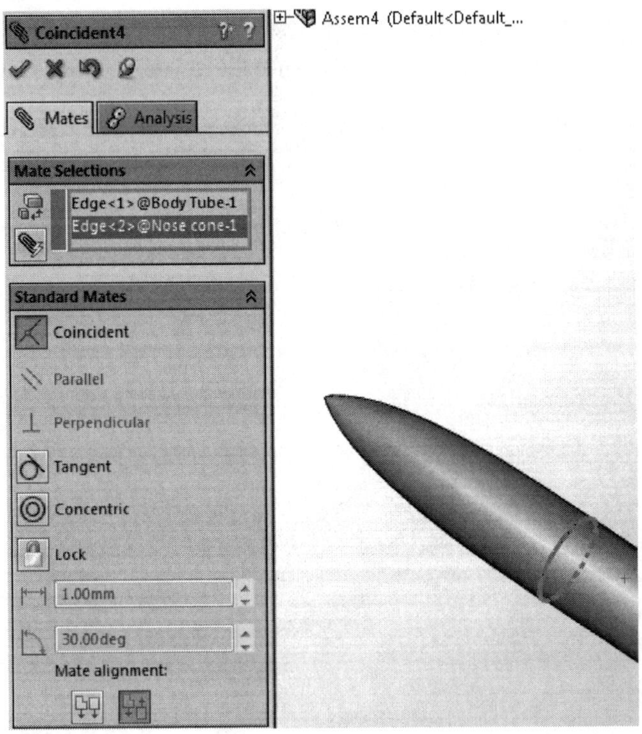

Figure 14.10c) Coincident4 mate of Nose cone and Body Tube

11. Select **Insert>>Component>>Existing Part/Assembly…** from the menu. Drag the **Engine Lock Ring** from the Open Documents: in **Part/Assembly to Insert** to the graphics window and insert the **Engine Lock Ring** beside the **Body Tube** and **Fins** assembly. Select **Insert>>Mate…** from the menu. Select the larger plane circular face of the **Engine Lock Ring** and the corresponding face of the **Body Tube**; see Fig. 14.11. Exit the **Coincident5** dialog. Select the circular outer edge of the **Body Tube** and the corresponding circular edge of the **Engine Lock Ring**. Set the **Mate alignment:**  **Anti-Aligned** so that the **Engine Lock Ring** is correctly mated on the **Body Tube**; see Fig. 14.12. Answer OK to the message that appears. Exit the **Coincident6** and **Mate** dialogues. Save the assembly with the name **Model Rocket Assembly**.

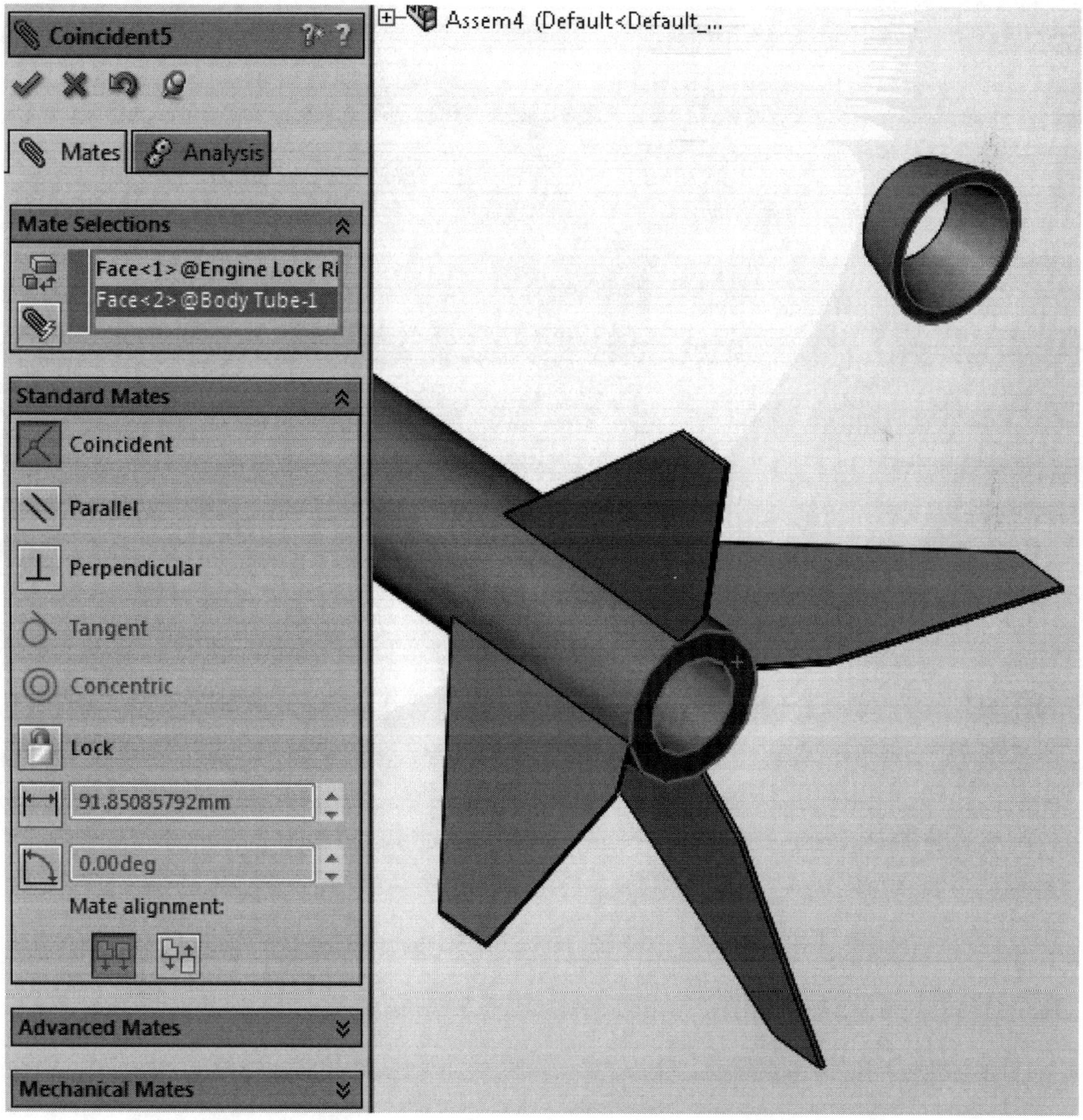

Figure 14.11 Coincident5 mate of Engine Lock Ring and Body Tube

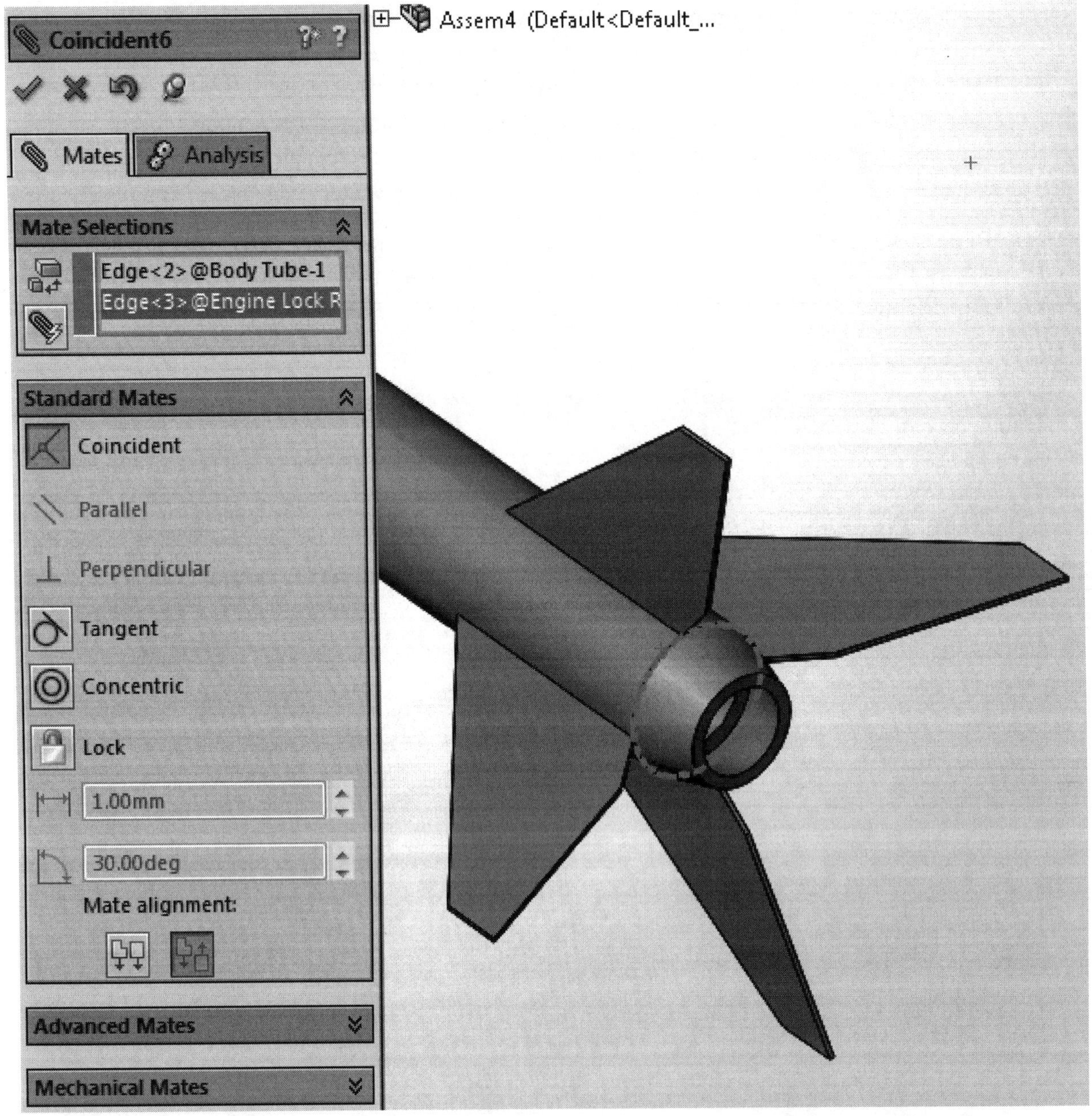

Figure 14.12 Coincident6 mate of Engine Lock Ring and Body Tube

Setting up the Flow Simulation Project for Model Rocket

12. If Flow Simulation is not available in the SOLIDWORKS menu, select **Tools>>Add Ins...** and check the corresponding **SOLIDWORKS Flow Simulation** box. Start the **Flow Simulation Wizard** by selecting **Tools>>Flow Simulation>>Project>>Wizard** from the SOLIDWORKS menu.

13. Create a new project with the following name: **Flow Past a Model Rocket**.

Figure 14.13 Entering configuration name

14. Select the SI unit system

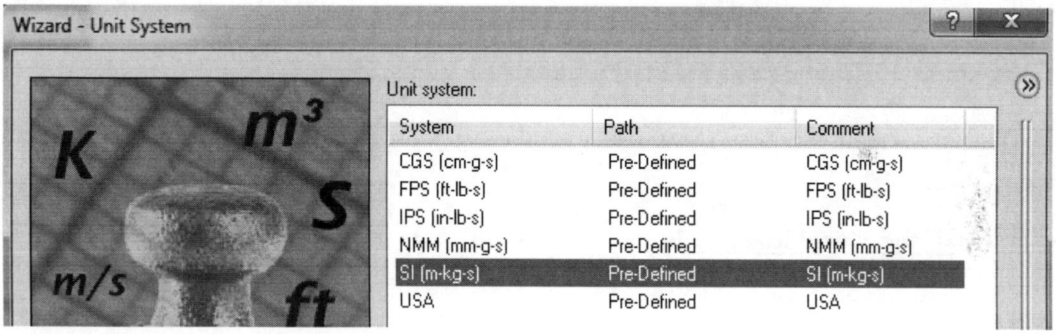

Figure 14.14 Selection of unit system

15. Select the **External Analysis type**.

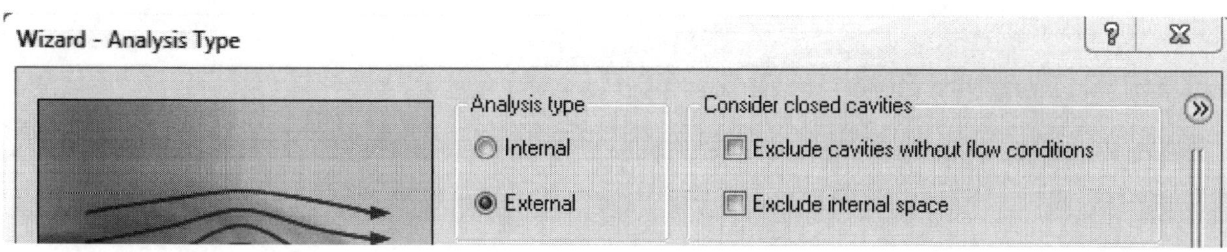

Figure 14.15 Selection of External Analysis type

16. Add **Air** as the default **Project Fluid** by selecting it from **Gases**. Choose default values for **Wall Conditions** and enter **-10 m/s** as the **Velocity in Z direction** as **Initial Condition**. Slide the **Initial Mesh** to **3**. Finish the Wizard.

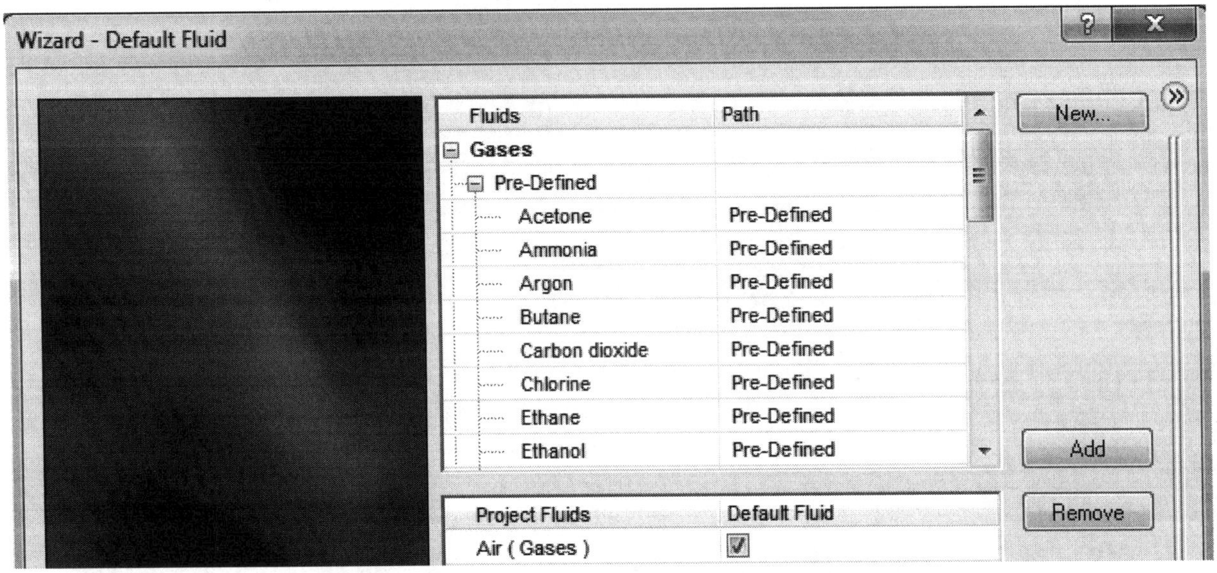

Figure 14.16 Adding air as the default fluid

Inserting Goals for Model Rocket Flow

17. Right click on **Goals** in the **Flow Simulation analysis tree** and select **Insert Global Goals...** Check the box for **Force (Z)**.

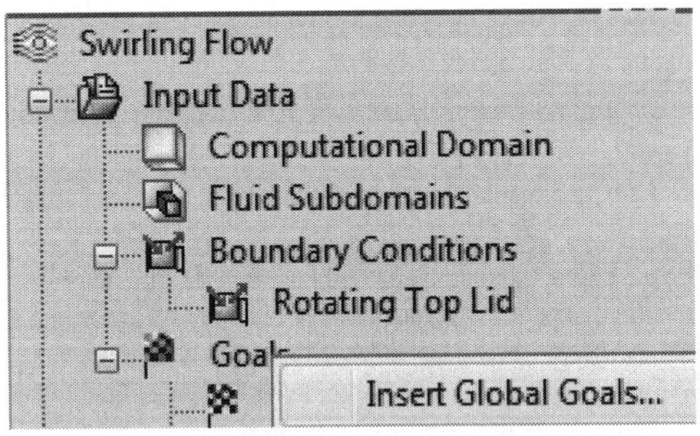

Figure 14.17 Inserting global goals

18. Right click on **Goals** in the **Flow Simulation analysis tree** and select **Insert Equation Goal…** Click on **GG Force (Z) 1** in the Flow Simulation Analysis tree. Enter the Expression as shown in Fig. 14.18. Select Dimensionless LMA for Dimensionality. Click on the OK button to exit the window. Rename the equation goal to Drag Coefficient.

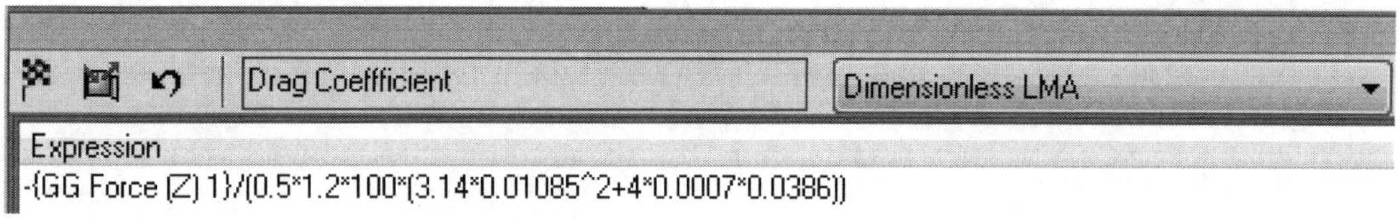

Figure 14.18 Expression for equation goal

19. Select **Tools>>Flow Simulation>>Initial Mesh** from the menu. Check the box for **Manual specification of the minimum wall thickness** and enter the value **0.0007 m**.

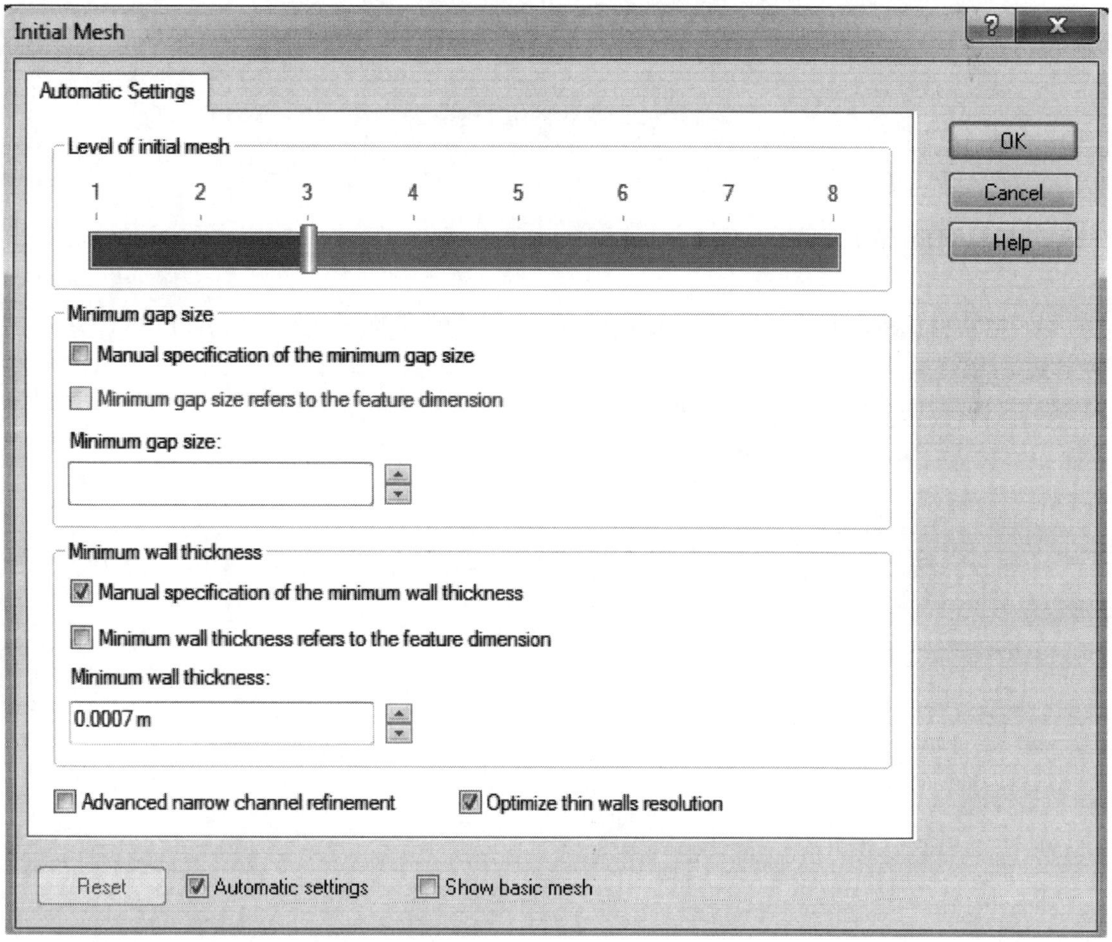

Figure 14.19 Specifying minimum wall thickness

Running the Calculations

20. Select **Tools>>Flow Simulation>>Solve>>Run**. Push the **Run** button in the window that appears.

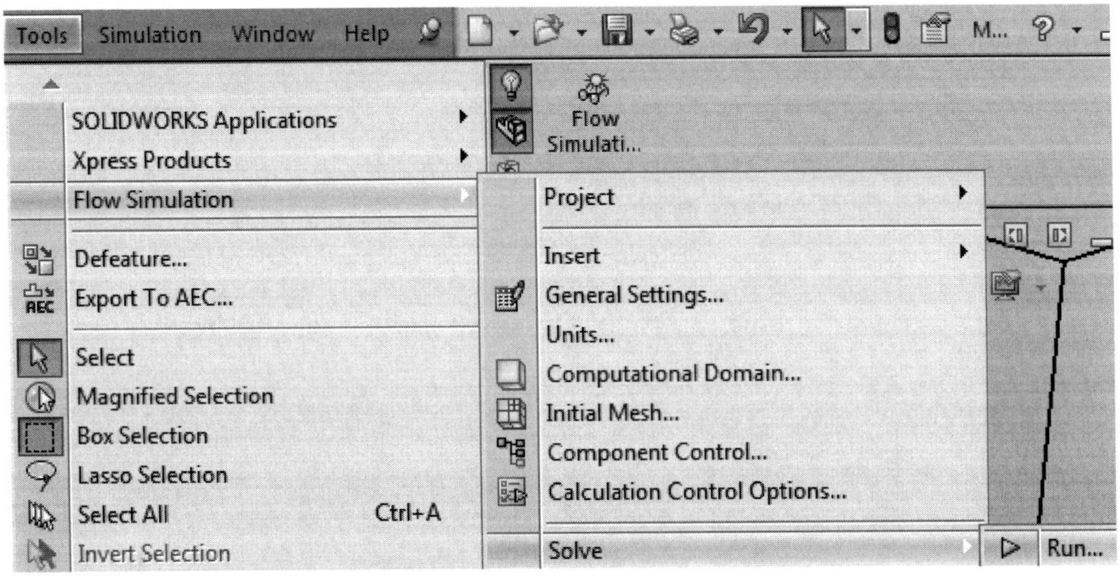

Figure 14.20 Starting the calculation for the flow field

21. Insert the goals table by clicking on the flag  in the **Solver** as shown in figure 14.21.

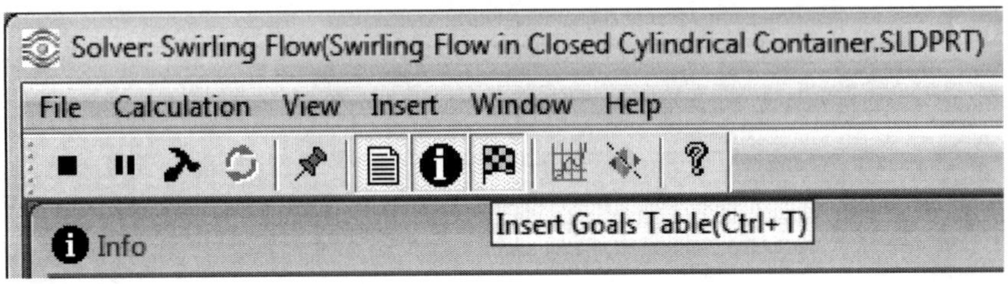

Figure 14.21a) Inserting goals

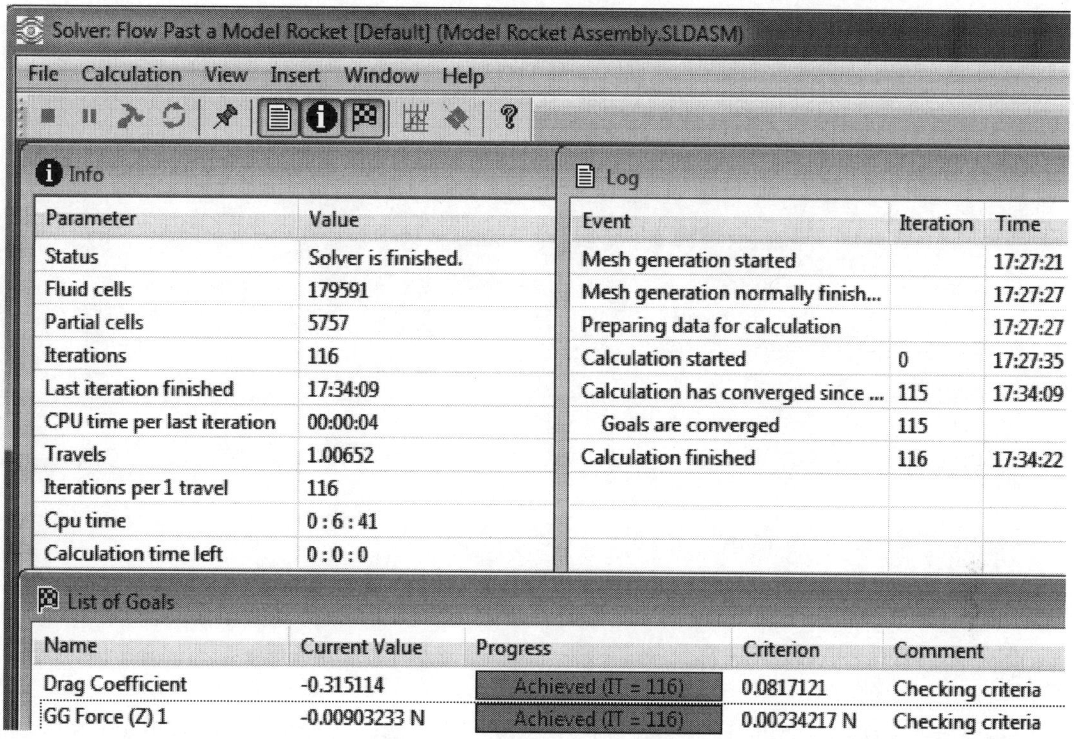

Figure 14.21b) Solver window

Inserting Cut Plots

22. Right click on **Cut Plots** and select **Insert**. Select the **Right** plane of the **Body Tube**. Select **Velocity** from the drop down menu in the **Contours** section. Slide the **Number of Levels** all the way to the right. Exit the **Cut plot**.

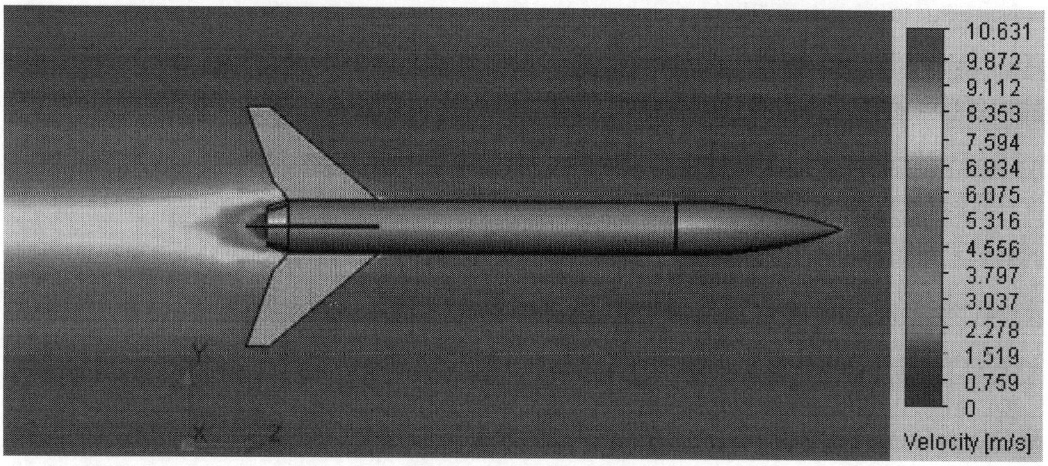

Figure 14.22a) Velocity field around model rocket

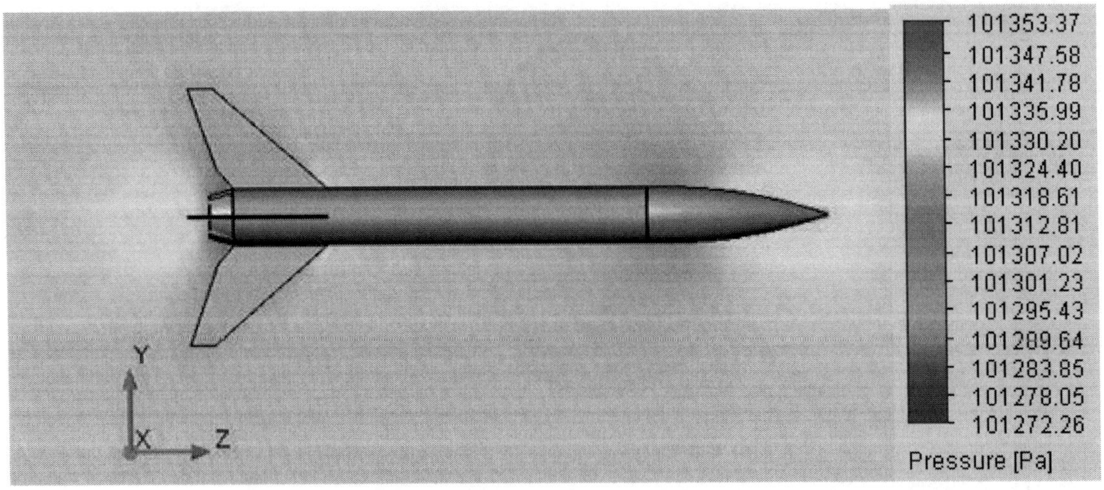

Figure 14.22b) Pressure field around model rocket

Reference

[1] Stine G.H. and Stine B., Handbook of Model Rocketry, 7th Ed., John Wiley & Sons, Inc., 2004.

Exercises

1. Run the flow case as described in this chapter for different velocities to see how the drag coefficient will change.

2. Run the flow case as described in this chapter for different fin shapes to see how the drag coefficient will change.

3. Run the flow case as described in this chapter for different mesh sizes to see how the drag coefficient will change.

Index

A

B

C

D

E

F

G

H

I

M

N

O

P

R

S

T

Y

Z